Developing Appropriate Curriculum for Young Children

Nancy P. Alexander
Associate Professor and Director NSU Child and Family Network
Northwestern Louisiana State University
Shreveport, Louisiana

Publisher
The Goodheart-Willcox Company, Inc.
Tinley Park, IL
www.g-w.com

Copyright © 2025
by
The Goodheart-Willcox Company, Inc.

All rights reserved. No part of this work may be reproduced, stored, or transmitted in any form or by any electronic or mechanical means, including information storage and retrieval systems, except as permitted by U.S. copyright law, without the prior written permission of The Goodheart-Willcox Company, Inc.

Library of Congress Control Number: 2023945848

ISBN 978-1-63776-683-5

1 2 3 4 5 6 7 8 9 – 25– 28 27 26 25 24 23

The Goodheart-Willcox Company, Inc. Brand Disclaimer: Brand names, company names, and illustrations for products and services included in this text are provided for educational purposes only and do not represent or imply endorsement or recommendation by the author or the publisher.

The Goodheart-Willcox Company, Inc. Safety Notice: The reader is expressly advised to carefully read, understand, and apply all safety precautions and warnings described in this book or that might also be indicated in undertaking the activities and exercises described herein to minimize risk of personal injury or injury to others. Common sense and good judgment should also be exercised and applied to help avoid all potential hazards. The reader should always refer to the appropriate manufacturer's technical information, directions, and recommendations; then proceed with care to follow specific equipment operating instructions. The reader should understand these notices and cautions are not exhaustive.

The publisher makes no warranty or representation whatsoever, either expressed or implied, including but not limited to equipment, procedures, and applications described or referred to herein, their quality, performance, merchantability, or fitness for a particular purpose. The publisher assumes no responsibility for any changes, errors, or omissions in this book. The publisher specifically disclaims any liability whatsoever, including any direct, indirect, incidental, consequential, special, or exemplary damages resulting, in whole or in part, from the reader's use or reliance upon the information, instructions, procedures, warnings, cautions, applications, or other matter contained in this book. The publisher assumes no responsibility for the activities of the reader.

The Goodheart-Willcox Company, Inc. Internet Disclaimer: The Internet resources and listings in this Goodheart-Willcox Publisher product are provided solely as a convenience to you. These resources and listings were reviewed at the time of publication to provide you with accurate, safe, and appropriate information. Goodheart-Willcox Publisher has no control over the referenced websites and, due to the dynamic nature of the Internet, is not responsible or liable for the content, products, or performance of links to other websites or resources. Goodheart-Willcox Publisher makes no representation, either expressed or implied, regarding the content of these websites, and such references do not constitute an endorsement or recommendation of the information or content presented. It is your responsibility to take all protective measures to guard against inappropriate content, viruses, or other destructive elements.

Image Credits. Front cover: FatCamera/E+ via Getty Images

Preface

Developing Appropriate Curriculum for Young Children focuses not just on the "whole child," but on the "whole classroom" and "whole community." Children do not arrive at the classroom door with the same abilities, experiences, or familial and cultural backgrounds. Thus, it is important for aspiring educators to understand that there is no one-size-fits-all approach to education. For each child to succeed, the teacher must understand each child's world outside of the classroom and plan how to use that information to the child's benefit.

Developing Appropriate Curriculum for Young Children introduces a streamlined focus on inclusion and familial and community involvement. They say it takes a village to raise a child. In this textbook, students will learn who is part of this village and how to utilize these villagers to promote equity and success for children. Rather than solely informing students about best curriculum practices, this textbook will guide students on how to apply these practices and build a learning environment that reaches each type of learner.

This textbook presents an integrated and a relationship-based approach to curriculum. Children learn best not in isolation but through interactions, explorations, and discoveries, with the support of caring adults in their lives. Providing a safe, secure, and comfortable environment full of rich and playful experiences is a primary focus of curriculum as described in this textbook—and the goal of the early childhood professional.

Reviewers

The author and publisher wish to thank the following industry and teaching professionals for their valuable input into the development of *Developing Appropriate Curriculum for Young Children*:

Derek Bardell
Professor, Education Department
Delgado Community College
New Orleans, Louisiana

Deborah Becker
Adjunct Faculty
Aims Community College
Greely, Colorado

Beverly Bennett-Roberts
Professor, Early Childhood
    Education and Special Education
University of the District of
    Columbia
Washington, D.C.

Heidi Broad-Smith
Early Childhood Education
    Instructor
Northern Maine Community
    College
Presque Isle, Maine

Susan Casey
Professor, Early Childhood
    Education
Stephen F. Austin State University
Nacogdoches, Texas

Priscilla Causey-Pope
Instructor
Bladen Community College
Dublin, North Carolina

Katie Champlin
Professor and Department Chair,
    Early Childhood Education
Des Moines Area Community
    College
Ankeny, Iowa

Jennifer Copeland
Chair, Division of Humanities and
    Education
Metropolitan Community College
Kansas City, Missouri

Susan Davies
Chair and Professor, Department of
    Counselor Education and Human
    Services
University of Dayton
Dayton, Ohio

Georgianna Duarte
Department Head
Indiana State University
Terre Haute, Indiana

Jannice Ellen
Professor
Community College of Vermont
Montpelier, Vermont

Christine Evan-Schwartz
Instructor
Kirkwood Community College
Cedar Rapids, Iowa

Melissa Fleck
Associate Professor
Early Childhood Education
Nashville State Community College
Nashville, Tennessee

Heidi Frankard
Professor
Metropolitan State University
St. Paul, Minnesota

Sherry Granberry
Instructor
Wayne Community College
Goldsboro, North Carolina

Julie Griep
Early Childhood Coordinator
Northeast Iowa Community College
Calmar, Iowa

Lisa Guenther
Early Childhood Education
    Instructor
Northeast Community College
Norfolk, Nebraska

Jeanne Helm
Professor
Richland Community College
Decatur, Illinois

Judi Holland
Program Director, Early Childhood
    Education
Colorado Northwestern Community
    College
Rangely, Colorado

Jeanne Hopkins
Department Chair and Professor,
    Early Childhood Education
Tidewater Community College
Norfolk, Virginia

Amy Huebner
Assistant Professor
St. Philip's College
San Antonio, Texas

Jamileth Jarquin
Professor, Early Childhood
    Education
Miami Dade College
Miami, Florida

Natasha Kile
Instructor
Northwest Arkansas Community College
Bentonville, Arkansas

Theresa Kohlmeier
Assistant Professor
University of Wisconsin-Stout
Menomonie, Wisconsin

Wendy Koile
Instructional Designer
Central Ohio Technical College
Newark, Ohio

Laura Kujo
Instructor, Teacher Education
CUNY Borough of Manhattan Community College
New York, New York

Debra Lawrence
Assistant Professor
Delaware County Community College
Media, Pennsylvania

Tami McCoy Leonard
Instructor
Hawkeye Community College
Waterloo, Iowa

Diane Lewis
Early Childhood Education Program Coordinator
Lakes Region Community College
Laconia, New Hampshire

Kerri Mahlum
Education Instructor
Casper College
Casper, Wyoming

Annmarie Malchenson
Education Associate Professor
HACC, Central Pennsylvania's Community College
Harrisburg, Pennsylvania

Lauri Marmorstone
Early Childhood Education Support Specialist
William Rainey Harper College
Palatine, Illinois

James Marshall
Instructor
Cabrillo College
Aptos, California

Meghan Martin
Professor
Quinsigamond Community College
Worcester, Massachusetts

Amanda McPherson
Adjunct Faculty
Pima Community College
Tucson, Arizona

Patricia Merritt
Professor Emeritus, Early Childhood Education
University of Alaska Fairbanks
Fairbanks, Alaska

Kerry Belknap Morris
Professor and Program Director, Early Childhood Education and Social Services
River Valley Community College
Claremont, New Hampshire

Dawn Sweeney Munson
Professor of Education
Elgin Community College
Elgin, Illinois

Debra Murphy
Professor and Program Director, Early Childhood Education
Cape Cod Community College
West Barnstable, Massachusetts

Jennifer Murray
Early Childhood Education Instructor
Richmond Community College
Hamlet, North Carolina

Kristina C. Norwood
Early Childhood Faculty
Iowa Western Community College
Council Bluffs, Iowa

Martha Page
Instructor
Elizabethtown Community & Technical College
Elizabethtown, Kentucky

Elvia Guerrero Parreira
Adjunct Professor
College of the Sequoias
Visalia, California

Kristen Pickering
Program Chair
Ivy Tech Community College
Indianapolis, Indiana

Ann Plourde
Professor
Hudson Valley Community College
Troy, New York

Tamara Rawlings
Instructor
Central Georgia Technical College
Macon, Georgia

Nicole Reiber
Department Head and Instructor
Coastal Carolina Community College
Jacksonville, North Carolina

Shelley Moira Rheams
Instructor
Delgado Community College
New Orleans, Louisiana

Jacqueline Rippy
Professor
Florida State College at Jacksonville
Jacksonville, Florida

Wilma Robles-Melendez
Professor, Early Childhood Education
Nova Southeastern University
Fort Lauderdale, Florida

Ardythe Rodriguez
Instructor
Riverside City College
Riverside, California

Rita Rzezuski
Professor
Bunker Hill Community College
Boston, Massachusetts

Tammy Schrickel
Instructor
Central Georgia Technical College
Warner Robins, Georgia

Jill Scott
Associate Professor
Abilene Christian University
Abilene, Texas

Monica Soublet
Instructor
Fresno City College
Fresno, California

Catherine Steinbock
Instructor
Eastern Wyoming College
Torrington, Wyoming

Amber Tankersley
Professor, Family and Consumer Sciences
Pittsburg State University
Pittsburg, Kansas

Sapna Thapa
Assistant Professor
University of Wisconsin-Stout
Menomonie, Wisconsin

Barbara Thomas
Instructor
Delgado Community College
New Orleans, Louisiana

Georgia Thompson
Instructor
University of the District of Columbia
Washington, D.C.

Josh Thompson
Professor, Early Childhood Education
Texas A&M University-Commerce
Commerce, Texas

Catherine Twyman
Instructor
Daytona State College
Daytona Beach, Florida

Shannon Vaughn
Instructor
Tri-County Technical College
Pendleton, South Carolina

Francis Wardle
Instructor
Red Rocks Community College
Lakewood, Colorado

Elizabeth Watters
Instructor
Cuyahoga Community College
Highland Hills, Ohio

Laurie E. Westcott
Instructor
Manchester Community College
Manchester, New Hampshire

Lisa White
Instructor
Athens Technical College
Athens, Georgie

Deborah Whitmer
Instructor
Shasta College
Redding, California

Dr. Brenda K. Williamson
Instructor
Durham Technical Community College
Durham, North Carolina

Jackie Zeckser
Instructor
Central Community College
Hastings, Nebraska

Elaine Zweig
Instructor
Collin County Community College
McKinney, Texas

About the Author

Nancy P. Alexander is Associate Professor at Northwestern State University and Director of the Child and Family Network, a child care resource and referral agency providing coaching and training throughout 16 parishes (counties). She is the former President of the North Louisiana Chapter of the Association for Talent Development and recipient of the Trainer of the Year Award from that organization. Nancy is a former board member of the Southern Early Childhood Association (SECA) and received the Outstanding Member Award from that organization. She is the former President of the Multicultural Center of the South and was honored during the Week of the Young Child by the center.

Nancy regularly conducts workshops and training sessions at national and regional conferences, such as the National Association for the Education of Young Children (NAEYC), Southern Early Childhood Association (SECA), and the World Forum on Early Care and Education. She was selected by the Shreveport Chamber of Commerce as one of the "One Hundred Women of the Century." She serves on a number of professional and community boards.

Features of the Textbook

The instructional design of this textbook includes student-focused learning tools to help you succeed. This visual guide highlights these features.

Chapter Opening Materials

Each chapter opener contains Learning Outcomes, a list of Key Terms, and an Introduction. The **Learning Outcomes** clearly identify the knowledge and skills to be gained by the student when the chapter is completed. **Key Terms** are terminology common to early childhood education to be learned in the chapter. The **Introduction** provides an overview and preview of the chapter content.

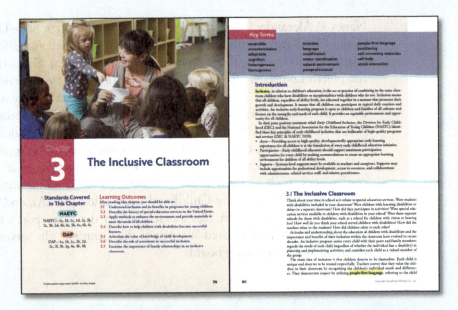

Additional Features

Additional features are used throughout the body of each chapter to further learning and understanding. **Teaching Tip** provides advice and guidance that is especially applicable for on-the-job situations. **Discovery Journeys** guide the reader through experiences with young children that have inspired and influenced the author and others to professional growth and insight in child learning and behavior. **Case Study** zooms in on specific early childhood education scenarios so that students can explore ways to respond and apply what they are learning. **From the Field** features provide advice and insight from active early childhood education professionals.

Teaching Tip

Applying Appropriate Language
As a rule, people-first, appropriate language puts the child before the description, uses respectful words, and describes what a child *has*, rather than what a child *is*.

Say	Instead of
he has autism spectrum disorder	he is autistic
he has Down syndrome	he's Downs or he is a Down's kid
children without disabilities	normal children
accessible parking	handicapped parking
she has a physical disability	she is crippled
he receives special ed services	he is in special ed
congenital disability	birth defect
child with a hearing impairment	hearing-impaired child
child with cerebral palsy	cerebral palsy child or CP child

Discovery Journeys

In the Family
Clarissa Willis, PhD, an author and a teacher who specializes in working with children with disabilities, shares this story about an event that strengthened her commitment and understanding of her role in special education:

I had worked in special education for many years, first as a teacher and then as a college professor, so I knew exactly what to say to a family who had a child born with a special need. Or I thought I did.

All my confidence in my knowledge went out the window one February night when my beloved sister-in-law called to say her baby, due in May, had come early and was being airlifted to a special hospital in Dallas. My husband and I rushed from Little Rock to Dallas, making the usual six-hour drive in under five hours.

In the hospital, my sister-in-law and her husband had just been informed that their daughter, who weighed just over one pound, would likely not make it. When it is your own family, everything you think you know about family empowerment does not seem to be enough.

As I looked at the tiny infant fighting to breathe, hooked up to machines, I heard the doctor tell the family, "She has cerebral palsy. She won't walk, talk, or be able to read. She will have very little ability even to feed herself or take care of other needs." Fortunately, today, doctors are more compassionate and less sure when a child is born what the outcome might be.

Lindsay did not die, nor was she impaired, other than having a problem walking. She went to public school and graduated, going on to earn both an undergraduate and a graduate degree. Today she works as an advocate for social services, finding foster home placements for children with special needs. I often say, "Lindsay didn't get the memo." Instead of focusing on what she would not be able to do, she went on to accomplish a lot.

I know that other children are not as fortunate as Lindsay, but I learned from this experience that some children have a built-in resilience that helps them defy the odds. After that experience I never dealt the same way with parents again. I now know that each family deals with adversity in their own way. My job became focused on helping families deal with what is happening in the moment, not what might happen in the future (Willis 2015).

Case Study

Joseph and the Relay Team
Joseph had a congenital condition that affected his legs, leaving him with limited control. However, following several surgeries, braces, and many hours of therapy, he was able to walk in an upright position. Although his mobility was slow and laborious, he participated independently in his second-grade classroom.

One day on Joseph's playground, the teacher observed a group of children in her class organizing a type of relay where they ran in pairs to the fence, creating a friendly competition between the pairs. Joseph was a part of the group, and when his turn came, one of the children announced, "If you race with Joseph, you have to walk to be fair." And that is just what the children did. Joseph's relay partner and the competing pair all walked rather than ran.

The teacher realized that the children had accommodated Joseph's abilities in their desire to include him. Inclusion was more important to them than winning. Often, Joseph was faster with his braces than the others who were walking; thus, he and his partner usually won the race. The teacher, who had Joseph in her classroom again the following year, saw that the new group of children again adjusted their activities to include Joseph in a similar way.

Consider This
1. What factors do you think motivated the children to make sure Joseph was included as an equal participant?
2. What experiences have you had that demonstrated children's acceptance of others with differences?
3. What actions or behaviors of the teacher may have affected the attitudes of the children?

Figure 3-7

Illustrations

Illustrations have been designed to communicate the specific topic clearly and simply. Photographic images have been selected to reflect the diversity of children, families, communities, and classrooms.

Expanding Your Learning

Checkpoint questions extend learning and develop students' abilities to use learned material in new situations and from diverse perspectives. **Consider This** questions appear within many features to develop higher-order thinking and problem-solving skills through application and transfer of learning.

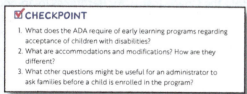

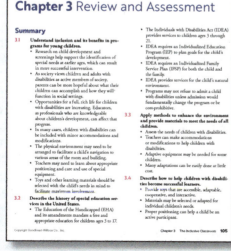

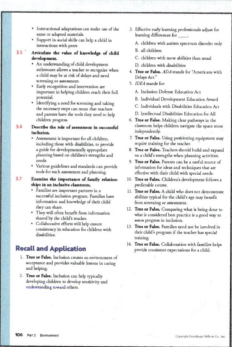

End-of-Chapter Content

End-of-chapter material provides an opportunity for review and application of concepts. The **Summary** matches the content to the learning outcomes for section-by-section review. The Summary provides an additional review tool and also reinforces important concepts presented in the text. **Recall and Application** questions extend learning and develop abilities to break down material into its component parts.

ix

TOOLS FOR STUDENT AND INSTRUCTOR SUCCESS

Student Tools

Student Text

Developing Appropriate Curriculum for Young Children walks students through the fundamentals of early childhood curriculum while correlating to NAEYC's developmentally appropriate practices for learners ages 0–8. The author explores how to build engaging and inclusive curriculum, then offers real-world advice on how future and current teachers can put these methods into practice in the classroom.

G-W Digital Companion

- E-flash cards and vocabulary exercises allow interaction with content to create opportunities to increase achievement.

Video Library

- Video assets enrich learning by capturing authentic examples of physical, cognitive, and social-emotional development of children. The videos were created in a developmentally appropriate learning environment and are rich in examples of child care best practices and effective classroom design. Videos are accompanied by assignable quiz questions that challenge students to identify the skill, stage of development, or best-practice endeavor that is being displayed in the video and think critically about the content.

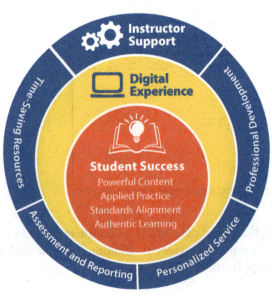

Instructor Tools

LMS Integration

Integrate Goodheart-Willcox content within your Learning Management System (LMS) for a seamless user experience for both you and your students. EduHub LMS-ready content in Common Cartridge® format facilitates single sign-on integration and gives you control of student enrollment and data. With a Common Cartridge integration, you can access the LMS features and tools you are accustomed to using and G-W course resources in one convenient location—your LMS.

G-W Common Cartridge provides a complete learning package for you and your students. The included digital resources help your students remain engaged and learn effectively:

- **Digital Textbook**
- **Videos**
- **Drill and Practice** vocabulary activities

When you incorporate G-W content into your courses via Common Cartridge, you have the flexibility to customize and structure the content to meet the educational needs of your students. You may also choose to add your own content to the course.

For instructors, the Common Cartridge includes the Online Instructor Resources. QTI® question banks are available within the Online Instructor Resources for import into your LMS. These prebuilt assessments help you measure student knowledge and track results in your LMS gradebook. Questions and tests can be customized to meet your assessment needs.

Online Instructor Resources

- The **Instructor Resources** provide instructors with time-saving preparation tools such as answer keys, editable lesson plans, and other teaching aids.
- **Instructor's Presentations for PowerPoint®** are fully customizable, richly illustrated slides that help you teach and visually reinforce the key concepts from each chapter.
- Administer and manage assessments to meet your classroom needs using **Assessment Software with Question Banks**, which include hundreds of matching, true/false, multiple choice, and short answer questions to assess student knowledge of the content in each chapter.

See https://www.g-w.com/developing-appropriate-curriculum-for-young-children-2025 for a list of all available resources.

Professional Development

- Expert content specialists
- Research-based pedagogy and instructional practices
- Options for virtual and in-person Professional Development

Brief Contents

PART 1

Basic Concepts ... 2
Chapter 1   Guiding Young Children's Learning ... 3

PART 2

Environment ... 48
Chapter 2   The Early Childhood Learning Environment ... 49
Chapter 3   The Inclusive Classroom ... 79
Chapter 4   Planning for Playful Learning ... 107
Chapter 5   The Basics: Safety, Health, and Nutrition ... 145
Chapter 6   Engaging Families ... 177

PART 3

Curriculum Areas of Focus ... 206
Chapter 7   Assessment: A Tool for Planning ... 207
Chapter 8   Language and Literacy ... 241
Chapter 9   The World We Live In: Social Studies ... 273
Chapter 10   STEAM: Science, Technology, and Engineering ... 301
Chapter 11   STEAM: Art and Music ... 337
Chapter 12   STEAM: Mathematics ... 379
Chapter 13   Back to the Great Outdoors ... 411

PART 4

Achieving Your Goals ... 446
Chapter 14   We All Belong: Becoming a Professional ... 447

Contents

PART 1

Basic Concepts 2

Chapter 1
Guiding Young Children's Learning 3
- 1.1 Infant and Toddler Brain Development 5
- 1.2 How Children Learn 6
- 1.3 Key Theorists and Their Contributions to Early Childhood.................12
- 1.4 Interactions That Support Learning........15
- 1.5 Promoting Cognitive Development........21
- 1.6 What Is Curriculum?..................... 24
- 1.7 Implementing Curriculum 38

PART 2

Environment 48

Chapter 2
The Early Childhood Learning Environment 49
- 2.1 The Physical Environment................ 50
- 2.2 Learning Centers....................... 53
- 2.3 Room Arrangement and Children's Behavior 65
- 2.4 The Social and Emotional Environment... 66
- 2.5 The Teacher's Role in the Environment... 72
- 2.6 Focus on Assessment of Program Practices.............................74
- 2.7 Family Matters 75

Chapter 3
The Inclusive Classroom 79
- 3.1 The Inclusive Classroom................ 80
- 3.2 Special Education Laws in the United States 84
- 3.3 Creating an Inclusive Classroom.......... 89
- 3.4 The Teacher's Role: Taking Steps Toward Inclusion............................. 92
- 3.5 Understanding the Role of Child Development Knowledge 98
- 3.6 Focus on Assessment of Program Practices and Involving Families........... 102
- 3.7 Family Matters 103

Chapter 4
Planning for Playful Learning.............. 107
- 4.1 The Importance of Play for Young Children 108
- 4.2 Types and Stages of Play 113
- 4.3 Cultural Influences on Play 121
- 4.4 Developmentally Appropriate Play Activities That Support Learning.........123
- 4.5 Adults' Role in Children's Playful Learning 133
- 4.6 Focus on Assessment of Program Practices.............................138
- 4.7 Family Matters: Understanding Playful Learning 141

Chapter 5
The Basics: Safety, Health, and Nutrition ... 145
- 5.1 Safety Outdoors...................... 146
- 5.2 Safety Indoors 153
- 5.3 Teacher Self-Care 157
- 5.4 Health 160
- 5.5 Nutrition for Young Children............ 164
- 5.6 Family Matters........................172

Chapter 6
Engaging Families 177
- 6.1 Building Positive Family–Program Relationships.........................179
- 6.2 Respecting Families' Cultural Background and Diversity................182
- 6.3 Family Matters........................ 191
- 6.4 Involving Families in a Program 196
- 6.5 Focus on Assessment of Program Practices............................ 203

PART 3

Curriculum Areas of Focus........... 206

Chapter 7
Assessment: A Tool for Planning...........207
- 7.1 The Purpose of Assessment 208
- 7.2 Assessment for Planning and Learning ...209
- 7.3 Recording Observations................ 212
- 7.4 Making and Using Portfolios............ 223

7.5 The Teacher's Role in Assessment....... 227
7.6 Using Observations and Assessments to Guide Behavior.................. 229
7.7 Evaluating the Program as a Whole...... 235
7.8 Family Matters.................. 237

Chapter 8
Language and Literacy................ 241
8.1 The 30-Million-Word Gap............. 242
8.2 Language Development.............. 243
8.3 The Teacher's Role in Fostering Language and Literacy Skills.................. 246
8.4 Guidelines for Reading Aloud.......... 259
8.5 Emergent Literacy................ 263
8.6 Assessing Program Practices.......... 267
8.7 Family Matters.................. 269

Chapter 9
The World We Live In: Social Studies....... 273
9.1 What Is Social Studies for Young Children?..................... 274
9.2 Developmentally Appropriate Concepts..................... 276
9.3 The Cultural Aspects of Social Studies... 290
9.4 The Teacher's Role in Social Studies..... 293
9.5 Focus on Assessment of Program Practices..................... 297
9.6 Family Matters.................. 297

Chapter 10
STEAM: Science, Technology, and Engineering................... 301
10.1 STEAM in Early Childhood Education... 302
10.2 Science in Early Childhood Education .. 304
10.3 Technology in Early Childhood Education..................... 307
10.4 Engineering in Early Childhood Education..................... 309
10.5 Science, Technology, and Engineering in the Classroom................ 311
10.6 The Teacher's Role in Science, Technology, and Engineering.......... 322
10.7 Establishing Science and Tinkering Centers..................... 325
10.8 Focus on Assessment of Science, Technology, and Engineering Practices..... 329
10.9 Family Matters..................331

Chapter 11
STEAM: Art and Music.............. 337
11.1 Art and Music for Young Children....... 338
11.2 Art and Music in the Curriculum........ 345
11.3 Stages of Development of Children's Art and Music Skills.................. 352
11.4 The Teacher's Role in Art............. 363
11.5 Focus on Assessment of Program Practices of Art and Music............... 373
11.6 Family Matters................... 374

Chapter 12
STEAM: Mathematics...............379
12.1 Developing Math Awareness...........381
12.2 Learning Mathematical Concepts...... 382
12.3 The Teacher's Role in Teaching Mathematics.................... 394
12.4 Focus on Assessment............... 405
12.5 Family Matters...................406

Chapter 13
Back to the Great Outdoors............... 411
13.1 The Importance of Outdoor Play for Young Children...................412
13.2 Equipment and Materials............. 420
13.3 Integrating Outdoor Time with Other Curriculum Areas................ 426
13.4 The Teacher's Role in the Outdoor Environment................... 432
13.5 Outdoors for Infants and Toddlers..... 436
13.6 Focus on Assessment of Program Practices.....................441
13.7 Family Matters.................. 442

PART 4
Achieving Your Goals............446

Chapter 14
We All Belong: Becoming a Professional ... 447
14.1 Is This Profession for You?............. 449
14.2 The Early Childhood Commitment..... 456
14.3 Professional Organizations and Resources.................... 461
14.4 Equity and Equality................ 467
14.5 Taking Care of Yourself as a Professional.....................469
14.6 Focus on Assessment.............. 473
14.7 Family Matters.................. 476

Glossary...................... 481
References.................... 485
Index........................ 488

Feature Contents

TEACHING TIP

Learning Characteristics of Infants	7
Learning Characteristics of Toddlers	8
Learning Characteristics of Preschoolers	10
Learning Characteristics of Young School-Age Children	11
NAEYC	24
NAEYC Teaching Strategies for Children with Special Needs	26
Questions to Consider When Selecting the Most Appropriate Curriculum	30
Creating a Theme Plan	36
Working with Mixed Ages	37
Seven Strategies for Implementing Curriculum	40
Applying Appropriate Language	83
Key Requirements for Providers	86
Encouraging Infant Play	124
How Teachers Hinder Play	132
Assembling Prop Boxes	135
When a Child Does Not Play	136
Theme Play	138
Barriers to Supervision	149
Holding a Fire Drill	152
Indoor Safety Checklist	155
Lead Exposure Concerns	157
Characteristics of a Healthy Child	164
Guidelines for Nutrition Education Activities	167
Respecting Confidentiality	196
The Continuity of Care Model	203
Setting Up Portfolios	223
Book Awards	259
Innovative Reading Programs	263
Incorporating Family	277
Steps in Engineering	311
STEM for Young Children	322
Setting Up Science and Tinkering Centers	326
How to Support Children's Creativity	342
Toddlers and Music	351
Examples of Musical Experiences	372
Celebrate International Mud Day!	413
A Different Approach: Forest Schools	416
A Different Approach: Adventure Playgrounds	422
Using Your Skills and Knowledge to Make Ethical Decisions	454
Roles Early Childhood Professionals Play	465
Eight Tips to Reduce Childhood Stress	470

DISCOVERY JOURNEYS

Cooks, Chefs, Conductors, and Supermarkets	39
I Learn from Children	67
In the Family	81
Finding Solutions for Frank	98
LaShonda's First Day	119
Play Supports Understanding	120
The Family Medical Book	122
The Croissant Rebellion	165
The Lettuce Wraps	171
Dudley's Mother	181
The Celebration	197
Welcoming Families	199
Are We Measuring What We Intend?	226
The Math Professor	235
The Green Crayon	251
Ironing Is for Girls	290
Girls in STEAM	303
Experiential Learning	306
The Winter Season	318
Soloman and *The Red Balloon*	344
The Circus Theme	350
Emmy and the Crackers	388
Understanding Fractions	391
The Paper Chain	392
The Neighborhood Fort	418
Dancing on the Playground	428
Fishing with My Father	443
A Career Niche	453
Rebecca Goes to Kindergarten	462
Lessons in Listening	477

CASE STUDY

Juan and the Raisin Boxes 9
Abigail 16
Seeing Beyond the Obvious 23
The Fallen Tree 33
Salina and the Fire Station Field Trip 42
Environment Influences Behavior 51
The Undesirable DVD Dilemma 61
Disaster in the Manipulative Area 65
Joseph and the Relay Team 97
Aaron 102
Playing with Infants 110
The Unaccompanied Minor and a Tropical Paradise 130
The Veterinarian Clinic 131
What Would You Do? 158
Environmental Change to Improve Communication 179
Celebrating Holidays 190
Emme and the Mean Turtle 211
Recognizing Colors 219
Anecdotal Records about Aidan 222
The Social Media Post 228
Conducting a Conversation—or an Interrogation? 250
On Fish and Phonics 255
Teach My Baby to Read 257
Building a Gate 283
The License Bureau 285
Making Rules 286
The Documentation Board 287
Holidays and Special Events 292
Tablets in the Classroom 308
The Cigar Box Ukulele 310
The Very Hungry Caterpillar 313
It's Getting New! 323
The Snow's Gone! 324
The Little Boy 346
Circle Time Transition 348
Recognizing Math in Early Childhood 382
Learning about Money 389
Kelly's Discovery 395
Communicating Children's Progress to Parents 408
Field Day Competition 426
First, Do No Harm 449
Scenarios You May Face 472
Professional Obligations 478

FROM THE FIELD

Michelle Galindo 72
Stefanie Echols 95
Toni Sturdivant 139
Susan Farmer 202
Jade Romero 268
Zlata Stanković-Ramirez 293
Lareasa Addison 462

Introduction

Being an early childhood teacher is more than a job or even a profession. Rather, it is a frame of mind and a way of being and doing that permeates one's daily life. It affects our relationships and interactions as a parent, a friend, or an employee. Growing the future is what we care about and what we value, whether the focus is on teaching children or teaching those who will teach children. It is a passion that manifests itself in concerns about equity, diversity, and opportunities for all children, regardless of ability, family structure, or any other characteristic.

This textbook is filled with stories and examples of early childhood education in action. They are real-life stories from my career or shared by friends and colleagues who, with a fascination for watching children grow and learn, are constantly searching for better understanding. The stories are descriptions of children's learning or behavior—occurrences that illustrate a principle or paradigm in young children's development.

It is hard to predict what the future holds. We have figured out how we can use existing technology in a developmentally appropriate manner. However, we cannot predict how technology will change what we do in the coming years as social media continues to evolve and artificial intelligence emerges. This text is a snapshot in time of cumulative best practices as principles for decision making about children. Even as new technology emerges, the developmentally appropriate principles provide a guide for the everyday choices we must and will make in the future.

In beginning your career working with young children, value your direct experiences with children. Use this textbook as a guide for what you should be noticing and staying alert to, and what you should watch for. Learn from what you read and reflect on, but also from what you see and hear from children around you. Observe what children know and can do, and use what you learn to guide what you do.

In crafting a guidebook on how to facilitate children's playful learning, I find it analogous to learning to play tennis or perhaps any sport. A book can give you information about rules, scoring, and even tips to improve how you play. For the most part, however, you will learn to play tennis only by watching and doing. You must go out on the court and pick up a racquet. This textbook is designed to provide much of what you need to know and understand about early childhood curriculum and practices, but conjointly to encourage you to put what you learn into practice by interacting with children.

Nancy P. Alexander

Part 1

Basic Concepts

Chapter 1: Guiding Young Children's Learning

Chapter 1

Guiding Young Children's Learning

Standards Covered in This Chapter

NAEYC
NAEYC—1b, 1c, 2b, 3a, 4a, 4b, 5a, 5c, 6e

DAP
DAP—3a, 3b, 4a, 4b, 4c, 4d, 4f, 4g, 5a, 5b, 5c, 5d, 5f

Learning Outcomes

After reading this chapter, you should be able to:

1.1 Explain infant and toddler brain development and how to nurture it.
1.2 Describe how children learn and how to support learning.
1.3 Identify key theorists and their contributions to early childhood.
1.4 Describe the value of interactions that support learning.
1.5 Identify a variety of methods to stimulate cognitive skills.
1.6 Identify indicators of a high-quality curriculum.
1.7 Explain how to implement a curriculum with fidelity.

Key Terms

affirmation
child-directed learning
child-initiated learning
closed question
constructivist learning
developmentally appropriate practice (DAP)
feedback loops
fidelity
multiple intelligences
National Association for the Education of Young Children (NAEYC)
open-ended question
parallel talk
scaffolding
scope and sequence
self-talk
teachable moments
teacher-directed learning
teacher-initiated learning
visual schedule

Introduction

A college student on the first day of their first early childhood class listens as the professor describes children's learning using an orange. The professor hands each student a sheet of paper with an outline of an orange and the printed word "orange" at the bottom. She then gives each student an orange crayon and asks them to color the drawing. When they finish, the professor asks her students what they learned about oranges from that assignment. Responses are slow in coming but include such statements as "staying in the lines," "recognizing the color," and "seeing the written word."

Then she passes around some actual oranges and asks her students to do whatever they want with them and see what they learn. The students examine, peel, smell, and taste the oranges. This time, when she asks them what they learned, the responses are much more enthusiastic. Classmates share that they became more conscious of the aroma, texture, and shape of the fruit. They sampled the bitterness of the rind, paid attention to the white fiber, and broke the fruit into its segments. They were aware of the size and number of the seeds, wondering if they could eat them. And of course, the sweet taste of the orange was more apparent as a result of the focus and exploration.

Any individual who plans a career in working with young children must understand children's development and how learning happens. This includes the characteristics of children at various ages and how children master the important skills needed for a lifetime. This foundation must be the basis for the hundreds of decisions about interactions and activities in a typical day of teaching young children.

While there is variation in what children can do at any particular age, young children are typically categorized as infants, toddlers, preschoolers, and young school-age to address expectations for different ages. For this textbook, consider infants or babies as children from birth to one year of age. The term *toddlers* describes children from one to three years, sometimes differentiated as younger toddlers or older toddlers due to the immense development that takes place at that age. The term *preschoolers* refers to children from three to five years. *School-age* in this textbook refers to children between five and eight years old. It is important to remember that while development, growth, and learning follow some predictable trajectories, each child is unique.

While physical development during these years is significant, the development of the brain in the infant and toddler years is even more amazing. These early years are the prime time for children's brain development, providing a foundation that is built for life. Significantly, this development depends on the quality and quantity of interactions with adults in the child's life.

1.1 Infant and Toddler Brain Development

Scientists and researchers report that most brain development occurs before the age of four (NAEYC n.d.). The newborn's brain is not fully formed, continuing to develop in the early years as stimulation is received and synapses are used and strengthened or pruned from nonuse. Thus, these early years are critical times in children's lives and essentially determine much of the child's future.

The infant brain absorbs information from the world around it at an amazing rate. The presence of a significant adult, touches, textures, sounds, smells, and tastes all stimulate the developing brain. The infant's brain is rapidly forming trillions of connections, or synapses, that allow learning to occur.

Studies suggest that children's ability to learn can increase or decrease depending on whether they grow up in a stimulating environment (NAEYC n.d.). If the parent or caregiver feeds the hungry infant brain good things (attention, caring, language, and stability), it grows strong. Feed it "junk food" (inattention, neglect, abuse, instability, or isolation), and a child's learning capacity is stunted, perhaps irreversibly.

Whether children spend most of their day with a family member or in a group program, the responsiveness of the primary adult in their life greatly affects their learning and ability to thrive. There are many ways adults can help nurture infant and toddler brain development. Fortunately, the process of supporting that development is easy, as you will see in **Figure 1.1**.

Helping infants and toddlers feel safe, secure, and free to investigate their world provides much of what they need for their brains to develop and for them to thrive. The next section looks at how children learn based on their characteristics by age.

Nurturing Infant and Toddler Brain Development

- Provide an environment free of hazards with responsive, affectionate adults.
- Be gentle; never shake or toss a baby in the air or treat a baby roughly.
- Point out, name, and talk about things around you. It does not matter if children do not understand; they are hearing names, sounds, and the syntax of language. Describe what you and the child see and do.
- Give children different objects, shapes, and textures to touch and handle.
- Remember that play and exploration are how children learn about their world.
- Play music and dance with babies. Clap, hum, or sing in time to the music.
- Listen to infants and pay attention to their attempts to communicate. Respond to coos, babbles, smiles, and gestures as well as to words.
- Share favorite poems, songs, and books.
- Avoid electronic devices. The American Academy of Pediatrics (AAP) advises no screen time for children under two and provides guidelines for children above two.
- Support children's efforts to become mobile.
- Enjoy time outdoors, appreciating the plants, animals, and weather.

Goodheart-Willcox Publisher

Figure 1-1 Fostering brain development is an important part of an infant/toddler teacher's job. Which poems, songs, or books would you share with children if you were an infant-toddler teacher?

☑ CHECKPOINT

1. Other than what you have read in this section, in what other ways do you think brain development can be supported?
2. Why do you think the AAP advises no screen time for children under two?

1.2 How Children Learn

Children's exploration of materials and their interaction with others are the foundation of learning. They learn through their senses and direct, hands-on experiences. Thus, it is essential that children have daily opportunities for such activities in an age-appropriate and individually appropriate manner.

Just as in the example of the orange, children's senses teach them about the world around them (**Figure 1.2**). Their senses bring information to their brain through what they see, the voices and sounds they hear, textures they feel with their tiny fingertips, aromas they smell, and foods they taste. Their senses help them develop the skills needed for a lifetime. Babies' ability to discriminate visually and auditorily (Mommy's face looks different from Daddy's, and their voices are different, too) will help them in time to compare and recognize letters, shapes, and sounds—all vital to becoming literate. Those pleasurable moments spent watching, touching, smelling, and tasting are preparing infants and toddlers for their future.

As they play with blocks, children learn to identify similarities and differences when they consider how some blocks are the same and some are different. They form concepts, see relationships, and make sense of the world as they ponder their surroundings. They learn to recognize cause and effect and figure out why things happen the way they do.

Zefirchik06/iStock/Getty Images Plus

Figure 1-2 All of a young chlid's senses are involved in an experience such as peeling and eating an orange. How does the experience of peeling and eating an orange compare to coloring a drawing of an orange or seeing a photo of an orange?

> **Teaching Tip**
>
> Children are born ready to learn. When adults talk, sing, and play with children, the children are learning in the way they learn best.

Domains of Children's Learning and Development

Children's learning and development are often categorized in domains: physical, cognitive, and social/emotional. Due to its importance, language is sometimes considered separately rather than as a component of cognitive development. The physical domain refers to fine and gross muscle use and coordination. Cognitive refers to thinking skills, including reasoning, problem solving, and logic. The social/emotional domain includes the development of all the relational and coping mechanisms needed for living in a social world. In the example of the orange, the experience included the physical activity of peeling the orange, cognitive skills in considering the makeup of the orange and the vocabulary to describe it, and the social experience of sharing and communicating with others.

Infant Learning

Infants first learn that the world is a good place (or, unfortunately, sometimes an unpleasant place) from the adults' reactions to them and from how well their needs are met. Infants regularly left alone in cribs or ignored may not develop a basic trust that they are important and will be cared for. Impersonal care can be detrimental to the development of a child's self-esteem and well-being. These youngest of humans greatly need the care and attention of adults. This confidence that one will be comforted and taken care of forms the foundation of a child's view of the world.

> **Teaching Tip**
>
> **Learning Characteristics of Infants**
> These characteristics are an important foundation of learning for infants:
> - Infants learn about the properties of materials by handling and exploring them.
> - They learn through their interactions with others and the responses of others.
> - Infants increase their motor skills through their efforts to obtain items they want by reaching, grasping, or becoming mobile.
> - They become aware of their own possessions and will often be comforted by familiar objects.
> - Infants begin to develop preferences and learn to make choices when offered items by adults.
> - They learn that they can make things happen as they repeatedly drop a spoon from a highchair, squeeze a toy, or shake a rattle.
> - Infants begin to develop self-sufficiency as they begin to use a utensil to feed themselves.
> - They respond to voices and faces through their interactions with others, learning social cues.

Toddler Learning

Toddlers are still dependent on adults to see that their needs are met and to gently guide them as they begin to develop more skills. They grow and change quickly, learning to walk, talk, feed themselves, toilet, and use materials of increasing complexity. A teacher of toddlers must understand that toddlers have a strong desire for independence yet are often frustrated when their motor skills do not allow them to do what they want. Furthermore, their verbal skills are not yet sufficiently developed for them to express themselves.

Toddlers need opportunities to use their newly acquired motor skills and language in a supportive and safe environment. They need adults who assist when needed but who understand their often strongly professed need, "Me do it!"

Toddlers are often reluctant to share toys. Consequently, duplicate toys are needed to reduce the frustration inherent among toddlers in groups. Toddlers need an adult to be a secure "home base" where they can get a reassuring hug, venture away to try newly developed skills, and return for reassurance that all is well in their world. It can be confusing to watch a toddler who is growing more independent every day, putting on shoes or feeding themselves, become suddenly dependent with strong emotional displays. The child is struggling between feelings of striking out on their own yet wanting to stay safe by your side.

When you understand the development of toddlers, you can understand why biting sometimes occurs. Toddlers who want an item or do not like something another child does may not have the language skills to communicate. But they do have the physical ability to express their desires by biting. Fortunately, with adult support and increased language skills, biting subsides, to the relief of those who work with children of this remarkable stage.

Teaching Tip

Learning Characteristics of Toddlers
Toddlers still have many of the characteristics they had as infants but are rapidly growing in many skills:
- Toddlers learn about concepts such as size, shape, and weight through hands-on activities using and comparing items.
- They have trouble taking turns with toys or sharing as they become increasingly aware of their own interests and possessions.
- Toddlers imitate others in play as they notice activities going on in their environment.
- They improve their fine and gross motor skills as they become increasingly mobile and strive toward independence in doing for themselves.
- Their sounds or gestures that result in action by others help them learn to communicate their needs.

When toddlers reach up with both arms and an adult picks them up, they learn how to communicate their desire to be picked up. When they go to the door and say "out" and someone goes outside with them, they learn to communicate their wish to go outdoors. When they attempt to put a large peg into a smaller hole, they learn about size and shape. When they select matching shoes to wear, they learn about pairs and uses of items (**Figure 1.3**). The case study "Juan and the Raisin Boxes" illustrates an example of how toddlers learn through their daily exploration and discovery.

Yaoinlove/iStock/Getty Images Plus

Figure 1-3 A preschooler selects and puts their shoes on without help. How does this experience build self-concept, independence, and physical coordination?

Case Study

Juan and the Raisin Boxes

Eighteen-month-old Juan toddled over to bags of empty food boxes sitting in a corner of his classroom. His teacher, planning to set up a grocery store play center, had temporarily placed several bags of items on the floor. Juan, in typical inquisitive toddler fashion, began removing boxes and dropping them on the floor beside the bags. Expressing delight in the experience of control he had, he gleefully explored the contents of the bags.

His teacher, watching from the sidelines, saw a small raisin box briefly catch Juan's interest. After a few seconds exploring the box, Juan deposited it on the floor with the other items. Continuing to remove items from the bags, he found a second raisin box and picked it up. Holding this second box firmly in one hand, he searched the floor for the one he had deposited earlier. Picking up the first box, he studied both carefully, turning them around and over in his hands. Juan's attention focused first on one, then the other.

It was apparent from the expression on Juan's face that he recognized that the raisin boxes were alike. This incident, a relatively brief one in the busy life of a toddler, was significant. At that moment, Juan saw that the two boxes were identical, and he recognized that he had seen others and they contained something he liked.

For years to come, Juan will be called upon to identify likenesses and differences in increasing complexity as part of his education. He will be expected to match items, first in pictures, then in letters, numerals, and other abstract symbols. Now Juan has an advantage. He was given the freedom to explore materials and allowed to make an important discovery for himself. He internalized a concept that, while clearly understood by him, was beyond his capacity to express verbally. He learned in a way far better than any worksheet or workbook could ever allow. His experience was that of real learning—the joy of discovery.

Consider This

1. Why was this event significant?
2. What did Juan's teacher learn about him by observing the activity?
3. How might this experience be used to inform additional planning for Juan?

Preschooler Learning

Preschoolers are increasingly independent and can usually play with others cooperatively. The years between three and five are a time of rapid growth in language acquisition, the social ability to interact with others, and motor skills, especially fine motor skills.

Experiences selected by the teacher should be appropriate for the age of the children and for individual children. For example, most preschoolers can use crayons and have reasonable control over their ability to mark where they want. Some, however, may need chunky crayons so they can better grasp them. While many activities and materials have suggested age guidelines, there is usually a range that may span several years. A knowledgeable teacher looks at children's developing skills to make decisions about what activities are appropriate for each individual child.

Teaching Tip

Learning Characteristics of Preschoolers

As children grow out of their toddler years, they gain many abilities:
- Preschoolers are interested in what makes things happen (cause and effect).
- They learn words in context and have rapidly expanding vocabularies.
- Preschoolers learn to match, identify, and classify items with increased details.
- They are curious and want to explore, sometimes taking risks.
- Preschoolers use their imagination in play and language.
- They ask a lot of questions. "Why" is a favorite word.
- Preschoolers are developing knowledge of numbers and need many experiences with objects.
- They are beginning to understand that pictures, letters, words, and numbers represent things and ideas.
- Preschoolers often take words literally.

Preschoolers often:
- Judge things by how they look. "We went on a walk to look for signs of spring and I saw a playground sign."
- Generalize from their experience. "Last year my teacher went home early and didn't come back. Today my teacher went home early so she will not come back either."

As children attempt to make sense of their world from their experiences and the language they have heard, their logic is often apparent. Consider these examples:
- Four-year-old Ashley saw some cows in a field and told her grandmother she wanted to buy a baby cow because they were all for sale. Her grandmother asked why she thought they were for sale, and Ashley quickly responded, "See the tags on their ears."
- Brandon, almost five, was on a play date at a cousin's house. He became upset when his aunt told him that his mother had called and would be late picking him up because she was "tied up at the office."

Consider This
1. Why do you think Ashley thought the cows were for sale?
2. Why would Brandon become concerned about his mother?
3. How do these examples illustrate young children's thinking?

School-Age Learning

As children become more confident in their abilities and can better express their needs, wants, and ideas, they enjoy projects and activities with small groups of peers. They show increased independence and less reliance on adults for daily tasks as they master many life skills, such as making their own lunch. They relish their mastery of technology and will approach new uses eagerly.

Eager to learn, school-age children actively seek books or information on topics that interest them as they become more adept at reading. They can use writing to communicate, such as writing stories or making lists or notes. They can use math skills in practical ways as they work on self-initiated tasks. As cognitive ability increases, their concepts of the past and possibilities of the future increase, fueled by constant curiosity.

While eager to be a part of the group, school-age children also enjoy solitary pursuits such as puzzles or crafts. Their attention span has increased, especially for topics of interest. Sports, too, may become a focus, as physical activity and teamwork appeal to them.

Teaching Tip

Learning Characteristics of Young School-Age Children
- School-age children still ask many questions as they seek to understand the world.
- They are developing a sense of self-confidence and mastery of their learning, becoming more self-directed and able to plan and carry out projects with minimum adult support.
- School-age children often have a sense of humor and enjoy riddles and jokes.
- They like to talk, use language to express their feelings, tell stories, or make plans, developing their oral language skills and acquiring new vocabulary and sentence structures.
- School-age children are still learning to read and write and are able to read and understand more complex books, both nonfiction and fiction.
- They are developing a better sense of time, including the distant past and future.
- School-age children enjoy collecting things and may spend much time sorting, organizing, and displaying their treasures.
- They enjoy problem-solving and skill-and-challenge games such as scavenger hunts.
- School-age children are better able than younger children to understand and appreciate differences of opinion and points of view.

Learning in Group Programs

In a quality early learning program, you will see happy, involved children. Teachers will be interacting with children and demonstrating a sincere enjoyment of them. There will be order, a pleasant sound level, and children exercising their freedom to move around. Adults will be involved in conversation with children, and children will be engaged with each other. While good-quality, appropriate equipment is important, the essential ingredients in children's learning are adult-child and child-child interactions and their relationships. A caring, responsive, well-trained adult is crucial to a child's development and learning (**Figure 1.4**). The adult should value play and exploration, curiosity, and creativity. These adults are the key elements in children's' learning—physically, socially, emotionally, and cognitively.

The classroom schedule should allow for a balance of large group, small group, and individual activities. This balance provides variety in children's experiences as well as much time for important interactions and experiences. The schedule and daily plan should offer opportunities for child-initiated activities as well as projects with the teacher serving as a facilitator and supporter. The teacher facilitates children's playful learning by providing materials and suggestions, arranging the environment, and selecting equipment and materials according to the concepts and skills needed by the children.

☑ CHECKPOINT

1. Can you give an example of something you learned by doing?
2. How would you explain to someone the importance of talking and interacting with infants?
3. What are ways to support learning with toddlers?

Sturti/Getty Images

Figure 1-4 A teacher gives a high-five to a second-grade child who is proud of the story they wrote. How does appreciation of creativity serve as encouragement for children's curiosity and their willingness to try new tasks?

1.3 Key Theorists and Their Contributions to Early Childhood

What is known about young children's development and learning is based on the work of visionary psychologists and child development specialists who studied and researched the topic. Knowledge of children's learning and strategies to support that learning are influenced by many researchers and theorists whose work has informed current practice.

Jean Piaget

Generally, the phrase *cognitive development* refers to the changes that occur in a person's concepts, abilities, and processes of learning to think and reason. Jean Piaget proposed the most widely known theory of childhood cognitive development in 1969. It was based on the idea that the development of this competence consists of four major stages, which are described in **Figure 1.5**. He also argued that a child's cognitive performance depended more on the stage of development the child was in than on the specific task being performed.

Piaget was a biologist, and he was interested in how an organism adapts to its environment (described as intelligence). He believed that behavior, an adaptation to the environment, is controlled through mental organizations, called *schemes,* that the individual uses to represent the world and designate action. Piaget became interested in how children think, becoming aware that young children's answers were qualitatively different from those of older children. It suggested to him that the younger ones answered the questions differently than their older peers because they thought differently. Piaget was one of the most influential researchers in developmental psychology during the 20th century. He believed that what differentiates human beings from other animals is our ability to perform "abstract symbolic reasoning."

His theory has two major aspects: the process of coming to know and the stages people move through as they gradually acquire this ability. Piaget believed that people use two processes to attempt to adapt: assimilation and accommodation. As people move through life, they increasingly adapt to the environment in more complex ways. Piaget also believed that:

- Children are born with a basic mental structure on which all learning and knowledge are based.
- Physical activity is crucial in the early stages of development.
- All early knowledge comes from the child's physical interactions with the environment.
- All humans seek order and are thus uncomfortable with contradictions and inconsistencies.
- Humans create "filing systems," called *schemas*, in which new information is added. Piaget identified four stages in cognitive development, which are described in **Figure 1.5**.

Many preschool and early elementary programs are modeled on Piaget's theory, which provides much of the foundation for **constructivist learning**, or learning that emphasizes the active role of learners in building their own understanding. Discovery learning and support of the child's developing interests are two main instructional techniques often used in programs for young children today that are attributed to Piaget. Teachers are encouraged to employ a wide variety of concrete experiences to help children learn, such as using manipulatives, working in groups to see another's perspective, and taking field trips.

Lev Vygotsky

Lev Vygotsky was a psychologist who strongly influenced our conceptions of how children learn. He was born in 1896 in Belorussia, and later began his career as an educator and a psychologist. After moving to Moscow in 1924, he set out to create what he hoped would become a new way to understand and solve the social and educational problems of his time.

Stage	Age	Description	Example
Sensorimotor	Birth to 2 years	Infants and toddlers begin to learn about the world through their senses. At first, learning relies on reflexes; but more purposeful movement later enhances learning.	 Daxiao Productions/Shutterstock.com
Preoperational	2 to 7 years	Toddlers and young children communicate through language. They recognize symbols and learn concepts. Both direct experience and imaginative play are keys to learning.	 Odua Images/Shutterstock.com
Concrete operational	7 to 11 years	Children learn to think logically. They can generalize, understand cause and effect, group and classify items, and suggest solutions to problems.	 Collin Quinn Lomax/Shutterstock.com
Formal operational	11 years and older	Children and adolescents master both logical and abstract thinking. This includes making predictions and considering "what if" questions.	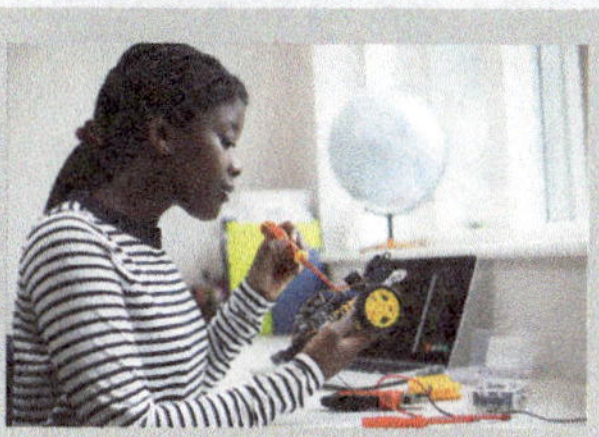 Daisy Daisy/Shutterstock.com

Goodheart-Willcox Publisher

Figure 1-5 Piaget's Stages of Cognitive Development.

His theory is based on the idea that child development is the result of the interactions between children and their social environment, including interactions with parents, teachers, siblings, and playmates. Those interactions also involve relationships with objects, such as books, toys, and cultural practices in which children engage. As a result of these interactions, children construct knowledge, skills, and attitudes and do not just copy what they see.

Vygotsky opposed the psychologists who believed that children's development occurs spontaneously and is not affected by education. He felt that learning could lead to development if it occurs within the child's zone of proximal development (ZPD). The ZPD represents skills and concepts that are not fully developed but will emerge if the child is given appropriate support. For skills and concepts outside a child's ZPD, instructional efforts may fail to produce developmental gains. He used the term *scaffolding* to describe an adult's supportive role in enabling a child to solve a problem, carry out a task, or achieve a goal just beyond the child's ability.

A parent who shakes a rattle just out of reach of an almost-ready-to-crawl infant is making use of the infant's ZPD (**Figure 1.6**). A teacher who turns a puzzle piece to help a child recognize where it fits is scaffolding the child's attempt to complete the puzzle. A parent who pushes lightly on a tricycle to help a child start pedaling is scaffolding within the child's ZPD.

Vygotsky recognized that what was needed to help children develop new skills and concepts took different forms for children at different ages. For example, fostering make-believe play with preschoolers could provide the same support that formal instruction offers for older students. Lev Vygotsky has contributed a wealth of ideas to early childhood education. Most importantly, he has demonstrated how children learn to understand the world around them through adults' interactions.

Maria Montessori

Maria Montessori (**Figure 1.7**), an Italian physician and educator, developed educational methods and materials based on how she believed children learn naturally. She opened her first Montessori school in Rome in 1907, then traveled the world and wrote extensively about her approach to education, attracting many devotees. There are now thousands of Montessori schools following her principles worldwide, and numerous others are influenced by her work.

Milan_Jovic/iStock/Getty Images Plus

Figure 1-6 An infant reaches for a rattle, held just out of reach. Why might the teacher hold the rattle just out of reach of the infant? How is this an example of a child's ZPD?

Wikimedia Common

Figure 1-7 Dr. Maria Montessori's work with underprivileged children in Rome led to many methods still followed today. What are some common practices in early childhood that are influenced by Dr. Montessori?

Maria Montessori was born in Italy in 1870. In opposition to the traditional expectations for women at the time, she entered an all-boys technical institute at age 13 to pursue a career in engineering. Deciding to become a doctor instead, she eventually gained entrance to medical school, becoming one of Italy's first female physicians. Maria Montessori initially focused on psychiatry, later developing an interest in education and educational theory. Her studies led her to observe and question the common methods of the day for teaching children with intellectual and developmental disabilities.

Upon her appointment as codirector of a new training institute for teachers in special education, Dr. Montessori approached the task by observing and experimenting to determine which teaching methods were most successful. She saw that under some circumstances, the children made unexpected gains. In 1907, she accepted the challenge to open a full-day program in a poor inner-city district of Rome. The students, between the ages of three and seven, were usually left on their own while their parents went to work. This center, the first of its kind in the nation, became the first Casa dei Bambini, or Children's House.

The children were interested in solving puzzles, preparing meals, and using the self-correcting learning materials Dr. Montessori had designed. She observed how learning in children is self-directed: They extracted knowledge from their surroundings, essentially teaching themselves. Using observation and experience gained from her earlier work, Maria designed learning materials and a classroom environment that fostered the children's natural desire to learn. She is noted for the development of child-size equipment and for popularizing the concept of children selecting what they do and learn. As the "Montessori Method" began to attract the attention of educators, journalists, and public figures, the popularity of her system grew, leading to the opening of the first Montessori school in the United States in 1911.

Howard Gardner

Howard Gardner is an American developmental psychologist known for his work at Harvard and for his theory of **multiple intelligences** described in his 1983 book, *Frames of Mind: The Theory of Multiple Intelligences*. According to Gardner's theory, humans have different ways of processing information rather than a single general ability. The theory is a critique of the traditional measures of IQ tests that typically account for linguistic, logical, and spatial abilities. Since 1999, Gardner has identified eight intelligences: linguistic, logical-mathematical, musical, spatial, bodily/kinesthetic, interpersonal, intrapersonal, and naturalistic. Gardner and colleagues have also considered two additional intelligences, existential and pedagogical. Many teachers, school administrators, and special educators have been inspired by Gardner's theory of multiple intelligences because it has provided the idea that there is more than one way to define a person's intellect. Gardner's theory of multiple intelligences resonates with many educators because it challenges the one-size-fits-all approach to education that invariably leaves some children behind. His work has significantly influenced the role of educators today.

☑ CHECKPOINT

1. Which of the theorists do you find most relevant to your work? In what ways do their ideas influence you?
2. Why is it important for a teacher to understand child development and what children are like at different ages?

1.4 Interactions That Support Learning

What is known about how children learn comes from the work of the many researchers who have contributed to our knowledge of development, the role of materials and approaches, and the importance of adult interactions with children. This section looks at what early childhood professionals can do to foster children's learning. In addition to planning based on what is known about how children develop, there are some specific ways of interacting with children that help build their cognitive skills.

Case Study

Abigail

Abigail looks at a piece of construction paper she left on a window ledge several days ago. "Look, Ms. Maria, it lost its color. It's not pretty anymore."

Her teacher provided information. "Abigail, I'm glad you noticed that. The sun faded the color. Sometimes when light shines on things the color will get lighter and fade, like this did."

In this situation, Ms. Maria acknowledged Abigail's efforts, reinforced her observations, supported her interest, and used new vocabulary about what happened.

Consider This

1. How could the teacher have responded to help Abigail figure out what happened rather than telling her?
2. In what other ways might the teacher have responded?

Steps to Quality Interactions with Young Children

For interactions that support learning, you can use specific strategies to help make the interactions effective. For one, be attentive to what the child is saying and doing. Connect and let children know that you are interested in what they are doing, saying, or thinking. Extend learning to stretch children's knowledge, skills, thinking, or vocabulary through feedback loops and conversations. Teachers can use specific strategies for quality interactions to help children develop the skills of reasoning and understanding the world around them. Following are some of those strategies.

Promoting Feedback Loops

Feedback loops are back-and-forth exchanges between a teacher and a child that increase the child's understanding of a topic or performance of a skill. Feedback loops are similar to a conversation but with fewer exchanges. For example, a child might say, "I'm going to put my doll in the bed." The teacher might respond, "I'll bet your doll is sleepy. Do you think she is sleepy?" The child replies, "Yes, she is," and leaves to put the doll in the bed.

Holding Conversations

A conversation with children is more than just asking a few questions for the child to answer. It is responding to a child's comment related to what the child has said and encouraging further communication. It is expanding on what the child said in a way that stimulates thinking and additional language use. A conversation involves many back-and-forth exchanges. The child says something, the teacher responds, then the child responds again, and the teacher follows up. The conversation continues with each response relating to and building on the one before. These exchanges increase a child's understanding of a topic as well as help children understand the give and take of conversations. See **Figure 1.8** for an example of a conversation exchange.

Conversations are valuable learning experiences. Here are strategies to hold quality conversations:

- Be nearby to focus on the child, and speak in a pleasant voice.
- Use language the child understands, explaining unfamiliar words through context.
- Relate new information to what the child already knows or has experienced.
- Ask thoughtful questions, and pause to give children time to answer or respond.
- Consider children's feelings, moods, and interests. Do not force a child to participate in a conversation or answer a question.

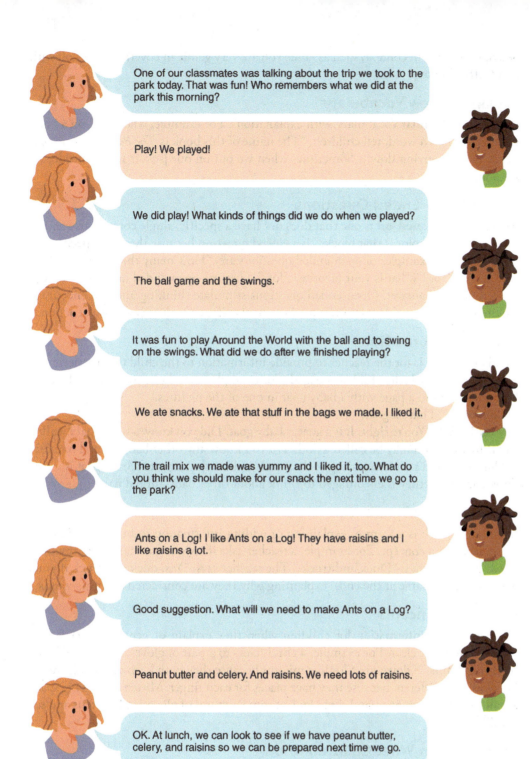

Figure 1-8 An example of a conversation between an adult and a child. Note that the adult does not directly correct the child's grammar. Why do you think that is?

Using Self- and Parallel Talk

Self-talk is describing what you are doing as you are doing it. "I'm going to help you with your jacket now." **Parallel talk** is describing what children are doing as they are doing it. "I see you are giving your baby doll a bath."

Self-talk and parallel talk are in unison with the action. A teacher who states what is being done at the time it is done helps children associate the action with the words. When a teacher states what the child is doing, the child associates the words with what is taking place. Engaging in self-talk and parallel talk provides opportunities to use many descriptive words in context, such as "I see you are very gentle in covering your doll with that fluffy blanket."

Explaining New Vocabulary

Introduce unfamiliar vocabulary with explanations. For example, when reading a book with an unknown word, tell children, "The name of this book is *The Pokey Little Puppy*. Pokey means moving slowly. Sometimes when we put on our jackets to go outside, we are pokey."

Asking Open-Ended Questions

An **open-ended question** is one that does not have a specific, single correct answer. For instance, "What color is that block?" is a **closed question** because there is a specific, expected answer. Examples of open-ended questions are, "How many things can you find that are red?" or "What is your favorite color?" They are open-ended questions because there is no right answer. Open-ended questions stimulate thinking and can encourage children to solve a problem, make a prediction, classify, or evaluate a course of action.

Providing Information

Another strategy is for the teacher to provide information to the child that is relevant to a situation in which the child is engaged. For example, a teacher reading a book about farm life comes to a page with a baby goat in one of the pictures.

Courtney: "That's a goat."

Miss Taylor: "You're right. It is a goat, a baby goat. Did you know a baby goat is called a kid? Just like you may be called a 'kid.' Do you know any other baby animal names?"

Thus, the child's understanding of the word "kid" as the name of a baby goat is introduced, and Courtney is encouraged to think about other baby animal names.

Giving Specific Feedback

Specific feedback is a form of explaining or adding information to build a child's understanding of a concept. For example, a teacher asks if anyone can name two rhyming words. Brandon says, "Duck and truck." The teacher says, "Yes, duck and truck rhyme. They sound the same at the end," explaining why they are considered rhyming words.

Clarifying Concepts

Teachers clarify information for children when they explain or gently correct it in a way that makes it clear. For example, a child refers to a pair of gloves as "mittens." The teacher explains, "Gloves are a lot like mittens because they both keep our hands warm, but gloves are different because they have places for each finger. Mittens have a big space for all the fingers on one hand. Let's look at some pictures of gloves and mittens and see the difference."

Expanding on What Children Know

Another strategy is for the teacher to expand on what children know with comments or questions.

Child: "The kitten wants some milk."

Adult: "Yes, the kitten does seem to want some milk. Kittens also eat solid food, like fish. Do you think the kitten would like some fish?"

Developing Analytical and Reasoning Skills

Teacher interactions with children can help develop skills in thinking and reasoning. Consider this example: A teacher shows some children two containers of markers; one container has more markers than the other. When asked which container contains more, Logan says that he thinks the one on the right does. The teacher asks why he thinks that, then asks how he might find out which container has more. Logan decides to count them.

Offering Encouragement and Affirmation

Encouragement and **affirmation** (acknowledging that something is true) such as, "You really worked on that," often motivate children to stick with a task longer than they might otherwise. For example, children are trying to build a corral for horses, but the plastic fence keeps toppling over. The teacher says, "You're really trying hard to make that fence stay together. And I bet you will figure out how to do it!" As a result of the teacher's encouragement, the children kept trying, and with a little more effort, they got their fence to stay by using playdough to hold it up.

Prompting Thought Processes

To promote children's thinking, teachers can ask questions that encourage children to see connections and to make observations and predictions. Two children are helping with snacks and have a tray of glasses filled with juice. Ming says there isn't enough, and they need more. The teacher asks Ming why she thinks there isn't enough. Asking children to explain their thinking with questions such as, "How did you figure that out?" or "Why do you think the boy is happy to get the new tricycle?" encourages children to think and explain their thinking.

Planning for Development and Learning

Teaching includes planning for what is important in children's development and learning. Here are some strategies that teachers can incorporate to facilitate children's learning through what they plan for each day.

Stating Clear Learning Objectives

The first factor to consider in planning is to determine the objectives. While an activity can be done just because it is fun, the teacher usually has in mind what is desired for children to learn. Are the scissors in the art center because you want children to improve their cutting skills? Do you want them to understand shapes, since you have provided construction paper for them to cut shapes? Or is your goal both? Stating the objective prior to an experience helps children focus on the desired outcome and understand the purpose of the activity.

Supporting Independence

When an environment is carefully arranged, children can take care of their own needs and access the materials they need. Make sure the supplies are accessible without adult help and that children know where to get anything they might need.

Supporting Autonomy and Leadership

Giving children opportunities to be responsible and to choose or lead activities builds confidence and decision-making skills. Some ways to allow children to be responsible include letting one child hold a book while another tells the story, or having one child explain to others how to use the new magnetic figures.

Encouraging Children's Engagement

Consider what materials, physical involvement, and language can be incorporated during an activity. Are they appropriate for the children's age and ability? Will the activity challenge them? In most cases, active engagement will follow when experiences are planned based on the children's interests and what you know about how they learn best.

Using a Variety of Modalities and Materials

Consider what auditory, visual, movement, and hands-on activities can be incorporated into each activity or experience. If you want children to learn about fish, would it be best to have a classroom fish for the children to care for, or simply show a photo and talk about fish (**Figure 1.9**)?

Comstock/Getty Images

Figure 1-9 A child has a turn to feed the fish in this classroom. What are some concepts or skills this child learns from the experience of caring for the fish?

Scaffolding

Scaffolding is the process of giving children a little help when needed but stopping short of doing a task for them. The teacher gives hints when children have trouble with an activity or seeing connections. For example, a teacher helps a child start the zipper on a jacket but then allows the child to complete the task.

Integrating Concepts

Consider what you have done recently that relates to the planned activity. Will the book about bears remind children of Teddy Bear Day last week when they brought their stuffed bears? Will they relate it to the song, "The Teddy Bear's Picnic," from yesterday?

Making Connections to the Real World

Connect activities to something in the children's lives outside of the classroom. For example, when you read the book *The Relatives Came*, children can tell you about relatives who visited them.

Including Opportunities for Creating

Provide materials for children to create something related to the activity that is their own idea. Could they draw a picture of themselves and their relatives who visited after hearing the story *The Relatives Came*? Could they act out a play or a puppet show of the story? Maybe make up a song about relatives? Creating something that relates to an experience provides opportunities for children to build on the experience in meaningful ways.

Advancing Language

Children can learn multisyllable words when the words are presented in context or with explanation. Consider how advanced language relates to the activity. Decide how the new words relate to familiar words the child knows and how you can explain what the new word means. In talking to a child on a tricycle, the teacher asks, "Where are you going in your vehicle? Did you know your trike is a type of vehicle?" or "What is your destination? Where are you going?" Using unfamiliar vocabulary in context helps children understand meaning.

Following these general strategies for supporting children's learning, this textbook addresses specific activities that promote cognitive development. These activities are listed under the age range for which they are intended. However, the development and needs of individual children should always be considered when planning activities.

☑ CHECKPOINT

1. How do open-ended questions build thinking skills?
2. Describe an example of scaffolding.
3. Why are conversations with children important?

1.5 Promoting Cognitive Development

Cognitive development comes both from interactions and from the many opportunities for exploration and discovery. See **Figure 1.10** for age-related ways to provide an environment for children to have those opportunities.

Creating an Environment That Encourages Exploration and Discovery

When you think of classrooms of many decades' past, visions of children at desks reciting by rote likely come to mind. A quality early learning program today looks very different. Children move about, engaging with other children and materials and talking about what they are doing. In general, it is a place where children explore and discover through intentionally selected materials and experiences guided by the teacher. Here are some of the ways an adult can set the stage for exploration and discovery in an early learning classroom:

- Organize and display learning materials logically by categories and attributes:
  "All the colored blocks go here. The animals go in the box on the shelf."
- Display materials that encourage children to make discoveries:
  "What did you see when you used the magnifying glass to look at the seashells?"
- Provide materials that encourage children to sort, classify, and order, such as buttons, bottle caps, parquetry blocks, and shells:
  "Tell me how you decided to separate the buttons."
- Provide materials that match the children's skill level and challenge them to extend their learning:
  "Here is a scale, a stamp and pad, and a mailbox for your post office."
- Offer open-ended materials:
  "You may use this fabric however you choose."
- Call attention to sensory experiences as children use materials and participate in routines:
  "How does finger paint feel when you spread it on the shiny paper?"
- Offer materials that encourage children to explore and make predictions:
  "What do you think will happen to the sand when you spray it with water?"

Helping Children Develop Problem-Solving and Other Cognitive Skills

Problem solving involves thinking of and trying out solutions to problems. It requires knowledge of how things work but also consideration of possibilities. Children learn to solve problems when faced with opportunities to figure out how to do tasks and how they can create items. Here are some ideas to create an environment that encourages problem-solving and other cognitive skills:

- Be patient and supportive as children explore and experiment.
- Accept and respect children's responses to challenges.
- Allow time for children to think about tasks and possible solutions.
- Scaffold by offering help a little at a time and only what is needed.

Age	Ways to Foster Cognitive Development
Infants  *Goodboy Picture Company/Getty Images*	• Play interactive games like Peek-a-Boo and This Little Piggy. • Tell the child what you are doing when you do it. "I'm going to pick you up, clean your face, and change your diaper." • Talk about what is happening in the environment. "Look at those leaves blowing! It's a windy day." • Comment on what the child is doing. "I see you have a big smile on your face this morning. You must be happy today." • Respond to infants' efforts to interact. When a baby smiles, smile back. When a baby coos or squeals, do the same or respond with words. • Offer toys and items with various textures, colors, shapes, and sizes. • Enjoy books together. Select books designed for infants that can be handled and even mouthed. • Sing simple songs such as "You Are My Sunshine" or "Five Little Ducks." • Talk to babies about what you think they are trying to communicate or accomplish. "It looks like you want the truck. Let me help you get it." • Respond to nonverbal cues such as gestures. • Talk during mealtimes, playtimes, and routines. Although infants cannot use words to communicate, hearing adult language is important for language learning. • Value floor time as a time for exploring and interacting.
Toddlers  *BananaStock/Getty Images Plus*	• Play "Follow the Leader" and "Simon Says" to help toddlers follow directions and learn to perform daily tasks. • Play along with dress-up and make-believe to spark imagination. Act out simple scenes from favorite stories together. • Use music and art to inspire creativity. Toy instruments, recordings, paper, paint, and crayons teach about sound, color, and texture. • Provide items for toddlers to organize and group by type. Grouping and sorting are the beginning of classification. • Provide building blocks and take-apart toys for toddlers to learn how things work. • Talk about what is happening at different times during the day, such as mealtimes, rest time, and outside time. • Follow the child's lead in play and make comments, describing what the child is doing. • Support budding language skills by "filling in the gaps" for children. • Ask many open-ended questions to encourage toddlers to explore language and learn to communicate. • Ask questions that involve children making choices and honing reasoning skills.
Preschoolers (3 to 5 Years)  *Andresr/Getty Images*	• Provide dolls, puppets, and playsets for children to explore different roles, situations, and feelings. • Explain the day's plans to help children understand routines and learn what to expect. • Include play in small groups to teach cooperation, sharing, and compassion for others. • Support children as they experiment and grow in developing language by listening and responding to their questions and comments. • Play simple board games together to teach how to take turns and follow rules. • Discuss situations depicted in books. Ask open-ended questions to build understanding and stimulate thinking. • Enjoy poems, riddles, and jokes together. • Model making up your own songs and encourage children's efforts to do so. Use a familiar tune with new words. • Encourage children to talk about their experiences.
School-Age (5 to 8 Years) *FatCamera/Getty Images*	• Provide many opportunities to use language: storytelling, conversations with peers, and written communication. • Use math in practical applications and challenges, such as figuring out what it will cost to purchase and set up a cage for a school hamster or how long it will take to go on a field trip. • Provide tinkering space to support planning, problem solving, and constructing. • Help them see things from other children's perspectives and begin to understand how their behavior affects others. • Propose activities that help them understand concepts of space, time, dimension, fantasy, and reality. • Make use of their increased attention span and memory. • Provide time for them to follow their interests and pursue knowledge and projects that they choose.

Goodheart-Willcox Publisher

Figure 1-10 Ways to foster cognitive development for each early childhood education (ECE) age range.

- Encourage consideration of multiple approaches to solutions.
- Model problem-solving yourself. Use "self-talk" as you figure out how to complete a task. Problem-solving opportunities can occur throughout the day as a part of children's activities.

Here are suggested steps to involve children with the process of figuring out how to do a task:

- **Discuss the situation.** What is the problem? "I see you are trying to get your paper trees to stand up, but they keep falling down."
- **Encourage children to generate many possible solutions.** "What might you do to make your trees stand up?"
- **Plan how to implement the most feasible solution.** "Do you want to try your idea of using chenille strips or popsicle sticks?"
- **Implement the plan.** "Do you want to show me how you use the popsicle sticks to hold up the trees?"
- **Assess the results.** Did the solution work? If not, what else might be tried? "Which do you think holds your trees up best? Is there anything else you want to try?"

Sometimes children surprise adults with their insight and demonstrate unexpected understanding, such as what happened in the "Seeing Beyond the Obvious" case study.

Case Study

Seeing Beyond the Obvious

The children in a kindergarten class had been on a field trip to a local farm, where they rode on a horse-drawn hay wagon, watched cows being milked, and saw tractors working in the cornfields. Montez, the teacher, had taken photographs of the trip, and the children dictated and wrote stories about the experience in their journals.

Montez had brought in farm magazines and placed them in the art area for collage constructions. She had farm-type clothes in the dress-up area, farm puzzles in the manipulative area, and a wooden barn with farm animals with the blocks. Some of the children even painted with bundles of hay and made prints with the corncobs they had brought from the farm. They read many books about life on a farm.

To conclude this project on farming, the class was making a large mural of things they would see on a farm. Satisfied with the two-week project, Montez watched to see what the children depicted in this concluding mural project. She planned to take photographs and make anecdotal records to put in their portfolios. Then, surprising after all her hard work, one of the younger children in the group, Kelly, drew some balls, dolls, and a tricycle on the mural. The teacher's first reaction was to wonder if Kelly had totally misunderstood the purpose of the project since all the other children were cutting out or drawing the typical farm animals, crops, barns, and implements.

Fortunately, Montez took time to ask, "Kelly, tell me why you chose to draw toys?"

"See," said Kelly, matter-of-factly and without even looking up from her work, "The children who live there could play with them." Kelly's response emulated the complete confidence that children have when they expect that everyone ought to see what they see.

Instantly, Montez remembered that the farm they visited was a family farm, and the children in the kindergarten class were very much aware that three young children lived there. She remembered, too, that some of the books she read were stories about children living on a farm. Montez was glad that she asked for an explanation. Kelly's answer showed insight and recognition of relationships that were not as readily apparent as the more expected and obvious cutouts and drawings of horses, cows, and barns.

From Kelly's teacher's point of view, she was helping children learn about farms. From Kelly's perspective, she made the association that farm families often included children who, like herself, would own and enjoy toys. Without communicating with Kelly and looking beyond her own expectations, Montez would not have realized that Kelly's seemingly inappropriate picture showed a depth of understanding that was not anticipated.

Consider This
1. Why is it important to ask children to explain why they responded in a particular way?
2. Why was Kelly's choice insightful and appropriate?
3. What would have been the effect if Montez had just told Kelly her drawing was wrong?

An effective teacher takes what is known about children's development and learning and creates a plan for each day's experiences. This plan, usually based on a curriculum, guides the *what*, *when*, and *how* of children's learning.

✅ CHECKPOINT

1. Why is knowledge of child development important in planning for children's learning?
2. Why is problem-solving an important cognitive skill?

1.6 What Is Curriculum?

At its simplest, curriculum is defined as "what is taught, how it is taught, and when it is taught." However, deciding what to teach—as well as how and when to teach it—is influenced by what knowledge and skills are viewed as important for young children. Selections are also influenced by the expected role children will have in making choices about what and how to learn and what organization of learning experiences is most likely to yield maximum results.

Curriculum includes everything that goes on in a program from the moment a child arrives until the child's departure. It is an ongoing process that requires teachers to think about child development, observe how children are learning, and make hundreds of decisions about the best ways to help them reach their full potential. Teachers plan, implement, observe, reflect, and adjust based on both group and individual needs.

> **Teaching Tip**
>
> **NAEYC**
> The National Association for the Education of Young Children (NAEYC) is the largest and oldest professional organization working for the well-being of young children. In a position paper, "Early Childhood Curriculum, Assessment, and Program Evaluation," the organization states, "Curriculum, [is] thoughtfully planned, challenging, engaging, developmentally appropriate, culturally and linguistically responsive, comprehensive, and likely to promote positive outcomes for all young children (NAEYC 2003)."

The components of curriculum are the content—what children are to learn—and the learning process—how children learn developmentally. A curriculum includes instructional strategies—how teachers teach young children—and describes the environment—what is needed and how the room is arranged for learning to happen. Lastly, a critical component of curriculum is assessment—how to know that children are learning and how to determine whether adjustments need to be made.

Overview of Effective Curriculum

A good curriculum provides a vision of what a program should look like and a framework for making decisions about how to achieve that vision. It provides teachers with a context for creating quality early childhood experiences.

Usually, a curriculum is based on or aligned with national or state standards or those established by a professional organization. These standards are collections of research-based and field-tested developmental indicators. A curriculum that is aligned with standards is one that includes experiences that help children reach the indicators of skills and knowledge identified as appropriate for various ages in the standards.

Most quality curricula provide a means of ongoing assessment as a basis for planning and individualization. This process of assessment is important in helping teachers know how individual children are progressing, what the children need, and how to best plan for them. It has provisions to adapt to meet children's individual needs and to provide for children with special needs. It should be based on research that acknowledges and supports diversity and equity. All these components assist teachers in working intentionally with daily plans and experiences by serving as a guide for selecting and conducting the experiences. A good curriculum makes provisions for enhancing family involvement and provides professional development for staff who will be using the curriculum. Most of all, an effective curriculum is developmentally appropriate and based on what is known about how children learn.

Basic Elements of Developmentally Appropriate Practice (DAP)

Developmentally appropriate practice (DAP) promotes optimal learning and development for children (**Figure 1.11**). It is an approach that focuses on each child, recognizing the child as an active participant in the learning process—one who constructs knowledge through interactions with others and the environment. The teacher serves as a facilitator, helping children make meaning of the various activities and interactions throughout the day. Creating a developmentally appropriate early childhood program is a process that emphasizes the whole child, providing many opportunities for independent exploration with concrete, hands-on experiences in all domains.

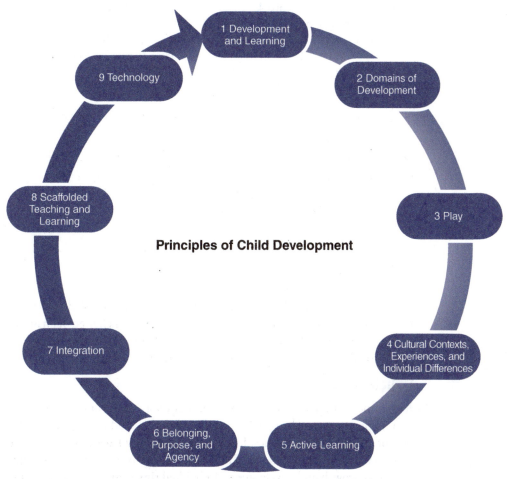

Goodheart-Willcox Publisher

Figure 1-11 Illustration of important considerations in education. How does this diagram demonstrate important areas of knowledge that are necessary for teachers?

Teachers guide and expand experiences through facilitated play and seek to expand and enhance learning by asking thought-provoking questions such as: "In how many ways can you show me about your trip this weekend? How did you think of making a sign to show that the dramatic play area is a bakery? What else tells people it is a bakery? How can you make your clay dog's ears stay on? What have you already tried?" Such thought-provoking questions promoting problem-solving and critical-thinking skills are important in young children's cognitive development.

The concept of DAP arose from the work of the **National Association for the Education of Young Children (NAEYC)** NAEYC is a large nonprofit association in the United States representing early childhood teachers, para-educators, center directors, trainers, college educators, families of young children, policy makers, and advocates. In promoting DAP to create high-quality experiences for children, NAEYC identified guidelines for teacher effectiveness. These guidelines reflect best practices in early care and education. DAP values individual children's interests and ability levels and practices that allow them to make choices and emphasize play and enjoyment. NAEYC offers the following ten effective teaching strategies for all children, including those with special needs.

Teaching Tip

NAEYC Teaching Strategies for Children with Special Needs

- Acknowledge with positive attention what children say and do. "You are such a good friend to help Victoria clean up the paint spill!"
- Encourage persistence and effort rather than only praise for the result. "I can tell you are really working hard at that task!"
- Be specific with feedback. "That was smart to use the stapler to attach the fabric on your cardboard house."
- Model desired behaviors and attitudes such as approaching problems and treatment of others. "Thank you for bringing the torn book to me. We can fix it now."
- Demonstrate a new task. "May I show you how to open that box?"
- Create or add a challenge. "You worked that puzzle really fast. Here are some with more pieces. Want to try a harder one?"
- Ask questions to encourage thinking. "How did you figure out that tape would work better?"
- Give assistance as needed. "Let me hold your sleeve, and you can put your arm through the opening."
- Provide information and facts. "The plant needs sun to live and grow, so I guess we should put it in the window."
- Give directions positively—tell children what to do rather than what not to do. "Let's walk in the room," rather than, "Don't run!"

Age-Appropriate

Programs for children should be based on professional knowledge of what is developmentally appropriate for each age group. Children grow and change in an anticipated sequence. A single age group (all 2-year-olds, for example) has different needs from a mixed-age group in a home day care, where the children may range from infants to school-agers.

Individually Appropriate

Each child is unique, and thus grows and develops according to their own individual pattern. A program that is developmentally appropriate addresses and celebrates the uniqueness of children. Personalities, learning styles, family backgrounds, and cultural heritages will vary greatly from child to child. While there is a general, anticipated timeframe for children's growth and development, individual timeframes will vary. You must understand individual interests, abilities, and family background before you can meet the needs of each child. Goals and objectives should be determined for individual children. Learning is best when new information builds on prior knowledge and each child has different experiences. Planning should center on the child, the family, and the child's everyday experiences.

Culturally Appropriate

Children cannot be separated from their family and culture. Developmentally appropriate practices mean that activities should respect family differences and wishes. Involve families in the program as much as possible, realizing that each family has a different way of contributing. Some families may choose to be very involved, and some may choose minimal involvement.

Child-Initiated and Child-Directed Learning

Child-initiated learning focuses on each child's interests, abilities, and learning styles, placing the teacher in the role of facilitator rather than director of learning. The child-initiated activity is distinguished from random activity. Children who choose or create an activity are likely to be engrossed in that activity, exploring materials with interest and curiosity, trying out ideas and involving themselves in their environment.

In **child-directed learning**, children carry out an activity as they wish, but within a framework provided by an adult who supplies the resources from which to choose. However, this does not mean that children should be allowed to do anything they want, whenever they want. It requires children to be active, responsible participants in their own learning. They choose what they will learn, how they will learn it, and sometimes how they will assess their own learning. The classroom environment and materials in the setting play a key role for this type of learning to occur.

Teacher-Initiated and Teacher-Directed Learning

Much of the difference between **teacher-initiated learning** and child-initiated learning is in who starts and controls the activity. In **teacher-directed learning**, children participate in activities designed and overseen by the teacher. The teacher is at the center of the learning process. In teacher-directed activities, the teacher decides what the children will learn, how they will learn, and how they will be assessed on their learning.

Creating an intentional and a planned framework for learning and providing materials and activities consistent with what is known about how children learn are the major tasks of the adults in a developmentally appropriate classroom. Teachers create learning opportunities in which children can have control and make choices based on their interests and abilities. They provide materials and supplies and ask questions that encourage inquiry, thought, discussion, and reflection by the child rather than expecting simple "right" answers. Teachers support the expansion of ideas by offering suggestions, providing information, and even participating in activities as a play partner.

Young children learn best by being immersed in their environment as active learners following their interests. For example, if a child is interested in frogs, the best way to teach about frogs would be to study a live frog, allowing the child to observe, hold, and care for the frog while guiding the child's learning through thought-provoking and open-ended questions. DAP requires that teachers follow the children's lead and allow them to discover answers for themselves. The least effective way to teach the child about frogs would be from a worksheet or another one-dimensional experience.

The term *developmentally appropriate practice* means teaching young children in ways that meet them where they are as individuals and as a group and supporting each child in attaining challenging and achievable goals that contribute to ongoing development and learning. The NAEYC's position statement *Developmentally Appropriate Practice* (NAEYC 2020), which forms the basis for DAP, defines six key aspects of good teaching (**Figure 1.12**).

Another consideration is how the curriculum provides for teacher intentionality, implementing learning experiences with purpose and intent. Teachers must know and understand why they are doing what they are doing. This understanding is crucial to implementing a curriculum with fidelity. The factors in **Figure 1.13** are interrelated and make up the educational components, or building blocks, of the program.

Six Key Aspects of Good Teaching

1. Creating a caring community of learners
2. Teaching to enhance development and learning
3. Planning appropriate curriculum
4. Assessing children's development and learning
5. Developing reciprocal relationships with families
6. Demonstrating professionalism as an early childhood educator

Goodheart-Willcox Publisher

Figure 1-12 Six key aspects of good teaching. Do you think any of these is more important than any other? Why or why not?

Building Blocks of a Developmentally Appropriate Program

- Goals for children's development and learning
- Experiences through which they will achieve these goals
- What staff and parents do to help children achieve these goals
- Materials needed to support the curriculum

Goodheart-Willcox Publisher

Figure 1-13 A developmentally appropriate program should have each of these. Is there anything else you feel should be included?

A Quality Curriculum

Usually, a program selects a comprehensive curriculum that addresses the whole child and all domains of development—physical, cognitive, social, and emotional, as well as the content areas of literacy, math, science, social studies, and the arts. A comprehensive curriculum provides goals and objectives to support both social and academic areas of growth. It includes commonly accepted skills and knowledge that children should acquire at various ages.

The content of an effective curriculum is interesting, inviting, and intriguing. It is play-based and focused on the interests of the child. The curriculum assists the teacher in setting up an intentional environment that builds on prior learning and experiences. The experiences that the teacher provides are thus planned with purpose and intent.

When an effective curriculum is implemented properly, children will flourish. You will see children engaged in play, interested in what they are doing, and actively using materials with respect and purpose. They will choose a task and follow it through to completion. They will be building language through conversation, and social and emotional skills will be apparent in interactions with peers.

A quality curriculum has activities that support multiple goals and build upon prior learning. For example, a teacher might first introduce a simple pattern of blocks—red, blue, red, blue, and so on. Later, the teacher could expand on that concept by making the pattern more complex, such as yellow, blue, green, yellow, blue, green.

A quality curriculum is likely to benefit children. It promotes a balance of planned experiences (based on helping children progress toward meeting defined goals) and spontaneous experiences (based on children's interests).

Benefits of a Quality Curriculum

There are many benefits to using a research-based curriculum, even with infants. First, a quality curriculum ensures that children have a variety of experiences, which might not happen if there is neither planning nor guides to follow. A quality curriculum also assists in balancing the activities for all domains of development.

When a curriculum is appropriate for the group of children and well implemented, children will be happy, engaged, and learning. A well-developed curriculum provides for repetition and reinforcement of content and skills with variety. Children are more likely to see and understand relationships when they are planned. Here are some other benefits of using a well-planned curriculum:

- Children are more likely to benefit from the experiences and stay engaged.
- Available activities and choices make planning easier for teachers.
- The experiences address all domains of development.
- Parents understand more about what children are learning.
- Preparation for substitutes is easier.

Following the curriculum plan can be a time-saver for busy teachers. Curricula that include activities and instruction can be a ready source of ideas, saving time in researching, locating, and planning appropriate activities. In addition, many curricula include adaptations of activities for children with different strengths and needs (**Figure 1.14**). The teacher can select activities or adaptations that fit the children's abilities to build on their strengths and needs.

With a quality curriculum, teachers have guidance about what should be happening in their classroom and in knowing they are meeting the educational needs of the children and the expectations of families. Most effective curricula provide both teacher-initiated work (including small-group planned experiences) and freely chosen, yet instructive, playful learning activities supported by teachers. A well-developed curriculum relates to *how* children learn, *what* learning looks like, *when* it is developmentally best learned, and *where* in the classroom environment the teacher creates learning opportunities.

An appropriate curriculum has benefits for all participants: It benefits the administrator, who has chosen a specific set of guidelines for staff, the children, and their families. It benefits the teacher, who understands the expectations for the children, and

Olesia Bilkei/Shutterstock.com

Figure 1-14 A child who has special needs completes an activity to encourage development of fine motor skills, an area of need identified by their teacher. How has the teacher included this child with their peers? What might the teacher do to further include the child with their peers?

the families, because they know their children are getting what is needed. Most of all, it benefits the children by providing optimum growth and development.

Choosing a Curriculum

Choosing a curriculum requires considerable thought on the part of administrators and teachers in an early learning program. First, consider whether it is based on child development and designed for the way young children learn. Does it require children to sit for long periods or do inappropriate paper work? Is it mostly teachers talking or giving children information? These factors do not represent the biological needs of young children. Other questions to consider in selecting the most appropriate curriculum depend on factors such as those shown in the Teaching Tip feature, "Questions to Consider When Selecting the Most Appropriate Curriculum."

Teaching Tip

Questions to Consider When Selecting the Most Appropriate Curriculum
- Is there research-based evidence to support the effectiveness of the curriculum?
- Is the plan balanced, including teacher-facilitated and child-initiated experiences?
- Does it match your goals and objectives for the children?
- Is it correlated with or aligned with state or national early learning standards?
- What additional or specific materials are required or recommended?
- Does it address the environment, such as how the room should be arranged?
- Is the cultural and racial diversity of families represented in the materials used and in the experiences?
- Does it support equity among children?
- Is there a family component to help families understand why their children are doing or not doing certain activities?
- Does it address active play, quiet play, and rest times?
- Are the children's interests, needs, and abilities the focus of planning? Are the children active participants in their own learning?
- What are the roles of the teacher and the children in the learning process?
- Are all domains of learning addressed?
- Is there guidance for differentiating instruction for various skill levels or children with special needs?
- Is an assessment system provided?

In today's world, it is important for the curriculum to address the psychological needs of children in addition to their cognitive needs. When considering a curriculum, you also want to determine how it addresses children's needs to feel secure and accepted and how it creates and supports a culturally responsive home-school connection and involvement.

Because development in young children does not proceed in discrete domains but overlaps, the curriculum must be holistic, encompassing all areas of development and ensuring continuity as children age. To effectively implement the curriculum, staff must recognize that the curriculum is intended to be used as a dynamic resource that unfolds in response to the developmental needs of each child in the program.

Types of Curricula

While there are many types of curricula, most can be classified into one of three types. The types considered in this text are described here.

Purchased Prepackaged Curriculum

A commercially available curriculum is prepared for the teacher, who is expected to follow a guide to teach and use the activities and materials included or recommended.

Often these additionally depend on standard classroom materials to conduct some activities. A research-based purchased curriculum provides teachers with security in knowing that they are providing children with a solid educational plan. Teachers sometimes need to know exactly what to teach and how to teach it.

Theme-Based Curriculum

Curriculum based on themes may be purchased or created by the teacher. The teacher chooses themes that are expected to be interesting and appropriate for young children and selects resources and activities based on the theme.

Emergent Curriculum

Emergent curriculum is based on the interests and needs of the children in the group. As children show interest in a topic, the teacher facilitates activities by providing materials and resources to support the children's exploration of the topic.

Children bring ideas into the classroom that promote topics of study for themes. A parrot brought from home can motivate children to focus on birds. A turtle found on the playground generates interest and becomes the catalyst for a study of reptiles and their characteristics (**Figure 1.15**).

There are many benefits to emergent curriculum because children tend to be more engaged when they are interested in their chosen topic and therefore gain knowledge, often at a complex, in-depth level. Children have genuine enthusiasm for learning because they are focusing on a topic of interest. Their enjoyment of learning helps create a lifelong love for learning. Fewer behavior problems occur, and the day goes better because children are productively occupied.

There are other types of curricula that are not discussed here. Each program must organize its resources, assess the children's interests, decide on the type of curriculum that best suits the program, and then use that curriculum to plan its approach. See **Figure 1.16** for some approaches that influence many programs today.

Creativa Images/iStock/Getty Images Plus

Figure 1-15 A child joyfully observes a turtle's movement. How might a teacher take advantage of this child's interest in the turtle to encourage language and literacy development?

Various ECE Programs and Their Characteristics

Program	Characteristics
Project Approach	A method of teaching in which an in-depth study of a particular topic is conducted by a child or a group of children. Based on the belief of supporting children's interests and drive to construct their own knowledge is important, the project approach is incorporated into the curriculum but may not always constitute the entire curriculum.
Reggio Emilia Approach	This method focuses on a child's natural development. It is child-centered and directed, taking the philosophy that learning must make sense to the child to be effective and meaningful. The approach was founded in the villages around Reggio Emilia, Italy, after World War II.
HighScope	HighScope is based on a system of children planning what they will do, carrying out the plans, and reflecting on what they learned; this is often referred to as "plan, do, review." The system grew out of the often-referenced Perry Preschool Project, which documented the system's effectiveness.
Montessori	Montessori is a system of teaching young children devised by Maria Montessori that emphasizes learning through the senses and guidance rather than control of the child's activity, encouraging self-education. The system makes use of unique materials designed by Dr. Montessori.

Goodheart-Willcox Publisher

Figure 1-16 Review the characteristics of these ECE programs. Which of these aligns the most closely with your values and ideas?

Finding Out Children's Interests

There are many ways to discover children's interests. You can observe them during play to determine what they are talking about, ask them and see what they bring up—for example, a family vacation at the beach.

Often, unexpected events will capture children's attention. While these experiences are not planned, they can be incorporated into the program in ways that comply with standards and curriculum goals. An astute teacher can use the children's motivation to include the event as a part of the curriculum by investigating what resources and activities in the curriculum relate to the topic, then analyzing the children's needs that can be addressed around the topic. Suppose a child comes in and announces that a kitten has come to live with them, and the other children begin to talk about their own pets. The teacher can find resources and learning activities about kittens and the other pets in the curriculum by reviewing what children need to learn as a result of their assessments and beginning a theme about pets to take advantage of the children's current interest.

Components of a Quality Curriculum

While you have seen the value of a quality curriculum, you have also seen that there are variations in approach. This section looks at the components that are generally accepted as determining a quality curriculum, in that the curriculum meets the needs of children and families.

Schedules and Routines

Schedules are important in conducting a curriculum because much of the curriculum for young children relates to the everyday activities in the classroom. Part of effective curriculum implementation is following a current, age-appropriate schedule. The schedule should be posted in the classroom in a space that can be seen by teachers, substitutes, administrators, families, and anyone else interacting with the children.

The daily schedule is created and used as a guide to tell everyone what they will be doing throughout the day. A **visual schedule**, or a schedule with photographs representing the major events of the day with time and simple text, can also be utilized by children as young as 2 (**Figure 1.17**). The schedule not only guides the day, but it also serves as a framework for the teacher's planning. Almost all activities represented on

Case Study

The Fallen Tree

Here is an example of an emergent curriculum experience. It was a rainy day at the child development center, and occasional booms of thunder meant children needed reassurance. As the children were looking at the weather and discussing the thunder and lightning, they heard a loud, roaring sound and watched a large tree fall and crash across the drive into the parking lot, clearly blocking the entrance. None of the teachers in the program had "tree falling" in their lesson plan that week, but that changed quickly.

The focus continued, with several classrooms taking mini-field trips out to see the fallen tree after the storm subsided. They watched as workers came to cut the tree into pieces so that it could be removed and the driveway cleared. At the request of several teachers, the workers cut some wood into large circles, making what the children referred to as *tree cookies*, which were taken into classrooms for further exploration. The children made tree rubbings, counted the lifelines of the tree, painted the slices, and rolled them around the room, even making chairs by sitting on stacks of them. One teacher located hard hats and orange vests, offering them to the children who became "tree cutters." Those tree cookies stayed in most of the classrooms for the rest of the year. If anyone noticed them and asked the children about the tree cookies, they told the entire story in great detail with much passion and sweeping gestures.

One child, however, did not enjoy the newly emerging topic. Christopher, a three-year old, had a hard time sleeping for days and cried whenever he was near a tree. His teacher took the following approach to the issue of the tree with Christopher and his class: They took a walk around the building and pushed on the large trees and shook the smaller ones so that he would know they were still sturdy and in the ground. Christopher's class talked about all the benefits of trees and how they help us. They collected items that had fallen from the trees. His teacher brought pictures that showed the roots of large trees and discussed how they help keep the tree upright and anchored in the ground. These activities helped Christopher recover from his fear of trees and enriched the learning for all the children.

This tree example is the reality of emergent curriculum. The teachers could not have predicted nor planned such a week. It was a natural event that the children talked about for months. The value of what they learned was unexpected but important—and it all grew out of an unplanned and unexpected event.

A baby brother or sister is born, a grandparent visits to show something from long ago, or a tree falls across the street. These things and more happen all around people regularly. Yet teachers may mistakenly stick to their weekly plans, missing the prime opportunity to build on what children want to learn.

Consider This

1. What concepts did children likely develop from the experience of the fallen tree?
2. What additional activities could relate to the incident?
3. What do you think about the teacher's handling of Christopher's reaction?

Alexandra B Dolgova/Shutterstock.com

Figure 1-17 This classroom poster shows the sequence of events of a child's day in picture form. How does such a chart help children understand time? Why is understanding what happens next important to young children?

the daily schedule are moments in which learning can be facilitated and, as a result, be incorporated into planning.

The schedule is one of the elements of the classroom that makes learning visible. It not only includes those activities typically associated with early education, such as circle or whole group time, center time, or outdoor time, but it also shows when smaller events such as routines and transitions will occur. Finally, the daily schedule provides predictability by listing the events of the day in order and providing approximate times when each activity should begin and end.

Consistent daily schedules are important because young children need predictability. They need to know what is going to happen now and what is going to happen next. It is important for routines and activities to occur in the same order each day. This order, or routine, is more important to children than the specific time at which the activities occur. For example, although ending circle time at exactly 9:30, washing hands from 9:35 to 9:45, and beginning snack time right at 9:45 is not necessarily important to children, doing these activities in this specific order (circle time, handwashing, then snack time) *is* important.

When children experience and can rely on elements of predictability such as these, their feeling of security increases, and they feel as if they have a greater sense of control. Typical routines such as arrival and departure, diapering and toileting, handwashing, and snack time and mealtime are integral parts of the daily schedule. These times are also opportunities for learning.

Transitions, or times between activities, are times in which curriculum-aligned activities can occur. Teachers can plan and establish ways to facilitate learning during these "in-between" times. Such activities might include singing a song while waiting for everyone to get their jackets on, describing items being served while waiting for lunch, or enjoying a quiet story while settling down for rest time. Planning for these times helps ensure that transitions are smooth.

Children coming together as a group at the beginning of the day is often called *group time*, *circle time*, or *morning meetings* (**Figure 1.18**). During these times, all areas of development may be addressed in a social setting. Songs, fingerplays, dramatic play, science, math, and physical activities can take place during group time. Group times can support themes and projects. During group time, planning should include alternating active and quieter experiences. For example, a teacher might sing a song with children, then read a story, conduct a fingerplay or action chant, and then tell a flannel board story.

During learning center and outdoor times, children are free to pursue their own interests and select the activities in which they will participate. Ample time should be allowed for children to become absorbed in their activity. When planning and implementing the daily schedules, teachers must consider how long it takes children to fully engage in an activity, how long they can maintain attention during an activity, and how long it takes them to transition out of one activity and into another.

A developmentally appropriate and well-developed schedule considers the characteristics of children as a group and as individuals. A schedule must be based on children's current level of development and learning in addition to their physical needs, interests, and skill levels. Teachers must consider what elements of a schedule are necessary to

FatCamera/Getty Images

Figure 1-18 Children participate in a morning meeting and discuss the events of the day. What else might children do during a morning meeting or circle time?

promote development and learning throughout the day, how long each of these activities takes, and the priority each of these elements has in the daily and even weekly schedule. For example, teachers know the importance of reading to children multiple times during the day; therefore, reading with children should be incorporated into the schedule at various points during the day.

Themes

For many teachers, using themes is a natural outgrowth of what is going on in children's lives. Teachers want to introduce children to their communities and assist them in making connections with the world around them. In the fall, teachers may introduce an apple theme or information about fall. In October, they read books about harvest time or how the weather is changing and the leaves are turning. In November, the topic of conversation and activities is often Thanksgiving. December brings discussions of celebrations and holidays.

Using a theme approach is one way to organize information for children. Focusing attention on one aspect of their environment assists children in becoming more knowledgeable and understanding of their world. Children may notice subtle changes in fall leaves, but they may not know that this time of year is a season we call *fall* or *autumn*. Reading books, telling stories, and introducing songs and fingerplays about fall help children attend to the seasonal changes during this time of year.

Other common preschool themes are home, family, pets, neighborhoods, friendship, the body, the five senses, health and safety, community helpers, transportation, shapes, colors, numbers, and the alphabet. The typical selection of themes relates to relevance to the child and the teacher's recognition that some topics are important for concept acquisition.

Themes can be used for a brief time, but they often last a week or two to provide an in-depth exploration of a topic. One theme often leads to another; for example, pets may lead the children's interests to wild animals, what veterinarians do, or categories such as birds or ocean creatures. The teacher's role in planning themes is to note children's interests by observing and listening to the children's discussions, questions, and play (**Figure 1.19**). Play cues can aid teachers in choosing new topics. By making a wide variety of toys and materials available to children, teachers can help them develop their own interests.

Planning for Themes

Some of the knowledge that children acquire happens when they ask specific questions in interactions with their teachers. These interactions are often referred to as **teachable moments**, and they are important in children's development. When children ask questions, the

ChristinaFelsing/iStock/Getty Images Plus

Bohdan Bevz/iStock/Getty Images Plus

Figure 1-19 A child examines a leaf from the playground. Later, the children use paper cuttings to depict their experience with trees in the fall. What else might the teacher do to take advantage of the children's interest in the leaf?

knowledge they acquire is relevant to them because they want to know the answers right then. Relevance is critical to the success of teaching and learning.

Listen to children and watch for their interests. A child who just got a new puppy is going to be very interested in anything about dogs. That child will want to hear stories about dogs, sing songs about dogs, and make dogs from playdough. The child might also make a dog pen in the block area or paint a picture of the new puppy.

Teaching Tip

Creating a Theme Plan

How does one go about planning to use a theme approach? The first step is to select the theme. Themes should be selected that relate closely to the child's immediate world. For example, activities associated with home, family, and neighborhoods hold the most meaning for very young children. As children develop, their knowledge base and interests expand, and their topics for themes can broaden. For the topic to be successful, there are several questions to consider:

- Does the topic address children's interests?
- Is the topic relevant to children's experiences?
- Is the topic age-appropriate and culturally appropriate?
- Are resources such as people to talk to, places to visit, objects or living things to observe and explore, books, songs, and other relevant materials available?
- Can children apply a variety of skills to exploring the topic?

The second step in creating a theme plan is to decide how to implement. This requires one to:

- Gather resources for information and activities.
- Evaluate the resources for age, cultural, and developmental appropriateness.
- Select or create an activity to introduce the theme.
- Decide which activities will be whole group, interest center, or individual activities.
- Decide on a logical and reasonable timeline.
- Gather needed materials and supplies.

The third step in using a theme plan is the actual implementation. This requires one to:

- Introduce the theme.
- Evaluate as you go, adapting or changing as necessary and making notes for reference.
- Communicate successfully with parents and other teachers.

Creating a Yearly Themes List

Look at your school year and plan to focus on themes that naturally fit certain months or seasons. For example, plants are a good theme for the spring because there will be much new growth and flowers will be blooming. Families is a good theme for the beginning of the year when you are getting to know new children and their families.

Concepts

Concepts are general ideas that foster understanding. Understanding that wheels are round is an example of a concept. Knowing that plants are living things and need water and sun are examples of concepts. As teachers plan themes of study, they should consider the concepts that they expect children to learn.

For example, pretend that you are a teacher who wants to teach children about good health habits, which is a popular early childhood theme. As you formulate concepts, you also think about how children will learn them. Do you have resources for developing activities and experiences? Do you have children's books in your classroom that will help children learn about healthy practices, or will you need to go to the library? What songs do you know or have you recorded about washing hands or sneezing into an elbow?

Generally, teachers think about school resources, possible literature, and community resources as they plan a theme. Once the resources are located, materials are gathered, and the activities are planned, it is time to implement the planned theme.

Teaching Tip

Working with Mixed Ages

Mixed-age groups are common in family child care and in some center-based programs. In such arrangements, there is a need to adapt activities due to the range of ages. Take, for example, tying shoes. Older children who have mastered this skill can help younger ones. The older child has the opportunity to develop verbal skills to communicate the steps to the younger child; thus, the younger child learns how to tie shoes. In many ways, the older children mentor the younger.

An older child may read a story to a younger child, pointing out letters and words as they read. The older child solidifies reading abilities, while the younger child develops listening and early reading skills. Of course, safety issues must be considered in mixed-age groups. For example, small parts that may be available to preschoolers would be a choking danger for younger ones. Here are additional considerations for mixed-age groups:

- A school-age child can be allowed more freedom than a toddler. Independence should be allowed as appropriate.
- Older children enjoy planning and conducting events such as puppet shows or art activities for younger ones, thus developing leadership skills.
- Older children can have their own activities while younger ones are resting or napping.
- Routines such as mealtime can be used to provide individual time with children.
- Children develop a sense of family with their classmates, who support and care for each other.
- Older children model problem solving, and younger children accomplish tasks they could not do without assistance—a dynamic that increases the older child's level of competence.

Use the range of ages for everyone to benefit. Encourage older children to help younger ones, but avoid depending so much on older children that they are not challenged themselves. Have a wide variety of equipment with a range of difficulty so all ages have toys and materials to use; for example, provide books with a range of difficulty. All children may enjoy books, but the story line and format of the books can make them appropriate for various ages. Open-ended materials such as LEGO® or DUPLOS® are very versatile and work with a wide range of ages.

Consider This

1. Give an example of ways to allow older children greater independence than younger children.
2. What are some ways in which children develop leadership in mixed-age groups?
3. How can you take advantage of routines to promote learning?

Curriculum Adaptations

A *curriculum adaptation* is the alteration of an activity or materials to facilitate or increase children's engagement. Adaptations may make it possible for children of different ages and abilities to benefit. These modifications are usually small changes that do not significantly affect the scope and sequence of the curriculum. They simply provide for more participation for the children involved. Even the best curricula and well-developed lesson plans will not always meet the needs of all children. Therefore, additional steps may be taken through modifications to facilitate development and learning for some children.

Children whose home language is not English will benefit from adaptations. Children may need activities adjusted to include instructions, labeling, explanations, and other elements in their home language to facilitate participation and learning. Most curricula have a variety of suggested activities from which to choose. However, all children may need and can benefit from modifications at some point to help facilitate their engagement, learning, and development.

Guidance for Differentiating Instruction

In the example in the case study "The Fallen Tree," children and teachers found ways to learn from that unexpected event, and children pursued different interests. How do you provide differentiated instruction for children of various ages, stages of development, abilities, and interests? One specific example is providing various types of puzzles with different levels of difficulty so children can select one that is challenging but achievable. Some puzzles have knobs or only a few pieces for children with coordination difficulties or younger children. Floor puzzles involve gross motor effort. Puzzles with numerous pieces can challenge more advanced children. There are many opportunities in your daily work with children to adapt activities so that all children can take part and benefit.

Perhaps you are a family child care provider and have toddlers and preschoolers. How do you meet their different needs based on their development? What if you work in a school setting? The children likely have a wide range of interests and abilities. Even if you teach in a kindergarten with all 5-year-olds, you may have a child with special needs. Too, any group of children, even if they are the same age, will have a range of abilities and interests based on their development and opportunities.

Curriculum for Infants and Toddlers

Yes, a curriculum is necessary for infants and toddlers. Within everyday routines, it is the interactions and how adults respond to infants with words, actions, gestures, and emotions that are critical to helping children grow and develop. These responses must be dynamic enough to move and flow daily with the infant's developing interests and changing needs.

☑ CHECKPOINT

1. How would you describe what constitutes a quality curriculum?
2. What do we mean by age-appropriate and individually appropriate?
3. How does child-initiated differ from teacher-initiated?

1.7 Implementing Curriculum

The successful implementation of any new curriculum involves thoughtful planning and work on many levels. Designing and implementing a long-term, well-articulated plan requires a shared vision with colleagues. Communication about the plan must be considered so that everyone knows what is expected and what resources are available to support the work. Curriculum requires a vision of what teaching and learning should look like and a thoughtful team that shares responsibility for developing, communicating about, implementing, supporting, monitoring, and evaluating the plan. The curriculum implementation plan should include:

- **Expectations.** A plan should describe what is expected and how people will be supported. Expectations must be reasonable and communicated clearly and consistently.
- **Resources.** Thinking about resources in the broadest sense—including materials, people, time, and money—is essential. Teachers must have convenient access to the materials needed to facilitate implementation.
- **Professional development.** Deepening teaching and learning requires a commitment to sustained professional development. All groups—teachers, teacher leaders, teacher aides, coaches, educational specialists, and administrators—need professional development and support designed to meet their specific needs to ensure that the curriculum is implemented with fidelity. Who will lead such professional development, as well as how it will be scheduled and funded, must be considered.
- **Working with families.** Families need to know why your curriculum provides for child-initiated activities and how this approach encourages learning. The plan should include how families can learn about and participate in the work of improving learning for their children.

Discovery Journeys

Cooks, Chefs, Conductors, and Supermarkets

Selecting and using a curriculum is very similar to the experience of cooking with a recipe. Like a novice cook, teachers with little early childhood experience might need a curriculum that specifies in detail what to do. This approach helps ease concerns about knowing they are providing the children in their program with a good educational plan. But the experienced cook or chef will take a basic recipe and what is known about food preparation and vary or alter it according to personal taste and dietary needs. In the same way, the experienced and knowledgeable teacher will use a more basic plan, and adapt, add to, and enrich the plan for the particular children and their learning needs.

Just as a conductor takes the musical score as published, yet may adapt it to personal taste, musicians' availability, and expertise, the teacher uses the curriculum as written but adapts it for individual children. Like the conductor, most of what the teacher does is designed to make all parts work together for a harmonious whole. Just as in a symphony, the whole orchestra plays—perhaps only the violins or wind section, or there is a solo from the first cellist—the children sometimes work together—sometimes in small groups, and sometimes alone—with the teacher as a facilitator.

Effective teaching of young children requires many of the same skills as both a supermarket manager and a symphony conductor. Just as a store manager stocks items in a logical manner with a detailed sense of organization, a successful teacher provides logical organization to learning centers. Just as the manager places tortilla chips near a jar of salsa to suggest relationships and make purchases convenient, the teacher places a book about trucks with miniature trucks in the block area or cards and envelopes in the writing area just before Mother's Day. Too, the manager must understand the customers and the culture of the shoppers. A local supermarket may not have stocked kale, quinoa, yucca root, or wasabi years ago, but those items are widely available now as interest in healthy eating has led customers to try new foods. A manager who wants to be successful must be aware of what the customers want and need, just as an effective teacher must be aware of what the children want and need and make those items and experiences available.

These analogies may help you recognize that working with young children requires much more than simply knowing what children need to learn. The type of curriculum, organization of the classrooms, and execution of the daily plan by the teacher are as important as the role of the chef, orchestra conductor, or supermarket manager in the success of those entities.

Consider This
1. How might teaching young children compare to running a restaurant?
2. What are other occupations you might compare to being a teacher?

Planning for Daily Experiences

Teachers plan the activities they want to use for children to develop the skills and understand the concepts important to the topic. An introductory activity that will catch children's attention is one way to begin. Often, a quality book will focus children's attention on the topic that the teacher is introducing, or a visitor to class can generate interest. In the case of a topic based on an event, such as the fallen tree in the case study, the event itself becomes the catalyst. With a healthy habits theme, you might invite a school nurse to visit and talk about the job, explaining what a nurse does at work. Often, someone with special equipment or paraphernalia or dressed in uniform will interest children.

Another approach to building interest in an upcoming theme or topic is to set up a discovery table. A discovery table is a spot in the classroom used to display objects and artifacts about a topic. Science and social studies materials or books that relate to the theme are popular. Children have opportunities to explore the materials independently, and teachers may plan an activity using the discovery table as a focal point (**Figure 1.20**).

Teaching Tip

Seven Strategies for Implementing Curriculum

Whether a curriculum is purchased or developed, it is important that it be implemented in the way the developers planned it. Here are seven strategies for successfully implementing the curriculum into the program:

1. Thoroughly read any manuals, guidelines, or directions provided with your curriculum, exploring the scope and sequence. Be sure you understand the design of the curriculum and how it is organized to implement the curriculum with fidelity and get the intended results.
2. Ensure that you have all the materials needed. If you do not have some of the items, what can you purchase or substitute?
3. Have a strategy and schedule for training. Training may be available online from the curriculum vendor, your local child care resource and referral agency, or another agency or individual.
4. Make a plan for communicating with families about your curriculum. Helping families understand what you are doing will encourage them to support your efforts.
5. Arrange for ongoing support through coaching and feedback. Learning new skills or ways of working takes time. Do you have a coach or mentor who can help? Can you help each other?
6. Consider how to evaluate your progress. Will you discuss progress at staff meetings? Will you use a checklist or other system to keep a record of what you have accomplished?
7. Set deadlines and responsibilities. Setting a deadline helps you stay on track with meeting your goals. Clear responsibilities help everyone share the work.

Consider This

1. Why do you think deadlines and clear responsibilities are important to this process?
2. How does evaluation of progress help with implementation?
3. How do coaching and feedback support fidelity of implementation?

lithiumcloud/iStock/Getty Images Plus

Figure 1-20 Children explore natural items and clay on this discovery table. *How might this discovery table serve as an introduction to a theme of fall? What else might the teacher have put on the table to encourage interest in fall changes?*

For the healthy habits theme, a discovery table might include medical kits, photos, books about nurses, and scrubs to try on. Miniature figures of nurses and doctors and toy medical kits are available through commercial suppliers and make appealing additions to a discovery table.

Activities are specific experiences planned to achieve understandings and developmental goals. Making a mural about a field trip, building a hospital in the block area, or dancing like butterflies are activities. Activities are encouraged and supported by the materials made available in the learning centers. By providing the materials and activities, teachers open the door to child-directed activities and playful learning.

Group or individual projects may be ongoing or brief. They might be child-directed or teacher-initiated. Allowing the child to set the pace and the means of exploration will lead to new ideas and experiences. Projects can be as simple as comparing the leaves from the plants in the classroom or as broad as bringing in community helpers to explain their work to the children.

Whatever is planned must be flexible to adapt to the needs of the children and opportunities unknown during initial planning. One way to provide flexibility is through the use of learning centers to support the theme. Learning centers can be supplied with materials that change according to changing themes and play an integral part in the curriculum when equipped with props related to current themes. In the case study "Salina and the Fire Station Field Trip," you can see how one experienced teacher plans and assesses the experiences.

Curriculum Fidelity

Whichever type of curriculum is used, it is important to implement it according to its guidelines. Quality purchased curricula are typically tested and researched prior to being put on the market. As such, the effectiveness of the curriculum is based on consistency in use.

Implementing the curriculum with **fidelity** is a key factor in using it appropriately. What is meant by curriculum fidelity? In a nutshell, fidelity means using the curriculum and following teaching practices consistently and accurately, as the developers intended. It means that the curriculum is responsive to children's and families' strengths, needs, interests, and cultural and linguistic backgrounds. Manuals, guides, and professional development support understanding and consistent implementation for fidelity.

When a curriculum is comprehensive for the age group with which it is used and is carefully chosen to align with desired standards, it should be followed as intended, because research on effectiveness has been based on systemic use. It usually includes activities or procedures to address all domains, or it may be based on a specific philosophy or system.

Curriculum fidelity does not mean doing everything on every page of the curriculum guide or administering every assessment or activity. It does not require that all providers have identical styles or that everyone be on the same page at the same time or even the do same activity on the same day.

Fidelity requires the following considerations:
- **Delivery.** Children's engagement is one of the NAEYC criteria for an effective curriculum. Does the adult conduct the teacher-initiated activities in a way that interests and engages children?
- **Setting.** The setting must support the curriculum. A curriculum based on learning centers requires scheduled time for children to use the centers. Is the environment supportive, and does it provide for a focus on children in the way the curriculum plan indicates?
- **Target population.** The curriculum for preschoolers is very different from the one for second grade. One for infants or toddlers differs from one intended for preschoolers. Is the curriculum being used with the correct age range?

Case Study

Salina and the Fire Station Field Trip

Salina, a preschool teacher, follows a theme-based curriculum that includes a module on Community Helpers. Salina noticed that children were excitedly discussing the various fire trucks that pass occasionally from a nearby station. She decided to use the topic from her school's curriculum and formalize activities related to fire fighters and their work. She found standards and benchmarks in her state social studies standards that relate to this topic.

Salina reviewed the standards and the suggested activities in the Community Helper module in her curriculum. She chose activities to develop concepts and skills she knew the children should learn and included plans for a field trip to the nearby fire station. Prior to the trip, she read books in group time about firefighters and trucks. In doing so, she addressed other state standards related to literacy. Prior to and during the walk to the fire station, Salina emphasized safety; thus, she also addressed standards related to safety.

While at the fire station, children saw and heard about the purpose of the various trucks and equipment used. They learned about the firefighters' jobs and how they work closely with the police to keep families safe. Children learned about fire and weather safety and how to report emergencies, addressing additional safety standards.

Once back in the classroom, Salina provided fire trucks, fire chief and police cars, wooden firefighter and police figures, and related items in the block center. She had plastic fire helmets in the dramatic play center and puzzles of various difficulties with firefighters and trucks on them in the math and manipulative center.

Children eagerly headed to the centers to use the props. Salina watched as they reenacted the field trip, built a fire station of blocks, and painted fire trucks with the red paint she provided at the easel. Her knowledge of children and their development led her to expect that the materials she provided would generate productive, child-initiated activities.

At circle time, Salina asked the children about their favorite fire vehicle they saw on the trip. She graphed the children's responses, thus addressing a math standard. She needed to assess what the children knew and had mastered to see what they still needed to learn. Here are the skills and how Salina assessed them from the experiences:

- **Understanding of graphing**—Children participated in an activity of graphing vehicles. Salina documented their understanding of this comparison more or less with a photo of the completed chart.
- **Understanding of more than and less than**—Salina watched for opportunities throughout the day to question more and less and used a checklist to record children's use of the terms.
- **Classifying**—Children demonstrated understanding of classification by completing an interest center activity classifying photos of vehicles, clothing, and tools used by firefighters.
- **Vocabulary**—Salina observed the use of new vocabulary in the block center, math and manipulative center, and dramatic play center as children reenacted their experiences. She made anecdotal notes in children's records and documented the vocabulary they used.
- **Sequence**—Children participated in completing a documentation chart (a poster with photos in the order that an event happened with captions describing what happened) by arranging photos of the trip in the correct order and dictating captions using the words *first*, *next*, and *last*.

Salina used the information for documenting learning and for future planning. This documentation served as an assessment of the experience. This scenario illustrates how one activity can relate to several standards and how learning can be reinforced through a variety of related and integrated activities.

For planning, Salina considered the children's interests arising from the experiences and reviewed curriculum material for related themes. For example, another community helper, such as a police officer theme, could grow from the fact that police and firefighters often work together. Safety might be another theme to develop next because some safety concepts grew out of experiences. For more information on assessment and the use of portfolios, see Chapter 7.

Consider This

1. How did Salina know that children are beginning to understand the work of firefighters?
2. How did the props Salina put in the dramatic play, block, and math and manipulative learning centers support children's learning and encourage child-directed learning?
3. What purpose did the documentation chart serve?

- **Professional development.** Many curricula have associated training either online or in person. To understand the curriculum, teachers must have the knowledge and skills to use it effectively. Has the teacher participated in specific training related to the curriculum being used? Has coaching and mentoring been provided to support ongoing improvement?

- **Teacher qualifications.** Knowledge of child development, standards, and assessment is needed to appropriately meet the needs of individual children. Does the teacher have adequate experience and qualifications, such as knowledge of child development, desired outcomes, and appropriate concepts?
- **Materials.** An effective curriculum must have the required materials available. Does the program have the necessary equipment and supplies, as well as any supplemental materials needed?

Accompanying assessments are designed with the expectation that the curriculum will be followed as intended for program monitoring or program evaluation. Fidelity is based on adherence to philosophy, approaches, goals, and objectives. It requires following the program's sequence and pacing and using the recommended equipment or materials. Making adaptations to the program should not significantly change its nature or intent.

Scope and Sequence

The sequence of activities is very important in the curriculum design. The curriculum guide or training materials should address whether activities should be in a particular sequence.

The National Center on Early Childhood Teaching, Development, and Learning states that an organized developmental **scope and sequence** outline what the early childhood curriculum focuses on and how the plans and materials support children at different stages of development (U.S. Department of Health and Human Services 2022).

They identify the scope as:
- encompassing the areas of development addressed by the curriculum, including breadth (development across all developmental domains) and depth (specific developmental goals), and
- being able to be applied across multiple learning experiences to facilitate engagement and sustain children's interest in exploring and learning.

The same document defines the sequence as follows:
- includes the materials and plans needed to facilitate learning experiences that support and extend children's learning across developmental areas and levels, and
- is made up of a progression from less to more complex, supporting children as they grow and develop.

According to the document, an organized developmental scope and sequence:
- helps staff support children's development of skills, behavior, and knowledge described in early learning and development standards.
- includes examples of materials, teaching practices, and learning experiences that support children at different levels of development.
- allows flexibility to respond to the needs of individual children, including dual language learners and children with disabilities and other special needs.
- provides information to staff that helps them plan and communicate with families and other education partners.

The scope and sequence are important in that they outline the learning experiences specifically for various levels of development and are a tool for planning experiences tailored to children's age and development level. Pacing is another important consideration when following the scope and sequence and in planning for and scheduling activities. Teachers must plan so that children will have the opportunity to experience the full curriculum during the school year.

Planning

Another essential element of curriculum implementation is planning. Teachers should follow the scope and sequence of the curriculum when making daily or weekly plans. Many curricula include a template for a daily or weekly plan designed specifically for that curriculum. Some centers create their own format that is unique to their program. Or a particular format may be used by a school system.

Basically, planning is the process of selecting activities and deciding when and how the experiences will occur. Lesson plans help the teacher make sure that the needed items are available.

Not only should these activities align with the curriculum, but they must also be developmentally appropriate—appropriate for the ages and abilities of the children in the classroom. Activities that are too hard can lead to frustration, and those that are too easy do not facilitate learning and development. Therefore, it is important to use the curriculum's scope and sequence to look ahead to see where children's development is heading and then intentionally scaffold their learning.

Curriculum, Standards, and Assessments

As the nation puts more focus on standards, curriculum developers are working to make sure their materials align with those standards (**Figure 1.21**). School systems, funding agencies, and other stakeholders may look at child outcomes to measure effectiveness. If the curriculum is not implemented as designed, the assessment tools used may not give a true picture of effectiveness.

Standards, curriculum, and assessment together help teachers decide how activities may fit together to benefit children's growth:

- Standards state what children should know and be able to do within a range of ages.
- Curriculum guides the activities that enable children to meet the standards.
- Assessments help determine if children have the specific knowledge and skills identified in the standards.

A quality curriculum that is aligned with standards is a roadmap for meeting the criteria of those standards. The assessment process is what gives the teacher the information needed to implement the curriculum effectively. Curriculum and assessment are also closely related. Most purchased curriculum include assessment tools to help teachers plan how they can best meet children's needs. Here are some considerations for including assessments as a part of the curriculum:

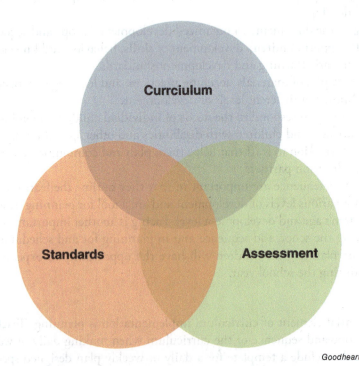

Goodheart-Willcox Publisher

Figure 1-21 This Venn diagram illustrates how the components of curriculum, standards, and assessment are used together to support children's learning. How are the three components related? In what ways should they each inform planning?

- Is the assessment based on the curriculum? If not, how do you know that children are learning what you intend?
- Is the assessment information used to build on children's strengths and identify areas where children need experiences from the curriculum or how to modify practices to best meet children's needs?
- Are the assessments used to communicate to parents how and what children are learning?
- If the curriculum is based on state standards, are you using an assessment aligned with state standards?
- Is the assessment system reliable and valid? Does it address the goals and objectives of the curriculum? For example, a curriculum that emphasizes social development should be accompanied by assessments of the children's ability to cooperate with others, make friends, and play with others.

In quality environments where children thrive, responsive adults understand developmental needs and know how to interact in ways that develop children's skills. Their interactions significantly impact young children's brain development. These effective teachers are able to follow children's interests, and above all, enjoy the challenges and rewards of working with young children.

Three fundamental considerations should guide teachers in their decision making about your early learning programs: Your curriculum must (1) reflect developmentally appropriate practices, (2) meet professionally created standards, and (3) be based on what is known about how children learn. The remaining chapters of this text explore more in depth the content of early childhood curriculum and other components of working successfully with young children.

☑ CHECKPOINT

1. What are some benefits of an emergent curriculum approach?
2. What are some benefits of a theme-based curriculum?

Chapter 1 Review and Assessment

Summary

1.1 Explain infant and toddler brain development and how to nurture it.
- Helping children learn involves the experiences and interactions they have with significant people and objects. Adults are important factors in stimulating brain development and thus children's learning.
- Promoting children's cognitive development includes creating an environment that encourages children to explore and discover; interacting with children in ways that help them develop confidence in their ability to think and solve problems; and providing opportunities for children to construct knowledge about their world.

1.2 Describe how children learn and how to support learning.
- Children learn through their senses and need experiences to understand the world.
- Infants learn through their senses and from the reactions of others.
- Toddlers grow and gain skills rapidly and need many opportunities to use their developing motor and language skills.
- Preschoolers gain abilities with increased motor and verbal skills.
- School-age children are more independent and in control of their learning.

1.3 Identify key theorists and their contributions to early childhood.
- Jean Piaget's work laid the foundation for understanding the need for concrete experiences.
- Lev Vygotsky used the term *scaffolding* to describe a supportive role for adults in children's learning.
- Maria Montessori is known for an approach to children's learning based on independence, choice, and self-paced learning.
- Howard Gardner held a theory of multiple intelligences: linguistic, logical-mathematical, spatial, musical, naturalist, bodily/kinesthetic, interpersonal, and intrapersonal.

1.4 Describe the value of interactions that support learning.
- Interactions encourage children to think about what they can and cannot do.
- Conversations, feedback loops, and open-ended questions encourage children to think and use cognitive skills.

1.5 Identify a variety of methods to stimulate cognitive skills.
- Interactions with books, singing, talking, and toys support children's learning.
- Simple games, dramatic play, music, art, and conversations with others are important in young children's development.

1.6 Identify indicators of a high-quality curriculum.
- A quality curriculum must be developmentally appropriate and implemented with fidelity.
- The National Association for Young Children has developed and published guidelines for quality curriculum.
- A quality curriculum provides for child-initiated and adult-initiated activities.
- A quality curriculum is research-based and follows developmentally appropriate practices.

1.7 Explain how to implement a curriculum with fidelity.
- Teachers must understand the scope and sequence, materials provided, and goals for children in the curriculum design.
- Coaching and professional development are beneficial in implementing a curriculum with fidelity.

Recall and Application

1. **True or False.** Children's brains are fully developed at birth.
2. **True or False.** Adult interactions with infants support the infants' brain development.
3. **True or False.** An example of self-talk is teachers describing their own actions.

4. ____ development is the process of learning to think and reason.
   A. Physical
   B. Social/emotional
   C. Cognitive
   D. Creative
5. **True or False.** The zone of proximal development (ZPD) refers to what the child already knows how to do.
6. ____ developed the use of child-sized equipment and materials.
   A. Montessori
   B. Piaget
   C. Vygotsky
   D. Gardner
7. ____ viewed intelligence as taking many forms.
   A. Montessori
   B. Piaget
   C. Vygotsky
   D. Gardner
8. **True or False.** Open-ended questions require only one-word answers.
9. **True or False.** Children primarily learn through interactions with people and objects.
10. **True or False.** The environment can support exploration and discovery through organization.
11. **True or False.** A play-based curriculum does not allow for adult-directed learning.
12. A quality curriculum should be based on ____.
    A. research
    B. intuition
    C. internet searches
    D. picture books
13. **True or False.** The teacher should not deviate from the plans in the curriculum manual.
14. **True or False.** Fidelity means adhering to the purpose, goals, and objectives of the chosen curriculum.

Part 2

Environment

Chapter 2: The Early Childhood Learning Environment
Chapter 3: The Inclusive Classroom
Chapter 4: Planning for Playful Learning
Chapter 5: The Basics: Safety, Health, and Nutrition
Chapter 6: Engaging Families

Chapter 2

The Early Childhood Learning Environment

Standards Covered in This Chapter

NAEYC

NAEYC – 1d, 2c, 3a, 3b, 4a, 4c, 5a, 5b

DAP

DAP—1d, 1e, 4b, 4c, 4d, 4e, 5a, 5b, 5d

Learning Outcomes

After reading this chapter, you should be able to:

2.1 Describe the characteristics of the physical environment in an early childhood classroom.

2.2 Name and describe at least five learning centers appropriate for preschool children.

2.3 Explain some ways in which the environment affects children's behavior.

2.4 Understand the social and emotional environment of an early childhood classroom.

2.5 Describe the teacher's role in preparing, supervising, and supporting children in learning centers and in the overall environment.

2.6 Identify specific guidelines for evaluating each common learning center.

2.7 Explain ways to communicate with families about appropriate environments.

Chapter opener image credit: kot63/iStock via Getty Images

Key Terms

aesthetics
dyad
environment
indirect guidance
learning center
picture symbol chart
tummy time

Introduction

Teachers must understand the impact the learning environment has on young children's cognitive, physical, and social/emotional development. The **environment**—the furniture and materials in the room and how they are arranged—greatly affects what children learn. The environment affects everyone. Look around you and notice how you and others react in various settings. A towering, majestic, gothic cathedral suggests quiet, reverent calmness; a cavernous skating rink or gymnasium brings to mind noisy, boisterous activity.

When creating an effective early childhood environment, teachers should consider both the physical space and the emotional climate. In this textbook, the term *emotional* generally includes social aspects. A classroom may be very well equipped with appropriate materials and activities, but unless children feel secure and comfortable there, the program will not be effective. Planning the environment entails looking at how space, materials, schedules, and routines can be used as resources for constructing interesting and enjoyable places for children.

The *indoor environment* includes everything that affects the child inside, all equipment, materials, interactions, and activities within the physical building. The *outdoor environment* encompasses all equipment, materials, and activities that happen outdoors. This chapter addresses the physical and emotional climate of the indoor environment. Chapter 13, "Outdoor Play and Nature," addresses the outdoor environment.

This chapter provides many practical suggestions for making the environment work for children through the materials selected and how they are arranged within the classroom. It addresses how to create an engaging, secure environment that encourages play, exploration, and learning.

2.1 The Physical Environment

The physical environment plays a vital role in young children's learning. The classroom environment is a major component of the curriculum for young children. For the environment to enhance learning, it must first be safe, healthy, and developmentally appropriate. Children's physical, emotional, social, and cognitive development should be supported by the environment. Following are some general guidelines for arranging the indoor environment to support children's learning.

Room Arrangement Guidelines

Following these guidelines will help ensure that the classroom is set up for safety and children's learning:

- Avoid arrangements that create hidden areas that hinder supervision. Ensure that teachers can see all areas without obstruction.
- Rooms that are slightly longer than wide are somewhat easier to arrange and encourage movement.
- Use tables, shelves, and learning center furniture to control traffic patterns and prevent interruptions of activities in the learning centers.

Case Study

Environment Influences Behavior

The impact of the environment on behavior was brought to life for Yolanda, a preschool teacher, by a public function in which she participated some years ago. Picture a large, community-wide planning event. Participants chose to attend one of several concurrent sessions according to their interests. In one session, the room was the appropriate size for the 20 people present. Chairs were in a circle, and interaction was excellent. Individuals, eager to share their ideas, interrupted each other with suggestions and comments in rapid succession. The facilitator was barely able to write fast enough to keep up with the brisk pace of the group's ideas.

Another session that same day was held in a large convention bay with chairs set up in an auditorium style. The facilitator had great difficulty getting any comments or suggestions from the audience. The chairs were set up far back from the facilitator, creating a somewhat intimidating situation. This distance, coupled with the lecture-expected setup in the much-too-large room, stifled interaction. The first room favored the exchange of ideas; the other inhibited interchange. This incident demonstrated for Yolanda the extent to which room arrangement affects participation.

Yolanda remembers this experience in relation to the importance of the environment for children. When arrangement affects adult behavior in such extreme manners, it is easy for her to understand that it can also affect children's behavior.

Consider This
1. How does expected behavior differ when attending a sports event in an arena versus a concert in a theatre?
2. In what ways have you seen room arrangements affect children's behavior?

- Include materials that are representative of the cultures of the children in the classroom. Familiar materials help children feel welcome and secure. The materials selected should avoid cultural stereotypes.
- Provide enough choices for children so that when they wish to change activities, they have a variety of options.
- Allow enough room between furniture for teachers and children to move easily. Consider space for wheelchairs and walkers if needed.
- Designate places for backpacks and jackets and for children to put items to take home.
- Leave an open space for active play.
- Put items in the area where they are to be used.
- Reduce clutter by storing extra materials in cabinets, closets, or drawers.
- Provide for private time in a quiet space.
- Place play materials on shelves so that the children can easily see and reach items they want.
- Label each learning center and post the number of children who can use it at one time to prevent crowding and maintain comfort.

Providing for Whole Group, Small Group, and Individual Activities

In most preschool classrooms, the beginning of the day includes time for the whole group to come together for what is commonly referred to as *circle time, morning meeting,* or *group time*. This time usually includes some welcoming activities, a review of the prior day's events, story time, and music, often ending with an introduction of any new materials or learning center arrangements. The space for circle time should have room for all the children to gather. Sometimes the floor is carpeted or has a rug in the designated area, because children typically sit on the floor for circle time.

Learning centers are distinct places where small groups of children can engage in self-selected activities. Other spaces may be arranged for individual children to provide a place to be alone (but still visible to the teacher). These alone places are important because interacting with others all day can be stressful for children. Individual activities might be blocks or a sorting activity on a small table with one chair (**Figure 2.1**), a bean-bag chair with a selection of books nearby, or materials in bins that are to be used on a small rug on the floor.

Making the Environment Convenient for Children and Adults

A key element in a well-functioning environment is that it is convenient for the children's use. Convenience is achieved by helping children understand expectations while giving them choices and control over what they do.

A convenient early childhood environment is one in which young children can easily see, find, and use materials with minimal adult assistance. A well-planned, functional environment makes the day go smoothly and is less stressful for both adults and children. Here are some ways in which you can create an environment that works well for both children and adults:

- Arrange objects or materials so that each one clearly stands out as an attractive choice (**Figure 2.2**).
- Ensure that surfaces are easy to clean and suitable for the activity in the area where they are located; for example, avoid placing a rug where children use water or paints.
- Choose activities that are child-directed. Doing so allows teachers to move around the room and interact in all centers as the children work independently.
- Use picture symbol charts to guide children's activities and help them know what to do. **Picture symbol charts** are reminders, such as a picture of handwashing to prompt children to wash their hands or a symbol for rain on a weather chart.
- Keep items that are used often, such as paper towels or tissues, within easy reach.
- Provide containers that make it easy for children to select and return the materials they use.

kate_sept2004/E+ via Getty Images

Figure 2-1 A 5-year-old builds with table blocks, exploring balance and comparing shapes. What other activities might children enjoy performing alone?

Jomkwan/iStock via Getty Images

Figure 2-2 The teacher in this toddler classroom arranged items to be readily accessible and to attract the children's attention. *Why do you think this arrangement would be inviting to children?*

Items should be near where they are expected to be used. For example, wherever you are likely to need masking tape or some water to mix paint, put the supplies in a place near where they will be needed. With items in a handy location, you and the children can avoid wasting time looking for what you need.

☑ CHECKPOINT

1. Reflect on an environment that affected your behavior. What about the environment affected you?
2. Other than the ideas from this textbook, what could you do to make a classroom convenient?

2.2 Learning Centers

As noted earlier in this chapter, learning centers are distinct spaces set up with related materials to encourage children to interact and work together or individually on a selected task. Learning centers, often called *interest centers* or *interest areas*, provide a concrete, practical approach to defining a curriculum. They provide a balanced collection of experiences that support child development through play. Learning centers provide a reference for developing and for seeing relationships between objects and materials.

The learning center approach supports the goals of early childhood education to develop children's desire to learn. Centers reflect what researchers know about how children learn best. They provide child-initiated and teacher-directed experiences, guided by the materials teachers provide. Once centers have been established, the curriculum can be maintained despite staff turnover or absences. Well-organized learning centers support teachers as well as children. Teachers spend less time performing maintenance tasks and resolving discipline issues. When the environment is set up thoughtfully and intentionally, the environment becomes a teacher.

Young children need choices to select and take part in activities and tasks that interest them. Multiple options allow children to follow their interests; thus, they will likely stay involved longer. Teachers can offer choices for children, providing activities to support all curriculum areas and encouraging children to experience a balance of activities that facilitate development. The defined spaces of learning centers encourage children to interact with materials and others, thus learning to:
- make plans and follow through on ideas.
- take turns, help each other, and cooperate.
- negotiate and solve problems together.
- build language and social skills.
- develop an understanding of relationships between objects and materials.
- learn from each other.
- build confidence in their skills and abilities.

Children can choose learning centers and the activities and materials throughout the day. These choices allow them to develop a sense of independence and control to pursue engaging activities. They learn through exploration and active involvement with the materials and their peers. As a result, they become more focused as they play, therefore learning more and increasing their attention span. Having multiple learning centers reduces conflicts over materials and activities and allows often-impatient preschoolers to choose other activities when one area is being used. Setting up a variety of learning centers allows children:
- many ways to develop skills.
- choices in what they want to do.
- opportunities to develop multiple intelligences and use their areas of strength to learn.
- to explore and express themselves in many ways.
- to engage in self-directed learning.

Learning centers offer materials that can vary from simple to complex, allowing children to:
- build on their prior knowledge and skills.
- address their different developmental needs.
- experience adequate challenges and mastery of skills.
- scaffold emerging abilities.
- participate in an individualized program to meet their unique needs and interests.

Organizing learning centers so that children can easily get the materials they want and return them when finished (Michigan Department of Education 2020):
- promotes feelings of competence and independence.
- reduces frustrating situations in which children must wait for help.
- allows children to carry out their own plans and ideas.
- provides teachers with more time to interact with children.
- frees teachers to observe how children use materials and interact with their peers.
- gives teachers the ability to assess each child's *learning* and make decisions on how to enrich each center to better meet children's needs.

Basic Learning Centers and Components

Certain learning centers are common in most early learning environments. These centers have stood the test of time in supporting children's learning. Although there are variations, the basic learning centers described in **Figure 2.3** are recommended for a preschool classroom, along with some recommendations of items that are usually included in each center. The number of children who can work without overcrowding in most classrooms is a suggestion. This number may vary based on the unique classroom space as well as other factors. Each learning center should be placed logically in the classroom with respect to other interest centers.

Common Early Childhood Learning Centers

Area	Description
Block and Construction Center  *PeopleImages/iStock via Getty Images*	The block area will likely be the noisiest in the room. Excited children interacting and wooden towers toppling generate noise that is likely to intrude on quiet areas such as the library. If the block area is near the dramatic play area, the activities often complement each other, and children use them interrelatedly. The area should be out of the line of traffic so that children passing by do not disrupt the building. Low shelves can provide a place for blocks that are stacked by size and shape with the larger ones on the lowest shelves. A low-pile rug can define the area and help stifle noise. The area should have space for about three to six children to comfortably use at one time. The area should contain not only blocks of varying lengths and shapes but also accessories such as trucks, cars, trains, traffic signs, and props related to construction. Often, wooden trains and train tracks and figures of people or animals are included. Periodically, materials related to curriculum themes can be added.
Housekeeping and Dramatic Play Center  *kiankhoon/iStock via Getty Images*	The housekeeping and dramatic play area is typically set up as a child-sized home setting. Because it is a popular area with much interaction, it is noisy and should be placed away from direct lines of traffic and quieter zones. There should be space and equipment for about three to six children to use the area comfortably. Equipment and materials should be relevant to the children's home lives, including diverse families and cultures. Some items to include are child-size furniture, a stove, a refrigerator, tables, chairs, a bed, dishes, pots, pans, utensils, dress-up clothes, mirrors, shoes, hats, books, magazines, telephones, and dress-up clothes.
Library and Listening Center  *RainStar/E+ via Getty Images*	The library center is an oasis in the classroom, offering a place for children to be alone or with a few friends. It is usually planned as a calming, quiet location and is thus best located away from noisy areas, protected from the line of traffic, and free of distractions. For it to function as a retreat, it need not accommodate more than two or three children at a time. This area should be cozy and comfortable and may be decorated or stocked based on current curriculum themes. The library area needs comfortable seating and a shelf or rack for displaying books. The area should include a variety of books rotated regularly, a small table and chairs, a child-size sofa and chairs, or beanbags. Many teachers include provisions for listening to audio stories or music with headphones.
Art and Creative Expression Center  *lostinbids/E+ via Getty Images*	An art area enables children to explore color, form, and texture through self-expression and creativity using a variety of media. The art area should be placed near a sink, if possible, since water will often be needed for cleanup. This area is somewhat of a buffer zone because it does not usually entail as much action as the dramatic play area but will not be as quiet as the library center. The art and creative expression area will need shelves for art supplies, a table with chairs for working, and hooks to hold smocks to protect clothing. The art shelf should include materials that the child may self-select at any time, such as crayons (including multicultural crayons), various types of paper, clay, playdough, white glue, paste, scissors, chalk, and cleanup supplies. There should be easels with paints and clean brushes, and supplies for pasting and gluing, making collages, stitchery, stamping, printing, etc. Each item may not be available every day, but they can be rotated.
Math and Manipulative Center  *M-image/iStock via Getty Images*	The math and manipulative area is a buffer zone and can be placed between noisy and quiet areas. It is usually comprised of low shelves holding an assortment of manipulatives and a table with chairs. Shallow containers are useful for storing the many small parts. The center should include a selection of table toys such as puzzles, lotto games, LEGO® and DUPLO® bricks, parquetry blocks, mosaics, number manipulatives, beads for stringing, lacing cards, peg boards, and table blocks. Three to six children can work comfortably in this center if there are adequate materials and the table is large enough.

Goodheart-Willcox Publisher

Figure 2-3 This chart includes descriptions of common learning centers. *What aspects of learning centers do you consider most valuable to young children?* *(Continued)*

Common Early Childhood Learning Centers (continued)

Area	Description
Science and Discovery Center  cheshka/iStock via Getty Images	The science area is also a buffer zone and can be placed between quiet and noisy areas. It will not be as lively as the dramatic play area, as a rule, but not as low-key as the library. A science area usually needs a table for a work space and a place for picture displays. The area should include magnifying glasses, seeds, plants, old clocks or radios, tools, magnets and objects to attract with them, water, funnels, measuring cups and spoons, materials for cooking experiences, tools for weights and measures, balance scales, and simple machines. The area might also include information on sea life, plants, animals, and insects; materials for pouring, mixing, and recycling; or any other items that represent the sciences. A science center should offer room for about three to five children.
Music and Movement Center  lostinbids/iStock via Getty Images	A music and movement center is usually a large, noisy space. Include recorded music, musical instruments (e.g., toy piano, autoharp, bells, triangles, rhythm sticks, wood blocks, tambourines, maracas, or stringed instruments). Include props for movement, such as scarves and sheer cloths. Allow ample space for three to five children to dance with scarves, use instruments, or march. Some teachers include means of listening to music individually such as headphones. Items for a pots and pan band will be popular. If the music area is adjacent to the active play area of the classroom, the active play area could be the space for dancing and marching.
Writing Center  SerrNovik/Getty Images	Pre-writing and writing experiences help children make the connection between writing and language. In some classrooms, writing experiences are included in the art area, but other teachers have a specific learning center for writing that includes a variety of writing materials, digital devices, and props. The writing center can be a place to make greeting cards and write notes for special occasions. It can also be a part of dramatic play if set up as an office. To integrate with curriculum experiences, the writing area might become a post office, selling pretend stamps, or a site for making books or writing individual stories. Usually, the writing center can accommodate two or three children and is considered a quiet area.
Active Play Area  FatCamera/iStock via Getty Images	In some programs, the only space for indoor active play will be an open area in the classroom. In others, a separate room will be set aside for indoor active play when weather restricts outdoor activities. Some early childhood programs may have access to a gymnasium. Gymnasiums, while enticing to children, have some challenges. Too much space can be overwhelming for children and encourage screaming and rough play. Additionally, it is more difficult to supervise a group of children in a large space. Masking tape or plastic cones can be used to establish boundaries.
Sand, Water, and Sensory Area  DGLImages/iStock via Getty Images	Some teachers include sensory activities as part of the art area. Others may set up an area specifically for sand or water play. Still, others may only have these activities outdoors or offer them on occasion. To avoid messes and overcrowding, control the amount of product on the table and limit the number of children who can play at the table at one time. Usually, three to five is a good number, unless the sand or water table is quite large. If a table specifically made for sand and/or water play is not available, large plastic containers will work to ensure children have access to these experiences. For sand play, include shovels, spoons, people figures, houses, vehicles, trees, and items to make landscapes. For water play, do not include glasses or cups, as children will be tempted to drink from them. Instead, use various measuring tools, basting tubes, and items that float, such as toy boats.
Maker or Tinkering Center  Paolo De Gasperis/Shutterstock.com	Maker or tinkering activities may be incorporated into the art or science areas or set up as a separate learning center if space permits. If established as an individual center, it can offer more opportunities for science, technology, engineering, and math (STEM) experiences. This area can include many recycled materials with which children can build and create. Up to four or five children can usually work together in a tinkering area, depending on their age and skills. Consider the maker or tinkering area near the art or science areas if it is a separate center. The three centers can often share resources.

Goodheart-Willcox Publisher

Figure 2-3 Continued

Establishing and Arranging Learning Centers

The success of a learning center depends on having developmentally appropriate items that children can use with a high degree of independence. For children to work uninterrupted, the overall placement of the learning centers in the classroom is important. The following general guidelines should be considered in arranging the classroom:

- Separate noisy areas from quiet ones. (For example, blocks and dramatic play can be adjoining, with library and manipulatives in other parts of the room.)
- Clearly define learning centers with boundaries of shelves, furniture, or rugs. Divisions help children stay involved and encourage the use of materials specific to each area.
- Display materials attractively and neatly at a height accessible to children so they can see available choices and retrieve materials themselves.
- Place learning centers near needed resources. (For example, place the art area near a sink and manipulatives near a table.)
- Arrange materials in an organized manner; label with pictures or outlines to show where items belong and to assist children in cleaning up their materials. Include both printed words and a picture, a shape, or an outline of the materials.
- Rotate and change center options as curriculum themes, children's interests, and individual needs change.
- Post the name of each center and the learning objectives to inform parents, volunteers, and visitors of the purpose of each center.
- Do not place teachers' supplies not intended for children in areas with the materials from which children may choose.
- Reduce visual clutter by storing materials not being used.
- Set up materials to allow children to explore independently.
- Use **indirect guidance** (the sounds, objects, visuals, and people in a child's environment that affect their behavior) so children know what to do. (For example, two chairs at a table with a board game tell children that two can play there together.)
- Rotate materials frequently so children do not tire of them.
- Preview learning center activities with children ahead of time. Introduce new materials and discuss guidelines for use of the materials as additions or changes are made.
- Limit the number of children per center if necessary. The number may vary depending on the size of the center and type of activity. Post the number as a reference. Some programs implement a "check-in" system. Each child has a "ticket," which is a small picture of themselves or their symbol with a piece of Velcro® on the back. They check in by attaching their ticket to one of the open spots on a board near the center. If there are no open spots, they must find another center.
- Provide materials that can be used in a variety of ways by children at different levels of development.
- Incorporate a traffic pattern that prevents children from interrupting each other's activities. Make sure there is ample room between furniture for you and the children to walk easily.
- Arrange your desk or work area facing the door and the center of the room for better supervision during naptime.
- Incorporate items and materials such as play food, posters, or clothing that reflect the languages and cultures of your students, their homes, and their community.
- Be flexible. If a room arrangement is not working, evaluate the situation and try another arrangement to produce the best setup for your room.

Learning centers are most effective when children have ample time to explore the materials. Rich play scenarios develop when children are provided stretches of time for participation in the centers. Provide at least one hour in the morning and again in the afternoon for learning center activities. Large blocks of time allow children to develop ideas and be creative. The time in learning centers is also a prime time for children to interact with their peers in social situations.

Classroom Considerations for Infants and Toddlers

Infant and toddler classrooms also have important room arrangement considerations. Not only is their equipment different from that of preschoolers, but their needs are different as well.

General Arrangements

To support infants' and toddlers' needs to move and explore, create an environment that supports their development and keeps them involved (Lally et al. 2004; Luckenbill et al. 2019):

- Plan furniture for basic needs: sleeping, eating, sitting, playing, walking, and climbing.
- Make it easy for infants to get up on surfaces of different heights by using risers and ramps to expand the use of the environment and increase opportunities for adults and children to relate eye to eye.
- Hang interesting objects from heights within sight of infants on the floor.
- Place safety mirrors (mirrors made of safe, shatterproof materials), pictures, and photos at the eye level of an infant on the floor.
- Supply space for **tummy time** (playtime for infants placed on a quilt or blanket on the floor) and gross motor movement (**Figure 2.4**).
- Provide adult-size furniture for feeding and cuddling infants and toddlers. High shelves and cabinets can store materials used by adults out of the reach of children.
- Provide motor experiences for active toddlers and those just learning to walk. Infants need something sturdy to pull up on, and toddlers need space to move around.
- Use tables and chairs that are the correct size for toddlers.
- Include equipment that may work for children of various ages in different ways. (For example, a low slide will be used competently by a two-year-old; a one-year-old will slide down it with assistance; and a nine-month-old will crawl under it.)
- Provide a corner or pit of pillows for toddlers' quiet time and rest that is protected from the active play of other children.
- Allow space for children to move freely through the room or in a designated area.

kuppa_rock/iStock via Getty Images

Figure 2-4 This infant classroom provides open space to support physical development. Why is it important that babies and children have freedom and space to move around?

Learning Centers for Infants and Toddlers

Even classrooms for older infants and toddlers can have materials arranged in simple learning centers. For example, manipulatives can be stored in one area, and riding toys can be grouped together in another. Such grouping helps children learn to recognize likenesses and differences, classify items, and know where items they want can be found. Learning centers for toddlers serve to organize materials and provide a variety of activities. For example, a toddler classroom might be arranged to include learning centers for:
- quiet, calm, relaxing activities, such as looking at books or cuddling stuffed animals.
- structured, teacher-guided experiences, such as music and read-alouds.
- discovery, with art materials and messy activities.
- dramatic play, with dress-up clothes or familiar home items.
- large motor activities, such as playing with balls and climbing on foam blocks.

Toddlers crave consistency but also need the ability to explore and try new experiences. Periodically, bring out new materials and rotate what is available. When you add a new item or activity, put something away that no longer holds their attention. Rotating toys or materials encourages children to refocus as they are attracted to the new items. For example, if you had the sensory table out in the morning, then cover it up and bring out a laundry basket full of soft balls or stuffed animals for the afternoon.

Sensory and motor experiences are important foundations of cognitive and physical development. Late in the day or when the weather prohibits outdoor play, toddlers may become restless and need some special change-of-pace activities. They may be tired and feeling sad as pickup time approaches, especially as they see their friends leaving. Here are a few suggestions of popular toddler activities for preventing or addressing the afternoon doldrums:

- **Chair line-up.** Toddlers love to line up chairs into long trains. Invite dolls and stuffed animals along on an imaginary ride, complete with sound effects.
- **Blanket caves.** Drape some blankets or large sheets over tables to create caves for toddlers to crawl into with supervision.
- **Afternoon fun box.** Prepare a special box for end-of-day time. The fun box is also useful for bad weather days when children would normally be outside. Put unique materials inside that the toddlers will look forward to. Vary what is in the box from week to week to keep interest high. Some possibilities are:
  - special manipulatives or toys reserved just for the fun box.
  - unusual art materials, such as sparkle crayons, stickers, wrapping paper, ribbon, and lace for collage.
  - special books not left out on the regular bookshelf.
  - scarves, wide ribbons, or streamers to use while dancing to lively music.
  - containers of different shapes and sizes with lids and some handles. Look for plastic containers with screw-tops to develop dexterity.
  - a covered shoebox with treasures, such as colored clothes pins, paper to tear, or interesting textures to feel.
  - kitchen utensils and items, such as wooden spoons and plastic bowls, to make a kitchen band and march.

Developmentally Appropriate Toys and Equipment

As children grow and develop, the toys and equipment they use need to change. They benefit from increasingly complex items that support their growing skills and abilities. Following are some suggestions for toys and materials based on developmental ages. You will want to incorporate more advanced items as children develop or replace previous toys and equipment with more complex ones as best fits the development of the children in your class.

- **Birth to 6-month-olds:** mobiles to watch movement, rattles, squeaky toys, soft items once they can grasp
- **6-month- to 1-year-olds:** soft animals, cloth or board books, dolls, soft balls, gym mobiles, music boxes

- **1-year-olds:** large foam blocks, doll and bed, blankets, telephone, small solid cars, vehicles for pushing and riding, large crayons, cloth books, storage shelves, stacking and nesting toys, pull toys, pop beads
- **2-year-olds:** simple climber and slide (**Figure 2.5**), rocking and riding toys, simple doll clothes, child-size furniture, play kitchen items, cars and trucks, books, bookcase, play table and chairs, simple puzzles, large wooden threading beads
- **3-year-olds:** doll houses, small dolls, furniture, play ironing board and iron, rocking chair, broom, dustpan, vehicles, easels, paints and brushes, blunt scissors, work and library tables, sand and water play table, wooden puzzles, plants, shopping cart
- **4-year-olds:** puppets, puppet theater, unit blocks, planks, slide, wagons, large climber and slide, clothesline and pins, aprons, child-size bed or cradle, carriage, dress-up clothes, clay
- **5-year-olds:** balls, skates, teepee or tunnel, tools, dominoes, card games, construction sets, board games, musical instruments, aquarium, science toys, craft supplies

In choosing items, select those that can hold up to heavy use. Children manipulate and use materials in unexpected and unintended ways. Unless the item can withstand heavy use, it may not be a sound investment. Good toys do not need to provide instant gratification. Winding up a toy and watching it move will not hold children's attention for long. Creating with construction materials will engage children much longer.

Good toys do not promote materialism, such as character dolls that entice children to beg to purchase numerous clothes and accessories. A simple baby doll with a blanket and bottle will provide hours of valuable dramatic play. Avoid items that glamorize and reflect destruction or violence. A good toy stimulates questions and presents problems for solving. The best toys are those that can be used in myriad ways. Apart from wooden puzzles, most toys should not have a right or wrong solution. The following are questions to ask about the materials and equipment being considered for a classroom:

- Is it safe for the ages that will use it?
- What areas of development will it support?

ChiccoDodiFC/iStock via Getty Images

Figure 2-5 The tunnel and slide in this toddler classroom provide for gross motor development. *What other items can support gross motor development indoors?*

- Is it developmentally appropriate for the children in the class?
- How many children can use the item at one time?
- Is it nonviolent, multicultural, and nonsexist?
- Does it add balance and variety to existing materials and equipment?
- Is it easy to maintain and keep clean?
- Is it durable enough to withstand frequent use?
- Is it suitable for the available classroom space?
- Can it be used with minimum supervision?
- Are there enough parts to maintain interest?
- Does it involve children in creative thinking or problem solving?

Case Study

The Undesirable DVD Dilemma

Meredith had always encouraged children to bring items from home to share with the other children, especially items that meant a lot to the child or represented something unique from the child's culture. Typically, Meredith offered a chance during circle time for children to introduce the items they brought. One day, a child brought an item that created a dilemma. Sophia, a 5-year-old, brought a DVD of a television show that Meredith knew would be a problem. The show, although intended for children, included much violence: karate kicks, punches, and other types of fighting. The message of the episodes was that violence was an appropriate way to settle disputes.

Meredith had worked hard to teach the children about communication and nonviolent behavior and to build an atmosphere of kindness and cooperation. She knew that if she let the children watch the segments, it might encourage aggressive behavior within the classroom. However, she didn't want to disappoint Sophia, who had brought a treasured birthday present to school to share.

Consider This

1. Should Meredith show the video anyway and take her chances?
2. Would it be best to talk to the children about why she could not show the video?
3. Should she tell Sophia's parents not to allow her to bring materials that could encourage aggression?
4. What else might Meredith do? Can you think of a solution that considers Sophia's feelings?

Paying Attention to Aesthetics

Aesthetics generally refers to a set of values relating to the appreciation of beauty and nature. Consideration of the aesthetics of the environment is important, as the early childhood field becomes increasingly aware of the role of beauty in children's lives (Duncan et al. 2010). The traditional classroom environment is typically rather institutional, with tile floors and sterile surfaces. Hard, laminated tables and plastic chairs add to the hardness of the room. Such surfaces tend to contribute to unpleasant noise due to the lack of sound-absorbing materials.

This institutional effect is partially due to the need for easy-to-clean and durable surfaces. However, there has been a growing awareness of the contribution of aesthetics to the pedagogical experience of young children. Architects, designers, administrators, and early education leaders are recognizing the effect that space, including its aesthetics, has on children. This emphasis on beauty in the classroom has evolved primarily from the Reggio Emilia Approach.

Reggio Emilia is a town in Italy that operates preschools with a philosophy that includes an emphasis on art, nature, and beauty. The Reggio Emilia Approach includes attention to light, color, softness, smell, and even sound. The philosophy includes the belief that beauty in the surroundings helps children focus and concentrate. A classroom's appeal to the senses, along with its organization, generate implicit and explicit messages that impact children's learning and well-being. When early childhood classrooms are planned to be aesthetically pleasing, young children will see the connection and importance of music, visual arts, and beauty in their educational environment.

While many programs operate in a site not planned with aesthetics in mind, there are many steps you can take to include beauty in young children's lives and make classrooms more aesthetically pleasing. How can you make such institutional settings softer and more inviting to children and adults? How can you make it more homelike and inviting? Here are some ways to add beauty to the classroom:

- Add plants and other natural materials to the indoor environment, preferably those gathered by the children (**Figure 2.6**). Items from nature that are attractively arranged, such as a dogwood branch, smooth river rocks, or colorful fall leaves pressed between book pages, can be interesting to observe and study.
- Select books with beautiful illustrations. Consider the illustrations as much as the story plot when selecting books. Caldecott Medal award books or honor books are desirable choices because these awards recognize excellence in picture-book illustrations. Caldecott Award-winning books include *Owl Moon*, *The Lion & the Mouse*, *The House in the Night*, *Kitten's First Full Moon*, and *A Chair for My Mother*. Provide nonfiction books with stories and illustrations depicting the beauty of various places and items from diverse cultures.
- Display posters and other works of art, such as photos of landscapes. Reproductions of museum-quality art are available inexpensively as posters. Frame and hang items at children's eye level for them to enjoy and appreciate.
- Use commercial teaching designs or anchor charts sparingly. Letters and numbers, shapes, and colors are often posted in early childhood classrooms, but such designs often add visual clutter rather than beauty. When they stay on the wall week after week, they lose any initial appeal they may have had for the children.

PhotoMavenStock/Shutterstock.com

Figure 2-6 Straw and reed baskets add elements of nature to this math and manipulative area. Can you suggest additional ways to use nature items indoors for aesthetics?

- Display children's artwork. This adds beauty to the classroom and encourages children to take pride in what they do. Chapter 11, "STEAM: Art and Music," provides suggestions for displaying children's art attractively.
- Display pottery and other artifacts with traditional cultural designs. Pottery, basketry, or weavings from various cultures can add earth tones and interesting textures to the environment.
- Use textiles with interesting designs and unusual colors. Children's environments need not be red, yellow, blue, and green. In fact, such colors may serve to create a busy rather than a beautiful environment.
- Include area rugs in the room to create more intimate gathering spaces. In the dramatic play area, a small rug can create a home environment. In the space where the children gather for circle time, a soft area rug can form a boundary for meetings. The rugs can be similar to those you might use in a home and need not be specifically created for children with bright colors and teaching designs.
- Consider placing colored plastic bottles (or clear plastic bottles containing colored water) along the top of a shelf where the light will shine through and reflect color on the walls and floor.
- Use decorative baskets or wooden bowls or boxes to hold toys or other items.
- Incorporate lamps to add coziness and provide relief from harsh fluorescent lighting, or add strings of lights that appeal to children.
- Include mirrors for children to see themselves or just as an attractive display.
- Consider the sounds in the classroom. The types of music and the noise level of the classroom affect the comfort of both adults and children.

Beauty can add joy and positivity to a physical space. Early childhood educators can use children's natural gravitation toward beauty by building an inviting learning environment that makes children want to be present and engaged.

In addition to what you put in the classroom, the walls themselves form the canvas for the artistic environment. Avoid using strong colors on walls. While an empty room with each wall painted a different color may appeal to some adults, consider what happens when the room is full of classroom equipment and materials, most of which may also be in bright primary colors. Add in children with colorful clothing, and the room can quickly become overstimulating. A better choice is to use a neutral color on the walls, natural wood for furniture, and let the color of the learning materials become the focus.

Avoid large murals on the wall. Children may enjoy murals of animals and cartoon characters, but the murals are permanent and do not provide the opportunity to rotate wall décor based on children's preferences or the curriculum. The mural may limit furniture arrangement and classroom flexibility because the furniture might cover some of the mural.

Planning for Supervision and Safety

Equipment in the classroom must be safe for the developmental age of the children using the materials, but supervision is also a critical factor in providing a safe environment. A teacher must be constantly alert to what the children are doing, what they need, and what potential hazards exist. The room must provide for children to be seen and heard; hidden areas or barriers that block adults' view should be avoided. Here are some additional tips for safety:

- Show children how to use materials and equipment safely.
- Discuss playing safely so children understand what to do and why.
- Involve children in establishing limits and remind them of those limits.
- Provide an uncluttered and organized play area; children and adults must be able to move freely without tripping or falling over materials.
- Remove broken toys, items with sharp, jagged edges, and other hazards.
- Base decisions on development and ability; age designations do not always fit all children.

The environment for young children needs to be both safe and responsive. **Figure 2.7** includes children's actions by ages, what you can do to make the environment responsive, and how that action helps children's development. Use this convenient guide for ideas on how to support children as they develop.

Planning a Responsive Environment

Ages	What Children Can Do	Ways You Can Arrange the Environment for Support	How This Supports Development
Young Infants	notice and watch what goes on around them	place pictures on the wall at child's eye level	encourages infants to focus and attend to objects in their environment
	reach for, bat, and poke at objects	hang mobiles where infants can see, touch, and kick them	shows infants they can have an impact on the world
	respond to being held and rocked	have comfortable places for holding infants, such as soft chairs and rockers	builds relationships and a sense of trust
	develop the ability to sit and crawl	install soft carpet or pads so infants can crawl comfortably	promotes physical development
Mobile Infants	pull themselves up to a standing position	be sure furniture is sturdy, with protected edges, and will not tip over easily; use mats with a variety of surfaces	allows mobile infants to explore in safety and builds large muscles
	push, pull, fill, and dump objects	offer a variety of playthings, including household objects	builds motor skills as well as coordination
	take comfort from familiar objects and reminders of home	display pictures of family members	helps children feel safe and secure; reduces separation anxiety
	sometimes need to be alone	create private spaces	helps children develop a sense of self and the ability to self-soothe
Toddlers	walk, run, climb, and play with objects and toys	arrange the space so toddlers can move around safely	allows toddlers to explore freely and independently
	sometimes want to do more than they can do	organize toys on low shelves and label with pictures	provides a variety of appropriate challenges so toddlers experience a sense of their own competence
	play alongside and with others	offer materials and activities that meet children's level of development; define areas where two or three children can play; provide duplicates of popular items	promotes the ability to engage in sustained and purposeful play
Preschoolers	enjoy playing with others, especially in small groups.	arrange interest centers with enough materials and supplies to accommodate several small groups of children at a time	physical presence and shared materials encourage social interactions
	prefer to choose their own activities	have enough interesting things to do so that children have a variety of options	supports decision making, which is an important skill and begins early
	learn through discovery and interactions	circulate among the learning centers and talk with children about what they are doing	talking with others builds language skills
	may have difficulty ending an activity when they are heavily engaged	give notices when learning center time is almost over or any transition is about to take place	helps children adjust to changes when they have time to prepare for them

Goodheart-Willcox Publisher

Figure 2-7 This chart suggests ways in which the environment can support children's development. *What are other skills children need to master that can be guided by the arrangement of the furniture and materials?*

CHECKPOINT

1. Why do you think learning centers have been common in early learning programs for so long?
2. Consider what makes an environment pleasant for you. Do you like plants, soft colors, comfortable furniture, or relaxing music? How do these things affect children?

2.3 Room Arrangement and Children's Behavior

Providing engaging and developmentally appropriate materials, equipment, and supplies goes a long way toward having a well-run classroom. How the items are arranged also contributes to a functioning classroom. Consider the number of children to determine how many learning centers and materials to include in a classroom. Increases in negative and idle behavior may occur in situations with a high density of children or inadequate resources, equipment, or interesting things to do. Good room arrangement often prevents potential discipline problems by helping to meet emotional, physical, and cognitive needs while keeping children happily engaged.

Case Study

Disaster in the Manipulative Area

Sydney, a first-year kindergarten teacher, was frustrated with her classroom. The children would not use the materials purposefully and often brushed the manipulatives and wooden unit blocks onto the floor, enjoying the racket they made. And the areas were always in a mess.

Seeking help, she contacted Allen, an experienced teacher she knew from her college days. His classroom never suffered from those issues. In his classroom, children used the materials creatively with focus and returned them to their proper place when finished.

Allen offered to come and look at her class in operation to see what he could do to help. After about 20 minutes of observation, he made the following recommendations:

- Place a table next to the manipulative shelves and teach children to take the items they wish to use to the table. This would stop the playing while standing at the shelves, which results in scrambling the many parts of the manipulatives.
- Find better containers for the manipulatives. When children tried to get what they wanted from the deep containers she was using, they often dumped everything out to find specific items. He suggested that dishpans would work better than the deep boxes she was using.
- Set a boundary for block constructions about two feet from the shelves. This makes it easier for children to get the blocks they want from the shelf without disturbing the construction going on in front of the shelves.

Sydney implemented the suggested changes and began to see the behavior improve. She consulted with Allen several more times about other learning centers and always got helpful suggestions gleaned from his years of experience.

Consider This

1. How did the space left between the rug for block construction and the shelves prevent the constructions in progress from being toppled to the floor?
2. Why do you think children's engagement with the materials reduced the discipline issues Sydney was experiencing?

Problems Related to Room Arrangement

Figure 2.8 addresses common room arrangement issues that may lead to or contribute to problem behavior. The undesirable behavior is listed in the left column, potential causes

Using Room Arrangement to Discourage Undesirable Behaviors

Behavior	Possible Causes	How to Change the Environment
Running in the classroom	too much open space: room not divided into smaller areas; long narrow spaces	use shelves and furniture to divide the space
Conflict over toys	few duplicate toys: children are expected to share too often; not enough toys or interesting activities	provide duplicates of toys; show children when it will be their turn (use an egg timer with a bell, a sand timer, or a list with names of children waiting for their turn)
Wandering around; unable to choose activities	overly cluttered room; choices unclear; materials and supplies inadequate, not interesting or too challenging	remove clutter; simplify the layout of the room and materials; add more activity choices
Easily distracted; difficulty staying with a task and completing it	undefined, open areas; children can see everything going on in the room; materials and supplies not set up attractively	use shelves or other means to define areas so children are not distracted by other activities
Materials used roughly; children resist cleaning up	unorganized materials on shelves; no order to display materials; not cared for by adults	make a place for everything; use picture labels to show where materials go

Goodheart-Willcox Publisher

Figure 2-8 This chart illustrates some ways in which the environment may contribute to undesirable behavior. Can you think of other negative behaviors that might be improved by considering the environment?

related to the environment in the middle column, and suggestions for practical solutions in the right column. Although room arrangement will not address all behavior issues, a carefully planned environment can reduce or eliminate many of them (NAEYC 2016).

Using Books to Guide Children's Behavior

Guidance in the use of learning centers can come from children's picture books that include a storyline about going to preschool, early learning centers, or specific activities such as art or music. Books such as *Preschool Day Hooray!* can serve as a means of introduction to each area, lead to discussions about how to use the centers, and help children feel confident in their individual pursuits. Often, too, the stories suggest activities for children and encourage their interest in each area.

☑ CHECKPOINT

1. What are some ways you can engage children in learning centers?
2. What are some books that you might use to guide children's behavior? How would you use them?

2.4 The Social and Emotional Environment

The classroom environment is much more than the materials and equipment provided and how they are arranged. The environment also includes the relationships and interactions between adults and children and among children. How children get along with each other, develop social skills for living and working in a group, and learn to use materials responsibly and with consideration for others are all parts of the emotional environment. Do children feel safe, cared for, and free to experiment? These are important questions to ask when assessing the emotional environment.

Adults in early learning environments are responsible for helping children learn necessary social skills through guidance and support in a comfortable and secure emotional environment. Adults help children work through disagreements and learn to manage strong feelings. Adults can also assist children in becoming comfortable and happy with friends as a way to support their growing social and emotional capabilities.

Discovery Journeys

I Learn from Children

In her book, I Learn from Children, *Caroline Pratt describes her own recognition of the importance of the environment and children's reactions on the first day of her "trial school" at Hartley House, which she opened in 1913.*

When they came on the first Monday morning, I was ready for them. There were blocks I had made, and toys I had designed and made myself; there were crayons and paper, and there was clay. I had laid them out carefully so the children would not only see them but could go and take what they wanted without asking. Nothing was out of their reach: everything was visible, accessible, and theirs for the taking. I had planned my display like a salesman, thinking of everything I knew about my small customers; anticipating the short reach of little arms, the tendency of piled-up objects to fall down and frighten a shy child away, the reluctance of a small child to hunt for something he needs. I made it all as easy and inviting as I knew how, and then I stood aside and let them forage for themselves.

I couldn't have asked for a more appropriate demonstration of my belief in the serious value of children's play. Michael was so deeply absorbed, so purposeful in his construction, that he might have been a scientist working out an experiment in a laboratory…

With blocks to help him, he was using all his mental powers, reasoning out relationships—the relation of the delivery wagon to the store, the coal cart loaded from the barge in the river and carrying its load to the home—and he was drawing conclusions. He was learning to think.

Consider This

1. What experiences have you had that contributed to your knowledge of the arrangement and children's accessibility of classroom materials?
2. Have you seen evidence of Caroline Pratt's influence on practices today?

Nurturing Children's Friendships

Young children who develop preferences for others in their group often keep these preferences as they grow. One good practice is to transition children to older classrooms in friendship groups. Rather than moving one child alone, try moving two or three who are friends at the same time. Transitions are easier for young children when they have a familiar friend with them.

Toddlers want to have friends and get along with others, but they are inexperienced. As with any other beginning skill, children will make mistakes as they try to figure out how to act (**Figure 2.9**). Helping children learn to have successful social relationships is one of the most important things that you can do to promote children's development. Social skills have a direct impact on children's ability to find success in school and in life.

How can you support social interactions? Create small spaces where two children can fit comfortably. Children love to sit in small spaces together. Larger groups can be overwhelming because children must interact with so many different personalities. Friendships start as **dyads**, or two children at a time. Large cardboard boxes work great for children to crawl into with a special friend. See what nooks and crannies you can create to help friendships blossom.

Consider having several smaller tables for children to sit at and eat together rather than one large group table. Also, consider a small table that can be used for dramatic play in which two children can pretend to eat together. Provide appropriate props, such as plastic dishes, pots and pans, and even tablecloths or placemats and napkins. Or, set up activities at a small table to give children a place to be alone or play with a special friend.

Another way to support a positive environment in which it is easy to make friends is to include activities that are more fun to do with someone or that require two to participate. Rocking in the rocking boat, rolling a ball back and forth, singing together, and

Figure 2-9 Conflicts over toys are a normal part of early interactions. *What can teachers do to help children have successful social relationships?*

blowing bubbles are good partner activities. Two children might share one large piece of fingerpaint paper. Through partner activities, children learn about the advantages of positive social contact with others.

Smoothing the Way

Teachers can help children learn social skills that they need to enter play and interact with others. Guide children on how to ask to be a part of a play activity by suggesting a role or task. Demonstrate how to compromise with others, to take turns in popular activities, and how to ask for what they want. Young children often need help in noticing the friendship bids or desires of other children. You might say something like, "Sandy has been watching you play with the doll. I think she wants to play with you. I bet the two of you could have fun with the doll together."

"Hanna, LaShaun asked you if he could have a turn with the wagon. Did you hear him ask for a turn? Can you let him know when you are through so he can have a turn, please?" And then later, notice when Hanna follows through with a statement similar to, "Hanna, you made LaShaun happy when you gave him a turn. Thank you for sharing with him."

One nice phrase to use frequently is, "That was a friendly thing to do. Letting Quinton use the blocks with you was very friendly, Jacobi." The more you notice and acknowledge the children's desirable behavior, the more they will repeat it and begin to understand the concept of friendly actions toward others.

Friendship Opportunities for Infants and Toddlers

With infants, the most important thing to be conscious of is providing them with access to each other. The infants should be able to see each other, make eye contact, smile, touch one another, develop interest in each other, and act on that appeal. Teachers can set up opportunities for infants to connect with others, such as sitting on the floor with a small baby nestled in their lap near other children who can come over to see the baby. Another example is a game of peek-a-boo with scarves, which is sure to generate interest from several children who will laugh together as you cover one child's face and then another's.

If infants and toddlers are in a room together, teachers should prevent toddlers from interfering with the play of infants by using barriers to keep them physically separate. A plastic swimming pool in which infants can be placed with attractive toys or foam blocks can separate infants from more active toddlers (Lally et al. 2004).

Adults must be available to smooth social attempts, avert conflicts, and help children move along the progression from solitary play to parallel play to associative, interactive play. Adults can encourage children and suggest ways they can successfully interact together. Even toddlers can be helped to develop social skills and friendships. For example, 20-month-old Mattie is holding a book that 19-month-old Eric wants. You might say, "Mattie, Eric likes that book too. Can you show him the pictures?" They then sit together and turn the pages, forming the beginning of a friendship.

The Environment and Children's Behavior

Children must feel comfortable and secure in their environment to gain the greatest benefit from their daily experiences. Adults are a vital component in creating a calm and responsive environment where children's needs are met. The emotional environment is good when the adults provide an orderly program in which children know what to expect. Teachers can provide a healthy emotional environment by (The IRIS Center 2015):

- having many one-on-one interactions with each child.
- being patient and giving children time to process what is said and how to respond.
- using many nonverbal clues—gestures, sign language, facial expressions, and changes in voice tone—to enhance communication.
- maintaining a predictable schedule.
- saying *yes* more than *no*.
- recognizing and acknowledging the positive qualities in children and their desirable actions.
- replacing undesirable behavior with a compatible alternative behavior.
- guiding children on what to do instead of telling them what not to do.
- giving children choices when possible. For example, saying, "It is time to clean up. Do you want to put away blocks or crayons?" When children have a choice, they are more likely to be agreeable.
- using the *when/then method*: "When your table is clean, then I will read the book." "When you clean up, then we will go outside."
- teaching children self-regulation skills.
- providing scaffolding to help them develop self-control.

Creating Private Spaces

Children in full-day programs are in a group setting for 9–10 hours per day. The constant need to react to, accommodate, and interact with others can be stressful for young children. In some programs, naptime is the *only* time of the day when the child is free from the constant demands of social interaction. Teachers can provide relief from this situation by making provisions for children to be alone (but supervised) throughout the day (**Figure 2.10**).

Some activities can be selected and set up for a single child. Placing a single chair at an activity indicates to the child that this is a place to work alone. Small rugs may be used on the floor on which individual children can place their materials. Such rugs also create boundaries and help children keep toy parts and related items together.

Recycled curtains, sheets, blankets, or large pieces of fabric can become tent-making material. Children can drape fabric over chairs, play equipment, or tables to create private places. Clothespins or masking tape will hold pieces together. Keep tent material in

timnewman/E+ via Getty Images

Figure 2-10 This girl takes advantage of this space to be alone and free of the distractions of a busy classroom filled with other children and activities. Why are private spaces important in a classroom?

a laundry basket and teach children to return the material to the basket when finished. All fabric should be washed regularly in hot water with detergent.

Large cardboard boxes may be used to create places to be alone. They are free, readily available, and come in a variety of sizes. They may be painted or decorated as an art activity. Remove any staples prior to use.

Creating places for children to be alone or with a few friends helps ensure that they can find solace during the day by having a means to remove themselves from the need to interact with many other people. Children can choose such spots when they are feeling overstimulated or just need time for quiet and calm.

Schedules and Routines

Schedules and consistent routines help children feel secure and provide a guide for the day's experiences. Knowing what will happen next is comforting to children. The daily schedule should include a balance of indoor and outdoor; quiet and active; individual, small group, and large group; large muscle and small muscle; and child-initiated and teacher-initiated activities. Breakfast, lunch, snack time, and naptime should be included in the schedule. Posting the schedule in the classroom will help ensure consistency and guide the teacher or substitutes in providing the sequence and necessary balance of activities.

For a classroom in which children are not yet able to recognize words, pictures can be used to create a visible schedule. The posted schedule can show children eating breakfast at a table, then circle time, and so on. A schedule allows children to recognize the sequence of events (**Figure 2.11**).

Since children usually function better in small groups, the schedule should avoid having large groups share a room for an extended period. Large groups of children together, even with many adults, can be overstimulating and make it difficult to engage children in meaningful experiences.

Figure 2-11 A visual schedule, such as this one for a part-day program, helps children understand the structure of the day. *How can the teacher help children recognize how this schedule guides their day?*

Following the schedule helps teachers avoid difficulties and provide for smooth transitions. Meals should be served according to the schedule to prevent children from becoming overly hungry.

Indirect Guidance of Children

Teachers can guide children's behavior through careful room arrangement and the way activities and learning centers are set up. The emphasis should be on creating an orderly environment in which children have freedom and can interact and participate in activities with a minimum of direct teacher involvement.

Organizing and arranging equipment for children's independent use, with minimum assistance from the teacher, encourages self-direction and self-confidence through a high-quality, carefully prepared physical environment. It is important to include activities initiated and controlled by the child. To do this, children need easy access to the materials. Indirect guidance while engaging children in meaningful activities is often the secret to guiding behavior.

☑ CHECKPOINT

1. How does a teacher create a positive social and emotional environment?
2. Why does a schedule help children's sense of security?

2.5 The Teacher's Role in the Environment

The teacher is responsible for setting up the environment and interacting with children to support learning as children work and play. These interactions provide guidance and help children develop social and cognitive skills. Interactions should be planned to scaffold children's learning through thought-provoking questions and providing information. Basically, the teacher's role includes setting up and maintaining the environment, interacting with children as they work and play, providing guidance, and evaluating what children are learning and how the centers meet their needs.

Maintaining the Environment

Teachers are responsible for providing materials and supplies that coordinate with the curriculum and are appropriate and safe. Teachers should instruct children on the proper use of materials and appropriate behavior within the learning centers, then reinforce the guidelines during center time. They can further guide behavior by taking part in an activity and modeling supportive behaviors for children.

It is inevitable that items will be damaged or need minor repairs. If a nut becomes loose on a tricycle and the teacher ignores it, it may fall off and be lost. The teacher then has a larger problem of finding a replacement that fits or not having the tricycle to use. There is also the risk that a child could be injured if the tricycle breaks or if they pick up the nut and swallow it. If teachers take the time to check items periodically and fix what they can, they save a lot of effort and keep the children safe.

Ensure that everything is returned to its proper place. It takes effort to teach children to put things back, but it pays off in the end. Be consistent in seeing that everyone returns things to the designated location.

Clipboards are useful tools to keep up with paperwork. Teachers often hang clipboards on the wall to have readily available to check attendance or keep anecdotal records. A roll sheet or anything used regularly is easy to find if kept on a clipboard.

From the Field

Michelle Galindo
Toys and materials are tools that support relationships with children. As we watch them play, we learn about their interests, individual development, and skills. Learning environment materials should reflect children's family experiences and the diversity of the world around them. For example, materials and books should represent diverse races, ethnicities, abilities, and family dynamics, including music and movement materials that promote the children's home languages.

Michelle Galindo, M.S.
Adjunct Professor, Child Development
Family Studies Department
Southwestern College
Chula Vista, CA

Michelle Galindo

Figure 2-12

Organizing, Displaying, and Storing Materials

Children may want to repeat or revisit their experiences. For example, after a trip to a fire station, they may want to build a fire station in the block area or involve firefighters in dramatic play. Having items organized and quickly accessible will allow you to reinforce the concepts and provide repetition opportunities.

Consider the local supermarket. Everyone knows that fresh corn is in the produce section; frozen corn is in the freezer with other vegetables; and canned corn is on the shelf. Children need this same predictability in their learning environments. They need to know where to find the items they want in logical places.

Classrooms are not unlike supermarkets, where featured items are highlighted and seasonal items are prominently displayed. Many times, items are located to suggest ideas. Spices and pie crusts might be next to the pumpkins as inspiration to make pies; vanilla wafers may be near the bananas, suggesting banana pudding; or shortcakes may be near the fresh strawberries. Similarly, teachers suggest ideas for children based on the materials they provide and arrange. When teachers put firefighter hats in the dress-up area and firetrucks near the blocks, they suggest to children that they may want to reenact the experience of visiting the fire station—and most of the time, the children will do just that.

Interacting with Children as They Work and Play

Teacher interactions are a key to supporting children's learning (**Figure 2.13**). During learning center time, teachers should be engaged in observing and listening to children, as well as participating in conversations to expand children's knowledge and skills. Effective teachers provide resources or information and suggest ideas to expand children's learning. They will move around to support a child who needs help with a collage project, offer suggestions to a block builder who may need a garage to complete her house, and help a child who wants to join a group in the housekeeping area. They encourage children to talk about their activities by asking questions or making comments, such as:

- "Look at you! You are trying so hard to scoot to that rattle!"
- "We're looking at the book together. See the puppy and the kitten?"

FatCamera/E+ via Getty Images

Figure 2-13 A teacher engages in conversation with a second-grade child while helping her with motor skills. Why are conversations and interactions with children important for their development?

- "Tell me about your painting."
- "How did you make your block construction?"
- "What do you do when you go to the grocery store?"
- "I notice you are making greeting cards. Are they for someone in particular?"
- "Tell me how you set up the pretend office."
- "What musical instruments do you think work best for that song?"
- "I see you have selected the parquetry blocks. What do you plan to do with them?"

For more information about interacting with children, review Chapter 1, "Guiding Young Children's Learning." Above all, teachers must be close by to support children's experiences. Effective teachers circulate around the room, checking in with children and engaging in many one-on-one conversations. They stimulate children's thinking through the questions they ask and their interest in what children are doing.

☑ CHECKPOINT

1. How can the teacher demonstrate interest in children's accomplishments?
2. Why is constant attention to organization important for a teacher?

2.6 Focus on Assessment of Program Practices

Assessment of the environment is an important ongoing practice to ensure that children have maximum learning opportunities embedded in the environment. An effective teacher observes what children are doing and adjusts appropriately in an informal manner, and also uses formal tools to ascertain what children need. During the span of a year, children's growth and learning will require many changes as they master new skills and seek new challenges.

Evaluating the Environment

A process of evaluation is important as a means of ensuring that the environment meets the needs of children. This ongoing process of collecting, reviewing, and using information about the environment and adult-child interactions can be used to improve teacher performance and child outcomes. Using the results of the evaluation can make the teacher more effective and create better classroom experiences for children.

A classroom environment assessment looks at the materials, equipment, space arrangement, program structure, and activities in the classroom. Such assessments should also look at the adult-child interactions throughout the day, including how the adults talk and interact with children and how those interactions support learning. Classroom assessments of the physical environment may be completed by the teacher, a fellow teacher, an administrator, or someone outside the program, such as a consultant or regulator.

The Environment Rating Scales (ERS) are widely used tools for assessing a classroom environment. Separate versions of the scales are published for early childhood (preschool), infant/toddler, school-age programs, and family child care homes.

Assessing What Children Are Learning

Teachers are responsible for noting what children are learning and how well the learning centers and activities meet their needs. They do this by observing and recording what is taking place in the centers and gathering other documentation. Then teachers are responsible for reviewing the information about how children use the centers, what they have learned, and communicating the information about the children's progress to families. Such assessments are vital tools for planning. For more information on procedures for assessing children's learning, see Chapter 7, "Assessment: A Tool for Planning."

Assessing Interactions

Interaction assessment is the ongoing process of collecting, reviewing, and using information about adult-child interactions and the physical environment to improve teacher performance and child outcomes. Such assessments may look at adult-child interactions throughout the day, analyzing how you converse with children and how you support them.

One commonly used assessment for adult-child interactions is the Classroom Assessment and Scoring System (CLASS). Separate scales are available for infants, toddlers, and preschoolers. Using this formal system requires training to ensure that scoring is consistent and ratings are completed with reliability. These scales and others are used as part of state quality rating systems.

☑ CHECKPOINT

1. What are some ways you could determine if children know how to complete a specific task?
2. Why are your interactions with children important in your role as a teacher?

2.7 Family Matters

Most families see an early learning center for the first time and think it looks like a playland. Indeed, it is, but there is a serious purpose for the arrangement and materials within. One way to help families understand the value of the various learning centers is to post information about how children benefit from participation in each area. For example:

Housekeeping and dramatic play center. In the housekeeping and dramatic play center, children learn:
- to cooperate and communicate with others.
- to play and carry out their ideas.
- to explore various roles.
- responsibility of caring for materials.

Block and construction center. In the block and construction center, children learn:
- teamwork and collaboration.
- to share ideas about what can be done.
- important math and science skills.
- problem solving and engineering skills.

Library and listening center. In the library and listening center, children learn:
- to recognize the value of books and care for them.
- prereading skills of letter recognition, using context clues.
- appreciation of books and stories as a source of pleasure.
- to use context clues to decode words.

Art and creative expression center. In the art and creative expression center, children learn:
- to express what they see and how they feel.
- fine motor skills important for learning to write.
- an appreciation for artistic creations.
- to use tools to accomplish tasks.

Math and manipulative center. In the math and manipulative center, children learn:
- many math skills through firsthand experiences.
- fine motor skills important for learning to write.
- cognitive skills related to numerical concepts.
- relationships of shapes, patterns, and sizes.

Science and discovery center. In the science and discovery center, children learn:
- about the properties of materials.
- to explore natural objects and scientific tools.
- to experiment with scientific concepts.
- to experience the joy of discovery.

Music and movement center. In the music and movement center, children learn:
- to appreciate music for enjoyment.
- gross motor skills and the value of physical activity.
- math skills related to beat and rhythm.
- fine motor skills from using instruments.

Writing center. In the writing center, children learn:
- fine motor skills important for school readiness.
- to understand the purpose of writing as a communication tool.
- to communicate their ideas to others.
- how writing is used in society.

Active play area. In the active play area, children learn:
- the joy of movement and accomplishment.
- gross motor skills from active play.
- coordination of movement.
- cooperation in group activities.

Sand, water, and sensory area. In the sand, water, and sensory area, children learn:
- to experiment with the properties of materials.
- to use the area and materials for calming and stress relief.
- how materials react as they pound, shape, or pour them.
- to appreciate the elements of the earth.

Maker or tinkering center. In the maker or tinkering center, children learn:
- to use tools to accomplish self-imposed tasks.
- to experiment with materials and tools.
- to participate in the engineering process.
- creative skills related to problem solving.

Another way to educate families about the importance and value of the environment is to hold an open house and allow them to experience the learning centers as the children do. Adults may indeed surprise teachers with their interest in clay or fingerpaint in the art area or their complex constructions with the blocks.

✓ CHECKPOINT

1. Why is it a good idea to help families understand how children benefit from learning centers?
2. What are some events you might arrange to help families understand the value of learning centers?

Chapter 2 Review and Assessment

Summary

2.1 Describe the characteristics of the physical environment in an early childhood classroom.
- The environment of an early learning center is comprised of both the physical and emotional environment.
- The physical environment includes all the materials and equipment and how those items are arranged.
- A well-arranged environment provides a framework for children's learning. Most early childhood centers use a system of learning centers that allows children to participate in various areas of the classroom based on their interests to reach planned goals for children's development.
- The emotional environment comprises relationships and feelings of comfort for the children and adults.

2.2 Name and describe at least five learning centers appropriate for preschool children.
- Learning centers are areas set up in the classroom for specific activities and types of play.
- Common learning centers for preschool children include housekeeping and dramatic play, blocks and construction, library and listening, art and creative expression, math and manipulative, science and discovery, music and movement, writing, and active play. Others that are often included or may be present periodically are the sand, water, and sensory area and the maker or tinkering space.

2.3 Explain some ways in which the environment affects children's behavior.
- The use of learning centers enriches the environment by providing a variety of experiences based on what researchers know about how young children learn.
- Learning centers provide opportunities for children to follow their own interests and to work with a small group of friends in child-initiated projects and play scenarios.
- Learning centers help children see relationships between objects and learn from explorations.
- Learning centers are often set up or provisioned with materials related to curriculum themes. This classroom arrangement supports an integrated, well-rounded curriculum.
- Learning center arrangement can influence how much children engage with the materials and become self-sufficient. Poor room arrangement can result in distractions and interference from others.
- The arrangement of furniture and the materials provided are important for infants and toddlers as well as for preschoolers.
- Materials for the classroom should be selected following developmentally appropriate practices by considering not only the age of the children but how they are progressing in development.

2.4 Understand the social and emotional environment of an early childhood classroom.
- The social and emotional environment provides for development opportunities as children work in small groups and build friendships.
- Appropriate schedules, designed to guide the daily activities, are important in ensuring consistency, meeting children's physical needs, and predictability in the sequence of the day.
- Guidance from the teacher influences the relationships among children. The teacher must model the behaviors desired in children and help them learn the skills to be a part of the group.

2.5 Describe the teacher's role in preparing, supervising, and supporting children in learning centers and in the overall environment.
- The teacher's role is to establish and maintain the physical environment and to provide support to children so that the environment is comfortable for them. The teacher is a facilitator who guides children by selecting and arranging materials and by interacting with them.
- The teacher is responsible for assessing children's learning as they use the materials.

- The teacher's role includes evaluating the learning centers to determine if changes need to be made and following a predictable schedule that helps children feel secure.
- The teacher's role also includes supervising and interacting with children in a manner that encourages and supports learning.
- Open-ended and thought-provoking questions help children express their ideas and develop cognitive and language skills as they participate in chosen activities.

2.6 **Identify specific guidelines for evaluating each common learning center.**
- Evaluation of the overall environment and individual learning centers can be conducted using commercially available tools or by comparing the criteria from a reliable list of quality criteria.
- Assessment is important to determine whether the program is meeting children's needs.
- Assessment can inform plans for improvement.

2.7 **Explain ways to communicate with families about appropriate environments.**
- Families new to early learning programs may expect a setting quite different from what they will see in a high-quality early childhood program.
- Communication with families may include formal or informal conferences, brief chats at drop-off and pickup time, newsletters, blogs, email or text messages, and telephone or web-based calls.

Recall and Application

1. An appropriate mobile infant environment includes each of the following *except* ____.
    A. a safe place to sleep, such as a crib
    B. climbing equipment
    C. low shelves for toys
    D. safety scissors

2. A well-arranged indoor environment includes all of the following *except* ____.
    A. consideration of traffic patterns
    B. arrangement for visibility and supervision
    C. rows of desks and chairs
    D. items near where they will be used

3. **True or False.** The arrangement of furniture and equipment should allow for teacher supervision.
4. **True or False.** Active play should be confined to the outdoors.
5. **True or False.** The math or manipulative area is a place for table toys.
6. **True or False.** Poor room arrangement can contribute to negative behavior.
7. **True or False.** Children can learn cooperation skills by working and playing in small groups.
8. **True or False.** Paying attention to traffic patterns in the classroom helps prevent interference in activities.
9. **True or False.** Learning centers offer opportunities for children to develop social skills.
10. **True or False.** Children need time and space to be alone or with a few friends.
11. **True or False.** Supervision should be considered in the placement of equipment.
12. **True or False.** Teachers should refrain from providing children with choices.
13. **True or False.** The key role of the teacher is to prevent misbehavior in the classroom.
14. The teacher's role in a center-based learning environment does *not* include ____.
    A. observing and listening to children in centers
    B. directing all of the activities
    C. interacting with children as they work and play
    D. modeling supportive behaviors for children
15. **True or False.** The Classroom Assessment and Scoring System (CLASS) is a tool for rating the interactions between adults and children.
16. **True or False.** The block area and the library area should be next to each other.
17. **True or False.** Once a dramatic play area is set up, it should not be changed.
18. **True or False.** One way to help families understand the value of learning centers is to plan a time for the families to participate as their children do.

Chapter 3: The Inclusive Classroom

Standards Covered in This Chapter

NAEYC

NAEYC—1a, 1b, 1c, 1d, 2a, 2b, 2c, 3b, 3d, 4b, 4c, 5b, 6a, 6b, 6c

DAP

DAP—1a, 1b, 1c, 2b, 2d, 2e, 2f, 3b, 3g, 4a, 4b, 4h

Learning Outcomes

After reading this chapter, you should be able to:

3.1 Understand inclusion and its benefits in programs for young children.
3.2 Describe the history of special education services in the United States.
3.3 Apply methods to enhance the environment and provide materials to meet the needs of all children.
3.4 Describe how to help children with disabilities become successful learners.
3.5 Articulate the value of knowledge of child development.
3.6 Describe the role of assessment in successful inclusion.
3.7 Examine the importance of family relationships in an inclusive classroom.

Chapter opener image credit: kali9/E+ via Getty Images

Key Terms

accessible
accommodation
adaptable
cognition
heterogeneous
homogenous
inclusion
language
modification
motor coordination
natural environment
paraprofessional
people-first language
positioning
self-correcting materials
self-help
social interaction

Introduction

Inclusion, in relation to children's education, is the act or practice of combining in the same classroom children who have disabilities or exceptionalities with children who do not. Inclusion means that all children, regardless of ability levels, are educated together in a manner that promotes their growth and development. It means that all children can participate in typical daily routines and activities. An inclusive early-learning program is open to children and families of all cultures and focuses on the strengths and needs of each child. It provides an equitable environment and opportunity for all children.

In their joint position statement titled *Early Childhood Inclusion*, the Division for Early Childhood (DEC) and the National Association for the Education of Young Children (NAEYC) identified three key principles of early childhood inclusion that are hallmarks of high-quality programs and services (DEC & NAEYC 2020):

- *Access*—Providing access to high-quality, developmentally appropriate early learning experiences for all children is at the foundation of every early childhood education initiative.
- *Participation*—Early childhood educators should support maximum participation opportunities for every child by making acommodations to create an appropriate learning environment for children of all ability levels.
- *Supports*—Systems-level supports must be available to teachers and caregivers. Supports may include opportunities for professional development, access to resources, and collaborations with administrators, related services staff, and relative practitioners.

3.1 The Inclusive Classroom

Think about your time in school as it relates to special education services. Were students with disabilities included in your classroom? Were children with learning disabilities or delays in a separate classroom? How did they participate in activities? Were special education services available to children with disabilities in your school? Were there separate schools for those with disabilities, such as a school for children with vision or hearing loss? How well do you think your school served children with disabilities? How did the teachers relate to the students? How did children relate to each other?

Attitudes and understanding about the education of children with disabilities and the importance and benefits of their inclusion within the classroom have evolved in recent decades. An inclusive program unites every child with their peers and family members; regards the needs of each child (regardless of whether the individual has a disability) in planning and implementing activities; and considers each child as a valued member of the group.

The main idea of inclusion is that children deserve to be themselves. Each child is unique and deserves to be treated respectfully. Teachers convey that they value the children in their classroom by recognizing the children's individual needs and differences. They demonstrate respect by utilizing **people-first language**, referring to the child

Discovery Journeys

In the Family
Clarissa Willis, PhD, an author and a teacher who specializes in working with children with disabilities, shares this story about an event that strengthened her commitment and understanding of her role in special education:

I had worked in special education for many years, first as a teacher and then as a college professor, so I knew exactly what to say to a family who had a child born with a special need. Or I thought I did.

All my confidence in my knowledge went out the window one February night when my beloved sister-in-law called to say her baby, due in May, had come early and was being airlifted to a special hospital in Dallas. My husband and I rushed from Little Rock to Dallas, making the usual six-hour drive in under five hours.

In the hospital, my sister-in-law and her husband had just been informed that their daughter, who weighed just over one pound, would likely not make it. When it is your own family, everything you think you know about family empowerment does not seem to be enough.

As I looked at the tiny infant fighting to breathe, hooked up to machines, I heard the doctor tell the family, "She has cerebral palsy. She won't walk, talk, or be able to read. She will have very little ability even to feed herself or take care of other needs." Fortunately, today, doctors are more compassionate and less sure when a child is born what the outcome might be.

Lindsay did not die, nor was she impaired, other than having a problem walking. She went to public school and graduated, going on to earn both an undergraduate and a graduate degree. Today she works as an advocate for social services, finding foster home placements for children with special needs. I often say, "Lindsay didn't get the memo." Instead of focusing on what she would not be able to do, she went on to accomplish a lot.

I know that other children are not as fortunate as Lindsay, but I learned from this experience that some children have a built-in resilience that helps them defy the odds. After that experience I never dealt the same way with parents again. I now know that each family deals with adversity in their own way. My job became focused on helping families deal with what is happening in the moment, not what might happen in the future (Willis 2015).

---

before using any other descriptive characteristics and referring to a child's disability only when it is relevant and necessary.

The Benefits of Inclusion

The positive benefits of establishing an inclusive early childhood program accrue for all the children within the program (both with and without disabilities), their families, teachers, and the community at large. In an inclusive learning environment, children with disabilities or other exceptionalities may:

- experience an environment that stimulates developmental progress.
- increase their social skills and language through interaction with peers.
- learn by participating in daily routines and challenging, interesting play activities.
- develop a better understanding of life outside their home.
- develop confidence and increase participation within their classrooms, homes, and communities.

In an inclusive classroom, children without disabilities may:

- learn about differences in human growth, development, and abilities.
- learn about diversity, patience, and helping others (Molina-Roldan et al. 2021).
- become more accepting of those who are different as they work and play together (**Figure 3.1**).
- observe perseverance, courage, and resilience in their peers with disabilities.
- understand how all children are similar in many aspects.
- cooperate with and care about others.

wavebreakmedia/Shutterstock.com

Figure 3-1 As these children work together on a group project, they learn to appreciate each other's contributions. In what other ways might a teacher help children appreciate others?

By enrolling their children in an inclusive early childhood program, families of children with disabilities may:
- become engaged members of the program.
- observe their child learn new skills and form friendships with others.
- develop relationships with other parents.
- develop positive attitudes toward their children's progress.
- gain understanding and a realistic perspective for interpreting their children's accomplishments and challenges.
- increase their knowledge of child development, age-appropriate activities, and accommodations.
- feel that they are valued and supported within the program and their greater community.

By enrolling their children in an inclusive early childhood program, families of children without disabilities may:
- have opportunities to teach their children about differences in development, abilities, diversity, and other individual differences.
- develop a greater understanding of people with differing abilities.
- develop relationships with other parents.
- become more sensitive to the needs of families with children who have disabilities.
- become advocates for community acceptance and integration.

By working in an inclusive program, the teachers and staff may:
- develop an understanding of the unique needs of all children.
- learn to value and appreciate individual differences.
- grow in their experience and abilities in working with all children.
- learn about helpful community resources and how to access them.
- enhance the program through partnerships with individuals and agencies in the community.
- develop positive, realistic attitudes toward inclusion.
- receive additional training, such as learning how to enhance social interactions, which will benefit all children.
- develop relationships with professional colleagues from various disciplines.

Language Is Important

The language people use reflects their attitudes and perceptions. Teachers can demonstrate commitment to including young children with disabilities in their early childhood program by what they say and how they say it. They may begin by adopting the term *inclusion* to talk about what they are doing, rather than using outdated terms such as *integration* or *mainstreaming*. Teachers should always use people-first language, emphasizing the child before any disability, such as "a child who uses a wheelchair" versus "a wheelchair-confined child" or "a child with autism spectrum disorder" rather than "an autistic child."

> **Teaching Tip**
>
> **Applying Appropriate Language**
> As a rule, people-first, appropriate language puts the child before the description, uses respectful words, and describes what a child *has*, rather than what a child *is*.
>
> | Say | Instead of |
> |---|---|
> | he has autism spectrum disorder | he is autistic |
> | he has Down syndrome | he's Downs or he is a Down's kid |
> | children without disabilities | normal children |
> | accessible parking | handicapped parking |
> | she has a physical disability | she is crippled |
> | he receives special ed services | he is in special ed |
> | congenital disability | birth defect |
> | child with a hearing impairment | hearing-impaired child |
> | child with cerebral palsy | cerebral palsy child or CP child |

To describe children who do not have disabilities, the terms *typical* or *typically developing* are frequently used. The term *normal* is generally discouraged because it can be hurtful to imply that other children are not "normal" (Research and Training Center on Independent Living 2020). For the purposes of this textbook, the term *child without disabilities* is used with the understanding that all children have unique needs.

The phrase *child with special needs* often refers to children with medical or developmental difficulties who need more assistance than most of their peers. However, the term has a broad meaning that includes a wide variety of exceptionalities and refers to children who may have disabilities as well as those who are gifted. In this textbook, the term *child with disabilities* is used instead. This phrase encompasses emotional, physical, or cognitive disabilities or delays and ranges from familiar diagnoses, such as Down syndrome or autism spectrum disorder, to some that are exceedingly rare. The degree of impairment varies with each child, even within the same diagnosed condition. In considering children with disabilities, it is important to remember that all children have their own unique strengths, weaknesses, and styles of learning.

Choosing positive, people-first language creates a healthy learning environment. Educators communicate this attitude to children, colleagues, and parents through the words they choose. Coworkers, parents, specialists, and therapists hear how educators talk about the children in their classrooms. All early childhood professionals must be considerate in the language they use.

Respectful language should also be evident in written materials, such as parent handbooks, brochures, letters to families, and bulletin board notes. These materials should visibly express educators' feelings about working with young children and their commitment to inclusion.

Teaching in an Inclusive Classroom

Early childhood educators do not need to be experts on every exceptionality but must be open to learning about them. Teachers should also focus on creating an environment that enriches the developmental needs of all children. Classroom materials should include positive examples of inclusion. Select books about children with different abilities or delays interacting with others and taking part in community life. Books that illustrate the challenges faced by children with disabilities can help foster understanding and empathy among all children.

Inclusive toys and materials are important in an early learning environment, too. Props and dramatic play materials are available that relate to disabilities, such as a doll with a hearing assistive device or a wheelchair. Posters and photos in the classroom should include people with disabilities. The goal is to show examples of inclusion as a common experience.

Effective teachers celebrate differences in all children. Children with disabilities may require unique methods, services, or equipment for learning. In recent years, **homogenous** programs that grouped children with similar diagnoses have shifted to more **heterogeneous** programs in which peers with a range of abilities and needs are grouped together. Every child is unique and thrives in an environment of acceptance, and all children benefit from having a range of abilities, interests, and needs represented in their classroom.

☑ CHECKPOINT

1. How does inclusion affect early learning settings?
2. How can you support the parents of children with disabilities?

3.2 Special Education Laws in the United States

To better understand the path to inclusion, it is important to understand the key laws in place to identify and protect the rights of children. Children with disabilities have not always had the protections and support for appropriate education that they now have. The timeline in **Figure 3.2** provides an overview of the progress of legal protections for children with disabilities. The laws were passed because families and child advocates recognized and made their voices heard regarding the lack of services and the significant role that early intervention plays in helping children reach their full potential.

Prior to Public Law 94-142 in 1975, local school districts could cite the absence of "services," "setting," or "professional expertise" as reasons to deny services to students with disabilities. Lacking legal protection, many children with disabilities did not have the educational programs and opportunities they needed. At that time, public schools in the United States accommodated only one out of five children with disabilities. Many states had laws explicitly excluding children with certain types of disabilities from attending public school, including children who were blind, deaf, or labeled "emotionally disturbed" or "mentally retarded." Before Public Law 94-142 was enacted, most children with disabilities in the United States had no access to the public school system. Many of these children lived at state institutions, where they received limited to no educational or rehabilitation services. Another 3.5 million children attended school but were "warehoused" in segregated facilities, receiving little to no effective instruction.

Individuals with Disabilities Education Act (IDEA)

The Individuals with Disabilities Education Act (IDEA) was originally enacted by Congress in 1975. At that time, the law was known as the Education of All Handicapped Children Act, or the Education of the Handicapped (EHA). The intent of the legislation was to ensure that children with disabilities would have the opportunity to receive a free

Timeline of Legal Protections for Children with Disabilities in the United States

Year	Legislation
1975	The Education for All Handicapped Children Act (EHA) (PL 94-142) mandated that local school systems serve children with disabilities ages 6 to 17 in a free, appropriate, and least restrictive environment.
1983	The Education of the Handicapped Act Amendments of 1983 (PL-98-199) encouraged programs under the EHA to expand services to preschool children ages 3 to 5 years old.
1986	The Education of the Handicapped Act Amendments of 1986 (PL 99-457) mandated preschool programs for children 3 to 5 years of age. Free, appropriate, public education was extended to this age group. This law also established the Handicapped Infants and Toddlers Program (Part H), directed to the needs of children from birth to 3 years of age.
1990	The Americans with Disabilities Act (ADA) of 1990 (PL 101-336) is a comprehensive federal civil rights law to protect individuals with mental and physical disabilities from discrimination. The Education of the Handicapped Act Amendments of 1990 (PL 101-476) amended the original wording of the EHA to people-first language (for example, changing *handicapped children* to *children with disabilities*) and expanded the definition of those with disabilities. It also renamed the EHA to the Individuals with Disabilities Education Act (IDEA).
1997	The Individuals with Disabilities Education Act Amendments of 1997 (PL 105-17) retained the major provisions of earlier laws. Early intervention services, now Part C of the law, explicitly called for delivery of services in *natural environments*.
2004	The Individuals with Disabilities Improvement Act (PL 108-466) reauthorized IDEA.
2010	Congress passed Rosa's Law (PL 111-256), which amended the IDEA and other federal laws to replace the term *mental retardation* with the term *intellectual disabilities*.

Goodheart-Willcox Publisher

Figure 3-2 This table outlines the timeline of legal requirements for educational opportunities for children with disabilities. Why do you think laws were needed to make such opportunities available?

and appropriate public education, just as children without disabilities have. In 1990, the EHA was renamed to IDEA.

The law has several parts. Part B of the law outlines regulations for services to children ages 3 through 21. Part B application programs are most commonly known as Special Education Services in local school systems. Part C addresses services for infants and toddlers with disabilities, birth to age 3, and their families. All states have a Part C program, but each state has a different name for its early intervention system. Additionally, different state agencies serve as the lead agency in the various states, which can make accessing the system confusing.

Under Part B of the IDEA, children who are eligible for services are required to have an Individualized Education Program (IEP). The IEP is designed to meet the unique educational needs of the child. It requires these services to be provided in the least restrictive environment. A team, including parents as equal members, is convened and collaborates on the development of the IEP. The goals and outcomes of an IEP relate to the child's progress in an educational setting.

Part C serves infants and toddlers from birth to age 3 with developmental delays or who have been diagnosed with physical or mental conditions with high probabilities of resulting in developmental delay. The services are designed to enhance development, recognizing the significant brain development occurring in the first three years of life. The law also focuses on increasing the capacity of families to meet the needs of their infants and toddlers. An Individualized Family Service Plan (IFSP) is developed to meet both the child's needs and the needs of the family. IFSP goals may be in nonacademic areas of development, such as mobility, self-care, and social/emotional well-being. In early intervention, services are to be provided in the **natural environment**, meaning places where the child would be or go if they did not have disabilities. This natural environment could be an early learning center, a school, or any other setting children might usually attend.

In addition to the home, services may be provided in an early learning setting or a school. Early intervention services are not therapy, and the child usually views the experiences as playing. The service provider models and teaches strategies to strengthen the child's motor skills, help with language use, or address the goals identified in the IFSP. With this approach, primary caregivers learn how to promote the child's development within daily routines and activities rather than in periodic, isolated therapeutic settings.

The IDEA ensures services for children with disabilities throughout the nation. The IDEA also governs how states and public agencies provide early intervention, special education, and related services to eligible infants, toddlers, children, and youth with disabilities.

Americans with Disabilities Act (ADA)

The Americans with Disabilities Act (ADA) of 1990 (PL 101-336) is a comprehensive federal civil rights law to protect individuals with mental and physical disabilities from discrimination. When Congress passed the Civil Rights Act in 1964, discrimination based on race, color, religion, sex, or national origin was prohibited, but people with disabilities were not included in the wording of this law. The ADA was passed in 1990 to guarantee individuals with disabilities equal access, protection, and employment. The act was in response to a growing insistence by the public to include people with disabilities in all aspects of community life. The ADA states that child care centers cannot discriminate against any individual—child or adult—because of a disability. This law ensures that children with disabilities have equal access to early learning centers and other programs and services.

Teaching Tip

Key Requirements for Providers

The goal of the Americans with Disabilities Act (ADA) is to consider what is reasonable to meet the needs of a particular person with a disability to include that individual in a specific program. The ADA seeks to be fair to early learning programs and not cause undue hardship while requiring the programs to make every effort to include children with disabilities. Thus, early learning providers must:
- not discriminate against individuals because they have disabilities.
- develop eligibility/admissions criteria that do not screen out or tend to screen out people with disabilities.
- decide on a case-by-case assessment what is required to fully integrate a child into the program.
- determine whether reasonable accommodations can be made to allow enrollment.
- make reasonable modifications to policies, practices, and procedures.
- comply with physical access requirements.
- eliminate eligibility criteria that explicitly state that children with disabilities are not included.
- eliminate admissions criteria, such as being toilet trained, unless it is made clear they do not apply solely to children with disabilities.

The ADA defines a person with a disability as a child or an adult who:
- has a physical or mental impairment that substantially limits one or more major life activities, such as self-care, manual tasks, walking, seeing, hearing, communicating, learning, or working.
- has a record of such an impairment.
- is regarded as having an impairment.

The ADA requires child care programs to remove architectural barriers when doing so is "readily achievable" and will not constitute an "undue burden" (ADA 1990). Court decisions continue to define the precise meaning of these terms, but in general, providers can understand *readily achievable* to mean something accomplished without excessive difficulty and *undue burden* to mean something that does not require excessive expense. The ADA also specifies that programs cannot:

- charge a higher rate for a child with a disability.
- deny admission because of an increase in insurance rates or cancellation of coverage.
- deny services because of a lack of staff training, if training is available at a reasonable cost.
- deny admission because of disability.

In making decisions about admission, each child must be considered individually. Early learning programs are not required to accept a child with a disability if doing so poses hardship to the program. According to the ADA, a child may be denied services by a program if:

- necessary accommodations are too expensive or difficult to accomplish. The program must consider available tax credits, resources available through local school and health programs, and other outside funding resources.
- the child poses a direct threat to the safety of others, such as a child with a severe emotional or behavioral disorder, if the situation cannot be remedied by reasonable methods or modifications.
- the child's needs would fundamentally alter the nature of the program.

Reasonable Accommodations and Modifications

The ADA requires that programs make reasonable accommodations and modifications to make their services available to individuals with disabilities. However, such changes are not required if they would significantly alter the nature of the program. Early learning providers may impose legitimate safety requirements necessary for the operation of the program based on real risks—not generalizations, stereotypes, or speculation. The ADA prohibits unnecessary inquiries about a child's disability. As a requirement for early learning programs, it is important to understand the difference between accommodations and modifications.

Accommodations

An **accommodation** is an adjustment that allows a child with a disability to participate in a program in a way that matches the child's learning strengths and abilities. One can alter the physical classroom environment, such as by widening the openings between shelves to allow for a wheelchair. A staff member can be trained to administer medication or adjust medical devices for a child who needs such help. Such an accommodation would not put an undue burden on the program nor alter its function significantly.

Adaptive equipment is available to help children take part in classroom experiences. Scissors with loops instead of finger holes can help children who have trouble using regular scissors. Fidget or sensory toys can help children who need sensory input in order to be attentive during circle time. Large, easy-to-grasp crayons can help children with coordination challenges. Materials can be adapted to facilitate use and increase participation in activities. For example, pencils can be fitted with special grips and holders to make them easier to grasp and control (**Figure 3.3**).

Making accommodations not only allows children to participate, but it also provides different ways for children to receive information or communicate their knowledge without altering or lowering the standards or expectations. With accommodation, children learn the same material as their peers, but the way they learn it may be changed. For example, a child with coordination challenges might be given additional time to complete written work rather than being assigned less written work.

nadisja/Shutterstock.com

Figure 3-3 A child with difficulty with fine motor control uses a device to make the pencil easier to grasp. What are other ways to accommodate a child's difficulty with fine motor control?

Modifications

A **modification** is a change to what a child is taught or expected to do in the learning environment. In education, modifications are changes to the content or the instructional level of subject matter or tests. Modifications may create a different standard for students with disabilities than for those without disabilities.

Accommodation and modification needs may be determined after the child's needs have been assessed—either formally through the IEP or informally between the program and the family—and vary for each child. Examples of reasonable accommodations and modifications include:

- providing a ramp for a child who uses a wheelchair to access the program.
- rescheduling snack time to accommodate a child with diabetes.
- providing extra rest for a child who tires easily.
- assisting with a leg or arm brace.
- providing visual or auditory cues for transitions.
- allowing extra time to complete routines.

Questions to Help Assess Individual Children

Prior to enrolling a child, it is important for the program staff to learn about the child from the family. The director or administrator may ask a series of preliminary questions upon a family's inquiry to better prepare to meet the child's needs, regardless of the child's ability level. In the case of children with disabilities, such information from families can be invaluable in planning for successful inclusion. The questions are not intended to be used to screen out a child or deny admission but to make an informed decision and plan. Some sample questions are:

- What type of program is the family expecting?
- What are the child's favorite toys, games, and activities?
- How does the family adapt activities or equipment at home?
- Is any special assistance used at home that would work in the classroom?
- Does the child need any special equipment?
- What self-care skills has the child mastered, such as toileting or eating?
- What opportunities has the child had to participate with other children?

☑ CHECKPOINT

1. What does the ADA require of early learning programs regarding acceptance of children with disabilities?
2. What are accommodations and modifications? How are they different?
3. What other questions might be useful for an administrator to ask families before a child is enrolled in the program?

3.3 Creating an Inclusive Classroom

For children with disabilities to fully participate in an early learning program, accommodations must be made to meet their needs. Children may experience physical, sensory, and cognitive challenges; have special healthcare needs; or present challenging behaviors that must be addressed. There are many ways to create an inclusive learning environment. Teachers and staff must look at the environment to determine accommodations for the children's instructional, social, and physical participation.

Considering the Environment

Sometimes only slight adjustments in the environment can make it possible for all children to participate fully in a program. Some adjustments are inexpensive and easily implemented. For example, building a ramp for access to the building and providing tables that are the right height for children in wheelchairs are achievable adjustments that facilitate participation and independence. Towel rolls, pillows, blankets, wedges, and bolsters are effective for positioning children who need assistance sitting upright. Implementing a room arrangement that is consistent and predictable will help children with limited vision. Providing a restful place in the classroom will benefit children who are easily overstimulated. Placing equipment to provide support for children who have difficulty standing alone can help them navigate the classroom more independently.

Some classroom environmental accommodations to consider include:
- making clear pathways and ensuring there is enough space for children to move around safely.
- organizing tables in the classroom for wheelchair or limited-mobility access.
- placing cubicles or coat hooks on the end of a row and near the door.
- arranging beanbags and chairs in the story area for children who cannot sit on the floor.
- accommodating playground participation by adapting equipment and activities.

Selecting and Adapting Toys

For young children, important skills are acquired through frequent interaction with play materials and peers. The give-and-take during learning center activities and routines provides opportunities to learn appropriate social skills and to use these skills in a variety of situations. Selecting or adapting toys with the goal of inclusion in mind can support interaction among all children.

Educators should start by evaluating their supplies. They should ask themselves how the materials may be utilized by children with disabilities and if modifications can be made to make the materials easier to use. Often, a small modification, such as making an item easier to hold, can make it more useful for children who have coordination or grasping challenges. If modifications cannot be made, inclusive items should be purchased. Materials that are designed for children with limited motor control are ideal. Puzzles with knobs are easier for children to manipulate than puzzles without knobs (**Figure 3.4**). Every other block in a set can be removed to help children who have

Figure 3-4 Knobs on this puzzle help this child with coordination. *What other considerations can you identify in selecting materials for children with disabilities?*

difficulty with sequential stacking. In selecting or adapting materials, consider the accessibility, adaptability, and interactive capacity of each item.

Accessible

Accessible equipment or toys should allow use by children of differing abilities. Each child can play in, on, or with the toy without help, although a child with limited motor ability may need occasional assistance.

Adaptable

Each child can do something playful with an **adaptable** toy, even if it is not the same activity. For example, a balance beam flat on the floor can be used by children with limited coordination.

Cooperative

When play materials involve cooperation with others, children need to communicate. For example, a child may sit in a wagon alone, but to go anywhere, they need to ask another child to pull them. To play a board game, one child must recruit another child. Materials designed for two or more children offer subtle messages that suggest playing together.

Interactive

Look for toys and consider arrangements that encourage children to be close enough to interact with one another while they play. When children are face-to-face, they can communicate with each other verbally and nonverbally (for example, through smiles, laughs, frowns, and hand signals). A large pan of sand or water can offer opportunities for several children to play and communicate about their activities.

Considering Activities

A classroom is a busy place, filled with materials and supplies that are designed to support children's learning. Just like materials, activities can be adjusted for the benefit of all children. The following procedures can help support inclusion:

- Use activities and materials that are accessible to all children in the program.
- Encourage each child to participate. Give assistance and support as needed.
- Treat all children with respect.
- When talking to a child, speak clearly and allow adequate time for a response.
- Point out the strengths of all children and emphasize similarities among them.
- Answer children's questions about a child with disabilities in a straightforward, sensitive manner.
- Be as consistent as possible in routines and interactions.
- Try using different cues to communicate.
- Help set goals and work toward achieving them.

Adaptive Equipment

The program may decide to invest in adaptive equipment or accessible materials that are shared by many children, such as a ramp or specialized playground equipment. The following are considerations when purchasing adaptive equipment:

- Identify whether the adaptive equipment is necessary and developmentally appropriate.
- Consider the degree to which the equipment may be intrusive in the early learning classroom.
- Determine a core set of materials and equipment to have available.
- Assess the appropriateness of any positioning equipment as well as the need for it (**Figure 3.5**). Children's needs for different pieces of equipment change as they grow and develop.
- Establish a storage area for the equipment when it is not in use.
- Plan to train staff to use the equipment properly and safely.
- Ensure that the equipment functions in a consistent and predictable way and is easily cleaned and stored.

✓ CHECKPOINT

1. How can inclusive toys support peer interactions?
2. When asking a child a question, why is it important to allow adequate time for a response?

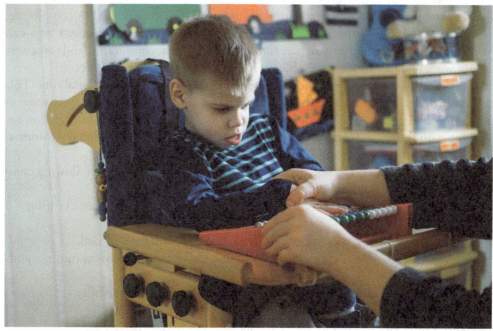

Iryna Imago/Shutterstock.com

Figure 3-5 This chair helps position the child so they can participate in a play activity. At what other time during the school day might this chair be useful?

3.4 The Teacher's Role: Taking Steps Toward Inclusion

How does the transition to providing an inclusive program take place? Sometimes, children arrive at a program with a diagnosis and a plan to address their learning needs. Other times, concerns arise after enrollment as the result of staff observations, screening, or evaluations. Early detection and intervention are essential to promoting optimal progress for children when they have challenges to overcome. The development of effective services and resources designed to address children with disabilities continues to evolve and improve as new intervention strategies are researched and evaluated.

When a child with disabilities enrolls in an early learning program, the program staff must decide whether the program can meet the child's needs. Communication with the parents or guardians, other educators, healthcare professionals, and related service professionals working with the child can help make the determination. Administrators and teachers should not react to preconceptions or stereotypes about what children can or cannot do or how much assistance may be required. They are often surprised at how easy inclusion can be.

Assessing the Child's Needs

A careful assessment can identify the procedures and adaptations needed to support optimal participation, recognize the skills the child has developed, and identify other skills that the child needs to learn. Accommodation ensures that the child will have access, is able to participate, and can develop independence in the early learning setting. Early learning programs may want to investigate available financial assistance opportunities for making accommodations and modifications, such as the Tax Reduction to Remove Architectural and Transportation Barriers to People with Disabilities and Elderly Individuals (Title 26, Internal Revenue Code, § 190) and the Disabled Access Credit for small businesses. Center owners and directors should consult their tax preparers to identify tax credits for which they may be eligible.

Early learning providers should establish good relationships with the child's parents and other caregivers. With a foundation of trust, families will provide direction about their child's needs. They can share tips and techniques they use to help their child be successful and safe. They have useful information regarding resources and contacts to aid in their child's inclusion. Early learning administrators can explore available options for additional staff training or financial assistance. Specialists can provide information and suggestions for accommodating a child's specific needs and ADA compliance. Teachers and administrators can take advantage of the knowledge of others who can help them provide the best experiences for the child. Parents, consultants, and caregivers should work together to set achievable goals that match the child's abilities.

There is a routine to follow when assessing a child with a suspected disability. This routine includes multiple steps, the first of which is to establish an evaluation team to assess the child and to develop an IEP, which will provide significant information for working with the child. Curriculum-based assessments can provide additional information about the child's skills and help set educational goals.

The team will identify the potential problem areas by considering the following components and planning for accommodations:

- Identify any necessary food substitutions, feeding techniques, and special eating and drinking utensils.
- Establish toileting routines, procedures, and types of assistance needed.
- Develop strategies for integrating the child into the existing classroom routines and activities.
- Modify the child's schedule in relation to the classroom daily schedule.
- Establish special healthcare routines and procedures.
- Identify strategies to support and teach socially appropriate behaviors.
- Determine the overall level of ongoing support necessary for the child to fully participate in the classroom in the most natural manner.

As part of the evaluation, the team may perform an environmental assessment, considering the routes the child will take to classroom areas, the bathroom, the lunchroom, the playground, and the classroom during arrival and departure times. They will identify areas that might be difficult or dangerous for a child with physical challenges or assistive devices and plan strategies for the child's movement throughout the day.

Once the needs of the child have been discussed, action plans can be developed and strategies designed to encourage participation. Some of these strategies include:
- providing a **paraprofessional** (a trained teacher's aide who works with children) for support to the child as well as the entire class (**Figure 3.6**).
- training appropriate staff in the child's needs, such as tube feeding, positioning, handling, or using adaptive devices.
- providing related services in the classroom (such as a speech pathologist planning an activity that involves others or the entire class).
- implementing a peer buddy system or other strategies to support friendships.
- assessing partial participation strategies.
- adapting the physical environment.
- modifying activities and materials.

The team should work closely with the child's parents and other caregivers as they complete the assessment and prepare for the child to enter the program. The parents and other caregivers can provide important information by visiting the facility and observing the program. They know their children's strengths and needs better than anyone and can offer valuable suggestions.

Welcoming a Child with Disabilities

Once the assessment is complete and the child is enrolled, a plan that focuses on the child's strengths should be put in place to optimize opportunities for participation. Recommendations from the assessment team can be a guide to make the necessary accommodations and modifications to the physical classroom.

Teachers also need to prepare the other children in the class for their new classmate. One way is to share children's books that include children with similar disabilities. This

DarioGaona/E+ via Getty Images

Figure 3-6 A trained paraprofessional assists a child with limited vision to complete a reading assignment. What specialized training might a paraprofessional need to be effective in working with children with special needs?

can stimulate a discussion about the child joining the class. Children can also create welcome cards or signs.

Try not to view inclusion as an overwhelming task. Many program accommodations and modifications are simple. For example, purchasing paintbrushes with long handles makes it easier for a child using a wheelchair to reach the easel. Large crayons are easier for a child with coordination challenges to grasp and use. Outlining pictures or shapes with white school glue helps a child with visual impairments identify images. These types of adaptations increase the child's opportunities to participate. If the child has an IEP in place, partner with the other professionals on the team for guidance and strategies to help the child succeed. As the child's teacher, you are an important member of the team and will share methods that work and how the child is progressing. Identify any needs the child may have and work with the team to find appropriate solutions.

Learning about Positioning

Positioning involves providing a child with external supports to help compensate for instability. Many children with severe or multiple disabilities require specific positioning for motor function and to promote normal muscle tone, stabilize body parts, and maintain alignment of their body. For example, supportive seating adapted for head movement and trunk support might offer a child the chance to practice head control during story time. The staff working with the child should be trained in positioning and handling techniques. Suggestions for training and skill development for proper positioning are:

- Ask parents for suggestions on positioning strategies based on their experiences at home.
- Ask a therapist to demonstrate ways to handle the child based on principles of good body mechanics and prevention of staff injuries.
- Involve occupational and physical therapists in developing strategies for positioning within the program.
- Determine how positioning can best be achieved using specially designed furniture, equipment, or supportive materials, such as towel rolls, pillows, or wedges.
- Develop a procedure and schedule for checking the child's position throughout the day to ensure correct and timely changes in position.
- Take videos or photographs of the child in positioning equipment and of the recommended carrying and transferring positions for review, new staff training, and procedure reminders.
- Provide staff with opportunities to handle and position the child to become comfortable with the process before needing to do it alone.

The position of a child should be natural for them and as similar to the way other children in the classroom are positioned as possible. A goal of positioning is to enable the child to participate with and have the same learning experiences as the other children. When an activity is conducted on the floor, position the child on the floor with appropriate supports, such as an adapted chair or an adult's body. Consider the best time of day for using certain equipment. For example, a child might be able to participate well in a stander at the art easel but may not be able to participate in the stander when others are playing on the floor in the block area. Follow the child's preferences when implementing positioning, and allow the child to select positions and areas where they would like to play. Provide opportunities for them to perform as much of the movement as they are able, even if it takes more time.

Making Structural Adaptations

Most curricula and instructional strategies assume that not all children need to be doing the same thing at the same time and that varying types and degrees of participation are appropriate. Early childhood special educators advocate for instructional goals and objectives to be embedded in the normally occurring routines and context of home

From the Field

Stefanie Echols

"Having opportunities to support students with and without disabilities simultaneously has been a privilege in my career as an early childhood educator. One thing that has been most enlightening is the realization that when we design an environment and make accommodations for children with disabilities, we improve outcomes for all the children in our classroom. Specifically, in an inclusive environment, students benefit from the influence of peers throughout their school day in a variety of naturally embedded social and academic situations. Children with disabilities gain natural peer models; typically developing children learn that differences are a part of life and we all need different things to succeed. Another way all students benefit from inclusion is because in most early childhood settings, support specialists and related service personnel "push in" to the classrooms where they can build relationships with, interact with, and provide enrichment activities to the whole group while still supporting the students on their caseloads inside the classroom."

Stefanie Echols, M.S. Ed.
Preschool Teacher, Special Education
Dr. James Mitchem Early Childhood Center
Valley View School District 365U
Romeoville, IL

Stefanie Echols

Figure 3-7

and early learning setting. Because children with disabilities may need more direct instruction, it is important to make adaptations that focus on maintaining an appropriate level of instruction, including purposeful participation in activities and educational achievement.

To make effective adaptations, teachers need to have a solid understanding of what is needed and decide how to maximize instructional inclusion of the child. All staff should be knowledgeable about the child's IEP objectives prior to planning the best path to inclusivity. Sometimes, even a carefully planned modification may not work, and a new plan will be needed. Three concepts provide general guidelines for instructional adaptations: (1) use the same materials and activities and have different objectives; (2) use the same materials and have adapted objectives; and (3) use the same activity with adapted materials and have the same or different objectives.

Same Materials, Different Objectives

Sometimes, the same materials and activities can be useful for meeting multiple objectives. While another child is working on learning classification by sorting objects by size or color, a child with motor challenges may participate in the same activity by naming the objects, grasping them, or taking turns with the peer. Both children benefit from the social opportunities as they work on their individual objectives.

Same Materials, Adaptive Objectives

Occasionally, a child with a disability will understand a concept but still struggle with the execution. For example, a child with limited motor control might be able to discriminate shapes or sizes but cannot physically sort them. The child might be able to indicate a shape or what size goes next by looking at or pointing to the one selected. If another child who is also learning to sort shapes or sizes takes a turn, then both children have the same objective but different means to demonstrate that ability.

Same Activity, Same or Different Objectives, Adaptive Materials

Sometimes it is necessary to physically adapt instructional materials to facilitate the child's participation. Following are some ways to adapt materials to increase stability and ease of handling:

- Add Velcro® fastener, tape, or nonslip material to prevent items from sliding on surfaces.
- Increase or decrease the size of materials as needed to support handling.
- Provide multisensory materials and components (for example, tactile, visual, olfactory, gustatory, and auditory).
- Arrange materials on lower or higher shelves if needed for easier access (**Figure 3.8**).
- Use adaptive devices, such as a mouth stick or universal cuff to hold paintbrushes or markers.
- Place play items within reach so the child can get them without assistance.
- Place materials on a vertical surface within a child's visual field or bring materials within a child's movement pattern.
- Provide materials that contrast sharply with surrounding work surfaces.
- Add handles or attach a string to materials so items can be picked up or retrieved.
- Group toys together to suggest a play theme. (For example, feeding utensils, such as a bowl and spoon, placed near a doll suggest feeding the baby.)
- Increase opportunities for children to interact. Provide enough materials that children can share but still have plenty for themselves. Having many parts of construction materials means there will be plenty for everyone.

Supporting Social Interactions

Successfully including children with disabilities in your classroom setting is achievable using strategies that provide development-enhancing opportunities. All children require attention to meet their individual characteristics and needs. Therefore, good, developmentally appropriate activities benefit every child. Children with disabilities may have specific needs based on their impairment, but all young children need support and encouragement as they learn to socialize and interact appropriately with each other.

Drinevskaya Olg/Shutterstock.com

Figure 3-8 In this classroom, materials are carefully arranged to be accessible to the children who will use them. Why is it important for children to be able to access materials independently?

Case Study

Joseph and the Relay Team

Joseph had a congenital condition that affected his legs, leaving him with limited control. However, following several surgeries, braces, and many hours of therapy, he was able to walk in an upright position. Although his mobility was slow and laborious, he participated independently in his second-grade classroom.

One day on Joseph's playground, the teacher observed a group of children in her class organizing a type of relay where they ran in pairs to the fence, creating a friendly competition between the pairs. Joseph was a part of the group, and when his turn came, one of the children announced, "If you race with Joseph, you have to walk to be fair." And that is just what the children did. Joseph's relay partner and the competing pair all walked rather than ran.

The teacher realized that the children had accommodated Joseph's abilities in their desire to include him. Inclusion was more important to them than winning. Often, Joseph was faster with his braces than the others who were walking; thus, he and his partner usually won the race. The teacher, who had Joseph in her classroom again the following year, saw that the new group of children again adjusted their activities to include Joseph in a similar way.

Consider This

1. What factors do you think motivated the children to make sure Joseph was included as an equal participant?
2. What experiences have you had that demonstrated children's acceptance of others with differences?
3. What actions or behaviors of the teacher may have affected the attitudes of the children?

Teach specific skills that will help children seek playmates and interact with others. Learning to look at another child when speaking or to say, "May I play with the blocks with you?" are skills that some children must be taught, especially if they have had little opportunity to be with others. Children with disabilities may be at a somewhat higher risk of peer rejection or exclusion in play than their peers without disabilities.

Teach peers how to interact with children with disabilities. Model acceptance through your own actions and words. Teach children specific skills about how they can best include a classmate with disabilities. Show them how to face a child with a hearing impairment so that the child can better understand what they are saying. Demonstrate how to help another child with tasks when coordination makes it difficult. Point out the similarities rather than focusing on differences.

Look for strengths. Provide opportunities and activities to support children's strengths and growing skills. Ensure that you treat each child as a valued member of the class rather than becoming focused on a child's delay or disability. Every child deserves to feel included, capable, and valued.

Model and coach appropriate behaviors. Sometimes, children with disabilities may have had limited opportunities to develop social skills through playing with others. Model appropriate play behaviors yourself by being a play partner with the child. Invite other children to join your activity. Acknowledge and encourage children's efforts and appropriate actions in their interactions with others.

✓ CHECKPOINT

1. How can you support social interactions in your classroom?
2. What is an example of a structural adaptation? When might a structural adaptation be necessary?

Discovery Journeys

Finding Solutions for Frank

Frank's family emigrated from Central America just a few years before he entered first grade. His family spoke little English, and at the time, there were no programs for English language learners at Frank's school. His father learned some English and pursued a career as a mechanic, while the family exclusively spoke Spanish at home. By the third grade, Frank was well behind his peers in reading and language skills. He had mastered enough oral language to meet his basic needs, but letter recognition and association with sounds eluded him. It was not a lack of ability that challenged Frank; it was the school's lack of support for his transition as an English language learner and the expectation for him to learn reading in a language he had not mastered orally.

In seeking classroom experiences that would be challenging but achievable for him, his third-grade teacher, Mrs. Chinara, borrowed from the work of Maria Montessori and her **self-correcting materials**. Mrs. Chinara created a series of matching cards and other materials with English words and corresponding pictures that applied to Frank's life. However, Frank had simply missed too much by that time to catch up to his peers by the end of the third grade. If Frank had the type of support available to children today, he might have become efficient in both languages by the third grade and had the benefit of being bilingual.

Consider This

1. What type of supports are available today for children who arrive at school with limited English language exposure?
2. What are the benefits to a child who is bilingual?
3. What are some ways a teacher can support children learning English as a second language?

3.5 Understanding the Role of Child Development Knowledge

Working successfully with young children requires an understanding of child development. Such knowledge helps early childhood educators recognize when a child's development may differ enough that assessment or consideration for intervention services may be needed.

Children's development usually follows a predictable course (**Figure 3.9**). The time required to master certain skills and abilities is often used to measure children's development and provide a guideline for measuring an individual child's progress. These skills and abilities are known as *developmental milestones*. Abilities such as sitting up, crawling, walking, saying single words, putting words together into phrases and sentences, and following directions are examples of these predictable achievements. Although not all children reach each milestone at the same age, there is a general timeframe for reaching these markers. The course of children's development can be traced using charts of developmental milestones. Some of the categories within which these behaviors are seen include:

- **Cognition**—thinking, understanding, reasoning, analysis, problem solving
- **Language**—both receptive and expressive abilities
- **Attention**—staying on task, noticing details, focusing efforts
- **Behavior and self-control**—impulsivity, temperament, turn-taking, delayed gratification, tolerating frustration
- **Motor coordination**—gross and fine motor skills, including jumping, hopping, throwing, catching, drawing, stacking
- **Social interaction**—response to social cues, initiating peer contact, participating in group play
- **Self-help**—dressing, washing, eating, toileting

Child Development Stages

Stage	Definition	Appearance
Prenatal	Begins at conception and ends at birth (typically 9 months later). The rate of growth at this stage is the fastest it will be in life. In this stage, a fetus grows from a single cell to a complete organism. Even before birth, babies can move, recognize the pregnant person's voice patterns, and react to strong stimuli.	 PeopleImages/iStock via Getty Images Plus
Neonatal	Also known as newborn, this extends from birth to 1 month. During this period, the baby physically adapts to life outside the pregnant person's body.	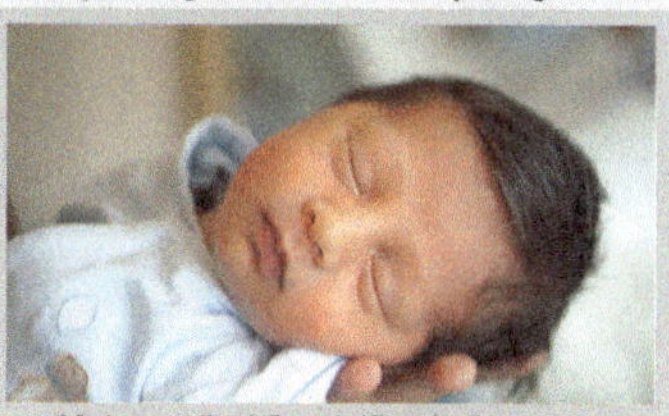 Mehmet Hilmi Barcin/E+ via Getty Images
Infancy	Begins at 1 month and continues to 12 months. The infant develops the foundation for motor, thinking, language, and social skills.	 MBI/Shutterstock.com
Toddler	Begins at 12 months and ends at 36 months (the child's third birthday). In the toddler stage, the child makes great strides in motor, thinking, and language skills and begins to be less dependent on adults.	 digital skillet/iStock via Getty Images Plus
Preschool	Begins at 3 years and ends at 6 years. During this stage, the child becomes more self-sufficient, spends many hours in play exploring the physical and social worlds, and begins to develop knowledge of one's self.	 LUNAMARINA/iStock via Getty Images Plus
School-age (middle childhood)	Begins at 6 years and ends at 12 years. This stage corresponds to the typical ages of children in the elementary school years. Achievement is the central goal of these years. School-age children become proficient in the basics of reading, writing, and arithmetic. They are exposed to many other learning opportunities, too. In school, children interact with peers more and learn through group instruction. Before the end of this stage, children have more stable feelings about themselves and know how others feel about them.	 LUNAMARINA/iStock via Getty Images Plus
Adolescence	Begins at 12 years and ends around 18 years. This stage corresponds to the typical ages of children in middle school and high school and is marked by the onset of puberty. Adolescence is the stage during which a young person develops from a child to an adult.	 Heather Preston

Goodheart-Willcox Publisher

Figure 3-9 This chart illustrates highlights in the typical development of children. Why is knowledge of child development important for everyone who works with young children?

Children do not always acquire skills at the same rate, and variations are to be expected. Many factors can influence development and learning, including available opportunities and variety of experiences. Cultural and environmental values and differences can influence how children are perceived and the encouragement of learning. A teacher may perceive a child who does not readily make eye contact as lacking in self-confidence. Yet in the child's culture, limited eye contact may show respect; the culture may consider maintaining eye contact an inappropriate way for children to interact with adults.

Limited exposure to the prominent language can influence the way children learn and interact. Situations may occur in which a child does not appear to grasp a concept when in reality the child may lack the language skills to understand what is being asked or taught. One way to help a child who is a dual-language learner is through pairing. For example, pair a child who is a dual-language learner with a child who speaks the same language, or pair a new child with a child who knows the program's routines to help them navigate the day.

Children with developmental delays, such as those who are progressing more slowly than their peers, may need activities adjusted to match their current level of development. Those who are more advanced in development may need more challenging tasks. For example, consider the adjustments that must be made for an early walker in an infant classroom.

Some children exhibit behaviors that fall outside of the typical, or expected, range of development. These behaviors emerge in a way or at a pace that is different from their peers. Culture and the environment contribute to the ways children behave. A child in a culture that does not value independence may not achieve the self-help skills expected in some other cultures. The child may rarely take the initiative and may instead wait for adult direction and always seek permission before starting an activity.

Directory of Conditions

In planning for an inclusive program, some knowledge of the common disabilities, disorders, and delays children might present is essential (**Figure 3.10**). There is a growing understanding that any and all disabilities may affect individuals along a scale from minimal or mild to severe. The greater the severity of a condition, the greater the likelihood for increased need for supports throughout life. Children with a severe disability often require ongoing, extensive support in major life activities to participate in integrated community settings, while children with a minor disability may need few modifications to fully participate in classroom activities. Children may also have multiple significant disabilities, including movement difficulties, sensory losses, and behavior problems. Because of this range of affectation, you may want more detailed information on any condition a child in your class presents as well as information on the child's specific abilities before forming a plan for meeting the child's unique needs.

Making a Referral

When providers have concerns about a child's development, having a partnership with the family is particularly important. Disabilities may not be recognized at birth but may become noticeable as a child exhibits a delay over time. Sometimes a child's disabilities are not recognized until they are in a group setting when a teacher notices that the child's development is behind that of other children in the group. What should teachers do if they have concerns about a child's development? First, before approaching the family, a teacher should document the concerns with clear, specific examples of the behavior the child is or is not exhibiting. Next, it is important to speak to an administrator for guidance or to jointly talk to the parents and ask if they have concerns. Sometimes, the parents voice their concerns to the teachers first and ask for input or opinions.

Teachers should not try to diagnose the problem. Instead, they can say something like, "I've noticed that Maya is having trouble sitting up and wondered if you saw that at home," or "Ishaan doesn't speak to anyone at school and doesn't seem interested in the other children," instead of "I think she has cerebral palsy," or "He may have autism spectrum disorder." Doctors and psychologists, not teachers, must make those kinds of diagnoses. If a

Common Childhood Disabilities, Disorders, and Delays

Condition	Description
Attention-deficit/hyperactivity disorder (ADHD)	ADHD is a chronic condition that affects millions of children and often persists into adulthood. Problems associated with ADHD include difficulty focusing attention, distractibility, and hyperactive, impulsive behavior.
Autism spectrum disorder	Autism spectrum disorder is a neurological and developmental disorder that is usually diagnosed during the first three years of life. A child with this disorder usually shows little interest in others and demonstrates a lack of social awareness. A child with autism spectrum disorder may seek a consistent routine and repeat unusual behaviors. Individuals often have problems with communication, avoid eye contact, and show limited attachment to others. Autism spectrum disorder can prevent a child from forming relationships with others, partially due to the inability to interpret facial expressions or others' emotions. A child may resist cuddling, may prefer to play alone, and will likely be resistant to change. Those with the disorder tend to exhibit repeated body movements, such as rocking or flapping hands, and often have unusual attachments to objects. Some people with this disorder excel at certain mental tasks, such as counting, measuring, art, music, or memory.
Cerebral palsy	Cerebral palsy affects muscle tone, movement, and motor skills, causing difficulty with purposeful movement. Cerebral palsy is usually caused by brain damage that occurs before or during birth or during the first few years of life. Treatment, therapy, special equipment, and sometimes surgery can improve a child's condition.
Deafness or hearing loss	Hearing impairment is defined by the IDEA as "an impairment in hearing, whether permanent or fluctuating, that adversely affects a child's educational performance" (1990). Deafness is defined as "a hearing impairment that is so severe that the child is impaired in processing linguistic information through hearing, with or without amplification" (IDEA 1990).
Down syndrome	Down syndrome is a set of mental and physical symptoms that result from having an extra copy of Chromosome 21. Many children with Down syndrome can function independently.
Emotional disturbance	An emotional disturbance is a condition in which children exhibit one or more of the following characteristics to a degree that adversely affects educational performance: A child may have an inability to learn that cannot be explained by intellectual, sensory, or health factors, or an inability to build or maintain satisfactory relationships with peers and teachers. There may be inappropriate types of behavior or feelings for normal circumstances, or perhaps a general pervasive mood of unhappiness or depression. Or there may be a tendency to develop physical symptoms or fears associated with personal or school problems.
Epilepsy	Epilepsy is a general term used for a group of disorders that cause disturbances in electrical signaling in the brain. A person with epilepsy is subject to seizures that may range from very mild to severe.
Intellectual disability	*Intellectual disability* refers to certain limitations in mental functioning, communicating, and taking care of oneself. These limitations, sometimes referred to as *cognitive impairments* or *developmental delays*, cause a child to learn and develop more slowly than their peers.
Learning disabilities	A learning disability is caused by a problem in the nervous system that affects how information is received, processed, or communicated. Various disorders affect the way verbal and nonverbal information is acquired, understood, organized, remembered, and expressed. Some common ones are dyslexia, dyscalculia, dysgraphia, and ADHD.
Speech and language impairments	Speech and language impairments are communication disorders such as stuttering, impaired articulation, or voice impairment, that adversely affect a child's educational performance.
Spina bifida	A child born with spina bifida has an opening in the spine. A healthy spine is closed to protect the spinal cord, a bundle of nerves that sends messages back and forth between the brain and the rest of the body. The condition may result in full or partial paralysis and bladder- or bowel-control difficulties.
Traumatic brain injury	A traumatic brain injury is caused by a blow or jolt to the head or a penetrating head injury that disrupts the brain's normal function. The severity may range from "mild," a brief change in consciousness, to "severe," such as an extended period of unconsciousness or amnesia following an injury.
Visual impairments	A visual impairment is any kind of vision loss, whether it is someone who cannot see at all or someone who has partial vision loss. Children with visual impairments are often delayed in physical and motor skills.

Goodheart-Willcox Publisher

Figure 3-10 This table describes some of the most common disabilities one might encounter in working with children. How might such a table be helpful to a teacher or for families?

parent asks about a specific disorder, teachers can certainly share any information or experience they may have with that condition or help the parent find more information. They can include information about the child's strengths and abilities in the discussion as well.

After speaking with teachers, parents may choose to seek medical advice from their child's healthcare provider or, if warranted, request a referral to the appropriate systems that provide services to children with disabilities. Usually, such systems are part of public school services. Early learning providers are important sources of information about children.

To make a referral, teachers do not have to know the diagnosis—they need only explain their observations and concerns. It is important for teachers to be specific. For example, "Adam is 16 months old and cannot yet sit without support," rather than a vague, "He is behind other children." A team of professionals will follow up on the referral with a screening. Then, if deemed appropriate, they will conduct an evaluation to determine if the child is eligible for services and which services are recommended.

☑ CHECKPOINT

1. Does inclusion apply to a child who speaks a language that the teacher does not understand?
2. What is the teacher's role in identifying developmental delays?
3. Do teachers need knowledge of common delays and disorders? Why or why not?

Case Study

Aaron

Aaron is 8 years old and has developmental delays. His parents try hard to give him the experiences most children without his challenges would have. However, they often find that their attempts lead to hurt and disappointment for themselves.

At a public park, some children laughed at Aaron's awkward attempts to climb the slide ladder. They referred to him as "that goofball" and taunted him until his parents asked him to walk with them to another part of the park.

"Why? I don't want to leave my friends," he wondered, with no understanding of the children's unkind intentions.

Other incidents also occurred. Upon their attempt to enroll him in a summer camp, his parents were told that he would not fit in because he was not yet reading and the children needed to read instructions. The parents learned of a birthday party held by family friends for their child who was the same age. Aaron was not invited.

Consider This
1. What examples of discrimination or lack of acceptance for someone with a disability have you witnessed?
2. How do you think the examples above made the parents' job harder?
3. What could a teacher do to help children be accepting of those with disabilities?
4. How do these situations reflect the need for more education and understanding about children with disabilities?

3.6 Focus on Assessment of Program Practices and Involving Families

Several areas of focus and many elements contribute to a quality program. These include the organization of physical space, an appropriate and adequate supply of materials, teacher qualifications, instructional strategies, collaboration among team members and families, and individualization and adaptations within daily routines.

Ideally, high-quality inclusive systems are intentionally developed from the beginning rather than after other aspects of the system are already in place. However, in some instances, existing systems and programs need to make changes to be inclusive of all children. Tools and resources exist to guide programs in implementing high-quality inclusive practices. However, inclusion alone does not guarantee desirable outcomes for children with disabilities. Assessing the program's effectiveness is an essential part of successful inclusion.

One means of program assessment is to compare an existing program with best practices. The NAEYC Early Childhood Program Accreditation Standards and Assessment Items relate to children with disabilities and can be applied to assess a program. Each standard can be rated as 1 (fully met), 2 (partially met), or 3 (not met) and used as a basis for ongoing improvement. Here is an adaptation of the standards that can serve as an assessment tool by using the 1–3 rating scale:

1. _____ Curriculum materials represent the diverse languages, ages, abilities, and genders found in society.
2. _____ Children with varying abilities have experiences similar to those of their peers.
3. _____ Assessment methods are sensitive to, and informed by, family culture and experiences, children's abilities and disabilities, and children's home language(s).
4. _____ Program staff ensure that all families are included in volunteer opportunities and program events, considering challenges that may be posed by family structure, socioeconomic circumstances, racial and cultural backgrounds, gender, abilities, and preferred language.
5. _____ Materials are selected and used in ways that depict a diversity of experiences, values, abilities, dress, and customs rather than singular representations of an entire group or selection of people.
6. _____ The program promotes positive relationships among all children and adults to encourage each child's sense of individual worth and belonging as part of a community.
7. _____ The program fosters each child's ability to contribute as a responsible community member.
8. _____ Teaching practices, curriculum approaches, and classroom materials do not present stereotypes, but instead respect diversity in gender, sexual orientation, age, language, ability, race, religion, family structure, background, and culture.

☑ CHECKPOINT

1. Why do you think it is important for children with varying abilities to have the same experiences as their peers?
2. How can you foster positive relationships among all the children in your classroom?

3.7 Family Matters

Providing a high-quality early learning program for children of all abilities requires an understanding of parent and family reactions and needs. When families learn about a delay in their child's development, the information may come as a heavy blow, leading to fear and confusion. Some may have noticed there have been problems since the child's birth. Others may have had no frame of reference to recognize that their child is not progressing at the same rate as others who are the same age. Some disabilities may go unrecognized until an astute teacher notices the child's difficulty in certain tasks.

Common Reactions

Upon learning that their child could have a disability, a parent's first reaction may be denial or anger directed toward the person who is delivering the news. Fear is another response. "What will happen to my child when he is 5 years old, or 25?" "Will my child be capable of living independently?" People often fear the unknown more than the known.

Families may be concerned about their child being rejected, how siblings may be affected, and whether they can provide the necessary care. The cost of potential medical care is a concern for many families. Memories of how children with disabilities were treated in their own childhood may come to the forefront. Guilt and concerns often arise about whether the parents themselves have caused the problem: "Did I do something to cause this? Did I take care of myself when I was pregnant? Is this situation hereditary? Does this mean my other children or grandchildren are likely to have the same problems?"

Some families may not fully understand what is happening and what will happen. Their confusion may cause sleeplessness, an inability to make decisions, and mental overload. Powerlessness to change what is happening or has happened is difficult to accept. Parents and guardians want to feel competent and capable of handling their own life situations, and that feeling may be absent when they are faced with raising a child with disabilities. They may feel that their child's disability reflects their own personal failure, challenging their own self-esteem. Their disappointment or inability to accept what they deem an imperfection can cause a reluctance to fully accept their child as a valuable, developing person.

Supporting the Families

As a partner in the child's growth and development, teachers can take many constructive actions to be a source of help and reassurance for the families of children with disabilities (**Figure 3.11**). Teachers can:

- let families know that their child is valued at school and that their development will be supported. They can inform families that they are trained, or plan to receive training, to support children with special needs.
- help families connect with other families, especially those who have experienced similar situations. Parents and guardians of children with disabilities may feel isolated.

sturti/E+ via Getty Images

Figure 3-11 A teacher and family review samples of work and discuss goals for the upcoming weeks. How do regular conferences help families and teachers to set reasonable and consistent expectations?

- keep a positive attitude of hope. A positive attitude is one of a teacher's most valuable tools for dealing with problems. Focusing on the positives diminishes the negatives.
- help families connect with resources to assist with the challenges they are having. Guide them in becoming advocates for their child.
- allow them to talk about their feelings and express their emotions. Some parents and guardians repress their emotions because they believe it is a sign of weakness to let others know how they are feeling.
- help families see that their child's development may be different from that of other children, but this does not make the child less valuable, less important, or less in need of love, nurturing, and parenting.

Chapter 3 Review and Assessment

Summary

3.1 Understand inclusion and its benefits in programs for young children.
- Research on child development and screenings help support the identification of special needs at earlier ages, which can result in more successful intervention.
- As society views children and adults with disabilities as active members of society, parents can be more hopeful about what their children can accomplish and how they will function in social settings.
- Opportunities for a full, rich life for children with disabilities are increasing. Educators, as professionals who are knowledgeable about children's development, can affect that progress.
- In many cases, children with disabilities can be included with minor accommodations and modifications.
- The physical environment may need to be arranged to facilitate a child's navigation to various areas of the room and building.
- Teachers may need to learn about appropriate positioning and care and use of special equipment.
- Toys and other learning materials should be selected with the child's needs in mind to facilitate maximum involvement.

3.2 Describe the history of special education services in the United States.
- The Education of the Handicapped (EHA) and its amendments mandate a free and appropriate education for children ages 3 to 17.
- The Individuals with Disabilities Act (IDEA) provides services to children ages 3 through 21.
- IDEA requires an Individualized Education Program (IEP) to plan goals for the child's development.
- IDEA requires an Individualized Family Service Plan (IFSP) for both the child and the family.
- IDEA provides services for the child's natural environment.
- Programs may not refuse to admit a child with disabilities unless admission would fundamentally change the program or be cost-prohibitive.

3.3 Apply methods to enhance the environment and provide materials to meet the needs of all children.
- Assess the needs of children with disabilities.
- Teachers can make accommodations or modifications to help children with disabilities.
- Adaptive equipment may be needed for some children.
- Many adaptations can be easily done at little cost.

3.4 Describe how to help children with disabilities become successful learners.
- Provide toys that are accessible, adaptable, cooperative, and interactive.
- Materials may be selected or adapted for individual children's needs.
- Proper positioning can help a child be an active participant.

- **3.5 Articulate the value of knowledge of child development.**
  - An understanding of child development milestones allows a teacher to recognize when a child may be at risk of delays and need screening or assessment.
  - Early recognition and intervention are important in helping children reach their full potential.
  - Identifying a need for screening and taking the necessary steps can mean that teachers and parents have the tools they need to help children progress.

- Instructional adaptations can make use of the same or adapted materials.
- Support in social skills can help a child in interactions with peers.

- **3.6 Describe the role of assessment in successful inclusion.**
  - Assessment is important for all children, including those with disabilities, to provide a guide for developmentally appropriate planning based on children's strengths and needs.
  - Various guidelines and standards can provide tools for such assessment and planning.

- **3.7 Examine the importance of family relationships in an inclusive classroom.**
  - Families are important partners in a successful inclusion program. Families have information and knowledge of their child they can share.
  - They will often benefit from information shared by the child's teacher.
  - Collaborative efforts will help ensure consistency in education for children with disabilities.

Recall and Application

1. **True or False.** Inclusion creates an environment of acceptance and provides valuable lessons in caring and helping.
2. **True or False.** Inclusion can help typically developing children to develop sensitivity and understanding toward others.
3. Effective early learning professionals adjust for learning differences for _____.
   A. children with autism spectrum disorder only
   B. all children
   C. children with more abilities than usual
   D. children with disabilities
4. **True or False.** *ADA* stands for "Americans with Delays Act."
5. *IDEA* stands for:
   A. Inclusion Defense Education Act
   B. Individual Development Education Award
   C. Individuals with Disabilities Education Act
   D. Intellectual Disabilities Education for All
6. **True or False.** Making clear pathways in the classroom helps children navigate the space more independently.
7. **True or False.** Using positioning equipment may require training for the teacher.
8. **True or False.** Teachers should build and expand on a child's strengths when planning activities.
9. **True or False.** Parents can be a useful source of information for ideas and techniques that are effective with their child with special needs.
10. **True or False.** Children's development follows a predictable course.
11. **True or False.** A child who does not demonstrate abilities typical for the child's age may benefit from screening or assessment.
12. **True or False.** Comparing what is being done to what is considered best practice is a good way to assess progress in inclusion.
13. **True or False.** Families need not be involved in their child's program if the teacher has special training.
14. **True or False.** Collaboration with families helps provide consistent expectations for a child.

Chapter 4

Planning for Playful Learning

Standards Covered in This Chapter

NAEYC

NAEYC —1a, 1b, 1c, 1d, 2b, 2c, 3a, 3c, 3d, 4a, 4b, 5c

DAP

DAP—3, 4, 5

Learning Outcomes

After reading this chapter, you should be able to:

4.1 Define play and describe how it benefits the young child.
4.2 Name and describe the stages and types of play.
4.3 Demonstrate cultural influences on play activities.
4.4 Describe developmentally appropriate play activities that support learning.
4.5 Explain ways that adults can support and extend play.
4.6 Describe how to assess play opportunities for young children.
4.7 Explain the importance of communicating with families about play.

Chapter opener image credit: olesiabilkei/iStock/Getty Images +

Key Terms

associative play	games with rules	role
constructive play	onlooker play	rough and tumble play
convergent thinking	parallel play	sensorimotor play
cooperative play	physical play	socio-dramatic
creative play	play	solitary play
divergent thinking	pretend play	social play
dramatic play	prop box	unoccupied play
fantasy play	props	visual perception
fill and dump	proximity	
fine motor skills	role play	

Introduction

When we think of play as a child's chosen and spontaneous activity, the idea of planning for play seems counterintuitive. Yet in early childhood, a teacher versed in a foundation of child development understands that play activities are often chosen by children based on the experiences occurring and the materials that are available. Experiences provide inspiration and motivation, and materials are often the catalyst for ideas. Thus, to plan for play entails providing an environment that supports playful learning, taking advantage of the important role of play in the lives of young children and their learning.

4.1 The Importance of Play for Young Children

From an early age, children play. It begins as physical movement for infants, such as joyfully waving arms and legs. Babies enjoy peek-a-boo and repetitive actions (**Figure 4.1**), such as shaking a rattle or squeezing a toy to see what happens, then moving on to playing with increasing sophistication as toddlers and preschoolers. Play remains important throughout the life span. Adults play sports and board games for recreation and amusement; they even "play around with" ideas to produce creative solutions.

In early childhood, play is the foundation for learning. Through play, children acquire the skills and knowledge to prepare them for adult life, including the development of imagination and problem-solving skills. It is a means of developing vital literacy and cognitive skills. Physical play, such as group games or climbing on playground equipment, helps to keep children's bodies healthy; play also has social and emotional benefits, helping children make friends and work through conflict.

What is meant by play? Is it aimlessly fiddling with materials? In contrast, play for children consists of intrinsically motivated activities engaged in for enjoyment. Play is a key tenet of cognitive development. Being allowed to experiment and explore through play provides children with the opportunity to construct knowledge. In this textbook, play is considered to be any activity into which children enter by choice, although the choice may be inspired by the materials provided or by suggestions made by an adult or other children.

In the NAEYC position statement, play is identified as "the central teaching practice that facilitates young children's development and learning." Key components of choice, wonder, and delight describe play as conceptualized in this text.

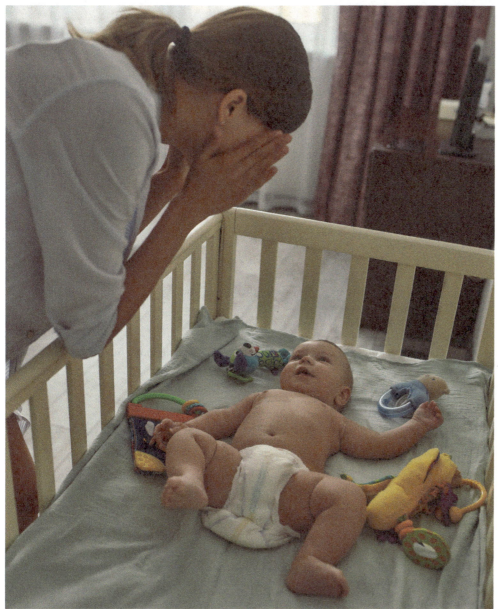

BAZA Production/Shutterstock.com

Figure 4-1 A caregiver plays peek-a-boo with an infant. How is the infant responding to the adult? Why are such interactions important?

Play is the basis of developmentally appropriate practice, and as you will see, each domain of children's development is supported through play. Thus, stimulating play environments that allow children to follow their own interests are important to support learning. The following sections detail some of the skills children learn and enhance through play.

Skills in the Physical Domain

Children make use of both their small and large muscles and support hand-eye coordination as they work puzzles, build with construction toys, or participate in group games. They learn how to handle and use materials and tools to accomplish tasks. During play, children are free to experiment and take physical risks in a safe environment, such as doing a forward roll for the first time or climbing to the top of the jungle gym. Children run, hop, skip, and jump for the sheer pleasure of the activity, and in doing so, they learn to control their bodies and build stamina (**Figure 4.2**). They talk with peers and adults about what they are doing, integrating language with their physical action.

Case Study

Playing with Infants

The following dialog demonstrates how an infant's focus can quickly change and shows how a teacher follows the infant's interests. Chris, the teacher, is on the floor with Olivia, barely 1 year old.

Olivia takes a toy sippy cup out of a toy bin and says, "Tup."

Chris: "You see the cup. Where's the baby? Maybe the baby wants the cup."

Olivia ignores this question and picks up a pop-up toy containing a plush tiger. She shakes the toy and hands it to Chris.

Chris: "Do you want me to open it?"

Olivia drops the sippy cup.

Chris opens the pop-up toy to show Olivia the plush tiger.

Chris: "This is a tiger. Do you see the tiger?"

"Gi-ger," says Olivia, reaching for the toy.

Olivia holds the toy out to Chris, who touches the top of the toy. "Do you want to push the tiger in again?" Olivia nods. "Goodbye tiger."

Olivia loses interest and crawls away to another bin of toys.

Chris puts the tiger toy aside.

Olivia takes a toy car and runs it along the floor.

Chris: "Are you going to drive the car?"

Olivia puts the car down and picks up a puzzle, touching a pig in the puzzle, and says, "pig."

Chris points to another piece and asks, "What's that?"

Olivia: "Tup" (although it is not the sippy cup).

Chris looks in the bucket. "Do you want the cup?"

Olvia dumps the puzzle on the floor and places one of the pieces on top of the frame. "Pig."

Chris: "Yes, that's a pig."

Olivia places two more pieces atop the puzzle and vocalizes. She wanders over to the bucket and pulls out a doll. "Tup," and returns to the puzzle.

Chris shows the child how to turn the pieces to match the holes in the puzzle. "See, they go like that. They fit in the holes. Each one fits in its own hole."

Olivia takes out a plastic box filled with small toy foods. She shows it to Chris.

Chris: "That's a box. Can you shake it? Can you open it?"

Olivia upends the box, but nothing comes out because the lid is closed. She hands it to Chris, heading off toward some foam blocks that caught her attention.

Consider This

1. How did Chris notice the child's interest and react to it?
2. In what ways did he extend the child's language?
3. How did Chris change the focus of comments in relation to Olivia's interests?

Skills in the Social-Emotional Domain

When children play with others, they learn to make friends, cooperate, compromise, and negotiate. They develop the ability to peacefully request what they want and to differentiate between their own and others' interests.

Children develop an understanding of social roles, gaining insight into how their own behavior affects their peers. (For example, "She won't play shopping with me if I hit her with the purse.") They learn empathy and gain insight into how others feel while clarifying and understanding their own feelings. They learn to express their feelings in a safe, nonretaliatory environment.

Children begin to assume responsibility by cleaning up and caring for materials, and organizational skills develop in the process. ("All of the K'Nex pieces go in this bucket; the DUPLOS® go in that bucket.") Play gives children a sense of mastery and control

Figure 4-2 School-age children create a collaborative game of running, improving coordination and stamina. What are some ways this activity might encourage children's development?

as they use their imaginations to create new worlds, build the tallest block skyscraper, or make up dance moves. They learn about the cultures of their peers as they engage in games and traditions from all over the world (**Figure 4.3**).

Play helps children deal with anxieties, giving them a sense of control over and understanding of what is happening. Playing hospital can help relieve anxiety about an

Figure 4-3 This 5-year-old and his teacher enjoy a game of parchisi, which is popular in the child's home culture. How does such a game provide opportunities for social development?

upcoming admission for surgery. Children can experience feelings of satisfaction and relief when anxieties are played through.

Skills in the Cognitive Domain

Children develop many cognitive skills through play. If you've ever played the game "Memory" (in which you match pairs of cards that are all turned face down), you know that children's games often help improve **visual perception** (the ability to perceive one's surroundings through the light that enters one's eyes) and memory skills that will be necessary for learning and reading throughout life. They also learn to use symbols to represent real objects, as when they use a plastic banana from the kitchen area as a telephone or a paper towel roll as a telescope.

Play helps children develop the ability to plan and assess outcomes and clarify information about the world. A baby learns that dropping a toy rattle will make the object fall to the ground—an early lesson in gravity. A toddler learns that the square shape fits in the square hole, and the nesting blocks stack better if the largest is on the bottom (**Figure 4.4**). A preschooler learns math with manipulatives by sorting items based on characteristics such as color and shape. They develop an understanding of patterns, one-to-one correspondence, and many other math concepts. Schoool-age children, too, use their reading, writing, and strategic thinking skills in their more complex play.

Through play, children experiment and draw conclusions by trying things out. They develop problem-solving skills as they attempt to construct a neighborhood from blocks. They must consider layout, height, which buildings to represent, how much space they have, how many blocks are available, and so on. Children use language to express their needs, thoughts, and ideas to others when they ask a friend to help make mud pies or express their pride and delight when showing the teacher how high they can swing.

Skills in the Creative Domain

Play is deeply linked to creativity. Through play, children generate new possibilities and ideas. They learn to extend and expand their ideas. Creativity involves making

Irina Wilhauk/Shutterstoack.com

Figure 4-4 A young child completes a toy with graduated rings. What concepts are developed by experiences with a seriated toy such as this one? How can the teacher adapt it for various ages or abilities?

Figure 4-5 A 6-year-old paints a box, creating a house to play in. What questions might a teacher ask to learn about the child's ideas for making the house?

unfamiliar uses of new or familiar equipment, using available resources in new ways and using their imaginations (**Figure 4.5**). As children play, they imagine the world as they would like it to be, creating visual images and exploring ideas in their own ways. Such experiences promote critical thinking and develop problem-solving skills that lead to seeing new possibilities and solutions, which we view as the foundation of creativity. Creativity consists of generating ideas and possibilities about how to perform a task and is supported by the testing of ideas.

Although we often think of creativity as it applies to artistic skills, creativity refers to many other areas: the engineering team that designs a new method of constructing a bridge, the medical researcher who finds a new use for an existing medication, or the homemaker who repurposes a decorative wrought iron gate into a headboard are all being creative. Creativity is the foundation of innovation and thus an important skill to support in young children.

✓ CHECKPOINT

1. What are some examples of playful learning in each domain that you have observed?
2. How might you explain to someone why play is so valuable to children?
3. How does play as described in this section differ from "letting children do whatever they want"?

4.2 Types and Stages of Play

As children grow and develop, they progress through commonly recognized stages of play and participate in various types of play. For an educator of young children, it is important to have a firm grasp on this aspect of their development. Teachers devote much time and thought to providing beneficial and developmentally appropriate play experiences for the children in their classrooms.

All play stages are important developmentally and serve a vital purpose. The baby does not have the physical skills necessary to move around and play with friends. The toddler does not usually have the verbal skills to say, "Let's play this game," or the social skills necessary to have a pretend tea party with another. Not until the preschool years do children have the social and language skills to be ready to engage in the complexity of more advanced dramatic play.

Children progress through these stages at their own pace, which may not correlate with their chronological age and may not be linear. One child may pass through the first stage quickly, while another may stay in the first stage for many months. Additionally, children may participate in different stages at different times; for example, older children may take part in solitary play. Many factors influence children's play, including life experience, exposure to television and movies, and family attitudes about play. The stages and types of play are examined in the following sections.

Stages of Play

Like all areas of learning, play is developmental in nature. Children move through a progression of stages in their play. The work of Mildred Parten is frequently cited when studying this topic, although her ground-breaking work was done in the 1920s. Current research in this area notes the following six stages: unoccupied play, solitary play, onlooker play, parallel play, associative play, and cooperative play.

Unoccupied Play

You can observe **unoccupied play** in infants from birth to 3 months. It is characterized by a child's lack of focus, no obvious story line, and an absence of language use. A child swatting at a mobile in a crib, giggling at a pop-up toy, or grasping, squeezing, and then discarding a ball are examples of this type of play. This play helps children to develop motor skills, depth perception, and tactile skills.

Solitary Play

Solitary play occurs typically between 2 months and 2 years of age. It involves children playing alone, often with a toy (**Figure 4.6**). The children are primarily interested in their

FatCamera/Getty Images +

Figure 4-6 A 1-year-old plays alone with blocks and tools, an example of solitary play. How might the child's activities be influenced by experiences and the materials available?

own activities in isolation; however, the play is more focused and sustained than what you will observe in unoccupied play. Infants are content playing by themselves or with a toy, while a toddler may play alone with simple puzzles, snap beads, or books.

During this stage, children will begin play narratives using objects to represent familiar items. They may use a block to represent a car or a telephone. They likely will not seek another child or adult to join them in looking at a book or picking up rattles.

Onlooker Play

Usually recognized at around 2 years, **onlooker play** involves a child showing interest in or watching what other children are doing without attempting to enter the activity. This behavior can result from children noticing others' activities and enjoying watching but not proceeding to take part. Even adults may engage in onlooker play, such as when they watch a sporting event.

Parallel Play

At about 2 to 3 years old, many children enjoy playing alongside another child. Although children may not interact, they will take pleasure in playing beside one another and engaging in similar or identical activities (**Figure 4.7**). This stage is known as **parallel play**. A parent walking into a classroom might assume that a child is "playing with a friend" because two children are simultaneously playing on rocking horses right next to each other. A closer look, however, reveals that the children are not interacting despite their physical proximity.

In parallel play, children often observe and copy each other. If one child is pushing a doll in a stroller, another child may follow suit. However, there is no communication between them as they engage in their pursuit. Parallel play is something of a transition that leads children into more complex and interactive associative play.

Associative Play

Associative play emerges around age 3 or 4 as children begin to acknowledge one another as they play. They now share, communicate, copy, and work with one another, although they are not yet sharing common goals in their play.

At this stage, children will talk to each other, asking questions about what the other is doing and negotiating the use of resources. For example, they may work together to split up the available table blocks so each will have plenty or decide who will use the arch blocks first.

FatCamera/Getty Images Plus

Figure 4-7 Toddlers playing side-by-side without interacting is an example of parallel play. How does parallel play differ from solitary play?

Cooperative Play

As its name implies, **cooperative play**, which occurs from about 4 years of age, involves interaction and cooperation between children in social groups. During this stage, you can expect children to approach each other and ask to play blocks, house, dress-up, and so on. Two or more children may also organically begin to play together. They will now have the same goals, assigning each other roles and collaborating in the activity. It is during this stage that friendships and social skills such as sharing, compromise, and turn-taking begin to develop: "You are my best friend!" or, if it does not work out, "You can't play with me!"

Cooperative play is often **socio-dramatic** in nature, meaning that it includes elements of imitative play and make-believe play; however, it stands apart from the earlier stages in that it requires verbal interaction between two or more children as well as the ability to make plans (**Figure 4.8**). For example, one child chooses to be a parent and the other child is the child; one child can be the doctor and another child is the patient. Because of its more complex story lines, socio-dramatic play requires a significant amount of time for children's ideas to materialize and develop.

Types of Play

In addition to the stages of play development, there are five commonly recognized types of play in which children engage: physical, social, constructive, fantasy, and games with rules. For infants and younger toddlers, play is mostly sensorimotor; they are learning about how they can act on the items in their environment to make things happen. A developmentally appropriate program provides for children to engage in various types of play throughout the day.

Physical Play

Physical play consists of activities that involve movement, especially gross motor skills that require the use of children's larger muscles. This play helps children learn how to control their bodies and coordinate their actions. Infants joyfully kick, grab, and roll.

FamVeld/Getty Images Plus

Figure 4-8 Two preschoolers who have created a socio-dramatic play scenario of a restaurant, pretending to be chefs, is an example of cooperative play. What are some ways socio-dramatic play encourage interactions, cooperation, and learning?

Older children learn how to run, throw, and catch and need many opportunities to play in both structured and unstructured activities. They need opportunities to exercise their bodies and use some of their seemingly endless energy. With so many children experiencing health problems today, especially obesity, it is essential for children to have regular opportunities to participate in many types of physical play.

Social Play

Social play includes activities with others. Groups of children acting out a trip on a bus or a day at the beach are examples of social play. Social play benefits children because of the need for collaboration, communication, sharing, and turn-taking. In social play, children are actively using their imaginations and ability to plan. Through social play, children develop language skills as well as important social skills.

When children are playing with friends, they practice cooperation, develop social skills, and learn about fairness. They learn how to make up after a disagreement and how to make and stick to rules, and they begin to develop a sense of humor. Children learn what works and does not work in a social atmosphere. Interaction with peers yields a different level of play than playing with adults who have authority over them.

Constructive Play

Constructive play involves any of the common construction toys such as LEGO®, DUPLO®, unit blocks, magnetic tiles, and similar items that are often used in a manipulative area (**Figure 4.9**). Constructive play occurs in a tinkering area where children use recycled materials such as cardboard boxes, paper towel tubes, milk containers, and other items to build and create.

Since they use their hands to manipulate the items, constructive play helps children develop **fine motor skills** and coordination. Children develop problem-solving skills as they figure out how to make their creations: How tall can the tower be before it falls over? What types of blocks should be used on the bottom versus the top for stability?

kate_sept2004/Getty Images

Figure 4-9 Children work together to create a model of their school. How does constructive play benefit children?

Working in a tinkering area, art area, manipulative area, or block area typically involves constructive play as children test to see whether cardboard, tagboard, or poster paper works best for the house they are building or decide whether staplers, masking tape, or paperclips make their airplane hold together best. They learn to use the tools of technology to accomplish self-imposed tasks.

This type of play can involve an element of dramatic play in miniature when themes are introduced through figures, animals, vehicles, and other props. For example, a group of kindergarten students might use recycled items to build a town complete with stories and dramatic interpretations of the figures who inhabit their imaginary world. Children may use blocks, miniature cars, and people to create situations related to their experiences. For example, a group of children might build a store in the block area and use small plastic figures to act out scenarios of shoppers.

Fantasy Play

Fantasy play is often seen as a part of social play. When children pretend, they are engaging in fantasy play. The child who puts on a cape and announces they are Wonder Woman or Superman is engaging in fantasy play. Groups of children using pretend food and a wagon to create a food truck are using their imaginations and creativity to create their own unique play scenario.

Games with Rules

Children become interested in formal games with others by about age 5. **Games with rules** are a more formal type of play in which the players must agree to follow an understood set of regulations or principles; they are a common form of play during middle childhood. (Think about games such as hopscotch, flag tag, wall ball, and red light/green light. The games only work if everyone agrees to follow the rules.)

Games with rules include play activities that have set procedures. Board games and card games fall into this category, as do many playground or group games (**Figure 4.10**). In early childhood, board and card games with simple rules, such as Candy Land,

Vladans/Getty Images

Figure 4-10 Two kindergarten children play a board game which requires following rules and taking turns. What other opportunities for learning do board games or games with rules offer?

checkers, Go Fish, and Guess Who?, become popular with children who are not yet reading. Such games reinforce social concepts of taking turns and fairness in following rules. Although children may alter the rules of a game, the participants abide by the set rules as they play together. Sports, from T-ball to soccer, are also examples of games with rules.

Game play is more structured in comparison to other types of play. Games usually involve two or more children or teams, competition, and agreed-upon criteria for determining a winner. Children use games flexibly to meet social and intellectual needs. For example, selecting a partner to play with may affirm friendship; disagreeing with an opposing team offers the opportunity to consider other perspectives or resolve conflict. Children learn reasoning strategies and skills from games such as checkers and Go Fish. In such games, children must consider offensive alternatives and the need for defense at the same time. Many board and card games additionally encourage awareness of mathematics and can be intellectually motivating parts of preschool and primary school curriculum.

Cooperative games are another type of game with rules. They are often adaptations of traditional games to emphasize participation and cooperation as a group, with no winner and thus no losers. For example, a version of musical chairs eliminates the removal of chairs, so the fun becomes the scramble to find a chair.

Discovery Journeys

LaShonda's First Day

The children were in learning-center time when LaShonda arrived at the 4-year-old preschool classroom where she was scheduled to observe as a part of her first early childhood education college class. She had returned to community college, having spent her adult years thus far helping to manage her family's business. She came prepared with her assignment, her background check, and an iPad to record her observations.

LaShonda expected to see the children coloring, writing their names, counting, and identifying shapes. Instead, she was surprised to see children actively engaged with materials and with each other. Two children were working on puzzles with letters and numbers; another was making patterns on a pegboard. Two more were at a writing desk and appeared to be making lists, while several others were on beanbags looking at picture books. A group of children were arranging items in a child-size kitchen to create a restaurant. Still others were on the floor with blocks, carefully stacking and balancing each block, gleefully laughing when the tower toppled noisily to the floor. Three others played musical instruments and danced in costumes. The sound in the classroom was unexpected, too. Not only were wooden blocks crashing, but conversation, laughter, and squeals of excitement filled the room. Children talked eagerly to each other and their teachers. It was far from the "sit-down-and-listen-to-the-teacher" environment she was expecting to encounter.

LaShonda had heard that "children learn through play," but she did not connect that idea with the concept of formal school learning, such as learning to read or doing basic addition. Over the months that followed, the phrase became increasingly meaningful as her experiences in her college course and teaching observation provided her with valuable opportunities to recognize the developmentally appropriate learning experiences children incur through play.

Consider This:
1. How do you think LaShonda's experiences led to her expectations in visiting the classroom?
2. In what ways do you think the observation affected her?
3. Why is the practice of observing in exemplary classrooms important in becoming an early childhood professional?

Rough and Tumble Play

Rough and tumble play often involves pretend wrestling or other physical contact between two children, usually accompanied by loud noises. Such play, popular among preschoolers and in the early primary grades, concerns some teachers who fear children may be hurt. However, proponents of the value of such play note that supervising adults should observe the facial expressions of the children for reassurance. A smiling or happy face means the children are playing and not engaged in a fight; a scowling or angry face indicates the opposite (Smith & Boulton 1990).

Another consideration is that roughhousing must take place in a safe environment such as on a gymnastic pad, and children must be evenly matched in physical ability. (In other words, a 7-year-old should not be wrestling a much smaller and less coordinated 3-year-old.) Supervision is important because a play tug might be interpreted as an aggressive act, and the rough and tumble play may escalate into an angry physical conflict.

In summary, play of all types contributes to children's development in numerous ways. The next section returns to the beginning of play, taking a closer look at the play of infants and toddlers.

The Sensorimotor Play of Infants and Toddlers

In **sensorimotor play**, infants experiment with body movements and objects. By 6 months of age, infants have developed simple actions through trial and error, and

Discovery Journeys

Play Supports Understanding

I liked having playground "duty" as a second-grade teacher. There was time to converse with children, observe their play, and interact with former and next year's students. Free of the constraints of traditional classroom activities, children's creativity flourished in those 20-minute periods.

One day on the playground, it was apparent some version of tag was underway. From the excited "I got you!" and reluctant treks to a circle drawn on the ground, I sensed this was not an ordinary tag game as I approached the group.

"It's God and the Devil," said a 7-year-old. "And this circle is Heaven, and the other is … down under," hesitating to use the word *Hell*. "Sheila's God and Mike's the devil, and right now Sheila's winning! See, when Sheila tags someone, they have to go to Heaven, and when Mike tags someone they go to 'down under,'" explaining the rules of the game.

It seemed logical to me. It was a dramatization of good and evil forces competing for mankind's souls. It was the children's understanding of religion portrayed in the way they knew best—through play. Their clear-cut dichotomy of right and wrong had led them to adapt a game of tag to depict their own version of religion.

Enjoying the memory of the display of second-grade imaginations, I shared the experience later with some upper elementary teachers in the lounge. "That's awful," one exclaimed. "Did you stop it?" asked another. While they were short of calling it blasphemous, it was clear that the other teachers did not share my opinion of the value of children's play and creativity in this expression of ideas related to religion. I couldn't bring myself to tell them how interesting I thought it was that Sheila— a girl—held the role of God. I've never seen children create this game again, and I wonder what they would call "down under" if they did it today. But on that day, in the heart of the Bible Belt Deep South, it made sense to me.

Consider This

1. Why do you think the teachers of the upper grades did not see the value of the game that the children had created?
2. What are some examples from your experience in which you or others have changed the rules of traditional games?
3. What are some experiences from your own childhood in which play has helped you express concepts?

they practice those actions repeatedly. Infants use actions such as pushing and grasping to make something happen. An infant pushing a ball to make it roll experiences the pleasure of movement and control. An infant grasping and releasing a toy to watch it drop enjoys the process. Children of this age like repetition. The baby in a high chair consistently dropping a spoon is enjoying the control of the action.

As children master new abilities, they begin to create more complex play activities. Older infants will not just push a ball, but will crawl after it and hand it to an adult. By pushing various objects, an infant learns that a ball rolls away, a rattle makes noise, and a mobile spins. At about 12 months, infants recognize that different objects need different actions. They will throw a ball but shake a rattle and grasp a squeeze toy. In interactions with adults, such as peek-a-boo, children learn to take turns and engage in sensorimotor play with others.

By the time they are toddlers, children's play shows a growing awareness of the functions of objects. The toddler puts a cup on the table and a bottle in a doll's mouth. Toddlers will repetitively fill a container and dump out the contents in a process often called **fill and dump**. During the last half of this year, toddlers begin to develop pretend play and may stir imaginary food and offer it to someone to taste. They may rock and feed a doll, treating it like a baby, or push a grocery cart and fill it with plastic food.

Sensorimotor play gives children opportunities to develop their small and large muscles and learn how to coordinate their muscles and brain. Children learn to use different muscles as they try new skills. Control of the small muscles of the hand is necessary for self-help skills, such as feeding oneself, and for future writing. This control is necessary for many technical skills they will need in later years, such as operating a computer or machinery. While these skills may seem years away for young children, the development of these abilities starts at a young age. These small movements of the hand are referred to as *fine motor skills*. Children use and develop these skills while playing in sand or water, putting together puzzles, cutting, stringing beads, and engaging in many other activities.

☑ CHECKPOINT

1. Why is it important for a teacher to understand the stages of play?
2. How might a teacher use knowledge of play to support learning?

4.3 Cultural Influences on Play

Another important aspect to consider is the effect of culture on children's play. Children around the world engage in play. The types of play may have many similarities, but they also vary. For example, in some cultures, children may roam and play freely, and parents are not concerned because the area is similar to a village in which people watch out for each other and each other's children. In others, children cannot go out alone due to safety issues, a lack of play space, or the inability of families to provide supervision. Additionally, the availability of toys and resources that may be lacking. Children living in urban areas have different experiences than those in suburban or rural areas, and those in cultures that value independence and play have different experiences from those in cultures that do not value play or children's independence.

Children usually incorporate their life experiences into their dramatic play. As such, it is important for early childhood educators to be knowledgeable of the cultural framework of the children in the program. For example, in a classroom of 4-year-olds, Liu, a child whose family immigrated from China two years prior, stopped to remove his shoes prior to entering the housekeeping area. In some classrooms, a child removing shoes might be asked to put them back on, but not in this one. The teacher was aware that Liu's family followed the cultural tradition of removing shoes when entering their home.

Discovery Journeys

The Family Medical Book

As I consider sensorimotor play and how important it is for infants, I am reminded of a book I own that is over 100 years old. When my grandparents passed away, one of the keepsakes I inherited was a fascinating home-remedy medical book nearly six inches thick with 1,500 pages. The book, *Domestic Medical Practice*, was intended as an encyclopedic volume of comprehensive home care for families at the time. As a college student majoring in education, I was enthralled by the information about children—especially the Baby Care section of the book. It was truly an historical documentation of how much more we now know about the importance of stimulating development than we did at the time the book was published.

This copyright 1913 book reflects the knowledge and beliefs of the care of children for its time. It includes extensive information about baby care and physical development, even addressing the influence of heredity and environment, although using now out-of-favor terminology in relation to children with disabilities. Although it devoted many pages to physical development, there was no mention of some of the factors we know are important in social and cognitive development. Most noteworthy to me is that the only reference to play is a statement that a young child might enjoy an item like a rubber ball. Of course, there was none of the information available today about brain development, the importance of interactions with babies, the value of play, or even cognitive development.

The book, for me, reflects the culture of the period. Looking at it today as a century-old artifact, it serves as a document of how much more we now know about children's development and why it is so important for those in the early childhood field to keep up with the research in our field. Although the environment was addressed as it affects children, social and cognitive development was neither recognized nor valued. Indeed, children were more likely to be engaged in labor or chores as soon as they were old enough, rather than playful learning.

Consider This

1. How have cultural changes contributed to how people care for infants and toddlers today?
2. What are some changes that could be attributed to today's mass media and the greater availability of information?
3. Where did you learn and adopt your attitudes about infants and play?

In another classroom, a group of children created a church scenario with roles for priests and parishioners. They used books as hymnals, baskets for collections, and a cup and saucer as a chalice and paten. Religion was an important part of their family's culture.

What are some ways one might respond to children's cultures? Materials such as pretend foods from various cultures, photos, dolls, and dress-up clothes can help children feel comfortable with familiar items. Family members might visit and share the music or artifacts of their cultures. Books that represent cultural traditions or ways of living help create an awareness and acceptance of variations.

☑ CHECKPOINT

1. What are some materials you have seen in classrooms or in catalogs that support cultural learning?
2. How might children's play differ depending on location and culture?
3. How can a teacher provide for children whose play opportunities at home are limited?

4.4 Developmentally Appropriate Play Activities That Support Learning

Creative Play

Play and creativity are closely intertwined. All types and stages of play can include creative opportunities. Here is a look at some ways creativity and play are related.

Creative play involves children using common, everyday materials in new and unusual ways. These play materials (depending on the age of the child) might include drawing supplies, glue, clay, crayons, paper, paints, recycled materials, scissors, and so on.

Children enjoy using such materials to make things by themselves and experience a sense of pride and accomplishment when a project is completed. Whether they are creating an igloo from recycled milk jugs or building a bird feeder from pine cones and sunflower butter, teachers help expand children's creativity by providing materials and being resourceful themselves.

As in constructive play, household discards and recyclables, such as empty margarine tubs, paper towel tubes, and packing materials, can be used for gluing and constructing (**Figure 4.11**). Yarn can be hair, pet fur, or a string for a kite. There is no right or wrong way to use creative materials, and this quality allows children the freedom to create new and unique objects or works of art. The most important part of creating is the process, not what the item looks like in the end.

Researchers see many relationships between play and creativity. For example, divergent thinking is one aspect of creative thinking that is encouraged through play. **Divergent thinking** is a process of looking at many ideas, much like brainstorming, to generate new ideas or find solutions. Children at play do this naturally when they imagine dozens of different ways to transform an empty box into a work of art or practical object. By contrast, many school experiences are based on **convergent thinking**, or looking to find the right answer. A question such as "How many ways can you make a picture of our field trip?" calls for divergent thinking, whereas "What do you call the hat that the firefighters wear?" requires convergent thinking.

Maria Symchych-Navrotska/Getty Images

Figure 4-11 A child works in a tinkering area to create a structure of recycled paper towel tubes. How has the child solved the problem of how to connect the tubes? What other recycled materials might be included in a tinkering area?

Dramatic Play

Much of the play of young children includes dramatic elements. These elements can include activities as simple as using a block to represent a car; however, dramatic play most commonly refers to play enactments carried out by children.

Dramatic play, sometimes called **pretend play** or **role play**, is a form of play in which children create scenarios. Many 3- or 4-year-old children will play specific parts or assume identities that reflect their ideas about the world around them.

In dramatic play, children carry out plans and use objects or props as part of their play scheme. Family-related themes are popular and common since home life (playing "house") is often familiar. Playing "school" is another popular choice. As dramatic play develops, objects begin to influence the roles that children assume. For example, miniature kitchen equipment or household implements stimulate family-related roles, while capes encourage superhero play.

Teaching Tip

Encouraging Infant Play

The quality of infants' play experiences depends mainly on the opportunities provided by adults, including parents and teachers. Enriching adult-infant interactions are important in helping children relate words to actions and in helping children continue to explore and evaluate what they can do. Here are some tips to enrich play for infants:

- Prepare the room so there will be no need to prohibit the child from any activity.
- Sit on the floor near the child, watching and waiting for an invitation to join in the play. Be aware of what the child is trying to do and facilitate these intentions in a supportive role.
- Repeat infants' favorite activities as often as possible. You will undoubtedly tire of them long before they will!
- While you are playing, describe what you are doing and what the child is doing or seeing to promote language understanding by associating the action with the words.
- Show delight in children's accomplishments. Smiles, clapping, and happy responses provide motivation for them to continue.
- Provide a variety of opportunities based on skill development. Offer activities the child can easily master, as well as those that provide practice for skills already developed.

Roles are identities that children assume in play. Some roles are necessary for a specific play theme. For example, taking a car trip requires a driver and passengers. Family roles, such as parent, grandparent, pet, and sibling, are popular and are integrated into play with themes related to familiar home activities. Children also engage in fantasy play, pretending to be doctors, firefighters, teachers, or athletes. They may even engage in fantasy and imagination by pretending to be dragons, knights, dinosaurs, fairies, sea creatures, or animals.

While some dramatic play is solitary or shared with adults, preschoolers' and older children's pretend play is more often in collaboration with other children. Players often make rule-like statements to guide behavior ("You have to finish your dinner."), and potential conflicts are negotiated. To maintain pretend play activities, children may benefit from a common set of experiences. For example, children may agree that "we sit down at a table" to play restaurant. However, this type of play also provides an opportunity to experience other cultural backgrounds and incorporate them into play scenarios. To continue the restaurant example, do we eat with our hands, a fork, or chopsticks? Do we sit in chairs or on pillows on the floor? What type of food will be offered and ordered at the imaginary restaurant?

Figure 4.12 describes how children engage in a dramatic play activity at a beginner level and then, with more skills, participate at a more advanced level. For example, toddlers

The Progression of Dramatic Play

Role Play	Beginning Level	Advanced Level
Role Chosen	Role relates to child's attempts to understand the familiar world (parent, child, pet).	Role relates to child's attempts to understand the outside world (teacher, police officer, doctor).
How Child Plays the Role	Child imitates one or two aspects of the role (child announces, "I'm the daddy," rocks the baby, and then leaves the house corner).	Child expands the concepts of the role (child announces, "I'm the daddy," feeds the baby, goes to a meeting, prepares dinner, plays with the pet, talks on the phone).
Use of Props	**Beginning Level**	**Advanced Level**
Type of Prop Needed	Child uses real object or replica of object (real or toy phone).	Child uses any object as a prop (block for phone) or a pretend prop (holds hands to ears and pretends to call a doctor because the baby is sick).
How Child Uses the Prop	Child enjoys physically playing with objects (banging receiver of phone, dialing).	Prop is used as part of play episode (child calls a doctor on phone because baby is sick).

Goodheart-Wilcox Publisher

Figure 4-12 This chart shows the progression of dramatic play.

will select roles to play centered on their family or pets. Preschoolers will expand to take on roles of community members in their broader world. A toddler may be the mother of a baby doll, while a preschooler may be a pediatrician.

In addition to the types of roles and props that vary by age and experience, other aspects of play vary, such as how the child engages in make-believe, the length of time in play, the types of interactions, and the language used. These differences are shown in **Figure 4.13** and **Figure 4.14**.

Support and Guide Learning During Play

A typical early childhood schedule includes numerous opportunities during the day to include rich experiences and interactions during play. To engage children effectively, informal talk must be interactive, with the give and take of conversation rather than interrogation.

Approaches to Play

Criteria	Beginning Level	Advanced Level
Make-Believe	Child imitates simple actions of an adult (child moves iron back and forth on ironing board, holds phone receiver to ear).	Child's actions are part of a play episode of make-believe ("I'm ironing this shirt now so I can wear it for the party tonight").
Time Spent in Play Activity	Fleeting involvement (child enters area, plays with doll, puts on hat, and leaves area)	Child stays in area more than 10 minutes (child is really involved in play episode and carries through on the theme).
Interaction	Solitary play (child acts out role alone with no apparent awareness of others)	Functional cooperation (child interacts with others at various times when the need arises to share props or have a partner in play) Cooperative effort (child acts out role cooperatively with others, recognizing the benefits of working together
Language—Verbal Communication	Verbalization centers around the use of toys ("Bring me that phone" or "I had the carriage first").	Dialogue about play theme—constant chatter about roles children are playing (restaurant scene: "What do you want to eat?" "Do you have pizza?" "Yup. We have pizza, cookies, and apple juice.")

Goodheart-Wilcox Publisher

Figure 4-13 This chart shows the various approaches to play.

Play Characteristics of Children Ages One to Eight

Age	Play Characteristics
One Year  Damircudio/Getty Images	• Children play reciprocal nursery games such as, "Where is baby?" and "peek-a-boo." • Children engage in mainly physical and exploratory activity. • Children pull objects in and out of containers.
Eighteen Months  Tassil/Getty Images	• Children climb on and move furniture. • Children play with pull toys, dolls, teddy bears, pots and pans, pounding toys. • Children fill and empty containers; they like to pour. • Children carry blocks around the room, pound them together, build a tower of three or four blocks.
Two Years  Sunan Wongsa-nga/Getty Images	• Children play with dolls and teddy bears, taking them for rides in carriages, feeding them, and so on. • Children play with sand and water, filling containers and then emptying them. • Children push wagons or carriages. • Children play with small items: cars, tools, beads, bottles. • Children fingerpaint and play with Play-Doh. • Children line blocks up or use them to fill wagons. • Children enjoy nesting blocks that fit into each other.
Two and One-Half Years  Yoainlove/Shutterstock.com	• Children engage in domestic play with dolls or teddy bears and housekeeping toys. • Children play with cars or wagons. • Children engage in sand and water play; they make pies and cakes with sand or mud and host tea parties. • Children enjoy bubble play. • Children paint with brushes and fingerpaints. • Children make cookies or cakes from Play-Doh. • Children begin vertical and horizontal building with blocks.
Three Years  FamVeld/Getty Images	• Children ride a tricycle. • Children push a wagon and pretend it is a vehicle, such as a fire engine or train. • Children swing and play on outdoor equipment. • Children engage in domestic play with dolls and household equipment. • Children play with imaginary playmates. • Children play house, store, and school with other children and simple equipment. • Children create art with crayons as well as paints. They may draw simple figures. • Children play in mud or sand, making cakes, pies, roads, tunnels, and so on. • Children build structures with blocks, using a diversity of shapes and sizes. • Children may combine blocks and other toys. They enjoy the construction more than play with the finished product.

Goodheart-Willcox Publisher

Figure 4-14 This chart characterizes the way children play at different ages. *(Continued)*

Play Characteristics of Children Ages One to Eight *(continued)*

Age	Play Characteristics
Four and Five Years  Real444/Getty Images	• Children are very interested in new experiences. • Children have a growing ability to cooperate with other children, working together to achieve a common goal. • Children are increasingly inventive in fantasy play and superhero play. • Children usually have a strong sense of fairness. • Children enjoy much more independence. • Children engage in pretend play that is increasingly complex. • Children like games with rules and are sometimes very rigid in enforcing them.
Six to Eight Years  People Images/Getty Images	• Children use their academic skills as a part of their play, making lists, menus, reading and writing instructions, and buying and selling. • Children's physical skills allow participation in games that require increased physical coordination and stamina. • Children often make their own variations of known games. • Children develop a sense of belonging through teams, clubs, and group activities. • Children's activities may continue over days such as a Monopoly marathon. • Children's crafts and collections are often a part of their play.

Goodheart-Wilcox Publisher

Figure 4-14 *Continued*

Age-appropriate language is key to this experience. Consider the tips in **Figure 4.15** to help children articulate what they are thinking and doing and encourage cognitive development.

You will find many opportunities to expand vocabulary and concepts as a part of children's play. For example, you might use words learned in another context during dramatic play. If children are creating a grocery store, you might ask them if they have some avocados on sale following a science experience about growing an avocado plant. Or, you might ask which fresh vegetables they have following a theme about nutrition. Look for opportunities to include math concepts as part of play activities. You might say, "I see four cups and two saucers. How many more saucers do you need so that each person will have a set for your dinner?" By observing children as they play

---

Age-Appropriate Language in Supportive Interactions

- *Infants*: When working with infants, support actions with words. As you handle routine needs such as changing a baby's shirt, take time to interact socially with the baby. Play a quick game of peek-a-boo or take turns hiding faces. "I'm hiding from baby!" or "Peek-a-boo, I see you!"
- *Toddlers*: With a group of toddlers, encourage their activities. For example, "Let's see how many of these blocks we can put in the bucket! Look what I can do!" while dropping blocks into the bucket. Offer the bucket to the toddler. Suppose the toddler takes it and turns the bucket upside down. Say something like, "Oh, look! You dumped them all out! What fun! Let's do it again!" and repeat the task.
- *Preschoolers*: Present simple problems as open-ended questions, such as "I wonder what you might use for a tablecloth?" to a child setting a table in the housekeeping area. Let the child think about it and figure out a solution, perhaps retrieving a doll blanket to use.
- *Kindergarten and older*: Encourage children to figure out solutions to problems encountered in everyday situations. For example, "How can we make sure everyone gets a turn with our new easel? What can we use to expand our obstacle course?"

Goodheart-Wilcox Publisher

Figure 4-15 Examples of age-appropriate language in supportive interactions.

and by interacting with them, you can scaffold their learning and help them find the right words to describe their discoveries, experiences, or ideas. For example, you might suggest to a child having difficulty making a construction of straws that taping two together might make their structure stronger. These suggestions will encourage children to continue their explorations.

The following are examples of what you might say to support learning and embed opportunities for development and learning during play:

- In the block area, two girls are making a pen for horses. "What kind of food do horses eat? Where do you think their food should go?"
- At the art table, a boy is dripping paint onto construction paper. "Look how your paint splashes and makes a design! Why do you think the paint drops from the straw and splashes like that?"
- Two children are making up a song about rabbits in the music area. "I hear you singing about how the rabbits hop, hop, hop. Can you think of some words that rhyme with hop?"
- A child in the tinkering area is using fabric to make a costume for a puppet. "How can you make the costume stay on the puppet? Are there any tools you might use?" (**Figure 4.16**)
- Two children are riding tricycles outdoors. "What is your destination today? Are you going to the park to play?"
- A child has a doll and a baby bathtub. The child fed the doll and picked up a nightgown. "Do you plan to give baby a bath before you put her to bed? What is baby's routine?"
- A child is seated in a chair, pretending to drive a car to the grocery store. Two other children are nearby but uninvolved. "I wonder if Natasha and Asia would like to go to the grocery store with you. What do you think? Would you like to invite them?"
- A child is making a dollhouse from a cardboard box and is looking for furniture to put in it. "Do you think you might use this (handing him a small box) for a bed or a sofa? What other furniture do you need?"

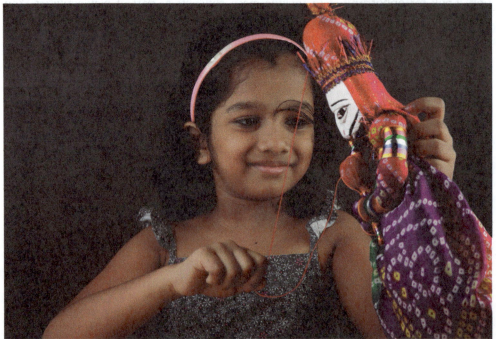

ajijchan/Getty Images

Figure 4-16 A third-grade student figured out how to repair a puppet, learning important life skills. How does a tinkering center encourage problem solving and other cognitive skills?

- A child is cooking with a wok in the housekeeping area. "I really like egg foo young, and I use a wok like that to cook it. Do you think you could make some for me?"
- A child looks in the cupboard in the housekeeping area but finds nothing there. "Looks like our cupboard is bare. We need to go to the store to get some groceries. Do you want to make a list? We need some masa so we can make tortillas."
- Two children are having a tense discussion about who is going to be the clerk in a pretend store. "I have been in stores where there are many clerks. What if I be the shopper and both of you be clerks? Or maybe you'd like to ask Lin to join us as another shopper. What do you think?"
- A child is in the dramatic play area, sitting at the table but uninvolved. "Hello, Laura. May I join you at the table? I'm thinking about having a glass of lemonade. Would you like some? We can visit while we have lemonade."
- Three children have created a shoe store with shoes from the housekeeping area. "I see you have a shoe store. When I go to buy shoes, they measure my feet to know what size I need. Do you want to measure your feet? I have a ruler you can use."

While play is certainly a child-led and child-centered experience, teachers should be prepared to guide children as they play. Guidance can be direct, such as through positive verbal expressions, encouraging words, clear directions, suggested options, redirection, or recognition of success. It can be nonverbal, such as a smile, nod, eye contact, **proximity** (nearness in space, time, or relationship), or modeling. It can be indirect through the organization and arrangement of materials such as using suitable containers and simplifying cleanup by labeling shelves with pictures or words.

Guidance may also come from adult participation, including interactions such as asking open-ended questions that encourage children's ideas (**Figure 4.17**). For example, when children are getting bored or frustrated, offer a new prop, suggest new roles, or provide new experiences. If a group loses interest in a pretend tea party, for example, offer some new dishes to try, provide some flowers to decorate, or invite a new guest to the party, and their interest will be renewed. Follow the children's interests by making additional items or props available to support their ideas.

romrodinka/Getty Images

Figure 4-17 Asking open-ended questions can help guide children toward new ideas. *What could you ask this child to enhance their play experience?*

Case Study

The Unaccompanied Minor and a Tropical Paradise

Jay

Jay, a very self-assured 6-year-old with a strong sense of authority, usually took the lead in most activities. An only child of divorced parents, he frequently traveled alone by air to visit his father in another state, undoubtedly a fact contributing to his strong sense of independence.

One day following a field trip to a local general aviation airport, play began to center on air travel. Jay, of course, took on the role of pilot and lined up chairs to set the stage for passengers. Other children began to board the pretend transport, fastening their seat belts and settling in for a flight. One passenger, Renee, decided that she wanted to be a flight attendant rather than a passenger. When she took a seat in the back row of chairs and firmly expressed her wishes, a very animated conversation commenced between Captain Jay and Renee.

"You have to sit in the front of the plane!" Jay declared, pointing to the front.

"No," Renee replied, "I'm going to sit in the back! That's where flight attendants sit!"

"Well, I know where they sit, and it's in the front!" demanded Jay. "I fly airplanes all the time. I'm an unaccompanied minor!" With great emphasis on the unaccompanied, he ended the challenge.

Having no rebuttal, Renee sighed, and deferring to Jay, placed an additional chair in the front of the plane and resolutely took her place.

The play continued for some time, with refreshment service and announcements about takeoffs and landings.

In a later conversation, it became clear that Jay did not know what "unaccompanied minor" meant. Sharing the event with his mother later that day, Jay's mother and his teacher decided that even though he probably did not understand the meaning of the terminology, when she checked him in, she referred to him as an unaccompanied minor and the flight attendants did the same. What he did know about the term was that it got him a lot of attention, so it must make him really important!

Mia

Mia had returned to her preschool following a family trip to Florida. In the block area, she was engaged in constructing several tall towers. When her teacher approached, she eagerly exclaimed, "Look Miss Kathy, I built a tropical paradise!" Following up on the statement, her teacher became aware that for Mia, a tropical paradise meant tall buildings. Miss Kathy realized from further conversation that Mia's family referred to the area of Florida they visited as a tropical paradise. Yet for Mia, the term was associated with the many condominiums that lined the Florida beaches.

Children learn vocabulary and language by using words and phrases that they hear. They often use the new words in social settings through dramatic play and other interactions with peers. In Jay's case, the meaning of "unaccompanied minor" was not clear, but the importance of the phrase was. Mia's concept of "tropical paradise" was vague, but with later experiences, it would be clarified.

In time, it is expected that Jay will come to understand that an unaccompanied minor is a child traveling without an adult, and Mia's concept of tropical paradise will refer to the environment of the area. But for now, the importance of the phrases is what matters. Their ability to use new vocabulary was expanded through both real-life experiences and opportunities to explore the use of new words and phrases through play.

What can teachers do to support this important process of learning to use language through play? They can provide time, space, support, and props that support social engagement. Opportunities for dramatic play should not end in preschool. Kindergarten, first grade, and beyond benefit from the opportunities intrinsic to dramatic play.

Consider This

1. What other events likely contributed to Jay's concept that an unaccompanied minor was important?
2. How would his experiences traveling alone support Jay's confidence and independence?
3. What could Miss Kathy have done to address Mia's concept of tropical paradise?
4. Can you think of a time when you heard children using a term they did not understand? Explain.
5. How does dramatic play provide opportunities for children to use new terms and build vocabulary and language skills?

Teachers should supervise by staying alert for sounds of dissension or disagreements among children. If dissension occurs and is not resolved by the children, a teacher might redirect the play by suggesting other activities or roles. Here are a few examples of how a well-placed suggestion can intervene and guide behavior by helping children focus on a new task:

- Three children are in a grocery store play area but are throwing pretend containers of food and sweeping them from the shelves with their arms. "Could you help me? I really need some boxes of macaroni and cheese (naming something available that is being misused). And I need a shopping bag to put it in. Could you help me find the macaroni and cheese, and give me a bag for it? I would really appreciate your help."
- Two children both want to use the toy doll carriage, and an argument is beginning. "Look, here is a shopping cart. I bet you could pretend that it is a baby carriage, and the two of you could take your babies on a walk together. I know you have good imaginations."

In *Developmentally Appropriate Practice* by the NAEYC, teachers are cautioned that the more the adult directs an activity or interaction, the less it will be perceived as play by the child. The document identifies play as a continuum ranging from self-directed play to direct instruction. Providing guided play opportunities is the challenge; neither end of the continuum is effective.

As a new teacher, you might wonder when you should sit back and allow children to play without adult interaction and when to become involved. Obviously (and as noted), safety is a key consideration. (For example, a toddler has broken a toy and small pieces could be swallowed.) Interaction can also help prevent play from becoming rough or out of hand. For example, moving close to an activity when voices are becoming loud or high-pitched, becoming a player, or making suggestions can add new interest or focus to the activity. Consider the following guidelines in deciding when to intervene:

Case Study

The Veterinarian Clinic

Mr. Hebert, a new kindergarten teacher, knew the importance of interacting with children during play. As a part of a project study on pets, the children set up a veterinarian clinic near the housekeeping center. They brought stuffed animals from home and created pens and kennels from unit blocks. Mr. Hebert brought in some animal carriers and set a table for examinations. He even provided a stethoscope and some lab coats and scrubs for children to dress the part of veterinarians and veterinary technicians.

The second day into the activity, a few children became rowdy and began throwing the stuffed animals. Knowing that his presence might refocus the play, he walked over to the area.

"What are you doing, Aiden? You are supposed to care for the animals, not throw them! Here, you be the vet, and Emmy and Isa can walk the dogs that are sick. Here are the leashes," directed Mr. Hebert as he handed the leashes to the two children. "Take them for a walk. And when you finish, put them on the examination table for a checkup."

Emmy and Isa took the leashes but shortly put them back on the hooks and took off to join some friends in the art area. Aiden put on a lab coat and picked up the stethoscope without enthusiasm. In a few minutes, Aiden, too, left to go to the library area to find a book about dogs. Mr. Hebert was left alone in the pretend vet office, not knowing what went wrong.

Consider This
1. Why did the children lose interest in the area and leave?
2. What could Mr. Hebert do or say to refocus the play successfully?
3. How could Mr. Hebert participate without taking over?

- *Observe First:* Watch to see what children are doing and how they are interacting. Look for opportunities to support problem solving and communication, such as encouraging children to tell you about their activities and plans. Open-ended questions are especially good for stimulating language and cognitive skills and learning more about what the children are doing.
- *Approach Thoughtfully:* To take part in children's play, suggest a role you might assume. For example, in a hospital setting, you might ask to be a patient. Ask permission to take part and wait for the children to indicate acceptance.
- *Expand Creatively:* You might use an assumed role to suggest additional activities. As a patient, one might say, "I think I have a fever." Children will produce something to use as a thermometer to enact taking a temperature or pick up a bottle and pretend to give medicine.
- *Interact Appropriately:* Use suggestions when involved in dramatic play in a way to ensure the children stay in control of their play scenario. Otherwise, you risk becoming directive and taking charge. Interact by participating, conversing, and demonstrating interest.

Participating in the activity can guide and enrich the experience, but it can also have the opposite effect and cause an abrupt halt to the activity. It is important that the teacher exit the play scenario once it is again going well. Staying in the activity too long can interfere with the children's control over the activities.

☑ CHECKPOINT

1. What are some examples of divergent and convergent thinking?
2. How would you explain to another teacher what we mean by playful learning?
3. Why might excessive teacher direction discourage children from play?

Teaching Tip

How Teachers Hinder Play
Sometimes teachers and other caring adults can restrict or inhibit children's play while attempting to guide and support their activities. Here are several examples of how that can happen so that you will not make these mistakes:
- Correcting children's activities. (This involves redoing or changing children's work; for example, straightening towers, rearranging materials, or showing where to put an item in a collage.)
- Encouraging competition by comparing. ("I'm only going to put the best art work on the bulletin board.")
- Teaching excessively. This means putting too much emphasis on concepts and skills. ("What color is that block?" "How many plates do I have? What letter does this start with?")
- Providing materials that are not age-appropriate (items that are too difficult or not challenging enough).
- Cutting the time short. (Children need time to become involved and time for ideas to develop and jell.)
- Assigning areas or roles rather than suggesting or allowing choices. ("Ethan, you be the police officer, and Emma can be the driver.")
- Providing an inappropriate supply of materials or choices. (Too few options diminish interest; too many make decisions difficult and clutter the room.)

4.5 Adults' Role in Children's Playful Learning

If play is the domain of young children and if children should exert a high level of control over their play, then you might be wondering: What is the role of the teacher? One veteran teacher explains his thoughts: "The teacher must make use of child development knowledge and be very intentional in what materials and experiences are provided." Another adds, "The teacher must have knowledge of what children need to learn and take advantage of opportunities. For example, when a child building a block tower notices how a block falls when it isn't balanced, that leads to questions and discussion about balance and gravity."

Teachers must create and develop an environment, both physical and emotional, that supports learning through play. This involves numerous decisions related to providing materials, organizing spaces, monitoring safety, allowing ample time, planning, and so on. In the sections that follow, you'll learn more about these essential skills.

Provide and Organize Materials

Teachers stimulate play ideas with the materials and supplies they make available to children. They also select **props** and arrange play setups to suggest play ideas and relate play to curriculum themes. For example, a teacher may provide grocery store items as part of a healthy foods theme in the curriculum.

Props are particularly important in fantasy and dramatic play as children assume roles and make sense of the world around them. Chairs can become trains, cars, boats, or houses. A table covered with a blanket or bedspread becomes a cave. Cardboard cartons convert into houses, forts, or stores. One role of the teacher is to be prepared to follow children's interests and see where they lead. Prop boxes are one way to respond to planned activities or unexpected interests.

Prop boxes can help teachers respond to children's interests. These are containers of related materials for use in dramatic play that can be used alone or as the basis for setting up a learning center. To make prop boxes, collect items related to a particular theme and store them in a sturdy container, such as a dishpan or laundry basket, for the children to use. **Figure 4.18** offers suggestions for popular prop boxes and items to include. Many of the items are free, inexpensive, easy to make, or readily available in an early childhood classroom.

Monitor Safety

The teacher is responsible for ensuring that play is safe and should, therefore, check materials and equipment frequently. For example, have any toys been broken in ways that leave jagged edges or protruding parts? Are toys for toddlers intact or have small pieces broken off that could be swallowed?

Teachers should provide appropriate supervision, anticipate potential problems, and educate children about safety. They should make children aware of any risks in physical challenges they set for themselves. For example, during sand play, the teacher should discuss the importance of playing with the sand (and building wonderful creations) in the sandbox because sand that is scattered outside means we have less to use, and sand that gets thrown about can wind up in a friend's eye.

Allow Sufficient Time

Teachers must allow enough time for ideas to develop and for children to take on roles. New teachers may underestimate the amount of time it takes young children to transition to a play space, acquaint themselves with the material, negotiate roles, and enact their ideas. Think of a meeting you have attended in which a group was tasked with planning an event. When the group initially arrives, some time is spent in greetings, discussing the task, and brainstorming possibilities before the group assumes roles and

Prop Box Ideas

Theme	Items to Include
Grocery Store	toy cash register, barcode scanner, play money, sacks or tote bags, empty food containers, plastic food, aprons, purses, wallets
Post Office	toy mailbox (or one made from a shoebox); stamps (stickers or those available in promotions); rubber stamps and stamp pads; envelopes; index cards; crayons; paper; shirt with US MAIL written on it; large bag (for mail sack); small boxes for packing, wrapping, and shipping
Kitchen	pots, pans, eggbeaters, spatulas, spoons, plastic dishes, canisters, cookie cutters
Laundry	clothesline, clothespins, doll clothes, small hand towels to wash, pan of water, soap, toy iron and ironing board **Note:** The experience of using a washboard and hanging clothes on a line may need to be introduced and explained.
Cleaning	whisk brooms, small mops, sponges, towels or clean rags, soap, spray bottles with water
Salon/Barber Shop	brushes, combs, cotton balls, scarves, ribbons, bows, barrettes, capes, empty hair spray cans, wigs, toy razors, magazines
Florist	various types of artificial flowers and greenery, plastic vases, Styrofoam
Water Play	shallow pan, toy boats, empty plastic jars and bottles, spray bottles, funnels, corks, bath crayons
Sand Play	plastic shovels, pails, transportation toys, flour sifters, funnels, molds
Gardening	gloves, toy rakes, plastic shovels, watering cans, laminated seed packages
Office	toy or discarded telephone, toy or old computer, paper, crayons, envelopes, old calendars, calculators
Dress-up	sturdy jewelry (not pins), gloves, shoes, hats, purses, wallets, belts, scarves, ribbons
Picnic	paper bags, paper and plastic dishes, plastic food or pictures of picnic foods laminated, tablecloths or sheets, basket
Doctor	strips of white cloth, stethoscope, white shirt or smock, disposable gloves, elastic bandages, adhesive bandages, cotton balls, scrubs
School	markers and small whiteboards, books, pencils and paper
Mechanic	assorted nuts and bolts, toy tools, tool belt
Firefighter	discarded vacuum cleaner hose or piece of water hose, shirt with FIRE DEPT written on it, plastic fire hats
Restaurant	pots, pans, eggbeaters, spoons, pitchers, salt and pepper shakers, tablecloths, aprons, notepads, pencils
Shoeshine Kit	soft cloth, small cans of clear polish, sponges, buffers
Farmer	shovel, rake, hoe, seeds, toy wheelbarrow
Painter	paintbrushes, buckets, white shirt and hat

Goodheart-Willcox Publisher

Figure 4-18 This chart suggests props that can be used for various dramatic play scenarios.

begins the actual work. Children, too, need time to settle in, think about what they want to do, and share ideas—all valuable experiences—before they engage in play scenarios.

Schedule a block of time of at least 60 minutes to encourage greater and deeper involvement in play scenarios, as these take time to develop. Additional opportunities can be provided by making use of rainy-day schedules and arrival times for additional playtime. Even outdoor time can be an opportunity for dramatic play, as described in Chapter 13.

Model a Love of Play

As noted earlier in this chapter, play does not end with early childhood. Teenagers, young adults, those in middle age, and senior citizens all love to play and enjoy recreation. If you reveal your own enjoyment and appreciation of play, you will show your

Teaching Tip

Assembling Prop Boxes

Putting together prop boxes is an easy task, but it takes some time and planning. Here are some suggestions for how to assemble them:

- Make a list of needed materials that can be donated by parents or local businesses. (Involving staff, children, parents, service groups, and members of your community in assembling these boxes will prove to be rewarding for all.)
- Send a list of materials that you need to families along with an explanation of why you need the items. Post a list on the parent bulletin board or classroom door, and cross out items when you receive enough. Request volunteers to contact local businesses for donations.
- Request parental help for materials that need to be made, such as aprons, vests, and tutus or other dance costumes. Also, local service organizations, such as the Scouts, religious or civic groups, or senior citizen groups, may help in making items such as placemats, tablecloths, or doll accessories for dramatic play.
- Make a list of materials that will need to be purchased. Check thrift shops and garage sales for special items such as galoshes for firefighters, hair dryers for the salon or barber shop, and briefcases to use for luggage or office play.
- Designate a storage place for the dramatic play prop boxes.
- Collect a sturdy box for each kit to be assembled. A copying service might donate their large boxes with lids, or you can purchase plastic ones. Try to ensure that the boxes are alike, so they are easy to stack and store.
- Label the lid and end of each box with large letters for ease of locating.
- Sort the material into appropriate boxes.
- Make an idea page and fasten it to the prop box lid of each box so that it can be used as a guide by substitutes, aides, and other staff. A list of items that go in the box is useful in having materials returned to the right box.
- Adapt and expand suggested materials and activities to meet the needs of your group and the resources that you have available.

Often a field trip to observe activities and collect materials is an excellent way to introduce a new prop box. For example, your class might tour a local restaurant to see behind the scenes what the employees do. Bring back a variety of items for your kit and set up a restaurant in your dramatic play area.

The teacher organizes materials and space by arranging the dramatic play area carefully to reduce wandering and encourage social interaction between children. Depending on the space available, it may be necessary to limit the number of children allowed in the area at one time to prevent problems from overcrowding.

Teachers should also take the lead in helping and encouraging the children to organize the play space. For example, each child should help to maintain the area so that it is orderly and ready to be used again. Additional information on organizing a dramatic play center can be found in Chapter 2.

Consider This

1. How can prop boxes help teachers react to children's interests?
2. What are some concepts that children learn from the organization of materials into prop boxes?
3. How can prop boxes support curriculum?

---

students how valuable it is. Your attitude can also support creative play when you interact with children in a way that demonstrates that you value their ideas and interests.

Here are some teacher actions that demonstrate an appreciation and enjoyment of play in the early childhood classroom:

- *Talk to children about their play.* Conversations with children demonstrate that you consider their activities important.

> ## Teaching Tip
>
> ### When a Child Does Not Play
> Sometimes a child may have difficulty playing or participating in play. Teachers may become concerned when children do not voluntarily take part in play with others. The following are suggestions for supporting dramatic play and tips for guiding children who may not readily participate in play activities:
> - Provide children with rich experiences so they have a basis for ideas and the experience for the behavior required in play situations.
> - Provide a supportive and encouraging environment. Encourage, but do not force.
> - For toddlers, use mirror play. For example, you blink … they blink; you touch the toddler's nose … the toddler touches your nose.
> - Pair preschoolers with good players to help them join in group play.
> - Select a theme that will be appealing based on the child's interests.
> - Suggest roles that might require little interaction, such as a stocker in a grocery store or a customer waiting for an appointment.
> - Teach the words to join in play. "May I play with the trucks with you?" or "Can I be the patient?"

- *Play with children and provide support for play.* No one is ever too old for a tea party! When adults engage in children's play, it tells children that play is valuable and that the adults enjoy spending time playing *with* them.
- *Create a playful atmosphere.* It is important for adults to provide materials that children can explore and adapt through play. Having a curious and inquisitive attitude conveys that you expect the same in children.

Use Themes in Planning for Play

One helpful planning tool is to use a theme, or a topic that children can explore in various ways, allowing them to see relationships, classify, use new vocabulary, and reenact events. For example, if your class visits the fire station or has an in-class visit from local firefighters for Fire Prevention Week, you might create a theme around the topic, providing fire helmets for dress-up, firetrucks in the block area, puzzles about firefighters and firetrucks, songs and books about firefighters, and science explorations about water pressure (**Figure 4.19**). This will reinforce concepts developed from the visit and can include all curriculum areas. Using a theme allows you to integrate curriculum areas tied together by a theme such as fire prevention or the work of firefighters.

Select themes with which the children are familiar and that are relevant to their lives and ages. For example, an outer-space theme is not appropriate for toddlers. A theme on pets or food is appropriate. Children should be able to draw from some type of experience in order to participate in dramatic play regarding the theme. For example, not all of the children in your classroom may have traveled on an airplane, but many have traveled on a bus (or seen older siblings ride the school bus). As such, an airplane theme might not be appealing, but a theme about riding the bus might be exciting for them.

Planning is equally important in supporting play for infants and toddlers because variety is important in the play of children of all ages. Using themes encourages the teacher to intentionally seek out new materials and experiences. For example, you might look for books, songs, and finger plays related to a theme of our bodies for infants. More information about selecting appropriate themes can be found in Chapter 1.

Hero Images/Getty Images

Figure 4-19 First-grade children question a visiting firefighter about what it is like to be a firefighter. What are some activities that would build on the theme of firefighters and their work?

Using Books to Inspire Play

Using themes to organize curriculum usually includes selecting books on the theme topic. These books can often provide inspiration for dramatic play. When children listen to a story, it often follows that they will reenact the story, especially if appropriate props are provided to support the action. For example, *The Keeping Quilt* by Patricia Polocco is a good example of a book that might be read during a theme about families. The book tells the story of the author's great-grandmother's immigration from Russia and how a quilt was made from clothing as a reminder of their former home. Over generations, the quilt was used by the family for many purposes, including a pretend tent and a cape by the author as a child. The cultural concepts within the story help children understand the variation in families, languages, religions, and traditions. With a few props, including a small quilt, children would incorporate the traditions and experiences depicted in their play, thus strengthening their understanding of culture.

Children's picture books are likely to inspire dramatic play. Just as books can frequently serve as catalysts for play activities, so can children's experiences away from school. Not only are they examples of children incorporating their experiences into play, but they also show children's use of new language skills in play.

☑ CHECKPOINT

1. Can you think of a story or book that inspired you and friends to engage in dramatic play?
2. What are some ways that teachers can demonstrate that they value play?
3. How might school-age children incorporate academic skills in their play?

Teaching Tip

Theme Play

When planning for play around a theme, consider the following tips:
- Select an activity to introduce the theme. A theme of "my school" might begin with a walk around the school to photograph and discuss the cafeteria, office, auditorium, and playground.
- Decide which activities will be whole group, learning center, or individual activities. Constructing a model of the school would be best as a small group activity in the tinkering area during learning center time. Reading *Miss Nelson Is Missing!* could be a whole group activity during circle time.
- Consider a reasonable timeline. One week may be enough time for most themes, but a theme of "my school" could expand into helpers in the school, such as cafeteria workers or maintenance staff, and thus be extended.
- Gather materials and supplies. What will be needed for children to construct a model of their school? What will you do with the photographs you take? Will you make a documentation board? What books are available based on the theme?
- Set up and display the materials and supplies. Arrange the materials in an attractive manner where they are most likely to be used. Will you place puzzles related to the theme in the manipulative area? What items can enrich the block area? Might props be added to the dramatic play area for it to become a school office or cafeteria?
- Introduce the theme and communicate expectations. For example, prior to a walk around the school, children may need to be reminded to use quiet voices so that other classes will not be disturbed.
- Take advantage of the teachable moments that occur. What do children notice? Are there signs that are good examples of environmental print? Were they curious about the equipment in the teachers' workroom?
- Evaluate as you go. Does the reading of *Miss Nelson Is Missing!* interest the children enough to lead into the work of substitutes? Do children have questions about substitutes or teacher absences?
- Adapt or change as necessary. After visiting with the cleaning staff, toy brooms, mops, and vacuums might be added to the dramatic play center.
- Make notes for future reference. Keep a clipboard handy to jot down additional ideas, interests of the children, and vocabulary to reinforce.
- Communicate successes to families. Social media photos, as well as blogs or emails, help families recognize the value of the experience. Let families know why the activity was planned and how it helped children.

4.6 Focus on Assessment of Program Practices

Every day, teachers make observations of children's behavior and development as they engage in play experiences. The purpose of observation is to use the information to document children's progress and to tailor instruction to meet their needs. A collection of children's work, along with their verbal comments about their work, are helpful and necessary to understand children and to support the need to facilitate learning. Documentation is also helpful in communicating with parents about strategies they can use at home.

From the Field

Toni Sturdivant

"Play provides the perfect opportunity for early educators to authentically assess children's learning in a variety of learning domains, including racial learning and feelings about human differences."
Toni Sturdivant, Ph.D., M.S. Ed.
Early Childhood Consultant
St. Hurst, TX

Toni Sturdivant

Figure 4-20

In addition to assessing children's development and learning, it is also important that programs consider how well they are incorporating best practices into their operations. Dr. Eric Strickland recommends questions (**Figure 4.21**) to evaluate how well programs provide opportunities for play for 4- and 5-year old children.

There are several other scales that can help measure the quality of play interactions. The Early Childhood Environment Rating Scale® is incorporated by many states as part of their quality rating system. One section of the scale is used to rate how well the environment contributes to play. The scale is used to assess a classroom as it exists and to show specific steps to improve.

There are separate scales for Early Childhood (ECERS-3™), Infants and Toddlers (ITERS-3™), and Family Child Care (FCCERS-3™). While the scales address all aspects of the environment, one subscale of each focuses on provisions for dramatic play. The chart below shows the ITERS scale that addresses the provision for play. The criteria are scored on the one-to-seven-point scale below.

Start from where you are. Assess the play value in your outdoor play area by asking:
- How do the pieces in our play area encourage children to interact as they play?
- Are there any pieces that are used more often than others?
- What can children really do in our outdoor play area?
- How many different kinds of play can happen in our outdoor play area? What equipment or props can we add to inspire additional and more imaginative kinds of play?
- Where do children spend most of their time in our outdoor play area? How can we make our children utilize all parts of the playground and in different ways?
- Do children have opportunities to change space?

Assess your programming for play—both outside and inside:
- Is it possible to move more curriculum experiences outside?
- Determine whether you allow adequate time for play. Ask yourself:
- Do children have uninterrupted stretches of time to play and discover?
- Are 15-minute bursts of activity punctuated by long periods of too much "teaching" and not enough child-directed learning?

When play is process-oriented, it helps children discover the joy, excitement, and satisfaction that come from their own imaginations. When we value play, we value children.

Goodheart-Wilcox Publisher

Figure 4-21 Examples of questions to ask when assessing the play value of an outdoor play area.

Instructions for Scoring: The Infant/Toddler Environment Rating Scale-3™ (ITERS-3™)

The ITERS-3™ is a tool used to rate the quality of early learning environments for children ages birth through 30 months (**Figure 4.22**). The tool is divided into subscales that rate different parts of the environment:

- Space and Furnishings
- Personal Care Routines
- Language and Books
- Activities
- Interaction
- Program Structure

The ITERS-3™ is an established and a trusted resource in early childhood education. It is used by directors and supervisors for evaluation purposes and is a mainstay in many teacher-training programs.

When scoring an item, always start reading from 1 (inadequate) and progress upward, scoring each indicator Yes or No (or NA where permitted).

Ratings are assigned as follows:

- A rating of 1 must be given if any indicator under 1 is scored Yes.
- A rating of 2 is given when all indicators under 1 are scored No and at least half of the indicators under 3 are scored Yes.
- A rating of 3 is given when all indicators under 1 are scored No and all indicators under 3 are scored Yes.
- A rating of 4 is given when all indicators under 3 are met and at least half of the indicators under 5 are scored Yes.
- A rating of 5 is given when all indicators under 5 are scored Yes.
- A rating of 6 is given when all indicators under 5 are met and at least half of the indicators under 7 are scored Yes.
- A rating of 7 is given when all indicators under 7 are scored Yes.

A score of NA (Not Applicable) may only be given for indicators or for entire items when "NA permitted" is shown on the scale and on the Score Sheet. Indicators that are scored NA are not counted when determining the rating for an item, and items scored NA are not counted when calculating subscale and total scale scores.

Overall, a rating of 1 indicates inadequate provisions for dramatic play. A rating of 7 indicates excellent provision for dramatic play. The chart can also be used for improvement by looking at the provisions for the next higher score and working to meet those requirements. The scale includes notes for explanation and clarification of the requirements.

*Early Childhood Environment Rating Scale®, Third Edition (ECERS-3™)
*Infant/Toddler Environment Rating Scale®, Third Edition (ITERS-3™)

Goodheart-Wilcox Publisher

Figure 4-22 How to score an infant-toddler rating scale.

☑ CHECKPOINT

1. Why is ongoing assessment important in maintaining quality and meeting children's needs?
2. Are you familiar with any checklists or scales that evaluate play experiences?
3. Why is observation an important tool for assessment?

4.7 Family Matters: Understanding Playful Learning

Parents and guardians who are unfamiliar with developmentally appropriate practices may need help understanding them and the teaching strategies in early childhood education. One way to help ensure that parents understand a play-based curriculum is to educate them about the value of play (**Figure 4.23**). This may be particularly important if the families in your program express a strong interest in kindergarten readiness and may wish to see drilling on numbers and letters to prepare for elementary school mathematics and reading.

A handout might be used in a family orientation or an open house or included as part of a family newsletter. To help potential parents understand the program philosophy before enrollment, it can be shared on a program website or on social media sites.

SDI Productions/ Getty Images

Figure 4-23 A teacher explains to a parent how her 8-year-old daughter has progressed during the school year. What questions might the parents have for the teacher?

Keeping records of children's progress and communicating the progress with families is necessary for them to understand what children are learning and how they are learning it in a developmentally appropriate, play-based program. During special or routine conferences, share examples of what the children learned. For example, "Josiah really enjoys participating in sand and water play. He was showing two other children last week how he could balance a particular toy by how much sand was on the other side of the scale. And he told me that he discovered he could use a funnel to make it easier to pour water into a bottle." Chapter 7 includes additional information on ways to share examples of children's progress.

☑ CHECKPOINT

1. How would you explain the value of play for infants and toddlers to families?
2. What are ways to help families understand the value of self-directed play?
3. Why do you think some families do not see the benefits of play?

Chapter 4 Review and Assessment

Chapter Summary

4.1 Define play and describe how it benefits the young child.
- Play is a central teaching practice and characterized by choice, wonder, and delight.
- Play is intrinsically motivated and consists of self-imposed tasks that often include exploration and discovery.
- Play may be inspired or suggested by the materials or interactions with others, but the key is that there is an element of control and choice on the part of the child.
- Many skills in all developmental domains are learned through play. People of all ages, from infants to seniors, participate in play in some form.
- Play is the basis of developmentally appropriate practice, and each domain of development is supported through play.
- The physical, social/emotional, cognitive, and creative domains are all enhanced through play.

4.2 Name and describe the stages and types of play.
- Most children will participate in various stages and types of play at various times in their development.
- The stages of play are related to the general ages of children and depend on the development of motor, language, and social skills.
- The types of play are general concepts of categories of play in which children engage.
- Children reenact their experiences and use play as a means of understanding their world.
- The play of infants is important in their growing understanding of their world.
- Adults can enhance infants' learning through interactions that enhance language and motor skills.
- Interactions with adults support infants' continuing involvement in play activities.

4.3 **Demonstrate cultural influences on play activities.**
- Developmentally appropriate practices include providing materials that allow children the freedom to explore and use them in their own ways.
- Activities that children choose for their own accord, those offered by an adult that build and expand on children's current knowledge, and group activities that provide social experiences support learning.
- Interest centers that provide a way to organize materials are a common means of integrating curriculum concepts.

4.4 **Describe developmentally appropriate play activities that support learning.**
- Creative play involves children using common, everyday materials in new and unusual ways.
- Divergent thinking is a process of looking at many ideas, much like brainstorming, to generate new ideas or to find solutions.
- Dramatic play, sometimes called pretend play or role play, is a form of play in which children create scenarios.
- It is important to use age-appropriate language when speaking to children.

4.5 **Explain ways that adults can support and extend play.**
- The teacher has an important role in providing children with rich play experiences.
- Teachers provide a safe environment that well-equipped and arranged and set up to inspire and support experimentation.
- The teacher's attitude toward play is important in achieving a supportive environment.
- The teacher's planning and interactions guide children's learning throughout the day.
- Although most activities in an early childhood program are child-initiated, teachers must use their knowledge of children's development and behavior to plan, assess, and guide the experiences in a safe, comfortable environment.

4.6 **Describe how to assess play opportunities for young children.**
- Questions such as those proposed by Dr. Eric Strickland can evaluate how well programs provide for children's play.
- The Infant/Toddler Environment Rating Scale-3™ (ITERS-3™) is a formal means of assessing how well the environment supports children's learning.
- Such scales can provide a baseline and guide for ongoing improvement in how the environment meets the needs of children.

4.7 **Explain the importance of communicating with families about play.**
- Communicating with families about the value of play is important to help them understand a developmentally appropriate approach to learning.
- Routine conferences can be a time to share what children have learned by presenting examples of how children have demonstrated what they have learned through play.

Recall and Application

1. **True or False.** Children learn problem-solving skills by playing.
2. **True or False.** In solitary play, children play near one another with similar materials but do not interact.
3. **True or False.** In parallel play, children play together with common goals.
4. **True or False.** Outer space is a good theme to use with toddlers.
5. **True or False.** For play to be meaningful, children must be old enough to share.
6. **True or False.** Themes should be selected according to children's interests.
7. **True or False.** The teacher can stimulate play by providing props, time, and space for play.
8. **True or False.** Open-ended questions encourage play.
9. **True or False.** The teacher's job is to tell children what to do when they play.

10. A teacher might help a group extend a role-playing situation by _____.

    A. telling children exactly how to play the role
    B. providing additional props
    C. making other children leave their play station of choice to join in the role-playing situation
    D. taking over one of the roles

11. **True or False.** Assessment of a program cannot be done when the program is based on play.
12. **True or False.** Assessment is an important part of planning for play to meet children's needs.
13. **True or False.** Children's play is not affected by their family's culture.
14. **True or False.** Communicating with families is important to help the families understand the value of play.

Chapter 5

The Basics: Safety, Health, and Nutrition

Standards Covered in This Chapter

NAEYC

NAEYC—2c, 2l, 3c, 5a, 5b, 5c, 6a, 8a, 9a, 9b, 9c, 9d, 10d

DAP

DAP—1d, 1e, 2g, 4b

Learning Outcomes

After reading this chapter, you should be able to:

5.1 Provide safe outdoor environments for young children.
5.2 Provide safe indoor environments for young children.
5.3 Describe effective ways teachers can care for themselves when working with young children.
5.4 Identify ways to maintain a healthy classroom.
5.5 Provide adequate nutrition and nutrition education for young children.
5.6 Engage families in understanding and supporting classroom practices.

Chapter opener image credit: SDI Production/Getty Images Plus

Key Terms

anticipation
childproofing
context
mandated reporter
neglect
physiological needs
pinch point
supervision

Introduction

It was a hot July day when a failure to follow established policy almost became a calamity for an early learning program and a tragedy for a child. For 40 years, the program had been housed in a community church, providing care and education for more than 150 children each year. Several veteran staff members, including the director who founded the program, had recently retired.

At around two o'clock, a mother arrived to pick up her child for a dental appointment. But the child was not in the classroom, and a search did not find him in the center. The class had returned from a field trip earlier that day so, fearing the worst, a staff member rushed to check the church van. The child was found asleep in the back seat of the van, sweating and dehydrated. Paramedics were called, and fortunately the child was unharmed after an overnight stay for observation. Both the van driver and the teacher failed to follow a key safety policy: to conduct a check of the van and complete a checklist that ensures that all children depart the van.

Both employees were investigated by Child Protective Services, and although no criminal charges were filed, both were terminated from employment. The incident was publicized, and as a result, the program was dissolved. Had the child not had a dental appointment that day, the situation would have been much worse.

Policies exist for a purpose: to take a proactive role in keeping children safe and healthy. Anyone responsible for young children must take policies seriously and realize that they must be constantly alert to the hazards that can cause injuries and illnesses and the policies that prevent children from being harmed.

This chapter examines these major components of children's well-being. The first of these aspects is safety. The text will address outdoor safety first, then indoor safety.

5.1 Safety Outdoors

The most critical skill of early childhood staff is that they can keep children safe, healthy, and well nourished. These key aspects of promoting good health, including proper nutrition and accident prevention, must be at the heart of all activities, curriculum, communication, and interaction, both in the classroom and outdoors.

Playground SAFE

The acronym SAFE is a straightforward way to remember important aspects of playground and safety for young children. **SAFE** stands for **S**upervision, **A**ge-appropriateness, **F**alls to surfaces, and **E**quipment maintenance. Although intended primarily for playgrounds, SAFE applies to many indoor safety issues as well (NPPS n.d.).

S = Supervision

What is meant by supervision? **Supervision** is the process of overseeing or guiding a person, an object, or action. It is a key to safety because better supervision equals fewer accidents and injuries. Supervision is more than simply watching children; it includes anticipating and preventing of potential problems, teaching safety habits, and assisting children when needed. **Anticipation** is a prediction of what might happen based on knowledge of children's behavior. It also entails being prepared, such as having cleanup supplies available because spills are common as children learn to do for themselves. Adequate supervision requires that adults be present, knowledgeable of children's behavior, alert to what children are doing, and able to recognize possible risks.

A = Age-Appropriateness

What do teachers need to know about children's physical development to determine age-appropriateness? Consider their strength, grip, height, weight, and coordination (**Figure 5.1**). What about their emotional development and propensity for risk-taking and exploration? Think about children's social development and how well they can cooperate and share. What about their cognitive development? How good are their judgment and caution, and how well developed are their decision-making skills? Will their inquisitiveness and creativity entice them to take unnecessary risks? Labels or other information recommending ages for equipment can be helpful, but teachers must still rely on knowledge of individual children.

F = Falls to Surfaces

Falls are one of the most common injuries on playgrounds. Therefore, teachers must consider the safety of the surfaces under equipment, especially those items that involve climbing. Asphalt, concrete, dirt, or grass are inappropriate under items where falls are possible. Commercially purchased mats or fill materials that meet safety standards—sand, wood chips, or shredded tires—are better choices. Also, consider Americans with Disabilities Act guidelines to provide an accessible playground.

E = Equipment Maintenance

Over time, equipment will require repairs or replacements. To maintain equipment, follow the manufacturer's guidelines. Be sure to consider the frequency of use and environmental factors such as weather exposure (NPPS n.d.).

The ABC of Supervision

Another helpful tool for remembering key supervision principles is this simple code: ABC. **ABC** is an acronym that represents **A**nticipation, **B**ehavior, and **C**ontext.

Rachasuk/E+ via Getty Images

Figure 5-1 This slide is the appropriate size for a child this age. Why is it important for children to use only age-appropriate equipment and toys?

A = Anticipation

An alert teacher uses knowledge of child development and behavior to anticipate (expect) and address potential perils by walking through areas to remove hazards before children are present and to eliminate visual barriers to supervision. During outdoor time, the teacher monitors equipment usage, because falls are a major cause of injuries. Know how children play; understand their skill level and the risks they are apt to take.

B = Behavior

Strategies to properly supervise children include making eye contact, watching all areas consistently to know what children are doing at all times, and listening for sounds indicating that children are becoming overexcited or that conflict may be developing (**Figure 5.2**). Prevent overcrowding by providing enough equipment and activities to engage all children. Limit the number of children using some equipment if necessary. Use proximity control by moving around to check on children and to stay close to challenging equipment.

C = Context

Teachers must consider the **context**, or the setting and circumstances, to adapt actions appropriately. To do this, they need to know how many adults are present, understand their responsibilities, and recognize the ages and skills of the children. They must assess the environment and how well it meets children's needs and constantly look for hazards to avoid or remove.

Certain times of the day and some activities may need particularly careful supervision because children are more at risk of accidents. Outdoor play and transitions such as arrival and departure times and restroom use are such times. Mealtime brings a risk of choking. New activities may need more supervision, because children will need guidance in safely using the materials (NPPS n.d.).

Zabavna/iStock/Getty Images Plus

Figure 5-2 These children are involved in a conflict. Which supervision strategy could you use to de-escalate the situation?

Teaching Tip

Barriers to Supervision

There are many barriers to supervision to consider and address. For example, a classroom may have furniture located where children cannot be seen, or the facility may have a room or playground in an L shape, so that part of the area is not visible. Adults may be distracted by administrative responsibilities, other adults, or even by involvement with individual children. Being rushed or hurried can cause adults to fail to pay careful attention to children's activities. Sometimes, hazards are not recognized by adults because of a lack of understanding of children's behavior or inadequate training in supervision. Too, programs may not have adequate policies or procedures related to staff/child ratios, job expectations, or responsibilities. Here are some common barriers to supervision:
- tall furniture that blocks a teacher's view
- equipment such as playhouses where children might be out of sight
- teacher distractions such as paperwork, other staff, or visitors
- extended focus on an individual child or group
- not being in proximity to children

Keys to Playground Safety

While both indoor and outdoor play require careful supervision, time outdoors usually involves more risk due to the higher activity level of children. Having at least two adults on the playground is best so that if one teacher is distracted, another adult is available to supervise the group. One adult should stay mostly in a location to see the entire play area. Other adults can be near the areas of greatest risk, such as climbing equipment or swings. Teachers supervising the playground should be circulating, moving around, and going where they are most needed. For example, if a large group of children are in a sandbox, a teacher should walk over and check in.

Factors that increase the risk of injury include equipment that is poorly installed, in the wrong location, or not age-appropriate. Equipment must be suitable for the age of the children using it, in good repair, inspected regularly, and well supervised. Additionally, failing to provide enough variety in equipment and activities often means children will become bored and more apt to create challenges by misusing equipment. A child who tires of a slide may decide to go down head first to increase the challenge. Here are keys to playground safety:
- Plan carefully for the location and installation of equipment.
- Check for and remove hazards.
- Make regular maintenance checks and perform regular maintenance.
- Minimize conflicts and crowding by providing duplicates of favorite toys, such as balls, buckets, riding toys, or wagons.
- Teach children safety habits.
- Provide adequate supervision.
- Count the children when outdoor time ends to ensure that all children go inside. Sometimes children hide or may try to remain on the playground after outdoor time is over.

Playground Safety Checklists

Using playground safety checklists can help teachers find hazards on a playground. If you find a hazard, fix it if you can. If you cannot fix it, make a note and report it to your administrator. Conduct safety checks at least once a month. Having different people do the safety checks helps find more hazards. The more people involved in watching for hazards, the more oversight is provided. Safety is everyone's business. Visit the National Program for Playground Safety's website for more information, including a playground safety report card (NPPS, n.d.).

Monitoring and Maintenance Outdoors

A monthly inspection of equipment should be made to locate any hazards or items that need to be repaired or removed (**Figure 5.3**). The inspection should check for:
- visible cracks, bending or warping, rusting, or breakage of equipment.
- faulty or broken hooks, rings, or links.
- worn swing hangers or chains, or open "S" hooks.
- missing, damaged, or loose swing seats.
- broken or missing supports or anchors.
- cement footings that are exposed, cracked, or loose in the ground.
- accessible sharp edges or points.
- exposed ends of tubing or protruding bolt ends that have lost caps, plugs, or protective covers.
- loose or missing bolts, nuts, or screws.
- splintered, cracked, or deteriorating wood.
- inadequate lubrication of moving parts.
- broken or missing rails, steps, rungs, or seats.
- openings that can lead to entrapment.
- chipped or peeling paint.
- pinch or crush points, exposed mechanisms, and moving parts.
- hard surfaces, especially under swings and slides, where resilient material has shifted or become packed.

Inspections should be made daily before children go outdoors to remove any hazards that developed overnight or during the weekend. Remove risks such as glass, rocks, or sticks; fire ants, bees, or other insects; animal feces; poison ivy or other poisonous plants; and trash and hazards, such as garden chemicals or paint.

Water Safety

Prevent access to any unprotected swimming or wading areas, ditches, or fishponds. Fencing around water areas should be at least 4 feet high with a self-closing, self-latching, adult-required gate. A child should never be left unattended in or near a pool or other water

SolStock/iStock/Getty Images Plus

Figure 5-3 A monthly inspection is necessary to make sure playgrounds are safe for children. What issues might the inspectors be looking for in the slide area?

location. Additionally, do not leave water, cleaning solutions, or other liquids in buckets or deep containers. Toddlers can topple into a large bucket while trying to reach an item within.

Sun Exposure

While protection from the sun is important, outdoor play is also important for children's development. The challenge is to find a way to provide for outdoor play while protecting children from ultraviolet radiation. Children can wear hats and appropriate clothing while outdoors, and teachers can apply sunscreen with parents' permission. Having plenty of shady areas on the playground will reduce sun exposure. If trees are not present, canopies can provide shade. Infants especially need shade because they are less mobile and their skin is more sensitive. Scheduling outdoor time in the early or late part of the day to avoid the hot noon and early afternoon sun can reduce sun exposure.

Transportation Safety

When programs provide transportation, either to and from home and school or for field trips, there are other safety issues to address, such as seat belts, safety seats, or booster seats. Using such equipment not only provides for safety but may also promote better behavior.

The vehicle must be kept in good running condition and properly maintained. Routes should be planned with safety in mind. Policies and procedures must require proper accounting for children as they board and disembark.

Every year, young children die from being left in vehicles because the driver failed to verify that all children exited the vehicle. Additionally, children have been left at field trip sites when they were not counted or checked before departure. A strict policy of accounting for children is critical to safety. Physically checking all seats and underneath seats in a vehicle is essential to ensuring that children are not left in the vehicle. Alarms can be installed in the back of a bus that require that someone walk to the back to disarm the alarm. The following are additional tips for ensuring safe transportation:

- When transporting children in vehicles, use appropriate car seats, booster seats, and seat belts that are properly installed (**Figure 5.4**).
- Avoid distractions when driving.
- Consider peak traffic times and the safest route when planning trips.

Eyecrave productions/E+ via Getty Images

Figure 5-4 This child has been secured in a seat that is recommended for the age group. What are some other precautions that adults should take when transporting children?

- Teach children to be alert to cars or to hold a grown-up's hand in or near a street or parking lot during loading and disembarking.
- If several vehicles are needed, such as parents helping on a field trip, travel in a caravan.
- Follow a system to ensure that all children are accounted for upon departure and arrival at the destination by a name-to-face check.

Emergency Preparedness

Being prepared, having a plan, and regularly practicing that plan helps ensure that staff will know what to do in an emergency. An emergency can be upsetting and frightening to children, so practicing a procedure can help ensure that the correct steps are taken if necessary.

Teaching Tip

Holding a Fire Drill

To hold a fire drill initially, such as at the beginning of the school year, plan as a group to ensure that all adults know the exits to use, the procedures to follow, and how to prepare children for the fire drill. Below are the steps to follow in initiating a first fire drill:

- Discuss the importance of drills with the children.
- Explain and show children what they are to do.
- Tell children to expect a loud noise. Let them hear the noise to see what it sounds like, so they will recognize the sound and know what it means.
- Be prepared to comfort any children upset by the noise of the alarm.
- Hold a "pretend" drill for children to practice what they should do.
- Conduct an actual drill a few days after reviewing the procedures with children.
- Review procedures again before the next drill.
- Record information immediately after the drill, noting the time it takes to vacate the building and any problems that occur. Discuss any problems with other staff involved and plan to address them.

Teaching Fire Safety

A teacher can help children understand fire safety as part of the curriculum. By including fire safety as a learning experience, you can help children be better prepared when a drill is needed. The following are some resources and activities for helping children understand this important topic.

Books to Read Aloud
- *Pete the Cat: Firefighter Pete* by James and Kimberly Dean
- *Clifford the Firehouse Dog* by Norman Bridwell
- *The Fire Engine Book* by Tibor Gergely

Songs to Sing
- "Hurry Hurry, Drive the Fire Truck" by The Kiboomers
- "Fire Truck!" by Ivan Utz

Manipulatives to Make Available
- Puzzles of firetrucks and firefighters
- Map cloth or rug with small vehicles
- Construction toys for building

Block Center Accessories to Include
- Firetrucks
- Wooden figures, including firefighters
- Posters of firefighters, firetrucks, and fire stations

Dramatic Play Props to Add
- Fire hats
- Blue shirts
- Recycled vacuum cleaner or water hose
- Rubber boots

Fire Prevention, CPR, and First Aid

States have various standards for emergency preparedness in early learning centers, such as fire safety, cardiopulmonary resuscitation (CPR), and first-aid training. Check your state and local regulations for what is required in the area. Most require that personnel check the batteries on all smoke detectors regularly and hold regular fire drills. Teachers are required to maintain CPR and first-aid certification and to keep a first-aid kit stocked and easily accessible.

Other Drills and Evacuations

Depending on the weather and other risks in your area, regulations may mandate additional drills or an evacuation plan. You may need to hold tornado or earthquake drills and develop an evacuation plan for flooding, chemical spills, or electrical or water outages. Active-shooter and lockdown drills are increasingly becoming part of safety plans. Consult with safety officials in your area for guidance in holding necessary emergency drills or evacuations. These drills can be introduced in a similar fashion to fire drills.

✓ CHECKPOINT

1. What are some ways to ensure adequate supervision of children?
2. What are some resources in your area to help with emergency preparedness?

5.2 Safety Indoors

Many of the hazards that are likely to occur in early childhood classrooms can be remediated or eliminated through well-planned procedures and processes. Clean up spills immediately; store towels near the art and water play areas to facilitate cleanup. Encourage children to clean up after themselves to prevent falls and tripping hazards. Watch for broken items or **pinch points**. Pinch points are places where a body part, such as fingers, can be caught between pieces of equipment.

Clearly define spaces for play materials. Mark areas where children may build with blocks or use other items, and teach children to respect these boundaries. Maintain a safe environment by watching out for potential hazards and avoiding or removing them. Here are some common ones:

- Prevent wet or slippery floors or other tripping hazards.
- Inspect plants and remove any that are poisonous, irritative, or have sharp leaves, stems, or thorns.
- Carpet or rugs should be easy to clean and low-pile and should not hide small objects that babies might put in their mouths.
- Check and clean air filters regularly to keep the air fresh. If necessary, install a humidifier to prevent the air from becoming too dry.
- Maximize children's contact with nature, such as having a small garden or animal feeder. Contact with the natural world can be calming and reduce stress.
- Check materials and equipment regularly for broken parts, sharp points, or edges, and remove them for repair or replacement.
- Make sure all electrical outlets are covered, and place appliances and cords out of reach of children (**Figure 5.5**).
- Arrange the room for clear exits.
- Take safety precautions in a calm, reassuring manner without overprotecting or making children fearful.
- Supervise children at all times, and never leave them unattended. Get any needed supplies and materials before starting work or during a break.

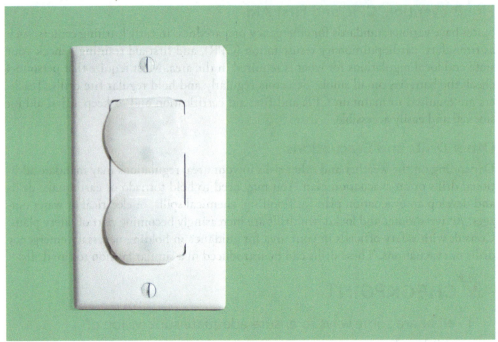

Blphotocorp/iStock/Getty Images Plus

Figure 5-5 This outlet has been covered so that children cannot insert their fingers or objects into the sockets. How will you ensure that all of these safety standards are met in your classroom?

Some hazards may not be commonly recognized, such as perfume or vanilla flavoring, which may be toxic to children. Choking hazards include popcorn, wieners and corn dogs, hard candies, grapes, deflated or popped balloons, Styrofoam, and small toy parts. Many of the foods that are choking hazards are snack-type foods; children walk around or play while eating them, increasing the risk. Have children sit at a table with an adult while eating, and be sure you know how to perform the Heimlich maneuver in a choking emergency.

Helping Children Develop Safe Habits

As an early childhood professional, your charge is to help children become aware of safety issues and to develop and practice safe habits. Many of these tasks can be accomplished during the day as you interact with children. Here are some ways to support safe habits through what you do and say:

- Convey to children in actions and words that safety is important and that you will help them to be safe.
  "Ayaan, let me help you tie your shoes so you will be safe on the playground."
- Scaffold children's developing skills.
  "Tommy, I'll stand next to the slide and help you go down."
- Remind children of safety rules as they play.
  "Jenny, let me help you move your toys back to the rug. You might get hurt playing near the door."
- Teach children how to obey safety rules by taking them on walks.
  "We're going to cross at the crosswalk where it's safe. Hold my hand when we cross the street."
- Use positive guidance techniques.
  "That hurts Theresa when you hit her with the spoon. Let me show you how to use the spoon to bang on the pots and pans."

Childproofing

Once a child becomes able to walk, many more hazards are accessible to them. This walking ability opens a new world of places to explore, such as tabletops, shelves, drawers, and

Teaching Tip

Indoor Safety Checklist

This checklist will help you find hazards within your classroom. Take a look around before the children arrive and frequently during the day.

Yes No

- ___ ___ Floors are clean, dry, and free of spills.
- ___ ___ Walkways are free of items that could cause tripping.
- ___ ___ All electrical outlets are covered or childproof.
- ___ ___ Electrical cords are out of children's reach.
- ___ ___ All carpets and rugs are clean and free of tripping hazards.
- ___ ___ Toys, materials, and equipment are clean and in good working order.
- ___ ___ Any soft items (for example, dress-up clothes, dolls, and pillows) are clean.
- ___ ___ Cots are clean.
- ___ ___ Heaters, registers, fans, and so forth are not accessible to children.
- ___ ___ The first-aid kit has been checked and is adequately stocked.
- ___ ___ The classroom is free of toxic plants.
- ___ ___ Cleaning supplies and staff's personal items are kept in locked storage.
- ___ ___ Food service areas are clean and sanitized.
- ___ ___ All furniture over 36 inches is anchored securely to walls or other surfaces.
- ___ ___ Sinks, faucets, counters, and soap dispensers are clean.
- ___ ___ Tissues, soap, and disposable towels are available and within children's reach.
- ___ ___ Bleach-and-water solution is fresh, and spray bottles are labeled.
- ___ ___ Handwashing procedures are posted.
- ___ ___ Spills are cleaned up immediately. Store towels near the art and water play areas to facilitate cleanup.
- ___ ___ Encourage children to clean up after themselves to prevent falls and tripping hazards.
- ___ ___ Clearly define spaces for play materials. Mark areas where children may build with blocks or other items. Teach children to respect these boundaries.
- ___ ___ The physical environment is clean and in good repair. There are no:
  - chipped, broken, or splintered flooring or tiles.
  - items with peeling paint.
  - broken windows or panes.
  - torn or frayed rugs or carpets.
- ___ ___ Furniture is clean and in good repair, free of:
  - protruding nails or screws.
  - torn padding or cushions.
  - broken table or chair legs.
  - sharp edges and splinters.

Consider This

1. In what ways might you assess your environment for health or safety?
2. What steps can you take to prevent injuries?
3. How might you determine whether you are prepared for emergencies?

---

surfaces previously beyond reach. Look at the environment from the child's level to plan **childproofing**. Childproofing refers to a thorough process of ensuring that an area has minimum risk to a child, including placing latches on cabinets and covers on electrical outlets. For the mobile child, a cabinet shelf is now a challenge that a curious toddler might try to reach. See **Figure 5.6** for additional safety steps to address related to doors, windows, and decks; the classroom and furniture; poison-proofing; and toys and clothing.

Responding to Accidents or Emergencies

Despite our best efforts, an accident will occasionally occur that must be dealt with. The nature of children's development means that skinned knees, scrapes, and bruises

Childproofing a Classroom

Area of Concern	Safety Steps
Doors, Windows, and Decks  Devenorr/iStock/Getty Images Plus	• Use doorstops and door holders to protect children from pinching their fingers. • Have sturdy railings on decks and landings. • Make sure openings in railings are not entrapment risks. • Cut off or tie up dangling cords on blinds.
Classroom and Furniture  Younggoldman/iStock/Getty Images Plus	• Prevent access to unsafe areas with safety gates, door locks, or knob covers. • Put locks or latches on accessible cabinets and drawers that hold unsafe items. • Keep trash cans inaccessible or use trash cans with child-resistant covers. • Never carry hot food or beverages and a child at the same time. • Keep breakable items away from the edges of tables and counters. • Remove clutter or protruding furniture that could cause you or a child to trip. • Attach corner and edge guards to furniture to avoid a hazard as a child grows taller. • Attach tall furniture, such as shelves and cabinets, securely to the walls to prevent toppling. • Do not leave anything in a crib that could help a child climb out. • Keep the crib sides up and latched when in use. • Put children to sleep on their backs. • Avoid bumper pads, pillows, or soft items where children can bury their faces.
Poison-proofing  Tiburonstudios/E+ via Getty Images	• Remove cleaning agents, medicines, vitamins, toiletries, mothballs, and other potentially toxic items and lock them up. • Keep purses out of reach. A purse may hold medicines or other toxic substances. • Prominently post the phone number of your poison control center.
Toys and Clothing  Baona/iStock/Getty Images Plus	• Select toys that are securely put together and in good condition. • Make sure toys are not too heavy. If a toy would hurt a child if it fell, it is too heavy. • Select toys that are appropriate for the child's age and physical skills. • Young children's clothing should have no buttons, beads, or other parts that a child could remove and choke on. • Young children's clothing should have no strings or cords longer than 12 inches that could be hung around a child's neck. Do not allow clothing with drawstrings.

Goodheart-Wilcox Publishers

Figure 5-6 Safety steps to take when childproofing a classroom. The next time you are in an early learning environment, check to see if each of these safety measures have been taken.

will sometimes happen. Hopefully, these incidents will be minor. To be prepared to respond to such situations, be sure first-aid supplies are available and know where they are stored. Be aware of and follow all regulations and established accident and emergency procedures of your state and those learned in first-aid and CPR classes. Keep parents' emergency phone numbers handy, and follow regulations or policies related to accident reports and parent notification.

Teaching Tip

Lead Exposure Concerns

Lead exposure can be another unrecognized risk, and even a small amount of exposure can have adverse effects on children. After being ingested, lead enters the bloodstream and is absorbed and stored in many tissues and organs, including the liver, kidneys, brain, teeth, and bones. Lead can cause serious health problems in children and can affect almost every system of the body, including the brain and central nervous system, causing (CDC 2023):

- headaches.
- memory problems.
- reduced coordination.
- learning disabilities.
- hyperactivity.
- increased sleeping and fatigue.
- hearing loss.
- muscle weakness, affecting mainly the upper extremities.
- seizures, coma, and elevated hypertension levels.
- abdominal pain.
- vomiting.
- anemia or low blood counts.

Consider This
1. Why do you think lead exposure is often not recognized?
2. What protections are now in place, such as regulations concerning paint on children's toys or equipment, to reduce lead exposure?
3. How are children exposed to lead?

☑ CHECKPOINT

1. What are the benefits of teaching children safety?
2. How might you integrate safety into the curriculum?

5.3 Teacher Self-Care

Caring for young children in a group setting is very demanding. It becomes even more challenging if the teacher is in poor health or has an injury. Thus, every teacher's goal must be to achieve optimum health and feel their best physically and mentally every day. This goal is most likely to be achieved in a positive environment in which health and safety practices are routine and factors contributing to illness and disease are reduced or eliminated.

Consider the many times during the day that teachers move or lift items in an early childhood classroom. Teachers may set cots down at naptime and stack them up afterward. They may move chairs for children to participate in activities and retrieve riding toys and other items from storage. Teachers who work with infants or toddlers lift children for diapering. A typical 1-year-old weighs around 20 pounds; a 2-year-old weighs about 25 pounds; and a 3-year-old, who sometimes may still need diapering, weighs around 30 pounds. A group of children with several diaper changes daily can translate to a lot of lifting and the potential for back injuries.

Preventing Back Injury

Many adults experience significant low back pain in their lifetime, sometimes caused by work-related injuries. Back injuries can create pain, medical expenses, and loss of work. Back injuries may occur in early childhood centers, where the physical requirements of

Case Study

What Would You Do?

Being prepared for common situations can help teachers respond appropriately and not be caught unprepared. Think about how you might prevent or respond to each of the following common problems.

1. Two preschool children arrive at school wearing jackets that have hoods with drawstrings. It is too cold to be outside without a jacket.
2. Christine (age 3) fell from a 2-foot platform onto the grass. She does not appear to be injured.
3. You are on the playground with toddlers and notice that the other teacher has taken her children inside, leaving you the only adult outdoors.
4. Sheryl (age 4) wore a dress that is so long you are concerned it is a tripping hazard for her. You call her mother, who tells you that Sheryl insisted on wearing the dress because it was a birthday present from her aunt.
5. Philippe (age 2) is playing near a small wading pool that older children have been using for water play.
6. Your school has little outdoor equipment for preschool children, so you take the children to the park across the street several times a week to use the equipment there. You arrive at the playground with your children and find broken glass near the play equipment.
7. Tyrell and Jamie (age 4) have created a game of climbing up the slide backwards.
8. Carlos (age 6) insists on standing up in the swing despite you telling him repeatedly to sit.
9. Annette, the mother of a recently enrolled 2-month-old, informs you that her daughter will not sleep on her back and wants you to put her on her stomach to nap.
10. Mr. Gregory's class is going on a field trip. He has a chauffeur's license and can drive the van himself. However, a parent failed to leave her child's booster seat at the center.
11. Ms. Johnson took several of her young after-school children outside with sidewalk chalk. There are no sidewalks, so they work in the driveway and plan to watch for cars.
12. Not all of Ms. Perez's preschool class can eat at the same table. Gonzalo and Marcia were especially good, so they got to sit at the "special table" out of sight of Ms. Perez. Gonzalo does not like being separated from his friend Don and keeps going back and forth from one table to the other to talk to Don.
13. Ms. Adams just rearranged her kindergarten room to separate her noisy play areas from her quiet library area. She moved a shelf away from the wall to serve as a divider, but now she cannot see children behind the shelf.
14. Xavier and Karen are the only children in the toddler class left to be picked up at the end of the day. They have been playing together well, so when the phone rings, Debbie leaves the room for a moment to take a call on the center's phone.
15. LaShonda took Darien's ball and threw it over the fence. Darien is mad and chases her.

Consider This

1. Which of the situations presented here could have been prevented?
2. How does a child's age affect what a teacher might do in these scenarios?
3. What other safety issues have you seen either in a classroom or at home?

---

the job are demanding and sometimes repetitive in nature. However, many back injuries can be prevented by following proper lifting and moving procedures.

The most common cause of low back problems comes from stretching muscles, tendons, and ligaments, which leads to inflammation, swelling, and pain. The following lists situations that have been identified as contributing to back injury and suggestions for reducing or preventing your risk of injury (NIH n.d.):

- Avoid awkward positions and forceful motions to move or reach around equipment or furniture, or to complete tasks in tight, cramped quarters.
- Use proper lifting techniques. Keep the item or child close to your body and avoid any twisting motion.

- Always lower the crib side before placing a child in or lifting a child out of the crib (**Figure 5.7**).
- Use comfortable chairs with good back support for rocking or holding infants or toddlers. Minimize time spent sitting on the floor with the back unsupported or in uncomfortable positions.
- Have the changing table at adult height. Use a stepstool for children to climb up to changing tables without being lifted when possible.
- When leaving the classroom with children who cannot walk well, use a multi-seat stroller rather than carrying children. Do not carry children if they can walk.
- Maintain a healthy, active lifestyle; get adequate sleep and regular exercise; and control your weight. Maintain proper posture to put the least strain on the back. Consider yoga, meditation, or other programs to maintain optimal mental and physical health.
- Wear appropriate footwear. Shoes should be comfortable, sturdy, and nonslip. Avoid sandals, flip-flops, and shoes with minimal support. Improper footwear can add strain to your back.
- Organize an efficient storage area. Keep the heaviest items at waist height; store only lighter items on high shelves. Use stepstools to reach high objects to avoid excessively reaching above shoulder height to obtain supplies.
- When removing items from high storage, ask someone nearby to take the items rather than stepping down a ladder or stool while holding the items.
- To transport trash or other items, reduce the size and weight of loads or use a cart. Making several trips is better than trying to carry too much.
- Avoid prolonged bending. Reduce or eliminate bending by sitting down to be at the child's level.
- Store wheeled toys, strollers, or other moving items where they will not cause tripping. Keep items that can become trip hazards off the floor.
- Promote education and awareness about injury prevention. Directors should educate and work with staff to prevent injuries and use accident reports to determine where and why an injury has occurred.

ANNA SUNGATULINA/iStock/Getty Images Plus

Figure 5-7 An adult has lowered the side of this crib so they won't strain their back when they pick up the baby. *What is another precaution you can take when lifting a child or a heavy object?*

Coping with Stress

Stress is an issue for everyone in early learning centers. It affects the staff, who have many responsibilities and sometimes limited benefits or resources to take care of personal needs. It affects children, who are influenced by stressors in the home or center, and it affects the families, who are juggling work and family responsibilities.

Paid leave for staff to stay home when ill, keep medical appointments, or take care of personal business without loss of income can reduce stress and make for a healthier workforce. Paid leave can reduce the temptation for staff to come to work when they may be ill because they cannot afford a loss of pay.

For children, a warm, nurturing environment can go a long way toward reducing stress. Additionally, some programs use deep breathing, meditation, and even modified yoga to help children learn to calm themselves. Chronic stress can lead to health problems, so helping both staff and children cope with stress pays off in terms of prevention.

☑ CHECKPOINT

1. What are some additional ways that you can protect yourself from injuries or illness?
2. What are some specific situations that cause stress in your life?
3. Have you tried yoga, exercise, or meditation to reduce stress? If so, what were the results?

5.4 Health

In addition to safety, protecting and supporting children's health is a primary requirement for programs for young children. This section of the chapter focuses on understanding why and how to create a healthy environment.

Keeping Children Physically Healthy

Keeping children physically healthy requires that providers consistently practice procedures to prevent the spread of diseases. When young children are in groups, there is a risk of spreading diseases as they handle items others have used or through coughing, sneezing, or close contact. Children are often careless with their own cleanliness.

As an early educator, there is much you can do to keep children healthy. State regulations and program policies often cover many of the appropriate steps that you should take to provide an environment that keeps children healthy and prevents the spread of disease.

Preventing the Spread of Disease

The following actions can do much to create a healthy environment and prevent the spread of disease:
- Perform a morning health check.
- Exclude children with signs or symptoms of a potentially contagious illness.
- Teach and implement regular handwashing (**Figure 5.8**).
- Practice proper diapering techniques and disposal of soiled diapers and clothing.
- Disinfect toys, cribs, eating areas, diaper changing areas, and restrooms.
- Separate food preparation area from the children's area.
- Do not allow sharing of food, plates, utensils, or drinks.
- Provide separate nap spaces for each child with 3-foot separations.
- Ensure proper storage and care of clothing, personal items, and bedding.
- Provide adequate ventilation and daily time outdoors.
- Require up-to-date immunizations.
- Clean toys, floors, rugs, walls, and baseboards regularly.
- Teach children to sneeze or cough into their arms.

Handwashing

How to Wash Hands	When to Wash Hands

HughStonelan/iStock/Getty Images Plus

XiXinXing/iStock/Getty Images Plus

1. Use warm, running water and liquid soap.
2. Wet hands, apply soap, and lather well, scrubbing between fingers and under nails.
3. Rinse thoroughly, letting the water run back into the sink.
4. Dry hands with individual paper towels or a blow dryer.
5. Turn off the water using a paper towel.
6. Dispose of used paper towels in a covered can.

- When entering the center and after playing outside
- Before and after eating
- Before serving food
- After diapering, using the restroom, or helping a child use the restroom
- After blowing your nose or helping a child blow their nose
- Before and after water play or handling animals
- If it is impossible to wash, use alcohol-based wipes or hand sanitizer.

Goodheart-Wilcox Publishers

Figure 5-8 Proper handwashing techniques. Why do you think it is preferable that children wash their hands with soap and water rather than use hand sanitizer?

Steps to Hygienic Diapering

If you are in a program that includes infants and younger toddlers, you will need to follow the steps necessary for the sanitary changing of diapers to prevent spreading illnesses to yourself or between children. Proper diapering should become a habit, performed automatically. Here are the seven steps to proper diaper changing from the Center for Disease Control:

1. Prepare by covering the changing table with a disposable liner, putting any cream to be used on a tissue, and bringing supplies to the area.

2. Place the child on the diapering surface, unfasten the diaper, and clean the child's diaper area with disposable wipes. Wipe from front to back. Keep soiled diapers and clothing away from surfaces that cannot be easily cleaned. Securely bag soiled clothing.

3. Remove trash, place used wipes in the soiled diaper, discard the diaper and wipes in the trash can, and remove and discard gloves.

4. Slide a fresh diaper under the child, applying cream if needed, then fasten the diaper and dress the child.

5. Wash the child's hands with soap and water, and return the child to a supervised area.

6. Remove the liner from the changing surface and discard it in the trash can. Wipe up the soil with damp paper towels or baby wipes. Wet the entire surface with disinfectant, following the instructions on the spray, fluid, or wipe.

7. Wash your hands with soap and water.

Cleaning, Sanitizing, and Disinfecting

Keeping children healthy means that adults must be conscientious about the tasks of cleaning, sanitizing, and disinfecting. These terms mean quite dissimilar things and involve distinctly different solutions. Cleaning and sanitizing cannot be done at the same time. The best practice in early learning programs is to clean, rinse, and then sanitize.

Cleaning involves scrubbing, washing, and rinsing to remove soil and debris using a solution of detergent and water. Cleaning removes most types of harmful germs.

Sanitizing means covering the cleaned area with a solution such as bleach and water. The recommendation is to leave the sanitizing solution on the surface to air dry.

Disinfecting is covering an already cleaned area with a disinfecting agent that is non-toxic for children, such as a stronger bleach-and-water solution. This practice kills any remaining germs on a surface. Follow safety guidelines for the solution used, and always store it out of reach of children.

Child Abuse and Neglect

All states have laws regarding child abuse. The laws generally define *abuse* as any of the following acts that seriously endanger the physical, mental, or emotional health of the child:

- the infliction, attempted infliction, or, as a result of inadequate supervision, allowing the infliction or attempted infliction of physical or mental injury upon a child by a parent or other person
- the exploitation or overwork of a child by a parent or other person
- the involvement of the child in any sexual act with a parent or other person, or the aiding or toleration of the child's sexual involvement with any person, or the child's involvement in pornographic displays, or other involvement of a child in sexual activity constituting a crime under the laws of the state

Neglect usually means the refusal or willful failure of a parent or caretaker to supply a child with adequate food, clothing, shelter, care, treatment, or counseling for any injury, illness, or condition as a result of which the child's physical, mental, or emotional health is threatened or impaired.

As a person responsible for young children, you are required by law to report suspected cases of abuse in most states. A **mandated reporter** is a person who is required by law to report suspected abuse or neglect. Mandated reporters include health practitioners, such as physicians, dentists, nurses, and others in the healthcare field; mental health and social service practitioners, such as psychologists, marriage or family counselors, social workers, and law enforcement personnel; and spiritual leaders, such as priests, rabbis, and ordained ministers. Others required to report suspected abuse or neglect include commercial film and photographic print processors who, in the course of their work, could come across pornographic photos or videos that include children. There may be penalties, such as fines or even incarceration, for failure to report. Make sure you know your state laws and center policies regarding child abuse reporting and know how to report suspected cases.

How do you know when a child might be suffering abuse? Here are some things to watch for that may indicate that a child has experienced abuse:

- bruises or welts, especially bruises in patterns that may have been made by a belt, strap, or human bite
- clustered bruises that may indicate repeated contact
- cigarette or rope burns
- loose or missing teeth
- frequent complaints of pain
- clothes that are inappropriate for the weather (sometimes done to hide injuries)
- frequent lateness or absenteeism
- unusual fear of adults
- malnourished or dehydrated appearance

- anxious, or outspoken, disruptive behavior or withdrawal (**Figure 5.9**)
- sexual knowledge inappropriate for the child's age

Another type of abuse is emotional, in which a child is frequently belittled or not provided attention that is needed for security. In this case, children may be verbally abused or have inappropriate demands placed on their capabilities. A child who is the victim of emotional abuse may show some of the following signs (Child Welfare Information Gateway 2021):

- generally unhappy, seldom smiles or laughs
- unusually disruptive, aggressive, or shy and withdrawn
- low self-esteem
- cautious around adults
- reacts without emotion to unpleasant statements or actions

Shaken Baby Syndrome

Sometimes, adults shake babies in an effort to get them to stop crying. This approach not only does not work but can do serious harm. A baby's neck muscles cannot fully support the head, and the shaking causes the vulnerable brain to collide with the skull, with the potential for permanent harm. At no time should babies be shaken, whether in anger or in an attempt to play.

Child Protective Services

To protect children from abuse or neglect, states have protective services policies intended to minimize harm to children and support families. Child protective services staff assess allegations of abuse or neglect to determine whether children need intervention. Where neglect is substantiated, these services provide support to enable family functioning or intervene until parents are able to provide a stable home. Protective services employees cooperate with law enforcement whenever criminal statutes have been violated to take appropriate steps to apprehend, bring to trial, and convict the perpetrator if found guilty.

Mixmike/E+ via Getty Images

Figure 5-9 Withdrawal or anxious behavior are both signs of possible child abuse. *What would you do if you noticed a child exhibiting these behaviors?*

✅ CHECKPOINT

1. What are some ways to maintain a healthy environment?
2. What are the physiological needs of young children, and how are they met in early learning programs?
3. Why is it important that an early childhood professional understand the responsibilities of being a mandated reporter?

5.5 Nutrition for Young Children

Maintaining good health requires proper nutrition. When you consider that early experiences related to food can influence lifelong habits, it is clear that an understanding of how to help children develop good habits is essential. This section addresses that important topic.

Early childhood is an exciting time of change. Children's bodies are growing, skills are being mastered, and attitudes are forming. Although every child is different, the following traits are common among young children and influence how they approach eating: Children have a natural curiosity, are striving for independence, have a need for security, and have limited attention spans that affect their eating behaviors. For children, eating may mean trying only a bite of squash today, maybe more tomorrow, or wanting a peanut butter sandwich every day for a week. Acceptable mashed potatoes

---

Teaching Tip

Characteristics of a Healthy Child

A healthy child requires an environment in which physiological needs, such as proper nutrition, adequate rest, and protection from diseases and accidents, are met. **Physiological needs** are those essential to life, such as oxygen, food, and water. However, there are other factors in ensuring that a child is healthy. Keeping children mentally healthy means that you must see that children are nurtured, valued, and contented.

Nurtured

Think about a time when you felt as if you did not belong. Maybe you did not make a sports team, were not invited to a party, or went to an event where you did not know anyone. Young children need help fitting in and feeling comfortable as well. Nurturing helps them feel they are wanted and belong.

Valued

Self-esteem is important in building one's confidence. Children build self-esteem through their interactions with others and the knowledge that adults care about them and will take care of them.

Contented

When children are nurtured and valued and their needs are met, a sense of contentment is generally present. This state of contentment helps them grow up to:
- be compassionate and accepting of themselves and others.
- be independent and secure in their thinking.
- be natural and spontaneous.
- possess a sense of humor.
- feel a sense of purpose.
- maintain meaningful personal relationships.

Consider This

1. Why is it important to nurture children?
2. How can you help children feel they belong in a group?
3. How can you help children feel valued?
4. What are some ways to promote children's self-esteem?
5. Why is self-esteem important in how we relate to others?

may become inedible if touched by zucchini. They will love carrots one day but refuse them the next. New foods may be refused with the common refrain, "I don't like it," even though they have never tasted it. Teachers should allow for individual and daily differences and not be overly concerned about children's changing preferences.

Young children explore their world by touching, seeing, hearing, smelling, and tasting. Most young children enjoy experimenting with new foods. A banana may be carefully inspected and squashed between the fingers of a curious 2-year-old. Children love surprises, such as a special fruit buried in gelatin or a heart-shaped sandwich served as a snack.

"Why?" becomes a frequent question, especially from 4- and 5-year olds. Because of their innate inquisitiveness, children may insist on knowing why the bread is brown before trying it. It is this curiosity that can be the catalyst for them to learn to enjoy an expanding range of foods.

Young children are striving for greater independence. Deciding whether to eat and what to eat is something they can control. They may accept toast only if it is cut into triangles or drink milk only if they can pour it themselves into a favorite glass. They may insist that an apple be whole, or soup be in a mug rather than a bowl. Four- and 5-year-olds enjoy helping adults select food at the supermarket, then taking part in preparing and serving it.

A Need for Food Security

Because they need the security of knowing that food will be available when they are hungry, children need structure in their lives. They need meals and snacks on a regular schedule and in known surroundings. They also need familiarity. Toddlers may insist on having their milk in a certain cup, their food cut in preferred shapes, or the same food for lunch for days at a time.

When they are hungry, young children will focus on food. When their hunger is satisfied, their attention turns elsewhere. Playing with their spoon becomes more interesting than eating the food before them when they are not hungry. Although parents may become concerned when a child leaves uneaten food on their plate, it is expected that children will lose interest in any activity after a brief time.

Many children spend extended hours in early childhood programs; thus, a major portion of food will be eaten at the center. Such programs have an obligation to not only provide nutritious food but also to help children learn to select healthy foods. A

Discovery Journeys

The Croissant Rebellion

It was the last day of a two-week summer camp at a local children's museum, and I had arrived just before lunch to pick up two children for a friend. The lunches for the camp were being prepared by the museum restaurant. Wanting to do something special for this last day and depart from the regular pizza, hamburger, and spaghetti fare, the kitchen had prepared a new croissant sandwich that was becoming popular with their adult patrons.

When the children saw the plates, I could tell there would be a problem. Frowns and puzzled looks were evident as the mostly preschoolers eyed the unfamiliar fare. A few poked at it while looking inside the croissant, and several asked the camp counselors about it, but none of the 20 or so campers even ventured to taste it. They clearly made their feelings about the strange food known.

When the chef and kitchen staff of the restaurant saw the untouched sandwiches, there was clear disappointment because they expected this to be a treat for the children.

Consider This
1. Have you witnessed children rejecting a food that you expected them to like?
2. Why do you think the children were not interested in the food?
3. What might the counselors have done to help the children accept the croissants?

well-balanced diet early on helps establish children's nutritional health for life. The overall goal of children's nutrition is to make sure they are eating the foods they need to maintain optimal health. These goals include the following:
- Eat a variety of fruits, vegetables, and grain products that are rich in vitamins and fiber.
- Include vitamin C-rich fruits and calcium-rich foods.
- Balance eating with physical activity.
- Develop children's willingness to taste new foods served at snack time or mealtime.
- Ensure that water is readily available and offered frequently.

The Teacher's Role in Nutrition Education

Adults responsible for young children can play a significant role in nutrition education and children's acceptance of nutritious foods. Your goal is to assist in the development of healthy attitudes toward food. The foundation established in the early years must be strong because eating habits that begin now can last a lifetime.

Adults should not discuss their own food preferences with children, especially if they are not fond of a particular food. Children are suggestible and will be more willing to try something new if the adults are enthusiastic about the food.

Children can learn to like a wide assortment of foods by eating with friends and family members who enjoy those foods. Children pick up subtle messages about how others view foods. A 4-year-old may be reluctant to eat turnips, a food his father is not fond of, whereas he eagerly eats cabbage, his father's favorite.

Here are some guidelines and suggestions for the adult's role in children's nutrition experiences:
- Be sure the foods you offer are nutritious. Avoid foods that are high in salt, fats, and sugar. Respect young children's strong dislikes of certain foods, and do not try to force them to eat something they resist. Forcing a child to eat will usually generate more resistance. As a rule, children dislike different foods mixed together, such as in casseroles where they cannot recognize individual items. Combinations of foods may be rejected, although macaroni and cheese and peanut butter and jelly are popular pairings.
- Serve meals and snacks on a regular schedule to allow children to develop a rhythm of hunger. Do not allow children to become overly tired before lunch or snack time. They may feel too tired to eat or even go to sleep at the table. Fussy eating, lack of appetite, boredom with food, and hunger at odd times may be signs that a child is following internal cues about when and how much to eat.
- Make mealtimes and snack times pleasant times for friendly conversation (**Figure 5.10**). Sit at the table and talk with the children to convey the idea that eating is a happy activity. Talk positively about the food yourself to set a good example, and take at least one bite of everything. Help children learn where food comes from. Help them grow, buy, prepare, and serve food to encourage acceptance.
- Be patient when offering new foods. If an unfamiliar food is not accepted the first time, offer it again later. The more children are exposed to new foods, the more likely they will taste them and eventually accept them. Always respect children's preferences. The color of the food, the plate, and the setting all influence appetite. Present food in appealing ways by combining colors, textures, and shapes. People enjoy food as a sensory experience, and that means it should be visually appealing.
- Offer small quantities of a new food with a familiar one without pressuring children to eat. Children can be overwhelmed by a serving that seems too large. They need smaller amounts to begin and then can be offered seconds. Serve a new food when children are with their peers; children often want to do what their friends do. Consider the health risks of childhood obesity. Do not encourage children to continue eating after they are full.
- Serve children who eat slowly first so that no one needs to be rushed to finish a meal or snack. If you cannot serve slower eaters first, allow them to finish while the other children get ready for rest time or go on to the next activity. Always be aware of food allergies children may have.

Figure 5-10 This teacher is making snack time a relaxed and social time for these children. *What else can teachers do to encourage children to have positive feelings about mealtimes?*

- Food preparation activities for young children are an effective way to introduce new foods and serving techniques. Learning to fix simple snacks can be a means of learning measurement, counting, and motor skills such as cutting, mixing, rolling, and stirring. Provide eating utensils and serving items that children can handle independently to encourage self-help skills and participation. Involve children in choosing snacks. When children have some say in what they eat, they will often eat items they otherwise might reject.
- Never use food as a reward or punishment. Withholding a dessert until all the vegetables are eaten may establish a preference for desserts and a dislike for vegetables.

Teaching Tip

Guidelines for Nutrition Education Activities

Early childhood teachers can plan specific activities to help children understand and select nutritious food. Children will eat foods that they might otherwise reject when they have been involved in preparing them. In planning food activities, consider food safety, cost, available equipment, and food allergies. Select nutrition activities that are suitable for the developmental level of the children. They should be involved in the actual preparation as much as possible. For example, a trip to the grocery store or farmer's market to purchase needed items can be a valuable learning experience. Include parents when possible. For example, ask them to share favorite food activities their family enjoys. Once the activity is completed, the food should be eaten soon while children are excited about the experience.

Consider This
1. What do children learn from food activities?
2. How do these activities provide good nutrition education and help children develop good eating habits?
3. In what ways can nutrition be integrated with other curriculum areas?

Food Preparation in the Curriculum

Including food preparation as a part of the curriculum provides an ideal opportunity for children to learn through real-life experiences, using and practicing skills in a relevant way. For example, take a field trip to a grocery store, farmer's market, or produce stand. Let children help select fruits and vegetables, count and weigh them, and then pay for the purchase. Afterward, set up a pretend grocery store or produce stand for children to replicate the experience in dramatic play.

Children can experience meaningful math, science, social studies, social skills, language, reading, and motor development by being allowed to plan, prepare, and enjoy their creations. Skills and knowledge embedded in food preparation activities can include language and literacy, mathematics, science, health and safety, social studies, social skills, creativity, and physical development (**Figure 5.11**).

Involving Children in Food Preparation

A child's involvement from the planning to the serving of a meal or snack stimulates interest in the activity and develops self-help skills. They learn about classification through activities such as identifying food groups. They can compare and describe

Food Preparation in the Classroom

Curriculum Area	Skills Learned from Food Preparation
Language and Literacy  3sbworld/iStock/Getty Images Plus	• Understanding that words on paper have meaning • Developing vocabulary using cooking, sensory- and culturally-related words, and scientific terminology • Following written directions • Writing directions for others to follow • Reading and authoring stories about the experience • Reading labels and directions
Mathematics  HappyKids/E+ via Getty Images	• Discriminating size and shape • Relating quantity to numerals • Using measuring tools and applying units of measure • Understanding and making use of time • Using addition, subtraction, multiplication, and division using whole numbers and fractions • Counting, classification, measurement, and weight • Using concepts of more than/less than; more/less, full/empty • Understanding one-to-one correspondence • Following the sequence of steps in a recipe
Science  JGalone/ E+ via Getty Images	• Observing physical and chemical changes and sharpening observation skills • Predicting, designing experiments, testing designs, drawing conclusions, recording results, and using the scientific method • Comparing raw, cooked, dried, and prepackaged foods • Discovering the nature of food, origin of food, physical properties of food, and food processing • Seeing relationships between types of foods • Learning to predict outcomes • Experiencing cause and effect

Goodheart-Wilcox Publishers

Figure 5-11 Tips on how to incorporate food preparation into the curriculum. Can you think of any ideas not listed here? *(Continued)*

Food Preparation in the Classroom *(continued)*

Curriculum Area	Skills Learned from Food Preparation
Health and Safety  Martin-dm/ E+ via Getty Images	• Understanding food sanitation and spoilage • Growing and using food plants • Practicing good hygiene and cleanliness • Recognizing food groups • Identifying healthy and unhealthy foods • Using cooking utensils safely
Social Studies  Triocean/ iStock/Getty Images Plus	• Experiencing and appreciating cultural differences in foods • Recognizing that people and their food are interdependent • Understanding the value of recycling
Social Skills  FatCamera/ E+ via Getty Images	• Cooperating • Following directions • Caring for equipment • Sharing and taking turns • Participating as a group • Developing feelings of competence, respect of other's work, and independence • Learning culturally appropriate manners
Creativity  Skynesher/ E+ via Getty Images	• Creating their own recipes • Writing stories • Designing packaging and ads for food • Creating a cookbook • Developing an awareness of color, form, texture, and shape • Writing songs and rhymes about food
Physical Development  JupiterImages/The Image Bank/Getty Images	• Developing small- and large-muscle coordination • Learning to mix, stir, and pour • Transporting items without spilling • Developing eye-hand coordination

Goodheart-Willcox Publisher

Figure 5-11 *Continued*

tastes and textures when you take advantage of opportunities to introduce vocabulary such as "crunchy," "chewy," and "tart."

Children as young as 2 years old can participate in serving themselves and will try new foods they might otherwise avoid. You can encourage self-feeding by providing finger foods for toddlers or older infants and letting them help with tasks such as spreading butter on toast. As part of encouraging children to develop self-help skills, accept spills as a learning experience. See **Figure 5.12** for some age-appropriate suggestions.

Is This Child Eating Too Little...or Too Much?

Many parents and early educators are sometimes concerned about a child's eating habits. For some, their concern is that the child is eating too little; for others, it is that the child eats too much. Children typically know best how much food they need. Parents and educators can help them meet their nutrient and energy needs by providing a variety of foods. Additionally, adults can support appropriate eating habits by:

- allowing the child to decide how much food to eat.
- offering small portions of food. Provide options for seconds, allowing children to serve themselves when possible.
- scheduling regular snack times and mealtimes that work best for the child and the family.
- allowing ample time for eating so that meals and snacks are not rushed.
- providing a comfortable setting and making the time enjoyable.
- not pressuring the child to eat.

Children Can Determine How Much to Eat

While parents and educators determine the selection of foods offered, children can determine how much food they need. For example, if a child has a small snack, the next snack or meal will be larger. Like adults, they may eat more at one meal than at another. By trusting their hunger cues, children can learn to choose an amount they can expect

Young Children and Food Preparation

Age	How They Can Help
Three-year-olds	• Pour liquids from small pitchers • Wipe tabletops • Scrub and rinse fruits and vegetables • Wash and tear lettuce • Snap green beans • Transport items from one place to another • Mix ingredients and pour liquids • Knead and shape dough • Put things in the trash • Shake liquids in a covered container
Four-year-olds	• Peel oranges or hard-cooked eggs • Mash bananas with a fork • Set a table • Cut parsley or green onions with kid-safe scissors
Five-year-olds	• Measure ingredients • Use an egg beater or a whisk
Six-to-nine-year-olds	• Select and read recipes and instructions • Calculate quantities needed • Use many appliances with supervision

Goodheart-Willcox Publishers

Figure 5-12 Tips on how young children can help with food preparation. Can you think of any ideas not listed here?

Discovery Journeys

The Lettuce Wraps

A mixed group of 5- to 8-year-olds in an afterschool program were accustomed to making their own snacks from available items. The items for the day were to be peanut butter (no allergies), cheese, and several types of crackers. However, a delayed delivery meant there were no crackers. The children quickly took charge of the situation and asked what other items they could have. The teacher named other items available, including lettuce. A 5-year-old announced to the group that they could put peanut butter or cheese on lettuce leaves and eat it like a taco! The others liked the idea, so lettuce wraps became the recipe for the day's snack, and it was consequently added to the snack rotation.

Consider This
1. Although this situation started out as a problem, how did the solution benefit the children?
2. How else might you encourage children to make healthy choices?
3. How do you think the children might have reacted if the teacher had made the decision and presented the idea of eating lettuce wraps to the children?

---

to eat. Adults can help build this trust by responding appropriately to signs that indicate when the child is hungry or satisfied.

Because children have both small stomachs and high needs for energy, they need to eat small amounts of food throughout the day. This is usually achieved by having three meals with nutritious snacks in between. Children's appetites may increase when they have growth spurts or are exerting themselves physically. Over time, the child's intake of nutrients and energy typically averages out, thus achieving a healthy balance.

Children with Small Appetites

Children who have small appetites and who typically eat less food need foods that are high in both nutrients and energy. When feeding young children, adults can offer:
- food without forcing the child to eat if they are not hungry.
- small meals with a nutritious snack between each meal.
- smaller portions with the option for seconds.
- nutrient-rich foods, including foods high in iron, such as meat, whole grain and enriched cereals, peas, and beans; energy-dense foods, such as peanut butter, cheese, high-fat yogurt; or whole milk.

Children Who are Overweight

Many young children are overweight, and the number is becoming a serious concern. Overweight children are at a greater risk for diabetes, high blood pressure, gallbladder disease, heart disease, and other health problems. Various changes in society have contributed to the increased incidence of obesity. These changes include a sedentary lifestyle, partially due to increased use of television, computers, and video games. Contributing to the increase are declines in outdoor play and activities such as walking to school that entail physical exercise.

Poor eating habits, fast foods, and preferences for high-calorie and high-fat foods add to the intake of more calories than needed for the activity in which children engage. While there is much you can do to provide appropriate food and exercise, educating parents and enlisting their help is necessary to fully address this aspect of health.

Food and Other Allergies

These days, many children have food allergies. These allergies may be caused by foods typically served in early learning programs, such as peanut butter, milk products, seafood, and some fruits. Before preparing snacks in the classroom, consider food allergies that children may have. Many states require that the allergies be listed where teachers have ready access to the allergy information. The teacher may send home a letter (**Figure 5.13**) that explains the role of snack preparation in the program. If a child has an allergy to a food that is being used, hopefully an alternative can be found and used for the activity.

✓ CHECKPOINT

1. Why do you think children are more willing to accept food when they have been a part of growing or preparing it?
2. How can food activities be integrated into the curriculum?
3. What are some ways to involve children in food preparation?

5.6 Family Matters

Parental support is necessary to encourage children to make healthy food choices and to help them maintain a healthy weight. Some parents may depend on fast foods or less healthy options or have little knowledge of their children's food needs. Childhood obesity prevention is a good topic for a parent meeting or an article to include in a parent newsletter. See **Figure 5.14** for a sample handout for a parent meeting or newsletter.

Childhood allergies are a topic of concern in many programs and require collaboration with families. Early learning staff must be knowledgeable of any child's allergy to prevent exposure. Parents must be asked upon enrollment about any known allergies their child might have and requested to provide medical guidance on treatment. The program policy regarding allergies should be communicated with families so snacks or treats provided by families do not accidentally expose children.

Sample Letter to Parents about Allergies

Dear Parents:

Snack preparation serves a significant role in our program. Besides providing nutrition for your child, snack time is a time when your child learns many skills and concepts, such as math, reading, writing, science, and social skills.

For us to provide appropriate food choices, please let us know about any food allergies your child has. If your child has a known food allergy, we will have an alternative snack to prepare. Please fill out, sign, and return this letter to your child's teacher. If your child has no known food allergies, write NONE, sign, and return this note. This information will be kept on file in your child's classroom.

My child is allergic to the following foods:

_____

_____

(Parent Signature)

Goodheart-Wilcox Publishers

Figure 5-13 A sample letter from a teacher to families about food allergies. *What else would you include in this letter?*

Sample Parent Handout or Newsletter

Staying Healthy

At (insert name of program) we work to support you in helping your child be healthy. Here are suggestions for ways you can help your child be more active and maintain healthy eating habits.

Plan Exercise for the Family

Family bike trips, active games, or weekend hikes make exercise fun. Children need to see their parents enjoying an active life. Play hopscotch, hide-and-seek, or jump rope; walk the dog; or build an obstacle course in the hall. Provide toys that encourage active play, such as balls, bats, bikes or tricycles, or scooters.

Tackle Television and Other Screens

Limit television watching and other screen time. Eating while watching television can become a habit and lead to overeating or focusing on convenience food. If your children beg for sugary, high-fat foods, they may be influenced by too many commercials.

Eat Meals as a Family as Often as Possible

Having a healthy family includes spending time together. The family meal is a wonderful way for everyone to be together, have conversations, and eat together. Make mealtimes pleasant by talking and sharing the activities of the day.

Plan Ahead

Serving meals at home requires planning. Before you do your shopping, plan your meals for the week. Make a list of ingredients you will need to prepare healthy, balanced meals. When fatigue kicks in and you want dinner on the table fast, your menu is planned and the ingredients are readily available.

Practice Healthy Eating

Prepare healthy meals and snacks and teach children about making healthy food choices. Allow your child to help make meals and snacks. Letting them help prepare food encourages them to try foods they might otherwise avoid and also teaches valuable life skills. Be a role model with your own food choices and exercise.

Routines and Rewards

Having a routine means having a set time for breakfast, lunch, dinner, and snacks. Once you have a routine for meals and snacks, mealtimes can be more relaxed. Most children are happier on a schedule and become hungry at regular times. Children need a meal routine just as they need a bedtime routine. Fruits and vegetables are great for snacking, too. Instead of rewarding your child with food, reward them with attention (hugs, kisses, and smiles) and playful activities.

Money-Saving Ideas for Better Health

Avoid temptations for high-fat, high-sugar foods by not bringing them into the house. Limit the number of processed, ready-to-eat snacks you buy, such as potato chips or cookies. Prepackaged and processed foods are generally higher in calories and fats and often more expensive than healthier items. Consider fruits such as apples, oranges, bananas, and melons, or vegetables such as carrots, celery, or nuts instead of bags of chips or boxes of cookies.

Water and Hydration

Offer water often. Water is inexpensive and healthy.

Goodheart-Willcox Publisher; (illustration) robuart/Shutterstock.com

Figure 5-14 A sample newsletter from a teacher to families that includes tips for children to stay healthy. How else can you involve families to help keep your classroom safe and healthy?

✓ CHECKPOINT

1. What are some other issues related to health, safety, or nutrition in which collaboration and communication are important?
2. How might you encourage parents to reduce fast foods for young children?
3. What are some suggestions you could give to families to involve their children in a more active lifestyle?

Chapter 5 Review and Assessment

Chapter Summary

5.1 **Provide safe outdoor environments for young children.**
- The acronym SAFE stands for **S**upervision, **A**ge-appropriateness, **F**alls to surfaces, and **E**quipment maintenance.
- Supervision is a crucial factor in providing safety for young children.
- Equipment and materials must be age-appropriate for the children using them.
- Falls to surfaces are a major cause of injury on playgrounds, but the risk can be reduced by using proper cushioning materials.
- Maintenance of equipment is essential because over time, both equipment and fall areas can become unsafe.
- The ABC of supervision stands for **A**nticipation, **B**ehavior, and **C**ontext.
- Supervision includes not just watching children but helping them learn safe behavior. It also includes an understanding of child development to ensure appropriate and safe activities. The supervisor *anticipates* what children might do based on their age and skills and recognizes what hazards exist. Knowledge of children's *behavior* at various ages is also important in providing a safe environment. The *context* of the setting must be considered when providing supervision.
- Water safety and sun exposure are important aspects of providing for children's safety.
- When programs transport children, adults must take additional measures to avoid injuries.
- Practice emergency preparedness for both natural and human-caused disasters.

5.2 **Provide safe indoor environments for young children.**
- The teacher is responsible for guiding children in developing safe habits.
- Childproofing can reduce the potential for injuries.
- Lead exposure is a serious concern for young children's health.
- All early learning staff should be prepared to respond to accidents or emergencies.

5.3 **Describe effective ways teachers can care for themselves when working with young children.**
- Adults caring for young children engage in lifting and need to know how to lift correctly to avoid injuries.
- Adults working in early childhood are faced with an elevated level of stress resulting from the constant alertness needed, the noise levels and activities, and the responsibility of the job.
- Specific strategies can help adults maintain a calm demeanor and the ability to cope with daily tasks.

5.4 **Identify ways to maintain a healthy classroom.**
- Observing proper protocols for sanitization and other health practices is important in preventing the spread of disease among groups of children.
- Handwashing, hygienic diapering, cleaning, sanitizing, and disinfecting are all means of maintaining a healthy environment.

- Children can be helped to learn good health and safety habits as a part of their daily routines.
- Knowledge of child abuse and neglect is required, because people who work in early learning programs are required in most states to report suspected abuse.

5.5 Provide adequate nutrition and nutrition education for young children.
- Children need nourishment on a regular basis.
- Providing adequate nutrition is a responsibility of adults who work with children.
- Teachers can integrate safety, health, and nutrition into the curriculum.
- Food preparation experiences can include math, science, and literacy.
- Food preparation activities can help children learn to select and enjoy nutritious foods that they otherwise might avoid.
- Obesity is a concern for children, even very young children, because of the health risks.
- Some children have allergies that require special consideration and understanding.
- Early learning staff must be knowledgeable of allergies to take appropriate precautions.

5.6 Engage families in understanding and supporting classroom practices.
- Engaging families is important so the teacher and families can work together for the nutritional benefit of the child.
- Some families may have little knowledge of young children's nutritional needs and will benefit from information provided by the early learning center.
- Communication with families about allergies is necessary to prevent accidental exposure.

Recall and Application

1. A major cause of injury to children is ____.
    E. other children
    F. falls from equipment
    G. sandboxes
    H. blocks
2. The best way to deal with injuries is to ____.
    A. tell your director
    B. prevent and know how to deal with them beforehand
    C. write notes to parents
    D. have good insurance
3. **True or False.** Most accidents children have cannot be prevented.
4. **True or False.** Active children will have injuries, and there is little adults can do about it.
5. **True or False.** Regular monitoring and maintenance are not needed if you purchase safe equipment to begin with.
6. The ABC of supervision stands for ____.
    A. anticipation, behavior, consistency
    B. age-appropriate, behavior, consistency
    C. anticipation, behavior, context
    D. ability, behavior, confinement
7. **True or False.** Knowledge of child development is important in supervision.
8. **True or False.** Good supervision is simply telling children what to do.
9. **True or False.** Supervision is the least important part of preventing injuries.
10. **True or False.** Sandals are okay for hot summer days if the playground is not concrete or asphalt.

11. **True or False.** Teachers should allow children to walk if they are able and avoid lifting when possible.
12. The most effective way to prevent infection is _____.
    A. using hand sanitizers
    B. handwashing
    C. wiping down surfaces
    D. wearing a hairnet
13. **True or False.** Children should always be encouraged to eat everything on their plates.
14. **True or False.** The nutritional habits that children learn during early years can significantly affect their future health.
15. **True or False.** Allowing children to plan and prepare simple nutritional snacks can promote learning in curriculum areas as well as promote nutrition.

Chapter 6

Engaging Families

Standards Covered in This Chapter

NAEYC

NAEYC—1a, 2a, 3b, 4b, 4e, 6b, 7a, 7b, 7c, 8a, 8b, 8c

DAP

DAP—1a, 2a, 2b, 2c, 2d, 2e, 2f, 2g, 3f, 3g, 4b

Learning Outcomes

After reading this chapter, you should be able to:

6.1 Develop positive relationships with families to work as a team for children.

6.2 Recognize and support diverse families and their needs and challenges.

6.3 Identify ways to communicate and interact with families of all children served.

6.4 Describe ways to actively involve families in a program.

6.5 Assess practices related to family engagement.

Chapter opener image credit: SDI Productioni/E + via Getty Images

Key Terms

blended family
Family Engagement Assessment and Planning Tool (FEAP-T)
LGBTQ+
multicultural
multiracial

Introduction

Societal changes and economics have generated a variety of family structures. With single parents, blended families, same-sex parents, guardianships, multigeneration families, and more, there is no such thing as a *typical* family. Families vary not only in their structure but also in their characteristics, resources, needs, and interests. Parents and guardians differ in how they approach their parental role and what they know or want to learn about parenting. A family's culture and origin can influence their view of parental roles and values. Parents and guardians tend to approach parenting in much the same way as they were raised themselves.

The term *parent* is broadly applied in this textbook as the person who has the primary responsibility for raising a child by providing shelter, food, and nurturing. This person may not be the child's biological parent. In most cases, the terms *family* and *parents* are used interchangeably to encompass those persons in the immediate family role who may be grandparents, aunts, uncles, foster parents, or legal guardians.

While outreach to all families is important, early childhood programs may need to plan special programs or initiatives targeted to meet the needs of specific parents or groups—for example, fathers, single parents, teen parents, or grandparents raising grandchildren. The better the staff knows, understands, and respects the parents in your program, the better the relationship they can form with their families.

All early childhood educators must communicate with and engage children's parents to work together effectively for the good of the child. Working together includes developing consistency in discipline and other expectations while respecting parents' rights to make decisions concerning their child. Involving families in the program helps them feel accepted by the staff and valued as a part of their child's education. Having families involved in your program promotes their continuation and support of their children's development at home. Understanding how and what a child is learning will help them provide consistency in home and school expectations.

As an early childhood educator, you play a special part in families' lives: You see the parents daily. You celebrate happy times and may be involved during difficult times as well. Your service gives parents an opportunity to further their education or to earn a living. You may spend more daytime hours with their children than they do. Parents will often look to you for support in child-rearing and consider your opinion if they have a specific question or concern regarding their child. You not only teach children, but by fostering relationships with families and involving them in your program, you are teaching them as well. A positive relationship between the educator and the parents is key in creating a team approach to early childhood education. Respect and trust must exist between the parent and the educator to effectively work together to best meet the needs of the child. Partnership with parents includes being honest, open, nonjudgmental, and respectful of families' diversity and culture. Parents must be viewed as significant partners in their child's early childhood experiences.

6.1 Building Positive Family-Program Relationships

The first step in building relationships with families is welcoming children and parents in a friendly, nonauthoritarian way from the beginning. Let parents know you are interested in and care about their child as an individual. When parents believe that staff members know and care about their children, they will feel more trusting. If developmental information is provided along with details from observations of children, parents will feel reassured about their children's development and well-being.

The second step in building trust and respectful relationships with families is open communication. Effective communication means that you do not interrogate parents. People are more open and helpful when they are not feeling defensive. Discuss, but do not criticize. Be a good listener. Demonstrate understanding and ask questions if you do not fully understand what parents are trying to communicate. Build an open relationship based on two-way communication and the sharing of ideas and solutions. Here are some additional tips for communicating with families:

- Help parents feel good about themselves and what they are doing for their children.
- Try to see the child from the parents' point of view.
- Do not compare one child to another.
- Avoid getting too personal; keep conversations friendly and professional.
- If parents need help with a problem, share or suggest resources that might help.
- Help parents build a support network with other families through center-wide activities and meetings.

Case Study

Environmental Change to Improve Communication

After several years of teaching in a toddler class, Olympia believed she had tried all she could to keep families informed about how their children were doing and what they needed. She was continually frustrated that many parents did not provide a change of clothes or other items their children needed. She was also discouraged that they often requested worksheets and drill work to demonstrate their children's learning, which were developmentally inappropriate for the children's young age.

One day, she left work disheartened because a parent she had wanted to talk to rushed in and out so quickly that she did not have a chance to tell him about his child's noteworthy achievement. Coincidently that evening, the instructor of her continuing education program told the class about how some teachers had tried moving their parent sign-in sheet from its location near the door to the far side of the classroom. They found that when family members had to walk into the room to sign in, they noticed what children were doing, talked more to the teacher, stayed longer, and were more apt to spend time interacting with their child about what was happening in the classroom.

Consider This

1. How do you think families might react to such an arrangement?
2. How might a teacher explain the reason for such a change?
3. What else might a teacher do to engage family members at arrival and departure times?

Off to a Good Start

The first step in creating a positive relationship with families is to make a good first impression. Greet and welcome families and their children by name on the first visit and daily at arrival. Friendly, positive greetings will set the stage for a good relationship between you and the parents. The following actions will help form a positive relationship and prevent misunderstandings and tensions between educators and families:

- Encourage parents to visit the classroom prior to enrollment so they can see your program in action.
- Have written policies and procedures to give to the parents at the time they visit or upon enrollment.
- Provide a thorough orientation to explain policies and procedures, and let the parents know what to expect in your program and classroom.
- Discuss communication options with parents and ask their preferences.
- Recognize that the parents are the child's primary caregivers and first teachers.
- Ensure that parents are knowledgeable about the program through visitation, conferences, meetings, and other activities.
- Encourage parents to be involved in activities to the extent that they are able.
- Share information about the program and the child every day upon arrival or departure.
- Schedule regular meetings with parents as well as additional meetings as needed.

Viewing the Parents' World

Getting off to a good start means that you must understand the families' concerns about someone else being responsible for their child. Consider how they might be feeling as they leave their child with you for the first time. In writing about parent–teacher conferences, Roslyn Ann Duffy (1997) lists the three main concerns parents want to address when meeting with their child's teacher: (1) whether the teacher knows and likes their child; (2) whether they can trust the teacher; and (3) whether their child is developing normally. These concerns provide a glimpse into a parent's world.

Do You Know and Like My Child?

Do you really know each child for whom you hold responsibility? How do you communicate your knowledge to parents? Some possibilities for reassuring parents that you know their child are parent conferences and conversations and regular information sharing, such as notes with details about a child's day, behavior, or interests. Daily conversations can be comforting as well as provide information about what their child is doing.

Can I Trust You?

What might help a parent feel trust in your program or in you as their child's teacher? Some factors that contribute to trust include a willingness to answer questions openly. Honest, clear, and tactful communication creates trust. Accessibility to what goes on in a program establishes trust. When families are welcome at any time with an open-door policy, they are more likely to feel trusting. Another factor in building trust is observing program staff respond to upset or misbehaving children with kindness and sensitivity.

Is My Child Normal?

Parents worry about their children's behaviors, but not all know when a behavior might be of concern. First-time parents often have no frame of reference as to expected developmental milestones. Or they may have limited contact with other families who have children of similar ages. Early childhood program educators can reassure parents about their child's development and behavior through parent education classes, brochures, handouts, or newsletters about development. Additionally, health and developmental screenings and progress reports can reassure anxious parents.

Barriers to Family Involvement

Sometimes, parents and teachers are not comfortable with each other. The teacher may dread the parent's criticisms or may feel financially at the parent's mercy. A displaced parent may remove a child from the center, creating an economic loss to the program.

Discovery Journeys

Dudley's Mother

Dudley was a 4-year-old only child, and his parents enrolled him in my preschool class as his first group experience. Dudley had undergone surgery that required a lengthy recovery and individual care for a few years. He was fully recovered and medically cleared to participate in an early childhood class. When I met with his mother, she was anxious about this new experience. Over the first few weeks, I frequently reassured her that he was doing well as she vacillated between continuing his enrollment or keeping him at home.

One rainy, gloomy winter day, she arrived late to pick him up. She was clearly upset about something and wanted to talk. She described her situation with a good deal of emotion. Before Dudley was born, she had worked in a laboratory and loved the challenge of her work in cancer research. However, family members had convinced her that she should return to school and become a teacher so she would be on the same schedule as Dudley. She did not want to be a teacher. This was not a career that inspired her. She felt she had given up a job that she loved and had already completed the education to do.

For about 30 minutes, we discussed how Dudley was doing in class—adjusting, learning, and, most of all, becoming increasingly independent. Dudley's mother was greatly reassured, and once she recognized that she had been led by others to a decision she did not like, she was able to express her frustration and dissatisfaction. A few days later, she updated her contact information to let us know she had returned to her job at the lab.

Consider This

1. How do you think the mother's family influence led to her unhappiness in her parent role?
2. Have family members ever tried to influence you to do something that you did not feel was right for you?
3. Why was it important that the teacher took the time to listen and understand the mother's frustration that day?

Parents also feel vulnerable to criticism. First-time parents can be fearful of a teacher's opinion. Parents may be seeking validation of their own worth by seeking the teacher's approval of their children. Parents may also fear making the teacher angry by speaking frankly and mentioning something they dislike about the center or what their child is doing. They may worry about reprisals against their child when they are not present. Friendly, open communication can allay such fears.

For both parents and teachers, past experiences and previous relationships may set the tone of what each expects of the other. In addition to pleasant memories, there may be emotional ones of being sent to the principal's office, staying after school, enduring authoritarian teachers, or having unreasonably strict parents. These memories may create a tense undercurrent for initial parent–teacher interactions. Therefore, teachers must put forth some effort and understanding if they wish to establish a rewarding relationship with the adults who are so important in their young students' lives. The most essential ingredients in a satisfactory relationship between teacher and parent are that the teacher has the child's welfare truly at heart and is genuinely concerned about the child.

Occasionally teachers have the impression that parents are too busy or are not interested in participating or being involved. Usually, however, parents are interested; they just do not know what to do. Communicating with parents as they drop off and pick up their children can help establish cooperative relationships. For example, giving parents ideas about interesting, free, or inexpensive developmentally appropriate activities they can do at home or in the community with their children can create a connection between home and center life.

Working with families in a positive way requires that teachers be accessible in two ways. First, because they care about the child, they need to be emotionally accessible.

Second, they must be physically available when the parent is at the center. Being accessible for more than brief conversations during the workday is difficult, but arranging schedules to be available occasionally for early-morning or late-afternoon meetings can provide time for more in-depth discussions. You may also consider after-hours calls when you and the parents can be free of work responsibilities.

☑ CHECKPOINT

1. What are some ways to make a good impression on families?
2. Why are good family relations important for the program and the children?

6.2 Respecting Families' Cultural Background and Diversity

Another way of building trust and acceptance with families is by demonstrating respect for their cultural background and family structure. Family structures and backgrounds are as diverse and unique as people themselves, and early childhood educators must support children's sense of belonging to their family. How can an early childhood program fulfill that central task? Teachers can demonstrate respect for families' cultural backgrounds and accept families as they are without judgment or bias in many ways, such as by:

- including photos of children with their families in the classroom.
- involving families in activities and making sure everyone feels welcome.
- using dress-up clothes and items from a variety of cultures in the housekeeping area.
- having pictures depicting different family units in the classroom.
- having a curriculum theme of families that depict diverse family compositions in books, posters, videos, and photographs.
- serving food from numerous cultures (**Figure 6.1**), especially from those cultures represented in the class.

Swirl/iStock via Getty Images

Figure 6-1 This toddler is having breakfast at her early learning program because she arrives at 6:30 so her parent can go to work. How does a breakfast program benefit the child and the parent?

- using inclusive language in communications so families are not made to feel different. For example, avoid terms such as *room mother*; instead, use more inclusive terms such as *room helper* or *room chair*.
- having information and resources available that are appropriate to diverse family structures and their parenting needs and issues. Brochures, pamphlets, and online resources can help parents get the information they need.
- getting to know parents as individuals.
- including books and stories that represent various family components, especially those present in your classroom.
- actively supporting the employment of center staff from various cultures.
- allowing children to use their home languages and providing opportunities for them to teach words and phrases from these languages to the class.
- respecting cultural traditions and ways of living.

While all families are different, particular groups and family structures have some characteristics and challenges in common. Early childhood programs can support children and their families by understanding their backgrounds and the challenges they may be facing. Many of the suggestions for supporting particular family backgrounds and structures are applicable to others. For example, suggestions for military families with an absent, deployed parent may be equally appropriate for single parents. The important task is that early childhood educators work not just with the young child but with the family as well.

Single Parents

The single parent who has full responsibility for the care and nurturing of a child is likely to have limited time to be involved with the program and may face restrictions caused by meeting financial obligations. The parent may simply lack adequate time or money. Other factors may come into play that affect the parent's ability to be involved, such as custody issues or juggling multiple children's schedules. Therefore, involvement opportunities should consider the limitations of many single parents. Suggestions include:

- accommodating their schedules and time limitations by arranging conferences or meetings at a time they can be available.
- suggesting ways they can interact with their child at home, especially during routine tasks. For example, when folding laundry, the parent may encourage a preschooler to match socks or hang clothing.
- communicating in writing or electronically to allow the parent to read information on the parent's timeframe.
- offering involvement opportunities that do not require extended time.

Fathers and Male Caregivers

Male role models within the family are important in the lives of children, but some fathers or other male caregivers may not feel comfortable or even welcome to actively participate in their children's early childhood programs. They may not recognize their significant role in raising children and may feel reluctant to become heavily involved in a typically female-dominated field. All members of a family have an important role in the healthy development of a young child and should feel welcomed and encouraged to take part in the child's education (**Figure 6.2**). How can an early learning program reach out to fathers and other male caregivers? Suggestions include:

- collaborating with fathers, grandfathers, uncles, and other male caregivers who are already engaged to encourage other males to volunteer as well.
- designing outreach activities and planning programs targeted at men, such as Special Grown Up Day, to indicate that fathers and other males are welcome. Make sure that families know that any male caregiver is included in the invitation.

Figure 6-2 This male parent is volunteering in his child's early learning classroom. What are some benefits of positive male role models in the classroom?

- finding out what skills male parents and caregivers have that can be useful to the school. Requesting help with a particular project can help them feel welcomed and valued. Sometimes, a personal request is more productive than a blanket appeal.

Multigenerational Families and Kinship Care

Those who work with young children recognize that an increasing number of young children live in families of either two adult generations or a grandparent and at least one other generation. In some cases, these families result from adults with offspring moving back home with their parents, grandparents, or other older relatives. These living arrangements often occur as the older adults respond to the needs of their children, grandchildren, great-grandchildren, nieces, or nephews.

In addition, 4 percent of all children in the United States—more than 2.6 million—are in kinship care, meaning relatives are raising children whose parents cannot care for them (AEFC 2020). The number of grandparents who are now raising a second family is increasing to the point that the term *grandfamilies* has been coined. These grandfamilies may develop due to economics, incarceration, mental or physical illness, death, military deployment, or numerous other reasons. The primary responsibility of rearing the children may be in lieu of the parents or in collaboration with them. Households in which grandparents assume full responsibility for their grandchildren are referred to as *skipped-generation* families. Here are some characteristics that affect many skipped-generation families:

- Many of the grandparents are still in the workforce themselves.
- Adequate space for children in the home may be unavailable.
- Resolving legal issues related to adoption, legal custody, or guardianship can be time-consuming and disruptive to family dynamics.
- Raising children without a legal relationship may limit the adult's access to services on behalf of the children, including school enrollment and necessary healthcare.
- They may feel apprehensive or presume that they will not understand and use correct parenting approaches or cannot help children with schoolwork because of generational differences.

One way to involve grandparents is to examine and revise program policies to accommodate the realities of children living with their grandparents. For example, grandparents who are retired may be available to be involved in ways that even the child's parent may not be, such as chaperoning on field trips or leading story time. Recognize that the grandparents' experience of school and early education may be very different from what happens at your program, and they may need more information about current methods, curriculum, and expectations.

Conversely, family dynamics may mean an absence of grandparents' contact with grandchildren due to geographic, relationship, or boundary issues. In these cases, grandparents may have limited means to be involved in their grandchildren's lives.

Teen Parents

Occasionally, grandparents rear children because the parents are very young. The young parents may have extensive support in their role and live with extended family, or they may have limited help and even be estranged from their families. They may have financial limitations due to unemployment or underemployment. Studies have reported that teen parents are less articulate and communicative and are perceived as less sensitive, less responsive, and more punitive than older mothers. How can a program help these young parents? Teachers can use knowledge and experience to teach and guide teen parents by demonstrating how to interact with children to facilitate attachment and engagement. Teen parents may also benefit from guidance that will help them learn to balance their life experiences with parenting demands.

Foster Families and Homeless Families

In the United States, more than 407,000 children were in foster care in 2020. Foster care is a temporary living situation for children whose parents cannot take care of them. While in foster care, children may live with relatives, with foster families, or in group facilities (AECF 2020).

Children entering the foster care system may have been victims of abuse, neglect, or other adverse experiences that hinder their social or emotional adjustment. Domestic abuse may have been present in their home, or their parents may have abused drugs or alcohol, engaged in criminal activity, or experienced physical, mental, or behavioral health challenges. The children may have moved from home to home and not had the consistency of care important in building a sense of security. For homeless families, many of the same insecurity issues also occur.

With both groups, there is a high probability that the children's education thus far has been sporadic. The family situations that led to the need for foster care or shelter residence may have also led to irregular school attendance. One main difference between the two situations is that in foster care, children are not with a parent and may be separated from their siblings. They may have limited or no contact with their parents. For homeless children in shelters, they are typically with at least one parent.

Children may be a part of several families during their time in foster care. What can you do to help families and children? Pay special attention to ensuring that the children are helped to fit in and make friends. Provide as much consistency in expectations and routines as you can by coordinating with the foster parent or shelter staff. You may need to assist in locating resources to help with school supplies or uniforms if needed. Recognize that the children may need help with some basic living skills, such as using utensils to eat or proper hygiene, if their experience in those areas is limited.

A subset of homeless families includes those who are displaced suddenly because of a natural disaster or loss of income. Following hurricanes, tornadoes, floods, fires, or earthquakes, many families are forced to start over in new locations with limited resources. Homes, jobs, businesses, schools, and whole communities may be lost, leaving nothing for families to return to. The emotional upheaval in the family can be significant, and mental health becomes a concern. For example, the massive evacuation of

South Louisiana and Mississippi families following Hurricane Katrina caused major disruption of livelihoods and the loss of belongings and loved ones, which lead to many relocated children engaging in troubling and, sometimes, destructive behaviors.

LGBTQ+ Parents

LGBTQ+ is an acronym for lesbian, gay, bisexual, transgender, queer or questioning, and other terms to describe a person's sexual orientation or gender identity. There were roughly 980,000 same-sex couple households in the United States in 2019, and most were married—around 58% compared to 42% unmarried. Children living in these households totaled 292,000 (**Figure 6.3**). These numbers do not include the many other gay, lesbian, bisexual, transgender, or queer single parents who are also raising children. Current estimates suggest that between 2 million and 3.7 million children under the age of 18 have an LGBTQ parent in the United States.

Children whose parents are gay and lesbian have historically been subjected to laws, social policies, and attitudes that challenge the stability of their families. However, according to the American Academy of Pediatrics, parents' sexual orientation is not among the factors that put children at risk (AAP 2013). Studies assessing the developmental and psychosocial outcomes of children in gay or lesbian households report that a family's social and economic resources and the strength of the parent-child bond are far more important than sexual orientation in affecting children's development and well-being. A large body of scientific literature demonstrates that children who grow up with gay or lesbian parents fare as well in emotional, cognitive, social, and sexual functioning as do children of heterosexual parents (WWKP 2015).

Military Families

Children often react to events, including a parent's deployment, based on the reactions and coping skills of their parents. This puts responsibility on adults concerned with children's welfare to consider the well-being of the adults who remain at home during deployments or in adjusting to relocations.

MBI/Shutterstock.com

Figure 6-3 This child has two male parents. How could a teacher help this child feel that her family is represented in the classroom?

Young children being raised by a single parent or both parents serving in the military face special challenges. These children are likely to be in the care of relatives for a time while their parents are deployed, and some of these relatives may not be adequately prepared for that role.

For young children in military families, deployment can interfere with the opportunity to develop and maintain relationships with a parent during a critical developmental period (Paris, et al., 2010). For a very young child, separation issues are especially a concern because a typical deployment period accounts for a relatively large proportion of the child's life. Parents who return home with injuries may be permanently disabled, creating added stress for the family and requiring additional readjustment periods. **Figure 6.4** identifies some of the behaviors that might be seen because of a parental deployment.

Military families often move their residence as the parent is transferred from base to base. As with other disruptions to routines, young children do best when parents and other caring adults prepare them for the change and demonstrate positive coping skills. These moves mean the loss of familiar adults and friends and require adjustments to new circumstances and environments.

Fortunately, the Department of Defense provides support through family service offices. These services aid family members who remain during deployment and help with the process of relocation. What can you, as an early childhood professional, do to help military families? First and foremost, establishing a secure, trusting relationship with the child and maintaining consistent daily routines are paramount. Keeping pictures, recordings, or other personal items of deployed parents in the center is helpful. You can help the child stay in contact with the deployed family member by sending cards, photos, or electronic messages. It is important to help children process their emotions in positive ways to avoid disruptive or unhealthy behaviors.

Adoptive Families

In the past, adoption was typically a secretive process with only basic information exchanged between the birth and adoptive parents through a social worker or other intermediary. In adoption agencies, social workers had most of the responsibility for matching the child to the adoptive family. Legal records were sealed, and a birth mother or adopted child faced many challenges in locating each other. Some adoptive parents made a choice not to inform their child of the adoption. In some cases, however, a grandparent or relative might legally adopt a child, and the birth parent is known to the child.

In the past, attempts were often made to match the birth and adoptive parents in attributes such as physical characteristics, religious preferences, and educational background. Now, with international and interracial adoptions being more common, adoptive children are more likely to know their history and have little resemblance to their adoptive families.

The adoption process has significantly changed. Searchable online sites allow a biological mother to select a family for her baby. Open adoptions, which include a relationship with both the birth and adoptive families, are more common. Ancestry search sites, social media, and genetic testing provide opportunities for birth and adoptive

Possible Responses of Young Children to Parental Deployment

Age Group	Possible Response
Infants (0–1 years)	listless or irritable mood, hyperactivity, apathy, refusing to eat, weight loss
Toddlers (2–3 years)	clingy and/or withdrawal behavior, sullen/sad mood, tantrums, sleep problems
Preschoolers (4–5 years)	clingy behavior, regressive behaviors, voicing fears, feeling guilt

Goodheart-Willcox Publisher

Figure 6-4 This table lists possible responses of young children to parental deployment. *How can a teacher help a child process these feelings?*

families to connect. Adults who were adopted as children can locate their birth parents or siblings. Adoption and the resulting extended families may be a source of confusion for young children. What can you do to support adoptive families? Suggestions include:

- finding out from the adoptive family what the legal obligations and preferences are regarding the involvement of the birth parents, if relevant to the program.
- following the child's lead on how to refer to family members.
- avoiding prying questions related to the circumstances of the adoption.
- following the parent's lead in referring to why the child is not with the birth parents.
- avoiding referring to the birth child as the "real" or "your own" child in familes that include both birth children and adopted children.

Incarcerated Families

Nationally, the number of children who have had a parent in jail or prison at some point in their childhood is around 5.1 million, and that is reported to be a conservative estimate. Among states, the percentage of children with an incarcerated parent varies dramatically, from only 3 percent in New Jersey to 13 percent in Kentucky (ACEF 2020).

Feelings Encountered by Children of Incarcerated Parents

According to the Prison Fellowship, an organization working to support families who have an incarcerated family member, having an incarcerated parent causes many confusing emotions for children (Prison Fellowship n.d.). This section describes some typical feelings that children of incarcerated family members may experience. These feelings may also apply to other situations in which a family member is absent, such as deployment or divorce.

Fear. Children fear being abandoned, never seeing their absent parent again, or being taken away from their caregiver. This fear may even translate to unfounded fears of specific people, places, animals, or activities.

Worry. Concerns about the well-being of the incarcerated parent are common, even if the relationship is troubled. Children may worry that their caregivers will not be able to take care of them or that there will not be enough food or money.

Confusion. Often, children are not told the truth about their incarcerated parent's whereabouts or the reason why the parent is incarcerated, leading to questions that children are afraid to ask. They become confused about what is true and what is not.

Sadness. The loss of a parent is not the only loss these children experience. They may have to leave their home, change schools, and lose contact with friends.

Guilt. Children sometimes feel responsible for their parents' behavior. They may express regret that they should have tried harder to stop their parent's drug use or blame themselves for not doing something differently. They might feel that their behavior or actions somehow caused their family member's incarceration.

Isolation. Family members may discourage the child from discussing the incarcerated parent. Social stigma may prevent children and their caregivers from talking about their situation. Well-intentioned adults may attempt to protect the children by avoiding conversations about the family member. The silence can leave the children feeling isolated.

Embarrassment. Children with incarcerated parents feel stigmatized, even when they know other people who have incarcerated family members. Older children may experience the shame and embarrassment of seeing a mother or father's picture in the news with a story about their arrest. They may have even been present during the arrest and witnessed their parent handcuffed and removed from their home.

Anger. Anger does not usually show up in the early days, but over time and after experiencing many losses and disappointments, anger likely emerges. Children of incarcerated parents have been deeply hurt.

Tips on Supporting Children of Incarcerated Parents

The National Resource Center on Children and Families of the Incarcerated maintains a Children of Incarcerated Parents Library that provides a variety of resources and free information for caregivers and people working with children of incarcerated parents. Establishing a trusting relationship, allowing children to express their emotions, helping them build resilience, and being careful not to condemn their incarcerated parents are some of the ways that you can meet these children's needs (Martoma 2020).

Multiracial or Multicultural Families

Multiracial (having parents or ancestors of different racial or ethnic backgrounds) children are one of the fastest-growing segments in the United States due to a rise in interracial relationships and marriages and an increase in transracial and international adoptions. For most multiracial and **multicultural** (having multiple cultures) children, growing up associated with multiple races or cultures is enriching and rewarding (**Figure 6.5**).

However, some interracial families still face discrimination in their communities. Children may also face pressure from society, peers, or their families to identify with only one race. However, with the increase in multiracial families, attitudes are changing. In the 2013 US Census, about 9 million Americans identified themselves as being of more than one race. Research has shown that multiracial children do not differ from other children in terms of self-esteem or number of psychiatric problems. In fact, they tend to be high achievers with a strong sense of self and of tolerance and diversity. Also, children with a true multiracial or multicultural identity generally grow up to be happier than multiracial children who grow up with a single-race identity (AACAP 2017).

However, multiracial children still face some challenges. Siblings in a multiracial family may have different racial identities from one another. Their physical features, family attachments and support, and experiences influence their racial identity with groups. Also, to cope with social biases, multiracial children may develop a public identity with the one race and a private interracial identity with family and friends.

What can early childhood professionals do to help multicultural or multiracial families and their children? They can assist children in developing skills to handle questions or address biases about their background. To do so, become familiar with the language, traditions, and customs of all family members. To provide a sense of acceptance, include books, pictures, and videos that portray multiracial individuals as positive role models.

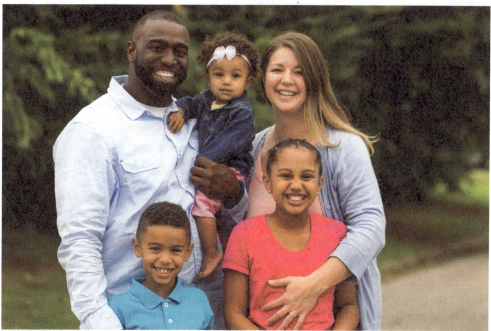

pixelheadphoto/iStock via Getty Images

Figure 6-5 In addition to being of different races, these parents also have two adopted children. What can a teacher do to make all families feel accepted and welcome?

Case Study

Celebrating Holidays

A common issue in early learning programs related to family expectations is holiday celebrations, particularly in a setting in which families differ significantly in religious orientation. Sarah and Taylor, both first-grade teachers, are new this year to a small private school. They often plan collaboratively, and as December approaches, they begin to address holiday plans.

For Sarah, there has never been a question about December. She has thick folders of ideas and activities based on Christmas and the symbols of Christmas—wreaths, candy canes, trees, Advent calendars, and a wooden nativity scene that she and the children set up. Where she worked before, parents often took charge of holding a huge Christmas party just before the school closed for the holidays. The children exchanged presents, and most of the parents and many grandparents attended the party.

Taylor reminds Sarah that not all of the children in the two classes celebrate Christmas. Three families are Jewish; two are Jehovah Witnesses; she believes another might be Hindu; and one child mentioned celebrating Kwanzaa. She wonders aloud if it is a good idea to emphasize Christmas, but Sarah is adamant that the school should support this holiday because it is so important to most of the children. "Besides, most of the families are Christian, and majority rules," Sarah says emphatically.

At an impasse, the two take their concern to the school administrator, seeking guidance. In the past, holiday celebrations had not been an issue for the school because, while family religions were different denominations, they were all Christian, so there was no official school policy about holidays. However, a new global business had located near the school, so the population in the school had become more diverse this year.

The administrator contacted some of the parent members of the school's advisory board, all of whom practiced different religions, to get their feedback and input. One parent expressed that she was not concerned because her family often addressed that issue by telling their children, "That's what some people believe, but that's not what we believe." She had no objection to Christmas celebrations, even though her family was not Christian.

Another parent was adamant that he had chosen this school over several equally good church-affiliated schools because he believed that religion should be a family matter and that such celebrations were inappropriate for the school.

One mother felt that since the majority of families were Christian that Christmas should be celebrated as usual, and the children would be greatly disappointed if it were not. "Why should most of the children do without it just because a few might not want it?" she challenged.

To address the matter and develop a draft for an official policy, the administrator set up a meeting to invite all of the families in the school to give input. As word spread about the meeting, some families threatened to withdraw their children if the school stopped the Christmas celebrations. Others threatened to withdraw their children if the school did not stop celebrating and take a neutral stand concerning religious holidays.

Consider This
1. How can the school respect the values of diverse families?
2. Would you mostly agree with Sarah or Taylor? Why or why not?
3. Why is it a good idea to have guidelines or policies available to parents prior to their enrollment?
4. What are some other ways that personal values and beliefs might influence a teacher's work with children?

Blended and Divorced Families

Higher divorce rates and changing family structures have led to an increasing number of **blended families** (families consisting of a couple and their children from this and all previous relationships). Each member of a newly blended family, including children, has experienced loss and faces adjustments to the new situation.

When a blended family is formed, the members may have no or little shared history or ways of doing things. They may have diverse belief systems, including different ethnic, religious, or educational backgrounds. A child may feel torn between the parent they primarily live with and the parent they visit. They may be aware of hostility between parents if anger or resentment over a divorce has not been resolved.

Children may exhibit strong feelings of being torn between two parents or two households. They may be uncomfortable with a member of the original family or the blended family. Additionally, the child may exhibit behaviors, such as directing anger toward a family member or openly resenting a stepparent or parent that they view as displacing their original parent in the household. The child may experience sessions of crying, sadness, or emotional withdrawal. They may even secretly or openly express hope that their parents will remarry and return to the former family arrangement.

Most stepfamilies, when given time to develop their own traditions and form new relationships, can provide emotionally rich and lasting relationships for the adults. These bonds can help the children develop the self-esteem and strength to weather the challenges of life.

What can you do to help children in blended families? It is important to communicate with the enrolling parent about any legal arrangements that affect the release of children or visitation arrangements that may include participation in the classroom. The noncustodial parent should not be excluded from participation if appropriate. It is also helpful to learn what the child calls the various family members and refer to them the same way.

The task of the early childhood educator is to recognize each child's unique family structure and how it may affect the child. Early childhood professionals must understand that all children have the same needs and the right to nurturing, security, and social support, regardless of their family situation. Children are in no way responsible for their living situation.

If the teacher blames the family when a child acts out, has emotional outbursts, or is struggling, barriers are created in the relationship. Even if unspoken, the family will sense disapproval. When feeling critical of a parent, seek to better understand the family's structure and challenges and try to find ways to guide and support them.

☑ CHECKPOINT

1. Consider some families you know. What makes them unique?
2. How can you demonstrate that you welcome all families in your program?

6.3 Family Matters

In the case study "Celebrating Holidays," the importance of communication was apparent as the administrator posed the question of religious celebration to the families of enrolled children. Effective communication is one key to a fruitful family–teacher relationship. However, establishing effective communication can take time and effort. Communication is challenging because individuals may interpret information differently and may have limited experience to appreciate the information being given. Therefore, it is important to be specific and give examples or illustrations of what you mean. Seeking input and feedback can help determine if understanding takes place.

Why is communication with families so important? Involving families in school and family partnerships supports understanding of what young children should do, what they need, and the educational goals of the program. Absent parents, for example, often miss important firsts and therefore want to know that their child has learned to pull up, taken a first step, or made progress in potty training.

How do teachers communicate with families? Programs for young children have a variety of options to get their messages across. For example, parents may be invited to observe a class session, watch videos of activities, and attend meetings or special events. They might receive a newsletter, an email alert, or a text message. They may be given

daily notes about what activities their child has participated in or other messages about the day. Here are a few other suggestions for strengthening communication:
- Send newsletters home weekly or monthly. Include pictures, short paragraphs, names, headings, and subheadings to make the newsletter attractive and easy to read. Newsletters can be electronic and posted on social media or websites.
- Involve parents in classroom activities when possible.
- Send home activity ideas to reinforce topics learned at school. Provide books or lists of suggested books to read to children at home.
- Send home positive notes about what the child has accomplished.
- Send children's projects home to stay connected with families and show that you value the child's work.
- Be available during drop-off or pickup times to talk. Encourage family members to talk about what the child does at home through open-ended questions. Demonstrate that you are interested in and care about the family through these conversations.
- Make periodic phone calls or send texts to let parents know about their child's progress.
- Hold special events such as Special Person's Day, or Open House.
- Hold conferences, both formal and informal.

Avoiding Jargon and Esoteric Terms

For clear communication, one must either avoid jargon and esoteric terms or explain what the terms mean. Jargon is technical terminology used within a restricted group or career field that is likely not understood by people outside that field. For the early childhood field, terms such as *perceptual motor development* or *peer interaction* may not be in the vocabulary of someone not in a similar field. Be sure the language you use is understood by others. Here are some examples of common jargon in the early education field that you may need to avoid or explain:
- developmentally appropriate practices
- emergent literacy
- project approach
- child-centered
- child-directed
- integrated curriculum
- circle time
- gross or fine motor skills
- manipulatives
- cognitive development
- standards
- assessment

Parent Conferences

Even though parent conferences can be time-consuming and difficult to schedule, regular conferences are effective tools for establishing and maintaining open communication. By holding routine conferences, you avoid the stigma that a conference means a child is misbehaving or not doing well. Regular conferences help you and the parents become a team. They provide an opportunity to stay informed and be active partners in the education of the child. Often, parents have something they want to ask or tell you but are hesitant to speak up. A routine conference offers them that opportunity. Holding conferences shows the parent that you care and want the child to do well. Both parties can better understand the child's needs so that a united effort can be made to address issues.

To arrange and conduct a conference, follow these steps:
1. Contact the families to let them know that you are scheduling conferences with all families and want to schedule one with them. The message should include the purpose of the conference, some possible meeting dates and times, and who will be attending. Or consider sending or posting a list of dates and times and letting families sign up. Providing options and flexibility increases the probability that parents will attend.

2. Prior to each conference, decide what to talk about and set one or two goals for the conference. Prepare an agenda to include at least the following:
   - how the child is progressing in each of the developmental areas
   - specifics about any areas of concern
   - goals you would like the child to achieve
   - suggestions you can offer for achieving those goals
   - questions you want to ask parents and the points you want to make
3. Prepare to explain your teaching philosophy and strategies and to describe what you have done to address any problems, if relevant.
4. Allow enough time. Parents sometimes need a few minutes to warm up.
5. Be prepared to share some of the following:
   - classroom expectations
   - lesson plans and types of activities
   - developmental checklists and observations you have completed
   - opportunities for parents to participate in your program
6. Allow time to answer any questions the families might have.

Guidelines for Parent–Teacher Conferences

Whether a conference is routine or needed to address a problem, you can do certain things to help ensure an effective outcome. Examples include:

Be prepared. Materials to share should be gathered and organized. Have portfolios, records, notes, and samples of the child's efforts readily available. Have written observations to refer to and show the parents that you have been documenting the child's progress.

Provide a comfortable setting. Adults who are not accustomed to the child-size chairs and tables may find them awkward and uncomfortable. See that adult-size furniture is available. Let the parent sit beside you rather than on the opposite side of a desk to eliminate a barrier between you and the parent (**Figure 6.6**). Sitting across a desk can be intimidating and may not convey approachability. Consider sitting at a table where you can spread out materials to review.

Weekend Images Inc./E+ via Getty Images

Figure 6-6 Parents review documentation of their child's progress as part of a parent conference. What are some ways in which you can make a parent conference productive?

Arrange for privacy and uninterrupted time. To establish open communication, privacy and your full attention are essential. If possible, arrange for child care during conferences to talk with the parent without interruption.

Start on time. Waiting can be stressful and create unnecessary anxiety for the parent. Be considerate of the time of the many working parents for whom the conference may mean lost wages or personal time off. Posting a schedule will help signify that an allotted time will be given and respected.

Greet parents warmly. Call the parent by name, using their preferred means of address. Conveying a sincere welcome can stimulate the desired rapport.

Open with positive comments. Begin the dialog with a description of something thoughtful or creative the child has done or an acknowledgement of a significant achievement. Opening with a child's strengths shows the parent that you see the child's good qualities. Relaying an amusing anecdote or a kind, responsible act can be successful in building rapport and cooperation before raising concerns. For example, "Alex told us the other day about helping his cousin learn to ride a bike. He's always helpful in class as well."

Be approachable. Be sure your expression and body language are friendly and your attitude is optimistic. Maintain good eye contact with the parent.

Maintain two-way communication. The purpose of a conference is interaction, so avoid doing all the talking yourself. Open-ended questions or statements will encourage parents to share their experiences. "Tell me about..." will generally produce more comments than "Does she ...?" Take care not to dominate the meeting. Make it easy for parents to ask questions or share their comments or concerns. Allow for occasional silence, which gives the parent an opportunity to digest information or think about a response. Your goal is to engage parents in planning the best ways to help their child, not to tell them what to do. Stick to the issue without becoming sidetracked. Remain focused on a solution and what is best for the child.

Provide information. Give parents the details and, when appropriate, additional resources they might need. Anticipate what might be helpful to the child or parent based on your recognition of interests or areas of concern. Express a willingness to seek information concerning unanticipated needs or identify a source of help. Give parents helpful materials to take home where they can review and consider them thoroughly.

End positively. End the conference with a message of hope. Summarize your agreement for a solution or course of action, and make sure you follow up on any agreement you make. Have notepaper to write down parent concerns, comments, and planned actions so you do not need to rely on memory of the conversation.

Talking about Difficult Issues

Sometimes, educators face a challenging concern that may be difficult to address. However, if you suspect there might be a developmental delay, vision or hearing problem, or other factors that should be evaluated, you have an obligation to address the issue. By discussing what you have observed and your concerns with the parent, you can help ensure that the child receives appropriate treatment and increase the effectiveness of intervention if it is needed.

In preparing for a conference where significant issues might be addressed, think through your concerns and how to best approach the matter. Consider what you will say and how you will express your observations and experiences with the child. Keep in mind that the parent may also be concerned or, as is sometimes the case with a first child, may not be aware that the child should be progressing or responding differently. Find out about resources in the community that might be helpful. Collect facts to share with the parent. For example, if a child is not responding to sounds as would be expected for their age, you might find information on hearing screening programs in your community. If a child is crawling significantly past the period when their same-age peers are walking, gather information on screening for developmental delays. Remember, however, that all children develop at different rates, and a developmental delay in one area may simply be the result of individual differences.

If several staff members are to be involved, avoid a "teamed-up" approach that can make the parent feel outnumbered or intimidated. Build trust by being professional and kind. Remember, the family may be facing challenges in ways unknown to you. Have empathy for them; acknowledge and recognize their important and demanding role.

Describe your concerns in a sensitive but factual way. Do not become judgmental or show evidence of blaming the parent for the issue or saying that they should have done things differently. Do not label the child with terms such as *slow, bad, aggressive, bully, rowdy,* or *shy.* Labeling may make the parent feel that you simply dislike their child and will likely discourage cooperation.

Review the issue and what you are doing about the situation during the day. Be specific and avoid putting parents on the defensive. Remember that you are there to address a concern and find solutions, so choose your words carefully. Are you making sure that the infant who is not walking yet has sturdy furniture to pull up on? Are you providing plenty of auditory stimulation, such as rattles, musical toys, or recordings, if you suspect a possible hearing loss? Are you providing a variety of activities that help children learn in a meaningful way?

Be sensitive to the parent's nonverbal questions, such as looks of confusion or disagreement. Listen carefully to understand what the parent is feeling and saying. Admit you do not know all the answers but are willing to make use of resources to help the family consider options.

Express your understanding of the parent's feelings if the parent becomes upset. Suggest that the parent discuss the matter with a pediatrician or healthcare professional. Offer to help in any way that you can by following the directions of the pediatrician or healthcare professional. Share with the parent situations in which intervention or remediation has been successful, if relevant. Tell about a child who made good progress once a plan was established and enacted.

Once you agree on a course of action, set a date and means of follow-up and put it on a calendar. Close with good points about the child and review the course of action on a hopeful and cooperative note. Agree to maintain communication and keep the parent informed.

Responding to Complaints

Family members may approach you with a complaint about the center, another teacher, an incident that has occurred in the classroom, or even a situation with another parent. At times, these complaints result from misunderstandings, poor communication of policies, or differences of opinion. However, the complaints need to be heard and addressed. They may have a valid basis, and, even if they are without merit, you should clarify and strengthen communication with the concerned parent. Here are some steps to address complaints when they arise.

1. Listen to the entire complaint without interrupting or defending. You may be the only adult to whom this parent can vent.
2. Try not to react defensively or in anger.
3. Ask for clarification until you understand exactly what the concern is. It is easy to misunderstand in emotional discussions.
4. Rephrase the concern in your own words to ensure that you understand each other.
5. Express your understanding of the parent's feelings.
6. Explain your program policy or position if that is the issue of the complaint. Help the parent understand the rationale for the policy.
7. Try to reach an agreement. Ask parents what they think will help. Sometimes all they want is to have someone listen and understand their frustration or concern.
8. Maintain confidentiality. Gossip hurts people, erodes communication, and eventually destroys the very foundation of trust.

Teaching Tip

Respecting Confidentiality

Failure to respect confidentiality can be detrimental to teacher–family relations. Consider the importance of confidentiality once the lines of communication are open. What are the ethical and legal aspects of respecting the confidentiality of sensitive information? What information would be considered confidential, and what information might be shared for the benefit of the child? For example, providing information about a child's behavior in a factual, helpful way to a mental health consultant might be acceptable, but providing that same information to a curious coworker is not. Respecting confidentiality is critical to maintaining parents' confidence in you. Here are some guidelines with respect to confidentiality:

- Share information only with people who can help.
- Be tactful and considerate in your choice of words.
- Protect records from the view of unauthorized people.
- Do not discuss matters in front of the child or others who have no need to know.

Consider This

1. How does respect of confidentiality build trust?
2. How do you feel when your confidence is betrayed?
3. What does a breach of confidentiality do to your relationship with the person?
4. How does failure to respect confidentiality harm the child?
5. How can it harm families' reputations?

☑ CHECKPOINT

1. What can parent conferences accomplish that newsletters or emails cannot?
2. Think about a time you were in a situation where you felt you were being blamed for something unfairly. How did you feel?

6.4 Involving Families in a Program

Much of a good family–school relationship depends on regular contact, which includes involving families in the program. There are many ways to involve parents in your programs, and opportunities may be one-time or ongoing. Possibilities range from donating supplies for art projects to serving on an advisory board. Here are some additional possibilities:

- volunteering help with tasks such as putting together equipment
- helping with a special day, an event, activity, or a field trip
- having lunch with their child
- learning-at-home projects
- being a resource person to talk about their job or hobbies
- contributing items such as art supplies, dress-up clothes, special treats, toys, or empty containers for storage and dramatic play
- serving on a policy or an advisory board
- helping with fundraising events, such as group garage sales, book fairs, charity events, and raffles

While most teachers agree that it is important to involve families, challenges exist even when the families want to be included. For example, they may take on responsibilities that they are ill-equipped to perform.

Discovery Journeys

The Celebration

During my first year as a second-grade teacher, a group of parents planned an end-of-the-semester celebration for the children in my classroom. The parents who were engaged in planning the event had not communicated with me, but I was delighted that they were planning the event.

On the day of the celebration, I could tell that none of the parents were knowledgeable about organizing an event for children on this scale. They had planned a game for the children that was more appropriate for older children, including the prizes. The mother leading the game began to give directions that may have been difficult for a group of adults to follow. "Divide yourselves into five groups," she told them, and then became frustrated when they could not follow the directions. She began to raise her voice, trying to get their attention. It was not long before misbehavior began to erupt as the children lost interest in a game they did not understand. Not wanting to offend the parents who had volunteered, I was unsure of what to do. I waited out the event but was unable to have the smooth dismissal that day that the children were accustomed to.

Consider This
1. What might the teacher have done to prevent the problem that occurred?
2. Why was it difficult to intervene?
3. What might you do to avoid the children's misbehavior?

Planning and Holding a Family Meeting

Family meetings can be a good opportunity to build an understanding of what children need. Meeting topics should be compelling and worthwhile to benefit families and attract parent participation. Family meetings could be sources of valuable information. Consider what will bring families out after work or on a weekend. A survey can help you determine which topics or events might grab their attention. Letting families select the topic or event that interests them will encourage their participation. To use a survey:
- Survey parents to identify the times and topics that suit them. Consider survey email programs or apps to gather responses.
- Allow about a week for the surveys to be returned. You may need to remind parents to return the surveys.
- Schedule the meeting at the time the majority selects. Of course, it will be impossible to find a time to meet everyone's preferences, but setting it at the time most preferable will increase the chances of good attendance.

If you are selecting a speaker, choose someone who can relate to the families in your program. You may want a counselor, a social worker, someone from the medical field, or a teacher. Depending on the topic, select someone with both knowledge and experience in the field. Some topics that might interest parents of school-agers include homework or study skill development. Some that might appeal to parents of preschoolers include discipline and guidance, moral development, or social and emotional development. Topics that might appeal to parents of infants and toddlers may be related to brain research and development- or health-related issues.

When you are planning a meeting or even looking for articles or information to include in a newsletter, consider these suggestions of topics that are usually of interest to parents of young children:
- the value of play and how children learn from play
- hands-on learning activities they can do at home
- types of age-appropriate play materials and experiences
- how to enhance language development through books and stories
- helping children put feelings into words and learn to understand and control their actions

- child development, children's needs, and individual differences in children
- helping children learn the difference between fantasy and reality, yet still enjoy using their imagination

Give families at least two weeks' notice of a planned meeting. Providing a yearly calendar of dates is even better. Ample notice allows parents to put the meeting on their calendar and adjust their schedule, if necessary, to attend. Additionally, provide reminders closer to the date of the meeting. You may want to both remind them verbally and give them a written reminder. Here are suggested preparations for holding a parent meeting:

- Enlist parents to help with refreshments or setting up arrangements. Having parents commit to helping will help ensure their attendance.
- Check with the speaker a few days before the session to confirm the date, time, and location. Provide directions to the site and any other helpful information, such as available audiovisual aids, room arrangement, and number expected.
- On the day of the session, remind all parents again of the event. Encourage participation by telling them more about the event.

Making the meetings interesting and fun will help boost ongoing attendance. When children are to be a part, they will encourage their parents to attend. Some suggestions for a variety of events that include the children as well as parents are described here.

Art Exhibit. Save samples of children's artwork to hold an art show (**Figure 6.7**). Writing what the children say about their paintings or drawings will make their work more interesting to families. Write their statements on an index card and post it near their artwork. Be sure that every child has something on display.

Field Day. Plan a field day, but hold typical outdoor activities, rather than competitive events. Water play, balloon toss, various ball games, Hula-Hoops®, and other activities can be even more fun when family members join in.

Picnic in the Park. Schedule a day to have families meet for a park picnic. You can schedule this activity during the week and have parents meet you during lunch.

Typical Day Program. Set up activity areas just as you do for the children. Let the family members participate with the children. You and other staff can help them understand how children use the various interest areas and what they learn from participation in each area. Posters describing what children learn placed near the area can help the parents see the value of what their children are doing.

Open-Door Policies and Video Access

Some states require that parents be allowed to visit anytime their child is in an early childhood program. Allowing parents to be freely present is referred to as an *open-door policy*. Such a policy can help parents feel welcome and reassure them that their child is in good hands.

Edgloris Marys/Shutterstock.com

Figure 6-7 A teacher has arranged a display of children's artwork for families to view at a special event. How does such a display encourage family involvement?

Some programs install video cameras in classrooms for parents to watch their child's activities during the day. Usually, the video is accessible online using a passcode issued by the center. Such cameras also provide documentation in the event of accidents or injuries.

Understanding Separation Anxiety

The fall months bring new children to the early childhood program, and these children often go through an adjustment period before they become comfortable as members of a new classroom. Children demonstrate various levels of adaptability to new situations and react differently. Some children may be upset for only a few minutes, whereas others may be upset for a few hours. Still others may take weeks to adjust. What can teachers do to make this adjustment smoother for the child, the parents, and the other children?

There are specific times in a child's life that are most likely to cause difficult transitions to new settings. For example, between 7 and 9 months old, many babies go through a period characterized by separation anxiety. At this age, they begin to recognize someone as a "stranger," and having strangers near creates anxiety (Kinsner 2021).

Separation anxiety can be stressful for families as well as for the staff. Children may become anxious, clingy, and easily frightened by unfamiliar people or objects. They have developed attachments to the important people in their lives and begun to understand that each environment is different. While very disturbing to parents, these behaviors are a sign that the child has reached an important developmental milestone and that those

Discovery Journeys

Welcoming Families

Betty Young stood at the door of her school as she had for several decades. Outside, parents and children gathered, waiting for the opening. Inside, teachers scurried around, putting last-minute touches on classroom arrangements to ensure that the rooms were ready for the children.

As if on an unseen and unheard signal, teachers were suddenly at their classroom doors, ready to greet children and parents. Betty stood at the entrance and greeted each parent and child as they arrived, inquiring about new siblings, illnesses, or absences. Notes and messages were exchanged. Young parents asked questions about their child's behavior and learning or parenting issues. Betty shared that she was in her second generation of children—some of the parents attended the school as children themselves and often commented on what they remembered. It was clear that the parents sought out and valued her knowledge and insight. Children stopped to describe weekend activities or adventures. She knew them all by name and extended a personal greeting to everyone.

The center's design reflected that families were welcome and encouraged to participate. At the entrance, there was a comfortable waiting area for family members arriving to pick up their children. The building included parent observation areas between each pair of classrooms. Parents scheduled times to observe their children and watch all of the experiences their children had.

Betty emphasized and practiced her belief that parents want to be greeted by friendly people and want to know who is responsible for their child. She advised that anyone in the early childhood field should always introduce the person who will be responsible for a particular child to the parent. She maintained that the friendliness and warmth of the staff were important to parents as they selected a program for their children. This belief allowed her to maintain full enrollment and provide a quality program for many years.

Consider This
1. Why is the personal greeting important for an administrator?
2. How does the building design demonstrate that families are welcome?
3. What is the value of providing opportunities for parents to observe their children in the program?

attachments have developed. Children may not understand that when a person is out of sight, the person has gone somewhere else; they are unsure whether that person is coming back. Objects and people exist to a young child only if they are present and visible; therefore, if their parents leave, they no longer exist. This phenomenon is known as *object permanence*, a concept that young children may not have developed. As children get older, their memories will begin to provide comfort as they learn that the caregiver will return.

These age ranges are only guidelines. Because of individual differences in children's development, some children may experience separation anxiety later in toddlerhood, and some may not experience it at all. Separation anxiety can be exaggerated for children experiencing other stresses in their lives, such as moving, a new care situation, the arrival of a new sibling, or relationship tensions within the family.

Separation is sometimes more difficult for the parent than for the child and involves mixed feelings for the parent. Families want their child to be independent, but at the same time, they may resent having the teacher take on a larger role in the child's life. To add to the confusion, the parent may also be struggling with feelings of guilt for returning to work. Parents sometimes demonstrate anxiety themselves, and their child may sense their discomfort. It may be the first time the child has been away from the parents, and this change may be emotional for them.

How can you help families with these transitions into a program? The following sections discuss tips for helping the families, the children, and yourself.

Helping Families

Talk with parents ahead of time about procedures to facilitate a smooth transition. Explain that children will feel better if the parent understands the child's possible anxiety but remains positive about the separation and the new facility. When it is time to leave, they should do so without hesitating but also without sneaking away. Sneaking away, while tempting, will only lead the child to be more guarded and resistant the next time. When the family arrives, help them feel comfortable and at ease. Some parents may find it difficult to leave, especially with their first child (**Figure 6.8**). You can help by being supportive and understanding. Here are additional steps to help families with this transition:

- Reassure families that an adjustment period is not unusual.
- Explain that the child feels the family's attitude and fears.

christinarosepics/Shutterstock.com

Figure 6-8 An anxious child has difficulty separating from her mother during arrival. What can the teacher do to help with this transition?

- For infants, encourage the parents to play peek-a-boo to help infants develop the understanding that even when things are not seen, they still exist.
- Suggest that the family begin talking about changes ahead of time and read books about separation to their child.
- Encourage the parent to ease into the transition slowly. Have the child visit the center with the parent and spend time with the child in the new setting. Both the teacher and parent should discuss what will happen in the new location, including activities, routines, and where the parent will be while the child is at the center.
- Ask parents to postpone changes to the child's life at home, if possible, when first enrolling to minimize the amount of change occurring at any one time.
- Set up separation situations before full-time attendance. Have the parent leave the room for a brief time and then return.
- Ask the parent to allow extra time on arrival to help the child settle in. Additional time at pickup can provide time to interact with the child about the activities of the day.
- Educate parents on how to leave the classroom. Be sure parents know to always say "goodbye" and to tell the child when they will return. Discourage parents who want to sneak out of the room.
- Suggest that parents take the anxiety seriously and react with respect and patience: "I know you are going to miss me, but I will come back to get you after lunch."
- Help parents establish a "goodbye" ritual, such as using a phrase or gesture. A high five or a fist bump, along with a regular "See ya later, buddy," can become a comforting ritual. Make use of classroom rituals such as a "waving window," where the child can wave goodbye to the departing parent.
- Consider a "no cell phone" policy at drop-off and pickup so the parent is not distracted from the child's transition needs or communication with staff.
- Because children are more susceptible to anxiety when they are tired or hungry, ask parents to try to schedule departures after naps and mealtimes.
- Explain how parents can prepare children before the separation occurs by reassuring them that they will return. Suggest using concepts that the children can understand, such as "I'll be back right after you have a snack" or "I'll be back after your outdoor time." Remind them to stick to that time or call if there is something that will delay their return.
- Encourage parents to try to keep any of their own anxieties, such as difficulty letting go or guilt about leaving, under control. Their distress may indicate to their child that something is wrong.
- A parent may fear being displaced in the child's affections. Sometimes, children will make comments to a teacher such as, "I wish you were my mother." Such statements may add to the parents' concerns. A good response by the teacher might be, "We are having fun and I like you too, but of course you already have a mother. I'm not your mother; I'm your teacher. I take care of you at school, and your mother takes care of you at home."

Helping Children

Once a child is enrolled, the teacher assumes responsibility for the child's day. Concentrate on getting the child accustomed to the routines of your program. The daily routine is a timekeeper for a young child. Consider how you might feel if you were in a situation where you had no idea what was going on, what would happen next, or when you would return home. Consistency in the daily routine gives the child a sense of time, what comes next, and a way to predict when their parent will return. The following are more suggestions for supporting the child's transition into the program:

- Realize how frightened and intimidated the child may feel.
- Help a toddler feel secure by providing much love and attention upon arrival.
- Young children learn faster when they receive the necessary attention and affection. Offer reassurance that the child is safe and that you will contact the parent if there are any problems.

From the Field

Susan Farmer

Families hold the key to a successful education. Creating strong relationships with families allows children to feel secure and loved. It also allows for open communication, teamwork, and the appreciation of one another.

Some measures that I have taken to promote strong family-program relationships in my classrooms are family interviews before school starts. Families are invited to come in, and we just engage in social conversation. I learn about their family, beliefs, and culture. I also invite parents to come and volunteer in the classroom to help students and the teacher.

Teachers and administrators can celebrate students' cultures by having a schoolwide culture night where students can showcase their culture. Family members can also come in and speak about their culture to students in the school. Also, incorporating multicultural literature into classrooms where students can see themselves in books is imperative.

Susan Farmer, M.S. Ed.
Intervention and Enrichment Coordinator
Valley View School District 365U
Adjunct Professor, ESL/Bilingual Department
Lewis University
Romeoville, IL

Susan Farmer

Figure 6-9

- Allow a new child to bring a special blanket, pillow, or soft toy for comfort during this transition period.
- Have a cozy chair in a comfort zone where the child can go and rest with a blanket or pillow when feeling sad. Initially, go with the child for reassurance.
- Get to know the child with the family's help. Find out about special interests and arrange activities around them.
- Talk about what will happen next so the child will know what to expect.
- Reassure the child and be nearby most of the day.
- Tell the child that after a certain activity, the parent will return.
- Read children's books that deal with transitions.
- Make a wall display of pictures of families, including the new child's family.
- Be ready for the child. Have a cubby, cot, or crib marked; have the parent's name on the sign-in sheet; and be prepared to spend extra time with the new child.
- Make a welcome sign or banner for the family in the lobby or the child's classroom. If the children in your group are old enough, let them assist in making the sign.
- Expect that the child may regress or have a delayed reaction at times, and be patient.
- Understand that the child may be angry, sad, or even ignore the parent upon return.
- Put yourself in the child's and parent's places. How do you feel in new settings?
- Do not expect the child to fit in immediately. Adjustment takes time.

Keep in mind that the other children may feel jealous of the attention you give to a new child. One way to combat this jealousy is by enlisting the other children to help you with the new child. They could do a puzzle together, show the new child where to put clothes and how to open the door, and so on. Point out how nice it is to have children who already know the routine and can help teach the new child. Encourage children to express their feelings. Help relieve some of the children's concerns by saying, "When Malcolm cries, I feel sad. But when he gets to know us better, he won't feel like crying anymore."

Helping Yourself

Helping a newly enrolled child adjust to the new setting can be stressful for you as you work to not only provide the help and attention the new child needs but also continue the daily program for the other children who also deserve your attention. The following are some ways to smooth the process:

- Plan activities that you like to do and that are familiar and enjoyed by the children, allowing for the extra time you need for the new child.
- Remind yourself that this period of anxiety is usually over in a few weeks.
- Get plenty of rest during these weeks so that you can be as patient, understanding, and loving as possible.

Teaching Tip

The Continuity of Care Model

The continuity of care model for early care and education reduces the stress and adjustments that children encounter. In most early childhood education programs, children move to a new classroom at least once a year. But the continuity of care model provides that the main caregiver remains with the same group of children for several years. This eliminates the need for the child to adjust to a new adult and new expectations yearly. The continuity of care model allows close partnerships between teachers and parents to flourish. When parents and teachers have worked together for a long time, it is more likely that a feeling of special friendship for the other significant adult in their child's life will develop. Parents feel more comfortable expressing concerns and are more likely to have a trusting, mutually respectful working relationship with the child's caregiver.

The continuity of care model eliminates the annual challenge for caregivers and parents to establish a new trusting relationship with each other. The trust that has developed over time continues, and energy is not expended on the task of developing new respect and understanding. Additionally, children stay with their friends and build close connections.

Consider This
1. How do separation issues differ from age to age?
2. How can parents help children prepare for starting an early childhood program?
3. What is one thing parents can do when they return at the end of the day?
4. Why should parents say "goodbye" and not just slip out?

✓ CHECKPOINT

1. What are some ways to involve families that is not described in your text?
2. Why is an understanding of separation anxiety important?

6.5 Focus on Assessment of Program Practices

A program's progress in supporting family engagement can be measured as a means of identifying strengths and areas needing improvement. One tool that can be used for evaluating and planning for improvement is the **Family Engagement Assessment and Planning Tool (FEAP-T)**. The FEAP-T was developed by the National Center for Children in Poverty (NCCP) in partnership with the Georgia Department of Early Care and Learning to help program staff identify specific, measurable actions they could take to strengthen family engagement practices.

The FEAP-T has two parts: a 16-item program assessment and planning tool to be completed by program staff and a 16-item survey to be completed by parents. The items in the program tool identify key family engagement practices.

Another way to assess the success of family engagement is to look at the section on family involvement in the *NAEYC Early Learning Program Accreditation Standards and Assessment Items* to determine how well each criterion is met. The score can provide a baseline rating, which, along with an action plan, can provide a means of assessing improvement.

Using an assessment instrument can be a means for a formalized method of determining how well a program works with families. The results will identify the strengths of a program and areas in which improvement might be needed.

☑ CHECKPOINT

1. What are some other ways you might assess your practices in family engagement?
2. How is assessment of your practices important in improving the quality of your program?

Chapter 6 Review and Assessment

Chapter Summary

6.1 Develop positive relationships with families to work as a team for children.
- The first step in building relationships with families is to welcome children and parents in a friendly, nonauthoritarian way.
- Open communication builds trusting, respectful relationships.
- Parents want to know whether you know and like their child, whether they can trust you, and whether their child is normal.

6.2 Recognize and support diverse families and their needs and challenges.
- Families are diverse and vary in their needs and interests.
- Accepting and working with families is important in creating a partnership to help the children reach their potential.
- Early childhood educators must be careful not to assume that children will share their values, ways of viewing situations, or experiences.
- One must respect families' cultural background, religion, or lifestyle.

6.3 Identify ways to communicate and interact with families of children served.
- Open, clear communication can often be a challenge, but it is a vital component in ensuring that families feel welcome and valued.

- Some ways to increase communication are to have regular conferences or meetings and provide daily notes or periodic newsletters about what the children are doing.
- The use of jargon and esoteric terms should be avoided unless the terms are explained.
- While there are many ways to communicate with families, one important method is to hold parent conferences.
- Family meetings involve planning and organizing materials to be the most beneficial for both you and the family.
- Respecting confidentiality is important for building trust and rapport with families.

6.4 Describe ways to actively involve families in a program.
- Involving families in the program can be helpful in building an understanding of what takes place in the early learning center.
- Understanding the program enables parents to support and expand the child's experiences at home.
- Open-door policies help families feel welcome and secure.
- Children's separation anxiety can be stressful for both the family and the child, but it can be prevented or reduced by coordination with the parent.

6.5 **Assess practices related to family engagement.**
- Assessment of a program's family engagement practices can be a basis for ongoing improvement.
- Two assessment tools are the FEAP-T and the NAEYC *Early Learning Program Accreditation Standards and Assessment Items*. The two tools provide a formal means of measuring practices and improvements.

Recall and Application

1. Which of the following is *not* a good way to form positive relationships with families?
   A. Try to see the child from the parents' point of view.
   B. Explain to the parents that if their child misbehaves, it is likely due to something they are doing wrong at home.
   C. Keep conversations friendly and professional.
   D. Help parents feel good about themselves and what they are doing for their children.
2. **True or False.** It is best not to post pictures of children's families in the classroom because they might miss their families and start to cry.
3. **True or False.** Respecting a family's cultural background is one way to build trust and acceptance.
4. **True or False.** A typical family consists of a mother, a father, and two siblings.
5. **True or False.** A monthly newsletter is all that is needed to communicate with families.
6. **True or False.** Regular conferences are not needed unless a child has behavior issues.
7. **True or False.** Respecting confidentiality means that you share information about a child or family only with those who can help or need to know.
8. Which of the following is *not* a desirable practice in working with families?
   A. having written policies and procedures to ensure communication
   B. using terms such as *room chair* or *special person day* to help family members feel welcome to participate
   C. assuming that all multigenerational families have the same needs
   D. respecting confidentiality
9. To address a parent complaint, you should *not* ____.
   A. listen to seek clarification
   B. ignore the complaint if you are right
   C. try to reach an agreement
   D. explain the policy
10. **True or False.** Family involvement is impossible because parents are working and too busy.
11. **True or False.** Consideration of the types of families enrolled is important in planning engagement opportunities.
12. **True or False.** One advantage of family engagement is that families can support their child's learning at home.
13. **True or False.** Separation from the parent can be challenging for some children.
14. **True or False.** Assessment is a means of identifying strengths and areas that need improvement.
15. FEAP-T stands for ____.
    A. Family Engagement and Planning Techniques
    B. Family Engagement Assessment and Planning Tool
    C. Family Engagement Assessment and Program Tool
    D. Family Evidence and Preparation Tool
16. **True or False.** Teachers can expect that all families will have the same approach to child-rearing.
17. **True or False.** If families are not involved in the program, it is likely because they do not care about their child's education.
18. **True or False.** An attitude of partnership underlies parent involvement.

Part 3
Curriculum Areas of Focus

Chapter 7: Assessment: A Tool for Planning
Chapter 8: Language and Literacy
Chapter 9: The World We Live In: Social Studies
Chapter 10: STEAM: Science, Technology, and Engineering
Chapter 11: STEAM: Art and Music
Chapter 12: STEAM: Mathematics
Chapter 13: Getting Back to the Great Outdoors

Chapter 7

Assessment: A Tool for Planning

Standards Covered in This Chapter

NAEYC

NAEYC —1b, 1c, 1d, 2a, 3a, 3b, 3c, 3d, 4b, 4c

DAP

DAP—2f, 3a, 3b, 3c, 3d, 3e, 3f, 3g, 4b, 4d

Learning Outcomes

After reading this chapter, you should be able to:

- **7.1** Identify the purpose and value of assessment.
- **7.2** Explain the role of assessment in planning.
- **7.3** Name and describe methods to record observations used to assess young children.
- **7.4** Describe the use of portfolios in assessment.
- **7.5** Explain the teacher's role in assessment.
- **7.6** Apply observations and assessments to guide behavior.
- **7.7** Explain the purpose of assessment of the program as a whole.
- **7.8** Prepare and conduct conferences with families to share assessment information.

Chapter opener image credit: SDI Productions/E+ via Getty Images

Key Terms

artifact	formative	portfolio
authentic assessment	hypothesis	qualitative measure
criteria	implicit bias	recording

Introduction

From the time Saul was able to stand, an annual birthday ritual consisted of standing at the bedroom door while his father put a mark on the door frame and wrote the date beside the mark. The ritual continued until Saul was in middle school when the family moved. The marks showed a lot about Saul—how he shot up in height some years and not so much in others. These marks were a type of assessment. They documented his physical growth each year and confirmed that his height was in the normal range for his age.

In a nutshell, assessment is the process of compiling information to mark progress over time. Just as the marks on the door identify Saul's growth in height, teachers use many methods of marking children's growth in skills. They see them cut with scissors and note progress in fine-motor coordination; they hear them retell a story and discern their ability to follow the sequence in the story, or they see them solve a problem to create a marble run.

7.1 The Purpose of Assessment

Assessment in early childhood education refers to an overall process of measuring and evaluating children's progress, usually according to developmental milestones or individual baselines. The assessment results can be used for planning children's experiences to support their learning and meet individual needs based upon culturally and developmentally appropriate practices. Assessment can provide documentation that children are learning and progressing as should be expected or that they may need intervention.

What are the benefits of assessment? Assessment shows growth of the child in each developmental domain. It helps the teacher tailor activities for the individual child's needs. The child benefits from an attentive, well-informed teacher who is prepared to make learning purposeful and effective (**Figure 7.1**). Additionally, an ongoing assessment process demonstrates professionalism and credibility for the program. Sharing assessment information with families helps them to better understand child development and how they might enrich the child's experiences at home.

Development is a dynamic process. Just as a child might seem inches taller following a school break, a child may have difficulty zipping his jacket on a Friday but return on Monday having successfully mastered the task. Assessments record what a child can do at one point in time, but they do not show the full range of a child's capabilities.

When a program receives public funds, documentation of progress or success is usually required. However, whether a program is publicly funded or depends solely on tuition, assessment plays a significant role in accountability. Families want to know that their children are developing and learning at an age-appropriate level. Assessment shows whether children are making the progress that one might expect in a quality program.

What happens if programs do not take the time to observe and assess the young children in their care? Most importantly, children may not make the progress they might have with better data for planning. Additionally, the program is unable to communicate factual information with parents and to help them understand their child's progress. Ultimately, a child who needs intervention may not get it, resulting in lost opportunities for remediation.

Prostock Studio/iStock/Getty Images Plus

Figure 7-1 A teacher plays a game with a child to determine what words she can think of that start with each letter. What do you think this teacher might learn about this child's additional needs from this playful activity with the letters?

☑ CHECKPOINT

1. Why is early identification important for children who may be at risk of disabilities?
2. How does assessment help one know if a child is developing as expected?

7.2 Assessment for Planning and Learning

Using assessment for planning allows teachers to think about the most appropriate experiences for children and provides a sense of order and structure to the day. If teachers assess properly, they can plan for opportunities that meet each child's needs and build on what each child has already mastered.

Reviewing the collected information about the children provides guidance in planning. An effective teacher uses knowledge of child development, each child's interests and skills, the effect of the environment, the children's cultural backgrounds, and the resources available to plan what will happen in the following weeks. Those plans may include:
- conducting activities to target children's developing skills and scaffold or enrich learning.
- making changes to the environment such as adding new props or materials to support children's interests.
- providing resources that build on children's experiences and expand their knowledge and skills.
- organizing special activities, including individual, small group, whole group, or field trips to expand and enrich learning.

Without careful observations, a teacher may miss details that are important to children's learning. A teacher may be aware of a child's interest in numbers, but the fact that the child has spent every morning for the past week lining up plastic numerals from 1 to 20 might be missed. Systematic observation would note the details of this child's interest and skill, whereas seeing that he is simply playing with a counting board would not provide this valuable information. By knowing what children know and can do, the teacher can plan appropriately. Careful and regular observations and recordings of children's behavior allow a teacher to:

- get to know children as individuals.
- plan the curriculum based on children's strengths and needs.
- measure and document each child's progress.
- identify problems that may need intervention.
- develop a strategy for dealing with challenging behavior if needed.
- collect information to share with families or specialists.
- evaluate the class environment and activities.

The Assessment–Planning–Learning Cycle

Using assessment as a formative tool for planning creates an ongoing cycle of assessing, planning, and learning. *Formative* simply means that the assessment is used primarily to note children's skills and knowledge and to plan learning experiences or make changes. For example, a preschooler who is showing interest in vehicles might enjoy puzzles or books about trucks or a field trip to an automobile museum. An infant who is beginning to crawl should be given extra time on the floor to explore and practice the new skill. Observation and assessment are part of the process of guiding children's learning and development. An intentional teacher follows a consistent cycle of assessing, planning, and learning.

After information is collected, teachers decide what to do based on the information, their understanding, and their interpretation of the information. They form a **hypothesis**, asking a "what if" question or making an estimate of what they believe is true. Each of the steps in the cycle—assessing, planning, and learning—leads to the action; they create a plan for future learning experiences. They implement the plan and observe the results. Then the entire process begins again: assessing how the plan works, recording what they observe, and evaluating their observations to create a new plan. Based on their evaluation and how well the plan is working, the process either produces a new plan or continues with the current one.

Observation as a Tool for Assessment

One key to assessment is careful observation by the teacher. Observing children is an ongoing process for those who work with children. They watch infants play and thrill at seeing them respond with cooing and laughter. They share stories with families about toddlers' first words and new physical skills. They notice how preschoolers learn to interact cooperatively with others. Observations are a useful way to get to know individual children—what they enjoy, what skills they are developing, and who they like to spend time with.

There is a significant difference between *watching* and *observing* children. *Observing* means paying close attention to the specifics of what is happening, while *watching* is usually superficial, without an attempt to remember. Teachers use observations to evaluate the source of behaviors and identify the proper strategies for addressing undesirable behavior. Proper observation means that they try to see what is happening, eliminating bias and expectations. These observations must be factual and free of cultural bias. Opinions, interpretations, and judgments are not part of the observation step.

☑ CHECKPOINT

1. Reflect on a time you made a decision based on what you saw a child do or say. Did you offer assistance? Did your decision encourage or discourage the child's interest?
2. How would you describe the difference between watching and observing in relation to assessment?

Case Study

Emme and the Mean Turtle

One day, in the art area, 3-year-old Emme drew what she told her teacher, Ms. Jo, was a "mean" turtle. Her illustration included a long neck and wide-open mouth with sharp teeth. When Ms. Jo asked about the turtle, Emme described how she and her grandmother were driving to school when they saw a turtle in the middle of the road. After stopping the car, her grandmother attempted to move the turtle to the side of the road. When she reached for the turtle, it extended its neck and snapped at her. Wide-eyed, Emme held her hands out to show how far the neck extended. She continued to tell how the surprise caused her grandmother to lose her balance and fall. But she was not hurt, Emme clarified. Her grandmother got a large box from her car and nudged the animal out of the road. "And then," Emme exclaimed, "we watched it walk to its home in the ditch."

From Emme's artwork and accompanying story, Ms. Jo observed that Emme recognized turtles, that they could bite, that being on the road was dangerous for them, and this one lived near water. To build on Emme's interest and what she had learned, Ms. Jo found photos online of different types of turtles to let Emme pick out the type that she and her grandmother had encountered. Identifying the photo of a snapping turtle, Ms. Jo and Emme discussed the differences in several types of turtles, their habitats, and what they ate. Later, Ms. Jo located a nonfiction book about turtles. While looking through the book in the reading area, Emme quickly picked out the snapping turtle from the dozens in the book, demonstrating that she had learned to recognize that type of turtle and could differentiate various features of turtles.

The next day, after considering what Emme might benefit from next, Ms. Jo followed up on Emme's experience by providing a wooden puzzle of a turtle to take advantage of her interest and to offer an opportunity for developing spatial perception. She read stories about turtles during circle time to stimulate language development. She knew that the puzzle and stories would stimulate conversations about turtles and help Emme understand more about animal characteristics.

Consider This:
1. What might Ms. Jo discern about Emme's literacy skills from this incident?
2. How did Emme's drawing of the turtle illustrate what part of the story was most important to her?
3. How else might Ms. Jo expand on Emme's interest in turtles?

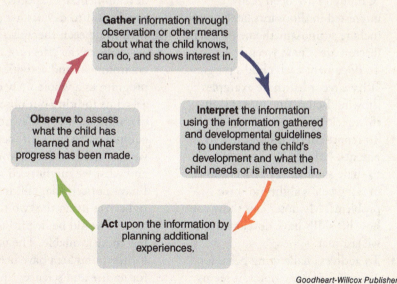

Figure 7-2 This graphic illustrates the steps in using assessment information. How does the graphic clarify the steps in the assessment–planning–learning cycle?

7.3 Recording Observations

For observations to be useful, teachers must have a consistent means of recording them. Teachers have many tools available for gathering information. Some, such as checklists, are easy and quick to use. Others, such as anecdotal records or journal entries, can require a greater time commitment. Some methods are less formal, such as notes or periodic entries in a log, while others are more formal, such as the use of performance checklists or tabulations of specific behaviors. A teacher's goal in selecting and using a tool or method is to identify children's growth and behavior, the program quality, and other valuable information (**Figure 7.3**). Types of tools commonly applied include:
- a tally or checklist, used to show interest or verify accomplishment.
- a rating scale, used to record a degree of accomplishment.
- anecdotal records, used to report an event or interaction involving a child.
- interviews with parents or children to gather information about a child's development, interests, likes, and dislikes.

Information-gathering tools need to be portable and convenient. In a classroom, children move a lot and the tools used to observe and record their activity must be easy to carry from place to place. A teacher might record on Post-it® notes or index cards and transfer them to a folder, notebook, or file at the end of the day. Preprinted forms on a clipboard are portable, making them a good choice. Hooks placed to hang the clipboards keep records easy to access, even on the playground. For a busy teacher, whichever format is chosen needs to be easy and convenient to use.

Why Observe and Record Children's Behavior?

- To determine each child's interests, strengths, and needs. "Juan likes to organize items on the science table. He sorts collections of rocks and shells in egg cartons."
- To plan an individualized program. "Children have been really interested in dinosaurs lately. I will include a dinosaur theme in several interest areas next week."
- To document each child's progress. "I have recorded three examples showing Bella's fine motor skills this week."
- To report children's progress to parents. "Ms. Fong, I would like to share some of my observations of Xingwen's ability to solve problems. My notes can show you how his skills have developed since we last met."
- To address challenging behavior. "In reviewing my notes, it seems that Jan hits other children when he wants to enter a group but does not seem to know how."
- To identify problems that may need intervention. "I have noticed that Aniyah has difficulty with some speech sounds that are developmentally expected for her age. I want to discuss her progress with the speech therapist."
- To evaluate the effects of the environment and activities on the program as a whole. "My director asked us to bring our observations of children's use of playground equipment to the staff meeting so we can discuss what is working well and what we might need to change. I have noticed that children often fight over using the two ride-on toys. It would be helpful to have a few more available. The new tools for the pond area have been useful for nature and science exploration."

Goodheart-Willcox Publisher

Figure 7-3 This list includes many reasons why observing and recording are important. Can you think of other reasons to observe and record children's behavior? Which do you consider the most significant reason?

The best method to use depends on the teacher's preference, what the teacher wants to learn about the children in the class, and what information the teacher wishes to record. The primary purpose of any observation is to collect accurate, objective, and useful information about a child. Teachers watch, listen, and write down what children do and say as events happen. The information they document, regardless of the method, is called a **recording**.

Note-Taking

Note-taking is essential to remembering the details of what one is observing. How does a busy teacher document important observations in an active classroom? Here are some tips:
- Carry a pad, index cards, or sticky notes and a pencil to take notes frequently.
- Clothes or smocks with pockets provide a place for note-taking supplies and free teachers' hands.
- Write down what you see, not what you think is happening.
- Include only facts, not opinions.
- Write in short phrases and abbreviate if desired.
- Always include the date and time in the notes.

Notice the difference between a note that says, "Mary cried all day because she missed her mother" and one that says, "Mary cried for 20 minutes. An hour later, she said she wanted her mother, to take her to the store with Sister." The difference between these two examples is that the first includes an assumption that Mary is crying because she misses her mother; the second one tells us she wants her mother to take her to the store. Observation notes should follow the second example, reporting facts rather than assumptions.

Tallies and Checklists

A tally or checklist is a useful tool to gather information about the frequency of a repeated activity or behavior. Every time a child engages in the activity, the observer marks it with a tally mark (**Figure 7.4**).

Sometimes tallying how often a child is doing a particular action or behavior can be helpful to a teacher. For example, a teacher could record how often a child is participating with others, playing with a particular child, or focused on an activity. To see

Tally Marks

Child	Activity	Observed
Amelia	Playing alone	ll
Knox	Playing alone	lll
Naima	Playing alone	llllll
Sybille	Playing alone	l
Zoey	Playing alone	lll
Amelia	Playing with others	lllllll
Knox	Playing with others	lllllll
Naima	Playing with others	ll
Sybille	Playing with others	llll
Zoey	Playing with others	ll

Goodheart-Willcox Publisher

Figure 7-4 This chart was used by a teacher who wanted to know if children were mostly playing alone or with friends. What can you tell about children's preferences by looking at the tally marks? What would be another way to use tally marks?

how well a new child is making friends, a teacher might tally how much time the child spends with others or alone. Then, over time, additional tallies can show progress or the need for additional effort to help the child make friends. A timeframe or context, such as an hour-long observation, or an observation at a certain time each day, such as interest center time, would make this information even more useful.

A record-keeping checklist can be useful in sharing information about a child's routine with families at the end of the day (**Figure 7.5**). For example, a teacher writes what the child ate; the number and types of diaper changes; notable events in the day, such as rolling over; any concerns, such as sleeping more than usual; and any items the family may need to bring. These may be paper forms given out at pickup or digital forms sent electronically at the end of the day. Either way, such lists are especially valuable for informing families of infants and toddlers about their child's day.

Simple, at-a-glance checklists are among the easiest tools for gathering information. Is something happening or not? When is it happening? Who is doing it? For example, a checklist would be a way to record the skills of a group of toddlers. All three items on the list in **Figure 7.6** are skills that should be acquired between approximately 15 and 18 months of age. The teacher simply checks off the skill when the child completes it.

An interest checklist (**Figure 7.7**) records children's choice of activities. Such checklists can tell the teacher if a child is participating in all activities or focusing on one or two areas. A teacher may place a checklist on a clipboard to record children's participation conveniently and quickly at various times during the day.

To add a **qualitative measure** (a type of measurement that involves judgment) to an interest checklist, you might rate the level of engagement in the activity. For example, you could rate a child's interest according to the following:

1 = Shows little interest
2 = Shows some interest
3 = Enthusiastic

Infant Daily Report

Child's Name _____ Date _____

Meal/Care Activity	Time	Amount	Notes
Breakfast			
Lunch			
Diaper change			
Rolled over			
Nap			
Other			

Goodheart-Willcox Publisher

Figure 7-5 Daily reports such as this are common in programs that include infants. Why do you think the information in this chart might be important to families?

At-a-Glance Checklist

Names	Drinks from Cup	Uses Spoon or Fork	Removes Clothing
Matthew	√		√
Andrea	√	√	
Raoul		√	√
Taylor		√	√

Goodheart-Willcox Publisher

Figure 7-6 A chart like this makes it easy for a teacher to document children's accomplishments. *What are some other self-help skills that could be documented with such a chart? How would this chart be helpful to families?*

Interest Checklist

Child	Art	Play	Sort
Greg	√√	√√√	
Joanna	√	√	√√
Todd		√√√	
Cleo	√		√√√
De Shaun		√√	
Beth	√√√√	√	
Carlos		√√√√	√
Lin Pei	√√		
Jean		√	

Goodheart-Willcox Publisher

Figure 7-7 This chart was created by a teacher who set up special activities in the art area, the dramatic play area and a sorting game in the math and manipulatives area. *What can you tell about the children's preferences from the chart? What might the teacher do with the information collected?*

Although children might be playing with blocks, their level of interest would offer useful information. Are they simply passing time, or are they actively engaged in the process? The fact that a child plays with blocks every day does not necessarily provide information about their level of engagement and learning. Determining the quality of play by rating the level of interest makes the information more useful.

Another version of an interest scale uses numbers with 5 representing high interest and 1 representing low interest. On a scale of 1 to 5, a teacher might rate a child's interest in a project, an activity, or event by circling the appropriate number to indicate the level of interest (**Figure 7.8**).

Teachers can build upon an at-a-glance skills checklist by adding a rating scale for items such as these:

1 = Not met (There is little evidence of the behavior.)
2 = Partially met (There is some evidence of the behavior.)
3 = Fully met (There is a great deal of evidence of the behavior.)

One way to organize the tallies or checklists is to create personal pages for each child in a loose-leaf notebook with a tabbed section for each child (**Figure 7.9**). The individual pages can be useful in communicating children's progress to parents.

A teacher can coordinate this record with developmental scales and use it as a benchmark for determining if a child is within appropriate developmental ranges for their age. For example: By age 5, children typically include six body parts in their drawings. If a 5-year-old includes only two body parts, a teacher may want to examine other areas of the child's development.

Interest Level Rating

Child's Name: _____ Date: _____

Interest in Earth Day card-making activity:

(High)   5   4   3   2   1   (Low)

Child's Name: _____ Date: _____

Interest in art center:

(High)   5   4   3   2   1   (Low)

Child's Name: _____ Date: _____

Interest in field trip to the wildlife preserve:

(High)   5   4   3   2   1   (Low)

Goodheart-Willcox Publisher

Figure 7-8 This interest chart has a numeric scale to measure the level of children's demonstrated interest in specific activities. How might the teacher use the information for planning additional activities?

Personal Page Checklist

Name: _____	Birth Date: _____
Colors: Can identify:	Date
Red	
Blue	
Yellow	
Green	
Other	
Counting: Can count to:	Date
1 only	
1–3	
1–5	
1–10	
Draws a person with:	Date
1–3 body parts	
3–5 body parts	
6 or more body parts	
Stacks blocks:	Date
3-block tower	
5-block tower	

Goodheart-Willcox Publisher

Figure 7-9 This is an example of a personal page checklist a teacher might use. What other skills can be documented on such a chart?

Grids

A grid can serve as an informal, quick means of recording information. Divide a single piece of paper into squares with one child's name in each square. Use the grid to jot down random information such as who a child plays with, a favorite song or book title, or an interest in a particular topic.

With many children in a classroom, remembering all the details noticed in a day can be difficult—or, more accurately, impossible. A simple grid, such as the example shown in **Figure 7.10**, provides a quick and easy means of noting details and ensuring that some information is recorded about each child on a particular day. At parent-conference time, the teacher can share information such as the names of playmates or activities that a child enjoys. For example, at a conference with Mei's family, the teacher can glance at the notes in the example grid and know to suggest play dates with Mei's friend, Rose.

The information in the grid can also be helpful for planning activities. For example:
- Noting Skylar's interest in spiders could lead to reading *The Very Busy Spider* or *Are You a Spider?* aloud or making spiderwebs of yarn in the art area.
- Manuel knowing the words to "The Itsy Bitsy Spider" would be a good reminder to let Manuel lead the group in singing the song at circle time.
- Kaya's fondness for *The Little Engine That Could* indicates an ideal time to put the wooden train set in the block area and find other books about trains that she might enjoy.
- The observation that Avania is playing alone might alert her teacher to find out what else is going on and why. Aviana may need help getting to know other children, or there may be a cultural or language barrier that is causing her to feel excluded.
- Recognizing that Evelyn is avoiding painting activities could suggest that she might need reassurance and a bit more adult attention to encourage her to try using the classroom easels.

Developmental Scales

Developmental scales (**Figure 7.11**) are charts that identify a list of skills that children of a specific age typically develop or learn through experiences. Early education teachers use developmental scales to keep track of important milestones in children's progress. A developmental scale may also be a checklist if it includes a place to check when a child demonstrates the skill. *Hopping on one foot three times, stacking four blocks in a tower,* and *stating first and last name* are examples of skills that might be included on a developmental scale checklist. The age range at which such skills are typically mastered by

Example of a Grid

Mei Favorite playmate: Rose	Rose Favorite playmate: Mei	Kaya Told the story of *The Little Engine That Could* from memory
Avania Played alone during interest center time	Skylar Says he loves spiders	Evelyn Did not choose to do the painting projects
Quianna Has not played with Naveen this week; playing with Skylar more	Manual Can remember all the words to "The Itsy Bitsy Spider"	Naveen Sat and attended story time for the first time

Goodheart-Willcox Publisher

Figure 7-10 This grid provides a place to randomly note information about each child. What might the teacher do with the information about Evelyn or Naveen?

Developmental Scales

Tiara Ramirez Age: 3 years, 4 months	Not Yet	Sometimes	Most of the Time
Personal and Social Behavior			
Knows full name			x
Knows home address	x		
Knows phone number	x		
Buttons and/or zips clothing without assistance		x	
Shows reasonable self-control in group situations			x
Accepts and follows rules			x
Accepts changes in routines			x
Can take turns			x
Plays cooperatively with other children		x	
Knows and uses names of other children		x	
Knows and uses names of adults			x
Physical Development			
Hops on one foot	x		
Jumps from standing position	x		
Runs			x
Gallops	x		
Skips	x		
Throws a large ball		x	
Catches a large ball		x	
Climbs, slides, swings on outdoor equipment			x
Alternates feet walking up and down steps			x
Rides a tricycle, steering and peddling	x		

Goodheart-Willcox Publisher

Figure 7-11 This developmental scale allows the teacher to rate the frequency or absence of a skill. How does this information help the teacher know what to do for children who have not mastered a skill? What if many age-appropriate skills are checked "Not Yet" or "Sometimes"?

children is the **criteria** for comparing each child's progress. Criteria are accepted standards against which children's skills are compared.

A teacher may post a list of skills that children may develop in each interest center. The list will remind the teacher of what the children are learning as they participate in the center. The list can also help the teacher focus on a specific skill while making anecdotal records. For example, a chart of math skills posted in the manipulative area can be used to record that a child is learning matching, seriation, or one-to-one correspondence. Recording is easier, faster, and more useful if teachers know what they are looking for and accurately describe what they are seeing.

Anecdotal Records

Anecdotal records are a step beyond tallies and checklists; they are brief, written narrative descriptions about children's actions. To be complete, anecdotal records must include:
- The observer's name
- The child's name and age

Case Study

Recognizing Colors

Tristin was a new teacher of 5-year-olds and used "personal page" checklists similar to the one in **Figure 7.9** to prepare for parent conferences. As Tristin reviewed the charts from the previous months, he noted that Ladarius did not have a check by green or red. This struck him as unusual since Ladarius seemed on track for his age in most other skills. Over the next several days, Tristin intentionally named those colors in conversation and gave Ladarius chances to identify the colors on his own. However, Ladarius continued to frequently mistake the two and seemed confused. Tristin knew that some people had difficulty distinguishing between red and green and decided to discuss the matter with Ladarius's parents during the upcoming conference.

Ladarius's dad told Tristin that he, himself, had a problem with those colors and had heard that the condition could be inherited. However, neither he nor his wife had noticed Ladarius's difficulty.

Because identifying colors is important in the curriculum for the early years, the three decided that it would be good for Ladarius to learn to read the color names on the paper labels of his crayons, especially red and green. Ladarius's parents also noted that they would discuss the observation with their pediatrician for additional guidance.

While it is beyond the scope of teacher observation to diagnose a condition, observational assessments can identify when a question arises about a child that should be explored further.

Consider This

1. What frustrations would Ladarius face if teachers were unaware of his difficulty in distinguishing colors?
2. How could Ladarius's condition cause problems in his education if it were unrecognized?
3. Would Tristin have realized the problem if he had not completed the checklist?
4. Why is it beyond the teacher's responsibility to diagnose a condition?

- The setting (where the activity is taking place and who is involved; for example, "In the library area, Carlos and Tonisha sit on the floor and look at books")
- The date and time. The date is important to examine growth over time. Dates allow teachers to know when a child started working on a skill and when the skill was mastered. The record establishes the baseline from which growth and change can be measured and evaluated.
- The behavior (what the child does and says)

To make objective anecdotal records, teachers should think of themselves as video cameras recording the experience. They should write only what they see or hear. They should not include opinions or what they think the child meant or intended. Here are additional guidelines:

- Teachers should not attempt to evaluate or analyze the child's behavior when they write an anecdotal record. However, a collection of anecdotal records, along with other information, can be helpful in measuring growth or patterns of behavior.
- Include the child's own words. By recording the child's actual words, anyone reading the record gains valuable information about what is going on as well as language skills. Analyzing the child's words later, after more information has been accumulated, can provide useful information about what the child is thinking. Put quotation marks around a child's words to easily identify them as the child's. Write the exact words the child says; do not paraphrase or "correct" them.
- Record the events in the order that they happen.
- Include details. Details provide valuable information about what a child is learning. For example, it is better to write, "William counted 1, 2, 3, 4, 5, 6, 8, 10," than to write, "William tried to count to 10." There is more information in the first example. Knowing which numbers he skipped allows his teacher to plan to help William learn to include those numbers when counting in sequence.

- Be positive. Look at what the child can do. Many things occur in the classroom, and teachers will learn more about an individual child if they write exactly what they see and hear.
- Know what is important to record. If a teacher records that a child is looking at a book, turning the pages in order, and moving a finger along the printed text, the child's behavior tells the teacher that they understand the construction of a book, the print has meaning, and they should read left-to-right and top-to-bottom in progression. Those understandings are important reading skills to record.
- Know how to use the information to look at a child's growth and change. When teachers look at a compilation of anecdotal records of one child over time, they are gathering information about how the child is changing. Documenting how the child changes is a primary reason for creating the records.

Making anecdotal recordings is a good method for gathering this kind of information into the child's portfolio, a system for collecting and organizing documentation of children's progress. See the example in **Figure 7.12**. Because these recordings are written without opinions about John's behavior, they can be used along with other documentation to show that John is having difficulty adjusting to separation from his father. Perhaps an intervention with John may be helpful.

Understand that one instance will not give a teacher an accurate picture of John's problem. Several such incidents, occurring over time, might suggest a pattern warranting intervention or other action. Anecdotal information can be shared with the parents to provide a constructive basis to create an individualized plan.

Maintaining Objectivity

Here are three different records of Taarush's activity in the water play area. Compare the three records, keeping in mind the need for objectivity and the guidelines for writing anecdotal records.

Example 1

"Taarush moved the water back and forth with the funnel. The water splashed inside and outside the water table. Some fell on other children's shoes. Taarush began to giggle."

This is an objective and accurate recording. It includes only the facts of what Taarush did (moved the water back and forth), what happened (the water splashed inside and outside the basin), and his reaction (Taarush began to giggle). Accurate recordings include all of the facts about what a child does, in the order they happen.

Example 2

"Taarush was bad today. He showed his anger by splashing the water on the floor and on other children at the water table. Then he laughed at them."

This example is not an objective recording. A label ("bad") is used, and judgments are made ("he showed his anger by splashing the water, and he laughed at other children"). The teacher could not know if Taarush acted in anger or why he laughed. A recording that he was "bad" not only labels Taarush but does not provide anything useful about his behavior since "bad" is a word that means different things to different people.

Example 3

"Taarush stood at the water basin looking to see if his teacher was watching him. He giggled and began to splash water on other children."

In this example, a statement was added that may not be a fact (looking to see if his teacher was watching him). If Taarush did indeed look for his teacher, the observer cannot know why without asking him. A fact is omitted ("Taarush moved the water back and forth with the funnel"). Another fact is written out of order ("He giggled and began to splash water"), which can change the meaning.

As the examples of Taarush's behavior indicate, what teachers say and the words they use are important in communicating with accuracy and objectivity when recording information. **Figure 7.13** is a list of subjective phrases to avoid when writing anecdotal records.

Example of an Anecdotal Record

Name: *John Joseph*   Date: *January 5, 2023*   Arrival time: *8:15 a.m.*   Location: *Classroom*

John ran into the classroom and threw himself down on the rug. His father walked from the classroom to the door. John screamed, "Don't leave me! I hate school. You're mean!" John's father continued down the hall. John started to cry and ran to the door. He yelled, "Come back!" He curled into a ball on the floor in the doorway and cried for three minutes. As soon as he seemed to be calming down, Ms. Smith (the teacher aide) interested him in the sensory area.

Goodheart-Willcox Publisher

Figure 7-12 This anecdotal record about John describes his behavior when his father drops him off. Why is it important to have the date on the record? Why should judgments not be made about one incident?

Informal Methods

In addition to tallies, checklists, and anecdotal records, observations may include narratives, such as notes in a journal, or a log of what took place each day. Observations provide a picture of what is happening in the classroom and help teachers record general class activities.

A classroom log records the activities of the whole group. A teacher might note: The children sang "Way Up High in the Apple Tree," walked to buy apples from the farmers' market, made apple butter, and decorated cards using stickers showing apples for a teacher who has been ill.

These informal observations give an overall picture of the classroom and activities. They provide information that teachers can use to plan formal observations for individual children or plan future lessons. Over time, a classroom log would show if one type of activity is occurring more frequently than others and might cause a teacher to ask, "Does our class go on walks frequently? If so, should that continue? Would more walks be beneficial?"

An informal record of a particular child's behavior might be a notation such as: "Lilia plays a lot with Angel and Quinton. She spends a long time at the water table with the boats and rarely finishes her sandwich during lunch."

If a child's behavior shows a pattern, that information can lead to even more questions: Why does Lilia play with Angel and Quinton exclusively rather than the other

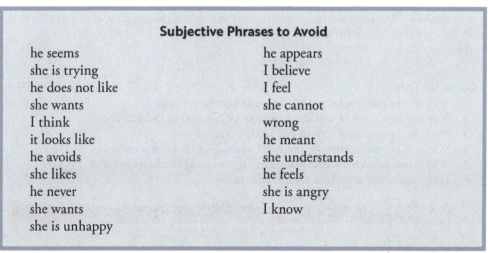

Subjective Phrases to Avoid

he seems	he appears
she is trying	I believe
he does not like	I feel
she wants	she cannot
I think	wrong
it looks like	he meant
he avoids	she understands
she likes	he feels
he never	she is angry
she wants	I know
she is unhappy	

Goodheart-Willcox Publisher

Figure 7-13 These phrases are not recommended for anecdotal records because they are subjective and reflect what the observer thinks about a child's actions. What are some other phrases that are subjective?

Case Study

Anecdotal Records about Aidan

The children in Gabriela's class sit on carpet squares during group meetings in the morning. Each day before the children arrive, Gabriela sets out carpet squares in the group area and places a check-in card with a child's name on each square. Upon entering the classroom, the children are responsible for going to the group area and finding the carpet square with their name card. They pick up their card and place it in a pocket chart nearby to indicate their presence that day. Then they return to the square on which they found their name card and sit down. Gabriela has observed and recorded Aidan's progress in mastering this task over time.

Name: *Aidan*   Date: *September 2, 2021*   Time: *9:00 a.m. Group Time*

Aidan came into the room and looked at the carpet squares with the names on them. He held up Tyrone's name and asked, "Is this my name?" He held up Lana's name next and asked, "Is this my name?" Rosita held up his name and gave it to him, saying, "This is yours." He put it in the pocket chart.

Name: *Aidan*   Date: *October 5, 2021*   Time: *9:00 a.m. Group Time*

Aidan came into the room, looked at the names on the squares, got Sofia's name card and checked in. Sofia picked up Aidan's name card and gave it to him. Sofia said, "You have mine; here is yours." Aidan checked in again.

Name: *Aidan*   Date: *December 22, 2021*   Time: *9:00 a.m. Group Time*

Aidan came into the room, went to the square with his name card, picked up his name card, checked in, and returned to the square that had his name card on it.

Name: *Aidan*   Date: *May 15, 2021*   Time: *9:00 a.m. Group Time*

Aidan came into the room, went to his square, got his card, checked in, and read the other children's names in the check-in pocket: "A.J., Tyrone, Danielle, Francisca, Ian, and now Aidan," he said. He returned to his square, where his name card was originally placed, and he said to Kevin, his neighbor, "You're sitting in the wrong place. You're in Ian's place." Aidan showed Kevin the carpet square with his name card on it.

Goodheart-Willcox Publisher

Figure 7-14 These anecdotal records show the progress that Aidan has made in recognizing his name and other children's names. What else might you learn about Aidan from these records?

Consider This

1. Why are the dates and times important in anecdotal records?
2. How does the series of records document Aiden's growth and learning?
3. How are the anecdotal records like a video camera?
4. Why is it important that the anecdotal records not be judgmental?
5. Why is one anecdotal record insufficient for assessing children's growth?
6. How might these anecdotal records be used?

children? Does Lilia use water play for soothing, or does she seem to be exploring something in particular, such as how to make the waterwheel turn? Is Lilia not feeling well, or does she not like the type of sandwich her mother is sending for lunch?

Observations give information by making it easier to notice what is absent. What is not happening can be every bit as important as what *is* happening. Consider what activities are not happening in the classroom. For example, if a teacher notes that children rarely use the unit blocks and seldom paint at the easels, should changes be made to make these activities more attractive? If so, how?

☑ CHECKPOINT

1. What are some reasons to use tallies or checklists?
2. Can you describe other situations in which various types of records could be helpful?
3. How could you make observation records easy and convenient to use in a classroom?

7.4 Making and Using Portfolios

As teachers move from the observation stage to the interpretation stage, one way of combining all the collected information about a child is through a **portfolio**. A portfolio is a collection of observation records and **artifacts** (examples of items children have created). These items are gathered by teachers and used to plan activities, add or change materials, and guide interactions with children. The information might be shared with specialists and parents. A portfolio helps teachers document what a child is learning when the materials collected are representative of the child's capabilities.

Portfolios are most useful when they contain documentation over time of children's progress. A child's writing sample at the end of the school year will be more accurate and have more detail than one from the beginning of the school year. It will show increased fine motor development and better understanding of letters and how they form words. For school-age children, a portfolio will show more evidence of proper grammar, punctuation, spelling, and sentence structure. Therefore, it is important that all portfolio items include dates to show this progress.

To ensure that portfolios have descriptive materials for each child, collect work samples and make recordings that:
- are consistent in what is collected.
- can be stored in an orderly and retrievable manner.
- are dated and properly identified.
- demonstrate growth or document reasons for concern in a child's development.

Teaching Tip

Setting Up Portfolios

One way to set up a folder system that is easy to use is to staple an index card with the child's first name in large print on the back page of a folder, letting it stick up about three inches above the folder. Alphabetize by each child's name, and store the folders upright in a file box or crate.

Fold art samples and paintings so the paint is inside the fold and not outside. Dried paint tends to crack and rub onto other work samples. Take photographs of items that cannot be filed, such as three-dimensional art or classroom experiences such as block constructions.

Before beginning to collect work samples for the children's portfolios, plan how the items will be stored. Teachers must have a way to store each child's materials neatly. Otherwise, the information will be disorganized and difficult to use. Consider the following ways to store the children's materials:
- Accordion folders or flat boxes
- Manila folders
- Scrapbooks
- Three-ring notebook binders
- Containers specifically designed for portfolio materials

As you choose your method for storing portfolios, keep the following in mind:
- Containers must be durable to withstand frequent use.
- The container can be divided into sections, so there are compartments for specific time periods or for categories of materials. The year might be divided into four-, six-, or nine-week intervals. This division helps establish a framework for looking at children's work in sequence and creates a timeframe for how often to collect materials.
- The system should offer convenient access for filing and retrieving materials. If teachers cannot get to each child's portfolio easily, they will accumulate piles of unfiled materials quickly. If children are old enough to help with filing, the system must be easy for them to use.
- Space is limited in most classrooms, so consider the space available.
- The container should ideally hold everything that will be saved for an entire school year.
- Individualize the containers by involving children in their decoration.

What to Include in Portfolios

It is helpful for teachers to decide at the beginning of the year which items they will collect and how often. Items may include:
- Developmental checklists
- Anecdotal records
- Art samples
- Interest checklists
- Writing samples
- Cutting examples
- Self-portraits (**Figure 7.15**)
- Math samples
- Dictated or written stories
- Photos of the child involved in activities
- Other documentation as events occur

Portfolio compilation is sometimes thought to be an overwhelming chore. In truth, a portfolio is simply a collection of materials that illustrate the developmental stages of the child. Establish deadlines and create reminders to collect children's work at various times during the year. Decide which can be collected over time and which can be gathered randomly. Items that are collected consistently throughout the year will demonstrate growth and change. At the end of the school year, teachers will have a collection of work samples showing each child's progress.

Digital Portfolios

Software programs are available to compile portfolio information in a digital format. Some assessment systems, such as Teaching Strategies GOLD®, provide a means of documentation online. Typically, examples of children's work are scanned and uploaded, where they can be categorized and accessed. Alternatively, milestones of development can be selected and marked as they are observed in children. Digital portfolios can reduce the issues related to storage and make the information available anywhere if

Figure 7-15 A first-grade child holds up a self-portrait she made before filing it in her portfolio. *How can self-portraits collected over time document a child's learning and development?*

the system is web-based. Digital portfolios can be easily shared with parents or others during videoconferences or in-person meetings. In addition, digital portfolios can be cumulative and document the child's progress over a multi-year period.

Published Assessment or Screening Tools

Another type of assessment involves the use of a tool that has been designed, researched, and tested for reliability. Most assessment and screening tools are administered individually to each child to record what the child can do in one or several sessions. School systems often give such assessments in preparation for enrollment or to evaluate school readiness. Some of these tools are designed to look at specific domains of development, such as the Ages & Stages Questionnaire®: Social-Emotional, Second Edition (ASQ®:SE-2), which considers social-emotional development. Others cover all domains, such as the Learning Accomplishment Profile™ (LAP). One benefit of a comprehensive tool is that it helps ensure that observations are made in all of the following areas of child development:

- Fine and gross motor development
- Cognitive development
- Language development
- Social development
- Creativity
- Self-discipline
- Self-help
- Self-esteem

While published assessment or screening tools are usually well researched, an important consideration is that no single tool should be used as the basis for major decisions regarding a child (NAEYC n.d.). Children are complex, changing beings and should be viewed as such.

Standardized Tests

Another type of published assessment tool is a standardized test. A standardized test is any form of test that (1) requires all test-takers to answer the same questions, or a selection of questions from a common bank of questions, in the same way, and that (2) is scored in a "standard" or consistent manner, which makes it possible to compare the relative performance of individual students or groups of students.

Most standardized assessment conditions have timed limits and require predetermined responses, and extended, focused attention (NAEYC n.d.). These demands create concern as to whether young children are developmentally able to understand the task and participate in the testing procedures. Preschoolers may not understand the demands of a standardized testing situation and may respond unpredictably to the conditions. Performance is highly influenced by children's emotional states and experiences. Young children may simply not be interested in the activity or tire of it prior to completion, thus making the results an inaccurate reflection of what they know and can do.

Some early childhood experts express concern about tests that do not follow how young children learn and how best to measure what they know and can do. This concern is mostly focused on paper-and-pencil tests, in which the tester may not have a rapport with the child. The concern is that young children may not respond to a stranger, and thus the process of test-taking may not give a true picture of what the child can do.

If using standardized assessment information to make decisions about children's progress, teachers need to make sure they are evaluating children authentically. Standardized tests may not provide the type of data that teachers need to design meaningful interventions. For example, these tests are graded on a set of correct answers that do not take individual children's experiences into consideration. Their designated correct answers may not recognize a child's thinking process or cultural background. **Authentic assessment**, in contrast, involves considering the child's ability to apply knowledge and skills in real situations or scenarios.

Discovery Journeys

Are We Measuring What We Intend?

Jessup is in the second grade. He was completing a worksheet on relationships and marking items that go together. One of the choices included a lamp, a clock, a flashlight, and a pair of scissors. When Jessup marked the lamp and the clock rather than the lamp and the flashlight, I was puzzled that he did not see they were both sources of light. Curious, I asked him to tell me why he selected the lamp and the clock as his answer. He replied confidently, "They are both on the table beside my bed." Jessup had made a logical association and identified a relationship that was not what the publisher of the worksheet had intended.

Shalonda, who is in the first grade, was completing a worksheet identifying the relationship between clothing and weather. The worksheet included a picture of a sun, snow, and rain and then a heavy coat, a bathing suit, a sunbonnet, rain boots, and an umbrella. Shalonda paired the pictures of the umbrella and the sun together. Where Shalonda lived, umbrellas were often used to provide shade on hot days.

In both instances, the children made logical, thoughtful choices based on their lived experiences, but those choices were not what the publishers had determined to be the correct answers. Were they wrong? No, they simply had different experiences from the authors of the worksheets.

Consider This

1. Have you had an experience in which the correct answer to a question might be incorrect in certain situations?
2. How do you think Jessup or Shalonda would have felt seeing their answers marked incorrect?
3. Why is it important that teachers ask children to describe their thinking?

✅ CHECKPOINT

1. Why is it important to put names and dates on all records?
2. What are some considerations in choosing a tool for recording a physical skill, such as skipping?
3. How might you organize materials for a portfolio?

7.5 The Teacher's Role in Assessment

As early childhood professionals, teachers need to implement a systematic approach to assessment. Assessment of children and classroom practices requires a planned and consistent means of gathering information. Teachers need to be knowledgeable of the limitations of any specific means of assessment so that the information is used in an appropriate way. The decisions that teachers make for and about children must be done with an understanding of the whole child, a recognition that children grow and change rapidly, and a practice that no single measurement be used as the basis of major decisions about a child.

Teachers should be selective in choosing assessment strategies with young children (**Figure 7.16**). Assessment requires establishing a relationship with the child, ascertaining if the task is familiar and comprehensible, limiting the length of the session, and considering the child's discomfort in the setting. The child's unique conditions, such as hunger or fatigue, can affect results. There is also the possibility of bias in the tester or the tool. Questions that may have no relevance to the child's experience at the time may be of little significance to a child who does not see any purpose in the questions.

When assessing young children, teachers may consider how each family's values influence the child's development. Some families may value manners and obedience over independence. Physical development may be a top priority for a family of athletes; academic skills may be emphasized by others. Many may be concerned that their child's social-emotional needs are being met and their child is making typical developmental progress for their age.

SDI Productions/E+ via Getty Images

Figure 7-16 A teacher aide is helping a third-grade child who is learning English as a second language. Why is the aide's good rapport important in assessing the child's language skills? How might she document the child's progress?

Best practice indicates that early childhood assessment should be an ongoing, dynamic system based on collecting authentic data in natural settings through a variety of methodologies. Assessment results should provide relevant information to contribute to planning activities and strategies, the design and implementation of interventions, and informed decisions.

Maintaining confidentiality is also part of being a professional in assessment, as it is in many other areas of working with young children. The goal is to document each child's progress over time, not to compare the child's results with those of their peers. Information about how a specific child is doing should be shared only with the child's family and other professionals who may be involved with the child.

Children's development is complex and ongoing. Therefore decisions about placement, retention, or interventions should not be based on any one assessment process. The purpose of most assessment is **formative**—to be used to understand each child and to plan for the child's expanded learning based on what has been documented.

Case Study

The Social Media Post

Sonia was excited about how well her second graders had performed on a recent schoolwide assessment. She was especially proud of how one child had done, scoring at a level that would make her eligible for the system's gifted program. She created a congratulatory post to MacKensie for scoring so high and put it on the class social media page.

That night, she received a text message asking for a conference from MacKensie's parents. She could tell from the curtness that they were not happy. The next day, MacKensie's parents came in and told Sonia they did not appreciate the post. They explained that they recognized MacKensie was advanced for her age, that she learned easily, and that she was very alert to what went on around her, but they felt she lacked the social skills and responsibility that are important for success. They did not want her recognized for a characteristic that she was fortunate to be born with. They felt it was more important to focus on what she did with the gifts and talents that she had. After all, they explained, having the ability to solve difficult math problems was of little use if one could not have a good relationship with team members at work.

Sonia appreciated their willingness to discuss their values with her and apologized. MacKensie's parents told her that they understood she meant no harm. Sonia removed the post immediately after the meeting.

Consider This
1. How did Sonia's values and the parents' values differ?
2. How might Sonia act differently in her approach to MacKensie's accomplishments in the future?
3. Do you think that teachers and school administrators give as much credence to social skills and development as they do to academics? Why or why not?
4. What are some considerations you should examine prior to posting on social media, even if the page is limited to other families in the class?

Using a Systematic Approach in Assessment

While there are many ways to observe and assess children, early education programs must have a systematic approach with a clear plan for the types of observations to be completed and a specific timeline of when they will be done. To ensure that observations are completed in a methodical, timely manner, teachers should:
- schedule time for recording of all children and set deadlines. Make assessment a part of the routine.
- maintain factual, accurate records.
- keep each child's best interests in mind to help the children succeed.

- recognize the importance of being objective and impartial, neither judgmental nor subjective.
- use the information in parent conferences to communicate and give examples of the child's progress to the family.

No matter how much information is gathered and recorded, it is only helpful when analyzed and applied. When designing systems, carefully determine what information to gather and why; consider how to use the information.

Interpreting and Using Information

Once teachers have gathered assessment data, they look at all the information about a child to identify what skills and abilities the child has mastered and what progress the child has made in achieving other skills. They must consider all variables regarding what they know about each specific child and typical child development. Interpreting and using information about behavior can include identifying and defining problems as well as figuring out the meaning of what teachers have observed. They might ask themselves questions, such as:

- What patterns have emerged in the child's performance or behavior?
- How does the child demonstrate age-appropriate expectations?
- Is there a concern? If so, who or what is involved with the concern?
- What plan of action is best based on observed information and appropriate expectations?

As teachers consider their role in assessment, they should remember the goals for the data they gathered. The information is essential for understanding each child, planning for the child's ongoing development, tracking progress over time, and identifying any concerns that might arise. Remember, too, the importance of sharing information and communicating with families to support culturally relevant learning.

☑ CHECKPOINT

1. Why is it not a good practice to make important decisions about children based on one assessment tool or record?
2. In what ways might assessment tools inform planning?
3. How can a systematic approach help ensure assessment effectiveness?

7.6 Using Observations and Assessments to Guide Behavior

While observation is primarily used in the classroom for planning learning experiences, it can also be an effective tool for addressing behavior or classroom management. Guiding behavior is an important task of early childhood educators, and teachers can use assessment tools to address behavior challenges. However, it is difficult to observe behavior without judgment. Every person has their own set of "mental filters" created from their life experiences. For example, a girl separated from her father through divorce may see raccoon cubs at the zoo and comment that they miss their father. The connection to her life experience is apparent. The connection may be less obvious if a teacher sees a child tearing up a piece of paper. The teacher might decide that the child is trying to get attention, angry over not getting to play with the blocks, or simply enjoying the process or sound that tearing paper makes. The observation is that the child is tearing paper. The teacher's supposition for why the child is tearing paper is a judgment based on personal perspective.

When teachers allow their expectations to affect what they see, it can invalidate their observations. For instance, teachers who expect a child to be rowdy will notice whatever the child does that is rowdy. Teachers who expect a child to be shy may be less likely to notice outgoing behavior. Teacher expectations can affect perception and not reflect what is actually happening (**Figure 7.17**).

NAEYC, citing the research of Dr. Walter Gilliam and the Yale Child Study Center, shows significant research documenting the **implicit biases** of early education teachers (NAEYC 2020). Implicit biases are attitudes that are unintentional and not recognized by the individual. Teachers who showed bias related to misbehavior and the severity of the misbehavior by race judged children more harshly. Length of expulsion or suspension actions also showed bias based on race. It is incumbent on teachers as professionals to work intentionally to avoid bias in their assessments and observations with objective data to avoid labeling children.

Applying these kinds of expectations and labels can be harmful. Once a teacher applies a label to a child—even if the label is a positive one, such as *creative*, *athletic*, or *smart*—that teacher, as well as other teachers and program staff, may observe that child's actions through the lens of that label, and fail to see other possibilities. Labeling a child creates a filter through which the child's behavior is viewed and interpreted, and the phenomenon can occur whether the behaviors are strengths or weaknesses.

Addressing a behavior requires tracking, or documenting the frequency and other factors related to the behavior. Knowing how often the behavior occurs and other facts about the behavior provide data to assess improvement.

Addressing Behavior with the Three Ws

After observing and documenting children's behavior, teachers can use the information they gathered to create a plan to guide certain behaviors. Behaviors tend to have patterns. The same behavior will often be repeated at the same time, in the same way, or under a similar set of circumstances. Observation can be a helpful tool for making decisions about how to best address undesirable behaviors. When dealing with challenging behaviors, patterns can provide clues to how to best address the behavior. Teachers ask themselves the three Ws—*what*, *when*, and *who*—while looking for patterns of behavior.

1. *What* is the behavior?
2. *When* does this behavior happen?
3. *Who* is involved?

Nimito/iStock/Getty Images Plus

Figure 7-17 A teacher talks to a child about why he pushed another child on the slide. How can teachers avoid implicit bias in observation and documentation to help guide the behavior of children?

What

What is the specific behavior? What is going on when the behavior occurs? What is the teacher's typical response to the behavior? What is the response of the other children?

1. Andy throws blocks.
2. Andy is sent to time-out when this occurs.

When

When does the behavior take place? When is it most or least likely to happen?

1. Andy throws blocks mostly at the end of the morning playtime, just before lunch.
2. Andy throws blocks after lunch, right before naptime.
3. Andy rarely throws blocks early in the morning.

These examples point to the possibility that the block-throwing may relate to being hungry or tired. However, answer the *who* questions before deciding upon a definite plan of action.

Who

Who is involved when the behavior occurs? Are specific children around each time, or does the behavior take place with random children? Are any adults present?

1. Andy throws blocks only when he plays with Dean.
2. Andy throws blocks, no matter who he plays with.

Depending on which of these answers is true, the choice of how to address the problem will be affected. If the combination of Dean and Andy is a consistent factor, then both Andy and Dean may need improved social skills or practice handling blocks appropriately.

If Andy throws blocks, no matter which child he is playing with, the problem may be more about his being hungry or tired. Anticipating Andy's vulnerability when hungry or tired could result in making sure he has a late morning snack or perhaps joining story time instead of taking out blocks at difficult times of the day. By gathering answers to the three Ws, teachers can identify patterns and use the information to better respond to the cause of difficult behaviors.

Assessing a Concern

When a challenging behavior occurs with a specific child, the temptation is to blame the child. However, impartial observation may reveal that the program, expectations, or environment are initiating the behavior. Try to identify why a challenging behavior exists. Start by analyzing the issues that are occurring in the classroom.

For example, several children are acting inappropriately during group time. They will not come when called without a good deal of prodding. The children poke at each other and are disruptive once they are finally gathered in the circle.

Identify What Is Happening

After identifying the main issue, look at it from different perspectives. If the issue is that the children will not gather in the group when asked to do so, consider what is going on right before group time.

- Are the children involved in activities that they enjoy more than group time?
- Are the transitions, routines, or expectations unclear?
- Can some children gather the group together and encourage them to become helpers instead of disruptors?

These questions look at the situation from the child's perspective. Answering these questions can lead to adjustments and potential solutions. Possibilities to consider are:
- Shortening group time or changing the time. Could group time be done at a different time of day?
- Giving a five-minute notice before calling children to group, thus allowing them time to adjust to a change.
- Offering a child the responsibility of ringing a bell to gather the group; this increases involvement and may improve cooperation.

Look for Environmental Factors

When an issue occurs, there may be other factors contributing to the behavior as well. Before assuming that the challenging behavior is due to willful disobedience, look at what may be contributing to the children's behavior by examining the environment and adult actions. Here are some other questions to ask for the group-time example:
- Do the problems result from interactions between adults and children or between peers?
- Is the teacher appealing to the children's diverse learning styles or a single learning style?
- Is group time not interesting to the children? What can be done to make it more appealing?
- Does the teacher demand compliance and get into power struggles? How can the approach encourage cooperation?

Look for a Teaching Moment

If changing the environment or improving interactions with adults does not help, then shift the focus to what is going on with a particular child. In some cases, rather than changes being needed in the environment or routine, teachers may need to work with an individual child to teach the desired behavior. The children may not understand the consequences of their actions. Teachers may use an approach such as, "Taking so long to gather quietly in the circle means we have less time to enjoy our story. Why don't we practice together how quickly we can gather in the circle to be ready for the story you chose?" The first step is always to examine what is really taking place before trying to determine why the behavior is occurring. Discovering the *what* and *why* of a behavior takes careful observation and questioning before teachers can identify workable solutions.

Rapid Change and Expectations

In fewer than five years, children grow from helpless infants who mostly eat and sleep and depend on others for everything to independently mobile beings who can express ideas and interact with others. These first years are times of rapid change. When working with young children, teachers must be sure their expectations are within the developmental abilities for a child's age. To expect an 18-month-old child to bathe alone would not only be unreasonable but also dangerous; yet sometimes adults expect children to do other things that are impossible for their age or developmental level.

Inappropriate expectations often create what are considered challenging behaviors. Examples include a toddler expected to resist touching a decorative vase; a 4-year-old expected to sit quietly for hours in a church service; or a 2-year-old expected to eat without making a mess. These are unrealistic expectations that extend beyond the children's developmental abilities and will lead to frustration for both child and adult.

Think about these expectations of children:
- Are they reasonable? Does the age and ability of a child influence the expectations?
- Do the expectations change as a child grows older and gains skills (**Figure 7.18**)?
- Is increased growth and competence supported?

Teachers who experience a persistent challenge in their classroom may need to examine their expectations. If their observation demonstrates a pattern, such as that challenging behaviors occur most often during circle time, they can use that information to examine their expectations.

Figure 7-18 A family child care provider encouraged this child to pour the cereal and milk. She knows that letting children do things for themselves can be messier and slower but important. What skills is this child learning? How does the adult's reaction encourage further efforts in self-help?

- Are children expected to sit quietly for too long and become restless?
- Are they not interested in the activities?
- Is there little variety in activities, so that children lose interest?
- Are the adults not enthusiastic enough to hold the children's attention?

If children in a program are failing to learn skills expected of their age, the adults may be expecting too little. Are the adults in a classroom of 4-year-olds still putting on and tying shoes, dressing children in jackets, and serving all the food? Teachers expect too little sometimes because it is easier or more efficient to do tasks for children. Teachers may find it easier to pour milk themselves than to have children spill it, but pouring milk for every child, every day, adds up. On the other hand, spending time showing children how to use a sponge helps them learn to take care of spills themselves. Doing these things for children only *seems* to be easier and less time-consuming than letting them learn to do it for themselves.

Is Intervention Needed?

All children develop skills in a similar order, but there is also variation in the time that specific skills are mastered. One child may walk at 11 months of age, and another at 14 months. Both are within normal developmental ranges. But when a child is still not walking at 17 months of age, an early childhood professional may begin to question why.

Adults working with young children provide valuable early warning systems for children and their families. Adults who spend all day with many children notice when one child's development or behavior seems unusual. By using effective observation and recording techniques, teachers need not rely on luck to notice what could be a delay or a symptom of a larger issue. Effective observation systems take the guesswork out of early identification.

Children who do not develop within developmental guidelines may need professional intervention, and the earlier they get it, the more likely it is that the issue can be successfully resolved. If a child lacks the skills that their peers already have, teachers may wish to consult with a specialist to determine the best steps to take (**Figure 7.19**). Most

Figure 7-19 A teacher shares assessment information with this second-grade girl and her mother. She believes the information suggests a need for further evaluation. *What suggestions would you make to the teacher about communicating with families about a concern?*

programs have a policy for how to communicate such matters to families. The policy might call for the concern to be discussed with the administrator or that a joint conference be held with parents. If there are no established procedures, the following steps can help teachers support the family:

1. Find out if a parent shares these concerns.
2. Determine what, if any, evaluations or consultations have already been completed.
3. Ask the parent's permission to have a public health nurse or other professional observe the child, or ask a parent to seek the advice of a specialist.
4. Work with the family and specialist to provide for that child's needs.
5. Seek resources that can provide appropriate services.

Technology Options for Observations and Assessment

Video recording and photographing are excellent ways to view and document interactions. A video captures actions and interactions and allows teachers to watch the recording repeatedly to observe subtleties. Teachers can also record a series of videos taken at separate times and look for changes that might be occurring over time. A series of photos of a child in the block area might show the increasing complexity of designs and constructions, and the same photos may also show that the same two or three children work together in this area regularly.

In one classroom, a 3-year-old girl was unable to complete many tasks related to numeral recognition. Her teacher video recorded her attempts and observed that the girl was under great stress while completing the tasks. The child had a pained look as she struggled to identify numerals. The child's grimaces helped her teacher understand that there was too much pressure on her or that the expectations were unrealistic at this point in her development. Watching the recording and looking at other documentation of the girl's struggles, the teacher recognized the need to build a foundation of first-hand experiences related to numeral recognition.

Technology changes quickly, with more choices becoming available regularly. Some technologies might be tempting to use but may prove to be less effective or more time-consuming than simpler methods. Using a computer or tablet to record observation details may take the focus away from the actual observation. However, an electronic device may make it easier to tabulate or compare large quantities of information.

For example, teachers may find it much easier to take quick notes on a clipboard using index cards, sticky notes, or labels they carry throughout the day rather than entering information digitally. However, if a series of notes are needed to document a behavior or to demonstrate progress, compiling the information digitally makes the data easier to access, read, and understand. If cumulative data is to be collected, then creating a table or spreadsheet makes the data easier to sort and analyze. Additionally, scanning examples of children's work, such as writing and art samples, can avoid the need to store paper items, yet make them accessible for conferences or consultations.

Adding any new technology or software requires some user training. Without training, the technology may be underutilized or ignored. Software can offer benefits such as online retrieval of assessments or templates specifically designed for early childhood; however, to get these benefits, one must be familiar with the software. When looking at investing in a new piece of technology to aid the assessment process, teachers can ask themselves, "Will this improve the process of observing the children, recording the data, and then analyzing the information?"

Discovery Journeys

The Math Professor

One of my own experiences exemplifies for me the futility of placing limitations on children's accomplishments based on any one factor. The experience demonstrated vividly for me that no one measurement or opinion should be used to judge a child's future.

As a graduate student, I tutored Lon, a third grader who had been diagnosed with dyslexia. At that time, I would have considered a college education unattainable for him, much less a doctorate degree, due to the reading limitations he faced. As I occasionally had contact with him over the years, I learned of his high school graduation, college graduation, earning of a PhD in Mathematics, and current employment as a tenured professor at a university.

Consider This
1. What would have happened if Lon had been perceived as a child with a limited future?
2. How might the tutoring and other resources have helped him achieve success?

☑ CHECKPOINT

1. How can assessment tools help teachers understand children's behavior?
2. Why is it important that teachers not make judgments about children's futures?
3. In what ways might technology help with assessment?

7.7 Evaluating the Program as a Whole

In addition to evaluating the children's progress and behavior, early childhood educators may evaluate the overall program for ongoing improvement through various types of accreditation programs. For example, the NAEYC's Early Learning Program Accreditation is an extensive program assessment tool. This system, based on self-assessment and professional validation, provides standards to assess and improve program quality. Program evaluation, when based on quality standards, can be a source for identifying professional development needs.

Teachers must learn to observe what is taking place without letting their beliefs or judgments intrude. This is one of the best ways to figure out what is working and what needs improvement in a program. For example, a stated goal of a program may be to provide all children with daily large-muscle challenges. Consider the following program scenario: There are climbing structures and large-motor equipment available on the playground. The children go outside twice daily for a total of at least one hour, weather permitting. The teachers engage in gross-motor activities, such as throwing balls, helping construct obstacle courses, and demonstrating how to safely use equipment.

It would be easy to think that these factors ensure that the children in this program are engaging in physical activities each day. It is only through objective observation that the teachers discover:

- William spends most of his time in the sandbox and does not engage in the various large-muscle activities at all (**Figure 7.20**).
- LaDonna never leaves the water table, even when a friend invites her to play ball.
- Lien sits in a swing most of the time she is outdoors.

By observing carefully and recording children's behavior over time, the teachers become aware that the stated goal of large-muscle development is not being met for these children as they believed. The temptation for teachers is to assume that what they expect to happen does indeed happen. However, careful observation and recording may tell a different story from what they believe is happening in the program.

☑ CHECKPOINT

1. How is evaluating the program different from assessing children?
2. What are some needs for improvement that can be identified through a program evaluation?

eclipse_images/E+ via Getty Images

Figure 7-20 William spends most of his outdoor time in the sandbox, a sedentary activity. *How can the teacher know if the goal of active physical development is being met in the program?*

7.8 Family Matters

Programs are increasingly using social media and other digital means to share information with families about their children's activities and progress. Daily emails are replacing paper notes, and digital newsletters can be produced quickly with online templates. Photos and videos can illustrate examples of activities and progress. Imagine the relief a distraught parent feels upon receiving a photo of a happy, involved child who was dropped off crying just a half hour earlier.

Teachers are sometimes reluctant to share assessment information with families. They may feel concerned about how the parent will react or unsure that they will say the right thing. Letting parents know at enrollment about assessment policies sets the stage for communication. Reporting at pickup time or sending a brief email that a child made progress in potty training is different from requesting a sit-down conference to review documentation about how a child is advancing overall.

Regular conferences to discuss a child's progress are easier if the policy is explained upon enrollment and can be viewed as a routine check-in rather than an indication of a concern. Here are tips for holding a conference specifically to share assessment data:

- Plan for the conference. With careful planning, a 20-minute focused session can convey a lot of information.
- Consider videoconferencing if an in-person meeting is not possible or convenient.
- Hold the meeting in a private setting. Assessment results are confidential information, and parents may have strong emotional reactions at times. These meetings require privacy so that teachers and parents can openly discuss the child's progress.
- Remember that the family has vast hopes and dreams for their child. Be kind and supportive.
- Have a written document to use as a guide. Make a list of topics to discuss, with notes about relevant examples.
- Provide an overview of the assessment's purpose and benefits. Even if this information is in the parent handbook, it may not have had the same significance then as it has now.
- Remind families that any one assessment tool is a snapshot and cannot portray the whole child, nor can it predict the child's future.
- A little friendly conversation can help set the tone of the meeting, but keep the focus on the child's development.
- Start with the child's strengths. A few positive examples can build rapport and reassure the family that you care about their child. Share examples to help the family understand what has been observed in the classroom.
- Clarify terminology and avoid jargon. Avoid statements that sound judgmental. A simple statement of fact, such as "Lanny can count to 10 now, but he should be able to reach 20," may be interpreted by a parent as "I don't do enough for my child."
- To end the session, provide information about what skills will be emphasized in the upcoming weeks, confirm any agreements to reconnect, and thank them for attending the meeting.

Assessments are important to track the development of young children, but they do not predict the future. Nor is it the teacher's role to diagnose issues of development. A teacher's unique relationship with children allows the teacher to see and understand children's progress. Teachers are vital in reassuring parents about a child's development or expressing concerns if a child's behavior signals some emotional distress or possibly an impairment or a delay.

Daily contact with children allows astute teachers to recognize accomplishments and needs. Making clear, unbiased assessments that are shared with parents helps them understand how their child is progressing. Parents depend on teachers for guidance. A diagnosis is not in teachers' realm of expertise, but they can use their knowledge of child development and individual children to help parents understand how their child is developing.

✓ CHECKPOINT

1. How can you help families understand that assessment is important for their child?
2. How can a portfolio help you show progress when meeting with parents?

Chapter 7 Review and Assessment

Chapter Summary

7.1 Identify the purpose and value of assessment.
- Assessment is important in planning and accountability.
- Assessment is needed to successfully build on what children know and can do.
- Without ongoing assessment, children who need intervention may not get it.

7.2 Explain the role of assessment in planning.
- A major purpose of early childhood assessment is to know what children can do in order to plan developmentally appropriate experiences to scaffold their ongoing learning.
- Close observation is a valuable tool for assessing young children.
- Assessment is part of planning a learning process rather than something done in addition to teaching.
- Assessment records should be factual, empirical evidence of skills and actions and should not include opinions or misleading information.

7.3 Name and describe methods to record observations used to assess young children.
- Educators need a consistent system of observation and recordkeeping to know if children are progressing as they should or if screening for possible intervention might be needed.
- Children's skills can be recorded and assessed in a variety of ways.
- The selection of the most effective tool depends on what information is to be gathered and how the information will be used.
- Tools may include notes, tallies that record the frequency of an activity, checklists that document skills, grids to gather a variety of information, developmental scales that identify skills that children of a specific age typically develop or learn, and anecdotal records that are a narrative of a specific event.
- Maintaining objectivity is important in the records that teachers keep and the information they gather.

7.4 Describe the use of portfolios in assessment.
- Developing portfolios is one way to collect information on children and store the information in an organized way.
- Records and artifacts gathered over time can show progress.
- Digital portfolios can make information available online.
- Published assessment and screening tools are available that provide a formal and more structured format for assessing children's progress based on standard ranges of expected developmental milestones.
- No single tool should be used to make major decisions about a child.
- Standardized tests may be inappropriate for young children because they are not based on how children learn and may be structured in a way that the children do not have rapport with the tester.

7.5 **Explain the teacher's role in assessment.**
- Teachers must be aware of the limitations of any specific means of assessment.
- Maintaining confidentiality is necessary in relation to assessment.
- Teachers should develop a systematic approach to assessment.

7.6 **Apply observations and assessments to guide behavior.**
- In addition to the role of observation and assessment for academic learning, assessment can also be a useful tool in managing behavior.
- Teachers must be careful to avoid biases.
- Tracking how often or when an undesirable behavior occurs can be used to measure improvement.
- Asking *what*, *when*, and *who* questions can guide a plan for addressing behavior.
- Environmental factors may contribute to unwanted behavior.

7.7 **Explain the purpose of assessment of the program as a whole.**
- One of the most respected systems of program assessment is the NAEYC's Early Learning Program Accreditation.
- Knowing what is done well and looking at what needs changing is necessary for improvement.

7.8 **Prepare for and conduct conferences with families to share assessment information.**
- Another purpose of assessment is to share information with families about children's progress.
- Teachers can make the sharing process more comfortable for the family and themselves by planning and being well prepared.
- A friendly approach by the teacher can help to build rapport and support cooperation.
- Clear communication skills and maintaining focus on the child's progress are important in using the time effectively.
- Families are typically happy to hear about their child's progress but may not understand technical terms and will need examples.

Recall and Application

1. **True or False.** Assessment is a useful tool for improving programs.
2. One important use of assessment is to determine if a referral for special services, or ____, might be needed.
   A. intervention
   B. punishment
   C. a teachable moment
   D. a portfolio
3. **True or False.** Observing and recording have no relationship to child development.
4. ____ charts can help teachers set appropriate expectations based on age.
   A. Cognitive
   B. Developmental
   C. Growth
   D. Behavior
5. **True or False.** Knowing what children know and can do should inform planning.
6. **True or False.** You should include the child's name and age, the date, the setting, and what happened in anecdotal records.
7. Which of the following is *not* a reason to assess children?
   A. to determine their progress
   B. to plan experiences
   C. to support learning
   D. to prove to the child's family that the child has been misbehaving
8. Which of the following is *not* an effective way for teachers to record their observations?
   A. behavior charts
   B. note-taking
   C. tallies and checklists
   D. developmental scales
9. **True or False.** Parent interviews are helpful when assessing children.

10. Teachers should be concerned about age-appropriate milestones when completing a(n) ____ checklist.
    A. assignment
    B. behavioral
    C. developmental
    D. school supply
11. **True or False.** Developmental scales compare children's development to common ages at which certain skills or abilities usually occur.
12. **True or False.** Important decisions about children, such as retention or intervention, should be based on one assessment tool.
13. **True or False.** The environment has no effect on children's behavior.
14. **True or False.** Observation is simply watching children's activities.
15. **True or False.** Observing and recording children's behavior can help teachers identify a cause or strategy for behavior.
16. The three Ws of addressing behavior are ____.
    A. what, when, and who
    B. who, what, and why
    C. where, when, and who
    D. when, who, and why
17. **True or False.** Assessment of the program is the same as assessment of children.
18. **True or False.** Program assessment can help achieve or maintain quality.
19. **True or False.** Parents may have values for their children that are different from those of the teachers.
20. The first thing a teacher should do in a parent conference about assessment is to ____.
    A. list the child's misbehaviors
    B. list the areas in which the child needs to improve
    C. discuss the child's strengths
    D. ask the family to apply more discipline at home
21. **True or False.** Portfolios provide a method to document a child's progress to families.

Chapter 8

Language and Literacy

Standards Covered in This Chapter

NAEYC

NAEYC—1a, 2a, 3b, 4b, 4e, 6b, 7a, 7b, 7c, 8a, 8b, 8c

DAP

DAP—1a, 2a, 2b, 2c, 2d, 2e, 2f, 2g, 3f, 3g, 4b

Learning Outcomes

After reading this chapter, you should be able to:

8.1 Explain the 30-million-word gap and why it is significant.
8.2 Describe strategies to encourage language development.
8.3 Identify how adult responses and interactions support language development.
8.4 Explain the role of reading aloud in language and literacy development.
8.5 Describe criteria in selecting materials and implementing strategies that foster emergent literacy skills in young children.
8.6 Identify methods for assessing program practices.
8.7 Describe methods to engage families in their children's literacy.

Chapter opener image credit: Prostock Studio/iStock via Getty Images

Key Terms

bibliotherapy
communication loop
emergent literacy
emergent writing
environmental print
expressive language
language
literacy
narrative skills
open-ended question
parallel talk
phonological awareness
receptive language
sequence

Introduction

The language development and growing *literacy* (the ability to read and write) of young children are remarkable. The process of a child learning to use words in an appropriate context and following the syntax of the language can be awe-inspiring when you consider the complex skills required. Understanding all the phrases and expressions that have very different meanings from what the words actually say can be humorous, as in Peggy Parish's classic book *Amelia Bedelia*. In the story, Amelia is told to "put out the lights," so she hangs lightbulbs outside on the clothesline. Instructions to "dress the chicken" are taken literally. The process of children learning all these nuances of language is a fascinating and amazing feat. As you look at this process, consider the intricacy of these skills and why and how educators must support their development.

8.1 The 30-Million-Word Gap

In a groundbreaking study, researchers Betty Hart and Todd Risley (Hart & Risley 2008) visited the homes of 42 families from various socioeconomic backgrounds to assess how daily exchanges between a parent and child shape language and vocabulary development. They found great disparities between the number of words spoken and the types of messages conveyed. The research determined that children from high-income families were exposed to approximately 30 million more words in the first four years than children from families on public assistance. Follow-up studies showed that these differences had lasting effects on children's performance later in life.

The children's vocabularies were derived from their parents' vocabularies. Not only were the words they used nearly identical to those of their caregivers, but the average number of words utilized, the duration of their conversations, and the speech patterns were all strikingly similar to those of their caregivers, too.

After establishing these patterns of learning through imitation, the researchers analyzed the content of each. They found that the number of words heard varied along socioeconomic lines. Children from families on welfare heard an average of 616 words per hour; those from working-class families heard 1,251 words per hour; and those from professional families heard 2,153 words per hour. Thus, children in better financial circumstances had far more language experiences.

The researchers looked at what was being said in these exchanges and found that children from higher-income families received many more words of praise compared to children from low-income families. Additionally, children from low-income families were found to experience far more instances of negative reinforcement compared to those from higher-income families. Children from professional families experienced a ratio of six encouragements for every discouragement. However, for children from working-class families, this ratio was two encouragements to one discouragement, and children from families on public assistance received an average of two discouragements for each encouragement (Hart & Risley 2008).

Of course, language development is much more than just the number of words heard. The quality of the interactions and the turn-taking in conversation are also important.

Dr. Jill Gilkerson and colleagues found that conversational turn-taking between the ages of 18 and 24 months was highly correlated with later language and cognitive skills. "When you're getting more directive, business talk, the short, directive sentences don't elicit this back-and-forth," Dr. Gilkerson said. That finding could explain, in part, why more total words are associated with better language skills for children. "We do know as the number of words increases," Dr. Gilkerson said, "so does the richness, the syntactic complexity, and the content" (Sparks 2017).

☑ CHECKPOINT

1. How does a family's socioeconomic status affect a child's language development?
2. What are some examples of encouragements and discouragements?
3. Why is it important to have conversations with children?
4. What is the difference between a conversation with a child and talking to a child?

8.2 Language Development

To better understand the impact that this gap has, consider how language develops. **Language** is any system used to communicate and share information, ideas, and feelings. Good language skills are important in school success because language provides the foundation for building the concepts necessary to bring meaning to reading. The goal in early childhood is to help children develop the skills to understand others and express themselves. These systems of language include unspoken communication (gestures, facial expressions, or other body signals), oral speech, written language, sign language, speech output devices, and communication boards.

Language is the foundation for many areas of development. It enables people to communicate their wants, needs, and information through engagement in social interactions. These communication skills begin at birth and, in a responsive environment, increase rapidly in the early years. Language supports cognitive development and reasoning, because knowledge is built on the ability to understand and describe items and concepts. Language has a direct tie to reading and writing. Marks on a piece of paper or in a book have meaning only because of the language that the marks represent.

Language is a system of symbols. The sounds made in speech and the marks on paper (or in digital form) are part of that system. Language is also a system of rules used to create new meanings. People can produce completely original sentences and understand statements they have never heard. This occurs many times during a single conversation. Language comprises a group of systems and standards that include what words mean, how to make new words (*friend, friendly, unfriendly*), how to combine words, and how to use appropriate word combinations in specific situations. For example, "Would you please put the trucks away?" could change to "Put the trucks away now, please!" if the situation calls for it.

Speech is the process of moving the right body parts correctly to make sounds that convey a specific message. In addition to learning the rules of language, young children must also learn the movements required for speech. Learning language is an awesome undertaking, and one that is frequently taken for granted. This is why an understanding of language interaction is important for teachers of young children.

Sequence of Language Development

As with other developmental domains, language and literacy emergence happen in age-related stages, although the specific timeline is significantly affected by the child's experiences.

Language is described as *receptive* (what they hear) and *expressive* (what they say), with receptive language emerging first. Children must hear and understand the meaning of words before they can use them appropriately. Children acquire language at various rates, but early learning professionals should be familiar with what is developmentally age-appropriate. Children may do some things much earlier than the chart (**Figure 8.1**) shows, although if a child is accomplishing the tasks much later than indicated, further evaluation may be necessary.

Receptive and Expressive Language

Receptive language describes one's understanding of what is said or expressed. Even before children can form words themselves, they are hearing language and learning how words make it possible to communicate needs, information, and ideas. Receptive language

Development of Receptive Language

Age	Expected Receptive Language Skills
At Birth  *Fly View Productions/E+ via Getty Images*	• Is aware of sounds, startles at unexpected noise, and becomes still in response to new sounds • Responds to sounds, especially familiar voices, and becomes quiet when picked up
0 to 3 Months Old  *fotostorm/E+ via Getty Images*	• Smiles when seeing familiar faces • Turns when hearing voices; quieted by a familiar voice • Cries, grunts, sighs, and blows bubbles • Feeding rhythms develop as "cues" • Produces first smile • Anticipates being picked up (excited arm-waving and kicking) • Makes non-crying noises, such as cooing and gurgling • Produces first laugh
4 to 6 Months Old  *PeopleImages/iStock via Getty Images*	• Recognizes and responds to familiar sounds, voices, and objects • Reacts to tones of voice; is upset by anger and cheered by brightness and jolliness • Begins to babble: "ga" and "goo" sounds joined together • Makes noises to show feelings of pleasure or distress • Responds to the word "no" and changes in tone of voice • Looks toward the source of new sounds
7 to 12 Months Old  *StockPlanets/iStock via Getty Images*	• Listens when spoken to and looks at the speaker's face when called by name • Likes vocal games • Recognizes names of familiar objects, such as "daddy," "ball," "milk," and "eyes" • Begins to respond to requests, such as "Give me the ball." • Understands signs; for example, a bib means food. • Responds to own name and other familiar names • Makes appropriate gestures, such as raising arms to be picked up • Claps • Plays peek-a-boo

Goodheart-Willcox Publisher

Figure 8-1 The expected rate of development of receptive language. What should caregivers do if they suspect a child has a receptive language delay? *(Continued)*

Development of Receptive Language (continued)

Age	Expected Receptive Language Skills
1 to 2 Years Old  *Fly View Productions/ E+ via Getty Images*	• Points to pictures that the caregiver names in a book and points to a few body parts • Follows simple requests such as "Push the car," and understands simple questions such as, "Where is the dog?" • Listens to stories, songs, and rhymes and likes to have favorites repeated • Understands games such as dropping and picking up a toy • Understands "give me" and "no"; follows instructions such as, "kiss the baby" • Enjoys songs, action rhymes • May produce first words—probably "dada," "mama," or "bye" • Engages in much expressive babbling • Plays with toys and objects and shows knowledge of what they are for • Laughs at humorous events, such as funny faces • May say two or three words but still engages in much speech-like chatter with no meaning • Continues to expand single-word vocabulary and includes words such as "more," "all gone," and "no," as well as some verbs and object names • Attempts to copy sounds, such as car and animal noises • Vocabulary increases gradually from 10 to about 30 words • Understands longer sentences • Recognizes objects and pictures in greater numbers • Can match familiar objects • Understands "more," "here," and "now" • Enjoys and follows simple stories
2 to 3 Years Old 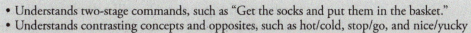 *kate_sept2004/E+ via Getty Images*	• Understands two-stage commands, such as "Get the socks and put them in the basket." • Understands contrasting concepts and opposites, such as hot/cold, stop/go, and nice/yucky • Recognizes sounds such as the phone or doorbell and may point to or try to get the caregiver to answer or attempt to answer themselves • Expands vocabulary from 30 to 60 or 70 words and joins some of them to make two-word sentences; makes up own words, tries to tell about things that have happened • Understands more concepts: "big" "small," "one," and "a lot" • Enjoys stories and remembers details • Can name pictures, match pictures, and define where things are—"in," "under," "over"
3 to 4 Years Old  *Eleonora_os/iStock via Getty Images*	• Understands simple *who*, *what*, and *where* questions • Can describe pictured actions • Understands size differences • Remembers events and can tell about them • Can put words into categories: "A cat is an animal." • Can anticipate • Tells you what they are going to do • Expands vocabulary to 500 to 1,000 words • Can construct many sentences that have proper grammar, with a few childish errors • Remembers nursery rhymes • Can play "Let's Pretend" games
4 to 5 Years Old  *SDI Productions/E+ via Getty Images*	• Enjoys stories and can answer questions • Understands nearly everything said to them in a familiar surrounding, such as home or school
6 to 8 Years Old *FatCamera/E+ via Getty Images*	• Can understand most new vocabulary from context • Able to retell stories with more detail • Can follow more complex directions • Enjoys riddles and jokes

Figure 8-1 Continued

is usually at a higher level than a child's **expressive language**, which is the ability to communicate ideas, information, and feelings to other people. Children understand much more of what they hear than they are able to express. For example, a child must understand what "Let's go outside" means before being able to express a desire to go outdoors. See **Figure 8.1** for a list of receptive language skills and the ages at which they typically can be observed.

☑ CHECKPOINT

1. What are some examples of unspoken communication?
2. How does oral language relate to reading and writing?
3. Why does a child's experiences affect their language?
4. How does your own receptive language compare with your expressive language?

8.3 The Teacher's Role in Fostering Language and Literacy Skills

How can you make sure the children in your early learning center acquire the language skills they need? The rhythm and the *syntax* of language in conversation, along with the vocabulary that you provide, will help these children understand the flow of both oral and written language. True engagement in the give-and-take of conversation allows children to practice communicating.

Because children's experiences greatly affect their language abilities, early childhood educators can play a key role in fostering language and literacy skills. Techniques differ according to the age group.

Talking to infants. Use the following methods to improve language skills in infants and children up to 2 years old:

- Talk to infants about what you are doing as you are doing it. "I am going to get the cup you need and put it here for you."
- Talk during mealtimes, playtimes, and routines. Value floor time as a time for exploring and interacting.
- Respond to infants when they make eye contact, babble, coo, or cry. Even though infants cannot use words to communicate, hearing adult language is important for their language learning. Respond to both verbal and nonverbal cues. "I see you want the ball."
- Interact with infants regularly by talking, singing, and playing.
- Label simple actions or feelings. "I think you must be tired."
- Read to infants and let them see how much you enjoy books.

Talking to toddlers. When working with toddlers (ages 2 to 3 years), employ these techniques:

- Ask toddlers questions geared toward their language level and expand on what they say.
- Speak slowly and clearly, avoid slang, use simple sentences, and repeat key words.
- Read aloud often. Choose both nonfiction books and storybooks with appealing, age-appropriate illustrations. As you read, point out unfamiliar words and discuss their meaning. Use the new words throughout the day.
- Ask toddlers to tell you what they are doing. "Tell me about the house you've just built with your blocks."
- Use prepositions routinely as you talk about what you are doing and what is happening. "I will put the crayons *in* the box *on* the shelf."
- Help children understand what opposites are. "Let's go *up* on the climber and then come *down* the slide!"

- Help children learn comparison words such as *big*, *bigger*, and *biggest*: "That is a big dog, and that one is bigger. Which is the biggest dog?"

Talking with preschoolers. Use the following techniques to increase the language skills and literacy of preschoolers (ages 4 to 5 years old):

- Use words that children do not know in context or with explanations. For example, ask a child riding a tricycle, "Where are you going? What is your destination?"
- Allow time for a child to respond after you ask a question (**Figure 8.2**). Adults sometimes jump in and answer for the child.
- Respond to children's comments in a conversational style. Talk *with* rather than *at* children.
- Ask children what things are for. For example, hold up a fork and ask, "What's this for?" A 3- or 4-year-old will be able to use the right verb in construction. "It's for eating." If you say, "What do we do with this?" they might say, "We eat with it."
- Suggest that children retell a story. Provide flannel boards, puppets, dolls, paper, crayons, and paint to recreate stories. Listen to see if children are using their new vocabulary in the correct context.
- Encourage children to discuss books they read at home and at school. Give them opportunities to use vocabulary from books.

Talking with young school-age children. More advanced techniques can be used with children ages 6 to 8 years old:

- Ask questions that call for evaluation and reflective thinking about stories children read.
- Encourage creativity in making up their own stories; use class technology to record their stories.
- Create class video blogs or newscasts about activities and events.

lostinbids/iStock via Getty Images

Figure 8-2 A teacher patiently listens to a child's response to a question about a family trip. How does listening attentively to children's responses encourage oral language?

- Read aloud books that may be too difficult for children to read themselves.
- Use newly introduced vocabulary frequently in conversation with children.

Vocabulary development correlates strongly to literacy development. Before starting kindergarten, a child is expected to understand and use thousands of words. Applying indirect and direct methods can help children build the vocabulary they need.

Indirect Vocabulary Learning

Indirect vocabulary instruction takes place casually. A child hears and learns new words in context from conversation, experiences, and interactions with others. Older children, who read on their own, can also learn new vocabulary from what they read. Emerging readers will hear or read new words in stories and relate the new words and concepts to what they already know. Because children learn by relating new information to what they already understand, it is important to provide them with new experiences and real-life learning opportunities. Regular and frequent interactions and conversations with adults are critical in language learning.

Direct Vocabulary Learning

In direct learning, a teacher provides intentional instruction to a student to teach vocabulary. Teaching vocabulary directly may involve asking a child to figure out an unfamiliar word by using clues from illustrations or context. For example, when a picture depicts a grandmother using a parasol on a sunny day, the teacher says, "Look, the grandmother has her parasol to keep the sun off. What does the parasol remind you of?"

Reading to a child is one of the most important language and literacy learning tools that caregivers possess. If a parent begins reading to a child for 30 minutes three times a week when the child is 6 weeks old, that child will have been read to for 387 hours by the time they reach kindergarten. Compare that to a kindergarten teacher who provides at most one hour per day of reading to children, or 180 hours of reading in a school year. It is impossible for a teacher to make up the difference from 180 hours of reading to 1,000 hours. Consequently, it is particularly important to communicate the message to families that reading from birth is essential to children's success. The families in your program can help their children immensely by reading to them at home.

Language Throughout the Curriculum

Language opportunities occur frequently throughout the day. Integrate and use reading in each learning center of your room, and incorporate conversation into various interactions. The vocabulary you use in the science area may be different from the vocabulary you use in the dramatic play area. Consider how you can transfer vocabulary from one center to another center or to another situation. For example, if a child used a magnifying glass in the science center, concepts and terms might be presented in the fine motor center as well. If you see a child playing with beads, you might say, "Those beads are so small, I think I need a *magnifying glass* to see them!" As you go through your day, note opportunities to transfer vocabulary and reinforce the experiences with words. The repetition of a word helps it to become part of the child's vocabulary.

Another way to encourage language skills is to provide opportunities for children to engage in conversations. Conversations with you and their peers can come naturally during play and at mealtimes. Small group areas such as the dramatic play center or block center are ideal for fostering conversations. Encourage children to put their actions, ideas, and feelings into words. Also encourage them to take turns talking and to listen when others are speaking.

When you help a child use language, you are encouraging cognitive development. Knowing the meanings of *large*, *larger*, and *largest* is important in learning math. Make a point of talking about what happened at the end of each day. Help children remember what occurred in the morning, after lunch, and after resttime. Conversations like this help build understanding of sequence and time. Ask children to tell you about the best thing that happened each day or what they liked most, providing experiences in comparison.

Whenever possible, be on children's eye level when talking to them. Such close contact helps you and the child focus and attend to the conversation. Sitting beside a child, bending down, or squatting will encourage valuable communication (**Figure 8.3**). Additionally, use your voice and face to emphasize a point, varying your tone and facial expressions to help communicate your message.

Children may enjoy playing language games at circle time, such as "I went on a picnic, and I brought…," in which they each add an item based on the alphabet. Rhyming games and singing also contribute to language development. Listen to a 3- or 4-year-old playing a game with a friend and notice how they imitate adults or make up nonsense words. Effective communication is an important social skill that helps children develop friendships as they interact with their peers.

Language Stimulation Techniques

The development of language skills depends on children's experiences in verbal interactions with others. A quality early childhood classroom provides many such experiences to build language skills throughout the day. This section describes some techniques that teachers find useful in engaging in conversations and stimulating language development with young children.

Self-Talk

Self-talk is a technique in which the adult describes what is happening while it is happening. Talking to children, even infants, about what you are doing is important for them to become familiar with language patterns and relate the words to the action. Self-talk also communicates respect. When a teacher tells a child what will happen before it happens, the teacher shows respect for the child. For example, an adult might happily say, "Look at you! I'm wiping your face, so you'll be all clean," while washing a toddler's face. Or, a teacher might say, "I will help you put on your coat, then we will go outside."

SDI Productions/E+ via Getty Images

Figure 8-3 The teacher sits beside a first-grade boy to engage in conversation about the book he is reading. How does sitting beside a child to be at eye level encourage conversation?

Case Study

Conducting a Conversation—or an Interrogation?

While the development of concepts is supported through conversations, sometimes adults become so focused on teaching concepts such as colors, shapes, numbers, and letters that language interactions deteriorate into drill or interrogation. Consider the following scenarios in which Warren, a 4-year-old, comes to school in a new jacket. Both examples begin with a comment from Warren, but then go in quite different directions.

Example 1: A Conversation

Warren: Guess what, Mr. Morrison? I got a new jacket!
Mr. Morrison: I see! That's really pretty! And it looks warm, too.
Warren: It's got flips!
Mr. Morrison: Flips?
Warren: Yeah, you know! Flips! Here, on the side. [Warren points to a flap on a pocket.]
Mr. Morrison: [realizing what Warren is trying to say] Oh, you mean flaps! I have a jacket with flaps, too.
Warren: Yeah, flaps!
Mr. Morrison: It looks like each flap has a snap, so you can fasten it.
Warren: Yeah, they do, so I won't lose things!
Mr. Morrison: What are some things you might put in your pocket, Warren?
Warren: If I had a phone, I could put it there, and it wouldn't fall out!
Mr. Morrison: I see. There's room.
Warren: My mother won't get me a phone, but I can put my toy cars in it.
[Warren heads off to put his new jacket in his cubby.]

Example 2: An Interrogation

Warren: Guess what, Mr. Morrison? I got a new jacket!
Mr. Morrison: I see! What color is your jacket?
Warren: It's brown!
Mr. Morrison: What are those things on the pocket?
Warren: I don't know.
Mr. Morrison: They are called flaps. Say, "flaps."
Warren: Yes, flaps!
Mr. Morrison: What is that on the flap? [Mr. Morrison points to a snap.]
Warren: I don't know.
Mr. Morrison: It's a snap. What letter does snap start with?
Warren: An "s," the snake sound.
Mr. Morrison: What shape is the snap? [Mr. Morrison points to the snap again.]
Warren: It's a circle.
Mr. Morrison: That's right! Now tell me how many snaps you have, then take off your coat and hang it in your cubby.
[Warren, happy to end the interrogation, bounds off to his cubby.]

Consider This

1. How do the two interactions differ?
2. Why is the first interaction more beneficial to the child's language development?
3. How does the first interaction develop reasoning skills?
4. Why do you think Warren was happy to end the second conversation?
5. Have you ever been in a situation in which you felt grilled? How did you feel?

Self-talk is particularly helpful in preparing children for transitions and can be a classroom management technique. "In 10 minutes, I will read the story again." Because the amount of language that children hear and the responsiveness of adults to children's language support overall language development, self-talk is an important skill for those who work with young children. Appropriate self-talk varies with the age of the child. Here are some examples:

Infants. Tell the infant what you are doing as you are doing it. "I'm changing your diaper. There you go, all nice and clean again."

Toddlers. Notice what toddlers are interested in and talk to them about it. "Yes, I see the truck, too. It's a red truck carrying groceries to the store. I hope it will go to the store where we shop for food."

Preschoolers. Talk to children during meals and about foods. "I'm eating my banana. Ruth, did you know the banana is a fruit, just like apples and oranges? I eat a big, yellow banana every morning for breakfast. What does a banana taste like to you? Is it good?"

Young school-age children. Talk to children about how to locate information. "I'll get the book about tigers, and we can find out where they live."

Parallel Talk

Parallel talk focuses on what the child is seeing, doing, or experiencing. This helps the child put word labels on behavior and, more importantly, connect the word labels into a phrase or sentence describing the action. Here are some opportunities for parallel talk:

Infants. Examples include: "You're shaking the rattle. Listen to the noise it makes." "Look at you, pushing that red ball!"

Toddlers. Examples include: "What a variety of colors! You really like using many colors, don't you?" "Garrett, I see you can rock quickly on that horse!"

Preschoolers. Examples include: "You and James are doing a wonderful job cleaning up the block area. And you're working rapidly." "Quinton, you painted a huge picture today. Do you want to take it home to Dad?"

Young school-age children. "Juan, that's a gigantic tower!" "Latoyia, I see you're using the zoo website. What are you researching?"

Both self-talk and parallel talk are opportunities to include descriptive words describing colors, quantities, shapes, or other characteristics in addition to naming objects. For example, referring to a bus as a big, yellow school bus or a button as a small, round button adds descriptive words that help build concepts. Using many descriptive words helps increase children's vocabularies.

Discovery Journeys

The Green Crayon

When kindergarten-teacher Molly's daughter, Bella, was about 15 months old, she managed to get a piece of broken crayon stuck in her nose. When Molly attempted to remove it, Bella pulled away and resisted, resulting in the crayon being pushed further into her nose. Molly was worried Bella might need surgery to get it out, so she quickly called the doctor. Molly's voice was stressed as she relayed to the nurse that, "My daughter stuck a green crayon up her nose, and I can't get it out!" Molly was told to bring her in right away. After the problem was solved with some special tweezers, the doctor told Molly that the staff was amused that, even in her stress, the kindergarten teacher role came out when she told them the crayon was green when explaining the problem!

Molly realized what a habit it was to use descriptive words. Molly never just said "truck" or even "firetruck," it was always "the red firetruck" or even "the big red firetruck." And she never asked, "Would you please pick up the block?" It was always, "Would you please pick up the red block or the square block?"

Consider This

1. What are some descriptive words you use frequently?
2. How does a teacher's use of descriptive words help children develop concepts?
3. What are some ways you can increase your use of descriptive words?

Expansion

Expansion takes what a child indicates or says and expands on it. When a toddler points to crackers or says, "cracker," the teacher might say, "Oh, you want another cracker?" If a child says, "Go buggy," the adult might say, "You want to go outside and ride in the buggy?" Expansion restates what the child says or indicates by adding words and making a complete and sometimes expanded sentence. The adult is thereby modeling structure and syntax for the child.

Expansion also involves facilitating learning concepts through language interactions. For example, if a child using scented playdough says, "Look, Miss Smith, I've made cookies!" Miss Smith might say, "I see you have, and your cookies smell good. They have a nice aroma. They smell like raspberries to me. Have you ever had raspberries? They're a lot like strawberries, but usually smaller." Miss Smith has introduced the terms *aroma* and *raspberries* in context.

As another example, a child building in the block area makes a pen for some rubber horses. The adult might introduce the terms *enclosure* and *corral* by commenting, "Emmie, I see you've made an enclosure for your horses. Did you know that a pen for horses is called a *corral*?"

Expansion is an important strategy because it responds to what a child initially says but adds to what was said. Expansion is an opportunity to create back-and-forth exchanges of conversation.

Open-Ended Questions

Open-ended questions are those that cannot be answered with one or a few words. A question that can be answered "yes" or "no" is not an open-ended question. Questions that ask "how" or "why" are open-ended because they can be answered in many different ways. Using open-ended questions during routines and play encourages children to express themselves, think critically, and express their ideas and feelings. Such questions also invite children to respond, reflect on events, and use their imaginations. Some examples of open-ended questions or directives are:

- Tell me about this.
- What else can you tell me?
- Tell me about what you want to make.
- What might this be used for?
- Why do you think that happened?
- What did you notice about this that is unusual?
- How are these things alike?
- Why do you believe that…?
- What might happen if…?
- How could we do that differently?
- How does that make you feel?
- Why do you think that happened?

Forming a Communication Loop

By responding to children, teachers help them learn important language and literacy concepts. One responsive strategy is to form a communication loop. A **communication loop** usually involves a statement and reaction that may continue back and forth. For example:

- A child expresses a need. "I can't finish my puzzle!"
- An adult responds to the child. "Here, let me turn some of these pieces. Now can you see where the blue one goes?"
- The child reacts to the adult's response, creating a loop of communication. "Yes. I can do it now."
- The adult responds to the child's reaction, continuing the loop. "Great! You can finish it now."

This communication loop not only builds language; it also assures the child that someone will help take care of their needs. The give-and-take of conversation is essential in teaching children that language is a tool they can use to get what they need or want and function in social groups.

Literacy: Learning to Read

Learning to read begins in infancy. A high-quality early learning environment can offer an enriching experience that increases a child's ability to learn to read. However, holding flash cards in front of a child or drilling on the alphabet is not usually the way to do it and can even be counterproductive. Rather, helping children learn to read involves:
- providing numerous interesting objects to explore and talk about.
- developing a stable sequence of events in the schedule and conversing about what is happening.
- encouraging children to use symbols, such as the icons used on a weather chart.
- exposing them to quality children's literature.

Language First

To read, one must understand words. Children gain receptive language skills and the ability to understand language when adults talk to them one-on-one in meaningful ways about what is happening. Adults respond to children's attempts to communicate first through their cries, grunts, and gestures, and later with their first words. Expanding on their language as they learn shows them how using language gives them power and control. To make the most of this important literacy learning opportunity, you must be conscious of your own language around infants and toddlers. You should use clear, descriptive words and speak to children directly as individuals rather than just making announcements to a group.

Objects

When infants pick up and examine objects, when they put things inside of containers, dump them out again, fit things together, and nest and stack things, they are learning about size, shape, and space (**Figure 8.4**). These are relevant concepts that lead to recognizing letters and their placement on a page. By manipulating age-appropriate toys, children build the finger muscles required to hold and use a pencil.

romrodinka/iStock via Getty Images

Figure 8-4 Manipulating items supports fine motor development in infants. Why are fine motor skills important in literacy?

Adults should provide infants and toddlers with a variety of interesting objects to handle and explore. This includes both toys and common items from around the house, as long as they are safe for children to handle and do not pose a choking hazard. In fact, infants and toddlers love handling items that they have seen adults use, such as pots, bowls, and other kitchen items. Focus on variety by rotating the toys and items that you make available. Put some items away and bring out new ones to keep the child's interest high and provide a variety of experiences.

Phonological Awareness

Phonological awareness is sensitivity to sound. It involves listening for the sounds in language. Activities can be tailored to help children recognize sounds that are the same or different. They can play with words, match rhyming word pairs, and identify repetitive sounds in an alliterative phrase. The following are some of the ways that a teacher can support phonological awareness:

- **Listening.** Listen for sounds and for differences in sounds, such as a tap versus a clap.
- **Rhyming.** Expose children to words that sound the same at the end, such as *cat* and *hat* or *truck* and *duck*. Songs and fingerplays are good opportunities for hearing rhyming words.
- **Alliteration.** Emphasize the same beginning sound in a song, poem, book, or fingerplay, such as "Willoughby Wallaby Woo." or "Peter Piper picked a peck of pickled peppers."
- **Words and sentences.** Help children understand that words make up sentences or phrases. For example, listen for and count the words in a phrase such as "Twinkle, Twinkle, Little Star."
- **Syllables.** Identify the syllables in a word. Try clapping the syllables in a child's name.
- **Onomatopoeia.** Call attention to words that sound like what they describe; for example, *pitter-patter*, *moo*, *quack*, *beep*, or *hiss*.
- **Blending and segmenting sounds.** Add and take away sounds in a spoken word. For example, remove the "c" sound in the spoken word "cat" and understand that what is left is the spoken word "at."

Experiences

Children become better readers when they are provided with a wide variety of experiences. Food preparation, nature walks, and seeing animals are all experiences that expose children to the broader world. These experiences help children learn language in the context of everyday life. Books become more interesting to children when they can connect them with the real world.

Sequencing

Sequences are orders of events or sizes. While people usually think of this as a math concept, it relates to reading as well. A consistent but flexible routine is important in developing this concept. Through the regular routines of the day, children learn that things happen in a certain, usually predictable order: Your caregiver puts a bib on you, you are fed, your face is wiped, and you feel full. You wake up, you make a noise, someone comes and gets you, and your diaper is changed. On the other hand, if a child lives in a chaotic environment in which they do not have a sense of what is going to happen next, this lack of predictability can make it more difficult to understand sequence.

Narrative Skills

Narrative skills involve the ability to tell a story or describe a sequence of events to others. Having numerous conversations with children throughout the day gives them opportunities to describe events in sequence and build narrative skills. Model narratives yourself as you converse with children during mealtime, center time, outside time, or during routines. Telling stories and describing events in sequence encourages children's use of narrative themselves.

Symbols

Learning to read involves using symbols. Letters are symbols for sounds, and words are symbols for objects or actions. Somewhere toward the end of infancy, children grasp the concept that some things stand for other things. You will see an infant put a toy phone to an ear. In their first attempts at dramatic play, such as feeding a doll, toddlers know that the doll is not real but represents a baby.

As children get older, they understand pictures as symbols. They can point to a photograph of their mother and say, "Mommy." They can look at a picture of a toy in a catalog or book and find the same toy on the shelf. They are learning that the shape on a flat piece of paper represents something three-dimensional and real. Children who have many experiences creating and using symbols are better equipped for later success in reading and math (Uttal & Yuan 2014).

Case Study

On Fish and Phonics

Five-year-old Keisha smiles with delight as she shakes the jar of fish food into the class aquarium. "Watch," she tells her friend Amanda. "The fish come to the top to eat. Watch how they eat!"

"See, that word says 'fish,'" she announces, pointing to the label their teacher placed on the aquarium.

Mrs. Copeland, their teacher, approaches, having noticed the girls' interest. "Would you like me to help you write a story about the fish?" she asks. "You can tell me about the fish, and I'll write down what you say."

"We have two fish," said Keisha.

"And they're both gold," chimes in Amanda.

"I wish we could get another, so we'll have three," added Keisha. "If we could, I'd pick out a really big one—one that can swim really fast!"

Mrs. Copeland wrote the girl's sentences in a notebook that she kept for recording children's stories. When they finished, they added pictures. Amanda drew the two fish, coloring them a bright orange. She then carefully printed her name in the upper left-hand corner of her picture. Keisha drew a bigger fish, like the one she wanted to get. Then they took turns reading the story to each other.

Mrs. Copeland helped them locate the letter "F" and recognize the sound associated with that letter. The girls noticed that "gold" and "get" started alike and began with the same sound. They learned that writing was a way to record what you said so you could repeat it the same way later.

Because they were enjoying this experience, each child wrote many of the words from the story during their activity time. They also asked their teacher for more fish stories. Mrs. Copeland selected *The Rainbow Fish* and some other library books about fish and helped the girls locate the words "fish," "food," and other words that started with the letter "F."

This was a *phonics* (matching sounds with letters) lesson for Keisha and Amanda. Their lesson happened when they were interested in something, and, as a result, they were more open to learning. Mrs. Copeland taught the letter sounds by helping the children recognize the letters and sounds at a time when they wanted to apply the knowledge. Their lesson, however, involved much more than phonic sounds. They learned about how books are made and the purpose of writing and became much more aware of the fish in the aquarium in their classroom. This was not phonics in isolation; it was phonics in the context of the children's experiences.

Mrs. Copeland knew the children needed phonics, but she also understood how children learn and how and when they learn best. She took advantage of their interest to teach a lesson on phonics in a developmentally appropriate way.

Consider This
1. Why is it important to notice what interests children?
2. How did Mrs. Copeland take advantage of the girls' interest in the fish?
3. What else might she have suggested to build on this interest in fish?

Daily Activities that Promote Literacy

As the research on literacy development continues to emerge, it is important to translate the findings into practical suggestions for supporting early literacy development. This section lists suggestions that promote early literacy in general and then by age group—for newborns to young school-age children.

General support. Teachers support children's literacy development in general when they:
- model reading and writing.
- share high-quality children's books and magazines, especially those related to children's interests.
- read stories more than once so that children can master the content and the use of language.
- tell stories—either traditional or invented—using puppets, flannel boards, or magnet boards.
- encourage children to enjoy books and magazines at naptime.
- share songs, rhymes, and fingerplays with children.
- help parents become involved in their children's literacy experiences. Welcome volunteers who can read to or take dictation from the children.

Infants. To support literacy development in infants, try the following suggestions:
- Introduce board- or cloth books with brightly colored pictures. Select books that reflect the child's own experiences with family members, animals, food, and so on.
- Read books that have rhyme, rhythm, or repetition, such as nursery rhymes.
- If an infant becomes restless or fussy while you are reading or looking at a book, put the book away for a later time.

Toddlers. Support toddlers using these methods:
- Add simple stories with a basic plot and one central character to nursery rhymes and favorite books, as toddlers' language abilities allow for greater listening capacity and understanding.
- Provide a warm, accepting atmosphere for reading by responding to children's requests for reading and rereading favorite stories. Respond to questions and comments about print, such as names, signs, and labels.
- Capitalize on children's developing interests, take short trips that relate to those interests, and read stories about similar events or places.
- Point out words on signs in stores, at the park, or when walking. Explain what the words mean as you name them.
- Create an environment that is supportive of early writing by making sure paper, crayons, and markers are available. Let toddlers help you write shopping lists.

Preschoolers. Use these techniques to support literacy development in preschoolers:
- Provide a rich literacy environment with high-quality books for children.
- Take children to the library. Limit screen time.
- Read aloud daily to the whole class, individual children, or small groups.
- Invite children to talk about books. Encourage them to comment and ask questions.
- Invite children to record their ideas as audio or on paper as drawings, tallies, or words.
- Provide writing materials and encourage their use as part of play.
- Plan activities that include recognition of letters, words, and numbers, such as cooking, mapping, or word games.
- Encourage social literacy experiences, such as sharing a book or writing with a friend.

Young school-age children. As young children develop more competence, consider the following techniques:
- As children are ready, suggest chapter books.
- Provide opportunities for children to locate information they need.
- Offer materials to summarize or retell stories that children read independently.
- Allow time for reading several times during the day.

Case Study

Teach My Baby to Read

As a teacher in a toddler classroom, Lucia works hard to plan activities that are developmentally appropriate for her students. She supports their language development by taking advantage of any opportunity to interact with each child individually. She reads books to them regularly, sings often, and follows their interests to engage in conversations.

At her routine conference with Amelia's mother, she was surprised by a request. Amelia's mom brought a set of flash cards and wants Lucia to use them with Amelia every day. She told Lucia that her cousin used them with her son, and he was accepted into one of the best magnet schools. She wants to be sure Amelia is accepted into the magnet school, too, and thinks the flash cards will help prepare her for the admissions test.

Parents usually want their children to become good readers. Society is heavily dependent on the written word, and parents recognize that being able to read is critical to their child's success. There has been much pressure to teach reading at earlier and earlier ages to give children a head start or to ensure that they do not somehow miss the opportunity. Moreover, some have taken advantage of parents' fears to promote expensive programs and toys that supposedly teach children to read. What is often not understood is that learning to read involves much more than recognizing letters and the sounds they make. Some of the materials available for purchase do not provide developmentally appropriate experiences. For example, one can purchase flash cards of the ABCs.

Yes, toddlers can learn the ABC song and even learn to recognize a letter shape and name it. While it looks impressive when they respond to a flash card, the child is just making a memorized response to a shape on a page. They might even be responding to something on the card such as a wrinkle or coffee stain. These activities have minimal relevance to learning to read. Children have plenty of time for letter recognition at an appropriate age. Even if these activities are not harmful per se, one concern is the time it takes to drill children to learn these responses. That same amount of time would be much better spent on truly valuable experiences, such as telling children a story, talking to them, or simply playing together.

Consider This
1. What do you think about Amelia's mom's request?
2. How do you feel about using flash cards with toddlers?
3. How do you think Lucia could best react to the request?

Environmental Print

Environmental print is an important way to support literacy development. **Environmental print** refers to the words and signs that are all around us. For young children, this often means the classroom labels and signs they see daily. When educators refer to print in and around the classroom and school, they support the development of print awareness, word recognition, and the purpose of written language. Here are some ways to help children develop print awareness through environmental print:

- Create a print-rich classroom by labeling containers and items with the name of the item and a picture. Talk to children about how the picture and the word represent the object.
- Use children's printed names often. Use name cards to show attendance, choose helpers, or conduct graphing or charting activities, or for children to identify which centers they choose. Have older children sign in by printing their name on a sheet or a board. Children will soon recognize their names and then their friends' names.
- Intentionally and strategically refer to print in and around the classroom. Say, "That sign says 'Office,'" or "This poster says, 'Wash Your Hands.'" Point out words on a morning message, chart, graph, or other writing in the classroom.
- Identify fun, interesting words in books. See the appendix for a list of children's books that focus on words.

- Take time to answer children's questions about words. For example, a child may want to know what the word on their backpack says.
- Write words that attract children's attention on index cards for their use. For example, a child might ask for the word *love* or *happy* to be written on a card to use in a message to a family member.

High-Quality Children's Literature

One of the best things teachers can do for literacy is to develop a collection of quality books written specifically for young children and read to them many times each day. It is never too early to begin reading to a child. By reading to infants, one can help children develop an appreciation of books and print at an early age and foster a lifelong passion for reading. Here are some reasons why early exposure to good books creates better readers:

- Children learn to associate reading and books with a positive emotional experience. They snuggle up to a favorite person and are entertained with attractive images and sounds.
- They learn how books work. They discover that books have a beginning, a middle, and an end; that they must turn the pages; and that the story goes from left to right.
- Children gain vocabulary and learn to focus their attention.

Selecting Children's Books

What do we look for in selecting books for children? And what determines quality and appropriateness? For all ages, consider the need to include diverse cultures, abilities, and absence of stereotyping. The following tips provide guidance in choosing books for various ages.

Infants. Choose cloth or board books with thick, easy-to-handle pages that can withstand wear. Books with large, clearly defined, brightly colored pictures of familiar objects and routines will help spark interest.

Toddlers. Choose stories with simple plots, familiar objects, and rhyming or repeated words.

Preschoolers. Choose books with humor, reality, exaggeration, and that explain how and why the events on the pages are happening. Books should also contain unfamiliar words to help expand children's vocabularies.

Young school-age children. Children will often be interested in a series of books with characters they like, wanting to read all books in the series. They like to use non-fiction books to learn how to do something or to learn about topics that interest them. Some will be ready to tackle chapter books.

☑ CHECKPOINT

1. How does reading to infants benefit them if they do not understand the words?
2. What are some benefits of talking to infants about what you are doing while you are doing it?
3. How do open-ended questions build language and cognitive skills?
4. What are some examples of environmental print one might see in a classroom?

Teaching Tip

Book Awards
Another way to select quality children's books is by looking at award-winning books. These books have been vetted by various groups to meet specific criteria and are usually a desirable choice. Here are a few of the annual awards for children's books.

The Caldecott Medal
The Caldecott Medal is awarded to the artist of the most distinguished American picture book for children published during the preceding year by the Association for Library Service to Children. The selection committee recognizes additional books as worthy of attention by designating them as Caldecott Honor Books.

The award honors Randolph Caldecott, one of a group of influential children's illustrators working in England in the 19th century. His illustrations for children were unique for their time in both their humor and ability to create a sense of movement, vitality, and action that complemented the stories they accompanied.

The Charlotte Zolotow Award
The Charlotte Zolotow Award is given annually to the author of the best picture book published in the United States. The award honors the work of Charlotte Zolotow, a distinguished children's book editor and author of more than 70 picture books, including classic works such as *Mr. Rabbit and the Lovely Present* and *William's Doll*.

The award, administered by the Cooperative Children's Book Center of the School of Education, University of Wisconsin-Madison, Zolotow's alma mater, may identify up to 5 honor books and 10 titles to call attention to outstanding writing in picture books. Eligible books may be fiction, nonfiction, or folklore and must be appropriate for young children.

Children's Book Award
The Children's Book Award is a national United Kingdom award for children's books selected entirely by children. Owned and coordinated by The Federation of Children's Book Groups, it is highly respected by teachers, parents, and librarians. Any child in the United Kingdom is eligible to vote for their favorite book.

Theodor Seuss Geisel Medal
The Theodor Seuss Geisel Medal, awarded by the American Library Association, honors the author(s) and illustrator(s) who made the most distinguished contribution to beginning reader books published in the United States during the preceding year.

8.4 Guidelines for Reading Aloud

The approach to reading to infants differs from that for reading to a group of preschoolers or school-age children. Even school-age children enjoy listening to a story, especially if it is an engrossing story that is above their ability to read themselves. This section lists some general guidelines for reading aloud to children and then specific guidelines for reading aloud according to children's ages.

General guidelines. Use these guidelines when reading to children of all ages:
- Find a comfortable pace and do not rush. Take your time, pause, and give children time to process the story. Do not overwhelm the child with too many words, rapid talk, or drilling questions.
- Keep eye contact with the children as much as possible to watch their responses (**Figure 8.5**).
- Introduce the book. Give a short sentence or two that relates the book to your children. "Billy, I know that you like kittens. This book is about a kitten named Stripes." "Yesterday we went to the park. This book is about some ducks who make their home in a big park."

Figure 8-5 A kindergarten teacher maintains eye contact while reading aloud to a group, holding the book for all to see. How does holding the book this way contribute to children's understanding and enjoyment of the story? How does eye contact help the teacher maintain children's interest?

- Make sure everyone can see the illustrations. Many teachers become adept at reading while holding the book to their side. Move the book around and share the pictures.
- Point to characters or objects as you read about them.
- Read with expression. Let your voice project anticipation. Use your voice and face to convey meaning. You may want to whisper certain passages or talk in a gruff voice to depict the character. The great big Billy Goat Gruff should talk differently from the wee little Billy Goat Gruff.
- Use introductory activities to launch the story. For example, to prepare to read *Millions of Cats*, ask children how much a hundred is, a thousand, a million. They will respond with a version of a whole lot, many, and so on. Then discuss how you are going to read a book about many, many, many cats.

Infants. When reading to infants, follow these guidelines:

- Focus on sound. New babies cannot see as well as adults, but their hearing is acute. Babies will respond to your excitement or funny sound effects.
- Read with the baby on your lap or while the baby wiggles on the floor.
- Share lullabies, short songs, and rhythmic books.
- Choose books with high-contrast colors, such as black and white.
- Babies like to look at familiar items. Look for books with pictures of babies and familiar objects in them.
- You do not have to read the book to make it a valuable experience. Simply talking about the pictures has value.

Toddlers. These guidelines apply to reading to toddlers:

- Choose books that offer an opportunity for conversation to support developing verbal skills.
- Let toddlers help you turn the pages. Keep study board books available for independent reading.
- Keep reading fun and make conversation pleasant. Never associate reading time with negative consequences.

- Engage children in the story by discussing the pictures, asking them to predict what will happen next, or to tell you how they think a character might feel or why they did something.
- Follow the toddlers' lead as to how long the story time should be. A story does not have to be finished to have value.

Preschoolers. Follow these guidelines when reading to preschoolers:
- Clarify and explain new terminology, relating new words to what they already know.
- Ask questions about the story, especially questions that call on children to predict or analyze.
- Do not just read stories and put the book away. Use stories as catalysts for other activities, such as providing puppets for children to retell the story. Put the book in the reading area for children to revisit the story and "read" on their own.

Young school-age children. When reading to school-age children, the following guidelines are appropriate:
- Discuss unfamiliar words that children encounter in their reading.
- Ask analytical questions and questions that compare or contrast characters or plots.
- Vary your expression and pace; this becomes more important because there may be fewer or smaller illustrations in books for this age group.

Holding Conversations about Books

Having conversations about books builds children's vocabulary, understanding, reasoning, and the language skills that lead to reading. When reading with preschool children, ask questions about the following:
- **The illustrations.** "What do you see on this page?" "What is happening in the picture?"
- **What happens next (predicting).** "What do you think the ducks will do now that they are at the pond?"
- **Relate to the children's experiences.** "It looks like the ducks are going to play in the water with their friends. What do you like to play with your friends?"
- **Identify the characters' feelings.** "How do you think the little duck feels now that she has to leave the pond?"

When to Read to Children

Many teachers primarily read to children during their circle or group time. However, there are many other opportunities during the day to read to children either individually or in a small group. Here are some of the additional times to enjoy books:
- at arrival time
- during learning center time
- while waiting during bathroom time
- during and after mealtimes
- before naptime
- at the end of the day

In addition, if you have readers in your program, consider setting aside a time for older children to read to younger ones.

Creating a Library Center in Your Classroom

A library center is an area of the classroom set aside for books and other language experiences. It is a place for children to be alone or with friends and to enjoy the world of literature. Additionally, it can be a place to relax in a soft, comfortable environment and get away from active, noisy areas. Here are some suggestions for making a library area enticing and relaxing for children:
- Include soft items such as rugs, pillows, and stuffed animals (**Figure 8.6**).
- Add nontoxic plants for a pleasant, homelike environment.

RainStar/E+ via Getty Images

Figure 8-6 Pillows and a rug provide a quiet, relaxing place to enjoy a story. *Why is it important to include soft elements in the environment?*

- Display story-related puppets, props, and toys to expand on stories. A puppet theater can encourage children to create and tell their own stories.
- Have a flannel board at children's height with an assortment of flannel board or magnetic items nearby for telling familiar stories or creating new ones.
- Display books with covers visible so children can easily select the one they want.
- Have a core of favorite books available, but add new ones frequently, especially those related to current themes.
- Once books are read aloud, put them in the library center to be available to children to enjoy again individually.
- Include recorded stories for children to listen to individually.
- Choose books according to past and current themes and projects. Consideration should be given to gender equality, culture, personal abilities, and race or ethnic background in the story line and pictures.

More information on setting up a library center is located in Chapter 2, "The Early Childhood Learning Environment."

☑ CHECKPOINT

1. How can maintaining eye contact while reading in groups help engage children?
2. Why does reading with expression help maintain children's attention on the story?
3. What are some ways to relate books to children's experiences?
4. Why is it desirable to have a reading area with books children can select on their own?

Teaching Tip

Innovative Reading Programs

The use of therapy dogs or other therapy animals is a growing trend in preschools and primary schools. Children can read to, talk to, or just enjoy comfort from these gentle creatures. Such animals must be well trained and healthy. Children who are having difficulty learning to read or using language may find it beneficial to interact with therapy animals. These interactions can reduce any anxiety that may be associated with reading.

The Reading Education Assistance Dogs® (R.E.A.D.) program improves children's reading and communication skills by employing a method of reading to an animal. R.E.A.D. companions are registered therapy animals whose owners or handlers bring them to schools, libraries, and other settings to work as reading companions for children. R.E.A.D. was the first program to utilize therapy animals to help children improve their reading and communication skills.

Reading to animals also helps children learn to love books and reading. More than 7,000 therapy teams have trained and registered with the program in the United States, Canada, the United Kingdom, Italy, France, Sweden, South Africa, Spain, the Netherlands, Norway, and other countries.

Bibliotherapy

Bibliotherapy is a system of using books and reading materials to aid in understanding emotions. At a basic level, it consists of selecting material relevant to life situations. The concept is based on identifying with others through literature and art. For example, a grieving child who reads or is read a story about another child who has lost a parent may feel less alone in the world.

In *A Chair for My Mother*, author Vera B. Williams tells the story of a young girl and her mother and their dedication to restoring their lives back to normal after a fire and the loss of all their possessions. The book emphasizes hard work, empathy, and appreciation, helping children to see that there is hope even after a tragedy.

Ira Sleeps Over, by Bernard Waber, is about a little boy named Ira who is excited to receive an invitation to sleep over at his friend Reggie's house. Ira's sister tells him that if he brings his teddy bear to the sleepover, Reggie will make fun of him and call him a baby. However, it turns out that Reggie has his own teddy bear. Realizing that Reggie will not make fun of him, Ira goes home to get his bear, then returns and falls asleep. The book helps children be comfortable and less afraid of being different.

8.5 Emergent Literacy

When children's brain development is supported through a responsive environment, literacy skills emerge from birth. From birth throughout the preschool years, children develop knowledge of spoken language. This is the first of the abilities that children need to be able to learn to read and write in school. **Emergent literacy** is a term used to describe the way children's literacy develops over time, beginning in infancy, as a result of children's experiences with spoken language, books, and print. Emergent literacy builds on what children know to promote later success in reading and writing. This includes exploring the sounds of language, building print awareness, and developing beginning writing skills. Students build comprehension skills, decoding skills, and phonological awareness.

Emergent Literacy by Age

As with many skills, literacy is predicted to emerge in a general timeframe, given good health and a nurturing, safe environment. This section reviews the developmental skills by age, beginning at birth, with suggestions for how development can be supported.

Infants. Children from birth to 12 months old will:
- imitate the tones and rhythms of the adults who talk to them.
- delight in listening to familiar jingles, rhymes, and chants.

- play along in games, such as peek-a-boo and "Pat-a-Cake."
- show interest in books that feature familiar objects.
- begin to name objects aloud.
- make animal noises, such as "moo" and "baa."

To encourage development of these skills:
- read simple picture books together and talk about what you see.
- tell stories and talk about daily events and routines.
- talk about what children are doing. "I see you are rolling the ball."
- read action rhymes and encourage children to imitate the movements being described.
- follow children's cues. If a child shows interest in an object, point to it and name it. "It looks like you want the block."

Toddlers. Children from 12 months old to 3 years old will:
- enjoy predictable songs and books, such as *Over in the Meadow* and *The Napping House*.
- understand that their written name signifies something special that pertains specifically to them.
- enjoy listening to stories, rhymes, and songs; doing fingerplays; and looking at books.
- scribble enthusiastically.
- like riddles and guessing games.

To encourage development of these skills:
- Play word and finger games such as "Eensy Weensy Spider" and "Where is Thumbkin?" to reinforce following directions, listening, and speaking.
- Share books that include repeated rhymes or phrases so children can join in.
- Encourage children to listen to sounds, words, rhymes, and poems.
- Look at and "read" books together.
- Provide art material such as crayons, markers, and large sheets of paper.
- Point to pictures or objects and describe to children what they are seeing. For example, "There's a dog. He is running."
- Talk with children about things that interest them in books. Some toddlers may not have the language to share what they see in books. Be sensitive to language differences and support developing language skills.

Preschoolers. A child from 3 to 5 years old will:
- begin to enjoy group activities and making friends.
- recognize many logos and signs in context.
- develop fine motor coordination to better facilitate writing and form some letters.
- understand that reading progresses from left to write and top to bottom.
- learn that print, rather than just pictures, carries the meaning of the story.
- understand that writing conveys messages and has a specific form and set of symbols.
- pretend to read, using visual cues to remember the words to favorite stories.
- recognize and name some letters and the sounds they represent.
- enjoy playing games involving written words and numbers.

To encourage development of these skills:
- Provide a rich variety of fiction and nonfiction reading materials.
- Choose age-appropriate picture books with clear story lines that relate to events and issues in the child's life.
- Point out words on signs or in the environment that begin with the same letter as a child's name.
- Offer wordless picture books for children to "read" to peers or adults.
- Encourage children to express themselves and use writing by asking them to take messages, make posters, or write stories.
- Encourage children to make lists of their favorite games and toys or what they plan to do.

- Post simple messages and read them to children.
- Encourage children to write their names and words they know.
- Be aware of the language level of each child. Ask children questions geared toward their level, and extend and expand on what they say.
- Support children as they experiment and grow in their developing language by listening and responding to their questions and comments.

Young school-age children. A child from 6 to 8 years old will:
- recognize, sound out, or identify an increasing number of words.
- enjoy writing and giving written messages to others.
- attempt to do their own writing, often using invented spelling and standard spelling using the words they hear.
- read or retell a story from a book using visual and print clues.

To encourage development of these skills:
- Support the love of books by reading together and sharing favorite stories.
- Encourage story dictation to practice writing.
- Involve children in reading signs, recipes, instructions, maps, and other print material they see and use every day.
- Encourage children to write words and read books with more complicated story lines.
- Play rhyming, board, and card games together.
- Introduce simple chapter books as children are ready.
- Learn ways to gather information and access resources in the community.

Emergent Writing

Emergent writing refers to a child's growing ability to use marks to represent words. It includes the ability to make marks on a paper, or the mechanics of writing. When toddlers make large circular strokes with a crayon, they are demonstrating the beginning of the fine motor skills required for writing. They develop a growing understanding that marks (or print) have meaning and that the marks represent spoken language.

The Stages of Writing

Just as other development areas have various stages, learning to write also follows predictable stages (**Figure 8.7**). The emergent literacy skills that young children develop are the foundation for later reading and writing success. Educators who intentionally engage with children and provide thoughtful and interesting language, literacy, and writing experiences provide children with a solid foundation for learning to read and write.

Supporting Emergent Writing

For preschoolers, provide writing materials in a dedicated writing center as well as in other areas of the classroom to encourage children's writing exploration. Materials may include paper, pencils, fat crayons, playdough (to use to form letters), stamps, and journals. For an interesting twist, children can use chalk and wet cotton swabs to write on dark construction paper. Provide many opportunities for children to see written language in use. Charts, names on cubbies, labels on items, and signs give children the chance to see that writing is important and that the marks represent words. They will begin to make associations about similar letters and sounds.

Talk with children about what they are creating. Ask open-ended questions, such as, "What can you tell me about your writing?" Model and integrate writing throughout the day. Write a daily message on the board and read it with children. Create charts and graphs, and make labels. When children see the meaning, value, and uses of writing, they will be more interested in the writing process.

Offer specific support as children move through the writing process. Many children will ask how to spell words. Take time to answer children's questions and guide them during these meaningful experiences. Use story dictation: Listen to and write down

The Stages of Writing

Example	Age	Stage
 summerphotos/iStock via Getty Images	15 to 30 months old	**Random scribbling.** Young children make random marks, or scribbles.
 jacoblund/iStock via Getty Images	2 to 3 years old	**Controlled scribbling.** With increased motor control, children begin to make repeated lines and patterns.
 Ann in the uk/Shutterstock.com	2½ to 3½ years old	**Lines and patterns/emergent writing.** Children begin to imitate letters in the environment, may make up their own letters, and use letter-like forms.
 Cmspic/Shutterstock.com	3 to 4 years old	**Transitional printing.** Children use their knowledge of letter sounds as they start to develop more conventional writing. Children may write one letter to represent a word and gradually add more letters to their words as they progress toward more conventional writing.
 Hakase_/iStock via Getty Images	3½ years old and up	**Conventional writing.** Children use more traditional spelling as they learn more about letters, letter sounds, and how to put letters together to form words.

Goodheart-Willcox Publisher

Figure 8-7 The Stages of Writing. Why is it important for teachers to know these stages?

children's ideas as they talk about a drawing or story. Read the story back to the child, calling attention to the words as you do. Many children will enjoy sharing their story with others.

Teachers should write children's names on their work, being careful to use the correct formation of the letters until children can write their names themselves. Children will learn to recognize their names sooner if the same form is always used. When children try to write their names, they should be supported in their efforts but never pressured.

Special Language and Literacy Issues

When children are learning a language other than the one primarily spoken in their home, they will need extra support in navigating between the two languages. Many learning materials are now available in several languages, and electronic translation programs can provide ready access to the new and most familiar language. Bilingualism is a highly desirable skill in our global society, and programs that assist children in becoming proficient in more than one language can help children build skills in both languages. The teacher's challenge is to differentiate instruction to ensure that these students are full participants while learning another language. A bilingual adult who can involve children in both languages along with many visual clues can facilitate this practice. Children who use sign language can benefit from similar adaptations.

When children are not developing skills as expected for their age, a referral for screening may be advised. There may be a hearing or other issue that will benefit from intervention if recognized. For additional information about children with special needs, see Chapter 3, "The Inclusive Classroom."

☑ CHECKPOINT

1. Why does reading depend on receptive language?
2. How do rhymes, songs, and fingerplays build literacy skills?
3. What are some ways to demonstrate the practical use of writing?

8.6 Assessing Program Practices

The *Early Childhood Environment Rating Scale*®, Third Edition (Harms et al. 2014) is a classroom evaluation tool that is widely used to assess the quality of the environment for children. It can also be used to determine a benchmark on which to base improvement. The scale uses the following criteria related to language and literacy as indicators of quality.

Helping Children to Expand Vocabulary

This section rates how staff talk to children in a way that builds their understanding and use of words. Examples of appropriate practices include using many descriptive words, explaining the meaning of unfamiliar words, and providing materials and activities that introduce words. The scale also rates the teacher's accommodations for children with special needs or whose home language is different.

Encouraging Children to Use Language

This section rates staff's interesting questions posed to children and their conversations with children during play. It rates the staff's positive responses to children's attempts to communicate and assistance in helping children communicate verbally with each other, such as teaching them the words they need. Also rated are communication activities that take place during both free play and routines including social talk about home and family life, activities in the community, feelings, and other non-school topics.

Staff Use of Books with Children

Rated in this section is the staff's use of books during whole group, small group, and individual activities. It includes accommodations for children who need additional support, such as those less fluent in the classroom language or those with developmental delays. The section rates the appropriate use of books related to current activities or themes and discusses the books' content. Also rated is the use of books to help answer questions and to provide information on topics of interest to the children.

Encouraging Children's Use of Books

This section rates the number and selection of books accessible to children and how they are displayed to encourage children's use. It rates the arrangement of a defined interest center with comfortable space and furnishings and the interest shown by the staff when children choose to use books independently.

Becoming Familiar with Print

Rated in this section are the staff's explanation and use of print as a tool, dictation taken by the staff of what a child says, and encouragement for the child to write. It rates the combination of visible print with pictures and those related to current topics. Also rated is the staff's frequent pointing out of letters and words when reading and calling attention to the letters or works in a manner that engages children. The scale rates the use of picture/word instructions that guide children through multistep activities such as handwashing or a food preparation recipe.

It is important for staff to balance listening and talking appropriately for the age and abilities of children during communication activities. For example, leave time for children to respond, and try to avoid answering for them. For children with limited communication skills, help them verbalize their thoughts. Also, link children's spoken communication with written language. For example, write what children dictate and read it back to them.

☑ CHECKPOINT

1. Why is it important to give children time to respond to questions or statements?
2. How can communication with children help develop cognitive ability?
3. What are some examples of materials that build literacy and reasoning skills?

From the Field

Jade Romero
Family engagement is important for all children. For ELL (English language learner) children, it is important to incorporate the children's home languages into school events, such as a Family Reading Night. Offer books in the children's home languages and encourage families to read them together. Give families information about the benefits of biliteracy. Model a read-aloud to show families ways to engage their children in reading. Offer individualized support. Help families identify areas of need and provide tailored strategies and resources to support their children's literacy development. Make use of public resources. Take advantage of free or low-cost programs offered by the local library or other community organizations that provide literacy-focused activities or resources and relay literacy information to families.

Jade Romero
Certified Elementary ESL Teacher
Robert C. Hill Elementary School
Romeoville, IL

Jade Romero

Figure 8-8

8.7 Family Matters

It is imperative that we share with families the important role that interactions play in language development. Families need to understand the value of talking and reading to their children.

Parent Newsletters

One way to communicate information about literacy to parents is to create parent newsletters. **Figure 8.9** shows a sample newsletter that might be sent home to families or posted on a program's website.

Book Bag Guide for Parents

Another way to encourage parents to support literacy at home is to institute a book bag project. To make book bags, use a tote bag or shopping bag to hold a book, a small notebook, and an activity sheet related to the book. Laminating the activity sheet will help it withstand frequent use. **Figure 8.10** is a sample instruction sheet for parents to include in the book bag.

Gateway Montessori School

February Newsletter

Emergent Literacy

Young children's emergent literacy skills are the building blocks for later reading and writing. From birth through the preschool years, children develop knowledge of spoken language; the sounds that form words, letters, and writing; and an enjoyment of books. You, as parents, are the best teachers to prepare your child for this important task. Here are some key facts to remember about children's progress in learning to read and write:

- Children get ready to read and write long before they start school.
- Young children have short attention spans but enjoy repeating favorite activities. Families can share these activities frequently.
- Parents know their children well and can take advantage of times when their child is interested and in the mood for sharing a story.
- Other family members can become involved so that the child will have several different people with whom to engage and learn.

Words are symbols that stand for items, actions, or concepts. The more words that children acquire and understand, the more adept they become at using these symbols. The more words that toddlers and preschoolers have in their vocabularies, the more complex their thinking can become. Therefore, everything you do to enhance language development also encourages intellectual development. Talk to children about the events that are happening during the day. Read books to them. Sing with them. Describe what you and they are seeing and doing. Encourage them to use words to express their ideas. Through these frequent exchanges, your child will master the beginning skills of reading.

Goodheart-Willcox Publisher; (icons) M.Style/Shutterstock.com

Figure 8-9 Emergent literacy skills foster children's success in reading and writing later in school. What can families do at home to promote a child's emergent literacy skills?

Gateway Montessori School

Welcome!

Studies show that reading to children gives them an advantage in school. You and your child are off on a new reading adventure that will prepare them for success. Have fun!

Every Friday, your child can choose a book bag to take home for the weekend. The book bag will contain:

- a book that is appropriate for reading to your child.
- directions for two activities related to the book.
- materials needed to complete the activities.
- a notebook to record your experience.

Set aside time for reading and doing the activities with your child. Identify a quiet spot where you and your child will not be interrupted. Read the book first yourself to become familiar with the story so that you can read with enthusiasm and make the appropriate growls, roars, squeaks, and special voices when you share the book with your child. Read the book using the suggested questions or activities to help your child develop comprehensive and reasoning skills.

Complete the activity together and use the notebook to record how your child reacted to the story, the activity, and your time together. Be sure all materials are replaced in the bag, and return it to school on Monday. Let your child's teacher know if there is any problem with the bag or its contents, or if you have any suggestions or comments about the book or the activity.

Thank you, and happy reading!
Mrs. Hernandez

1

Book Bag Activity Sheet

In this book bag, you will find:

- the book *Good Night, Gorilla* by Peggy Rathmann.
- questions to ask your child about the story as you read it aloud.
- directions for two activities related to the book.
- a small flashlight and a set of keys.
- a collection of small plastic animals.
- a notebook to record your experience.

This book has only a few words, and the pictures tell the story. When you read the book to your child, talk about the pictures, naming the animals and describing what they are doing. Ask your child questions such as:
- Why do you think the zookeeper had a flashlight?
- How did the gorilla get the zookeeper's keys?
- What did the gorilla do with the keys?
- What does the mouse do with the banana?
- Do you think the armadillo is a baby? Why or why not?
- Do you think the zookeeper knew the animals followed him?
- How did the zookeeper's wife feel when she turned on the light?

Activity One: Use the flashlight, keys, and plastic animals to retell the story. Which animal does the gorilla let out of its cage first? Which one is let out second? Which animal is let out of its cage third? Which animal is let out fourth? Which is the last animal let out of its cage?

Activity Two: Look at the book and see if you can find:
- items the gorilla plays with.
- a bunch of bananas.
- items the elephant plays with.
- a toy giraffe and a toy hyena.

2

Goodheart-Willcox Publisher; (icons) M.Style/Shutterstock.com

Figure 8-10 Sending home newsletters is one way for teachers to help families get involved in their children's education. *How does Mrs. Hernandez's letter encourage family involvement?*

☑ CHECKPOINT

1. Why is it important to involve families in children's language development?
2. How can an activity based on a book reinforce concepts and language?

Chapter 8 Review and Assessment

Chapter Summary

8.1 Explain the 30-million-word gap and why it is significant.
- Children who receive few or no positive verbal interactions with adults are often behind in vocabulary and other language skills important to succeed in school.
- Children in lower-income environments hear far fewer words than those in more financially secure families.

8.2 Describe strategies to encourage language development.
- Language is any system used to communicate and share information, ideas, and feelings and is basic to other areas of the curriculum. It is highly based on the child's experiences, especially in conversations.
- Receptive language describes a person's understanding of what they hear and see, and expressive language is the ability to communicate ideas, information, and feelings to others.

8.3 Identify how adult responses and interactions support language development.
- Language and literacy experiences can be integrated into all areas of the curriculum and all learning centers.
- One advantage of the learning center approach is that a word learned in the dramatic play area, such as *kale*, might be used in the art area as a child draws a picture.
- An early childhood professional can foster both receptive and expressive language through indirect and direct methods.
- Adults can promote language through using self-talk and parallel talk, expanding on what children say, asking open-ended questions, and forming communication loops that lead to conversations.
- Open-ended questions encourage children to talk and give longer answers than questions that can be answered with *yes*, *no*, or other one-word answers.
- Literacy involves objects, narrative skills, experiences, sequencing, phonological awareness, and symbols. Numerous opportunities occur throughout the day to provide experiences with literacy.

8.4 Explain the role of reading aloud in language and literacy development.
- Reading aloud can be more effective if adults take time to prepare for the reading. Readers should read the story ahead, learn to vary their voice, and make sure that all children can see the illustrations.
- Literacy can be encouraged by creating a library center in the classroom that provides a place for a child to engage with books alone or with a few friends.
- One way to encourage literacy is by paying attention to environmental print, including signs, labels, and other examples of print used purposefully in the child's environment.

8.5 Describe criteria in selecting materials and implementing strategies that foster emergent literacy skills in young children.
- Educators who intentionally engage with children and provide thoughtful and interesting language, literacy, and writing experiences provide children with a solid foundation for learning to read and write.
- Select quality children's literature with appealing stories and illustrations. Noting and reviewing books that have received awards is one way to choose books for children.
- Learning to write progresses through stages, just as other developmental areas do.
- Bilingualism is a highly desirable skill in our global society, and programs that assist children in becoming proficient in more than one language can help children build skills in both languages.

8.6 Identify methods for assessing program practices.
- The Early Childhood Environment Rating Scale® is an assessment tool that measures how well a program meets the needs of children. The section of the scale for language and literacy can help one measure the effectiveness of programs and provide a guide to improvement.

8.7 Describe methods to engage families in their children's literacy.
- Family engagement in supporting their child's development in language and literacy is important because families can provide many more opportunities for their child to hear stories and engage in conversation than a teacher can provide in school.
- Families can help their children develop an understanding of print at an early age to make connections between words and meaning.
- By engaging children at an early age by reading aloud and allowing children to observe those around them engaged in reading activities, families help foster a lifelong passion for reading that leads to benefits in all areas of development as they grow older.
- Language skills are critical to a child's future success and development in many areas. Adults must pay attention and respond appropriately to children's attempts to communicate. By responding to children, adults can help them learn language that will help them later become happy and productive citizens.

Recall and Application

1. **True or False.** The 30-million-word gap refers to the number of interactions that a child hears at school.
2. **True or False.** There is a positive relationship between the size of a child's vocabulary and the child's future reading ability.
3. **True or False.** A child's experience with spoken language has little impact on emergent literacy.
4. **True or False.** Open-ended questions are questions that can be answered in many ways.
5. **True or False.** Self-talk and parallel talk add descriptive words and help expand language skills.
6. **True or False** As children listen to you read a book to them, they build vocabulary in an indirect manner.
7. **True or False.** When asking questions to help build vocabulary, it is best to use questions that can be answered by *yes* or *no*.
8. A communication loop includes each of the following *except* _____.
   A. the child's attempt to communicate
   B. taking turns in talking
   C. the adult responding to the child
   D. answering for the child if they are taking too long
9. **True or False.** If you read a book aloud, there is no value in discussing the book because the children have already heard the story.
10. **True or False.** Reading aloud should not be restricted to circle or group time.
11. **True or False.** Any book that includes large pictures is appropriate for a toddler.
12. **True or False.** Predictable books encourage cognitive skills.

Chapter 9

The World We Live In: Social Studies

Standards Covered in This Chapter

NAEYC
NAEYC —1b, 1c, 2a, 2c, 3b, 4a, 4b, 5a, 5c, 6e

DAP
DAP—1a, 1b, 1c, 1e, 2a, 2b, 2c, 2e, 2g, 4a, 4b, 5c, 5e

Learning Outcomes

After reading this chapter, you should be able to:

9.1 Describe the concept of social studies as it applies to young children.
9.2 Identify appropriate components of social studies for early childhood.
9.3 Explain the cultural considerations in teaching social studies.
9.4 Explain the role of the teacher in designing and guiding social studies experiences.
9.5 Identify ways to evaluate social studies opportunities offered.
9.6 Describe ways to involve families in activities.

Chapter opener image credit: fstop123/E+ via Getty Images

Key Terms

documentation board
ecology
economics
empathy
stereotyping
visual schedule

Introduction

First-grader Jasmine loves to have playdates with her friend Betty. Betty lives with her family above their neighborhood grocery store. When Jasmine visits, she and Betty are each allowed to select a soft drink from the cooler. Jasmine is envious because she thinks being able to grab a soft drink anytime she pleases would be a wonderful way to live.

Jasmine's other friend, Vicky, lives downtown in a second-floor apartment, close enough to walk to movies. Jasmine imagines that Vicky must go to the movies anytime she wants, and this seems like a wonderful way to live. Going to the movies is an occasional treat for Jasmine.

When Jasmine's cousin, Melanie, visits from West Texas, she and her family stay at a hotel with a swimming pool. Jasmine is once again envious, wishing she could wake up and hop in a pool on a hot summer day.

While these ways of living seemed very different and more desirable to Jasmine, as she grew older, she recognized that her perceptions were wrong. Betty did not get soft drinks anytime she wanted them; Vicky did not get to go to the movies whenever she wanted; and while Melanie enjoyed the swimming pool, it certainly was not an everyday occurrence. In many ways, Jasmine and her friends were much alike. The soft drinks, movies, and swimming were occasional treats, rather than a daily experience.

The ways in which people live and work in groups are the essence of social studies for young children. Like Jasmine's perceptions, both adults' and children's perceptions may be incorrect. This chapter takes a closer look at what social studies entails and how people are all more alike than different.

9.1 What Is Social Studies for Young Children?

Social living requires people to develop a sense of cooperation, fairness, and other skills necessary for getting along with others. It involves creating or following a structure of governance and responsibility. These skills begin in the early years, as children learn how to relate to others in their environment. The toddler who gently pats the arm of an upset child, the preschooler who shares the blocks with another to enjoy building together, and the school-age child who follows the rules of a playground game are practicing the skills of living in society.

Social studies is the curriculum area pertaining to how people live together in the social world. Young children are interested in the similarities and differences between people and how people interact with the natural world of animals and plants. Social studies is the study of how lives are alike and yet different, and includes an appreciation of those similarities and differences. For example, children in most cultures live in families, celebrate holidays, play games, and practice religion. However, the types of families, holidays, games, and religions vary greatly.

For young children, social studies begins with a focus on themselves, since that is the world of the very young. Self-concept, therefore, is a logical starting point in early childhood social studies. To help young children have a positive view of themselves, help them accept their feelings, recognize the range of emotions they experience, and learn that others have similar feelings. Help them understand that what they say and do affects others in their social world.

From one's self, the child's world extends progressively to family, friends, the neighborhood, the broader community, and eventually the world (**Figure 9.1**). A successful social studies curriculum guides the child through these entities.

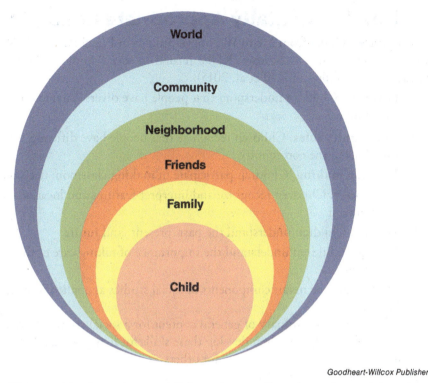

Goodheart-Willcox Publisher

Figure 9-1 This graphic shows how a child's understanding about the social world expands with experiences. How should this progression inform the experiences you provide for children?

For infants and toddlers, the social studies content is self-development. Adults support this development by providing toys, materials, and experiences to encourage exploration and interactions. Infants and toddlers play alone, beside others, and then with others, developing their understanding of themselves through nurturing guidance from families and other significant adults. In these early years, teachers encourage respect for others and provide opportunities for exposure to varied ways of living. They teach respect by singing songs and reading stories from various cultures, displaying pictures that reflect different types of families, and modeling an appreciation for all family backgrounds. Even toddlers develop an understanding of classroom community responsibility through putting toys away and sharing materials.

In the preschool and primary years, social studies poses a structure well suited for theme-based curriculum content, activities, and experiences organized around a topic with many opportunities for exploration and investigation. Such content provides a means for acquiring planning, cooperation, and problem-solving skills and for developing interpersonal coping skills and strategies.

In developing these social concepts, teachers first focus on what children know and can do, then help them expand their understandings to the broader world around them. In today's world, young children must learn to operate in a society that values respect for diversity, equity, and appreciation of differences.

✓ CHECKPOINT

1. Do you think a theme approach works well with social studies? Why or why not?
2. What experiences have you had with people who live differently from you?
3. How does social studies for infants and toddlers focus on them and their families?

9.2 Developmentally Appropriate Concepts

In her article, "Going from Me to We: Social Studies in Preschool," Polly Neill includes six key developmental indicators (KDIs) related to social studies. The KDIs that she identifies are as follows (Neill et al. 2015):

1. **Diversity.** Children understand that people have diverse characteristics, interests, and abilities.
2. **Community roles.** Children recognize that people have different roles and functions in the community.
3. **Decision making.** Children participate in making classroom decisions.
4. **Geography.** Children recognize and interpret features and locations in their environment.
5. **History.** Children understand the past, present, and future.
6. **Ecology.** Children understand the importance of taking care of their environment.

Overall, these are the major components of social studies as applied to young children's curriculum.

The following is a summary of general content for a social studies curriculum. Overall, social studies helps children develop these skills for living (**Figure 9.2**):

- A healthy self-concept and respect for others
- Self-control and independence
- Ways of relating to and working with others
- An understanding of the purpose and need for rules
- Attitudes and skills to live in a democracy
- Respect for other people's feelings, ideas, and property
- An understanding of the roles that people have in life
- Recognition of the various types and value of work
- Appreciation of the past and its relationship to the present

Preschool and primary-age children can develop a sense of civic responsibility through exploring rich thematic topics such as food, clothing, shelter, money, communication, family living, and transportation. Using such themes, children and teachers can form hypotheses, gather information, summarize, and draw conclusions. Children can organize information with pictures, maps and charts, or other methods, depending on the child's skills and interests. Not only do children use the skills of social scientists in these investigations, but they also learn about civic engagement as they read, manage, and display data for others.

Following is a closer look at a common sequence of themes in curricula for young children. Curriculum plans often follow a succession of myself, my family, my friends, my neighbors, and then my community. Teachers build on children's developing understanding of themselves as part of the world.

Develop Children's Social Understanding

- Assist children in basic social-emotional growth and skills.
- Collaborate with families.
- Foster the development of integrity as children learn to interact responsibly with others.
- Demonstrate an anti-bias and inclusive approach.
- Emphasize cultures that are represented in the community.

Goodheart-Willcox Publisher

Figure 9-2 These suggestions provide an overview of how teachers can focus on children's development of social understanding. How do these factors contribute to children's understanding of their world?

Myself

Young children first learn about themselves as they experience what they can do and how adults react to them. Infants whose needs are met, who are cuddled and responded to, learn they are important, loved, and valued. Those who do not receive such support may not develop the positive self-concept and trust necessary to relate constructively to others. Children develop self-understanding and respect as competent human beings through acceptance, and they develop respect for others' similarities and differences and an appreciation of their own cultural and ethnic background. Young children develop skills to interact positively with others and an understanding that there are many ways of living. However, the best way for them to gain these characteristics is in how they are treated by others and how important adults in their lives respond to them.

My Family

The child's family provides the safety and security needed by a young child. Quality programs create emotionally safe environments when they promote awareness of and design curriculum that respects diversity, supporting inclusion and acceptance of everyone. Educators have been aware of the importance of diversity education for many years. Diversity education begins with what teachers model and how well they relate to those unlike themselves.

The view of family has changed in the past few decades to become increasingly broad. Today, a family can no longer be defined solely as two adults of the same race or opposite gender raising one or more children. Adults can keep children emotionally safe by modeling accepting, inclusive behavior, and respecting and supporting their familial origins. Families may include adopted children, grandparents, stepparents and siblings, extended family, or family friends. There may be more than one ethnicity, nationality, religion, or language spoken within the family. There may be one, two, or several parents and caregivers, including stepparents and same-sex parents. Yet all families have a common goal—to raise healthy, happy, and well-loved human beings. Educators are role models who must stretch their definition of family to include all people who come together to love, guide, and support children.

Teaching Tip

Incorporating Family

A wise teacher incorporates the family into the classroom and curriculum to connect the child within the family to the classroom. For example, a teacher might demonstrate acceptance and support of family situations and cultures by:

- displaying pictures of each child's family on a bulletin board. Displaying these pictures demonstrates that each child's family is unique and welcome. A group picture of all of the children along with the teachers may be displayed to model inclusion.
- taking photos that show the children and their families in the classroom, at home, and in the neighborhood and posting them around the room or, with permission, to a class blog or website. Such activities help develop the attachment that is the basis of a sense of belonging in the community.
- including photos of families in child-made books to bridge the home, school, and community.
- reading books that depict different cultures and family structures.
- providing puzzles and learning materials that include children and adults of different races, ages, genders, capabilities, and settings.
- incorporating dolls and puppets with various physical features for dramatic play.
- including food, toys, artifacts, and music associated with different cultures.

My Friends and Neighbors

The next social relationship to develop is that of friends and neighbors. As children form friendships within the classroom or in their neighborhoods, they are learning to relate to a broader society. They learn that activities might be more enjoyable when others are included and that friends and neighbors can be helpful to each other.

Social learning and self-concept, including character development, can be supported during children's playtime. While constructing a block structure together, young children learn to negotiate, solve problems, and cope with strong feelings.

A teacher can incorporate many ways to help friendships develop. One way is by teaching children how to engage with others. Helping children understand friendly behaviors such as sharing, cooperating, and showing consideration for others helps them build friendships. For example, an adult says, "Julie, you might ask Chloe for help. I noticed that she knew how to open the paint jar she was using. I bet she would be happy to help you."

Although children gravitate toward other children—even infants want to be near other infants—they may need help in learning how to approach another child and interact. Asking for a toy rather than grabbing it, helping another child with a challenging task, or just being kind to another encourages friendships. As children begin to play together in groups, they sometimes need specific help in knowing what to say and how to join a group already engaged in play. Adults can help the process by teaching children the words to gain entrance into a play group. One way is to help a child learn to suggest a role. For example, 4-year-old Sonya is watching a group of classmates play grocery store, clearly wanting to join but not knowing how. Her teacher suggests, "Sonya, why don't you ask to be a shopper? Here's a tote bag. The grocery store I go to always has many shoppers." The teacher helped Sonya participate by encouraging her to take on a role in which she could be a part of the activity. Here are additional examples to encourage positive social behavior and friendship:

- Mr. Jack asks, "Allan, would you mind getting the paper for Branson? You're taller, and that would be helpful to him."
- Ms. Adams acknowledges, "LaTrenna, I saw how you helped our new student by showing her where to put the puzzles. Thank you so much for helping her."
- Leif says, "I see you're watching Mae build with the linking cubes. Do you think you'd like to make something together? You can ask if you might work with her on a project if you'd like."

Valuing Self and Others

Each of us has a racial and cultural identity. It is crucial for understanding who we are. It is important to recognize the following concepts when working in early childhood:

- Group identity influences self-concept and helps individuals see themselves in relation to others.
- Children are connected to their cultural background. They build self-esteem and cultural pride through identification with their traditions. Cultural pride is part of forming positive self-esteem.
- Children need a strong sense of self to appreciate others. They learn to value and enjoy diversity if adults teach them by example and words—by what they do and say. What people do always speaks louder than what they say.
- Children can learn the importance of valuing others. A child's circumstances, age, and needs determine the types of strategies to use.
- No one culture is superior or inferior to another. The cultures are simply different—a key point to remember and emphasize in your work with young children.
- Children can be helped to understand that there are many ways to do things. For example, all cultures have unique ways to dress, speak, play, celebrate holidays, and worship.
- Diversity is important to all segments of the population and affects many aspects of people's lives. In society, race, culture, and ethnicity impact the way people work, live, and relate to others.
- Although there are many differences in cultural groups, there are also many similarities.

Learning Empathy

An important part of friendship is **empathy**, the ability to feel the emotions of others (**Figure 9.3**). Even infants are empathetic by instinct. We are meant to be social beings and therefore respond to the mood of the group. Any teacher of infants will tell you that one vigorously crying baby will quickly lead to a room full of crying babies. Even the young can show empathy, and educators often see comforting behaviors from children toward others. An 18-month-old will offer a crying 10-month-old a pacifier, bottle, or favorite toy. The 10-month-old stops crying, and the 18-month-old is praised by the caregiver for being such a good helper and friend. Thus, the caregiver reinforces this prosocial comforting behavior, and the child is more likely to repeat the action for which praise was given. Adults do things for their friends because it makes both of them feel good. Infants are beginning to learn the concept and satisfaction of helpfulness.

Children learn empathy from how they themselves are treated. A child who was never comforted or treated with kindness may have difficulty showing empathy to others. Feelings of empathy are there by instinct, but children learn what to do about those feelings from the adults around them. Consequently, showing empathy to a child in distress not only calms the child but is an important modeling technique that helps children learn appropriate reactions to others.

Specific Social Skills

Social skills are behaviors that enable people to relate to others and interact socially in a positive and productive manner. What are the main social skills that people need as adults? When you consider those skills closely, you will see that many of them begin in childhood. The following are major social skills that children can develop in early childhood settings that will serve them well as adults:

- Cooperating and working with others begins as children learn to share and take turns, cooperating in play and cleanup tasks.
- Showing empathy and compassion for others is demonstrated as children invite another child to play and show concern for other children's feelings, by being helpful, kind, and considerate toward others.

RuslanDashinsky/E+ via Getty Images

Figure 9-3 A playmate shows empathy for a friend who was disappointed at being left out of a game. How can a teacher help children consider others' feelings in their interactions? What might a teacher do to acknowledge the child's empathic response?

- Being a responsible citizen emerges as children understand and follow simple rules, care for materials, and respect other people's property.
- Being an honest and a trustworthy person begins as children learn to understand the basic concepts of right and wrong.
- Appreciating diversity and their own culture is expressed as children develop self-esteem and show pride in who they are and what they have done, learning culturally appropriate manners and behaviors.
- Participating in social groups starts with children learning to navigate small groups of playmates in learning centers and outdoors.
- Collaborating with others develops as children learn to express their ideas, listen to others' ideas and suggestions, ask for help when needed, and say "no" politely when not accepting an invitation.
- Being a disciplined and confident individual begins when children try new things and show confidence in most daily situations, such as meeting a new friend or playing outside on a challenging swing.
- Inventing or initiating games with simple rules that one can share with others occurs. For example, a child might suggest, "Let's bury these rocks in the sandbox and see who can find the most."

My Community

Being part of the community, whether in a city or country landscape, brings new and different sounds, smells, and experiences to children's developing sense of location. The communities in which children live, as well as the quality and quantity of their involvement within the community, vary greatly. A child living in a city apartment has different experiences from a child living in a rural area (**Figure 9.4**), and both of those are different from a child that lives in a populated suburban area. A city child not allowed to go outdoors alone has different experiences than a city child allowed to navigate public transportation independently. Both of these are different from a rural child, whose playground may be forests and fields.

Although children may have experiences in their community such as buying groceries, that experience is distinctly different depending on whether the store is a neighborhood supermarket, mega-mart, local convenience store, or bodega. It also varies according to how much the accompanying adult manages to experience while shopping there. The child in a car picking up an online grocery order has less exposure to the process of selecting and purchasing food than a child going to a farmers' market and participating in making purchases.

Imgorhand/E+ via Getty Images   MBI/iStock/Getty Images Plus

Figure 9-4 Children's experiences vary, depending on where they live. How does the experience of children in a rural area differ from the experiences of children in a large city?

Thus, children enter the classroom with mixed concepts of community. Teachers can support and expand children's concepts of community by providing opportunities for exploring and being part of the larger school environment and community.

Plan visits to different classrooms around the school so children can share experiences with other children. Having common experiences links people and places and helps children make social connections outside of their families and classroom.

- Organize schoolwide family evenings. Families and children can participate in events together outside of school hours and develop a connection to the school while getting to know other students and families.
- Host schoolwide activities such as multigenerational family dinners or cultural celebrations to highlight commonalities and differences in traditions. Such events demonstrate that each family's culture is valued and respected.
- Determine which places in the community are familiar to the children. Consider other facets of those places that children can explore to develop a deeper understanding of their community. Most children are unaware of what happens behind the scenes in their favorite locations, such as a bakery, dollar store, or supermarket.
- Plan field trips in children's neighborhoods to local stores, parks, and museums. Involve children familiar with the destination site to assist in planning the excursion.
- Nurture children's awareness of their location by planning project-based investigations of the local environment. Begin the investigation by inviting children to share what they want to learn about the community. Watch to see what attracts their attention and what they are curious about.

Exploring how a local bakery produces their favorite treats adds depth to children's learning experiences and strengthens their understanding of what it takes to make their treats available. In-depth exploration helps children think about the environment and develop more personal connections. The longer time spent on an exploration project benefits students with disabilities and dual language learners who may need additional time to process information. Explore issues of accessibility with children. Have them assess whether they can easily enter stores or use equipment independently. Point out the uses of multiple languages on signs or in written materials (**Figure 9.5**). As children learn about their community, they will develop an understanding of the challenges that some people face in navigating to get what they need or want.

GWengoat/iStock/Getty Images Plus

Figure 9-5 Pointing out signs written in more than one language is one way to help children notice the diversity of their communities. What is another way to help children notice and value diversity?

Through exploration of the community, the various roles that individuals play become apparent to young children. The teachers, principals, cafeteria, and maintenance personnel are seen doing their work. The firefighters, police officers, and mail and parcel carriers are seen completing their jobs. The deli clerk, baker, stocker, cashier, and server are observed in everyday tasks. The concept of community encompasses knowledge about the people in it, and this knowledge expands the child's world.

Learning Geography

Even young children can begin to understand some basics of geography. They learn the terminology for geographic features, such as lake, hill, city block, and highway. They can draw maps and make replicas of an area using unit blocks. Here are additional ways to help children begin to develop an understanding of geography:

- On a walk, talk with children about the things they see, such as fountains, streets, or unique buildings. Discuss their locations in relation to other items. For example, "The library building is right across the street from the park," or "Did you notice that the statue is in the center of the park?"
- Take photos of familiar buildings and locations to make a map of the school or neighborhood. Children can glue the pictures on the map and label each location.
- Post photos of familiar buildings and landmarks in the block center, tinkering area, and other learning centers to suggest incorporating the buildings into the activities.
- Encourage children to make and use maps in conjunction with other activities. Block play can incorporate a model of their classroom, school, or neighborhood. Drawings can include local landmarks.
- Invite children to consider and describe their surroundings with questions such as:
    - What buildings are near the school?
    - Why is it important that there is a special place for buses to pick up children?
    - Is the auditorium far away from or near the cafeteria?
    - How could you rearrange equipment on the playground?

Becoming a Good Citizen

Becoming a good citizen begins when children are young. Understanding the need for and value of rules is one of the facets of a civilized society. Children learn about the need for rules in life by seeing the benefits of organization and routines in their classroom. Daily life in the classroom offers many opportunities for children to learn the importance of rules in groups. Teachers can talk to children about how rules help people live and work together in groups, but it is clearer when children experience the benefits. Through such experiences, children are building foundational understandings of civic responsibility.

People in the Community

As children progress in the development of social understandings, they begin to appreciate the concepts of living in a community and the roles that people in the community play. Consider asking families to share examples of what they do for work or play, or even hold video conferences with family members from different parts of the world. Be open to the possibility that field trips to unusual places may provide valuable experiences and learning, as the example of an out-of-the-ordinary field trip in the "Building a Gate" Case Study feature demonstrates.

The Economics of Work

Even economics has a place in a young child's social studies learning. **Economics** is the study of scarcity and its implications for the use of resources, production of goods and services, and growth of production and welfare over time. It includes complex issues of concern for equity and equality.

Case Study

Building a Gate

Tonya, a preschool teacher, was concerned about a shy child, Dustin, who was being raised by his grandparents. During a group-time discussion about the work that people do, Dustin mentioned he wished they could visit his grandfather's fence business. Wanting to support the child's relationship with his grandparents, Tonya took a chance on arranging a field trip to the grandfather's business.

When the class arrived, it was clear Dustin's grandfather enjoyed children and could talk confidently with them. He demonstrated and described the process of installing fence posts, even letting the children take turns using the post hole digger. He had arranged an area of soft dirt and small spades to let them dig. He asked thought-provoking questions about how long they thought it would take to dig the hole with a spoon or a scoop instead of the spade. Dustin's grandfather showed them how he measured and made a gate to fit an opening, providing an example of using math in the real world. He showed how he stretched the wire to make it taunt and talked about why wood should not touch the ground.

For days following the trip, the children built fences in the tinkering area to use with block constructions, drew pictures in the art area, and talked about the experience. Not only was there much learning in this experience, but Dustin was more confident in his interactions with the other children as they talked about the adventure. The message? A valuable field trip can lead to unexpected places.

Consider This
1. How did the trip affect Dustin, and why?
2. What factors made this unique field trip especially valuable?
3. What might be other unusual trips a class could take?

Helping children experience and understand the availability of goods, services, and money is the beginning of teaching economics. Some children may have an allowance or receive holiday money and learn to save for a special item they want.

There are many opportunities during the day in which learning about both work and money can take place. Children in the dramatic play area often incorporate buying and selling in their play. For example, a grocery store center involves purchasing food, and a pretend veterinarian office will spawn a need to determine the cost of services. Here are some examples of how the economics of work can be a part of the curriculum:

- While the children are playing store, Teacher Tim asks how much an item will cost, then pays for the item. He asks for change and pretends to put the change in a wallet. He suggests that the children make a sign to tell other customers what each item costs.
- While a group of children are exploring coins with a magnifying glass, the teacher talks with them about the pictures on the coins, using the names of the coins in the conversation.
- Children contribute pennies to a penny jar for a future purchase. Each day, they count the pennies to be added to the jar and mark a chart to show their progress.
- As a sorting and classification activity, children sort pennies, dimes, and nickels.
- Children take on the roles of workers in their dramatic play.
- The children and teacher look through catalogs or online to see how much a needed item will cost.
- Children create their own money, credit cards, and checks to use in the dramatic play area. They pay for items using toy cell phones.

My World Ecology

As children progress in gaining a broader understanding of their world, **ecology**, or the impact of humans on the Earth, becomes important. Ecology addresses human relationships with the environment and how humans impact it. How can you help children develop values about conserving the planet and caring for the environment? One idea is to allow time for children to explore everything outdoors—mud puddles, trees, sticks, rocks, parks, and playgrounds—and to personally appreciate the value of nature. Help children pay attention to their environment in new ways by going on a listening walk. Take a digital camera or an audio recorder with you to document observations through pictures, videos, and sound recordings. Participate in ecological activities such as Arbor Day, Earth Day, or International Mud Day.

Ecology is included in social studies because it deals with people's responsibility to care for the environment. Ecological concepts appropriate for young children include recycling, conserving water and energy, and protecting the environment. Actions as simple as turning out the lights when leaving the classroom and not running water wastefully teach ecology. Recycling should be a routine part of every day (**Figure 9.6**). Saving construction paper scraps and other materials to use for collage or art projects teaches ecology. Children whose families practice recycling can be helpful in getting others into the habit. Here are a few examples of what ecology looks like in practice:

- LaDonna reminded Shannon to turn the water off when she filled the glasses.
- During snack time, Mia told the others to save their scraps so they could put them in the composting bin.
- Jacob looked in the scrap bin for a piece of construction paper and told his teacher he didn't need to use a new piece because he was only cutting a small triangle.

Democracy and Government

Children participate in the process of democracy when they work as a group and share in decision making about rules or activities. They learn to respect the concept of majority rule and begin to develop a sense of fairness. Children can vote on which game they want to play when they go outdoors, which book they want read to them, or even

Rawpixel/iStock/Getty Images Plus

Figure 9-6 Children in this school take great pride in their recycling program. How can a teacher encourage understanding and appreciation of ecology?

which song they will sing first. When children are asked to vote, the options must be acceptable.

Children learn about responsibility as they clean up and care for their environment. Another way to help children understand responsibility is through the use of a job chart. A job chart that lists classroom responsibilities provides opportunities for children to take leadership and assume responsibility. Children choose or are assigned jobs on a rotating basis. Job charts help integrate responsibility into the daily routine and give children the opportunity to contribute to the organization and upkeep of the learning environment. The Case Study "The License Bureau" provides an example of how democracy and government concepts can be included in the classroom.

Case Study

The License Bureau

Quinton, a 4-year-old, had gone with his mother to renew her driver's license at the local Department of Motor Vehicles. While there, his mother explained what she was doing, and the two conversed about why people had driver's licenses. He saw people taking a card with a number, waiting for their number to be called, and then going to a window and being helped by clerks. He was fascinated by the activity of filling out paperwork on clipboards, getting eyes checked, and having photos taken.

The next day at his preschool, Quinton created his own simulated license bureau in the housekeeping and dramatic play center. He engaged other children with details about his trip and what he had witnessed. For several days, the dramatic play focused on applying for and receiving driver's licenses. His teacher furnished a small camera, supplies for making numbers, eye charts, licenses, and clipboards for records. Children sat and waited until their number was called. Their eye checks were conducted, paperwork completed, photos taken, and licenses were issued.

Following the license bureau dramatic play experience, children incorporated their driver's licenses in their play with wheeled toys on the playground. They proudly showed off their licenses to others. Officers conducted license checks, stopping tricycles and wagons to check for possession of licenses. The teacher followed the experience with opportunities to address traffic safety.

Consider This
1. Why do you think the experience at the bureau was so important to Quinton that he was talking about it the next day?
2. In what ways did the teacher support the children's developing concepts about the process of governance in society?
3. What new vocabulary could the children learn through this experience?

Making Decisions

As part of living in society, individuals frequently need to assess situations and make decisions about actions to take, weighing and comparing options. Decision making is an important skill for young children and begins simply as a request for them to select an activity in which to engage. Not only does giving children choices respect their interests, but it also helps them learn how to consider available options. Including children in classroom decisions strengthens their sense of belonging. The fact that the space and materials belong to them and that they are free to use them fosters an emotional attachment to the environment.

What does it look like to involve children in making decisions and in operating a democratic classroom? The "Making Rules" Case Study feature provides one example.

Case Study

Making Rules

A teacher gathers the preschoolers for a morning meeting, asking them to help decide what rules the group should follow so everyone can be happy and safe. The children begin making suggestions, and the teacher aide records the suggestions on a chart as children state them. Their suggestions are:
- Do not run in the classroom.
- Do not ever hit anyone or fight.
- Do not take items that belong to someone else.

The teacher then helps the children focus on what they *can* do instead of what they must *not* do, leading them to state what should happen instead. The rules were reworded as follows:
- Walk in the classroom.
- We only make friendly touches.
- We are kind to our friends.
- We ask permission if we want to use something that someone else has.

Consider This
1. What are the benefits of having children help make rules?
2. How does helping to make classroom rules relate to social studies?
3. What is the value of having the rules stated, in a positive manner, of what *to* do rather than what *not* to do?

History

Young children begin to understand history as they develop a sense of time and change. They talk about events that happened in the past and make plans for the future. Help children remember activities by putting together classroom photos and documentation boards and creating books of classroom activities or special events. Recalling and reflecting on previous project-based activities in which children interacted with peers and the environment leads to a deeper connection to the activities and people who took part. It helps children develop a sense of time and chronological order of the past.

Documentation boards help children organize information into chronological order and represent events that have already taken place. A documentation board is a display showing events in the order they occurred. Usually, they are a poster board with photos showing the steps in an activity or event along with captions or written descriptions of the photos. See the Case Study feature "The Documentation Board" for one teacher's experience in working with her class to create a documentation board.

A **visual schedule** posted in the classroom helps children develop a sense of time passing and the order in which daily events occur. It is important for young children to know what to expect each day in the classroom. A visual schedule is a comforting reminder for children that they know what will happen next.

Resources in the Community

In any community, there are many social studies resources: public facilities such as libraries, businesses, cultural events, and people who are considered to be community helpers and the work they do. Making use of those resources might include planning a field trip or arranging for a visitor from community sites.

Museums, Libraries, Parks, and Recreation Opportunities

What are available local resources (such as experts, materials, and venues), and what questions might children ask about them? What might children learn that is appropriate to their ages? Most communities have public services that provide learning resources that can be incorporated into curriculum themes. Museums often have special programs to

Case Study

The Documentation Board

During a class morning meeting, Mrs. Lin began the documentation board by saying to the children, "I have pictures of our trip to the pumpkin patch yesterday. Can we put the pictures in the order of what happened so we can remember our trip?"

She showed the photos, including one of her reading *The Pumpkin Book* by Gail Gibbons two days prior to the trip. She asks the children which picture shows what took place first. After some discussion, the children agreed that reading the story happened first. Mrs. Lin put the picture in the upper left-hand corner of the poster board. Mrs. Lin and the children continued to talk about the photos and posted them in sequence, ending with photos of the carved pumpkin and then eating the roasted pumpkin seeds. Later, they added photos of the rotten pumpkin in the compost pile. Once the photos were posted, the children dictated descriptions of what was happening in each photo, and the teacher wrote their words under the related photo. The children loved sharing the event with their parents by telling the story of the pumpkin experience. Using the photos as reminders, they could tell the story chronologically and associate the written words with the photos.

Consider This
1. How does a documentation board help children understand time and sequence?
2. What social skills did the children exercise in making the board?
3. How were language and literacy skills developed in the project?

---

support education. Libraries today have much more than books. Many provide special programs for schools that integrate with curriculum themes. Introducing children and families to these special programs and opportunities can encourage families to expand their children's understanding of the social world.

In addition, parents can be wonderful assets by sharing their experiences and knowledge. Is there a spot on the playground for a classroom garden? Teachers can recruit volunteers to help children plan and create a garden. Engaging children in group activities with a common purpose reminds them that they share the space with others.

Having families and others come into the classroom and taking field trips requires planning to make the experience meaningful. The following sections discuss matters to consider when planning a field trip away from the school. Much of the information is applicable to planning for visitors as well.

Field Trip Planning and Preparation

A field trip away from the school requires careful preparation. A field trip might be as simple as a walk around the block with teaching staff to look at the neighborhood. Or it might include a bus ride that involves parent chaperones. What does a teacher need to know about taking children on a field trip? Here are some planning tips for field trips:

- Visit the site yourself to become familiar with any safety concerns, discover the learning opportunities, and ensure that the trip is age-appropriate.
- A few days before the field trip, conduct activities that relate to the trip, such as going on a pretend trip and addressing safety issues.
- Children might wear T-shirts or nametags with the name and phone number of the school for group identity.
- Maintain the required ratio of children to adults and have parent helpers accompany you if extra supervision or assistance is desired.
- Take a sign-in sheet, emergency information, a first-aid kit, and a fully charged cell phone.
- Carry a tote bag to conveniently hold the items you need.
- If going by car, car seats or boosters must be provided for children as required by law.

- Ensure that everyone has a buddy and knows to stay with their buddy and an adult.
- Never leave the school facility without securing permission slips.

Permission slips are a critical requirement for every field trip. Be sure to request permission slips from the parents for the specific trip, not just generic permission to go on field trips. Distribute permission slips about two weeks before the scheduled trip. Two or three days prior to the day of the trip, remind any parents who have not returned them. The permission slip should include the following:

- why you feel the trip is beneficial and information about what children will learn
- the form of travel and any specific safety precautions you plan
- the time you will be leaving and the time you expect to return
- what the child will need to bring, if anything

Following the trip, furnish materials and activities that integrate the field trip experience into the curriculum. For example, include puzzles, dress-up clothes, music, or art related to the trip in learning centers. Let children draw pictures or make cards to send to any volunteers, hosts, or the people they met.

Field Trip and Visitor Ideas

Arranging for visitors to come to the classroom is another way to have children experience their community, either to supplement field trips or if field trips are not possible. Arranging for visitors may include having parents demonstrate music from their culture, or a visit might be scheduled through an agency that provides educational events, such as a public safety outreach program. Here are some ideas for both field trips and visitors:

- Police station or police safety officer (**Figure 9.7**). Children learn that if they are lost or need help, a police officer or a firefighter can help them. They can learn about the police and their function in the community, as well as details about the work they do to help people stay safe.
- Fire station or fire safety officer. Children can learn about firefighters, their job details, how firetrucks work, how firefighters keep everyone safe, and the importance of fire prevention.

kali9/E+ via Getty Images

Figure 9-7 A police safety officer laughs at the jokes and riddles of these third graders. Why is it important for children to view the officer as helpful?

- Humane Society or animal shelter. A field trip to the local Humane Society or animal shelter or inviting an outreach representative to come to the classroom can teach children how important it is to take care of animals. They can learn the duties and responsibilities of pet ownership and the work of an animal shelter.
- Library or library outreach agent. This field trip or visitor can encourage children to appreciate books and library assets. They will learn about the many resources available in libraries.
- Greenhouse or garden center (**Figure 9.8**). This field trip or visitor can help children understand how and why people grow plants. They will learn why plants grow better in a greenhouse and how to care for the different plants and flowers. They gain an appreciation for what it takes to have healthy food year-round.
- Zoo or zoo representative. Children will learn about the job of the zookeepers and what it is like to work in a zoo. They will learn about the different animals, their habitats, and the food and care the animals need to keep them healthy.
- Safety village. Some cities have a miniature town designed to teach safety. Children will learn safety practices such as wearing bicycle helmets, using seat belts, crossing streets, riding bicycles safely, and fire safety, as well as various rules and laws and the consequences when these are not followed.

☑ CHECKPOINT

1. Why does instruction in social studies start with the child and progress to the community?
2. What organizations or agencies in your community could be good resources?
3. How might a teacher include technology in social studies?

SDI Productions/E+ via Getty Images

Figure 9-8 Parent volunteers help build a vegetable garden on the school grounds. How does the experience of growing vegetables relate to economics and ecology?

9.3 The Cultural Aspects of Social Studies

Teachers and children alike are the products of their culture. Attitudes, beliefs, values, and ways of relating and interacting are all influenced by culture. It is easy for individual teachers to see their way of behaving as the "right" way and work to ensure that children behave the same.

For example, in some families, being respectful is shown by terminology such as "yes, ma'am" or "no, sir"; yet in others, these terms might be seen as subservient. Making eye contact is viewed as disrespectful in some cultures, but it is expected as a show of respect in others. Individuals working with young children must recognize and support those differences in cultural practices.

Generations and Families

Because people today are living longer than in the past, there are more families that include great-grandparents in the extended family. These relatives are often in good health and are active participants who want to be a part of their great-grandchildren's lives. More grandparents are raising their grandchildren, adding to the variety of family styles and the need to include opportunities for extended family involvement in early childhood programs.

Increasingly, educators today are recognizing the importance of depicting a variety of familial structures in children's books and photos and avoiding outdated stereotypes. In planning activities, you must be cognizant of the family structures of the children enrolled.

Stereotyping

The term **stereotyping**, as used in social studies, describes the perception that groups of people will all have characteristics in common. Stereotyping presents the concept that one specific way is best and others are somehow inferior. Such ideas—for example, that the housekeeping area is for girls and the blocks area is for boys—are outmoded and restricting. As the world recognizes the need to encourage girls in the sciences, you must avoid actions that imply that activities or eventual employment are limited based on gender, family origin, or other personal characteristics.

Children develop views of stereotypical behavior based on what they hear and see. Adults who work with young children must be aware of how stereotypes limit children's opportunities. The Discovery Journey feature "Ironing Is for Girls" describes an experience with a newly enrolled child that makes it clear how children's opportunities are limited when expectations are based on stereotypical roles.

Discovery Journeys

Ironing Is for Girls

Stephen, a 3-year-old, was happily ironing a dress-up vest in the housekeeping area when I walked by. Accustomed to commenting on what children are doing to bolster language development, I said, "Stephen, it looks like you're ironing today." Unexpectedly, Stephen abruptly dropped the iron, exclaiming, "No. No, I'm not! I'm not ironing! Ironing is for girls!" and quickly took off to another area.

What happened that caused Stephen to react that way? In Stephen's home, ironing was considered a task that only women do. At only 3 years of age, he had already learned that this was not a desirable task for boys, although he found it fun. In his home, there was a distinct division of tasks, and he was already attuned to those strict divisions.

Consider This
1. Why do you think Stephen reacted as he did?
2. What are some examples of stereotyping you have observed?
3. How can a teacher intentionally or unintentionally influence children's concepts of appropriate roles and tasks?

Creating More Inclusive Holiday Programs

Holidays can be a time of confusion for many school programs. Should teachers allow frightening costumes or hints of the occult at Halloween? Should they include the religious nature of winter holidays—candles, dreidels, and Santas—or just snowflakes? As an educator, what should you celebrate? What should you ignore? The need to be culturally sensitive as well as culturally relevant can lead to a flurry of political correctness and sometimes a lack of substance. How can you create activities for holidays without stereotyping certain groups? What is and is not appropriate? How can you include children who may be the only one or part of a small group that has the same religious beliefs? The answer comes in many forms, each as individual as your own program; however, here are some ideas to facilitate your efforts in creating culturally relevant, inclusive holiday programs.

Communicating with Families about Holidays

You must have open and honest communication with families about holiday matters. Permission slips and policy statements are ways to keep parents informed as holidays approach. Encourage parents to ask you questions, seek information about plans for celebrations, and offer suggestions.

Assure parents that their children will be engaged in other, separate activities if they decide not to allow them to participate in holiday-related events. The goal is not to exclude children and make them feel left out, but to offer participation within a framework of celebrations while respecting parents' preferences. Consider asking parents to be guest speakers on holiday topics with which your staff is unfamiliar or to attend a staff meeting and provide information about family traditions.

A survey of the children and parents can generate a list of the holidays they actively celebrate at home. Some families may have strong belief systems that eliminate or magnify certain holidays. What and how do your children's families typically celebrate? Who objects to Halloween, and what aspect is objectionable? How much exposure to other faiths do parents want their children to have? With which holidays are you and other staff members familiar? Which do you feel comfortable discussing and celebrating? These are matters that need to be addressed to provide a culturally sensitive learning environment.

The emphasis should remain on teaching children about people in the world around them. By providing a forum through which they can learn about belief structures and cultural traditions other than their own, you help children be more open to differences, less biased, and better equipped to interact with others.

One key to having an inclusive holiday program is to create activities for holidays that allow children to personalize the activity and share it with others. Perhaps a child in the group celebrates Hanukkah and can talk about the activities that take place at home. Include parents or grandparents who can share information about celebrations from their childhood, possibly in other countries.

Utilize community members and parents as additional resources to create an authentic explanation of holidays. Teach children about lesser-known holidays in other cultures, regardless of whether they are celebrated in your region. For example, you might look at the different origins of a Santa figure or explain how pumpkins grow and why harvest celebrations exist in many cultures. The key is to align your views of what is appropriate with those of the families.

Building Community through Similarities

Help children understand that people of all cultures have many similarities. For example, all cultures celebrate holidays, although the holidays have different significance and are celebrated in many ways. Holidays are usually a time to focus on family and close friends and share and spend time with loved ones. Ask children to compare various holiday celebrations with the goal of finding similarities among several cultures.

One similarity of holidays that can be considered is that all cultures have traditional food, usually dishes created using items readily available in the original country. These dishes may have evolved as generations adapted and were influenced by other cultures. For example, Louisiana's popular Creole and Cajun dishes mostly evolved from the readily available seafood, sugar cane, rice, and pecans, with French, Spanish, and African influences. The Mexican time-honored tradition of preparing tamales at Christmas significantly involves family and close friends completing the preparation together.

Case Study

Holidays and Special Events

Holidays and cultural events are important in most people's lives, and they often consist of traditions in which children are active participants. Since children's concepts of expectations are typically formed around their own experiences, consider the following scenarios that describe three children's views of separate holiday celebrations.

One Christmas, Angela, a 6-year-old, asked when her grandparents were going to come over to spend the night. The year before, an ice storm hit the town a few days before Christmas. Power was out, and her grandparents' home was left without light or heat. Angela's house had a fireplace, although no power, so the grandparents spent several nights there during the outage. The evenings included telling stories around the hearth and making hot chocolate by heating water in the fireplace. In Angela's experience, the overnight stay was perceived as a part of Christmas since the two events happened concurrently. Thus, she expected the same thing the next year and was disappointed when the experience was not repeated.

Maddy, born on July 4th, thought fireworks were an expected part of birthday celebrations until she was 5 years old. For several years, she believed the fireworks were part of her birthday celebrations rather than associating them with the Independence Day holiday.

Maria, whose family was from Mexico, brought photos to her preschool of a family celebration, Día de los Muertos, or the Day of the Dead. Her teacher, unfamiliar with the holiday, was concerned that the pictures of skulls and death symbols would upset the other children. Not recognizing the cultural significance of the holiday to Maria and her family, she would not let Maria share her photos. For Maria, it was a day to have extended family time, special snacks, and share fond memories about ancestors who were no longer living.

Consider This

1. Why do you think Angela's experience became associated with the Christmas holiday and Maddy's birthday with fireworks?
2. How did Maria's view of Día de los Muertos differ from that of the teacher?
3. How could cultural understanding change how the teacher handled Maria's photos?

Another similarity is that most holiday celebrations have music associated with them. Consider how music adds to the traditions we associate with special days. The musical accompaniment to New Year's Eve fireworks complements the event. Mardi Gras music, the Mariachi music of Cinco de Mayo, or the enthusiastic marches of Independence Day all contribute to the festivities as they accompany ceremonies and festivities. Encourage children to recognize and enjoy different types of holiday music and traditions.

Finally, remember that gifts are often part of holidays. Guide children to understand that giving gifts is often a way of showing appreciation to family and close friends. Review gift-giving traditions in several holiday celebrations and look for similarities. Provide materials and encourage children to make gifts for their friends and appreciate gifts from others.

Identifying similarities in celebrations will help children understand that people are more alike than different. Even though the food, music, and gifting may differ, the fact that these traditions are typically a part of holidays makes it clear that the celebrations are more alike than different.

☑ CHECKPOINT

1. How does stereotyping limit children's opportunities?
2. Why is it important to focus on similarities rather than differences?
3. What are other materials or activities that help children appreciate differences?

9.4 The Teacher's Role in Social Studies

The role of the teacher in relation to social studies involves planning experiences that help children develop concepts about the world and behaviors that are valued in society. Some of the ways to accomplish the goals of the social studies area include:

- **Build on what children already know.** For instance, after experiences related to home and family, expand experiences into the community and focus on how each child's family is part of a community with other families.
- **Develop concepts and processes.** Rather than focusing on isolated facts, develop understandings. For example, create maps depicting the classroom or the neighborhood as a means of understanding the geography of how people live and how they depict location.
- **Provide hands-on activities.** Give children many opportunities to experience the social studies topic of history. For example, let them make photo charts showing how they have grown and changed by bringing photos of themselves as babies or toddlers to compare with current photos.

From the Field

Zlata Stanković-Ramirez

Often, we see a "trip around the world" approach to "celebrating" the various cultures of the children we serve. This can signal to a young child that their culture is something exotic to be considered only once a year. The best way to incorporate the various cultures of the children's families in your classroom is to do the following:

- Ask the parents to share popular kids' songs and rhymes from their culture. Incorporate the songs and rhymes into your typical routine so that all the children can truly learn and familiarize themselves with their friends' cultures, and all of children will feel included daily in their school life.
- Work with the parents to incorporate beloved children's games from their culture or country and have them become part of playtime for all the children to enjoy.
- If you are able, purchase children's books or have the parents donate a few to incorporate into your library and have them available and accessible for all of the children.
- Ask for toys, items, and artifacts that are common and dear to your children's cultures and add them to your environments for all children to explore.

Zlata Stanković-Ramirez, PhD
Assistant Professor of Instruction/Psychology
The University of Texas at Dallas
Dallas, TX

Zlata Stankovic-Ramirez

Figure 9.9

- **Include practical social studies experiences.** Provide opportunities for children to address problems or make decisions by voting on or choosing classroom activities.
- **Capitalize on children's interests.** Take advantage of unplanned and unexpected opportunities. A child with a new puppy wants to learn all about how to care for puppies. In this way, the curriculum of social studies connects children with one another and deepens their understanding of their social world.
- **Support family diversity.** Ensure that the family members of each child are greeted warmly and respectfully. Encourage staff and children to adopt appropriate language that includes and supports different kinds of families, free of language that might inappropriately discriminate. Create opportunities for children to include family representations, bring in photographs, or invite family members for a visit or to share special expertise.
- **Focus on living in the social world.** Have books and other materials available that include diversity and a broad view of how people live. As children learn about themselves and other people who share their world, they will discover that they are more alike than different.

Teaching Prosocial Behaviors and Social Skills

One way to support social relations and skills is through affirmation when children show desired social interactions. Here are some examples of comments that can help children learn to recognize effective social skills and make such skills a habit:

- "I can tell you enjoy helping your friends."
- "LaDarian likes it when you share your cars."
- "I feel good when I see you help others."
- "That was nice of you to walk Taylor to the car with the umbrella to keep her dry."
- "You were helpful in cleaning up today."
- "Maria appreciated how you helped her with the heavy wagon."

In addition to what you say to children, there are many other ways to promote positive social skills and teach specific skills. For example, you can:

- have small group activities and learning centers to encourage cooperation.
- select materials and activities that require working together, such as heavy blocks, rocking boats, board games requiring two or more players, long jump ropes that need two throwers, and wagons for pulling.
- teach children the words that promote prosocial behaviors. "Why don't you ask Melee if you can build with her?" or "Can you tell Jarod that you would like a turn with the truck when he is finished?"
- provide a nurturing environment and model appropriate social behavior.
- use stories and pictures of children sharing and working together.
- display children's work where they can enjoy and be proud of it.
- place low mirrors in the room to build self-concept.
- praise sincerely; never belittle or discourage.

Making Your Program Multicultural

Respecting the various cultures and types of families in your program is important in helping children feel that they belong. Exposing children to artifacts and activities of other cultures helps to build familiarity and acceptance of others. See **Figure 9.10** for various cultural experiences that can be included in an early learning program.

Making Your Classroom Multicultural

Classroom Area	Multicultural Ideas
Snack  romrodinka/iStock/Getty Images Plus	• Use different cooking and eating utensils: wok, pasta maker, chopsticks, or tortilla maker. • Serve a variety of foods: beans, pita bread, fish, corn or flour tortillas, rice, spaghetti, sushi, or unfamiliar vegetables and fruits. • Create different eating environments: sit on pillows or on blankets, or stand to eat around a table.
Dramatic Play  FatCamera/E+ via Getty Images	• Include cultural attire in your dress-up clothes. • Act out stories, legends, and folktales from around the world. • Use dolls and clothing that are culturally diverse. • Include pretend foods and cooking utensils from other cultures.
Music and Movement  FatCamera/E+ via Getty Images	• Try meditation, yoga, or other relaxation exercises. • Select music from various cultures to listen to and look for different rhythms and instrumentation. • Learn and participate in cultural dances. • Play popular games from other cultures. • Learn familiar songs such as "Hokey Pokey" or "Frère Jacques" in several languages.
Art  allanswart/iStock/Getty Images Plus	• Consider art projects from diverse cultures. • Use multicultural crayons, markers, paints, paper, or chalk. • Offer different art media: paint with bamboo or small branches, make paint or dye from natural items. • Create artifacts similar to those traditional in other cultures.
Group Time  MBI/iStock/Getty Images Plus	• Tell stories, fables, legends, and poems common to other cultures. • Use different languages to greet and say "goodbye" to children. • Plan an international festival to celebrate the cultures of the families in your program. • Take field trips that are multicultural in nature, such as a trip to a museum or festival.

Goodheart-Wilcox Publishers

Figure 9-10 This chart presents many ways to support inclusion of cultures. What other ideas can you add? (Continued)

Making Your Classroom Multicultural *(continued)*

Classroom Area	Multicultural Ideas
Math and Science  *Siarhei SHUNTSIKAU/iStock/Getty Images Plus*	• Include counting activities using items from diverse cultures. • Learn to count in another language. • Use puzzles that depict children or adults of other cultures. • Make maps of the school or neighborhood.
Geography, History and Current Events  *FatCamera/E+ via Getty Images*	• Read about different cultures throughout history. • Make maps, flags, currency, and other cultural items. • Look at stamps, postcards, newspapers, coins, and other items from around the world. • Write to pen pals in other countries or communicate over electronic media. • Encourage students to bring items from home that represent their culture.

Goodheart-Willcox Publisher

Figure 9-10 *Continued*

Supporting Social Studies Concepts

Teachers have many opportunities in daily classroom activities and routines to help children learn social studies concepts and integrate the concepts with other areas of the curriculum. Here are some examples:

- Mr. Ho asked a child about plans for choice time. "Clanton, what is your plan for today?" Clanton replies that he wants to use the iPad to learn more about the things at the library that yesterday's visitor talked about. Mr. Ho extends Clanton's thinking by further questioning, "What service are you most interested in?"
- As part of a study of community helpers focusing on the work of firefighters, Miss Rizzo talks to a small group of children about the need for an evacuation plan in case of a fire. Together, the group draws a map showing how to exit the classroom and where to gather on the playground. They place the map on the wall at their height and describe its purpose to the rest of the class.
- In the tinkering area, Mrs. Alonzo says, "Levi, tell me about your building. I noticed Ava helped you with it. How did you decide what you wanted to make?" Levi tells her he is making the building they saw across the street from the school when they went on a walk.
- While setting the table for snack time, Ms. Wallace asks, "Myra, would you please see how many spoons we need and get them from the cart, please?" Myra did so and was happy that she was selected to help.
- Rachal pulls down a Mexican *serape* from the dress-up shelf and wraps it around her. "Look, Miss Betsy, I look like the people in the pictures!" she proclaims, pointing to a book cover of dancers in Mexico.
- Iva lines up the dolls and stuffed animals in rows of chairs. "I'm the teacher," she says, and passes out a book to each. "It's time for reading," she explains, pointing to the schedule.
- After one of the children brought in some crickets from a fishing trip with his dad, the class set up a cage to feed, watch, and listen to them. They read *The Very Quiet Cricket* and talked about how crickets are a part of nature and how some cultures consider them a sign of good luck. After a few days, they took the cage outside and watched the crickets hop away.

CHECKPOINT

1. Why are the words and actions of teachers important in the cultural aspects of social studies?
2. What are other important tasks of a teacher in reference to social studies?
3. How might an adult know what interests children?

9.5 Focus on Assessment of Program Practices

A program benefits from regular assessment of how well it meets its own goals as well as the established standards that represent the consensus of best practices within a field. One organization, the National Council for Social Studies (NCSS), makes the following recommendations for early childhood programs in its "Early Childhood in the Social Studies Context" position statement.

- Young children have the capacity to use the skills of reasoning and inquiry to investigate social studies concepts as they explore how people interact in the world.
- Early childhood is a time when the foundations of social studies are established, and curricular standards should explicitly attend to engaging and developing young children's capacity for citizenship, democratic or civic activity, and participation in decision making, as well as critical disciplinary literacies.
- As teachers set the tone for children's social studies learning, it is critical that curricular and instructional decisions embrace diversity and social justice while intentionally contesting bias and inequity.
- Young children need multiple and varied opportunities to engage in social studies inquiry.
- Early childhood educators should receive social studies-specific professional development that includes guidance on how to teach social studies to young learners to cultivate bias-free and discrimination-free communities.
- There is a need for the social studies community to engage in further research on early childhood social studies curriculum and instruction (NCSS 2019).

These recommendations can serve as the basis for an assessment of the social studies curriculum in individual classrooms or throughout the school. One way to use the statement as an assessment is to gather artifacts and data that provide evidence of activities and methods that mesh with these statements. Another method is to reflect on each recommendation, and consider how well you believe the principles are met.

CHECKPOINT

1. How might you find out how much children are engaging in social studies activities?
2. Which social studies recommendations do you consider the most important?
3. In what ways can early childhood programs build a foundation for citizenship?

9.6 Family Matters

Describing the center or school policy and practices in teaching social studies to families, especially prior to or at the time of enrollment, can prevent misunderstandings and support collaborative relationships with families. See **Figure 9.11** for a sample letter that can be used to help families understand the goals related to social studies. Similar communications may be included in newsletters, parent letters, blog posts or websites, social media, text, or emails.

Note to Parents

Dear Families,

Early learning center enrollment is often a child's first experience of community outside the family. Social studies learning begins as children build friendships in the school setting and participate in making choices and decisions within the classroom. In time, their circle grows beyond the school, into the neighborhood, and eventually around the world.

Preschool is a safe, caring community with an orderly structure that responds to children's interests and abilities. Each child is valued as an individual with a unique culture and approach to learning. When children play games, construct in the tinkering area, or work together in small groups, they learn cooperation, empathy for others, acceptance of differences, and how to make decisions. They learn to share, take turns, and be responsible for tasks. In essence, they learn to be reliable citizens of their classroom community.

Children develop an understanding of their neighborhood by observing their surroundings: homes, banks, firehouses, police stations, restaurants, theaters, religious buildings, schools, playgrounds, and parks. They observe the stores in the area that provide the goods they need, such as groceries, clothing, and household items. They develop an understanding of the various jobs that people do and how available services help everyone.

Children in our program take field trips to visit firehouses, police stations, senior citizen centers, and animal rescue centers. In the classroom, they discuss what they saw and learned. They reinforce those concepts through their play. They may set up a grocery store or firehouse in the dress-up or block area and reenact the experience, using the information they have learned as components of their play.

We observe holidays to teach children about cultural differences and help them understand the value of traditions. At Thanksgiving, children talk about the things they are grateful for and how sharing a meal together strengthens friendships and makes us happy. On Abraham Lincoln's birthday, they build log cabins, examine pennies with a magnifying glass, and listen to stories about Lincoln's life as a child. On Martin Luther King Jr.'s birthday, we address the importance of respecting others' rights, peaceful cooperation, and fairness to all.

Children learn to appreciate the traditions of others by understanding the customs of religious and ethnic holidays: Christmas, Diwali, Passover, Ramadan, and Kwanzaa. Our focus is on developing a respect for those whose traditions and practices may be different from their own. Parents, grandparents, or other family members are welcome to share symbols, music, and traditions of their holidays with the class.

Children learn about their history and other cultures through books available and read in the classroom. Teachers read stories about children growing up or living in other countries. Stories feature people of all ages and various ethnic groups, as well as people with disabilities. Children often act out the stories, learn some words in another language, and enjoy the music of other cultures.

Parents, grandparents, and others, such as police officers, firefighters, dentists, doctors, or artists, may visit to share stories about their jobs. A parent from another country or culture might visit in a traditional costume, tell a native tale, or teach a dance, game, or song from their culture. They might prepare a favorite recipe to taste, and explain how it is made and the source of the ingredients. Children may draw pictures or write stories about the visit to reinforce what they learned.

Our approach to social studies, and our approach overall, is one of valuing the broad range of human experience within our school family. We hope that you will take an active role and share your culture with us.

Sincerely,

Miss Riona

Goodheart-Wilcox Publishers

Figure 9-11 This letter to families explains the program's approach to social studies. Why is the information in this letter important to share with families? What else might you add to it?

☑ CHECKPOINT

1. What are some additional ways in which families might be engaged in social studies activities?
2. What do you consider the best way to communicate with families?
3. What are some pros and cons of various means of communication with families?

Chapter 9 Review and Assessment

Chapter Summary

9.1 **Describe the concept of social studies as it applies to young children.**
- Social studies is the curriculum area that focuses on how people live together in the social world, focusing on similarities and differences between people and their interactions with the natural world.
- For young children, social studies begins with self-concept, helping them accept their feelings, recognize emotions, and understand that their actions affect others.
- In infants and toddlers, social studies content focuses on self-development, with adults supporting this through toys, materials, and experiences.
- In preschool and primary years, social studies provides theme-based curriculum content, activities, and experiences, allowing children to develop planning, cooperation, problem-solving, and interpersonal coping skills.

9.2 **Identify appropriate components of social studies for early childhood.**
- Children's social concepts begin in infancy and expand as their knowledge of their world expands. First, these concepts center on themselves, then progress to family, and then to friends and neighbors.
- As they grow and their contact with others increases, children learn skills that are important in developing friendships and relationships.
- Teachers can help children develop friendships through specific strategies in what they say and do and through the guidance they provide for children.
- The child's understanding of one's self is an important step in developing empathy and concern for others.
- Many important social skills needed as adults begin in childhood.
- Children's neighborhoods become more significant as their world expands. An effective teacher plans experiences that allow children to exercise their growing curiosity about the world around them.
- As children explore their school, community, and areas outside of their home, they begin to see people at work and develop an understanding of the jobs that people do and the benefits of the work performed.
- Children learn to be good citizens through activities such as recycling, caring for the environment, being concerned for others, and being responsible for classroom tasks.
- Teachers can provide opportunities for children to vote as a way of making decisions. Such experiences are the beginning of understanding democracy and government.
- Children need opportunities to develop the skills of making decisions, and these skills start in simple ways.
- Children can learn about the sequence of time and history through documentation boards, marking time or changes in relation to time passing.
- Field trips and invited visitors can help children understand their community. Field trip experiences can be integrated with other areas of learning.

9.3 **Explain the cultural considerations in teaching social studies.**
- Children are a product of their family culture. Understanding the families' values, beliefs, and traditions is important in providing an environment of acceptance and respect.
- Stereotyping should be avoided in the interest of helping children see that they are welcome in all activities and helping them recognize that there are many ways of living.
- Holiday celebrations are a function of family cultures. Developing a policy about celebrations can be helpful for programs when families' religious beliefs are diverse.
- Diversity in holiday celebrations is broad, but there are many similarities. Most cultures have food, music, traditions, and often games associated with them. Focusing on the similarities can be helpful in family relations related to holiday celebrations.

9.4 Explain the role of the teacher in designing and guiding social studies experiences.
- Many opportunities occur to integrate social studies concepts with other curriculum areas throughout the day.
- The role of the teacher in relation to social studies involves planning experiences that help children develop concepts about the world and behaviors that are valued in society.
- One way to support social relations and skills is through affirmation when children show desired social interactions.
- A multicultural early childhood program helps children feel welcome in the classroom. Books, posters, music, snacks, and dress-up clothing should be representative of various cultures.

9.5 Identify ways to evaluate social studies opportunities offered.
- Ongoing assessment helps a teacher or program determine if goals are being met or are not met as well as desired.
- An important function of assessment is that it documents a need for changes that will improve the program.

9.6 Describe ways to involve families in activities.
- Social studies goals create many opportunities for including families.
- Involving families in contributing their expertise to the class can enrich the relationships and help families feel welcome.
- Having clear policies that are communicated to families related to field trips, objectives for children's learning, and holidays can open important doors to collaborative work on behalf of the children.
- Teachers can support children's family relationships by communicating with families and including them in classroom activities.

Recall and Application

1. **True or False.** Social living requires a sense of cooperation and fairness.
2. Social studies is best described as the study of ____.
   A. how people live together in the social world
   B. the major wars that have been fought throughout human history
   C. plants and animals
   D. communism and democracy
3. **True or False.** Helping children understand the relationship of themselves to family, home, and community is a part of social studies.
4. **True or False.** Children under 3 years old are too young to learn any social studies concepts.
5. Young children's understanding of social studies begins with ____.
   A. community
   B. themselves
   C. sharing
   D. family
6. **True or False.** In all cultures, making eye contact when talking or listening is a way to show respect.
7. **True or False.** Even young children can begin to understand some basics of geography.
8. Many cultures' holiday celebrations have the following elements in common *except* ____.
   A. food
   B. music
   C. traditions
   D. gift exchanges
9. **True or False.** Allowing children to vote on activities helps them learn about civics and government.
10. Which social studies skill can *best* be guided by what the teacher says and does?
    A. listening
    B. prosocial behaviors
    C. writing
    D. math
11. **True or False.** Including cultural items in learning centers and routines can help children understand diversity.
12. **True or False.** Assessment is not important if you know you are using a good curriculum.
13. **True or False.** Professional organizations frequently provide information about best practices in a field.
14. **True or False.** Communicating with families about social studies is needed only when a problem occurs.

Chapter 10
STEAM: Science, Technology, and Engineering

Standards Covered in This Chapter

NAEYC

NAEYC—2b, 2c, 3b, 4a, 4b, 4c, 5a, 5b, 5c, 6e

DAP

DAP—1a, 2b, 2c, 2f, 3a, 3d, 4a, 4b, 4c, 4d, 4e, 5b, 5c, 5d

Learning Outcomes

After reading this chapter, you should be able to:

10.1 Describe the relationships among science, technology, and engineering as components of STEAM.

10.2 Identify the goals of science with young children.

10.3 Describe appropriate use of technology in early childhood.

10.4 Explain the benefits of tinkering as a means of engineering skill development.

10.5 Describe how to integrate science, technology, and engineering throughout the early childhood curriculum.

10.6 Define the teacher's role in science, technology, and engineering.

10.7 Set up a developmentally appropriate science and tinkering center.

10.8 Describe how to assess a science, technology, and engineering part of the curriculum in early childhood.

10.9 Demonstrate ways to involve families in science, technology, and engineering.

Chapter opener image credit: BigZenDragon/iStock/Getty Images

Key Terms

classification	observation	STEAM
comparison	paradigm	STEM
engineering	prediction	technology
experience chart	process skill	tinkering
exploration	quantitative	transferable
hypothesis	science	variables
inference	screen time	

Introduction

Margaret looked at the science section of her textbook in preparation for her upcoming college early childhood education class and was caught between feelings of apprehension and anxiety. She remembered all too well her high school science classes, where she often felt she did not understand the information presented by the teacher or what she read in her textbook. The vocabulary was unfamiliar and confusing. She considered science beyond her ability to comprehend and questioned why it even needed to be a part of the early childhood curriculum. After all, how much can such young children understand? And what did she, as an adult, need to know about science?

Walking into class on the dreaded day, she was surprised at what she saw. The classroom was set up in "stations" for her and her classmates to explore. There was a place to use magnifying glasses to observe pine cones, rocks, katydid shells, and other items of nature. A second station included prisms, mirrors, and flashlights to explore light. Another contained a hamster, an ant farm, and a bug cage to contemplate. And one more clearly popular spot, judging from the classmates gathered around, was a tank with colorful fish, snails, and other sea life.

During most of the class time, the undergraduate students explored the science stations, chatting about what they saw and did. The last part of the class was devoted to enthusiastic group discussions on how the experiences related to teaching science in early childhood. The instructor had set up the stations as they would see them in an early childhood classroom to give the students an opportunity to explore and discover as children would.

For the first time, Margaret enjoyed science in a way that was relevant and understandable to her. She approached the rest of the class with eager anticipation.

10.1 STEAM in Early Childhood Education

Future educators are likely aware of the acronyms STEM and STEAM. Many people believe that these are concepts that originated in education to describe and discuss learning in fields such as science and mathematics. The National Science Foundation (NSF) began to use the acronym SMET for science, mathematics, engineering, and technology in the 1990s. In time, *STEM* replaced *SMET* (McComas 2014). **STEM** stands for "science, technology, engineering, and mathematics."

Published by the White House Office of Science and Technology Policy, the 2022 Progress Report on the Implementation of the Federal Science, Technology, Engineering, and Mathematics (STEM) Education Strategic Plan reported on a federal plan based on a vision for all Americans to have lifelong access to high-quality STEM education. The vision included making the United States a global leader in STEM literacy, innovation, and employment (USDE 2022). The plan identified three overarching goals: (1) build strong foundations for STEM literacy; (2) increase diversity, equity, and inclusion in STEM; and (3) prepare the workforce for STEM skills.

Supporting these goals is an approach to curriculum that educates students in the four disciplines—science, technology, engineering, and mathematics—in an interdisciplinary and applied manner. Rather than teaching the four disciplines as separate and discrete subjects, STEM integrates them into a cohesive learning **paradigm**, a model or system based on real-world practical applications.

When you consider the subject areas in STEM, it becomes apparent that early childhood programs have been hard at play while governments and associations were in discussion. Children look at leaves under magnifying glasses and compare natural materials, such as rocks and soil. They mix substances together to see what happens and create castles and rivers at the sand and water tables. These are young scientists at work. Regarding technology, young children use computers as well as an assortment of tools and simple machines, such as gears, wheels, levers, and pulleys. These fledgling engineers are busy in the block area, the manipulative area, and increasingly in the classroom tinkering or maker area. Math activities are common in early childhood programs where children are counting, matching shapes and making patterns in a manipulative area, or measuring ingredients in a cooking project.

More recently, art (including music as an art form) has been added to the discussion, creating the acronym and concept of **STEAM**. STEAM depicts the interrelationship of the arts with the technical and scientific fields. Art incorporates shape, contrast, perspective, light, shadows, and colors, thus tying visual art to mathematics and engineering. In music, counting, rhythm, scales, patterns, symbols, time signatures, tone, and pitch are mathematical in nature. These elements of mathematics, along with the science of sound, create the music that people enjoy.

Discovery Journeys

Girls in STEAM

Consider some stereotypes that have kept many students from pursuing STEAM occupations. Current efforts to engage young girls in science, technology, engineering, and math pursuits stand in stark contrast to lost opportunities resulting from social attitudes that designated those subjects for boys while Jody was growing up. As a young child, Jody was fascinated by model trains. At age 5, she got lost at the state fair because she waited to see a model train on display come through the tunnel *just one more time!*

Jody wanted very much to have her own model train and create a world of paper mâché mountains with tunnels, bridges, houses, and stores crafted from balsa wood. She envisioned lakes made from mirrors and crumpled cellophane, and she hoped to sculpt clay figures to live in her miniature railroad town. But Jody never asked for what would have been the catalyst for many hours of creative enjoyment because, simply, trains were for boys. It was not just the technology of the train's operation that Jody missed out on, but the many engineering challenges of creating the geography in which it would operate.

Fortunately, attitudes about women in STEAM fields continue to evolve, and young girls grow up today with role models and encouragement to enter these fields. Early childhood educators have tremendous power to encourage and normalize girls' interests in the sciences by making the suggestions offered in the text accessible to all children.

Consider This
1. Have you had experiences in which you felt activities were not available to you because of your gender?
2. What might cause girls to avoid science, technology, or engineering in the early childhood arena?
3. How have your own actions possibly discouraged or encouraged girls' interest in science, technology, or engineering?

This chapter explores the first three areas of STEAM: science, technology, and engineering. The following chapters will explore art—including music—and mathematics. Given that discussions of STEAM topics are evolving, each area will be discussed in the sections that follow.

☑ CHECKPOINT

1. How are the components in STEAM related?
2. How do young children make use of science, technology, and engineering?

10.2 Science in Early Childhood Education

When people think about science, they may envision scientists on television crime dramas wearing pristine white lab coats and oversized goggles conducting experiments with test tubes and petri dishes. Or they may remember their high school or college physical science or biology classes. People's experiences with formal science education may make them excited to share their interests with children or may leave them feeling underprepared or unqualified to do so. **Science**, however, simply refers to the process of methodically exploring through observation and experiment; it involves paying attention to what exists or is happening, predicting what might happen if specific changes are made or actions are taken, testing predictions under controlled conditions to see if they are correct, and trying to make sense of the experiences. In the context of early childhood education, teaching science does not require an advanced degree in chemistry or physics but rather a desire to help children explore the world.

Because science involves exploration, investigation, prediction, problem solving, and discovery, it is highly applicable to young children. Imagine visiting an early childhood program on a beautiful spring day. Toddlers play outdoors while making bubbles with a wand and are delighted to see them glide through the air. Two 4-year-olds are disagreeing about which item will sink first in a tub of water: a small rock or a large stick. Other children throw balls and watch them fall, watch feathers floating gracefully to the ground, or blow dandelions to see the seeds spread. These children may not understand why the wind blows or grasp the concept of gravity, but they do witness the effects. This is the heart of science for young children.

Science education in early childhood settings does not consist of sit-down lectures about matter or molecules; it involves imparting skills in organic ways. For example, young children should be developing the key **process skills**, or the skills that scientists use in their work, and the competencies for solving scientific problems. These skills are a set of broadly **transferable** abilities: abilities that are necessary to many disciplines and reflective of the behavior of scientists (NARST n.d.).

- **Observing.** Young children are naturally curious and want to know "why." **Observation** consists of using the five senses to gather information to understand how things work.
- **Predicting.** A **prediction** is a reasonable guess or estimation of what will happen under specified circumstances. For example, asking a child, "If you have two plants, one that you water and another that you do not, which plant will keep growing?" would be asking a child to make a prediction (**Figure 10.1**)."
- **Exploring.** Opening a door, climbing into a box, or shaking a small tube are all examples of **exploration**. In this context, *exploration* refers to children examining an object to see what it does and what they can do with it. Children want to see what happens to an item when they act on it or change it.
- **Understanding.** Once children have explored an object of interest, they develop understanding. This does not mean that a child will comprehend all aspects or uses of that object, but they have gained some familiarity with it.

FatCamera/E+ via Getty Images

Figure 10-1 Second-grade students carefully measure the water for each plant. They have measured the height of the seedlings each day for a week. What science process skills are involved in this experience?

- **Comparing**. A **comparison** is an analysis of similarities and differences in objects. As children develop skills in observation, they naturally begin to compare likenesses and differences. Comparison is the first step toward classifying.
- **Classifying**. **Classification** involves grouping and sorting according to categories, such as size, shape, color, or use. To classify, children need to compare objects and develop subsets. Even the infant who rejects mashed peas but readily accepts applesauce is beginning to classify foods into the categories of "like" and "dislike."
- **Measuring**. A measurement is a **quantitative** description made by an observer. Quantitative measurements relate to the determination of quantity and involve using numbers, distances, time, volumes, or weights. For young children, measuring might be as straightforward as "two shakes" of cinnamon or a "handful" of playdough.
- **Communicating**. Communication in science refers to the skill of describing attributes, processes, or events in words, charts, or graphs. Clear communication requires that information be collected, arranged, and presented in a way that others comprehend. Children using a weather chart to record the weather are communicating and reporting data (**Figure 10.2**).
- **Inferring**. An **inference** is an educated guess about an object or event based on data or observations. For example, a child might conclude, or infer, that it is chilly when noticing people wearing coats.
- **Hypothesizing**. A **hypothesis** is a formal conditional statement about a person's beliefs regarding the outcome of what is being investigated. A child might hypothesize that a block tower will be stronger if large blocks are used on the bottom and small blocks on the top.
- **Controlling variables**. Determining which characteristics in an investigation should be consistent to conduct an experiment is the process of controlling **variables**. For example, asking children, "If a plant grows in the window, will it also grow in the closet?" could lead to an investigation by controlling the placement of the two plants while providing the same amount of water and soil to both.

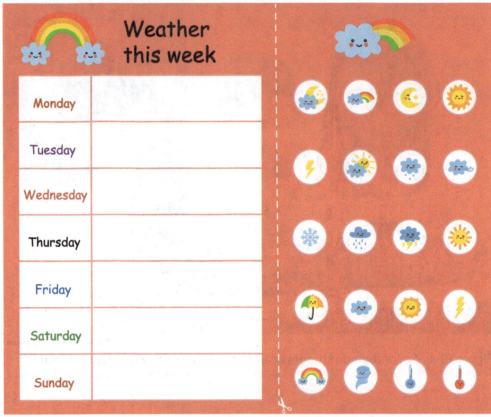

Milyausha Shaykhutdinova/iStock/Getty Images Plus

Figure 10-2 Children can use this chart to document the weather. How might this activity encourage children to communicate with one another?

Discovery Journeys

Experiential Learning

The value of firsthand experiences in learning, as exemplified by process skills, was made clear to Chenille a number of years ago when her daughter, Tenisha, was in the fifth grade. Tenisha had a homework assignment to read a chapter and answer questions about convex and concave lenses in her science textbook. Chenille reminded Tenisha that her preschool class used magnifying glasses to burn paper—a lesson Tenisha readily recalled. She drew upon that experience as she completed her homework and in the class discussion the following day. She told Chenille that only two other children in the class had a similar experience with lenses; most students did not really understand what a convex lens in a magnifying glass could do.

This conversation with her 10-year-old daughter deepened Chenille's understanding of the importance of hands-on learning. Tenisha's grasp of the principles of lenses came not from her fifth-grade reading assignment but from her experience seeing the effects in action as a preschool child.

Consider This

1. Consider a scientific concept you learned from a hands-on experience. How was your understanding of the concept different from what you may have been told about it or read about it?
2. Why do you think the fifth-grade teacher did not take advantage of providing firsthand experiences in class?
3. Consider concepts of plant growth, water properties, and temperature. How can you provide hands-on experiences to help children grasp these concepts?

Young children are observing, comparing, measuring, classifying, and communicating on a regular basis. They often conduct experiments by asking relevant questions and by striving to figure out how things work and how they can affect materials. These important science process skills can be integrated into the curriculum in many ways.

☑ CHECKPOINT

1. Why do some teachers feel ill-prepared to teach science?
2. How does science education relate to what is known about how children learn?
3. In what ways do the key process skills of science support cognitive skills?

10.3 Technology in Early Childhood Education

The second letter of the STEAM acronym refers to technology. This term often suggests the many electronic devices that people use in their work and daily lives. While these are certainly examples of technology, in its broadest form, **technology** is the application of scientific knowledge for practical purposes. Experts can use technology to produce innovative goods or services, carry out goals such as sending a spaceship to the moon, or solve problems related to ending disease or famine. But technology is not limited to such lofty goals; it is usually applied more generally, as in the use of basic tools such as levers or wheels. When considering this broader definition, it is apparent that young children use technology regularly each day. Cutting paper with scissors or playdough with a plastic knife is using technology, as is applying paint with a brush, using a balance scale to compare weights (**Figure 10.3**), or fastening a jacket with a zipper or buttons.

That said, the use of electronic technology is widely discussed in early childhood education as doctors, psychologists, teachers, parents, and others concerned with the welfare of children worry about the amount of **screen time** (time using tablets, smartphones, televisions, video games, and other screen items) in which young children engage. Many

faithhoca/E+ via Getty Images

Figure 10-3 This teacher is facilitating children's exploration of a balance scale. What questions might the teacher ask to help children think about what is happening?

early learning center licensing regulations restrict children's screen time. The American Academy of Pediatrics (AAP) recommends no screen time for children under 2 years of age and issues cautions about its use with other young children (AAP 2020).

The key issue for incorporating technology seems to be determining best practices for using technology to add to and enhance children's learning and exploring in developmentally appropriate ways. General recommendations are that teachers consider the American Psychological Association (APA's) guidelines for using technology as well as the NAEYC's and Fred Rogers Institute's Technology and Interactive Media as Tools in Early Childhood Programs Serving Children from Birth through Age 8 position statement. In using technology with young children, teachers must be knowledgeable of the concerns about the excessive use of technology, and they must know how to integrate and supplement playful learning in a developmentally appropriate manner. In addition, it is recommended that, considering the dynamic nature of electronic devices and capabilities, teachers stay up-to-date on research and professional recommendations regarding screen time issues.

Effective uses of technology and media are active, hands-on, engaging, and empowering. Appropriate technology gives the child control and provides adaptive scaffolds to ease the accomplishment of tasks. Teachers play an important role in supervising, guiding, extending, evaluating, observing, and, when needed, limiting the use of technology by young students. They should utilize technology and media in an active, hands-on, engaging, and empowering manner as one of many options to support children's playful

Case Study

Tablets in the Classroom

Ms. Alverez was concerned when she was informed that her school had recently purchased four tablet computers and wanted her to use them in her preschool class. She knew that many leaders in the field had concerns about screen time. She worried that the children would have conflicts over who would get to use the tablets at any given time. She feared that the tablets would reduce opportunities for social interactions among the children. Her concern led her to think about what she could do to prevent discord.

When introducing the tablets to her class, Ms. Alvarez was up-front about how the children would need to share and take turns. She assured them that they would each get to enjoy time with educationally relevant technology, the school's basic text-writer program, and a photo album app that she had loaded onto the tablets. She showed the children how she made a list of their names and would know who had not had a turn. She believed that if they understood their turn was coming, they would not be anxious about missing out.

After a few days, she was pleasantly surprised that children began to use the tablets as part of their play scenarios. Two children in the block area used a tablet to find pictures of bridges for ideas on how to design a bridge they were building. Another child used a tablet in the veterinarian-themed dramatic play area, checking in patients and video-calling pet owners to report successful treatment and make discharge arrangements. Another child pulled up a digital version of *Hondo & Fabian* and "read" it to two other children.

When Ms. Alverez recognized that the children were incorporating the tablets in their activities in a developmentally appropriate manner, she realized that technology could enrich and expand their learning. She saw how tablets have become another tool to be incorporated into playful learning scenarios.

Consider This
1. How do you think Ms. Alverez's introduction of the tablets prevented the anticipated conflict?
2. Why was it important for Ms. Alverez to prepare the tablets with resources prior to letting the children use them?
3. In what other ways might children use the tablets as part of their daily activities?
4. What else can a teacher do to encourage social development in using digital technology?

learning. Interactive media can be developmentally appropriate by facilitating communication with families, supporting learning across language differences, and providing adaptations that support the inclusion of children with disabilities (DAP 2020).

☑ CHECKPOINT

1. Why are there concerns about the use of electronic devices in early childhood?
2. How might electronic devices be used appropriately in early childhood classrooms?
3. In what ways can technology strengthen home/school connections?

10.4 Engineering in Early Childhood Education

The letter "E" in STEAM—**engineering**—is the process of building machines and structures. In many classrooms, engineering is encouraged by a place called a *tinkering area* or *maker space*. Such an area usually consists of tools and materials that encourage construction and creation of items by using recycled materials or construction toys, such as DUPLO® and LEGO®, many types of blocks, magnetic tiles, and so forth.

Tinkering refers to playing around with materials and becoming familiar with their properties and what they can do. It is a first step toward engineering. You can imagine how a 4-year-old might start tinkering with paper towel tubes, fabric, and tape and eventually figure out how to utilize them to construct a miniature tent for the block area.

Tinkering and engineering in early childhood involves allowing children the freedom to explore materials and what they can do with or build from the materials (**Figure 10.4**). Cardboard tubes, taped together, become a marble raceway; paper cups attached with wire become a castle; fabric squares stapled to a dowel convert to a flag. Increasingly,

Hispanolistic/E+ via Getty Images

Figure 10-4 A kindergarten child tinkers with a construction toy. What might the child construct? What are some skills used in the process?

as the early childhood field recognizes the importance of engineering and the skills and attitudes that can be developed at young ages, the early childhood curriculum is expanding to include a tinkering or maker space as a regular part of the early learning classroom.

By participating in tinkering, children are learning many analytic skills that will help them throughout their lives, including how to:
- identify a problem.
- make plans.
- use tools and materials.
- estimate and measure.
- find solutions.
- use language to describe a problem and suggest a solution.
- cooperate with others.
- develop confidence and self-esteem.
- evaluate outcomes.

✓ CHECKPOINT

1. What might a teacher do to encourage problem-solving skills in the tinkering area?
2. Why is it important to have a wide variety of materials available?
3. How can the tinkering area integrate with other curriculum areas?

Case Study

The Cigar Box Ukulele

The process of learning through tinkering is described in this story of 6-year-old Yvonne. Yvonne loved visiting her grandfather, Pappa, because he was always repairing and making things. She liked hanging out with him in the garage he used as "his space." On one visit, Yvonne brought her toy ukulele with a broken neck that she hoped he could repair for her. She watched as he carefully used a glue gun to reattach the neck, adding a piece of plastic to reinforce the section where the break had occurred.

Waiting for it to dry, Yvonne began playing with the stack of cigar boxes her grandfather kept for storing numerous small parts: screws, nails, tacks, and other items. "Pappa, can I use this? Can I make a ukulele?" she asked, picking up a cigar box.

"Well, what would you need?" asked Pappa.

"This box and some wires," Yvonne answered. "I need some wires."

"See what you can find," responded Pappa, pointing to the assorted rolls and collections of wires on a nearby shelf.

She chose several, and Pappa helped her use pliers to attach them to the box with eye hooks. The first wires she used made a very dull sound, which was not what she wanted. When she tried thin copper wire, the sound was a little better but still not to her liking. Then she had an idea. "What about rubber bands? Wouldn't they work?" she asked.

Finding some rubber bands in her grandfather's stash, she experimented with various strengths and sizes until she created an instrument that she could play.

Consider This
1. What do you think Yvonne learned from this experience?
2. How would the experience have been different for Yvonne if Pappa had made the ukulele for her?
3. What science concepts were learned or reinforced in Yvonne's experience?
4. How do you think her grandfather's interest in tinkering and materials motivated Yvonne to create her ukulele?

Teaching Tip

Steps in Engineering

The following guide can be used to help children think through a problem they want to solve and brainstorm or plan solutions and processes.
1. Define the project: What is the problem?
2. Generate solutions: What are some ideas for fixing the problem?
3. Make a plan. Draw or sketch your idea.
4. What materials do you have or need?
   - tools and materials to build with
   - several means for connecting items
   - materials to sculpt and mold
   - items for decorating
   - tools to work with fabrics and textiles
   - tools for marking or writing
5. Gather the materials needed to build or create the solution you planned.
6. Build or create your idea for fixing the problem.
7. Test your solution or try your creation to see if it works.
8. Does it work? What does not work? What changes might make it work better?
9. Revise to improve it.
10. Share your creation with others.
11. Talk about how you made it.
12. Listen to others' ideas about how it might be improved.

10.5 Science, Technology, and Engineering in the Classroom

Opportunities abound for coordinating the science, technology, and engineering components of STEAM in early childhood education. Experiences involve language and literacy as children read and talk about what they are doing; they involve social-emotional learning as children work with others to achieve a shared goal, negotiate roles, or share materials (**Figure 10.5**). These opportunities take place in the classroom, on the playground, and in the community. The following sections detail various methods, themes, and activities that will assist you as you introduce and incorporate STEAM into your curriculum.

Integrating Science, Technology, and Engineering with Other Curriculum Areas

The historic division of educational topics into discrete subjects is somewhat forced. You cannot read the *Little House on the Prairie* books of Laura Ingalls Wilder (literature) without appreciating the experiences of women (sociology) in the Midwest (geography) in the late 1800s (history). In routine daily life, most topics are interrelated. For example, in planting a garden and then preparing a special meal with the produce you have grown, you make use of science (selecting the location to provide conditions for growth), technology (the tools for digging, cutting, or mixing), engineering (staking the tomatoes and trussing the turkey), math (measuring, temperature, and timing), and art (the presentation of the food and garnishing). The same idea holds true in the early childhood classroom, where the literature that teachers read to children, the music they play, the outdoor activities, and the food preparation all integrate with science, technology, and engineering in meaningful and memorable ways. Consider these intersections in the sections that follow.

Figure 10-5 Two children discuss how they can use the materials. *What are some benefits from children working together on shared goals?*

Language and Literacy

The world of STEAM integrates well with reading and writing. Vocabulary, object naming, **experience charts** (written stories complied by children describing an event the class has experienced), documentation boards, and dictating or writing stories about STEAM-based experiences all encourage early literacy. When children ask "what" questions, they are linking science to language and cognitive skills. Teachers promote this connection by asking children to provide their own explanations for what they observe. For example, why do puppies grow bigger but stuffed animals do not? Or what do the children think will happen if they mix the colors together?

Teachers respect the wonder and awe that children have for their environment when they help them express that wonder with language. Use new vocabulary in context and encourage children to verbalize their ideas. Young children can understand and use such multisyllabic, adult-sounding words as "dehydrated" and "evaporated" as easily as they can learn "dried" when the words relate to their own rich experiences. That said, the vocabulary of science and engineering should not be introduced as any type of "lesson" or directed task but rather modeled in an appropriate context. In this way, children can interpret meanings and associate words with the concepts being explored. The teacher who casually comments to a child, "I see you have made your tower *stable*, so it won't fall down," is teaching the vocabulary of engineering in context.

Children's literature is bursting with additional opportunities to integrate science, technology, and engineering into the curriculum. From animals or seasons, trucks that go, and buildings that touch the sky, teachers can offer their young students many occasions to question, infer, and discuss, with books as the catalysts. The Case Study feature "The Very Hungry Caterpillar" describes one teacher's method of incorporating STEAM and literature.

You might be wondering about the role of technology programs (apps or software) that claim to increase early literacy. Alphabet programs do not necessarily build the connection needed for language development and may be little more than electronic worksheets or flash cards, presenting information in isolation. Look instead for ways to

Case Study

The Very Hungry Caterpillar

Juan always enjoyed introducing his kindergarten students to the process of metamorphosis as part of his curriculum theme on insects. This year, he requested and received a butterfly hatching kit, which included a form to submit to receive the caterpillars. He projected the form on the class SMART board, and the children helped him fill in the address and other information needed for the caterpillars to be shipped to the school.

His students waited as patiently as 5- and 6-year-olds can for the caterpillars' arrival. During the wait, he read stories about butterflies and insects during circle time, and the children perused picture books related to the topic. One of the books that Juan read to them was *The Very Hungry Caterpillar* by Eric Carle, a story about a caterpillar who ate through increasing numbers of fruits and other foods each day. Juan carefully selected questions to help the children predict, infer, and discuss what happened in the story of a caterpillar eating and eating, building a cocoon, and eventually turning into a beautiful butterfly. Juan guided the children in understanding what a *cocoon* is and explained that what happened to the caterpillar was called *metamorphosis*. Later, after the caterpillars arrived at the school and the children began watching them change, he enjoyed hearing them use the same scientific terms that came out of their discussion of Eric Carle's classic story.

Consider This

1. Why do you think Juan let the children take part in completing the form to order the caterpillars?
2. What questions could he have asked to help children understand why the caterpillars had to be ordered and were not included in the kit?
3. How does this book incorporate math concepts? How does it relate to science?
4. What other books might Juan have selected?

---

include alphabet experiences within a framework of child control and choices, problem solving, experimentation, exploration, and connection to the child's real world.

Mathematics

Science and tinkering experiences offer many opportunities to use math skills. Measuring, comparing, organizing, and classifying are math skills frequently required in science. Charting the growth of plants in a garden or counting how many cucumbers are ready to pick is a relevant use of math for young children. Checking the weather can involve comparing the number of sunny, cloudy, and rainy days in a week.

The need to measure is clearly apparent in engineering. The supports for a bridge in the block area must be equal, and two half units can replace one unit block.

Art

Visual art creation encompasses many elements of science as well as engineering. When children blend two colors to create a third, they are conducting both an artistic experiment and a scientific experiment. When they use pencils, rulers, stencils, brushes, and molds, they engage in engineering and learn to use tools purposefully.

Even something as commonplace as playdough in the early childhood setting can be an accomplishment in art, engineering, technology, and science. Tools for playdough can be employed to create food objects such as sushi, spaghetti, hamburgers, or even ice cream. Other tools make hair or facial features on figures. Molds can even transform playdough into cars, igloos, spaceships, and dinosaurs. Basic tools such as plastic knives and scissors, rolling pins (**Figure 10.6**), or cookie cutters provide experiences with technology. As children play, they increase their skill and comfort in utilizing and mastering tools, building, experimenting, designing, and creating.

mzoroyan/iStock/Getty Images Plus

Figure 10-6 A 3-year-old uses a rolling pin to make cookies from playdough. How does this activity relate to science? To technology? To engineering?

Music and Dance

Musical instruments allow children to experience the movement of air and vibrations to create sound. An early learning environment need not be stocked with expensive instruments to offer a beneficial intersection of music, science, technology, and engineering. Filling glasses with differing amounts of water and tapping them with spoons gives children insight into how music works. They can even construct and create their own instruments in a tinkering area—paper towel rolls to make kazoos, paper plates for tambourines, or paper mâché and rice for maracas.

Dance offers a wonderful opportunity to discuss science as well. How do our bodies move the way they do? Why does a scarf play in the air when we dance with it (**Figure 10.7**)? What does it feel like when we spin? How might we use our bodies to depict a seed sprouting or a flower blooming?

Teachers can also play songs about science. For example, "The Science Song" by The Learning Station has an upbeat tune that encourages children to dance along. It includes the words "hibernation," "migration," "evaporation," "gravity," and "metamorphosis," with descriptions of what the terms mean. The call-and-response format makes it easy for children to enjoy these multisyllabic words. Another song, "World of Wonder" by Jack Hartmann, illustrates how plants, animals, weather, insects, and the world around us are full of wonder. The song can be a catalyst for discussion about the many wonders in the world.

Play

Teachers do not need to focus on a particular content area for children to begin to understand science and technology. Children begin to understand scientific concepts such as volume and conservation when they measure water and sand. They explore buoyancy with toy boats and learn about properties as they build and sculpt with wet and dry sand.

Blocks are an excellent way for children to begin to understand gravity and simple machines such as ramps. They discover stability and balance (essential concepts in engineering) while playing with unit blocks or DUPLO® to create a skyscraper or a

FatCamera/E+ via Getty Images

Figure 10-7 This first-grade student dances to music with a scarf. *What will the girl learn about the movement of sheer material? How does this experience involve science?*

whole town. When children are finished building, the teacher can take a digital photo to have a permanent record of the construction.

During dramatic play, children are often problem solvers, figuring out how to complete a task and use various tools. They use brooms to sweep the floor. They use spoons to stir in pretend ingredients and markers to make a sign for a make-believe store. And they often use phones or pretend barcode scanners as part of their play scenarios.

Science opportunities abound during outdoor play. Outdoor time provides occasions for children to recognize and predict weather, practice balancing, and experience friction while riding a tricycle. Even the activity of swinging encompasses science. As children learn to pump and notice how the swing gradually comes to a stop when pumping ends, they are encountering the physics of motion. A slide is technology: It is an inclined plane, which is a simple machine that uses gravity to assist in moving items. When children go down a slide, they are using technology and experiencing the force of gravity (**Figure 10.8**). The tricycles and wagons they use are also technology: They are propelled by pedals and wheels.

Themes

Another common way of integrating science, engineering, and technology into the curriculum through the use of broad topics or themes. Many curricula are built around a theme approach where activities and experiences focus on a general topic relevant to young children. Themes can be a framework for planning and helping children generalize, develop concepts, and see relationships. Common science-focused themes are described in the sections that follow.

Our Bodies

The human body is a popular theme in early childhood programs. Every time children perform movements (e.g., dance, yoga, swinging, climbing), they are learning about the functions of the human body and thus science. Body-part identification activities, such as "Simon Says" and "Heads, Shoulders, Knees and Toes," connect movement with

Figure 10-8 A kindergarten child enjoys the sensation of going down the slide. What might be learned about speed, motion, and gravity?

knowledge of the physical body. Teachers can even address body-part identification with infants by naming body parts while providing care. For example, "I'm going to tickle your foot! (**Figure 10.9**)" or "I'm going to wipe your mouth now!" Another way to teach body parts to infants and toddlers is to play such games as "This Little Piggy" and "I've Got Your Nose."

Figure 10-9 An infant responds to his mother talking about what she is doing. How does self-talk support language development and understanding? How does it relate to science?

Plants and Animals

Teachers should plan many opportunities throughout the year for children to observe the growth of plants. For example, children can be actively involved in the planting process and in caring for the classroom plants. They can build seed collections or gather leaves for sorting and classifying. And do not forget the value of a garden for growing flowers or vegetables.

Animals are tremendously appealing to young children. Caring for classroom animals (such as hamsters, guinea pigs, or betta fish) can contribute not only to knowledge about the animals but also to the development of empathy toward living things. Children are frequently excited to grow butterflies in an enclosure and release them (**Figure 10.10**) or watch tadpoles turn into frogs and hop away—reminding children that animals do not "belong" to us and that we should care for them in a way that makes sense for their species. Many local zoos, farms, and aquariums are equipped to work with early childhood centers and schools via class trips or visits to educate students about caring for animals and introduce them to unfamiliar animals.

Seasonal Themes

Teachers can provide materials in the science or tinkering centers related to the four seasons. They can encourage children to bring items that they find in their environment that are typical of the current season. Some teachers create boxes called "Signs of Spring" or "Signs of Fall" into which children deposit their treasures, such as flower buds or colorful fall leaves. Teachers can also display pictures of appropriate clothing—for example, winter hats, coats, and mittens for winter or shorts, sandals, and T-shirts for summer.

Heather Preston

Figure 10-10 These insect homes allow children to observe for several days and then release the insects outdoors. Why is it important for children to learn to respect nature by releasing insects or animals into their natural habitat?

Discovery Journeys

The Winter Season

Having spent his teaching career in the southern part of the United States, Rowan often questioned the relevance of snowmen and snowflakes that so frequently adorn classroom bulletin boards and window decorations as representative of winter. In the South, it is not unusual for children to reach the age of 3, 4, or 5, never having seen a snowfall remotely like the scenes depicted on calendars for December or January. Winter in the South is mostly gray with barren trees and shrubs. More wet than white, the weather mostly requires no more than a jacket. Snowsuits and even mittens are unknown to many children. When there is snow, it is usually brief, turning quickly to slush.

Do photos of snowy landscapes depict winter for everyone? When we consider what is developmentally appropriate for young children, the winter focus on snow may be foreign and abstract for some. Thus, teachers should be prepared to discuss how seasons are different in various places.

Consider This
1. What are other topics where children's experiences differ based on where they live?
2. What foods might be unfamiliar depending on children's geographic location?
3. How might a teacher build on children's experiences related to seasons?

Community Helpers

Children love learning about the different people who work in their community: police officers, firefighters, doctors, nurses, mail carriers, and librarians, to name a few. Teachers can arrange to have community helpers visit the classroom or take the children on a field trip to see community helpers in action. Technology such as digital cameras might be used to record experiences with community helpers and the equipment they use. Children might engineer their own versions of a fire station or police precinct with blocks. Remember that there are many community helpers whose work and equipment would interest children.

Transportation

Transportation themes are a natural pairing with science, technology, and engineering. A ramp enables children to pull wagons easily up into the storage area. Inspired by stories or songs about trains, children might create a pretend train using cardboard boxes taped together. Digital cameras can record a parade around the playground and create a presentation for families. Busses, trucks, and cars enhance play in the block area while a small train set in the manipulative area encourages fine motor skills. Boats added to the water table inspire activities there. Consider the many opportunities to create a miniature world for the vehicles to operate within the sand area.

Sample Activities

Although most science, technology, and engineering involve learning through exploration and discovery, teacher-initiated activities provide children with valuable experiences. Most of the activities listed in this section will be appropriate for 3-year-olds and older but may be enjoyed by younger children with adaptations and appropriate supervision.

When preparing for these activities, teachers should ask themselves a few important questions: What skills, knowledge, or concepts might children gain from participating in each activity? How can children construct their own knowledge as a result of taking part? What materials are needed? How will you lead the children to understand the desired concepts? What vocabulary should you know and introduce? What questions might you ask to encourage children to describe their thinking or summarize what they are observing? What can you do to facilitate their exploration? This preparation will make it possible to respond to the interests of the children and follow their lead as the activity evolves.

Ramps and Pathways

Ramps made from blocks, tubes, molding, or even taped-together paper towel tubes offer opportunities for engineering. Children can create paths for marbles, small cars (**Figure 10.11**), or other items using their science, technology, and engineering skills to create simple or complex structures. Such constructions can provide hours of experimentation and exploration related to gravity, angles, momentum, and speed.

A marble run is another version of ramps and pathways that children can create. A marble run can be made from cardboard tubes cut in half lengthwise and attached to a bulletin board at angles to create a path for a marble to roll from one tube to another.

By providing the materials for ramps and pathways and encouraging children's exploration, the teacher can facilitate children's learning about gravity, the relationship of inclines to speed, and the momentum of items as they travel.

Prisms and Rainbows

Let children investigate the sun's rays through prisms both inside and out. Place prisms in an area that receives sunlight or set up a sprinkler outside on a sunny day. Encourage children to change the placement of the sprinkler to see what happens as they vary the location.

Provide a solution to make bubbles, and look for the rainbows in the bubbles. Suggest that children explore many tools that might make bubbles other than the wands that come with purchased bubble solutions. Some possibilities are wire coat hangers twisted into a variety of shapes, colanders, or slotted spoons.

Sweet Potato Plants

Provide some sweet potatoes, glasses or jars, and toothpicks (**Figure 10.12**). Explain that the sweet potato can grow into a plant, but it must be partially in water and partially out.

FatCamera/E+ via Getty Images

Figure 10-11 A kindergarten child built a ramp with unit blocks and is using it to see how fast the car will travel. How are unit blocks useful for developing science, math, and engineering concepts?

arcimages/iStock/Getty Images Plus

Figure 10-12 Children have placed three sweet potatoes in water and are watching for changes. *How can the children document the changes they observe?*

Ask children to figure out how they can put the potato where it will be in water halfway and out halfway by using the items you provided. In time, they will see that the toothpicks can be stuck in the potato horizontally and balanced on the rim of the glass or jar. They can then add enough water to cover the bottom half of the potato. Mark the level of the water so they can see that it evaporates and determine when to add more. Watch for the roots and vines to sprout.

Wave Jars

Let each child fill a small plastic bottle or jar half full of water with some food coloring. Then fill it with light-colored corn oil. Seal the lid using a hot glue gun. Let children shake their jars to create waves and watch how the oil and water react. For variety, offer small plastic fish or decorative items such as beads or sequins to include before sealing. While young children may not comprehend the differences in density and the molecular attractions that cause this phenomenon, they will experience the results of it.

Vegetable or Flower Garden

Work with children to create a plan for a garden to grow flowers or vegetables. Before you start, consider what plants need to grow—water, soil, and sunlight. Children can look for the best locations for the garden based on the number of hours of sunlight needed. Popular and easy-to-grow options will depend on your United States Department of Agriculture (USDA) Hardiness Zone and soil type, but may include cherry tomatoes, cucumbers, lettuce, violets, marigolds, and herbs such as basil and rosemary. Older children may be able to help measure and draw garden designs to determine how many plants can fit in your space. Be sure to enlist families if you need assistance, such as with building a raised bed.

Be sure that children participate by using appropriate garden tools. They can use watering cans during a dry spell, tools for chores such as weeding, and help stake and tie the plants as they get larger. Harvesting, of course, is the most enjoyable part (**Figure 10.13**). Students should certainly sample the foods they grow. Guide their experiences with questions such as: How does a tomato look on the inside? What do the seeds feel like? How does it smell? Help children enjoy the beauty of the white and red sliced radishes and the bright orange of homemade carrot juice. Let them draw or fingerpaint to capture their impressions of the vase of flowers from the garden now sitting in a sunny spot of the classroom.

FatCamera/iStock/Getty Images Plus

Figure 10-13 A parent volunteer engages in conversation about the vegetables they have grown in the school garden. Why is creating and maintaining a garden a good experience for children? What can they do with the carrots they are harvesting?

Homemade Ice Cream

Food experiences offer wonderful opportunities to use science and technology. Children may use measuring cups, whisks, mixing spoons, decorating tools, and numerous other utensils.

One popular option (depending on allergies and dietary needs) is to make simple homemade ice cream. Provide a can with a lid, a larger can with a lid, duct tape, rock salt, and ice. You will need sweetened condensed milk and flat, flavored soda.

Put the soda and condensed milk in the smaller can in a one-to-one ratio. Attach the lid and seal it tightly with duct tape. Place it inside the larger can, and fill the larger can with ice and rock salt. Put the lid of the larger can on with duct tape as well. Have children roll the can back and forth to each other. Once frozen, enjoy!

Photography Activities

A digital camera (whether a separate device or one used via a mobile phone or tablet) can be an incredibly valuable resource for artistic and technological endeavors in the early childhood classroom. Consider the following suggestions:

- Take photos of children's projects and creations around the classroom. This attention demonstrates that you value their work.
- Create portfolios for each child, including pictures of their block constructions, three-dimensional artwork, or other projects you wish to document. Take videos of children's outdoor play to create a portfolio of gross motor skills that documents increases in abilities in jumping, climbing, running, or other physical skills.
- Use photos as starters for children's literacy experiences. Take a photo of something that interests a child and let them dictate a story about it. Make personalized books using the children's ideas and interests.
- Create mystery photos by having children take close-up detail photos of ordinary objects and ask their peers to guess what the objects are from seeing the small part.
- Let children create "scenes" with small figures, toy vehicles, and other miniature objects, and snap a photo. Children will busy themselves setting up the perfect scene for the photo, using engineering and problem-solving skills in the process.

Through the process of taking photographs or preparing scenes or objects for a photo shoot, children begin to learn about composition and other photography essentials. Early on, you may find they are upset that they chopped off a friend's head or made the photo blurry because they were moving while snapping the picture. Encourage them to try using the camera to experiment with distance, color filters, and lighting conditions to see how they affect the end product.

☑ CHECKPOINT

1. How can science, technology, and engineering be incorporated into a transportation theme?
2. What are other skills that children might develop that are common to science, technology, and engineering?
3. How does use of a digital camera help children notice details?

10.6 The Teacher's Role in Science, Technology, and Engineering

Teachers must understand how children learn if they are to guide their experiences in science, technology, and engineering. They must have a sincere desire to provide opportunities in the way children learn best. Having an inquisitive nature and the ability to enjoy a spirit of adventure and sense of discovery with children are integral parts of the process of science and engineering. Effective teachers will understand the appropriate use of technology in children's lives and how to integrate that technology into other areas of the curriculum. The competent teacher understands their role as a guide rather than an imparter of knowledge, as a facilitator of thinking rather than a conveyor of information, and as a supporter of learning rather than a controller.

The sections that follow will explore the role of the teacher in enriching STEAM education by asking thoughtful questions, motivating scientific and engineering exploration, and taking advantage of opportunities and children's interests.

Teaching Tip

STEAM for Young Children

The following are useful teacher guidelines for planning and conducting an effective program in science, technology, and engineering for young children:

- Set up and maintain science and tinkering areas.
- Provide a wide variety of materials for age-appropriate activities and exploration.
- Take time to introduce the equipment when you first put it out. Keep the guidelines simple, but be sure that children understand safety precautions and know how to use the technology. Let children help decide what the guidelines will be.
- Create an environment that supports wonder, curiosity, and experimentation.
- Model practical uses of technology by calling attention to your use of a calculator to add numbers or how you print photos of their art or block constructions.
- Set out items or materials to suggest activities for children. For example, display a sample book or photo puzzle that a child has made using a digital camera and a computer, along with the necessary supplies for making individual books or photo puzzles.
- Encourage children's questions and attempts to answer their own questions.
- Support children's growth through questioning and discussion that encourages wondering, thinking, and reasoning skills.
- Observe and assess the program and children's progress to expand their knowledge and skills.

Asking Thoughtful Questions

As children explore and use materials in science or tinkering areas, well-thought-out questions scaffold their reasoning and problem-solving skills. Asking questions that encourage children to think about their experiences and projects can help them understand and see possibilities or solutions. As a facilitator, your role is to help children figure out and decide what to do, not to tell them what will work.

Here are some examples of questions that are useful in helping children develop critical-thinking and reasoning skills to support engineering and scientific thinking:
- What do you think will happen if ____?
- How can you make it more stable?
- What can you do to make it stronger?
- Tell me how you ____?
- What did you notice about ____?
- How could you change your design so that it ____?
- What tools could you use to ____?
- Why do you think it keeps ____?
- What other way could you use the item you created?
- How could you make it faster? Slower?

In addition to asking questions and engaging in conversations, restating children's comments encourages deeper conversations. For example, "Quinten said he thought the new fish would eat all of the food we put in the tank because it is bigger than our other fish. What do you think the fish will do?" Or "Jacinta wants to see if the two of you can make a ramp that will send a marble clear across the room. How do you think you might do that?" Such questions elicit ideas that help children understand that there may be many ways of accomplishing a task and many solutions to a problem. Through the conversations you have with children, you will support their curiosity, expand on their ideas, and guide them to conceptualize, use vocabulary, and learn to find answers to their own questions.

Motivating Scientific and Engineering Exploration

Often, children will have ideas of their own about what they want to create, and the supportive teacher will encourage such ideas. However, one way you might motivate children to participate is to suggest a problem that might be solved in the science or tinkering area. Many children's books suggest ideas that promote tinkering. For example, after reading *If I Built a Car* by Chris Van Dusen, you might suggest children build a fanciful car themselves.

Everyday experiences offer opportunities to use problem-solving and engineering skills. After seeing a bird pick up a twig on the playground, you could suggest children consider and plan how to build a nest themselves. Seeing a melted crayon on the sidewalk can lead to exploring the effect of heat. Finding the water in the turtle's bowl at a lower level can generate interest in what made the water disappear.

How do teachers intentionally provide guidance and facilitate children's playful learning? The Case Study feature "It's Getting New!" provides an example of how one teacher set up an encounter for children to explore the concept of chemical changes.

Taking Advantage of Unplanned Opportunities and Children's Interests

Experienced teachers recognize that when children are interested in a topic, they are motivated to question, explore, and experiment, creating an opportunity where they are actively seeking information and answers. Skilled teachers respond to that interest by providing resources such as books or tools, time, and support for children to pursue that interest.

While teachers can plan events and situations that motivate children to experiment and explore, many unplanned occasions for discoveries occur regularly in our daily lives

Case Study

It's Getting New!

When a group of 4-year-olds arrived at their early childhood program one morning, they found a science table with a few pennies in a basket, two small bowls—one with water and one with vinegar—and some small pieces of cloth. The teacher watched from a distance as the group gathered around the table. The children immediately recognized the coins as pennies, and several noted Abraham Lincoln's profile on the coins. They wondered about the clear liquids in the bowls, and one child commented on the "pickle" smell.

"It's vinegar," contributed another, proud that he had recognized and named the smell. "My mommy uses it. It goes on lettuce."

Soon, as the teacher had anticipated, one child put a penny in the water. In time, another penny was placed in the vinegar. The children watched, intrigued by the change in the coin that was placed in the vinegar.

"It's getting new!" one child exclaimed as they observed the chemical reaction taking place. Just as the teacher expected, all of the pennies were soon dropped in the vinegar and "shined." As other children approached the table, the teacher was ready with more "old" pennies in her pocket to add to the dwindling supply. Two children, having satisfied their curiosity, left to pursue other activities. Some children were content to watch but did not participate. A few used a small magnifying glass to get a close-up view of both the "old" and "new" pennies. Several delighted in telling peers that the vinegar makes pennies shiny, but the water does not. Two busied themselves with seeing how many pennies they could shine, counting and carefully stacking the finished products. Others engaged in conversation about their purchasing experiences and shared their knowledge of the value of other coins.

Each child participated at a level of involvement appropriate for that individual's interest. The children followed their natural curiosity uninterrupted, and the teacher taught science in the best way possible by allowing them to question, experiment, and draw conclusions. Her lesson certainly taught them something about chemical changes but also supported language development, math, social skills, and, most of all, curiosity and exploration.

Consider This

1. How did the teacher predict what the children were likely to do?
2. What might the teacher have done if the activity had not interested the children?
3. What science vocabulary could have been introduced to the children?
4. How could the teacher expand on the experience?

with children. How might you use unplanned opportunities to guide children's learning in science, technology, and engineering? The Case Study feature "The Snow's Gone!" illustrates how one teacher took advantage of a child's fascination with melting snow to create a spur-of-the-moment learning opportunity. Teachers can help children develop science process skills through their innate curiosity about the world around them. They can respect the wonder and awe that children have for their environment and help them express that wonder with language.

☑ CHECKPOINT

1. How do thoughtful questions help children develop cognitive skills?
2. Why is it important to take advantage of unplanned opportunities for learning?
3. What are some books that might suggest a problem that motivates children to participate in science or tinkering, or use technology?

Case Study

The Snow's Gone!

"The snow's gone! It's all gone!" was the disappointing observation made by 3-year-old Ming, who had experienced snow for the first time.

The teacher, Mrs. Joe, could have reacted by merely stating, "It melted. It turned to water because the temperature rose, and it got warmer." Instead, she remembered a shady portion of the playground where some snow remained, not yet affected by the rise in temperature. Recognizing the opportunity to take advantage of the child's curiosity, she suggested that the class go out to see it.

Mrs. Joe gave the children time to notice the wetness from the melting snow and allowed Ming to bring a bowl of snow inside to observe. After a few minutes looking at snowflakes through a digital microscope, she asked, "What do you think will happen if we also put some in the freezer where it's cold like the weather was yesterday? And how about one in the classroom as well?"

For the next several hours, Ming periodically checked the bowl of snow placed on a tray in the classroom and the other bowl in the freezer, eagerly sharing with friends the exciting news that the snow in the freezer did not turn to change to water, but became ice, while the snow on the table did.

Ming had a question, not stated as such, but a wonder recognized by this astute teacher. Mrs. Joe resisted the temptation to offer a simple explanation. Instead, she helped Ming find an explanation by conducting an experiment in a manner appropriate for a young child. She did not give answers but led Ming to find answers by providing a responsive environment and guidance on making associations.

Consider This
1. What else could Mrs. Joe have done to help Ming understand what was happening?
2. What science vocabulary could she have introduced?
3. Why was this a better experience for the child than if the teacher had conducted a demonstration of why water freezes and melts?
4. How might Mrs. Joe have expanded the experience?

10.7 Establishing Science and Tinkering Centers

In many early childhood classrooms, teachers dedicate specific spaces to science and tinkering. While the goals and materials of both areas may overlap, the science area is likely to focus more generally on exploration, while the tinkering center will focus on constructing or creating with recycled or inexpensive consumable items. These centers are not designed for all children in the class to occupy at one time, but for children to come and go independently or in small groups as their interest ebbs and flows. Effective science and tinkering areas have materials arranged to attract children's interest, help them recognize possibilities, and inspire them to experiment.

A science center can be open-ended, offering free exploration of materials and their properties, or it can be designed to encourage children to discover a specific phenomenon or solve a specific problem. For example, a water activity may have the goal of understanding the properties of water and consist of a large pan of water with various items for pouring and filling, along with objects to help children conclude whether certain items will float.

Similarly, a tinkering area may focus on children's exploration of materials, but at times it may be set up for children to solve a particular problem such as building a strong bridge or measuring specific items. It might be as simple as a table with a balance scale and items of different weights to compare (**Figure 10.14**).

The Teaching Tip feature "Setting Up Science and Tinkering Centers" offers some general guidance for teachers. Teachers will also need to consider their goals for the

Figure 10-14 Two girls work at a science table exploring the balance scale. What skills can children learn from a balance scale?

centers, the types of items they need to include, and where to source those items. Those topics are addressed in the sections that follow.

Science and Tinkering Center Goals

Teachers want their students to explore, think independently, find solutions, and create. This is true across the curriculum. But what specific goals might a teacher have for their class in terms of science and tinkering? Here are some common goals other early childhood educators have identified. They want their children to:
- acquire basic STEAM concepts through exploration and experimentation.
- learn to use tools and manipulate equipment and materials.

Teaching Tip

Setting Up Science and Tinkering Centers

The following are useful teacher guidelines for setting up science and tinkering centers for young children:
- Define the areas using shelves and tables.
- Select and provide safe, age-appropriate materials and tools.
- Display materials attractively and at an accessible height for children to see the choices available.
- Include only items the children are free to use.
- Set up the areas near needed resources such as water, light, or storage.
- Make sure you can supervise the areas from anywhere in the room.
- Consider the traffic pattern so other children will not interrupt the activities in the centers.
- Use containers that make it easy for children to select, use, and return items.
- Group items to show relationships. (For example, place all seashells or all types of tape together.)
- Rotate materials available for variety and new experiences.

- develop skills in identifying and solving problems.
- learn to formulate and test hypotheses and draw conclusions.
- develop classification skills.
- use units of measurement.
- participate in the proper handling and care of plants and animals.
- develop positive attitudes toward living things, their interrelationships, and the environment.
- use and extend the vocabulary of science.
- discuss plans and share ideas with others.

Items and Equipment for Science and Tinkering Centers

What types of items and equipment do teachers generally want for their science and tinkering centers? For science, start with a child-size table, one or two chairs, and some low shelving. Add an assortment of free or inexpensive items that children can explore, including nature items such as leaves, twigs, rocks, pine cones, or seashells. For tinkering, almost anything that can be glued, stapled, taped, wired, or otherwise attached to make a construction is a great start. Older children even enjoy using tools to disassemble nonworking small appliances. Those items must be prepared for safety by removing any batteries or electrical cords. Taking apart items such as hair dryers, irons, radios, mixers, or toasters provides skills in using tools and insight into how the items work.

Figure 10.15 and **Figure 10.16** offer suggestions for engaging science and tinkering items for preschool and school age children. Many of the items could also be used for younger children as long as safety is foremost. For example, you would need to omit any small parts that younger children might put in their mouths.

Items to Include in a Science Center

Furniture		Tools	
Small table and chairs		Scissors	
Low shelving		Child-safe knives	
		Tweezers	
Light, Vision, and Sound		**Objects from Nature**	
Magnifiers	Flashlights	Animals	Rocks
Loupes	Color paddles	Ant farms	Leaves, pods, and seeds
Microscopes	Tuning forks	Butterfly gardens	Plants
Kaleidoscopes	Xylophone and other musical instruments	Bug cage	Seashells
Mirrors and lenses		Aquarium	Pebbles
Prisms		Terrarium	Sand
		Soil of various types (sandy, clay, and peat)	Wood bark
			Driftwood
Measurement		**Simple Machines**	
Tablespoons, teaspoons, cups, etc.	Measuring tapes	Gears	Ramps
Balance scales	Hourglasses	Pulleys	Pendulum
Rulers	Compasses	Wheels and axles	
Miscellaneous		**Taste and Smell**	
Magnets and magnetic toys		Vinegar	Baking powder
Wood		Baking soda	Sugar
Wire		Salt	Food coloring

Goodheart-Wilcox Publisher

Figure 10-15 This chart lists many items commonly used in science areas. What else can you think of that you might add?

Items to Include in a Tinkering Center

Adhesives	Tools and Containers	Materials and Supplies
Tape of all types (masking, painters' duct, florist, etc.)	Tape holders (handheld or desktop), multi-roll dispensers	Cardboard tubes, sheets, boxes of many sizes
Staples, brads	Staplers (regular and long-reach)	Paper or plastic cups, plates, bowls, bottles, small wooden or plastic spoons, straws
White glue in various forms (bottles, sticks, dots, paste)	Q-tips®, craft sticks, brushes	Paper of all types (manilla tagboard, poster board, construction paper in many colors, tissue, crepe paper and streamers, wax paper, aluminum foil, colored and clear cellophane)
Wire of various types (twist ties)	Containers for sorting and organizing	Fabric of many types (sheer, textured, fleece)
Hook and loop closures (self-adhesive and glue-on)	Scissors	Rubber bands of various sizes
Yarn, string, thread, cording	Dispenser or basket for balls of yarn	Paints, crayons, markers
Velcro®	Measuring cups and spoons	Recycled plastic, packing materials, Styrofoam pieces

Goodheart-Wilcox Publisher

Figure 10-16 This chart shows items that might be included in a tinkering center. What else might be added?

While these charts offer common suggestions to get started, teachers should evaluate other factors when deciding what will go in their centers. They can ask themselves the following questions:

- Are the materials safe and sanitary for the ages using them? Are plants non-toxic? Are any of the items so small that they can be swallowed by very young children? If activities involve food, are provisions made for separate spoons or individual serving dishes? Will children with allergies or disabilities be able to participate?
- Are the materials open ended and versatile? For example, water play provides opportunities to explore measurement, floatation, evaporation, and so on. A supply of cardboard tubes, paper cups, or wooden sticks can be used in endless ways.
- Can the materials be used independently by children with minimal adult assistance? Can children answer questions for themselves such as, "What happens when I blow up a balloon and let it go?" "How is sand different when it is wet?" "How can I make this stack of cups taller?"
- Are materials arranged to encourage communication among children? Are there materials to record information, such as notepads or digital cameras? Children quickly learn to cooperate and work together in order to complete an activity. Is there ample workspace for several children in both the science and tinkering areas?
- Is there a variety of materials for children to select according to their personal interests? Having many options is particularly important for tinkering. When a child needs to make an axle for a truck, the right item might be a recycled wooden chop stick.
- Do the materials encourage "what if" questions? A magnet activity (**Figure 10.17**) invites children to predict what will happen if they attempt to pick up various objects—a pencil, a paper clip, coin, or plastic lid. Such an activity lends itself to experimenting and finding out what happens. Building a stronger home for the three pigs encourages children to consider the properties of various materials and structures.
- Are the materials appropriate for the children's maturity? Keep in mind that children's maturity levels can change quickly as they age. For instance, children in a pre-kindergarten class will be able to handle activities in May that they could not in August of the previous year.
- Do the materials stress process skills, the fundamental skills emphasized in science explorations? Consider how the materials might help develop those skills.

Sturti/ E+ via Getty Images

Figure 10-17 Third-grade children show their delight that their predictions were correct about what the magnets would pick up. *Do you think the children would have been as excited if the teacher had just told them what would happen rather than letting them test their ideas?*

For additional information on setting up a science center or a tinkering center, see Chapter 2, "The Early Childhood Learning Environment."

✓ CHECKPOINT

1. What are other items that might be added to a tinkering center?
2. What are ways and reasons to establish a science or tinkering center?
3. How can a teacher ensure that items are safe for children to use independently?

10.8 Focus on Assessment of Science, Technology, and Engineering Practices

Ongoing assessment in all early childhood areas, including science, technology, and engineering, can be the catalyst for ongoing program improvement. Assessment helps teachers see where equipment or supplies might be needed, to consider changing how an area is arranged, and to analyze the benefits for the children.

Teachers must be constantly alert to how children are functioning in the science or tinkering center and in using technology. Children's success in using materials, making observations, formulating provocative questions, and creating ways to test their ideas should be carefully observed; their abilities to see relationships, describe what they see, and make inferences should be noted. Teachers must be alert to the sometimes subtle signs that children are losing interest, then determine whether the activity should be varied, expanded, or ended.

The following section illustrates a tool that can help you better evaluate and plan for your program needs.

Science Area and Program Assessment

Figure 10.18 offers one means of assessing a science program to determine areas that need improvement. It is an easy-to-use checklist developed and used to help early childhood programs appraise their approach to the STE portion of STEAM. The questions offer a broad range of experiences to ensure children have the skills related to common standards and goals for early childhood. Although it is a yes/no binary checklist, there will often be cases where the response is somewhere in between. For example, perhaps children are exposed to *some* firsthand, sensory experiences but not as *much* as the teacher or program would like. In that case, another option of "somewhat" or "partial" might be added, or space could be included for notes.

Science, Technology, and Engineering Program Assessment

Yes	No	Assessment Question
		Are children exposed to many firsthand, sensory experiences?
		Is exploration of objects encouraged?
		Are food preparation experiences provided frequently with an emphasis on good nutrition?
		Are activities located as to not interfere with others?
		Are the science and tinkering areas clearly defined with boundaries?
		Are field trips planned to expand children's view of the world? Are visitors invited to the classroom to share information?
		Is there adequate preparation and follow-up for field trips or visitors?
		Are children learning the vocabulary of science?
		Do materials and supplies relate to a theme or to children's current interests?
		Are new activities developed based on the interests of individual children?
		Are opportunities provided for learning through guided discovery, problem solving, imitation, etc.?
		Do children care for and observe animals of several types?
		Are children involved in suggesting and planning activities?
		Are experiences provided to help children learn about their bodies?
		Do children have access to water and sand activities frequently?
		Are experiences provided to help children learn about simple machines?
		Are children involved in nature experiences such as planting seeds, caring for plants, nature walks, raising vegetables, etc.?
		Is technology used to supplement and enrich firsthand experiences?
		Are electronic devices easy to use and controlled by the children?
		Do the equipment, materials, and supplies encourage children to construct and build?
		Are adequate and versatile equipment and tools available and in good shape?
		Are materials changed often to stimulate and maintain interest?

Goodheart-Wilcox Publisher

Figure 10-18 Assessment is important for knowing if you are meeting your program goals. How can an assessment chart like this be used to support ongoing improvement?

CHECKPOINT

1. How might you use your state standards to develop your own assessment of your science program?
2. Why is ongoing assessment important?
3. What skills in science, technology, and engineering do you consider most important?

10.9 Family Matters

Helping families understand the role and value of science, technology, and engineering is an important role of an early childhood teacher. As in other areas, those topics are part of a broader home-school connection in which families and teachers work together to support children's learning and development.

Figure 10.19, **Figure 10.20**, and **Figure 10.21** are sample letters that teachers might share with families to ensure they are aware of the creative and fun things their children are doing in the classroom. Teachers can edit these to fit a variety of formats: printed notices or newsletters, email, blog posts—however they choose to communicate with families in their programs.

Vegetable Garden Note

To Our Families:

Our science program offers many opportunities for parental involvement. One of the most popular is our annual vegetable garden.

Each year, the children gain valuable life skills as they plan and care for the garden, taking responsibility for watering, weeding, and caring for the plants. They spend time watching the plants grow, making observations about what they see, and imagining what they think will happen next. When the vegetables are ready for harvest, the children prepare and eat the foods they have grown. Families often report that they were surprised to find their child eating a new vegetable—one that would not have been tried without this experience at school!

The garden is not only an excellent science activity, but we also read stories on related topics, draw pictures of garden plants and their insect friends, write about our experiences, and use math to measure as the plants grow.

Families in our school have been instrumental in assisting with this task in past years, and we are now seeking volunteers. Specifically, we would be grateful for your support in:

- purchasing a packet of seeds from the list posted on our bulletin board or donating seeds from your own garden.
- providing a bag of one or two cubic feet of garden soil.
- volunteering for a one-hour shift to prepare the garden.
- donating or lending any gardening tools to adults or children.
- providing snacks or beverages on work days.

Please sign up on the attached sheet if you can help this year. I appreciate your support!

Thank you!

Miss Lupita

Goodheart-Willcox Publisher; (illustration) Gvardgraph/Shutterstock.com

Figure 10-19 A newsletter or family letter is often used to communicate with families. *What are other ways a program can communicate effectively with families?*

Technology Use Policy

To Our Families:

We are frequently asked by family members how we handle technology (including tablets, computers, online educational games, digital cameras, and so on) in our classroom. The question is an important one, and we wish to communicate our procedures to avoid confusion.

First and foremost, we believe that children learn best when they have real, tangible experiences in the physical world around them. We want children to use all of their senses to engage in their environment. We also want them to interact with the classroom adults and their peers in ways that are appropriate for their age and development. This quote from the National Association for the Education of Young Children's Developmentally Appropriate Practices position statement summarizes our practices in relation to technology use:

> "When truly integrated, uses of technology and media become normal and transparent—the child or the education is focused on the activity or exploration itself, not the technology."

When we use technology, our goal is always to foster children's natural wonder and creativity. For example, in our classroom, we really enjoy digital cameras as technology that is easy and versatile for children to use. When we give children cameras, they see the world differently. Photography is about documentation and communication; children are often excited to share their work with their families. A digital camera makes it easy for children to explore their world and document what they see and do. The technology becomes normal and transparent, so the child is focused on the exploration.

If your child expresses interest in our photography activities, you may find the following list of activities helpful to try at home. These activities provide means for children to experiment with digital media possibilities.

Photo Puzzles
Glue a printed photo onto a sturdy piece of tagboard. Cut the picture into pieces to create a puzzle. To support social skills, let children make a puzzle from a photo of a friend as a gift or share a photo puzzle of themselves with friends.

Family Trip Fun
Even ordinary trips to the park can take on a completely new aspect when children take a camera along to document the trip. Consider the possibilities at a zoo, a farm, or just a walk around the block.

Make a Photo Journal
Take photos of interesting things you and your child see as you go about your day. The photos may be as simple as a small wildflower or a pretty leaf. Help your child organize the photos on a poster or in a scrapbook, adding captions to each. On another day, complete a similar project called "My Home" by focusing on items around your home and/or yard. These projects can be springboards for much conversation and will open your eyes to what your child considers important.

Wearable Photos
Print photos your child takes on transfer paper and make T-shirts or other clothing items from the photos.

Collecting with a Camera
With a camera, you can collect objects you cannot own. Perhaps your child likes vehicles. You could work with your child to take photos of planes, trains, cars, and buses and collect them to create a slideshow or print them to hang up in a collage.

Thank you for your support. I hope you enjoy using technology as a tool for learning as much as we are enjoying it at school!

Miss Katya

Goodheart-Wilcox Publisher; (illustration) HappyPictures/Shutterstock.com

Figure 10-20 It is important to share information with families about your use of technology. How does this information help parents support their child?

To Our Families:
You may not think of your children as engineers, but they are! They construct bridges and buildings in the block area, make complex marble raceways, and solve problems such as how to build a strong house after reading *The Three Little Pigs*. They build kazoos from paper towel tubes and figure out how to attach bells to paper plates to make tambourines. They are truly amazing and keep us inspired every day.

To encourage children to think creatively and solve problems, we have a tinkering area where they can use a wide variety of materials to engineer their creations. Much of the material in the tinkering area is recycled, and we invite you to contribute to our supply. We can use all types of cardboard, plastic, wire, masking tape, and almost anything else that is clean and can be attached to other items or used to attach items.

We have placed plastic bins at the school entrance marked "Tinkering Center" for you to place your donations. Our tinkering area is very popular, and we use a lot of material! We appreciate your regular donations throughout the year.

Thank you!

Mr. Lamar

Goodheart-Wilcox Publisher; (illustration) YummyBuum/Shutterstock.com

Figure 10-21 The value of engineering in early childhood may not be understood by families. What other ways might you help families understand?

✓ CHECKPOINT

1. How did the requests for help from families serve to inform them about the value of the experiences?
2. What are other ways to involve families in science, technology, or engineering?

Chapter 10 Review and Assessment

Chapter Summary

10.1 Describe the relationships among science, technology, and engineering as components of STEAM.

- STEAM is an acronym for Science, Technology, Engineering, Art, and Mathematics.
- All components of STEAM involve exploration and discovery, problem solving, and the development of critical-thinking skills.
- The components of STEAM are interrelated and overlapping in early childhood programs.
- Many popular activities in early childhood programs make use of science, technology, and engineering in the way that children learn best—through hands-on exploration and discovery.
- The STEAM experiences in a quality program contribute to the development of those thinking skills and abilities that will serve children throughout life.
-

10.2 **Identify the goals of science with young children.**
- Some activities may not be recognized as a part of science.
- Teaching science is teaching thinking skills, and the very nature of science makes it a vital component of any curriculum plan.
- The key process skills of science are adaptable to other curriculum areas.
- Experiences are most effective when integrated into the curriculum to help children see connections and understand concepts.
- The teaching strategies used to help children learn through exploration and discovery are cultivating the methods of the scientist. The tinkering experiences lead to engineering.

10.3 **Describe appropriate use of technology in early childhood.**
- Technology use includes more than electronics.
- There are concerns about screen time expressed by the NAEYC, the AAP, and others.
- Electronic use with young children requires careful attention to ensure that devices are used in a developmentally appropriate manner based on what is known about young children's learning.
- Media can be a tool for learning if used judiciously, with developmentally appropriate practices as the overriding factor in decisions about how it is used.
- Electronic devices can supplement hands-on experiences but should not supplant them.

10.4 **Explain the benefits of tinkering as a means of engineering skill development.**
- Tinkering is a precursor to engineering and allows children to explore the properties of materials to see what they can construct with the materials.
- Engineering, as applied to young children, includes attaching materials, testing constructed structures, and forming concepts about building and creating with a variety of materials.
- Engineering involves problem solving, a skill that is transferable in all curriculum areas.

10.5 **Describe how to integrate science, technology, and engineering throughout the early childhood curriculum.**
- Science and tinkering centers provide opportunities in small groups that support language experiences.
- Science, technology, and engineering can be integrated with other curriculum areas through reading and writing, mathematics, art, music and dance, and play.
- When children talk or write about what they are doing, they are developing literacy and language.
- Engineering involves measuring, counting, and many other mathematical skills.
- Books can be used as catalysts for ideas and information.
- Another common way of integrating science, engineering, and technology into the curriculum is through the use of broad topics or themes.
- Although most science, technology, and engineering involve learning through exploration and discovery, teacher-initiated activities, such as building ramps and pathways, growing a flower or vegetable garden, and photography activities, provide children with valuable learning experiences.
- Science, technology, and engineering activities build small motor coordination.

10.6 **Define the teacher's role in science, technology, and engineering.**
- The teacher's knowledge of how children learn must inform their scientific experiences.
- A major role of the teacher in STEAM experiences is to provide opportunities for children to identify problems, make predictions, experiment to seek solutions, and analyze their success.
- The teacher's role is to support children in using materials and communicating in a way that promotes cognitive skills.
- Thoughtful, open-ended questions can help children develop critical-thinking skills and learn to express their thoughts.
- Although children's curiosity will usually motivate them to explore and experiment, the teacher can set the stage for such activities through the use of materials and events.
- Science or engineering activities can be facilitated by the teacher through planned experiences or by taking advantage of unplanned events that attract children's interest.

10.7 Set up a developmentally appropriate science and tinkering center.
- Specific science and tinkering areas in the classroom provide encouragement for children to freely explore and experiment.
- The way the areas are set up, organized, and provisioned are important considerations in determining how effective the areas are in meeting these goals.

10.8 Describe how to assess a science, technology, and engineering part of the curriculum in early childhood.
- The materials and supplies provided and how they are arranged can engage children and allow for their independent use.
- It is important for the teacher to regularly assess the program and to use formative evaluation to adjust teaching strategies and materials available.
- Such assessments provide for ongoing improvement and allow one to better meet both the program needs and the individual needs of young children.
- A checklist based on standards is one way to assess the STEAM program.

10.9 Demonstrate ways to involve families in science, technology, and engineering.
- Engaging families in an early learning program helps them understand the value of science, the appropriate use of technology, and how tinkering leads to engineering skills.
- Families benefit from information about science and how to support children in learning science.
- Suggestions about appropriate activities can help families understand how digital media can best be used.
- Involving families in creating opportunities for children's creative tinkering is one way to build home-school connections.

Recall and Application

1. **True or False.** The letter "T" in STEAM stands for "tinkering."
2. **True or False.** Science, technology, and engineering require many of the same skills.
3. **True or False.** Science is a collection of facts that one must memorize.
4. **True or False.** Process skills are the skills that children learn through science exploration.
5. **True or False.** Technology in early childhood refers only to electronic devices, such as computers.
6. **True or False.** Software and apps that drill children on the alphabet and numbers are the most effective use of technology since these are skills children need to learn.
7. **True or False.** The main use of digital cameras in early childhood programs is to take photos to identify cubbies.
8. Which of the following is *not* a true statement about technology use?
    A. Professional judgment is needed to determine if a specific use of technology is developmentally appropriate.
    B. Effective uses of technology are active, are hands-on, give the child control, and support children's learning.
    C. Children should be allowed to use electronic technology as much as they want since it is known that they can learn important skills from it.
    D. Interactions with technology and media should support creativity, exploration, pretend play, and active play.
9. **True or False.** Children learn how to use materials by tinkering.
10. **True or False.** A tinkering area is expensive to create.
11. **True or False.** Tinkering supports the development of fine motor skills and coordination.
12. **True or False.** The concepts of color and texture fall under both science and art.
13. **True or False.** Asking open-ended questions about what a child is doing at a computer can expand language skills.
14. **True or False.** There are many opportunities during the day to integrate science with other curriculum areas.
15. **True or False.** The teacher can stimulate problem-solving and thinking skills by asking thoughtful questions.
16. **True or False.** Everyday experiences can often be a catalyst for science exploration.
17. **True or False.** All science activities should be suggested and directed by the teacher.
18. **True or False.** Observation and prediction are scientific concepts too advanced for young children to understand.

19. Which of the following is *not* a good example of a thoughtful question to stimulate children's thinking?
    A. What tools could you use to ____?
    B. What is the name of this shape?
    C. What other way could you use the item you created?
    D. How could you make it faster? Slower?

20. **True or False.** Materials in a tinkering area should allow for individual differences, such as abilities and interests.

21. **True or False.** Science activities are best restricted to the science center and not integrated into other classroom areas to avoid confusing children.

22. **True or False.** Materials in the science center should be designed for one purpose and used only for that specified purpose.

23. **True or False.** In a tinkering area, children should learn to make something by following the teacher's example.

24. In a tinkering center, children can learn each of the following *except* ____.
    A. how to use tools and materials
    B. how to evaluate outcomes
    C. how to find solutions
    D. how to follow directions

25. **True or False.** One purpose of assessment is to know when an activity should be expanded or ended.

26. **True or False.** One way to assess a program is to use a checklist.

27. **True or False.** Involving families in the science program can help them understand the value of STEAM.

28. **True or False.** Parents need not be informed about screen policies because they might object.

Chapter 11

STEAM: Art and Music

Standards Covered in This Chapter

NAEYC
NAEYC—1a, 1b, 1c, 1d, 2a, 2c, 3a, 3b, 4a, 4b, 4c, 5a, 5b

DAP
DAP—1b, 1d, 2a, 2b, 2c, 4a, 4c, 4d, 4e, 4h, 5a, 5c, 5d

Learning Outcomes

After reading this chapter, you should be able to:

11.1 Identify the importance of art and music in curriculum for young children.
11.2 Explain how art and music can be integrated into the rest of the curriculum.
11.3 Describe the developmental stages of children's art and music skills.
11.4 Explain the teacher's responsibilities in implementing an effective art and music program.
11.5 Describe methods for assessing the art and music program.
11.6 Examine the role of the teacher in connecting with families.

Chapter opener image credit: SDI Productions/E+ via Getty Images

Key Terms

aesthetic	interlacing	rhythm
analytical	media	tempo
collage	model	three-dimensional
creativity	pitch	transition

Introduction

While the concept of STEM (Science, Technology, Engineering, and Math) has been widespread for a number of years, the concept of STEAM, with the letter "A" representing the arts (including music), is newer. STEAM better represents the interrelationship of the five areas. Too, this evolution results from recognition of the importance of a creative mindset in STEAM experiences. The creative and **analytical** (reasoning) skills developed through art and music are important to foster the innovation and evaluation required in science, technology, engineering, and math.

Generally in the field of education when we refer to art, we think of the visual arts. However, for this text, music is included as a component of the arts. Like the visual arts, music has many facets of mathematical and scientific principles. Music includes patterns, time measurement, and repetition, which are all mathematical elements. Creating music, like science, involves problem-solving and analytical skills, including an understanding of how sound is produced and perceived.

The process of exploration in art parallels the exploration in science. Exploratory art experiences inspire curiosity, stimulate analytical skills, and lead to understanding the properties of various materials—skills we often identify as components of science. For example: What happens when paint colors run together? How can one construct a tower from craft sticks and tape? How does clay respond as we squeeze and shape it? What is the best way to attach pieces of cardboard to make a house for a miniature figure? How many ways can I make sounds with a tambourine? Can I make the sound of the flute louder?

When we think of visual art in early childhood, what typically comes to mind are activities such as easel painting, drawing, or sculpting playdough or clay. While these activities are certainly artistic experiences that young children should have often, we must ensure that children have ample experience with the elements of art. These art elements are line, shape, form, color, and texture. When you consider what young children do with art **media** (the materials used), they clearly are using those elements (National Gallery of Art n.d.).

When we consider music, we often think of simple songs that children learn and sing, but music also includes the exploration of sounds and their patterns. How do sounds differ among instruments? How do you change the sound an instrument makes? How does a bell make a sound? What other objects make sounds? What are the sounds of nature? Even an infant explores the sounds of a rattle and quickly learns to intentionally reproduce what they hear (**Figure 11.1**).

The value of art and music is not in the finished product but in what the children are doing and learning. A key message is that the process is more important than the product. A second key message is that whatever the child creates, whether a painting or their own version of a song, should be the child's work and not the teacher's.

11.1 Art and Music for Young Children

Why are art and music important in early childhood? Art can help children learn problem-solving skills as they make choices about media, tools, and subjects. They develop fine motor skills and hand-eye coordination through cutting, sewing, drawing, painting, and modeling. As children work cooperatively with others in art experiences, they learn the social skills of sharing, taking turns, and adapting to the group. They develop

Figure 11-1 These two toddlers react to a teacher's actions and enjoy the sounds they are able to make. *How do you think a teacher might engage the toddlers to imitate actions?*

language skills by describing their creations and talking about their enterprise as they work. Math, science, and reading skills come into play as children learn about the sequence of actions, cause and effect, and how to work with the various media and tools.

Art and music are much more than something teachers have children do to produce an object to send home or a fun activity to perform. Art and music foster the development of children in many ways. When young children engage in art and music activities, they:

- explore the properties of materials and experiment with what they can do.
- express thoughts and emotions.
- use their imagination, creativity, and problem-solving skills.
- feel a sense of accomplishment and begin to see the value of their own and others' work.
- see the beauty and uniqueness of their environment.
- try new ways of doing things and make their own choices about how to approach a task.

Creativity and Young Children

Every child naturally has some element of **creativity**. Creativity involves the use of one's imagination and seeing new possibilities—common traits in young children. A teacher's role should be to maintain the natural creativity that young children have—rather than try to "develop" creativity in them. Why is it important to be concerned about preserving children's creativity? Society places a high value on contribution to the fields of art, science, and technology with the end result of preserving creativity in young children. The importance of creativity puts responsibility on early learning programs to furnish many opportunities for creative expression. Children are reaching out at a young age, exploring and experimenting with all media. Creative experiences can foster emotional health and enhance self-esteem by giving children an outlet to express their emotions.

Art and music allow for firsthand experiences in other curriculum areas. In art, children learn to integrate math skills such as color, shape (**Figure 11.2**), seriation, classification, and ordinal and cardinal numbers. Art activities permit children to engage in self-selected use of skills. Music provides occasions for children to use and create rhyming schemes, which are important literacy skills. Both help develop planning and analytical abilities.

Teachers should make ample materials freely available and cultivate their own ability to stand back, letting children explore and utilize the materials. Teachers should also support children's production of ideas, recognizing and acknowledging their value by asking thought-provoking questions that encourage their creative thinking.

Gajus/iStock/Getty Images Plus

Figure 11-2 This two-year-old is experimenting with paint by making circles. Why do you think he is using his fingers?

Crafts and Digital Media

Some classrooms rely on crafts rather than creative art. Crafts have a predefined outcome, such as making a spring basket following specified instructions and steps. The teacher, often using a **model** (a sample) to follow, gives instructions by demonstrating how to construct the product. Creative art, on the other hand, should reflect a teacher's hands-off attitude. Creativity is taking what we know from our experiences and putting that knowledge together into new ideas, new products, or new uses.

With creative art, the teacher might suggest an idea, but is primarily responsible for providing a wide variety of materials and time for art and music experiences. In creative art, the process and outcome should be determined by the child's efforts rather than the teacher's intent.

Software and applications are available to create digital illustrations using electronic means. While such media can provide unique experiences, one must consider goals and developmentally appropriate practices in choosing when and how to use them.

The Creative Process

Experts tell us that there are four steps in the creative process. In this context, whether children are exploring items in the science area, making up lyrics to a song, creating a cardboard construction, or combining ingredients to create a new dish for a special meal, the process is similar. All areas of STEAM include creativity as an essential ingredient.

- **Preparation.** The first step in the creative process is preparation. This step includes all of one's skills, knowledge, and understanding. It includes trying out and exploring materials and their properties to understand how they work.
- **Incubation.** The second step, incubation, refers to a time when one is consciously or subconsciously thinking about the problem or the desired outcome.
- **Illumination.** The third stage is illumination, a word for the "idea" or "sudden insight" when one thinks of a way to do a task or accomplish a goal.
- **Verification.** The last stage, verification, is the stage where a product or system is created, evaluated, and revised.

For children to utilize their creativity, we must allow time and resources for them to progress through these stages. They need time to learn how to use the materials, think about what they want to do, and try out many ideas. They need large blocks of time where they are free for such explorations and analyses. And they need plenty of time to try out, revise, and redo, if necessary, their solutions.

Cultivating Creativity

The early childhood years are critical to many areas of development, including the preservation of creative thinking and development of self-confidence. Art can support children's confidence and creativity because there should be no right or wrong way to complete an art task. All ideas are acceptable, and children's unique works are reflections of themselves. Similarly, music supports creativity because the song or tune a child makes up is their own product.

To fully cultivate children's creativity, a teacher must have enthusiasm and appreciation for children's creations, understanding that there are many ways to approach a task or goal (**Figure 11.3**). Children need acceptance of their efforts, encouragement, and support to try their ideas. Most children will be very self-motivated and simply need time to think, solve problems, and access to a wide variety of materials. Some may need encouragement to explore the media. See the Teaching Tip feature, "How to Support Children's Creativity," for helpful guidelines.

Benefits of Art and Music

To answer the question of why art and music are important components of the curriculum, one must address their benefits to children. Many of the benefits of visual art overlap with the benefits of music. The following sections discuss several of the desired skills which art and music experiences can encourage.

Attention Span

Art and music activities can help children lengthen their attention span. When children choose and engage in activities they enjoy, they will stretch their attention span to new lengths because of their interest.

Nazar Rybak/E+ via Getty Images

Figure 11-3 The teacher shows interest in the girl's construction project and scaffolds her thinking about possibilities. Why is it important that the teacher not just tell the child what she should do?

Teaching Tip

How to Support Children's Creativity

- Interfere as little as possible. Scaffold the child's efforts rather than doing it for them.
- Avoid coloring books, coloring sheets, and models for children to copy. Copying takes away from the process of self-expression. Anything a child might learn from a coloring book or coloring sheet can be learned in a more meaningful way. Learning to stay within the lines is not a reason to use coloring pages. Children can master staying within the lines they make themselves and will be more motivated to do so.
- Understand that it is the process of creating, not the product, that matters most to the young child. The work does not have to be something recognizable or look like a specific object. There does not need to be a finished project; it is the act of creating that is important. Children are often satisfied with the activity itself and do not desire a completed product.
- Allow plenty of time and opportunity for children to use the materials to provide a satisfying experience. Have materials available most of the day, not just during a designated "art or music" time. Allow time for children to be absorbed in work. Continuing an activity as long as they are interested prevents a child's thought process from being interrupted and allows for the development of ideas.
- Learn how to talk to children in ways that enhance the child's creativity. Comment on the pleasure the child is feeling or ask them to tell you about what they are working on. Ask questions that call for divergent thinking, such as "How many ways can you...?" or "How many uses can you find for...?" to encourage creative thinking.
- Grant a child who is reluctant the right to refuse. Art or music should never be forced or required. Observing others can be valuable.
- Allow ample time to play. Through play, children test ideas, experiment with materials, and assume a variety of roles.
- Provide an atmosphere of acceptance. Knowing an accident or a mistake will not bring ridicule or reprimand gives children the security to approach new experiences without fear.
- Value originality and self-expression. Treat children's ideas with respect; share their delight in discoveries.
- Provide privacy and space for time alone. Children need time to think; they need time away from constant social interaction.
- Avoid stereotyping. All activities should be available to all children, not supported or restricted based on gender or other factors.
- Help children become more sensitive to the environment. Encouraging the use of all of the senses helps children become more alert and responsive to their experiences.
- Provide an organized variety of supplies, sound makers, and found or recycled materials. Having access to many materials to freely use permits children to follow through on their creative ideas.
- Educate families on the value of children's creative efforts. Having work and ideas appreciated at home encourages children's future attempts.

Language Skills

Most activities that encourage children to converse with each other or use words foster language development. Singing and musical games encourage conversations and the use of new vocabulary. Some art activities, such as modeling, fingerpainting, and using easels arranged side by side, facilitate conversations as children work alongside each other. Participating in musical activities such as "The Farmer in the Dell" encourages shared language (**Figure 11.4**). Even picture books related to art and music can build vocabulary and literacy as well as motivate children to create. A list of books with a theme of art or music can be found in the Instructor Resources section of this text.

PeopleImages/iStock/Getty Images Plus

Figure 11-4 This teacher leads a song where children clap when they hear certain words. How does music enhance language and literacy?

Social-Emotional Skills

Art and music activities provide an appropriate outlet for feelings. For children, art materials such as modeling dough and clay, fingerpainting, and **collage** (an artwork made of gluing or pasting materials on a flat surface) using various textures provide outlets for emotional expression and release of tension or stress. Music, too, can provide an outlet for feelings. Singing together can build a cooperative spirit and create shared experiences that build friendships. Lullabies can be calming and soothing, helping children to relax.

MaryAnn Kohl, a nationally known author of numerous books on process art, tells the story of how she learned the value of art as a means of emotional expression for young children in the Discovery Journeys feature "Solomon and *The Red Balloon*" on the following page.

Pre-Reading and Prewriting Skills

In art activities, children develop skills of visual discrimination, perception, and memory. Both art activities and songs with finger or hand movements develop hand-eye coordination and fine motor skills. These skills are necessary for readiness to read and write.

Physical Development

Art and music activities primarily help children develop small muscles and coordination, but children can also develop large muscles when both large brushes and large paper are used or when songs call for sweeping movement. Children can improve their fine motor control by working with small paintbrushes, cutting with scissors, pasting or gluing, and singing songs with finger or hand movements (Mayesky 2002).

Self-Expression and Pleasure

Perhaps the most significant benefit of the arts for children is that self-expression is encouraged. Children can express emotions and work out issues of concern through art and music. For example, children draw items that are important to them, and a song can express happiness or sadness. They can achieve the satisfaction that comes from experiencing success.

For optimal results in these different areas, children's explorations should not be censored by adults; their works should be accepted and valued. With such acceptance,

Discovery Journeys

Solomon and *The Red Balloon*

Mrs. Kohl's kindergarten class had just watched the French film *The Red Balloon*, a touching and beautifully rendered wordless children's classic. They were preparing for recess when Solomon, a brown-eyed Native American boy, approached Mrs. Kohl and requested a private word.

"Mrs. Kohl," he said in a whisper, "I need to draw about that movie."

Mrs. Kohl's heart rate was buzzing. "Of course, you do." She smiled gently. This beautiful child with dark eyes and hair-like feathers rarely expressed any interest in school activities or projects and had not bonded with Mrs. Kohl, though she reached out to him daily. Mrs. Kohl's thoughts were racing to capture this moment, to allow it to be meaningful for him, and to tread gently so that it might be a springboard for future learning and communication.

Mrs. Kohl excused the others to the playground and helped Solomon find a large, fresh sheet of drawing paper and a box of unbroken crayons with the points still intact. He packed everything off to the reading corner tent to work alone.

As he worked, Mrs. Kohl reflected on this child, who often chose fighting over playing and lived a pretty tough life, which he acted out daily. But today, *The Red Balloon* touched his heart, and he couldn't keep his feelings inside.

Mrs. Kohl could see him through the entry of the tent. He was working with purpose—elbow and arm moving resolutely across the wide paper, filling it with expressions from his heart. He drew about the story of *The Red Balloon*, who befriends a small boy, and about how that boy loses his friend.

His drawing was not the blonde French child in the film; it was a brown, strong boy running on a rocky beach with a huge, red, smiling balloon in tow on a heavy rope—a rope that would never come untied or let a balloon break free. His clouds were gray with rays of sunlight spilling out from behind. The sea breaking on the shore was choppy, with two fish jumping and smiles on their silvery faces. The boy was running with surprise and joy on his crayoned face. Mrs. Kohl could tell that this boy would never let his balloon go and would never lose his gentle friend.

When the drawing was finished, Mrs. Kohl saw Solomon start to cry. He cried silently—shoulders shaking and tears spilling down his cheeks. Mrs. Kohl did not interrupt but waited nearby, anxious to soothe his hurts.

When he left his drawing in the tent and walked toward Mrs. Kohl, she knew she was being allowed a rare gift in this child's life. Mrs. Kohl remembers thinking, "I will make a difference to this child. We can build from this together. We're going to make it this one year we have together."

As the other children returned from recess, Solomon and Mrs. Kohl gathered up his drawing and supplies, but neither of them was the same. They had begun.

Consider This
1. Why was Mrs. Kohl's response to Solomon's request so important?
2. What do you think touched Solomon about the movie?
3. What do you think Solomon's picture reflected his feelings?

---

children gain confidence in their abilities to express themselves and demonstrate their creativity. The Case Study feature "The Little Boy" that follows on page 346 provides insight into the outcome of insensitivity toward children's efforts.

As in art, high-quality musical experiences contribute to helping children grow and develop socially, physically, mentally, and emotionally. Music has numerous positive impacts on our daily lives. From lullabies, sing-alongs, nursery rhymes and more, music can help build an intimate connection with children, enhance their fine and large motor skills, and impact their overall happiness. Just like language, music is a shared, an expressive, and an inventive way to be together. It can be a powerful force in the lives of young children and families in the following ways:

- Music is a universal language that can be enjoyed and appreciated by all.
- Music encourages laughter, creativity, and movement.
- Concepts and vocabulary can be learned through music.
- Music can relieve tension, lift spirits, improve moods, and be calming and relaxing.
- And mostly, music is fun, enlarging the capacity for pure enjoyment.

✓ CHECKPOINT

1. What does it mean that the value is in the process, rather than in the product when referring to art for young children?
2. Why are art and music experiences important for young children?
3. What are some similarities you see in art and music?

11.2 Art and Music in the Curriculum

When exploring the benefits of music, it is important to note that all cultures have music. Humans have an inborn need to create melodic and **rhythmic** (repeated) sounds. Music helps children respect and appreciate individuals of various cultures (**Figure 11.5**). For example, you might invite families to teach songs or chants from their childhood. You might record them singing a lullaby or ask them to share any lap games or chants that their culture uses with babies.

Recordings of popular songs, such as "Hokey Pokey," can be found in several languages. Using a familiar song in another language helps children recognize the words and appreciate that children of other cultures have similar interests to theirs.

Visual art, too, can be found that is emblematic of various cultures. A Japanese scroll is quite different from a Monet painting. The art of the Southwest United States has typical colors that symbolize the area. Both art and music are means of communicating the shared values of cultural groups.

Music is connected to the basic learning process and cognitive development beginning in infancy. Some brain research suggests that early exposure to music, especially classical music with its intricate and repeated patterns, can help children develop cognitive and mathematical abilities.

FatCamera/iStock/Getty Images Plus

Figure 11-5 These children are experimenting with musical instruments from various cultures. How does it benefit children to hear music from different cultures?

Case Study

The Little Boy
Self-expression is an integral part of the creative process. However, sometimes educators and families knowingly or inadvertently discourage creative expression. Over time, children can begin to feel their work is inadequate. Adults may be intimidated by art and make such statements as "I can't draw" or "I'm not an artist" as a result of feeling inept themselves. Consider the following poem by Helen Buckley, describing the effect of a teacher's uninformed approach to art on one small boy.

The Little Boy
By Helen E. Buckley

Once a little boy went to school.

He was quite a little boy. And it was quite a big school.

But when the little boy found that he could go to his room by walking right in from the door outside, he was happy. And the school did not seem quite so big any more.

One morning, when the little boy had been in school a while, the teacher said: "Today we are going to make a picture."

"Good!" thought the little boy. He liked to make pictures. He could make all kinds: Lions and tigers, chickens and cows, trains and boats—and he took out his box of crayons and began to draw.

But the teacher said: "Wait! It is not time to begin!" And she waited until everyone looked ready.

"Now," said the teacher, "we are going to make flowers."

"Good!" thought the little boy. He liked to make flowers, and he began to make beautiful ones with his pink and orange and blue crayons.

But the teacher said, "Wait! And I will show you how." And she drew a flower on the blackboard. It was red, with a green stem.

"There," said the teacher. "Now you may begin."

The little boy looked at the teacher's flower. Then he looked at his own flower. He liked his flower better than the teacher's. But he did not say this. He just turned his paper over and made a flower like the teacher's. It was red, with a green stem.

On another day, when the little boy had opened the door from the outside all by himself, the teacher said, "Today we are going to make something with clay."

"Good!" thought the boy. He liked clay. He could make all kinds of things with clay: Snakes and snowmen, elephants and mice, cars and trucks. And he began to pull and pinch his ball of clay.

But the teacher said, "Wait! And I will show you how." And she showed everyone how to make one deep dish.

"There," said the teacher. "Now you may begin."

The little boy looked at the teacher's dish then he looked at his own. He liked his dishes better than the teacher's. But he did not say this, he just rolled his clay into a big ball again, and made a dish like the teacher's. It was a deep dish. And pretty soon the little boy learned to wait and to watch, and to make things just like the teacher. And pretty soon he didn't make things of his own anymore.

Then it happened that the little boy and his family moved to another house, in another city, and the little boy had to go to another school. This school was even bigger than the other one, and there was no door from the outside into his room. He had to go up some big steps, and walk down a long hall to get to his room. And the very first day he was there, the teacher said, "Today we are going to make a picture."

"Good!" thought the little boy, and he waited for the teacher to tell him what to do. But the teacher didn't say anything. She just walked around the room. When she came to the little boy, she said, "Don't you want to make a picture?"

"Yes," said the little boy. "What are we going to make?"

"I don't know until you make it," said the teacher.

"How shall I make it?" asked the little boy.

"Why, any way you like," said the teacher.

"And any color?" asked the little boy.

(Continued)

Case Study (continued)

"Any color," said the teacher. "If everyone made the same picture, and used the same colors, how would I know who made what, and which was which?"

"I don't know," said the little boy.

And he began to draw a flower. It was red, with a green stem.

Consider This
1. What do you think the author of the poem wanted to tell us about appreciating children's creations?
2. Why do you think the first teacher approached the activity as she did? Are her actions typical in the lives of young children?
3. Do you feel adults who stifle children's self-expression are merely guilty of not knowing any better or are they trying to mold children into conformity?
4. How could a similar story be told about creativity in music?

Many songs provide repetition of vocabulary or actions. Repetition helps children remember the words and actions. Consider the classic "The Wheels on the Bus" and how the repetition of both the words and the actions makes it easy for children to learn. In art, children reproduce the experience of what they have seen and use the vocabulary of what they have heard. Yet, in an early learning classroom, subjects are not taught in isolation but integrated in a way that reinforces children's learning and understanding.

Art is a natural activity to integrate with all other curriculum areas. A teacher may select materials that reflect current themes, such as paint colors to reflect seasons. Clay can encourage modeling pets for social studies; labeling, conversing, and writing about artwork support literacy. Using shapes and patterns in collage reinforces math concepts. The art itself supports the fine motor development necessary for writing. Children may paint to music and react to the types of music, or they may make up a song about something they have created.

Music for Classroom Management

While music for its own benefit is valuable for young children, teachers often use music to manage daily routines for children. The major uses of music as a classroom management strategy are for:
- keeping children on a schedule.
- **transitions** (switching from one area or activity to another).
- gaining or holding children's attention.
- a change of pace.
- relaxation, reducing stress, and calming.

Maintaining a Schedule

"Come to Circle Time" or "Prepare for Lunch" songs are excellent signals to children that routine activities are approaching. The songs may be transitional in nature, but they are also timekeepers that announce what is next in the daily schedule. Teachers usually first introduce songs they intend to use as transitions for children to become familiar with the purpose of the song and follow the teacher's lead. The children will prepare for or move on to the next activity when the teacher simply begins singing once they are familiar with the song's intent.

Conducting Transitions

Specific music can signal the beginning or end of a routine activity. For example, a call-and-response song might announce group time, a sing-along tune might signal morning snack time, a clean-up song can designate the end of learning center time, or a lullaby can prepare children for naps. Music can be an effective way to occupy children while they are waiting, such as for snack time or lunch. Familiar songs contribute to a predictable routine that helps children know what to expect.

While there are many songs commonly used for such purposes, it is not necessary to select music specifically written with that intent. Consider Native American chants as soothing accompaniments to naptime. A Sousa march or calypso music will energize clean-up time. An instrumental classical piece might indicate the transition to or from lunch or snack time. Play or sing the same song at the same time each day, and soon children will respond to the transition without being verbally reminded. Consider this Case Study titled, "Circle Time Transition."

Case Study

Circle Time Transition

Mrs. LeBlanc begins her usual "Circle Time" song while her 4-year-olds gather for the routine morning group time. She makes new words to the tune of "Three Blind Mice." Her created song allows children sufficient time to finish their early arrival activities and join others in the circle. She sings:

Circle Time, Circle Time,
Come and join me, come and join me.
We'll chant some rhymes and read a book.
We'll sing some songs, come take a look.
We'll play some games here in our nook.
Circle Time, Circle Time!

Mrs. LeBlanc's song is an example of music used as a classroom transition. When teachers need to move children from one activity to another, a transition song provides a signal and encourages orderly movement. Her song serves an important purpose in her classroom. She uses it as a routine transition to move children from individual activities into group time. Teachers like Mrs. LeBlanc use music as a classroom management strategy.

Songs as transitions are useful because they can indicate a scheduled activity such as going outdoors, getting ready for lunch, or preparing to go home. Mrs. LeBlanc invented the "Circle Time" song by making a parody to use for the transition to circle time. Many teachers use invented songs at some point, either for transitions or to communicate information to children when no other song is available. More information about creating songs will follow later in this chapter.

Consider This
1. How does a song serve as a transition to move children from individual activities into group time?
2. What are other songs that Mrs. LeBlanc might use?
3. What other times can music be used as a transition?

Gaining and Holding Children's Attention

A transitional song that prepares children for what is happening next can additionally serve to capture children's attention. Mrs. Leblanc's "Circle Time" song catches children's attention, announcing morning group time and calling them together. During group time, singing or playing a song that children like and know well serves to regain attention if they become restless. Call-and-response songs that request participation from children are useful for gaining or regaining attention. Using a song with motions provides a movement break between more sedentary times such as storytime or discussions to allow children to refocus.

Providing a Change of Pace

Music serves us well when children need a change of pace. When children are working in interest centers, their activities are individualized and allow them to stay engaged as long as they like. During circle time or other group experiences, inserting songs to break up the session keeps children engaged longer as a group. Leading children in an active song or rousing march around the room creates a pleasurable break in the group time or during the day.

Music for Relaxation

One of a child's first exposures to music is often when it is used to calm and soothe them as an infant. Not coincidently, all cultures have lullabies. Throughout history, families have lulled children to sleep by singing. Experienced infant caregivers report that when several children start crying at the same time, singing or rhythmic chants help stop the crying. Holding a crying infant close to one's chest and singing is often effective in comforting a fussy baby (**Figure 11.6**). An older infant or toddler, distressed when a parent leaves, can be comforted by cuddling and singing more often than with spoken words. The singing voice seems to make a child feel safe and cared for in those situations.

Because music is mood-altering, it offers wonderful possibilities for relaxation. When music is used to encourage relaxation, the child is exposed to a world of quiet, peaceful music in contrast to what is commonly heard on the radio or television. This exposure can result in a greater appreciation for **aesthetics**, or a heightened awareness and sensitivity to beauty.

There are many children's recordings available for resting or quiet times. However, teachers are not limited to those selections. The music that teachers enjoy can be enjoyed by children as well. Children can enjoy a wide variety of music, not just music intended for them.

For relaxation, choose slow-paced and soothing selections. Ask children to lie or sit comfortably with their eyes closed, sometimes just to listen and other times to listen for specific repetitions of elements. Use peaceful music in conjunction with imagery or deep-breathing exercises. Try some recordings of instrumental music with nature sounds such as rain, ocean waves, or birds chirping. Harps and other stringed instruments can be especially relaxing and calming.

Help children recognize how some music can be very calming, such as the music selected for rest time. Other music can be exciting, such as the music selected for parades.

kate_sept2004/E+ via Getty Images

Figure 11-6 A teacher uses music to calm a fussy baby. What are other uses of music with infants and toddlers?

For an example of music creating certain moods, see the Discovery Journeys feature, "The Circus Theme."

Music and Movement

When a very young child hears lively music, they will often move their body from side to side in an endearing dance. Children's nature requires that they move. Music and movement are natural partners and a wonderful way to have fun together. When children are free to move, their whole bodies will match the mood of the music, displaying beauty, grace, and energy.

Movement activities can support physical development while giving children a chance to move between teacher-led group activities. Music activities that involve movement are useful to provide physical exercise on inclement weather days.

Purposeful Music

Some people have music playing for prolonged periods in the background, thinking it is soothing to children. However, continuous music is usually not a good idea. Just as your mind tunes out a scent that you initially notice, children tune out continuous music and no longer pay attention. Too, background music can make the environment overstimulating, add auditory clutter and distraction, and cause children to talk louder to be heard.

Music should be played consciously and with intention, not just as background noise. When children are alert and relaxed, play an instrument or recorded music and enjoy it with them. Move to it. Clap hands. Shake rhythm instruments. Dance. Pay attention to it.

Discovery Journeys

The Circus Theme

As a kindergarten teacher, I often include music related to themes in the curriculum. I played the "Toy Symphony" to accompany children's projects on favorite toys. I used Aaron Copland's "Rodeo" with a western theme.

As an outgrowth of children's interest in an upcoming Shrine Circus, I built activities and assembled materials around a circus theme. I gathered books about the circus, and located some clown costumes, hoops, balls, and animal masks to enrich the circus experiences. I set out puzzles of clowns, trapeze artists, and other performers. I was specifically happy to find a recording of circus calliope music to add to the atmosphere.

During the next week, children created tricks with hoops and balls, worked on the puzzles, and enjoyed books about the circus. They built a circus ring in the block area, with rubber animals and people performing in the ring, painted circus posters, and made collages—all activities leading up to the culmination of a classroom circus the children planned.

Overall, my class was pretty orderly. However, on the day of the classroom circus performance (to which another classroom had been invited) matters certainly got out of hand! The children in my normally orderly classroom became quite unmanageable and unruly. What went wrong?

Although well intentioned in providing music related to children's experiences, I played circus calliope music. Consider the intention of circus music—to excite people about the upcoming experience. And that is exactly what the music did! It was so overstimulating for the children that they became excited and boisterous to the point of being almost unrecognizable. The children's reaction highlighted for me the influence of music on the mood, emotions, and activity of children. And I resolved to either change the selection of music I would use with future circus themes or alter the way I used it.

Consider This
1. What about the music affected the children's behavior in such as an extreme manner?
2. Could one use calliope music in another way to avoid overstimulating the children?
3. What other types of music might affect children's behavior in a similar way?

Art and Music for Infants and Toddlers

Art and music are not just for preschoolers or school-age children. We should be enjoying both art and music with infants and toddlers. Not only are there many benefits, but art and music add joy to the day. Infants and toddlers will respond happily to the music around them. Infants are developing their senses, which will guide them in both art and music. Toddlers will often explore art materials and what they can do with them. The Teaching Tip feature below lists some ways to incorporate art and music in programs for infants and toddlers.

Teaching Tip

Toddlers and Music

Here are some guidelines to help you plan and conduct a music activity with toddlers:
- Keep it short—under 10 minutes.
- Make participation voluntary; do not force anyone to take part.
- Combine music with movement. Look for songs that encourage movements such as swaying, hopping, and jumping.
- Repeat familiar songs regularly. Children do not learn a song from hearing it once. They enjoy repeating familiar songs.
- Consider singing at a slower pace than you might normally sing.
- Objects can help hold toddlers' attention. Invite toddlers to wear hats and wave ribbons, scarves, or pom-poms while they sing or dance. Let puppets, dolls, or soft animals participate with you.
- Offer toddlers a large hoop to hold on to and play "Ring Around the Rosie" or other simple musical circle games.
- Try shadow dancing. Put a bright light behind children so that they cast shadows on the wall, and let them dance while watching their shadows.
- Give toddlers all of the same rhythm instruments to help prevent conflict.
- Do not expect toddlers to play a rhythm instrument and march at the same time.
- End music time with a slow, calming song to settle down afterward.

What about art for the very young? Toddlers love to mark with crayons. They may make one mark and discard the paper, so even scrap paper is a valuable commodity for toddlers. They will need larger crayons because they tend to press hard on regular ones and become upset when they break. All the sensory activities described can be enjoyed by toddlers with recognition of the temptation for toddlers to put items in their mouths. Toddlers often find using their fingers to paint is easier than using brushes or other tools. Here are tips for successful art with toddlers:
- Provide large crayons or crayons made specifically for toddlers.
- Tape paper to the table to make it easier for toddlers to use.
- Consider separate materials for each child since toddlers do not share well.
- Allow children to experiment and explore play dough.
- Do not expect a creation. The goal is to explore the properties.

✓ CHECKPOINT

1. What experiences have you had with music used as a transition technique?
2. Other than children's music, what type of music have you used or seen used with young children?
3. Why is constant background music not desirable for a classroom?

11.3 Stages of Development of Children's Art and Music Skills

Now that we have looked at the importance of creativity and the benefits of art and music, we will address the development of children's art skills (**Figure 11.7** and **Figure 11.8**).

Drawing Stages

Skill	Characteristics
Uncontrolled Scribbling *mturhanlar/iStock/Getty Images Plus*	Scribbling refers to making random marks. Children start scribbling as early as 13 months. The marks have more to do with movement than with art. Toddlers are often surprised to find that a crayon or paintbrush will make these marks.
Controlled Scribbling *aykut karahan/iStock/Getty Images Plus*	Children demonstrate a greater variety of scribbles. Arcs get smaller as children begin to use their wrists. They repeat actions they like and may make endless lines in a rhythmic manner.
Named Scribbling *SorinVidis/iStock/Getty Images Plus*	There may be no doubt in the child's mind about what they have made. Adults, however, may not recognize the drawings. Drawings are symbols of objects, events, or experiences that were significant to the child. This is a major step because the child is using abstract thought and sees the relationship between the marks on the paper as a symbol or object.
Forms Basic Shapes *Cavan/iStock/Getty Images Plus*	As physical and mental development progress, scribbles begin to take on the configuration of shapes. Six basic shapes are made: (1) rectangle (including square), (2) oval (including circle), (3) triangle, (4) Greek cross (+), (5) diagonal cross (x), and (6) a variety of other shapes in a catchall category.
Early Representational *Heather Preston*	The drawings begin to look like the objects they represent, but they are often distorted in size. Usually, the most important part of the drawing will be much larger than the rest. By this time, the child will have changed the grip on the drawing instrument to one similar to an adult grip.

Goodheart-Willcox Publisher

Figure 11-7 Drawing stages. Most children will progress through these stages when they have opportunities to use art materials. *How can this information influence your planning and the experiences and materials you offer? (Continued)*

Part 3 Curriculum Areas of Focus

Drawing Stages *(continued)*

Skill	Characteristics
Makes Mandalas Heather Preston	Children often combine two of the shapes they can make, such as a Greek cross and a diagonal cross. Combining an oval or rectangle, they make what are called mandalas.
Makes Suns larisa_zorina/iStock/Getty Images Plus	Children frequently make a combination of an oval with lines radiating from its rim. Most early attempts at sun figures include some kind of marks in the center of the figure.
Makes People Heather Preston	One of the first pictorial figures that young children draw is a person. They typically draw it as one large head-body oval or circle with two lines for legs and/or two for arms. Circles or dots represent eyes and sometimes a nose and mouth.
Draws Animals, Flowers, and Trees  galamoments/E+ via Getty Images	After children learn how to draw a person, they will begin drawing animals, flowers, and sometimes trees. A tree is likely one or two lines for a trunk and a circle for the limbs and leaves.
Preschematic  Helen_Field/iStock/Getty Images Plus	Objects become more relative to size. There is a right side up to the drawing, and a base line is often included. A base line at the bottom of the work may be green for grass, and another one higher on the page may be blue for the sky. By this time, children are using their wrist and fingers and have mastered an adult grip on the drawing instrument.
Makes Pictorial Drawings  portishead1/E+ via Getty Images	These drawings will be representations and not reproductions. Young children draw what they know rather than what they see.

Goodheart-Willcox Publisher

Figure 11-7 Continued

Clay or Dough Stages

Age	Skills with Clay
Age 2  *dcdp/iStock/Getty Images Plus*	Beats clay, pulls it apart, puts it back together
Age 3  *supersizer/E+ via Getty Images*	Forms balls, often makes snake shapes
Age 4  *Nadezhda1906/iStock/Getty Images Plus*	Forms balls, begins to make something, may still pull and punch holes
Age 5  *Viktoria Hnatiuk/iStock/Getty Images Plus*	States what they are going to make, first attempts at planning a creation

Goodheart-Willcox Publisher

Figure 11-8 Most children will progress through these stages when they have opportunities to use clay or dough. What are some differences in the way dough and clay respond to children's efforts?

The development of children's music skills will be addressed later in this chapter. As a rule, children typically progress through various stages as they grow and gain new skills, such as using scissors (**Figure 11.9**). Just as children develop physically following predictable patterns, so do they develop in their use of materials. Knowing what can be expected at various ages informs the curriculum and planning.

Art Processes

Basic art processes for children include applying, forming, constructing, and interlacing. Children should have regular experience with each of these processes. The sections that follow give examples of how we can provide these basic art experiences and incorporate them into the curriculum.

Cutting Stages

Age	Skill Level
Age 3 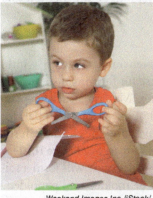 Weekend Images Inc./iStock/Getty Images Plus	Experimentation time; holds paper and cuts random snips by closing scissors; may be unable to open scissors to repeat the cut; may tear paper to finish
Age 4  ziggy_mars/iStock/Getty Images Plus	Able to cut straight lines forward without experiencing forward movement of the helper hand; able to cut simple curves and angled lines with one direction change without moving the assisting hand on the paper to reposition; cuts straight lines, wide zigzags, and long curves
Age 5  Wavebreakmedia/iStock/Getty Images Plus	Able to cut simple curves and angled lines (one direction change) while moving the assisting hand on the paper to reposition; mastery of basic shapes
Age 6  RobMattingley/E+ via Getty Images	Can cut simple lines with more than one direction change; can cut complicated shapes with straight and curved lines; mastery of previous skills; introduction of two-direction short curves, connected short curves, narrow zigzags, and small circles
Age 7  M-Production/iStock/Getty Images Plus	Can cut intricate designs and designs within designs

Goodheart-Willcox Publisher

Figure 11-9 Cutting stages. Learning to use scissors involves the development of hand-eye coordination. *How can this information influence and guide the experiences you provide?*

Applying

Materials are applied to other surfaces in various ways or attached with materials such as glue or tape. These activities include drawing with crayons, markers, or chalk; painting, and collage. Applying can include pasting, gluing, stapling, taping, or any method that involves attaching or affixing one material to another.

Forming

Materials are modeled into new forms, usually **three-dimensional** (having width, height, and depth) figures or items. Materials that children use for forming also provide tactile experiences, which are important for sensory learning. Materials such as play-dough and clay encourage exploration of new sensations. Although various materials for forming can be purchased, many teachers make their own. Involving the children in the process adds to the integration of science and other curriculum areas. See **Figure 11.10** for two recipes for making your own dough and clay. The clay in this recipe will form a solid object as compared to pottery clay which, like dough, can be molded and remolded.

Children can use the dough on trays or vinyl place mats to help keep tables clean. To maintain interest, add accessories such as rolling pins and cookie cutters. Try cookie cutters that are seasonal or related to themes. Cookie cutters in the shapes of letters and numbers contribute literacy and math experiences. Heavy plastic cookie cutters are easiest for children to use; metal ones may bend out of shape, and light plastic ones can break with use.

For more variety throughout the year, add flavoring extracts to scent the dough. Try lemon or banana extract with yellow dough; strawberry or peppermint with red dough; chocolate or vanilla with brown dough; or coconut or pineapple with uncolored dough. The aroma adds to the pleasure of the experience.

Recipes: Colored Dough and Play Clay

Colored Dough

Items needed:
- 3 cups of flour
- ¾ cup salt
- tempera paint or food coloring
- 1 cup of water

Sift flour and salt together in a large, deep bowl. Mix tempera paint or food coloring with water and add gradually to the flour and salt mixture. Knead as you would bread dough until the mixture is smooth and easy to handle. The more the mixture is kneaded, the smoother it becomes. If the dough becomes sticky, add more flour. Add more tempera paint or food coloring to get the desired color. When not in use, store the dough in a zip closure bag or other airtight container and refrigerate. Children can help make this dough or even make it themselves. Keep ingredients on hand, always ready to make a fresh batch. Children can be provided with individual portions if desired.

Play Clay

Items needed:
- 1 cup cornstarch
- 2 cups baking soda
- 1 ¼ cups cold water
- 1 tbs. corn oil
- food coloring if desired

In a medium saucepan, stir together the cornstarch and baking soda. Add water, oil, and food coloring if used, and stir until smooth. Cook over medium heat, stirring constantly until the mixture reaches the consistency of slightly dry mashed potatoes. The mixture will come to a boil, then start to thicken, first in lumps and then in a thick mass.

Turn it out onto a plate and cover with a damp cloth. Let the mixture cool until it can be handled. Knead thoroughly on a surface dusted with cornstarch until it is smooth and pliable. If the clay is not to be used immediately, store the completely cooled clay in a zip closure bag or a container with a tightly fitting lid. The clay may be kept in a cool place for up to two weeks but should be kneaded thoroughly before use. This recipe may be cut in half if less is desired.

Goodheart-Willcox Publisher

Figure 11-10 These two recipes can be activities themselves when children participate. *What are skills children might learn when making these recipes?*

Using dough is a safe way for children to work off aggression or tension. Keep a supply of dough available to give to a child who is having a difficult day and help them work out anger or stress. Children do not need to make something to enjoy using the dough. Squeezing, rolling, pounding, and exploring its properties may be all that they want to do.

Constructing

Materials are put together in such a way that a three-dimensional object is formed. Materials for construction may include paper, cardboard, wood, or any found or natural objects. LEGO® or other construction toys and blocks also provide opportunities for construction. In creating three-dimensional constructions, children gain knowledge of relationships and how objects can look quite different depending on one's view. Some ideas for three-dimensional art include box construction, hats, and aluminum foil sculptures.

Box Construction

Provide an assortment of small boxes of various sizes. Paper clip boxes, small cereal boxes, and jewelry boxes all work well. Provide several means to connect the boxes such as colored or plain masking tape, transparent tape, nontoxic white glue, or staplers. An assortment of markers, crayons, or items to glue on the boxes can inspire ideas for decorations.

Once children have made constructions, talk to them about their project, asking them to look at the construction from several angles to see how it is different. Take digital photos from different angles and let them compare the photos and match them to the correct side of the construction.

Hats

This project helps build cooperation since children must work together to complete the hats (**Figure 11.11**). Each child will need a partner to make a hat on the partner's head. Provide some construction paper, glue, scissors, and markers or crayons. Show children how to form the construction paper into a hat shape. Each child can decorate their hat using an assortment of flowers, ribbons, natural objects, or other adornments.

Aluminum Foil Sculptures

Provide sheets of aluminum foil cut to about 14 to 18 inches long or purchase precut sheets of foil. Suggest that children experiment with a sheet to see what they can create. Provide markers if they want to add details to their sculpture. If they have difficulty making their sculptures stand, provide some playdough or clay to support their work.

kali9/E+ via Getty Images

Figure 11-11 Children enjoy making hats for a special event. How does this activity support creativity and engineering?

Interlacing

Interlacing includes any type of weaving, lacing, knotting, sewing, or any means of creating by attaching materials in such a manner. The following sections provide some suggestions for interlacing experiences for children.

Grill Weaving
A metal grill or wire shelf hung either from the ceiling or on the wall can be a frame for weaving. Materials to use include crepe paper streamers, fabric strips, vines or flexible twigs, yarn, or ribbons.

Container Weaving
Weave plastic berry baskets and onion or orange bags with yarn, ribbon, rickrack, or chenille strips.

Styrofoam or Paper Plate Weaving
Interlace Styrofoam plates or trays by making holes with a hole punch around the edge.

Of the basic art processes, drawing, painting, and collage are the most common experiences in early childhood programs. Of these, painting using easels is often a concern of teachers, primarily because of the potential mess or the additional preparation involved. Let us look at painting specifically and how to incorporate it successfully.

All about Easel Painting

Easel painting is one of the most valuable art experiences for young children. Easel painting allows children to make bold strokes on large sheets of paper. However, some early childhood educators do not take full advantage of the possibilities of easel painting or may be reluctant to provide it to children due to inadequate space or other concerns. Some suggested materials and tactics to successfully include easel painting are discussed in the sections that follow.

Paint
Tempera paint is a versatile medium in an early childhood program. It comes in a liquid form or may be available as a powder to be mixed with water. Have a separate brush for each color of paint to keep colors true. As young children use paint, they will inevitably mix colors. The muddy paints will not be as appealing as bright, fresh colors. Separate brushes reduce the mixing that muddles the colors. Provide fresh paint regularly to maintain the appeal.

Containers
Select heavy, wide containers that will not tip easily to hold the paint. Put only a few inches of paint in the containers at one time. You can always add more paint as the children need it, but a small amount will be easier to clean up if there is an accident. Or purchase paint holders specially designed to prevent spills that are available at many school supply companies.

Paper
Paper may be purchased in rolls or sheets in diverse sizes from school supply companies. Since it is the process of painting, not the finished product that is important, almost any type of paper can be used, including recycled newspapers or wrapping paper. For most painting experiences, large sheets are preferred.

Easels
Floor-standing easels designed for children may be purchased, but one can get started by hanging cardboard on a fence. Painting outside eliminates concerns about spills. Tabletop easels are also available for purchase.

MartinPrescott/iStock/Getty Images Plus

Figure 11-12 A child wears a smock to protect clothing while painting. What else has the teacher done to support successful easel painting experiences?

Smocks
Painting smocks (**Figure 11.12**) are available for purchase but a recycled shirt, worn backwards, will protect children's clothing from most painting activities. Clothespins make it easy to fasten shirts in the back and encourage children to help each other. Have spare shirts or smocks available to replace as needed.

Procedures
Teach children to wipe the brush on the edge of the container to reduce dripping. Make sure children know what to do with their paintings when they finish. Do they put them in a certain place to dry? Is there a place to hang them? If they paint outside, they can simply hang completed artwork with clothespins or lay paintings on the grass.

What to Expect
If children have not painted before, they will often cover the paper with paint as they explore the medium. Children will go through the same stages with painting that they do with crayons—the painting equivalent of scribbling, repeating patterns, naming their work, and then painting a picture.

Labeling and Describing
Write the child's name or encourage them to write in the upper left-hand corner of their paper to help develop left-to-right progression. Writing one's name lets children see the purpose of writing in a relevant way. Another option is to write the child's name in the bottom right corner as an artist might sign their work.

Ask children to tell you or others about their paintings to encourage language development. Write their comments on an index card to display beside their work. Notes such as "This is my dog eating his food" helps families interpret artwork as the child intended.

What Can Children Use to Paint?

Easel brushes specifically manufactured for tempera paint are available from school supply companies. Look for handles no longer than 8 inches. Long handles are more difficult for children to control and more likely to tip the paint container. Watercolor brushes do not hold enough paint to provide a satisfying experience, and brushes intended for oil or acrylic paint are expensive. Easel brushes are not the only thing children can use to paint, however. Many possibilities are recycled, inexpensive additions to your art supply shelf. Consider these other materials to apply paint:

- kitchen basting brushes, makeup brushes, and toothbrushes for drip or spatter painting
- sponges and dishwashing sponges
- pine boughs or other leaves or branches
- rubber stamps
- wood scraps
- Q-tips® (**Figure 11.13**)
- string and yarn
- straws for dripping paint
- feathers and feather dusters

Try putting paint in the following containers and applying it to paper. Add a little water to thin the tempera for these applications:

- stamp moisteners
- small squeeze bottles
- roll-on deodorant bottles
- shoe polish container (the type with a foam applicator)
- bingo daubers

4u4me/iStock/Getty Images Plus

Figure 11-13 A child uses Q-tips® to make a design. What other items not listed can be used to apply paint?

The Special Benefits of Sensory Art Experiences

Busy children are happy children, and sensory experiences will readily engage them. Children will remain actively involved for extended periods when they choose what to do and how to do it. Time spent by teachers in providing and valuing children's sensory experiences is time well spent—time invested in good experiences and learning. One valuable sensory art experience is fingerpainting.

Purchased fingerpaint paper or slick shelf paper may be used if a finished product is desired, but the real value of fingerpainting is in the sensory experience of the activity. Children will enjoy using a tray or just fingerpainting on a tabletop. You can make a print of table creations by pressing a piece of paper over the design.

Arrange the fingerpainting near a water source for easy cleanup. The activity will be easier to supervise if only two or three children are working at a time. Explain that there will be enough time for all to have a turn to participate. Limit the number of chairs and trays or workspaces available to the number of participants you want at any one time as indirect guidance.

You can make your own fingerpaint by mixing liquid starch with a small amount of tempera paint and a little liquid soap.

Stages of Development of Children's Music Skills

As described earlier in this chapter, children progress in art skills in a predictable pattern and sequence. As with all developmental stages, there are general ages at which they will enjoy or achieve skills and abilities. This developmental progression in music also occurs in young children in a predictable pattern. The following chart, "Musical Abilities by Age" (Sarrazin 2016), identifies the expected behaviors and appropriate activities to guide a teacher in planning based on children's development (**Figure 11.14**).

Musical Abilities by Age

Age	Musical	Appropriate Activities	Limitations
0–1 year old (Infants)	Enjoy: • Hearing melodic contour in voice • Being sung to • Hearing a variety of styles of music	Enjoy: • Being rocked, patted, and stroked to music • Responding to rhythmic play and body touch songs • Bouncing or jumping to music • Experimenting with gestures, clapping, and pointing • Playing with rattles and bells	Cannot use language or sing
1–2 years old (Toddlers)	• Are aware of musical sounds • Demand repetition • Experience delayed response during music time	• Create their own made-up songs • Sing simple 1- to 2-word songs • Enjoy voice inflection games • Enjoy making random sounds on instruments • Improvise their own lyrics to traditional songs • Respond to musical stimuli • Perform rhythmic movement and movement patterns • Clap to music, steady beat • Move and respond to signals and sound and silence games	• Cannot sing "in tune" but can maintain melodic contour Developmental Issues: • "Centering" (pre-operational stage) can fix a child's attention on one perceptual feature. • Difficulty seeing the larger transformational picture of some activities as attention is diverted by one feature

Creative Commons

Figure 11-14 Most children will progress through these stages when they have opportunities to experience music. *How can this information influence your planning and the experiences and materials you offer?* (*Continued*)

Musical Abilities by Age *(continued)*

Age	Musical	Appropriate Activities	Limitations

3-year-olds	• Prefer to sing beginning on their own pitch
	• Increasing ability to match pitches
	• Sense of musical phrasing
	• Increasing expressiveness in voice
	Enjoy:
	• Manipulating objects while creating songs
	• Repeated songs
	• Having their own movements/ideas copied by others
		• Reproduce recognizable songs
		• Explore musical sounds with their voices and instruments
		• Random exploration of xylophones, percussion instruments, and voices
		• Maintain a steady beat
		• Handle mallets and drum beaters
		• Move spontaneously to music
		• Respond to sound and silence games
			• Cannot reverse thought (i.e., can't reason back to the beginning)
			• Cannot play a repeated xylophone pattern
			Developmental Issues:
			• Responds to abstract or iconic musical notation:
			  ▪ Pictures
			  ▪ Hand signs
			  ▪ Movement/motions
			• Cannot respond to formal music notation (i.e., notes on a staff)

4-year-olds	• Awareness of beat, tempo, volume, pitch, and form • Sing a wide variety of songs • Sing in D–A range • Critique their own song-making efforts • Aware of tonal center	• Perform individualized musical exploration and play; large motor movement is best • Have the ability to step to a beat • Repeat short movement sequences, simple rhythms, echo, pitch contour, melodic fragments, formality within phrases, key stability, and categorization of instruments • Symbolic "pretend" play, songs with stories, acting/pretending • Can perform some musical analysis such as hearing form (AB, ABA) or distinguishing song phrases	• Experience difficulty in group musical activities or coordinated instrumental play • Cannot perform a steady beat on xylophones • Have trouble discriminating between musical genres
4–5-year-olds	Able to classify sounds as: • High–low • Loud–soft • Fast–slow • Smooth–disconnected (legato–staccato)	• Can reproduce sounds and patterns vocally and with instruments • Able to play simple, repeated instrumental accompaniments to songs and improvise on simple classroom instruments • Improvement in stepping to the beat • 5-year-olds can learn simple dance steps • Organize sounds that express a story or accompany a song Prefer: • Action songs and fingerplays (imagination) • Silly word and rhyming songs	• Require many opportunities to match pitches and order direction of musical sounds in terms of going up, going down, and staying the same

Creative Commons

Figure 11-14 *Continued*

1. Which of the art processes have you observed in use in a classroom?
2. Why are three-dimensional constructions helpful for children?
3. What would you consider the most important art materials to include in a classroom?

11.4 The Teacher's Role in Art and Music

Understanding the typical stages through which children progress in both art and music is important in fulfilling one's role as a teacher. From a procedural standpoint, a teacher's role in art is to set up an art area for the children and provide a wide variety of materials to use. However, a teacher's role involves more than that. The teacher must ensure that the work is the child's and not determine the outcome nor correct or attempt to improve children's artwork for adult appeal. Here are guidelines for providing successful creative art experiences:

- Allow adequate time and space. Crowding invites spills and conflicts. Limit the number of children in an area at a time if warranted.
- Be comfortable with the materials yourself.
- Offer a variety of materials; provide plenty of paper and supplies of all types.
- Have materials ready and arranged where children can access and select what they want easily (**Figure 11.15**).
- Protect children's clothing when necessary.
- Reduce interference from others through consideration of boundaries and traffic patterns.
- Be sure children understand any restrictions.
- Interact appropriately; show interest and give meaningful praise.
- Ensure safety. Use blunt or safety scissors, and nontoxic materials, and watch for small parts that might be swallowed by younger children.
- Be open to and prepared to accept messiness.
- Recognize and acknowledge the process rather than the product.
- Include a place to display children's art.
- Avoid coloring pages or adult-made patterns or models. Do not impose your own standards.
- Enjoy art yourself; provide an atmosphere of acceptance and approval.
- Avoid drawing for children, even if they request it.
- Realize that during the time children work, they acquire important experience.
- Let children develop their own techniques through experimentation.
- Do not discard a child's work in the child's presence.
- Avoid comparing or favoring one child's art over another.
- Interpret the value of art experiences to families.

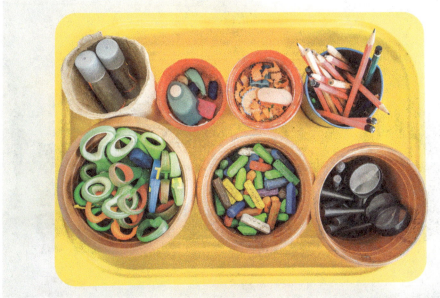

Creative Circle Studio/iStock/Getty Images

Figure 11-15 The teacher selected and organized these materials and put them out for the children to use. *How does arranging and organizing materials suggest ideas for children? How does it encourage them to clean up?*

Setting up an Art Area

Grouping art materials in an area of the classroom where children can work uninterrupted encourages children to pursue their own interests and work individually or in small groups. The art area usually includes easels and a table for art activities. Near the table, there should be a shelf with art materials organized and displayed. Preferably, this area should be near a sink to facilitate cleaning up. The area should be out of the line of traffic to avoid interruptions from others.

Some materials, such as crayons, construction paper, and scissors, are staples and should be available every day. Other materials can be rotated. Variation in materials supplied keeps children interested in the area. Additional information about creating and supervising an art area can be found in Chapter 2, "The Early Childhood Learning Environment."

Talking to Children about Their Art

It is difficult for some people to know what to say to children about their artwork. Sometimes they try to be supportive by saying, "That's pretty," "I like your picture," or "You did a good job." Conversely, they may say nothing at all. Children, however, need us to talk to them, to model language, introduce vocabulary, and encourage conversation (**Figure 11.16**). We want to communicate to children that we are aware of their work and help them develop their own observation skills. Sentences like, "That's pretty" do not help children with any of these skills. Such remarks do not say anything about what the child did or about the specific piece of artwork.

Another common adult comment about children's artwork is the question, "What is it?" Although we have all seen abstract painting, adults are conditioned to think of art as representing something. However, young children do not always think of their artwork as representational. Sometimes adults think they recognize something specific in the child's artwork and say, "Oh, you've drawn a flower," or "Is that a bird?" The problem in such situations is that the adult is imposing ideas on the child. The child may agree simply to please the adult, yet the child may not have been trying to make anything at all and, instead, just enjoying the use of the medium. Such statements send a message that artwork should show something realistic.

FatCamera/E+ via Getty Images

Figure 11-16 A teacher converses with two children about what they are doing. What might she say to encourage them to continue the discussion of their work?

In many cases, children are just interested in the process of creating and learning to control their strokes with brushes or crayons. Just the very creation of marks on the page may be satisfying for young children. It does not have to be anything, just marks on the pages—or as very young children may say, "It's scribbles." However, to early childhood educators, it is developing the hand-eye coordination that is required for writing and creative self-expression.

If we should avoid general words such as "pretty," "good," and "nice," asking "What is it?" or naming the work for the child, then what should we say? You can describe what you see. For example, you can ask the child about what you noticed, such as:

- What colors were used—were they dark or light?
- How do the lines go—are they horizontal, vertical, or diagonal? Zigzag, curved, or straight?
- How many different colors, strokes, or collage pieces were used?
- What is the same or different from another artwork the child has done?
- What happened when the child tried something new? Did the paint run together, creating a new color?
- What specifically do you like about the artwork? Was it the bold colors? The wide strokes? The place where colors ran together?

If you talk to children as described, you are telling them that you are looking carefully at their art piece, sending a powerful message that you are interested in the work. You are giving children new vocabulary and supporting language development. You are helping them look closely at their own work, developing observation and evaluation skills. And you are enabling them to realize what skills they possess, developing feelings of confidence and competence. None of this happens when you say, "That's pretty," or ask, "What is it?"

For many adults, giving descriptions is a new skill that requires practice. Describing what you see does not mean saying what you think the child felt, wanted to create, or liked. Looking at a scribble made with heavy black and blue lines, some might say the child was angry. However, one cannot know if this is so. Anger is the adult's association with dark colors, but perhaps black and blue just happened to be the colors the child picked up. Heavy, circular strokes might make an adult think of anger when a child is just experimenting with motion. These are judgmental comments. Nonjudgmental, descriptive statements about the same picture might be:

"You used a lot of blue and black."
"You filled up most of the paper."
"You must have pressed hard to make those heavy lines."
"Your hand went round and round to make these circles."
"Most of the lines go around, but this blue one goes up and down. It's vertical."
"You have a lot of wiggly black lines on this side."

In discussing what to ask children, try "Would you like to tell me about your picture?" or "How did you decide what you would paint today?" You might ask, "What did you enjoy about doing that?" or "How did you do this part here?" These questions are open-ended and allow children to tell you as much or as little as they want.

Displaying Children's Artwork

Exhibiting children's work for a few days in the classroom is one way to demonstrate our respect and appreciation of their work. Displaying quantities of children's art can be a challenge since numerous works can easily become visual clutter.

Art displays can show children and families the importance of this aspect of the curriculum, as well as highlight the value of creativity and self-expression. Taking the time to put the art on the walls in an aesthetically pleasing manner shows that you care about the creations the children make. The sections that follow offer some suggestions for displaying children's art.

Taping

To tape crayon work or paintings on walls, roll a small piece of masking tape with the sticky side out. Put a roll of tape on the back of each corner and several extras across the top if the paper is large. Taping in this way prevents the tape from showing and detracting from the art. Line up the tops of the paper and leave even spaces between sheets for balance and order in the display. While it may take a few minutes longer, the effect is more appealing than a haphazard arrangement.

Frames

Show appreciation for children's efforts by giving their art the extra attention of a real frame. Purchase picture frames that are the size of the paper usually used in your classroom. Alternate children's work in the frames. Sometimes framing shops will give you scraps of mat boards or pieces cut in error to frame children's art. Alternatively, mount children's artwork on larger pieces of construction paper that can serve as frames. You may also use pieces of poster board or sheets of wallpaper as frames.

Clotheslines

Run a cord through the metal spring holes in clothespins. The clothespins will slide along the cord to the desired location. Attach the cord firmly to the wall, tight enough to avoid sagging. To hang artwork, simply clip it with the clothespins and display it in a line. (**Figure 11.17**). As an added advantage, preschoolers can hang completed projects themselves.

Magnets

Use magnets to hold smaller works on file cabinets or metal doors. Magnets make it easy to post artwork quickly. As a bonus, children love arranging and rearranging the artwork themselves.

Bulletin Boards

Group smaller projects together on a single bulletin board to make a composition that is neater than many individual pieces on the walls.

SDI Productions/E+ via Getty Images

Figure 11-17 A teacher has hung a cord to hold children's artwork. What are other ways to display children's art?

Keeping Clean with Art

Teachers sometimes avoid valuable art experiences because they are concerned about the mess and the time it takes to clean up. However, there are many ways teachers can make cleaning up easy. No one should omit art because it might make a mess.

Take It Outside

Make easel painting a regular part of the outdoor activities. Special easels are available that attach to fences, or you can just take your standing easel outdoors. Taking painting outside means that you need not worry about spills. For fingerpainting, just move a table outdoors and when done for the day, a water hose makes a quick cleanup.

Be Prepared

Set up materials in a manner to prevent mishaps and to facilitate cleanup. Put a plastic tablecloth, shower curtain, or even a beach towel under easels to protect flooring. Inexpensive drop cloths from home improvement stores can be cut to the size you need. Use masking or painter's tape to hold your floor protector in place. Even newspaper or large sheets of paper will work, but paint will sometimes seep through newspaper. If the easel is near the wall, consider taping clear vinyl to the wall where paint might be splashed.

Keep several towels, a supply of cloths, and large sponges accessible for wiping up. Terry cloth or other absorbent fabrics work best for cleaning up spilled paint. Smaller hand towels are best since large towels are difficult for children to handle.

Use trays for activities such as playdough or collage. Trays make it easy to keep materials together and are easy to clean up.

Protect Clothing

Purchase smocks or wear a recycled shirt, worn backwards, to protect clothing from painting activities. Ensure your smocks or shirts are easy for children to put on and to take off. Sleeves on shirts should be short so they do not get in the child's way. Provide enough shirts or smocks near the area so that clean ones are available as needed. Children are less likely to use them if they are not conveniently accessible.

Let families know that they should not dress children in their best clothing since art and other potentially messy projects are integral to your program. Explain that while you try to control messes, some spills will occur. When a child does get paint on clothing, tell the parent and remind them to pretreat the spot and wash it right away. Tempera paint is usually washable but can become a permanent stain if not washed out soon.

Your Role in Music

As with art, the teacher in early childhood has a significant role in helping children enjoy and learn from music. Planning for music in early childhood is much more than selecting which songs to sing or which musical games to play. The following sections discuss some ways to provide rich musical experiences.

Provide Variety

Play all types of music. Look for music that you like and that is appropriate for your age group. But go beyond children's recordings and play other genres of music as well. Many classical pieces provide interesting rhythms, loud and soft dynamics, and rich sounds. Look for appealing dance music and rhythmic recordings; even consider polka, waltz music, or lively swing. Try jazz, blues, or folk genres. The only genres to avoid might be hard rock or heavy metal, which can be irritating and jangle nerves.

Sing and Sing Often

Children will join you if you start singing. It is a great way to communicate. You can even talk to children in a singsong voice about what you are doing. It does not have to rhyme; just make it up as you go along.

Introduce Children to Musical Elements

There are many musical elements that young children can and should experience including tempo, volume, pitch, mood, and rhythm. The following sections discuss ways to include these musical elements in an early childhood curriculum.

Tempo

Tempo is the speed at which music is performed. The best way to introduce tempo is by contrasting the extremes—very slow and very fast. Once children can recognize and move to fast and slow music, you can begin introducing the more challenging concept of the continuum from very slow to very fast and the reverse (**Figure 11.18**).

Volume

Volume refers to the loudness or softness of sounds. Many people incorrectly associate big or high movements with loud music and small or low movements with soft music. However, volume is better equated with a movement's strength or weakness (or firmness or gentleness). The best way to introduce volume is by contrasting extremes, from forceful to gentle movements. Once children can move to loud and soft music, begin introducing the continuum from soft to loud.

Pitch

Pitch is the highness or lowness of a musical tone, so the use of high and low movements is appropriate. Asking children to "move in the high space" (such as on tiptoe with their hands in the air) or "move in the low space" (bending down with hand movements low to the floor) can help them understand the highs and lows of pitch.

Mood

Music can help set the mood throughout the day and become a signal for various activities. For example, if a teacher wants children to begin to settle down, they can play soft music at lunch to prepare them for naptime. Feelings are often conveyed by music. Young children notice the mood of a song and respond to it. This ability is due to the sensitivity of the young child's ear and willingness to demonstrate a physical response. Ask children to move the way the music makes them feel. Does it make them feel happy? Sad? Tired? Excited?

FatCamera/E+ via Getty Images

Figure 11-18 Children clap to the tempo of a music selection. What are other ways children can experience the concept of music tempo?

Rhythm

Rhythm consists of the concepts of beat and meter. To help children understand rhythm, pass out some musical instruments and keep a pair of rhythm sticks for yourself. Pick a beat and tap it out with the rhythm sticks. Let children with instruments join in. Others can clap, snap their fingers, make up words, or even dance to the beat. Have one of the children create a beat for everyone to follow. Play distinct types of music and let children respond. Ask: "How does the music make you feel? Do you want to clap your hands, tap your feet, sway, or march?"

Overall, your role as a teacher includes making children aware of how different music affects them. Engage in conversations about how they react to certain songs, the musical elements involved, and why they think the songs evoke the responses they do.

Setting up a Music Center

Learning centers offer children opportunities to explore their interests individually or in a small group. A classroom music center allows children to listen to music of their choice, play instruments, and experiment with sound at their own developmental levels. Many teachers also provide space for moving to music. Additional information about establishing and supervising a music center can be found in Chapter 2, "The Early Childhood Learning Environment."

Equipment for the Music Center

The following items are often included in a music center:
- a way to play recordings: virtual assistants, technology devices, or CD players
- headphones so that children can listen without disturbing others
- percussion instruments—maracas, tambourines, castanets, finger cymbals, triangles, wood blocks, rhythm sticks, toy pianos, and xylophones (**Figure 11.19**)
- miscellaneous sound sources: cans, plastic or cardboard containers filled with beads or sand, coffee can or oatmeal box drums, or assorted sizes of metal mixing bowls and spoons
- items to classify and for sensory experiences, such as objects to hit, pluck, blow, scrape, and make quiet and loud sounds

Collab Media/iStock/Getty Images Plus

Figure 11.19 Even these two 15-month-olds can use this percussion instrument. *What are some skills these toddlers are learning?*

- a container with scarves, streamers, elastic bracelets or anklets with bells, and dolls or stuffed animals to become dance partners; create prop boxes with different items to rotate to maintain interest and entice children to the area
- nonbreakable mirrors so that children can observe their movements
- an ever-changing selection of books to read or look at while listening to music

If You Cannot Sing or Play an Instrument

What if you cannot hold a tune or feel you have a terrible voice? Children will not care; they will just be happy that you are singing and will gleefully join in. You need not be an expert in the field of music or even have an experienced singing voice to offer your children valuable musical experiences. Children will not judge you on the quality of your singing, instrument playing, or musical creations. Children learn much from your example and your enjoyment of music. In early childhood, attitude is more important than skill. Here are some ways to provide rich musical experiences even if you feel you cannot sing or play an instrument:

- Use recordings or videos for music experiences.
- Purchase or make simple rhythm instruments—drums, sticks, bells, wood blocks, and so forth.
- Record or purchase diverse types of music, such as classical, jazz, pop, new age, or zydeco, and listen or dance to them.
- Invite children to draw what they feel is happening in the music or move how the music makes them feel.
- Have children make up a story about what they imagine when they listen to a selection of instrumental music.
- Dance to different types of music (fast and active, slow and relaxing) using scarves or streamers.
- Record familiar sounds such as a phone, a door closing, a vacuum cleaner, water running, and so forth. Have children listen and guess what the sounds are. Cut out pictures of the objects that are making each sound, and have children match the objects to the sound.
- Encourage children to experiment with different sounds that their bodies can make (click, snap, clap, stomp, swish, rubbing, etc.). Use the tune of "Old MacDonald," changing the words to parts of the body.

Musical Experiences

Five aspects of musical experiences should be part of every child's life: (1) moving, (2) listening, (3) singing, (4) playing, and (5) creating. Note that there is considerable overlap and interrelatedness among the five aspects.

Moving

Beginning as babies, we are led to movement when we hear music. Many traditional children's songs passed down through generations are those that have games or movements attached to them.

Listening

There is a difference between listening and hearing. The latter requires little concentration; the former does. To really listen, one must pay attention and focus the mind on what is being heard. The ability to pay attention is a learned skill, and active listening is required if children are to make sense of their environment. Playing music in the background for long periods of time with no specific purpose can easily become a distraction rather than a pleasant accompaniment.

Singing

The stages of vocal expression, beginning in infancy, move from cooing and babbling to chanting to singing. Because most children love to sing and often break into spontaneous songs, music often becomes a part of every program where there are children, even when it is not consciously planned.

Adding hand motions and other actions to songs can enhance listening and add greater meaning to the lyrics. If children are reluctant to sing, actions may entice them to participate. However, some children may have difficulty singing and following movements at the same time. Learning to do both simultaneously is a developmental process, and teaching the words before adding the actions may help support this process.

Playing

Playing instruments and exploring environmental sound should occur early and often in a child's life (**Figure 11.20**). Both contribute to the child's overall music experience and provide an awareness of sound that can enrich daily living. Like singing and moving simultaneously, playing and moving at the same time is more challenging than doing either separately. However, when children reach the stage where they can do both, one will enhance the other. For example, marching while playing a rhythm instrument enhances enjoyment and a sense of rhythm.

Creating

Children may make their own instruments or invent their own dances. They may create songs or chants using tunes they know. Their invented songs usually include repetition but not necessarily rhymes. The main factor is that the creation process is their own and that it delights and satisfies them.

Creating and Using Invented Songs

Invented songs, sometimes called piggyback or parody songs, are new words set to familiar tunes. Teachers of young children use invented songs often in their classrooms. Sometimes, invented songs are used because the teacher cannot find a suitable song for the topic. Or they find lyrics but cannot read music and therefore do not know the tune. So they make up a song to a familiar tune.

Using a familiar tune helps the teacher develop and remember the words in an invented song and when children recognize the tune, they learn the song fast. Creating a parody song requires that the teacher match the words to a known tune. For example, Mrs. LeBlanc's "Circle Time" song was easily adapted to a tune she knew well.

Liderina/iStock/Getty Images Plus

Figure 11-20 These children explore musical instruments. They experiment to see what the sounds are like. How does this experience relate to other curriculum areas?

Teaching Tip

Examples of Musical Experiences

The following are suggestions for using music throughout the day:

Moving
- Use music with actions, both whole body and fine motor.
- Let children show with movement how the music makes them feel.
- Provide opportunities for children to move to a variety of musical types.

Listening
- Identify environmental sounds or various instruments.
- Take a listening walk.
- Echo the rhythms heard.
- Use the four voices: (1) whispering, (2) speaking, (3) singing, and (4) shouting.
- Make body sounds: tapping, clapping, patting, stomping, and so forth.

Singing
- Encourage children to make up songs about everyday experiences.
- Record children's voices and play the recordings.
- Offer both spontaneous and structured experiences.

Playing
- Experiment with how different instruments sound.
- Teach children the names of instruments and the proper way to care for them.
- Make and use homemade instruments.

Creating
- Create movements to go with music.
- Create music with or without instruments.
- Create parody songs.

Try an activity yourself. What if you need a song about seeing a yellow flower on the way to school? Teachers who do not know a flower song can think of words and music to create the song. First, the teacher might think of a tune they know and like, such as "Oh! Susanna." Then they think of words that fit the tune, such as, "I came to school this morning, and guess what I did see?" Next, they think of words that rhyme with "see," such as, "I saw a yellow flower, so beautiful to me." Then they continue with variations of the second line, "Oh, yellow flower, you're beautiful to me." And they repeat the lines to make the words fit the tune. Now they have a song about a yellow flower to sing with the children!

☑ CHECKPOINT

1. What are time and space considerations in planning for art or music?
2. What are some benefits of special art and music learning centers?
3. Have you ever made up a song? Did you use a tune you already knew?

11.5 Focus on Assessment of Program Practices of Art and Music

Providing a rich music or art program relies on ongoing improvement. An effective teacher will include formative assessments to determine what is working well and where improvements may be needed. Checklists based on commonly accepted practices or standards are one way to assess a program. **Figure 11.21** and **Figure 11.22** are checklist tools to assess the music and arts component of the curriculum.

Assessing an Early Childhood Art Program

This checklist can be used to assess your visual art program:

_____ Are there stimulating and quality materials for children to use?
_____ Are the materials representative of various cultures?
_____ Does the program provide many opportunities for child-initiated and child-directed expression and exploration?
_____ Are children engaged in creating and reflecting on their own art?
_____ Do the art experiences build upon curriculum goals and skills and connect across subject areas?
_____ Does the program emphasize the process of art and not depend on finished products?
_____ Are art materials and activities offered outdoors?
_____ Are children given many opportunities to choose to participate in art throughout the day?
_____ Does the schedule allow children time to repeat and practice new skills?
_____ Do adults engage children in conversation about their work?
_____ Is children's work respected and cared for?
_____ Are families included in art offerings and helped to understand the value of art for children?

Goodheart-Wilcox Publisher

Figure 11-21 This checklist can be used to determine how well your art program is meeting the needs of children. What else might you add to the checklist?

Assessing an Early Childhood Music Program

This checklist can be used to assess your music program:

_____ Is there a variety of musical experiences available throughout the day?
_____ Is music an integrated part of the curriculum, utilizing recordings, individual and group singing, instruments, creative movement, and dancing?
_____ Is a music player available that children can use independently?
_____ Does the supply of recordings include a variety for quiet listening, active movement, and rhythmic activity, as well as songs to sing?
_____ Are there props, such as scarves or streamers with which to dance?
_____ Are there sufficient musical instruments available for experimentation with sound and the creation of music?
_____ Is the emphasis on enjoyment more than performance?
_____ Are various types of music used, including music from other cultures?
_____ Is music used as a motivator for other tasks, such as cleanup or transitional time?
_____ Is there ample space where children can move about freely for movement activities?
_____ Are music experiences broadened to the outdoors?
_____ Do families participate in the music? Have you helped them understand the role of music in the curriculum?

Goodheart-Willcox Publisher

Figure 11-22 This checklist can be used to determine how well your music program is meeting the needs of children. What else might you add to the checklist?

✅ CHECKPOINT

1. How does a formal assessment practice benefit an art and music program?
2. What are questions you might ask teachers to determine how effective a program is?
3. How might you record children's responses to an art and music program to ascertain necessary changes?

11.6 Family Matters

There are many ways you can engage families to be actively involved in supporting art and music in your program. When families understand and recognize the value of the arts in early childhood, rewards are in store for all concerned. They might share a recording of their favorite music or a selection that represents their culture. A parent might play a musical instrument or demonstrate an art process. Families can enjoy songs and art activities if you send them the words of classroom songs or your art recipes. Families and children learn more about the creative process through this collective exploration.

Consider sending information home to help families understand your philosophy about supporting children's creativity for a consistent approach. See **Figure 11.23** and **Figure 11.24** for sample letters that explain one program's approach to art and music.

Holding a Family Art Fair or Music Fun Day

One way to help families understand children's creativity and to involve them in your program is to hold an art fair or music fun day. At an art fair, children's art processes, projects, and products can hold high appeal for families. Adults participating in art experiences with their children remember their own childhood delight from a brand-new box of sharp-pointed crayons. For a music fun day, rather than having children in a performance, have them show the families songs and musical activities they have been learning and invite family members to participate with them. They might also make and play musical instruments with their families in a multigenerational rhythm band.

Holding an art fair or music day for families can be a rewarding exhibition that gives families an opportunity to both see and sample the techniques their children have been enjoying. An effective way to set up an art fair is to arrange stations where families participate in the various processes. An extra benefit is that the children gain experience in planning, organizing, and conducting an event, using literacy, collaboration, and other skills.

Let children decide which art projects or music activities will be offered. Help them decide on the specifics of their project: If they want to do collage, will it be fabric, torn paper, or other materials? Which musical activities will they include, and how? Allow groups of two or three to choose a different art process or song to teach families. If many want to do the same thing, help them think of variations. For example, if too many want to use playdough, one group might use cookie cutters and rolling pins, another might use scissors and table knives, and a third group might use scented playdough to make pretend cupcakes or cookies.

Help children plan a schedule for the event and volunteer for the necessary tasks. Guide them in deciding about name tags, greeters, and other tasks. Let children choose which of their own projects they want to display. Do they want to show the collages or tambourines they made? Or will they demonstrate a new song they created?

A week or two before the event, let children make invitations and take them home. Help them set up exhibits in the classroom, along with numbered worktables where they will be stationed with appropriate materials. As families arrive, provide name tags with numbers to indicate initial project locations. Encourage families to participate in several child-led workshops.

Dear Families,

In our classroom, we encourage every child to design, draw, explore, and create. These activities help children develop fine motor skills, hand-eye coordination, and social skills; understand sequencing; and increase language skills. Children take pride in their accomplishments. Please continue to encourage your child's creativity at home by praising their hard work and displaying their creations. Below is information about how to encourage your child's art and the practices that we follow in the classroom.

Do's and Don'ts of Art

Do's of Art	Don'ts of Art
• Do ask your child to talk about their artwork; discuss the colors, forms, textures, patterns, and space. "Tell me about your picture." • Do regard your child's art as self-expression. • Do realize that during the time your child works, they acquire important experiences for growth. • Do display your child's artwork. • Do let your child develop their own techniques by experimentation. • Do encourage your child to respect others' expressions.	• Don't correct or try to improve your child's art for adult appeal or impose your own standards. • Don't regard the final product as more significant than the process. • Don't hang only the "best" example of your child's artwork. • Don't compare your child's art with another's art. • Don't make comments that minimize your child's artistic expression.

Looking forward to an art-filled year!

Miss Tracey

Goodheart-Wilcox Publisher; (illustration) Antonov Maxim/Shutterstock.com

Figure 11-23 This letter provides guidelines to help families respond to children's art. How might you also use these guidelines with staff members?

Dear Families,

In our program, we encourage every child to enjoy music in many ways. Through music, children develop skills such as recognizing rhyming words, increasing vocabulary, working as a group, and physical coordination. Please continue to encourage your child's fun with music at home by sharing and supporting their interest and talking with them about music. Below is information about how to encourage your child's interest in music that we follow in our program.

Do's and Don'ts of Music

Do's of Music	Don'ts of Music
• Do enjoy music with your child. • Do remember that making up songs can be fun and creative. • Do try a wide variety of music. • Do talk about how the music makes you feel. • Do discuss favorite songs and why they are favorites. • Do remember that music is about enjoyment.	• Don't expect your child to learn a song with only a few exposures to it. • Don't require your child to perform for others. • Don't expect perfection. Music is about enjoyment. • Don't belittle your child's efforts at playing, singing, or creating music. • Don't compare your child's efforts with others'.

Thank you for your support!

Mr. Marco

Goodheart-Wilcox Publisher; (illustration) Antonov Maxim/Shutterstock.com

Figure 11-24 This letter provides guidelines to help families respond to children's music. How might you also use these guidelines with staff members?

Following the event, invite children to recall and write about their families' experiences and comments during the event. Post the comments and display families' photos for all to admire and enjoy and to document the event.

Involving families has many benefits for an early childhood program. Working together for the benefit of the child creates support for the program as well as consistency for the children.

☑ CHECKPOINT

1. How does it benefit children when a program communicates well with families?
2. Why is it important to include children in making plans for special events such as an art fair or music fun day?
3. What are some additional ways families can be involved in the art and music program?

Chapter 11 Review and Assessment

Chapter Summary

11.1 Identify the importance of art and music in the curriculum for young children.
- Visual art and music are part of STEAM and play a vital role in young children's learning and development.
- Children make use of the elements of art in many early childhood activities.
- Creativity is recognized by society for its value.
- Crafts are different from creative art in that crafts have a predefined outcome and follow a model or instructions.
- In art, children need a wide variety of materials to express their emotions and ideas and the freedom to do so.
- There are four steps in the creative process: (1) preparation, (2) incubation, (3) illumination, and (4) verification.
- Both art and music give children opportunities for creativity and self-expression.

11.2 Explain how art and music can be integrated into the rest of the curriculum.
- Including music and art from other cultures can enrich an art and music program and help children appreciate other cultures.
- Art integrates with other curriculum areas and includes many of the skills commonly thought of in science and engineering.
- Art supports fine motor development necessary for writing.
- Music is an important part of the early childhood curriculum, contributes to children's learning, and can play a role in classroom management.
- Music can stimulate or calm children, encourage movement, and support social development.

11.3 Describe the developmental stages of children's art and music skills.
- Children progress through recognized stages in their drawing, cutting, and modeling skills.
- Basic art processes for children include applying, forming, constructing, and interlacing.
- Easel painting is one of the most valuable art experiences for young children.
- Children develop skills in musical abilities in a predictable sequence and pattern based on generally recognized ages.
- The stages in art and music can be used as a guide for planning developmentally appropriate experiences.

11.4 **Explain the teacher's responsibilities in implementing an effective art and music program.**
- The teacher's role in art is to support children's efforts through the provision of materials, time, an appreciation of their work, and an accepting attitude that encourages exploration and creativity.
- An art center and a music center allow children to engage in art and music and follow their interests.
- Conversing with children about their art is an important teaching role.
- Teachers can provide rich musical experiences for young children by providing a variety of music, singing along with the children, and introducing the children to musical elements.
- A teacher's primary task is to share an enjoyment of music with children, not necessarily to have a good singing voice or play an instrument.
- If children are to fully experience music, they should explore it as a whole and be given opportunities to listen, sing, play, create, and move.
- Displaying children's art demonstrates respect for their work and helps educate families on the value of art.

11.5 **Describe methods for assessing the art and music program.**
- Checklists of commonly recognized criteria or standards can be used to assess an art and music program.
- Quality programs are created from formative assessments that lead to ongoing improvement.

11.6 **Examine the role of the teacher in connecting with families.**
- Communication with families about how to support children's creativity at home helps build a successful program.
- Music can develop awareness of rhyming words, expand vocabulary, and contribute to language and literacy.
- Involving families and others can increase children's cultural understandings and help families recognize the value of art and music in children's lives.

Review Your Knowledge

1. **True or False.** Self-expression is an integral part of the creative process.
2. **True or False.** Music can help bring calmness to overstimulated children.
3. Art and music develop all of the following skills in young children *except* ____.
   A. social skills and problem-solving skills
   B. language skills
   C. problem-solving skills
   D. note-taking skills
4. **True or False.** Art and music can reinforce concepts children learn in other areas.
5. **True or False.** Singing songs can help children learn new vocabulary by introducing them to new words.
6. **True or False.** Young children do not have sufficient coordination to dance to music.
7. **True or False.** Art and math share no common concepts.
8. **True or False.** Toddlers can easily play an instrument and march at the same time.
9. **True or False.** Preschoolers have difficulty playing percussion instruments.
10. Art activities for children ages 2 and under ____.
    A. are not needed since other types of development are more important
    B. should focus on sensory stimulation and exploring with materials
    C. should concentrate on fine muscle development
    D. should only include crayon activities
11. **True or False.** Teachers should always make a sample of any project they want the children to do.
12. **True or False.** Teachers must be able to draw in order for children to produce creative artwork.
13. **True or False.** To offer children valuable musical experiences, a teacher should be an expert in music and have a good singing voice.
14. **True or False.** Teachers should use only music written specifically for their classroom's age group.

15. **True or False.** An effective teacher provides children with a variety of musical styles and cultures.
16. The role of the teacher in the art program is to ____.
    A. offer a variety of materials and interpret the value of the process of art to parents
    B. make sure the children do not cut themselves or get paint on their clothing
    C. teach the children how to color in the lines
    D. ensure the children have something to take home to their parents
17. **True or False.** Assessing the music and art components of the curriculum requires the aid of an artist and a musician.
18. **True or False.** If a program follows a good curriculum, assessment is not necessary.
19. **True or False.** Some educators and parents unknowingly discourage creative expression.
20. The role of the teacher in the art program does *not* include ____.
    A. making sure the children have something to take home to their parents
    B. offering a variety of materials
    C. interpreting the value of the process of art to parents
    D. ensuring materials are safe

Chapter 12

STEAM: Mathematics

Standards Covered in This Chapter

NAEYC

NAEYC—1c, 2b, 3a, 4a, 4b, 4c, 5a, 5b, 6c

DAP

DAP—2a, 2c, 2d, 2e, 2f, 3a, 3b, 3c, 3d, 4b, 4c, 4d, 4e, 4g, 4h, 5a, 5d

Learning Outcomes

After reading this chapter, you should be able to:

12.1 Explain how mathematics is included in the daily lives of young children.
12.2 Identify children's experiences that develop mathematical concepts.
12.3 Describe strategies and techniques for teaching mathematics to young children.
12.4 Identify methods for assessing children's mathematical learning.
12.5 Describe ways to communicate with families and involve them in their children's learning.

Key Terms

attributes
graphing
labeling
one-to-one correspondence
parrot
rebus
seriation
symmetry

Introduction

Mathematics, commonly referred to as math, is the final component of the acronym STEAM. Math relates to science and the other components of STEAM in many ways. Calculations are a critical part of science, engineering, and technology for comparing and documenting outcomes, precise measurements, and accurate processes. Math is related to art and music, as proportions, balance, and patterns are components of both. Art includes the use of shapes and perspective, and music consists of mathematical repetitions and cadence.

Mathematical knowledge and skill are widely recognized as vital components of children's learning. However, the many mathematical concepts important to young children are not as commonly recognized, at least by those outside the field of early childhood. The concepts learned in early childhood lay down the foundation for children's futures and will be used throughout a lifetime. Consider counting, for example. The ability to count and understand the base ten system, upon which the U.S. number system is built, is the foundation for adding, subtracting, multiplying, dividing, and all other mathematical calculations. Children will one day need to use this skill in their daily life tasks, such as purchasing items, fulfilling work requirements, or managing finances. What about cooking? Would one be able to follow a recipe without learning the basics of measurement (**Figure 12.1**)? Following directions of all types requires knowledge of sequence, and often, timing. When introducing math concepts to young children, teachers are building the children's entire math foundation—a critical stepping stone for their successes in life.

What are the concepts young children need to learn? We would not expect most young children to understand quantities of thousands, but we would expect most preschoolers to be able to demonstrate an understanding of **one-to-one correspondence** (counting a group of objects by assigning one number to each object and only counting each object once) by putting one spoon in each bowl in the housekeeping center. We may not expect them to determine the area of a square or circle, but we would expect them to be able to identify items that are square or round.

Counting, recognizing numerals, and identifying shapes are part of most early childhood curricula. Math concepts, however, are much broader than just these skills. This chapter will explore how to develop math awareness, teach math concepts to young children, create a math-rich environment, assess mathematical knowledge, and connect with children's families to communicate what children are learning.

ktaylorg/E+ via Getty Images

Figure 12-1 Learning about measurement is necessary to master a major life skill: cooking. *What other skills are improved by understanding measurement?*

12.1 Developing Math Awareness

To many adults, math is the most abstract of the curriculum content areas. Some adults may dislike math because they failed to do well in the subject during their own school years. Perhaps they had difficulty on standardized tests that concentrated heavily on math. Some adults may associate math with tasks they view as unpleasant or tedious, such as completing tax forms or staying within a budget.

Children, however, do not view math in the same way as adults. For children, math is not abstract but rather relies on concrete experiences such as the exploration of objects and the gradual understanding of objects' properties and relationships. Cognitive concepts of classification, **seriation** (ordering), numbers, time, and space are developed through firsthand experiences with items in the child's environment. Thus, children are acquiring mathematical knowledge when they sort, stack, and compare manipulatives; explore sand and water; set the table for snack time; or hear rhymes and stories, such as *The Three Little Kittens* or *Goldilocks and the Three Bears*. They are learning math when they distribute one napkin to each child at a table or figure out if there are enough plates in the housekeeping area for each child. Children learn even more math in the block area as they compare sizes and shapes, substitute, and build with the various sizes and shapes of blocks. **Figure 12.2** summarizes some of the many ways that young children learn math.

Although Figure 12.2 shows many ways that children are learning math in typical classroom activities, these experiences are not always recognized as mathematical learning. The Case Study feature "Recognizing Math in Early Childhood" illustrates the phenomenon of math in the lives of young children.

✓ CHECKPOINT

1. Why are firsthand experiences important in math for young children?
2. What are some children's books you are familiar with that include math concepts?

Children Learn Early Math by...

Method	Examples
Hearing the language of math	• Adult asks if the child wants more milk • Adult uses descriptive words such as big, heavy, or round • Adult describes what is taking place, such as "here are both of your socks," or "here are your two shoes" • Adult refers to next, soon, after lunch, or when we go outside • Adult talks about the routines, "First, we wash our hands, then we eat."
Seeing, touching, and handling	• Sees items in various colors, shapes, and patterns • Has access to items that are alike but are different sizes or weights • Plays with toys such as shape sorters or simple puzzles • Plays with snap beads that are different shapes or colors • Sees a mobile with different birds on it • Feels a doll blanket that is fuzzy and soft
Engaging in one-to-one correspondence experiences	• Watching as an adult puts one sock with one shoe or one cookie on each napkin • Playing with toys where one peg goes in one hole or one puzzle piece goes in one opening • Putting one cup with one saucer or one spoon in each bowl • Giving each child a napkin
Classifying and creating patterns through activities	• Sorting items by size, shape, color, or texture • Clapping rhythms: fast, fast, slow; fast, fast, slow • Playing with snapping beads or arranging toys in patterns, such as red, blue, yellow; red, blue, yellow • Reading books that include number or shape concepts, such as *Chicka Chicka Boom Boom*

Goodheart-Willcox Publisher

Figure 12-2 These are some of the ways that children learn math. Do you think any of these are more important than the others? Why or why not?

Case Study

Recognizing Math in Early Childhood

At an early learning center open house, a parent asked Ms. Martin, a teacher who worked with toddlers, if she "taught math" to the 2-year-olds. The parent was thinking of math in the traditional way—simplifying it to basic counting and recognition of numerals and shapes.

Unfortunately, Ms. Martin seemed to view math in the same way, as she replied that math is not taught to toddlers. This exchange raises questions about the difference between the adult perspective of math and the actual components of math.

Many of the activities in **Figure 12.2** were part of Ms. Martin's curriculum, but she did not recognize them as math learning. Further, she missed an opportunity to explain the value of such experiences to this parent. Unfortunately, when administrators or parents insist that math be part of the curriculum, teachers like Ms. Martin may resort to developmentally inappropriate methods, such as using workbooks and flash cards. Lack of knowledge of the spectrum and application of math can prevent the incorporation of the developmentally appropriate math experiences described in **Figure 12.2**.

Consider This

1. What might a teacher who understands developmentally appropriate practices have said to this parent?
2. What are some ways to educate adults about firsthand experiences in learning math?
3. Why do you think many adults focus mainly on counting, recognizing numerals, and knowing shapes as math skills?

12.2 Learning Mathematical Concepts

If you ask the public what children need to learn in school, most people will mention reading first, then math. When referring to math, they are usually talking about recognizing numerals and counting. Yet math concepts are far more complex than those two tasks. As children go about their daily lives, exploring and discovering items around them, they are exposed to the world of mathematics. Moreover, mathematics has become increasingly important in this technological age, calling for more understanding of how best to teach math at an early age.

Equations, fractions, and ratios may be among the concepts many adults envision when they further consider mathematics from their high school experiences. But, of course, the math concepts appropriate for exploration with young children begin with the basics. They include:

- **Number awareness and recognition.** This involves identifying numbers and distinguishing one number from others (**Figure 12.3**). Parents usually recognize and acknowledge this skill, along with counting, as important math knowledge for young children.
- **Counting.** Counting often begins with rote memorization, which then evolves into an understanding that numbers correspond to quantities. Meaningful counting requires recognition of a relationship between the numbers and the items being counted. This concept is referred to as *one-to-one correspondence*. One-to-one correspondence describes the matching of one item with another. Examples of one-to-one correspondence are one sock to one shoe, one jacket for each child, or one peg for each hole. This math concept is essential in understanding how numerals represent one additional item and that, for example, the symbol "5" represents five items. Children can begin to understand one-to-one correspondence when performing tasks such as making sure each child gets a cracker, matching cups to saucers in the pretend kitchen, or putting one doll in each bed.

Figure 12-3 This child needs to have number recognition to find the house with the number 22 on it. What are some other ways that teachers can encourage number recognition?

- **Quantitative concepts.** Examples of quantitative concepts include big and little, long and short, wide and narrow, more and most, same size, same length, same width, or same amount. The development of these concepts relies heavily on the contextual use of language.
- **Basic geometry.** Geometry begins with the ability to identify shapes such as circles, squares, and triangles, and then three-dimensional objects such as spheres (balls) and cylinders (cans) (**Figure 12.4**). Geometry for young children, however, does not involve the processes of determining diameters or square footage.

Figure 12-4 By playing with these blocks, this child can begin to understand basic geometry. What are some other ways that young children can learn basic geometry?

- **Simple computation.** Simple computation includes addition and subtraction by combining and separating sets of objects. Provide opportunities during the day for children to add by combining sets, by finding out how many more of an item are needed, or by looking at how many red blocks one has, how many blue ones, and how many altogether.

Number Awareness, Recognition, and Counting

Recognizing numerals and counting are two of the first concepts that adults will recognize as math. It is important to realize, however, that an understanding of one-to-one correspondence must be achieved before counting is meaningful. For example, a child might count a group of six blocks as one, two, three, four, and five without recognizing that each number means an additional block.

One-to-one correspondence is a separate but related skill from counting. A child is capable of rote counting without understanding the relationships between the numbers and the quantity. In other words, children sometimes **parrot**, or say words they do not understand. Pointing to items that are being counted can help children understand one-to-one correspondence. For example, when counting how many children are in the room, say the numbers aloud while pointing to each child.

Between the ages of 1 and 2, most children will understand the concepts of "more" and "enough." For example, when children want more cookies, they will say "more." They may also say "no more" when they have enough. This association of words to quantity concepts is an important foundation in children's understanding of math.

Some 2-year-olds may understand words such as "one" and "two" and follow simple directions, such as "Take one cookie" or "Choose two crackers." Many 2-year-olds will also know they are 2 years of age and hold up two fingers to illustrate (**Figure 12.5**). Toward the end of their second year, some may try to recite number words in sequence, but as they count higher, they often say numbers out of sequence. By their third year, many can count 5 items, some can count to 10, and a few can accurately count to 20.

Many 4-year-olds can tell what number comes after a given number in a sequence up to 10 or more. For example, if asked, "What comes after 1-2-3-4-5?" most 4-year-olds can answer "6," although they may not be able to tell you that 6 comes after 5 without counting 1 through 5 again. Given two numbers between 1 and 10, many 4-year-olds can identify which number is larger.

kali9/E+ via Getty Images

Figure 12-5 This child is trying to hold up two fingers to tell his teacher that he is 2 years old. At what age might this child learn to count in sequence?

During the second half of their fourth year, children usually understand when given a group of items (such as a set of blocks) that if they give one away, they will have fewer. Children of this age will also understand that if given another item, they will have more. Throughout these early years, however, many children will believe that a single cracker broken into many pieces is more food than the same unbroken cracker.

Quantitative and Qualitative Concepts

Quantitative concepts are those properties that allow us to describe and compare items based on measurable features. Quantitative concepts give us the language to talk about such features as size, amount, and weight. For children to develop an awareness of quantitative concepts, it's important to take advantage of opportunities that arise in everyday activities. Skills such as counting, seriation, recognizing patterns, graphing, money, statistics, probability, and basic geometry are all factors in quantitative concepts. Qualitative concepts are the subjective qualities of characteristics such as color, texture, or appearance.

Sorting and Classifying

Sorting and classifying items refer to the organization of objects into sets, or groups, based on one or more similar characteristics. The characteristics might be similar colors, shapes, or even the way the objects are used.

By the age of 3, many children begin to recognize how to sort or classify objects into sets. For instance, they may group all soft, fuzzy animals into a box; stack all of the square wooden blocks together on a shelf; or park all of the big trucks beside the wall.

Four-year-olds can sort a group of items by one or more characteristics (**Figure 12.6**). For example, they can separate forks, knives, and spoons; organize a group of socks by color and size; or sort buttons by color, size, and the number of holes.

Many opportunities to sort and classify materials occur during daily activities in an early childhood classroom. Look for opportunities for children to sort and classify to develop these skills. **Figure 12.7** shows some of the sorting and classifying math concepts that preschool children might be expected to learn.

Marnya Auramchuk/iStock/Getty Images Plus

Figure 12-6 This child is sorting the objects by color. What other characteristics could they sort these objects by?

Sorting and Classifying Skills that Children Need

Concept	Skills
Color	Items can go together that are the same color.
Number	There are the same number of items (pairs or sets of four).
Shape	Items may all be round, square, triangular, and so on.
Material	Items are made of different materials, such as wood, plastic, glass, paper, cloth, or metal.
Pattern	Items have different visual patterns, such as stripes, dots, or flowers.
Texture	Items feel different from each other: smooth, rough, soft, hard, fuzzy, wet, or dry.
Function	Some items have the same function, or they are used for the same task (a group of forks and spoons are for eating; a group of pencils and crayons are for writing; or a group of toy instruments are for playing music).
Association	Some items work together (knife and fork), come from the same place (animals from a farm), or belong to a special person (the boots and helmet of a firefighter).
Class name	Items belong to groups (children and adults to "people," horses and pigs to "animals," oranges and bread to "foods," or cars and trucks to "vehicles").
Common features	Items have something in common, such as feathers, legs, or wheels.

Goodheart-Willcox Publisher

Figure 12-7 The sorting and classifying skills that children need. Which of these skills do you think children acquire first?

Comparing

Comparing items is a skill that adults use regularly in their daily lives. One might compare the price of two different brands of salad dressing or the overall cost of a car, depending on how long it is financed. Children learn comparing skills as they handle objects, observe differences and similarities, and hear the language of such comparisons. Recognizing items' likenesses and differences is also an important pre-reading skill. Opportunities abound in most classrooms for making such comparisons.

Ordering and Seriation

Seriation is arranging objects by size or, in some instances, characteristics. Arranging objects from smallest to largest, shortest to tallest, or lightest to darkest is seriation. Putting items in a graduated sequence builds an understanding of relational changes (**Figure 12.8**). Think of nesting blocks or cups, Russian dolls where each doll is inside one just a bit larger, and so on. Using vocabulary that reflects order and seriation helps children build these understandings. Look for opportunities to use words throughout the day such as those in **Figure 12.9**.

Recognizing and Creating Patterns

Recognizing patterns is an important skill, because numbers follow distinct and predictable patterns. Toward the end of their first year, many children figure out that there is an order or a pattern to their days. For instance, they will recognize that after dinner, bedtime is soon to follow. They begin to learn that their school day rest time succeeds lunch, and after rest time, they have a snack.

Posting a schedule helps children learn to see that their daily routines are predictable because they follow the same sequence. For more information about creating visual schedules, see Chapter 2, "The Early Childhood Learning Environment."

By the middle of their second year, children will understand that night and day follow a continuous cycle. They become aware of fabricated patterns, such as color patterns on rugs, floor tiles, or clothing. Throughout their second year, many children will figure out how to follow a simple repeating pattern by stringing large beads in alternating colors or stacking colored blocks in repeating patterns.

Figure 12-8 This toy gives children the opportunity to practice placing objects in a graduated sequence. How does this help children understand relational changes?

Order and Seriation Vocabulary

- Big, bigger, biggest
- Few, fewer, fewest
- First, second, third
- Large, larger, largest
- Small, smaller, smallest
- Last, next, then
- Many, more, most
- Thick, thicker, thickest
- Thin, thinner, thinnest

Goodheart-Willcox Publisher

Figure 12-9 These vocabulary words help children understand order and seriation. Why is it important for children to understand these words?

During their third year, some children learn to follow a simple sequence of familiar events. For example, they can describe the steps they follow in taking a bath: First, plug the drain, then run the water, remove clothing, get in the tub, apply soap, rinse the soap off, and finally get out, dry off, and dress (**Figure 12.10**). They may not include all of the steps, however.

During their fourth year, many children will follow and even make their own simple repeating patterns. If shown a color pattern of red, blue, yellow, green, red, blue, yellow, green, children will predict that another red should come next. Many 4-year-olds can follow and make their own sound patterns, such as clap, clap, stomp, clap, clap, stomp.

Graphing

When guided by an adult, many 4-year-olds can understand simple graphs and use the information to answer questions. Children can sort in a variety of ways, such as color, use, or other common attributes, and then make a graph representing their findings. They can graph simple concepts such as how many children like green apples and how many like red apples (**Figure 12.11**). **Graphing** for children involves pictorially representing numbers on a chart. To graph, children must understand that one picture or symbol

fstaop123/iStock/Getty Images Plus

Figure 12-10 Bath time is an opportunity to teach children sequence of events. *What are some other opportunities to teach this concept?*

Discovery Journeys

Emmy and the Crackers

When 5-year-old Emmy asked for some crackers, her teacher, Miss Lucia, told her she could get four from the box. Shortly thereafter, Emmy wanted more, and knowing it was nearing lunchtime, Miss Lucia told Emmy that this time she could get three crackers. Quickly devouring those, Emmy asked again for more, and Miss Lucia reduced the number to two. When Emmy came back once more, she counted backwards and announced, "Four, three, two, and now I get one more! And I guess then I get zero!" Emmy's ability to see what the next step would logically be demonstrated that she understood the pattern that had emerged.

Interesting to Miss Lucia was that she did not intend this as a mathematical lesson but was using it to engage Emmy prior to lunch. How many intentional and unintentional chances do we have each day to support children's math learning in a practical way when we are alert to the opportunities?

Consider This

1. Why was this a good experience for Emmy?
2. What examples have you seen of children learning math concepts in everyday activities?
3. What questions might Miss Lucia have used to scaffold Emmy's response if this were a planned activity?

represents one choice. The more symbols, the more people made that choice. **Figure 12.11** includes some questions to ask about the apple graph.

Money Value

At age 4, children will begin to recognize and learn the names of coins. They will understand the role that money plays in daily life, such as buying items. Dramatic play activities offer opportunities to include experiences using money. For example, a pretend grocery store can include items with price tags, play money, a cash register, and even a scanner and self-checkout counter.

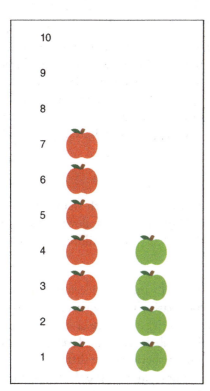

Apple Graph
1. Did more people like red or green apples?
2. How do you know?
3. How many more liked them?
4. Did fewer people like red or green apples?

Goodheart-Willcox Publisher

Figure 12-11 This simple chart documents how many children prefer red apples and how many prefer green apples. What concepts or skills are accomplished by graphing?

Case Study

Learning about Money

In the 1960s, prior to the institution of a specific math program in a school district, developers wanted to determine what math skills children possessed prior to attending school. Their plan was to assess the math skills of children in lower-income families and compare the results to those in more middle-class or affluent families. This would provide a baseline for intervention that would focus on improving math readiness. Historically, in the school system, children of lower-income families scored lower on most readiness skills.

The results were predictable in most abilities, such as number concepts, but in understanding the value of money, a significant difference was apparent. The children in the lower-income families showed a much better understanding of the value of coins than those in the higher-income families. As researchers explored the reason for such an unexpected outcome, they became aware of several factors. The children frequently walked to local stores to make purchases. They collected glass bottles in their neighborhood and were paid in coins by returning them to the store and soon learned how much more they needed to buy a special treat of ice cream or candy. Those experiences led to their understanding of money value.

In contrast, interviews with the families of the other children indicated that treats were generally bought and paid for by the adults rather than the children, and rarely with coins. Thus, those children lacked the experience of using money in the way that the others had.

Consider This
1. Why do you think the researchers were surprised at the findings about money?
2. What does this example demonstrate about the value of firsthand experiences?
3. How do you think the use of credit and debit cards and other electronic payment methods may have now affected children's understanding of coins and money?

Statistics and Probability

Between the ages of 3 and 4, children can begin to organize items into categories and compare the results to answer a question. During their fourth year, many children figure out that some ideas can be predicted or understood based on prior experience. For example, a young child given a cloth ball may expect it to bounce and may try to bounce it, whereas an older child will know that it will not bounce. Some preschoolers begin to understand the likelihood or chance of an event happening. For example, they know that it is unlikely that snow will fall in the summer.

Basic Geometry

Young children use geometry often in their lives as they play with shape sorters, work puzzles, draw, paint, and create three-dimensional objects. The following sections discuss some of the basic geometry concepts and skills that young children develop.

Recognizing Shapes

Following are some basic geometry concepts and skills that are developed in the early years. A preschooler can recognize at least the four basic shapes: square, circle, triangle, and rectangle. Some children will also be able to identify an ellipse, a rhombus, an oval, an octagon, or a pentagon. With shapes, as with numbers, concept development occurs in progressive stages. First, children must discriminate between the difference in a shape as compared to other shapes. Then, **labeling** (giving a name to the shape) occurs. This stage is followed by matching shapes of various sizes or colors and sorting according to **attributes**, or characteristics of an item.

Between 1 and 2 years of age, many children figure out how to match same-size shapes with each other. Some will be able to match same-size circles to circles and triangles to triangles (**Figure 12.12**). With increased experience, they can match different sizes of the same item, such as pairing a small circle with a big circle.

During their second year, many children learn how to stack three or more blocks to make a tower. They can complete simple insert puzzles, placing a single item in each opening.

Many 4-year-olds will naturally make shapes that show **symmetry** (balanced proportions, similarity of placement) without necessarily understanding the concept. For example, they might make a structure of blocks where one side is identical to the other because it appeals to them. They might draw a picture with a similar tree on each side of a house. There are numerous opportunities during the day to refer to the shapes of various items. A teacher might provide paper shapes for a collage activity, ask a child to select the round beads, or ask a child to pick up the square tiles.

Understanding Space Concepts

Space concepts involve knowing how one object exists in relation to others. During their third and fourth years, many children begin to understand most of the following directional words:
- Where (on, over, under, in, inside, out, outside, into, top, bottom, above, below, in front, in back, behind, beside, by, next to, between, left, right)

tam_odin/iStock/Getty Images Plus

Figure 12-12 Shape recognition is an important skill of basic geometry. Is this an appropriate toy to teach shape recognition to children? Why or why not?

- Which way (up, down, forward, backward, around, through, to, toward, from, away from, sideways, across)
- Distance (near, far, close to, far from, further)

The teacher's frequent use of this terminology in context helps children understand these concepts.

Understanding Fractions and Percentages

Understanding that an object may be made of parts helps children build a foundation to understand fractions and percentage concepts. Cutting a sandwich in half, putting triangular blocks together to make a square, or dividing a box of crayons among several children helps build the concept of parts and whole. Words such as part, whole, divide, share, pieces, some, and half support the concepts of fractions.

Discovery Journeys

Understanding Fractions

My parents were fond of telling stories about my introduction to fractions when I was five years old. One day, two friends were at my house and with only one soft drink available, I endeavored to share it with them. I poured half of the bottle into each of their glasses, but was surprised when there was none left for me!

Another time, while eating dinner with my extended family, I was asked to find out how many people wanted a piece of pie. I counted and reported six. When the pie was served, there was none for me because I had not counted myself! Fortunately, once the error was recognized, family members shared pie with me.

Consider This
1. Do you remember a time you made a similar mistake?
2. At what age do you think a child would most likely divide the soft drink by thirds?
3. What other experiences will help children understand fractions?

Measurement

Measuring is an important life skill and is necessary for many tasks in daily life. Measuring volume and temperature is essential in cooking. Measuring temperature and taking the correct dose of medicine is critical in healthcare and in numerous other tasks. Even common experiences of purchasing clothing or choosing what to wear for the day requires measurement of size and weather temperature.

Distance, Length, Volume, and Weight

During their first years, many children learn how to judge short distances. Infants learn to adjust their reach to pick up an object. During their third year, they may display an understanding of distance by stepping over a small object or taking long steps as they walk.

Between the first and second year, many children explore quantity by filling and emptying containers. This process is common in toddlers and is often called fill and dump. Some 2-year-olds will learn to correctly use words such as big or small, fast or slow, and heavy or light to compare two entities. For instance, a child might say, "My sister is a baby. She's small. I'm big." or "The block is heavy; the cloth is not."

During their third and fourth years, many children compare the length of objects. They might take two blocks, place them side by side, and see that one is longer. They will be able to compare objects using words such as bigger or smaller, heavier or lighter, taller or shorter, and faster or slower. By the end of their fourth year, some children may discover how to measure an object such as a book or picture by using a number of smaller objects, such as crayons lined up end to end.

The understanding of how units can be used as a means of measuring is illustrated in the following Discovery Journeys feature.

Discovery Journeys

The Paper Chain

A group of second graders decided to make a long paper chain with a large supply of paper strips left from an earlier project. They taped, glued, and stapled the strips together. As they worked, they checked to determine if their chain was as long as the bulletin board, discussing the possibility of hanging it there. Noting the ample supply of paper strips, they opted to continue their work and soon were measuring to see if it was as long as the classroom. Seeing that it was, they set another goal: to make it long enough to go across the hall into another classroom. Once completed, they decided to count the number of links and proudly announced that their chain was 427 links long! Agreeing to each take a part home, the next problem was to determine how to divide the chain among the four. They addressed the challenge by folding and cutting the chain in half and then in half again to have four relatively equal parts. Their self-imposed task involved a very practical use of counting, measurement, fractions, and equality.

What was the teacher's role in this activity? The teacher provided the materials, time, and place for the children to follow their interests. As they worked, the teacher talked with them about what they were doing, showing interest and support for their effort while using questions to stimulate their thinking about how they might connect their links and what they might do with their chain:

- What are all the ways you can join the links together?
- How can you tell if it is long enough to drape on the bulletin board?
- What are some ways you can divide the chain so everyone gets an equal part?

For me, this experience of watching the self-imposed task solidified the value of allowing children to take the lead in their learning and to set their goals and follow through on projects. It confirmed the value of the teacher's role as a facilitator in providing time, materials, thought-provoking questions, and most of all, showing interest in what the children were doing.

Consider This

1. Why do you think self-imposed tasks might engage children longer than teacher-required tasks?
2. How did the teacher's actions expand on what the children learned?
3. What else might the teacher have done?

Time and Sequence

Many 4-year-old children will understand time concepts such as morning, afternoon, night, earlier, and later. Concepts related to measuring time include much more than just knowing how to read a clock. It involves such terminology and concepts as shown in **Figure 12.13**.

Time and Sequence Measurement Terminology

A long time ago	Early	New	Second	Today
Already	Fast	Next	Slow	Tomorrow
Always	Holiday	Now	Sometime	Week
Before	Hour	Often	Sometimes	Weekend
Birthday	Late	Old	Soon	When
Calendar	Minute	Once	Speed	While
Date	Month	Present	Then	Year
Days of the week	Never	Season	Time	Yesterday

Goodheart-Willcox Publisher

Figure 12-13 These vocabulary words are important when teaching time and sequence. *What are some ways you could incorporate these words during the day?*

Teachers can support children's learning of time concepts by intentionally using the vocabulary in context, such as "Soon it will be 11 o'clock and time to get ready for lunch. Then it will be rest time."

Informal Measurement

Consider the words in **Figure 12.14**, which represent opportunities for measurement experiences that occur as part of daily classroom activities. Use these words intentionally when talking to children and sharing examples with parents of how their children understand and use these concepts.

Unit Blocks and Mathematics

Although there are numerous types of blocks available, unit blocks offer much learning value, especially in the area of math. What is it about unit blocks that make them such an important part of an early childhood classroom? To begin with, they are proportional in size to a basic block called a unit, thus the name unit blocks. The basic block is considered the unit and all other blocks are proportional, e.g., two or four units long. Other shapes, such as wedges, squares, and arches, are also based on the size of that unit so that all blocks work together. This feature helps children understand the basic relationships in mathematics. Unit blocks are usually made of hardwood with a natural finish and can therefore be expected to last many years. Typically, an area of the room will be set aside for a block learning center where there will be easy access to the blocks on shelves and space for construction on the floor.

How does the teacher maximize children's activities in the block area? First, provide a background of experiences that suggest possibilities for the children to pretend, such as a trip to the doctor's office or the fire station. Accessories enhance block play and suggest ideas for construction using the blocks. For example, vehicles and traffic signs enhance the building of roads, rubber or wooden animals inspire the creation of a farm or zoo, and wooden or rubber people suggest community or home life scenarios. These accessories offer ideas for use of the blocks in a way that relates to themes.

Many free or recycled materials enhance block play. Cardboard can be used as roofs, fabric becomes tents, and tile, vinyl, or carpet samples make floors for the buildings.

Pictures and posters can stimulate play ideas as well. A large photo of a highway construction site may suggest ideas about road building. A poster of a family shopping for groceries might motivate children to build a grocery store.

Sometimes teachers avoid block play because they fear that it will get out of hand. A few simple guidelines such as these can help prevent that from happening.

Simple Guidelines for Block Play

- We build with blocks, not throw them.
- You may knock down only the tower you build.
- You may build as tall as you are.
- We keep the blocks on the carpet.
- We build away from the shelves and others.
- We take only what we will use.

☑ CHECKPOINT

1. How does a teacher support math experiences?
2. Why is the vocabulary of math important?
3. How does an understanding of child development inform the materials and experiences we should provide for children?

Informal Measurement Terminology

Big, little
Cold, hot
Fast, slow
Fat, skinny
Heavy, light
Higher, lower
Large, small
Later, sooner (earlier)
Long, short
Loud, soft (sound)
More, less (fewer)
Near, far
Older, younger (newer)
Tall, short
Thick, thin
Wide, narrow

Goodheart-Willcox Publisher

Figure 12-14 These terms describe informal measuring terminology. In what areas of life will this vocabulary be important?

12.3 The Teacher's Role in Teaching Mathematics

The teacher's key role as an early childhood professional in relation to math is to create an environment that is full of opportunities for children to explore math concepts in relevant ways. This role includes interactions that use the vocabulary of math and scaffold children's development of concepts. The role includes setting up a math or manipulative area and integrating math into all learning centers and areas of the curriculum (**Figure 12.15**). The teacher is responsible for assessing children's progress and assessing their program to plan for children and identify changes that should be made for program improvement.

Creating a Math-Rich Environment

Routines such as checking attendance, recording the weather, or preparing snacks can all add opportunities to understand and use math in a functional way. Teachers can enrich the environment by ensuring adequate materials for learning math. They can further enrich the environment by intentionally including math learning opportunities in various learning centers and engaging in frequent conversation with children about math concepts using relevant math vocabulary.

Math and Food Preparation

Children will learn math in a valuable way when teachers use food preparation as a teaching tool. Some of the math concepts that a child can learn from food activities are counting, measuring (**Figure 12.16**), one-to-one correspondence, fractions, and shapes. In addition to learning math, children are also learning important and beneficial life skills. Pouring, stirring, and squeezing develop motor skills and eye-hand coordination. Conversing about what they are doing increases children's vocabulary and develops language skills.

hiphotos35/iStock/Getty Images Plus

Figure 12-15 Before school, this teacher placed these math manipulatives on a child-size small table. What are other ways you can encourage children to play with math manipulatives?

Case Study

Kelly's Discovery

Eighteen-month-old Kelly toddled over to the container of empty food boxes sitting in a corner of her early childhood classroom. Her teacher, planning to set up a grocery store play center, temporarily placed several sacks of items on the floor. Kelly, in typical inquisitive toddler fashion, began removing the boxes and dropping them on the floor beside her. Expressing delight in the experience of control, she gleefully explored the sack's contents.

Her teacher, watching from the sidelines, saw a small raisin box catch Kelly's interest. After a few seconds of exploring the box, Kelly deposited it on the floor with other items. As she continued removing items from the sacks, she found a second raisin box and picked it up. Holding this second box in one hand, she searched the floor for the one she had dropped earlier and picked it up. She studied both carefully, turning them around and over in her hands. Kelly alternated her attention by focusing first on one raisin box, then the other.

While Kelly did not yet have the language skills to describe her recognition that the two raisin boxes were alike, it was apparent from her actions that she had made that discovery. She not only recognized the raisin box, but she also remembered that she had already put one aside that was exactly like the second one. This incident, a brief one in the busy life of a toddler, was significant. At that moment, Kelly recognized that the two boxes were identical.

For years to come, Kelly will be called upon to identify likenesses and differences with increasing discrimination as part of her education. She will be expected to match items, first in pictures, then in letters, numerals, and other abstract symbols. Now Kelly has an advantage. She was given the freedom to explore materials and allowed to make an important discovery for herself. She internalized a concept that, while clearly understood by her, was beyond her capacity to express verbally. She learned in a way far better than any later worksheet or workbook could provide. Her experience was that of real learning—the joy of discovery.

Consider This
1. How did the teacher understand that Kelly recognized that the boxes were alike?
2. Why was this recognition significant?
3. What might the teacher do to expand on Kelly's experience?

Jupiterimages/The Image Bank/Getty Images

Figure 12-16 These children are measuring ingredients as they prepare food. Other than measurement, what math concepts can be learned from food preparation activities?

Preparing food is fun for children. When they have a hand in preparing the food, they often try food items they might otherwise not eat. The following are suggestions for successfully incorporating food preparation into the classroom curriculum:

- **Use or adapt recipes to maximize children's involvement.** When possible, use individual serving recipes or revise recipes so children can do most of the work. Make, or have the children make, **rebus** cards using pictures and words for children to follow. A rebus card is an instruction card using pictures to show the steps in a task (**Figure 12.17**). It is intended to be understood with minimal or no reading skills.
- **Provide proper utensils for children to use so they are familiar with actual measuring tools.** Families might donate sets of plastic measuring cups and spoons so there will be enough for classroom use. Label the tool, such as ½ cup or 1 tsp., if not already marked. These symbols help children associate the written measurement with the quantity and the utensil.
- **Include food activities often by letting children make their own snacks.** Snacks can be as simple as putting a piece of cheese on each cracker.
- **Use the language of math when interacting with children as they work.** **Figure 12.18** shows some math words that children learn through food preparation.

Portishead1/E+ via Getty Images

Figure 12-17 This rebus card will help this child and her classmates remember to wash their hands. What other instructions can be communicated on a rebus card?

Food Preparation Chart

Add	Measure	One-third	Separate
Combine	Minutes	Ounce	Tablespoon
Cup	More	Pint	Teaspoon
Hours	One-fourth	Quart	Temperature
Ingredients	One-half	Recipe	Time

Goodheart-Willcox Publisher

Figure 12-18 These are common terms used in food preparation. Can you think of any other words to add to this list?

The Vocabulary of Mathematics

The ability to use mathematical words is important for children's understanding of math concepts. When the vocabulary is used in connection with experiences, it makes sense to children. The words in **Figure 12.19** should be used frequently by teachers as they explain activities, identify objects, converse with children, and even sing songs and read stories.

Extending Math Learning throughout the Day

When children are engaged in activities, take the opportunity to extend their math learning. Provide instructional support by asking questions such as the following:
- How did you figure out that the puzzle piece goes there?
- What do you think will happen if we add more? What if we take away some?
- What do the objects in this set have in common?
- Why do you think that car went faster than the other one?
- Are these shapes alike or different? How are they alike? How are they different?
- I see a pattern. Do you see it?
- How many more do you need to make 10?

Supporting Math Learning through Conversation and Interactions

Much math learning can occur in context throughout the day when adults talk to children using math terminology in meaningful situations. To engage children effectively, this informal talk must be interactive with the give and take of conversation rather than drill or an interrogation. The following are some tips for conversing with children to support math learning:
- **Use age-appropriate language.** Talk to children about the math they experience throughout the day. **Figure 12.20** shows some common math words and phrases to use when talking with children of different ages.

Mathematical Vocabulary Words

Time	Measurement	Size	Position	Amount
Date	Cup	Big	Up	Set
Clock	Pint	Little	Down	Group
Calendar	Quart	Fat	Here	One, two, three, etc.
Second	Gallon	Thin	There	Pair
Minute	Ruler	Tall	Top	Dozen
Hour	Inch	Short	Bottom	Cent
Day	Foot	Long	Far	Nickel
Week	Yard	Heavy	Close	Dime
Month	Mile	Light	Right	Quarter
Year	Scale	More	Left	Dollar
Season	Pound	Less	Inside	How many
After	Ounce	Greater	Outside	How much
Before	Thermometer	Full	First	Whole
Today	Degree	Empty	Last	Half
Yesterday			Middle	Part
Tomorrow				

Goodheart-Willcox Publisher

Figure 12-19 These are some math vocabulary words. Can you think of any other words to add to the list?

- **Include many opportunities to count or add.** Count the number of green tiles on the walls of the gym or the number of cracks you step over on the sidewalk. Once children can add, look for opportunities to do so as a part of other activities. You might say, "I see two plates on the table and three plates on the shelf. How many plates does that make?"
- **Look for opportunities to solve problems.** Math problem solving can be included in everyday events, such as determining how many children are absent or how many more blocks are needed to build a road from the shelf to the table. For example, ask a child, "How many apples do you think we need to buy so that everyone has half an apple?" The answer will require figuring out how many people will get apples and how many half of that number will be.

Math Talk by Age Group

Age	Math Talk
Infants  Goodboy Picture Company/ E+ via Getty Images	When an adult hides their face behind their hands and says, "One, two, three, peek-a-boo! I see you," the baby hears the language of counting and learns to anticipate seeing the adult's face following the counting.
Toddlers  gradyreese/iStock/Getty Images Plus	A teacher looks out the window with a toddler and says, "Let's count how many birds we see! I see one. I see another. That makes two. Do you see one more?"
Preschoolers  Kiwis/iStock/Getty Images Plus	Discuss simple addition problems such as, "I wonder if we get two more balls if that will be enough for our group?" Let the child think about it and decide. The key is engagement in conversation rather than a question-and-answer drill. A teacher conducting a food preparation activity with a group of children says, "How many crackers do I need in order to have one for each person? What if we need two for each person?" Even wrong answers provide opportunities for learning. A child might say that three and three are five. A response of "Show me" might result in the child showing the three objects and then three more and discovering the error. Letting children think about a problem and talk through solutions helps them determine where they made mistakes without adult corrections. Asking questions and listening is often the best course of action when children do not answer correctly.
Kindergarten and older  Caiaimage/Robert Daly/ iStock/Getty Images Plus	Ask older children to help with the math encountered in everyday situations. A teacher might ask, "Ashleigh, can you help me count how many blocks are in your tower?"

Goodheart-Willcox Publisher

Figure 12-20 These are the anticipated math-talk skills by age group. Do you think all children will understand these words at the expected age? Why or why not?

- **Ask open-ended questions to sustain math talk.** The goal of a math conversation is to help the child figure out solutions. Instead of simply telling a child how many apples are needed, ask open-ended questions and listen carefully to the child's responses. Be ready with follow-up questions that can extend and deepen the discussions. For example, a way to expand the discussion about apples could be to ask a question such as, "How can we divide this apple so that each person gets half?" Taking time to think about a problem is an important problem-solving strategy.
- **Allow ample time.** Discussion about problem-solving experiences, such as how many apples are needed, takes time, but such interactions are wonderful opportunities for cognitive development. Think about additional typical classroom situations involving math that warrant conversation. Consider what you would ask or say and how you could extend the math conversation with children. For example,
    - Sam says, "I have more crayons than you, Ginny." "No, you don't," responds Ginny. "Yes, I do!" counters Sam.
    - Juanita is trying to put a round peg in a square hole. She is beginning to look upset.
    - Taylor wants a turn on the rocking horse that Emma is on. She says, "Emma has been on it all morning!"

Learning Math with Manipulatives or Table Toys

Many early childhood classrooms will have a learning center for manipulatives or math because children learn a great deal of math from the manipulatives they use. **Figure 12.21** shows some examples of manipulatives useful for teaching math concepts to young children (Geist 2016).

Children can use manipulatives alone, with a few friends, or with an adult. Often, manipulatives will have many parts and can be used in numerous ways. Let's examine why manipulatives are important for young children:

- Children learn math skills such as matching, classifying, putting items in order according to size, color, or shape, comparing sizes, recognizing shapes, and seeing patterns. Their fine motor coordination improves from using manipulatives (**Figure 12.22**).
- Children need to handle items. Starting with the infant who reaches eagerly for a rattle, children of all ages learn from objects they can explore and manipulate.
- Children develop self-esteem as they experience the satisfaction of successfully completing a task, such as a puzzle. Therefore, it is important to ensure toys are available for children that are challenging but achievable. Items intended for older children, such as difficult puzzles, may leave younger children frustrated when they are unable to complete them. A puzzle that cannot be finished due to missing parts will also deny children the sense of satisfaction.

Examples of Math Manipulatives

Balance scales	Magnet board and numerals
Bristle blocks	Pegboards and pegs
Counting items	Pop beads
Cube blocks	Puzzles
Geoboards	Seriated items
LEGO® bricks and other construction toys	Shape sorter toys
	Snap beads
Lotto or bingo games	Soft blocks

Goodheart-Willcox Publisher

Figure 12-21 This is a list of manipulatives that can be used for math. Can you think of any items to add to the list?

Figure 12-22 This child is practicing her fine motor skills by using these math manipulatives. *What other skills can children practice by using math manipulatives?*

- When children use manipulatives with others, they learn to cooperate, share, and take turns. Playing beside and with others is important for a child's social development.
- Children develop creative thinking and problem-solving skills as they experiment by using items in various ways. They can build with LEGO® bricks, take their building apart, and build again.

Math for Infants and Toddlers

Even infants and toddlers are developing math concepts through their experiences and environments. Infants and toddlers develop math skills:
- through hearing the language of math, such as when an adult:
    - asks if the child wants more milk.
    - uses descriptive words such as big, small, and round.
    - makes comments such as "here are both socks" or "here are your two shoes."
- by seeing likenesses and differences through:
    - items that are alike (for example, the same color) but are varied shapes and sizes (**Figure 12.23**).
    - shape sorters.
    - simple puzzles.
- through seeing and touching items in various colors, shapes, and patterns, such as:
    - snap beads that are all the same shape but different colors.
    - a mobile with several types of birds on it.
    - a blanket or garment in a black-and-white striped or polka-dot design (**Figure 12.24**).
- through books that include number or shape concepts such as:
    - *Chicka Chicka 1, 2, 3* by Bill Martin Jr. and Michael Sampson
    - *Round Is a Tortilla: A Book of Shapes (A Latino Book of Concepts)* by Roseanne Greenfield Thong.
    - *My Very First Book of Shapes* by Eric Carle.

Tetyana Linnik/iStock/Getty Images Plus

Figure 12-23 This basket and objects represent an opportunity for children to recognize characteristics that objects have in common. At what age do you think a child could understand the directive, "Place all of the blue objects in the basket"?

Halfpoint/iStock/Getty Images Plus

Figure 12-24 Babies love the contrast of black and white, like the stripes on this adult's shirt. Why do babies like strong color contrasts?

- through one-to-one correspondence such as when an adult:
  - puts one sock with one shoe.
  - provides toys where one peg goes in one hole.

Combining Language and Literacy with Math

Many children's books can be found that include math concepts. In addition to the many counting books, there are books about concepts of shape, size, and seriation. Most stories provide opportunities to discuss events in order, such as what happened first, next, and last. Predictable books such as *Over in the Meadow* or *The Napping House* include examples of patterns and addition.

Math and Engineering

Whether tinkering is taking place in the art area or in a separate center, a tinkering center provides valuable opportunities for children to use math in their engineering projects. Math is a key component of tinkering because parts often need to be cut or shaped to fit together. Structures may need parts that are the same size to be stable. Tools such as rulers, calipers, tape measures, and framing squares provide opportunities to determine length or width using different tools (**Figure 12.25**). Digital or balance scales may be used when projects require a specific quantity of material (**Figure 12.26**).

Car Race

One way to incorporate measurement into engineering is to create ramps for toy cars to race on. To suggest an engineering experience, provide similar toy cars and items to create ramps and roads. Encourage children to roll toy cars on a flat surface to see which will travel farther. Then suggest they create ramps to see if the cars will go faster and farther. How can they change the ramps to make the cars faster? Ask children how they can tell which went farther without using a ruler or tape measure. They will likely use an item such as a unit block. Ask children, "How many unit blocks long is the distance

Renata Angerami/iStock/Getty Images Plus

Figure 12-25 Math manipulatives. What skills can children learn by using these manipulatives?

Figure 12-26 This child uses a scale to weigh manipulatives. What is the child learning from this activity?

that each car traveled?" "How many crayons would it take to equal that distance?" Encourage investigation by using yarn to compare the farthest distance with the nearest. Then measure the distance with a standard ruler, yard stick, or tape measure. Use math words such as longer than, shorter than, how many, how far, measuring, length, distance, and so forth.

Incorporating Technology in Math Learning

While we know that technology should not replace experience with real objects, some uses of technology can enhance a math program. For example, digital cameras can capture items that are big or small or be used for a shape scavenger hunt, increasing children's ability to notice details of their environment. Credible websites can provide information about items that catch children's attention. The teacher's "Let's find out!" approach to children's questions may lead to a search on a zoo website to learn how tall a giraffe stands or how much time it would take to travel from the classroom to the ocean.

Photos of a process can document the steps in the procedure. For example, making a photo schedule shows the order of activities in the day. Photos of a field trip can show the order of the experience.

Technology should supplement rather than be used in lieu of real-life experiences. Caution should be exercised to avoid software programs that are mostly electronic worksheets. Technology should not be used with an intent to serve as the math curriculum itself.

Setting up a Math and Manipulative Center

To set up a math and manipulative learning center, find a place to display the manipulatives at the child's eye level on low, open shelves. Toys should be accessible to children without their having to ask someone to get them (**Figure 12.27**). If the manipulatives have many small parts, store them in a container such as a basket, shoebox, or dishpan so children can easily carry items to a table or designated spot on the floor. The way materials are displayed and stored will influence how the children use, learn from, and take care of them (**Figure 12.28**). For more guidance in setting up and using a manipulative area, see Chapter 2, "The Early Childhood Learning Environment."

FatCamera/E+ via Getty Images

Figure 12-27 This child is working with these manipulatives independently. Why is it important for children to have access to developmentally appropriate toys?

Tetyana Linnik/iStock/Getty Images Plus

Figure 12-28 The children in this classroom are responsible for keeping these science materials neat and clean. What skills do children learn by caring for classroom materials?

✓ CHECKPOINT

1. How does food preparation include mathematics?
2. Why is conversation important for children to develop math concepts?
3. What are some concepts learned from manipulatives or table toys?

12.4 Focus on Assessment

Every day, teachers make observations of children's behaviors and cognitive development. The purpose of observation is to use this information to document progress and tailor instruction to meet the needs of individual children. A collection of children's work along with their verbal comments about their work is helpful to understand what children know and what support they may need to facilitate their learning. Documentation is also helpful in communicating with parents about strategies they can use at home to help their child succeed in school (**Figure 12.29**).

To assess mathematical skills effectively, teachers must first understand the skills that children need to learn and when they should learn them. The general categories and some of the specific skills are found in the NAEYC standards and your state has standards that early learning programs must follow.

Though observations may be regularly taking place, are those observations being used to guide instruction? One strategy in determining understanding of a concept is to ask a question that will prompt a child to explain his or her thinking. Juanita Copley's article, "Assessing Mathematical Learning: Observing and Listening to Children," provides many examples of probing questions that can help teachers improve the quality of their observations and assessments of student learning (Copley n.d.).

Once a child reveals their thinking, the teacher can determine whether further intentional experiences around that skill are necessary. If students need more practice to master certain skills, Copley suggests providing them with a variety of different experiences related to those skills. For example, if children have difficulty explaining why measurements are different when units of varied sizes are used, arrange for a variety of measuring experiences with different-size units. In this way, assessment is used to determine instructional strategies and improve student learning.

Questions similar to these can be used to assess children's understanding:
- How did you know that the next peg should be green in the pattern?
- What do you think will happen if you put the largest block on the top of your tower?
- How did you figure out that you needed four more napkins?
- How are these blocks alike? How are they different?
- What did you use to know how much the plant grew?

Dusan Stankovic/E+ via Getty Images

Figure 12-29 This teacher is documenting her observations of her students. How can teachers use documentation to improve their teaching skills?

☑ **CHECKPOINT**

1. How does assessment inform planning?
2. Why is careful observation an important tool in assessment?
3. Why is it helpful to have children explain their thinking?

12.5 Family Matters

Parents and other family members can participate in the math program in a variety of ways. At a minimum, they can contribute to the classroom material. In the following examples, parents are not only asked to contribute but are also being educated about how children learn math.

Building Collections

See **Figure 12.30** for a sample parent letter that an early childhood teacher might use to involve families and explain how the materials support math skills.

Math Take-Home Bags

Math take-home bags can be an effective way to involve and educate parents. Math bags offer parents activities they can easily do at home, along with information about what their children are learning through the activity. **Figure 12.31** is a sample letter for parents that describes the bags and includes a card insert with an activity.

Seashells, Seashells

Put an assortment of seashells in the math bag, making sure the shells are assorted sizes and shapes. Enclose the card shown in **Figure 12.31**.

Food Preparation

Parents can be involved and educated by contributing to or participating in food preparation with their child. See **Figure 12.32** for a sample notice to include in a parent letter or newsletter.

Dear Families,

We are collecting items to use in our math program. Could you help your child collect items from this list? The children will use the collections for counting, sorting, classifying, patterning, comparing, and other math-related activities. Items needed for our math program include:

bread tabs	magnets	pom-poms
buttons	measuring cups	seashells
clothespins	old keys	small plastic figures (animals or people)
dominos	plastic bottles and lids	small toys
empty thread spools	playing cards	spoons and forks
golf tees	polished rocks	

The experience of contributing to the classroom helps children realize they are valued members of our class. Sharing one's materials with others and having others share with them helps children appreciate the cooperative effort that is necessary to build a learning environment. Thank you for your help.

Sincerely,

Miss Kallin

Goodheart-Willcox Publisher

Figure 12-30 Newsletters like this are a great way to communicate with families. *What are some other effective ways to communicate with families?*

Dear Parents,

We are asking you to help your child with important math skills by participating in the following:

We will be sending math take-home bags for you to use to review important math concepts with your child. The bags will include activities focusing on a variety of math processes: sorting, classifying, comparing, patterning, graphing, estimating, counting, and measuring. Simply follow the instructions on the card enclosed in the bag.

Thank you for your help!

Sincerely,

Mr. Michael

Dear Parent:
Please have your child complete the following activity to explore the important math concepts of classifying and comparing. The entire activity should be fun for your child and not take more than 10–15 minutes to complete.
1. Ask your child to lay the shells out on a table and sort them as desired. Your child may sort them by size, shape, or even some other characteristic.
2. Talk with your child about why they sorted the shells in this way.
3. Discuss with your child how the shells are alike (same shape, for example) and how they are different (different shapes, colors, or different sizes).
4. Talk with your child about how they are classifying the shells by size or type and how they are comparing them.
5. Ask your child to separate the smaller shells and count the set of smaller shells. Ask them to count the set of larger shells. Then have them put all of the shells together and count them all.
6. Help your child build math vocabulary by talking about which shells are the smallest and which are the largest. Show your child two shells and ask which is smaller, then three or more and ask which is the smallest. Do the same with larger and largest and bigger and biggest.
7. Look for other items around your house to do a similar activity. Remember, the activities should be fun!

Goodheart-Willcox Publisher

Figure 12-31 Newsletters like this are a great way to communicate with families. What are some other effective ways to communicate with families?

Dear Parents:
In our classroom, we will be preparing some of our own snacks. Food preparation can be an important math learning experience that is fun for children. Some of the math concepts that children learn from food activities are one-to-one correspondence, counting, measuring, fractions, shapes, and sequence.

To involve the children for maximum learning, we need many measuring cups and spoons. If you have extra plastic or metal utensils that you can donate, we would very much appreciate them. We also invite you to visit our classroom to see the activities in action and let us know how your child likes these experiences. Please encourage your child to talk about the activities. We will share our recipes and instructions with you in our monthly newsletter so that you can repeat the activities at home.

Thank you for your help.
Sincerely,

Miss Patel

Goodheart-Willcox Publisher

Figure 12-32 Newsletters like this are a great way to communicate with families. What are some other effective ways to communicate with families?

Keeping records of children's progress in math and communicating that progress with parents is necessary for parents to understand what and how children are learning in a developmentally appropriate program. The Case Study feature "Communicating Children's Progress to Parents" demonstrates this fact as it is related to maintaining enrollment in the program.

Case Study

Communicating Children's Progress to Parents

"Derrick will not be returning next fall," Mrs. Williams told Mike Hernandez, the director of the early learning center that 3-year-old Derrick attended.

"I'm sorry to hear that," Mr. Hernandez replied. "Is there a problem? Has anything happened that I'm not aware of? Derrick has progressed so much in the year he's been with us."

"That's just it," commented Mrs. Williams. "I don't think he has progressed as much as my sister's girl who's in preschool in another state. They visited last month, and my niece could count to 100 and name all of the shapes—even trapezoids. She brings home a stack of math and reading worksheets every week, and I'm afraid Derrick won't be ready for kindergarten. He's really had a good time here, but my niece is the same age, and he can't do nearly all of the things she can."

"Why don't you have a seat and let me show you Derrick's records? Maybe we haven't kept you as well informed as we should have," Mr. Hernandez said, pointing to a chair, which Mrs. Williams accepted.

Mr. Hernandez opened a file drawer and removed Derrick's portfolio. One by one, he reviewed the contents with Derrick's mother, emphasizing those related to mathematics.

"Here's a photo of him using the blocks from last week. The teacher's note shows he estimated the number of blocks that it would take to make a road as long as the shelf. Then he got the yardstick and a ruler and figured out that they were both 4 feet. She describes how he built other things using that measurement for reference. You know, that's pretty amazing for a child his age."

"I remember that day," responded Mrs. Williams. "When I picked him up, he was all excited about the long road he built. He said he made it as long as the shelf, then twice as long, and then three times as long. I didn't think about it being math, but I guess it is. I thought he just had fun playing with the blocks."

"When children learn through play, the learning is relevant and meaningful to them. They don't tell you exactly what they're learning because they may not realize that they're learning math skills. The children simply have an idea and need to figure out how to follow through on their idea with the teacher's help. And estimating and measurement are important math skills. It's clear from his teacher's notes that he really understands the concept of linear measurement and estimating length."

"Here's a checklist of some of his other accomplishments," continued Mr. Hernandez, bringing out a checklist of skills that Derrick's teacher had completed for his portfolio. "According to this, he's certainly within the expected range for skills in math. All of these are checked off, which means his teacher has observed him using the skills during activities.

"Did you know that he is especially good at recognizing and making patterns? His teacher saw evidence of that, according to this anecdotal record. It describes a complex pattern he made with the parquetry blocks and also with the cube blocks. Since mathematics is based on patterns, understanding patterns provides a solid foundation for math."

"Here's a record about a conversation the teacher had with him that shows he has a good understanding of time. His teacher notes that he identified the time that school starts and ends with no hesitation. He could also talk about minutes and hours," Mr. Hernandez explained.

"I've noticed that he looks at the clock when we're in the car. The other day, he told me that we had only 10 minutes to get to school! I was surprised that he knew that," responded Mrs. Williams.

"Some people don't realize that math is a lot more than just counting and recognizing shapes. Children need to learn about sequence, measurement, patterns, and a whole lot more. Many times, children can count to 30 or more but don't understand the one-to-one correspondence. When they don't understand that each number stands for an item, then they may count very high, but it's just repeating words without understanding—sort of like saying words in a foreign language without knowing what the words mean," clarified Mr. Hernandez. "We stress meaningful counting rather than just rotely saying number words."

"Let's look at some more," he continued. "Here's a copy of his story about a graphing project. After several children got into a discussion about what they liked most with peanut butter, the teacher helped them make a graph. Here's a photo. It seems three liked peanut butter with bananas best, and four of them liked it with jelly more, with two opting for honey! Here, Derrick even wrote his name—at least his first four letters—beside the jelly jar picture representing his preference. Graphs like this are excellent ways for children to understand abstract concepts in a useful way. The children learned that each picture represents one child who liked that item most, and they learned how graphs work."

"He told me about making a picture of who liked jelly with peanut butter, but I thought it was some sort of art project," Mrs. Williams contributed.

"Let's look at the screening his teacher just completed. Here's the math section. He's right on target for his age and above in some skills. I don't see anything that would make me concerned that he would not be ready for kindergarten. Why don't we make an appointment for you to come back? I'll ask Derrick's teacher to meet with us and talk more about his progress. Would next Monday work?"

(Continued)

Case Study (continued)

"Why, yes, that would be great. I do want to hear more about what he's done. You've already reassured me a lot. This has been very enlightening and helpful. I'll see you again Monday."

This scenario illustrates an all-too-common issue in early learning programs. Mrs. Williams judged Derrick's program on what she saw (and did not see) and compared it to what her niece was doing. The anecdote illustrates the importance of documenting children's progress and of regular and frequent communication with parents.

Consider This
1. What could Mr. Hernandez have done to prevent Derrick's mother's plan to send him to another program?
2. Why is communication with families important in programs for young children?
3. What other ways are portfolios helpful in providing a quality program for children?

Chapter 12 Review and Assessment

Chapter Summary

12.1 **Explain how mathematics is included in the daily lives of young children.**
- For children, math is concrete, exploring properties and relationships.
- Many math opportunities and experiences occur daily in realistic, practical ways from which children can learn the functions and purposes of math.
- Math for young children is much broader than counting and recognizing numerals and shapes.
- Children's understanding of math concepts varies by age and experiences.
- Sometimes adults do not recognize either the various components of math learning or the examples of math that occur in the daily life of young children.

12.2 **Identify children's experiences that develop mathematical concepts.**
- Math for young children includes number awareness, recognition of numerals, counting, and qualitative and quantitative concepts.
- Concepts of classification, seriation, time, and space are developed through firsthand experiences in the environment.
- Children learn about math as adults converse with them about what they are seeing and doing, asking thoughtful questions that stimulate children to think about what they are seeing and doing.
- Mathematical concepts such as geometry, measurement, and others begin in early childhood as children are provided experiences that develop those understandings.
- Teaching young children involves strategies that respond to their great curiosity and interest and those that provide for handling concrete materials.
- Unit blocks are extremely valuable for learning about size, quantity, space, length, shape, and equality.
- A block area should be carefully set up to maximize children's use of the center.

12.3 **Describe strategies and techniques for teaching mathematics to young children.**
- Math can be incorporated into food preparation for snacks.
- Children's math learning is supported and enhanced by conversation that helps children learn to think, explain how they came to a conclusion or describe how they might solve a specific
- Opportunities for math abound in learning centers such as the block, housekeeping, and dramatic play areas.
- Pegboards, beads, parquetry blocks and cube blocks enable children to follow and make patterns. Seriated cups and dolls develop the concept of graduation and seriation.

- Even infants and toddlers are learning math through their environment, experiences, and interactions. As they learn to recognize similarities and differences, they are building a foundation for future math understandings.
- Math can be integrated into other curriculum areas in ways that support integration of learning. Such integrations additionally provide for practical use of math in real-life situations.
- Many manipulatives, often called table toys, provide opportunities for children to develop many math skills through self-directed, hands-on exploration.
- A math or manipulative center is a way to organize manipulatives for independent use by children.

12.4 Identify methods for assessing children's mathematical learning.
- Documenting children's progress is important in knowing what concepts and skills children have mastered and for which they may need additional experiences.
- Assessing the mathematical component of the curriculum is important in planning to meet the needs of individual children and to gather data to consider changes or improvements.
- Sharing assessment documentation with families helps to educate them on what is important in young children's learning and can build support for programs.
- National or state standards can be a basis for assessing a program.

12.5 Describe ways to communicate with parents and involve them in their children's learning.
- Educating families about math learning in early childhood is important so that they recognize the value of a developmentally appropriate math program in a quality early childhood program.
- Families can support and enhance the opportunities for their children when they understand how young children learn math and what math concepts are appropriate for their age.

Recall and Application

1. **True or False.** Playing with manipulatives is a mathematics experience for children.
2. Each of the following is an example of children understanding one-to-one correspondence *except* _____.
   A. putting a plate at each chair on the doll table
   B. asking for another bottle so each doll can have one
   C. asking friends to play
   D. giving a friend a buggy so each can have one
3. **True or False.** A math-rich environment means that a classroom has a lot of worksheets and flash cards.
4. **True or False.** Children learn math in the block area when they build with blocks of assorted sizes and shapes.
5. Which of the following is *not* an example of an understanding of measurement?
   A. Michael lines blocks end-to-end to see if two tables are the same size.
   B. Elaine stacks one block on top of another.
   C. Ming Lee tells you how tall she is.
   D. Manny puts the big doll in the big bed and the small doll in the small bed.
6. **True or False.** Food preparation activities include math learning opportunities.
7. Which activity is *not* developmentally appropriate for toddlers?
   A. Asking each child to identify a shape the teacher holds up
   B. Providing simple puzzles
   C. Asking children to take four crackers at snack time
   D. Asking a toddler to find all of the blocks that are red
8. **True or False.** One way to assess math understanding is if children can memorize the order of numbers.
9. **True or False.** Recognizing shapes and counting in order are the most important math skills for young children.
10. **True or False.** Showing and explaining how children learn math through firsthand experiences is helpful to families.
11. **True or False.** Parents should leave the job of teaching math up to the teachers.

Chapter 13

Back to the Great Outdoors

Standards Covered in This Chapter

NAEYC

NAEYC —1a, 1b, 1c, 3b, 4b, 4c, 5a, 5b

DAP

DAP—1d, 2b, 4b, 4c, 4d, 4e, 4f, 4g, 4h, 5b, 5c, 5f

Learning Outcomes

After reading this chapter, you should be able to:

13.1 Describe why outdoor play is important for young children.

13.2 Identify what equipment and materials should be provided to support social, physical, emotional, and cognitive development.

13.3 Explain how to integrate outdoor time with other curriculum areas.

13.4 Describe the role of the teacher in maximizing outdoor experiences.

13.5 Identify ways to provide outdoor time for infants and toddlers.

13.6 Describe one way to assess the outdoor environment for ongoing improvement.

13.7 Explain why and how to communicate with families about the benefits of outdoor time.

Chapter opener image credit: eclipse_images/E+ via Getty Images Plus

Key Terms

field guide
fine motor development
gross motor development
loose parts
myopia
nature-deficit disorder
play space
zone system

Introduction

Daily, in early learning centers, children line up on cue to go outside for "recess." Teachers all too often spend that outdoor time enforcing restrictions against standing up in swings, sliding down a slide head first, or engaging in rough-housing play. The underlying assumption is that this outdoor time is a break from learning and that it is a time for children to simply exert physical energy in order to return sedately to the more valuable activities in the classroom. Such a perception of outdoor time fails to recognize the learning that happens when children have the freedom to pursue self-selected activities. Indeed, a playground does give children much-needed physical activity, but more importantly, for young children, it can be an outdoor learning laboratory with experiences that are infinitely exciting and challenging—mentally, socially, and physically. Or, in the case of elementary school, outdoor time provides a release from focused attention as well as opportunities for physical movement.

Outdoors, children can observe nature. They can hang bird feeders, cultivate radishes, search for cicada shells, or watch the communal, determined behavior of ants. They can develop interpersonal skills of collaboration and conflict resolution that are needed to build an obstacle course or construct a playhouse. Children can explore the arts and enjoy the beauty of nature. Even dramatic play takes on new dimensions outdoors.

Obesity is becoming increasingly prevalent, even in young children, and can lead to many other health problems. Obesity typically results, in large part, from insufficient physical activity. Since children are usually more physically active when they are outdoors, the absence of outdoor playtime is a contributor to childhood obesity.

When children's programs fail to take advantage of this prime opportunity to engage children in worthwhile outdoor experiences, teachers may become rule enforcers. Their primary function becomes stopping objectionable behavior rather than stimulating playful learning. In addition, the early childhood field is becoming aware of another issue that stems from a lack of outdoor time: nature-deficit disorder.

13.1 The Importance of Outdoor Play for Young Children

Nature-deficit disorder is a term coined by Richard Louv in his 2005 book, *Last Child in the Woods: Saving Our Children From Nature-Deficit Disorder*. The term describes how humans, especially children, are spending far less time outdoors, and this is resulting in a wide range of behavioral and other issues. While nature-deficit disorder is not a clinical term or medical diagnosis, it is a description of the costs of isolation from the natural world. The concept has caught on with educators and parents who remember their own outdoor experiences from childhood. Many adults have fond memories of camping in the backyard, building a tree house or fort, or attempting to dig to the center of the earth in neighborhood vacant lots. The issue of nature-deficit disorder has prompted a movement to reconnect children and nature.

The success of *Last Child in the Woods: Saving Our Children From Nature-Deficit Disorder* inspired the creation of the Children & Nature Network, co-founded and chaired by the book's author, Richard Louv. The Network's mission is to encourage and support people and organizations working to reconnect children with nature. Louv, an award-winning journalist, cites extensive research from practitioners of many disciplines on attention disorders, obesity, reduction in creativity, and increased depression as problems associated with a nature-deficient childhood (Louv 2005).

In addition to the Children & Nature Network, other organizations and initiatives have emerged to encourage efforts to inform and support individuals and organizations working to advocate for more time for children in the natural world. See the Teaching Tip feature "Celebrate International Mud Day!" to learn about a fun, albeit messy, initiative that encourages outdoor play.

Teaching Tip

Celebrate International Mud Day!

International Mud Day was developed in 2009 by two members of the Nature Action Collaborative for Children: Gillian McAuliffe from Australia and Bishnu Bhatta from Nepal. Bhatta mentioned that there is plenty of mud for children to play with in Nepal, but they rarely did so, because they did not have enough clothes to be able to get them dirty. McAuliffe brought this story back to her school in Australia, and a group of 7- and 8-year-olds decided to raise money to buy play clothes for the Nepali children.

Since then, International Mud Day, celebrated annually on June 29, has grown in popularity, connecting children around the globe with a love of playing outside and getting dirty. Visit the National Action Collaborative for Children's website for resources to help plan a Mud Day for the children in your life.

vm/E+ via Getty Images

Figure 13-1 Joyful children enjoy experiences with mud during International Mud Day activities. What experiences did you have with mud or dirt as a child?

Causes of Nature Deficit

To address the nature deficit, one must first look at the source of its origin. Louv attributes the causes of the phenomenon to the following three issues (Louv 2005).

1. **Parents keeping children indoors for safety.** Growing fear of "stranger danger," fueled by the media, keeps children indoors rather than outdoors. The concern leads to a focus on supervised and regimented sports over imaginative play, even when children are outdoors.

2. **Loss of natural surroundings in a child's neighborhood.** Many neighborhoods, parks, and nature preserves have restrictions on the types of activities allowed. Open space is limited or nonexistent, street traffic adds risk, and neighborhood common areas are carefully landscaped. Vacant lots, a common play area for past generations, are less available in developed neighborhoods (**Figure 13.2**).

3. **The appeal of technological entertainment.** With the advent of increased access to television, computers, video games, and other technological entertainment, children have more enticement to stay inside. The addictive nature of screen items promotes sedentary activity, even if devices are taken outdoors.

NoSystem images/E+ via Getty Images

Figure 13-2 This family's life in a large city provides limited opportunities to experience nature. What are barriers to outdoor play that children experience in your neighborhood?

Results of Nature Deficit

According to a study at the University of Illinois (Kuo 2019), interaction with nature reduces symptoms of attention-deficit hyperactivity disorder (ADHD) in children. Exposure to natural settings in after-school and weekend activities may be widely effective in reducing ADHD symptoms. The following are some of the results of nature-deficit disorder in the study.

- Lower grades in school seem to be related to nature-deficit disorder. Studies of students nationwide show that schools using outdoor classrooms produce significant gains in social studies, science, language arts, and mathematics.
- Studies by other researchers throughout the world suggest physical activity and nature exposure are important for good health. They report positive impacts on mental health and well-being associated with natural environments and a reduction in sadness and negative emotions.
- Even very young children are suffering from overweight and obesity at an alarming rate.

Lack of exposure to bright light at outdoor levels among children contributes to **myopia** (nearsightedness) due to the absence of chemical signals that prevent elongation of the eye during growth. Scientists even found that children who spend time outdoors reduce the risk of developing myopia later in life.

An expanding body of evidence suggests that nature-deficit disorder contributes to diminished use of the senses, concentration difficulties, and higher rates of physical illnesses.

Research suggests that nature deficit weakens ecological understanding and stewardship of the natural world. Recent studies focus not solely on what is lost when nature experience is lacking but significantly on what is gained through more exposure to natural settings, including nature in urban settings (Oh et. al 2017).

Benefits of Nature Exposure

Because the natural world is filled with amazing sights, sounds, and textures, it is the perfect resource for young children to develop an appreciation of beauty. Nature's sounds can be soothing. Reading, listening to stories, and just relaxing outdoors are calming (**Figure 13.3**). Even the outdoor smells can be pleasant. Consider the aroma of freshly mowed grass and the scent of wild honeysuckle or other blossoming plants.

Figure 13-3 An 8-year-old enjoys the pleasant aroma and sounds of nature. Why do you think being outdoors can be calming and relaxing?

Children learn their values from the important adults in their lives. When children are primarily indoors, they learn sedentary habits. Being outside together can bring families closer. When families spend time outdoors, they have opportunities to bond and engage in conversations about the natural world around them.

Time outdoors gives the human body opportunities for vitamin D production, which helps strengthen bones. There is evidence that time spent in natural light improves sleep by regulating sleep patterns. Getting enough sunlight can even boost the immune system and help fight disease. Research has found that participants who spend time each week walking in the woods experience lower levels of inflammation (Oh et al. 2017). Going outdoors gives people's eyes a break from staring at a computer, television, or smartphone.

Nature comes in many colors, from the autumn leaves to the pink and orange sunsets, to seafoam green or clear blue waters, to multicolored gardens. Spending time outside provides a chance to be inspired by all of the beautiful sights, smells, and sounds of the natural world.

Capitalizing on Nature in a Playground Setting

Programs that operate mostly indoors can work to include the benefits of nature on playgrounds or even indoors. Louv says that while nature should not be considered a cure-all, adults should see the woods, streams, fields, and hills around their homes as assets that can keep children focused, confident, healthy, and balanced (Louv 2005). According to Louv, schools should not just teach about nature in the classroom. They should send children out to nature—even if just to a patch of woods behind the school (Louv 2005). He believes these mini-field trips should be viewed as an integral part of learning. Here is a sampling of ideas that support child–nature connections on playgrounds or nearby locations:

- **Invite native flora and fauna.** Maintain a birdbath or hummingbird feeder. Designate part of the playground for native plants. Plant butterfly-attracting bushes.

Teaching Tip

A Different Approach: Forest Schools

As educators and others become aware of the need for more nature experiences, "forest schools," or "outdoor schools," have developed. These are programs that operate totally or mostly outdoors. While the idea of outdoor preschool programs is not new, the movement seems to be taking hold, especially in areas with mild weather and/or a culture that supports time outdoors. Some states have created regulations governing such programs, and others are beginning to draft regulations and licensing standards.

vm/E+ via Getty Images

Figure 13-4 Children in a forest school make a mural about an activity they just completed. What are some benefits to outdoor art experiences?

- **Help children discover a hidden universe.** Find a scrap board and place it on bare dirt. Return in a day or two, lift the board, and see what life found shelter there. Identify the creatures with the help of a **field guide** (a book with illustrations and descriptions to identify plants or animals).
- **Revive old traditions.** Make a collection of interesting leaves, rocks, or flowers. Keep a terrarium, an aquarium, or an ant farm. Lie down and watch the clouds move across the sky, changing shapes. Search for pretty stones, leaves, nuts, plants, flowers, or leaves. Suggest that families collect lightning bugs at dusk, observe, and then release them.
- **Make nature time a new tradition.** Provide time for daily nature experiences and unstructured interaction with the natural world.
- **Take a hike.** Go outside and walk regularly. With younger children, take your time and stop often. Take infants out in strollers or buggies into the neighborhood.
- **Invent your own nature games.** Help children be attentive during walks with "I Spy" games. Find items in a category such as birds, insects, snails (**Figure 13.5**), footprints, or other signs that an animal lives nearby.
- **Encourage children to build a fort or hut.** Provide the raw materials—sticks, boards, blankets, large boxes, or ropes—and let children be architects and builders. The older the children, the more complex the construction can be.
- **Plant a garden.** Choose seeds that mature quickly and are large enough for children to handle. Young gardeners can help grow food, share it with others, or donate to a food bank.
- **Grow flowers to enjoy.** A landing, deck, or terrace can accommodate large pots for a mini-garden.

Louv suggests that adults view reconnection with nature not as a chore or an extracurricular activity but as an antidote to the stress in their own lives—as a type of therapy, widely accessible, with no side effects or cost (Louv 2005).

Developmental Benefits of Outdoor Play

In addition to remediating or preventing nature deficit, what are other ways outdoor play contributes to children's growth and development? Clearly, physical development, especially **gross motor development** (the development of large muscles), is fostered outdoors, where children are free to run, jump, and climb, building the large muscles of their legs and arms. Outdoor time is also an open invitation for social and emotional

romrodinka/iStock/Getty Images Plus

Figure 13-5 A toddler stops to pick up a snail while on a walk. How can the teacher explore the outdoors with infants and toddlers?

development, providing opportunities for making friends and playing cooperatively. Cognitive development, too, flourishes when children have the freedom to explore.

Social-Emotional Development

The social-emotional benefits of outdoor time are not as widely recognized as those of physical development. However, when you look closely at the potential of well-equipped playgrounds and carefully planned outdoor time, the social-emotional development opportunities are abundant. Here are some to consider:
- Learning and demonstrating social skills—joining in or leading an activity
- Sharing and taking turns on popular equipment—asking for or offering the use of a wagon or a turn on a swing
- Negotiating compromises and cooperation—working together to build a fort, engaging in dramatic play with others
- Expressing creativity—inventing games, participating in art, sand, and water play
- Enhancing self-esteem, confidence, and pride in physical abilities—climbing the slide ladder alone for the first time
- Gaining independence in learning to use equipment—mastering a balance beam or peddling a tricycle
- Cooperating in group games—learning and following rules

Cognitive Development

As with social-emotional development, cognitive opportunities are not as widely recognized as physical development opportunities. A closer look, however, reveals the cognitive benefits listed here:
- Making decisions—choosing activities in which to participate and how to participate
- Planning and following through on ideas—building sand structures
- Solving problems and experimenting with new ideas—creating an obstacle course
- Reenacting life experiences—using a tricycle as a truck or car in dramatic play

Discovery Journeys

The Neighborhood Fort

I always believed that problem-solving, cooperative, and cognitive skills could develop through outdoor play. This belief was supported one morning on my way to work when I noticed a small fort on a vacant lot. At first, the "fort" was just a stacked pile of small tree trunks about 4–5 feet tall. As the weeks passed, branches were added to make a roof. I noticed changes to the fort mostly on Mondays, leading me to infer that children were doing this work over the weekends.

I was fascinated to see the fort built, rebuilt, and becoming more complex. One Saturday afternoon, I passed the lot and noticed several school-age children working on it. I parked my car, walked over to them, told them I was a teacher at the local school, and was interested in what they were building. They were happy to let me look inside, where they had set up beanbag chairs, a rug, and a makeshift table. One explained they had brought the logs from a construction site about five blocks away, describing how hard it was to drag them so far. They explained how it took three of them to transport a log until they realized they could pull them on wagons.

One of the older boys even showed me his father's hatchet that he used to remove unwanted branches. The children shared information about a tree house nearby that was built by teenagers and recommended that I go see it because it was "really cool."

Summer came, and I no longer passed the lot daily, only occasionally, continually fascinated by the engineering and collaboration of this self-imposed project. Whoever mowed the lot respected the work and mowed around it; however, one August day, it was all over. The logs were piled near the street. Did the children tire of the project? Did the lot owner decide it was too risky? Did someone consider it unsightly? Or did the beginning of school limit the children's available time to work on it?

A few months later, a realtor's "for sale" sign appeared, and no evidence existed of the unique construction. Even later, a house was built on the site. Although years have passed and the children would now be adults, whenever I go by that location, I still marvel at the children's ingenuity. Yet I am a bit saddened as the availability of vacant lots diminishes in areas where children are growing up and opportunities for such experiences concurrently diminish.

Consider This
1. Were you ever part of a group that built a fort or tree house in a vacant lot?
2. What do you think are the benefits of such an activity outdoors?
3. How could we provide for similar experiences on a playground today?

- Learning about science—observing changes in the weather, seasons, and plants (**Figure 13.6**)
- Using math skills and concepts—counting how many hops, bounces, or rope skips
- Developing communication skills and increasing vocabulary—talking with others during play, teaching and explaining games
- Observing many cause-and-effect relationships—seeing changes in nature and materials

Physical Development

While the physical opportunities outdoors are more apparent, the variety of physical development opportunities might not be. Even some very experienced early childhood professionals might not recognize the prospects for **fine motor development**, the use of smaller muscles in their hands and fingers. Consider the variety of physical development possibilities identified here:

- Developing and refining large and small motor skills—picking up a stone and hopping on a hopscotch, sorting pine cones by size
- Developing hand-eye coordination—throwing and catching a ball (**Figure 13.7**)
- Improving balance and coordination—walking a balance beam or navigating an obstacle course

SrdjanPav/E+ via Getty Images

Figure 13-6 A teacher holds a child up to select and admire the beautiful fall leaves. What else might a teacher do to encourage the child's interest in the leaves?

andipantz/iStock/Getty Images Plus

Figure 13-7 This toddler is developing the motor control and eye-hand coordination needed to throw a ball. What are ways a teacher can encourage other gross motor skills?

- Increasing spatial awareness—judging distance and controlling one's body moving through space
- Exploring and discovering what their bodies can do—finding new ways of moving, attempting new physical challenges
- Improving health—benefiting from fresh air, exercise, and reducing the possibility of obesity
- Increasing stamina and physical endurance—climbing, running, and jumping

Outdoor time can also be an additional opportunity to integrate curriculum. The playground can provide abundant opportunities for playful learning, offering not only the freedom for more physically active play but also space for typical early childhood activities. The outdoor environment is best viewed as an extension of the indoors, thus an integral part of the curriculum program. It should provide a stimulating resource for learning rather than a recess from learning.

☑ CHECKPOINT

1. What are the concerns resulting from insufficient time outdoors?
2. What are some benefits of nature exposure for children?
3. How can you include experiences with nature in your school setting?

13.2 Equipment and Materials

Selecting equipment and materials for a playground requires consideration of safety. All playground equipment must follow safety requirements; this is the number one priority when planning outdoor experiences. The following are other important considerations in planning and supervising a playground for young children:

- Equipment should be designed to match the size and skills of the children using it.
- Check regularly for any broken parts and materials around equipment and for any maintenance needs.
- The playground should be free of blind spots for ease of supervision.
- Fences or other enclosures must be sturdy and at least 4 feet high.
- For climbing equipment 4 feet or higher, there should be 8–12 inches of shock-absorbing materials on the ground below.
- Plan for areas of shade, such as trees or covered areas.
- Locate the sand area a good distance away from the building entrance to reduce tracked-in sand (**Figure 13.8**).

LightFieldStudios/iStock/Getty Images Plus

Figure 13-8 This sand area is located away from the building entrance and away from other activities. What are other considerations in setting up sand play?

- Plan for active and quiet areas and places for individual and group play.
- Provide a water table for water play.
- Consider the traffic flow and arrange equipment with clear pathways.
- Specify a riding area for tricycles and other wheeled toys that does not conflict with other activities.

Supplementing Permanently Installed Equipment

Good, multipurpose playground equipment is important for gross motor development. Such outdoor equipment is expensive, but when viewed over its expected lifetime of use, that equipment becomes an investment. In addition, permanent equipment can be supplemented with a variety of learning center experiences, such as water play, sand play, gardening, dress-up, art, and many more.

Most everything that takes place indoors can happen outdoors. In fact, moving an existing indoor activity to the outdoors can revitalize it, opening new possibilities for stimulating children's imaginations in the new location. A dress-up area can easily be set up on the playground. In an early learning center or private preschool setting with a protected play area, simply keep a collection of dress-up clothing wherever outdoor equipment is stored. Art and even manipulatives can offer more choices. Blocks, too, work outdoors and open exciting new possibilities for imaginative use.

Teachers can use their imaginations to decide which other materials they can move outdoors. Undeniably, some effort is required to transport materials, but there are multitudes of benefits for the children and teachers alike. Time spent providing a variety of activities outdoors will be returned in the amount of engagement. Happy, occupied children who are challenged by equipment and interesting materials are far less likely to seek challenges in undesirable, aggressive, or unsafe ways (Brussoni et al. 2012).

Loose Parts

One way to address adequate materials and variety is to include many loose parts. **Loose parts** are materials that can be moved, carried, combined, put together, and taken apart in a variety of ways. They come with no specific set of directions, and their usage is determined by the children. Loose parts are adaptable in a multitude of ways to support imagination, skill development, competence, and creativity in an open-ended manner. Loose parts may be natural materials such as rocks, pine cones, pebbles, shells, and sand (**Figure 13.9A**), or manufactured items, such as hoops, balls, boxes, or blocks (**Figure 13.9B**). Some play equipment manufacturers are even creating configurable systems to encourage outdoor play with loose parts.

A   *Elena Abrosimova/iStock/Getty Images Plus*

B   *waraphorn-aphai/iStock/Getty Images Plus*

Figure 13-9 These children are using loose parts on their playground. How do loose parts enhance outdoor experiences?

There is a growing interest in loose parts play as a means of stimulating imagination, cooperation, and interaction among children. These open-ended play experiences support problem solving and are child-centered. Children involved in using loose parts for play can experience exploration that occurs naturally, without adult intervention or direction. Besides exercising the creative mind, loose parts encourage using math principles. For example, as children interlock and count pieces and identify physical properties, they are using math skills.

Large commercially available loose-parts systems encourage interaction because the pieces require cooperation among children to connect. A myriad of ways to join the pieces provides open-ended play experiences that are widely varied and inclusive of children of all abilities.

Integrating Loose Parts Into the Curriculum

Another value of loose parts is their adaptability. They can be fashioned for use according to individual interests and abilities and incorporated into many areas of the curriculum.

Integrating blocks, balls, rings, cones, and other manufactured small parts into the play space stimulates imaginative play, brings learning and the classroom curriculum outdoors, and keeps the experience new and fresh. By giving children the time and freedom to direct their own play and move items around, teachers can help facilitate playful learning in its highest, most beneficial form.

Nature provides loose parts that engage children, such as pine cones, seedpods, small stones, and leaves. Natural elements provide for open-ended play that emphasizes unstructured exploration with diverse materials. The level of complexity and variety that nature offers invites varied and more complex play. Loose-parts play can encourage many skills, including:

- creativity and use of imagination.
- understanding the properties of materials.
- cooperation and social interactions.
- planning, organizing, discussing, building, and designing.
- communication and discussion.
- translation of ideas to concrete examples.
- moving, learning, and having fun together.
- problem solving.

Teaching Tip

A Different Approach: Adventure Playgrounds

Adventure playgrounds, popularized in the 1970s and 1980s, consist of a wide assortment of discarded or scrounged materials where children can build and create using real tools such as hammers, saws, and drills. The concept developed as an approach to play areas that gave children maximum opportunities for constructing and working cooperatively. Typically, an adventure playground is staffed by play leaders who supervise and assist in the children's activities. Such playgrounds are primarily intended for school-age children.

Irina Belova/E+ via Getty Images

Figure 13-10 A child uses tools for wood construction with guidance from an adult. What are other adventure playground concepts or experiences that you can adapt for your playground?

Many of the valuable principles inherent in adventure playgrounds can be incorporated into the playgrounds of early childhood. Include an extensive variety of loose parts, materials, and activities to encourage exploration, creativity, and construction.

Activities

Although children should have ample basic equipment to use on the playground, plenty of interesting loose parts will encourage them to pursue their own ideas. A teacher might also suggest ideas that the children can carry out. Here are some possibilities for activities that might be suggested or encouraged by teachers:

- Build an obstacle course using rope, chalk, blocks, tires, sawhorses, boxes, hoops, or boards.
- Use paper and crayons to rub textures from brick, asphalt, bark, and so forth.
- Introduce parachute play for lifting, falling, and running inside and out. The parachute can also be attached to a fence or structure to become a tent.
- Ask children to close their eyes and talk about what they hear.
- Invite some ants to a picnic; put out different types of food (peanut butter, cheese, crackers) on plates near an ant hill and return to determine the ants' favorite food.
- Cut the bottom from plastic milk bottles by cutting them at an angle, starting below the handle, to make scoops for catching and tossing balls or beanbags.
- Make pinwheels and provide scarves for streaming on windy days (**Figure 13.11**).
- Make a punching bag from an old pillowcase filled with foam.
- Set up a small tent or make one from sheets for pretend camping. Provide cooking utensils and dishes, a sleeping bag, and sticks for a campfire.
- Paint small stones gold. When children are not around, bury the stones in the sand area for a treasure hunt.
- On a warm day, let children wear swimsuits and paint themselves with washable paints. Provide a mirror so they can check their progress. Rinsing off the paint is easy with a water hose.
- Have children practice rolling a ball into a box at the bottom of the slide.
- Purchase multicolored fish gravel, and before children go out to play, spread it around the play area. Provide small paper cups or boxes for children to gather their treasures.
- Cut plastic shower curtains into squares to make mats for sitting.

Wavebreakmedia/iStock/Getty Images Plus

Figure 13-11 A child uses a pinwheel to test how hard the wind is blowing. What are additional ways that children can enjoy and learn about wind?

Dramatic Play Activities with Wheeled Toys

Wheeled toys can be valuable assets when incorporated into dramatic play activities (**Figure 13.12**). Add some props, and the wheeled toys will stimulate many playful learning experiences. Activities can be planned to reinforce the curriculum, such as vehicles for work-related themes. For example, ambulance drivers, police officers, and firefighters relate to safety or community helper themes. A farmers' market or produce stand can relate to a health theme, and a car wash and gas station can relate to transportation themes.

Wheeled Toy Activities for Dramatic Play

Theme	Props	Activity
Ambulances	Medical bags, white shirts, medical instruments, blankets, pillows	Suggest the assistants administer first aid to tricycle accident victims and transport them to the hospital.
Car wash	Buckets and soapy water, washcloths, sponges	Make a "Car Wash" sign and post it near the props. Don bathing suits or old clothes and wash tricycles, wagons, and other wheeled toys. "Car wash" is an amusing way to cool off during hot summer days. Leave items in the sun until well dried to prevent rusting.
Chuck wagon	Poster board, tape, metal or plastic cups, spoons, pie tins, buckets, cowboy hats, bandannas, chef's hat	Convert a wagon to a chuck wagon by bending poster board in an arch to form a cover. Attach the cover to the sides of the wagon with tape. One child can be the cook, while the others are cowboys or cowgirls. Change props, and the chuck wagon becomes a covered wagon for pioneers.
Delivery people	Cardboard boxes, hats, plastic or silk flowers, pizza boxes	Select the appropriate props for your current theme or follow the interests of the children. Children take orders and use props and wagons to deliver them to customers.
Drive-in movie	Table or booth, tickets, popcorn, microphone, show-and-tell items	Plan for "show and tell" or a talent show. Let children make popcorn and take it outdoors to eat while watching the show from their tricycles. Some children can sell tickets and refreshments to riders. (Note: Popcorn can be a choking hazard for younger children. Puffed corn snacks are a safe alternative.)
Farmers' market or produce stand	Baskets, sacks, tote bags, straw hats, bandanas, plastic fruit and vegetables	Wagons can be farmers' trucks. Children can ride tricycles to the farmers' market or stop at a roadside stand to bring items to sell or make purchases.
Firefighters	Fire hats, hoses, bells, small ladder, blue shirts	Let children paint a box with red tempera paint and put it in the wagon to turn it into a firetruck. Children can put out fires or rescue plush cats from trees, bushes, or play structures.
Gas station	Boxes with hoses attached or toy gas pumps, play money	Child customers can pump gas for their vehicles.
Obstacle course	Plastic jugs with water, wood blocks or dowels, rope, hoops, crates, tires	Arrange a course through which children can ride wheeled toys. Giving a variety of instructions can stimulate sequential learning. For example, "Ride to the green jug around the blocks and between the milk crates." Start with a simple course and add additional obstacles to make it more challenging.
Parades	Paper bags or paper plates, crayons or markers, string, tape, ribbon, balloons, crepe paper	For a circus parade, have children draw the animals they want to be on bags or plates and attach them to the front of their tricycles. For a Fourth of July parade, have children decorate tricycles with red, white, and blue ribbon, crepe paper, and balloons. Use star stickers to add a nice touch to fenders and wagon sides.
Police officers	Hats, whistles, pads and pencils, badges	Suggest that children patrol the play area and watch for safe drivers. They can write tickets for unsafe tricycle riders. Add traffic signs to extend the activity and include literacy experiences.

Goodheart-Willcox Publisher

Figure 13-12 This chart illustrates ways to encourage dramatic play related to wheeled toys. What are other dramatic play ideas that could involve wheel toys? *(Continued)*

Wheeled Toy Activities for Dramatic Play *(continued)*

Theme	Props	Activity
Repair people	Toolboxes (can be made from shoeboxes), play tools	Children can carry toolboxes and travel around to repair other toys.
Riding to music	Recordings of lively music	Place music outside while children are triking. Marches and polkas are especially stimulating for this activity. Try some slow music, such as waltzes, to vary the pace. For variety, turn the music off, and children must stop. Start the music for them to ride again.
Taxi, bus, or shared-ride drivers	Hats with "driver" written on them, wallets, play phones	The driver can pick up customers, collect money, and transport them to their destination. Pretend money and dress-up clothes add to the fun.

Goodheart-Willcox Publisher

Figure 13-12 *Continued*

Beanbag Activities

Beanbags are inexpensive, versatile items to add to playgrounds. They can be purchased or easily made and used to increase motor skills, hand-eye coordination, and manual dexterity. Beanbags should be loosely filled for easy gripping. Here are some activities using versatile beanbags:

- Toss beanbags into a cardboard box or from hand to hand as a beginner's activity.
- Toss beanbags back and forth to one another like balls.
- Cut holes in the shape of circles, squares, and triangles in a cardboard box to toss beanbags through. The holes can provide an opportunity to refer to shapes. Make the holes large to begin with and change to smaller ones as children become more skilled.
- Balance beanbags on your head and walk around without letting them fall. Perform other movements such as hopping, jumping, or walking on a balance beam.
- Make a target on the ground and toss beanbags at it.
- Use a beanbag as a marker for hopscotch.

Storage on the Playground

Ideally, there will be a storage building to hold items such as dramatic play props and riding toys. Additionally, it is desirable to have hooks for Hula-Hoops®, jump ropes, or items that can be hung on the walls of the building. Provide large, heavy-duty shelves to hold containers for smaller toys.

In a facility without outside storage, dress-up items may be transported to the playground. A small trunk or suitcase filled with dress-up clothes can be carried outdoors, placed in an accessible location, and then opened to display items to attract children's attention. Laundry baskets work well as containers. Be sure containers are large enough to hold a variety of interesting articles and lightweight enough for children to carry to and from the storage area or classroom.

Wagons can transport blocks, manipulatives, and even books from the classroom or storage to the outdoors. Children love pulling a wagon loaded with materials they want to use. Purchased net bags or pillowcases, especially king-size ones, can be filled with balls and transported by children.

☑ CHECKPOINT

1. What are safety factors to consider in planning and supervising your playground?
2. What are the benefits of adding loose parts to your playground?
3. Why is storage on the playground important?

Case Study

Field Day Competition

The preschool where Sophie was employed traditionally held a field day every spring. As a new teacher, she asked a co-teacher, Courtney, what to expect. Courtney explained that each class had their own activities, but that there were relays where all classes competed. The winning class was awarded a pizza party.

Sophie had learned in her early childhood classes that cooperative games were better for young children than competitive games such as relays. She had recently read an article that pointed out how, in many cases, the children who were eliminated in such games were the ones who needed the experience most. She had seen children crying and upset when they were put out in games because they still wanted to play. As a result, Sophie adopted a philosophy of planning cooperative games and activities for her class. She had created her own version of no-elimination musical chairs so that all of the children could enjoy the game as long as they wanted. She liked musical games, such as "Little Sally Walker" and "Go In and Out the Window," where everyone participated cooperatively. She let the children work together to make their own obstacle courses and then have fun navigating the courses. She often used parachute activities because they involved children all working together to reach a goal.

After thinking about how hard she endeavored to build a community of children who cooperated and collaborated on activities regardless of physical abilities, she felt she could not support a traditional field day, complete with winners, losers, trophies, and ribbons. She especially disliked the highly competitive relay, resulting in a pizza party that left all of the others out.

Consider This
1. How do you feel about competitive events for young children?
2. What could Sophie do to follow her beliefs?
3. What are other activities that are noncompetitive?

13.3 Integrating Outdoor Time With Other Curriculum Areas

How do teachers make outdoor time into a "learning laboratory" and make maximum use of the time? One important way is to link curriculum activities with the outdoors. This section will provide ideas to help teachers get started.

Housekeeping and Dramatic Play

Outdoor equipment and appliance boxes can be transformed into boats, planes, automobiles, castles, or forts for dramatic play. Blankets, sheets, and other props enrich the play experience. A housekeeping area can be constructed of cardboard boxes, or a stove-sink-refrigerator set can be moved outdoors periodically. Children can pretend to cook with all of the natural materials around them—leaves, pine cones, and sticks—if teachers keep small pots and pans handy in the outdoor storage unit or transport them from indoors.

Some dress-up items tend to stimulate more active, noisy, or aggressive play than is usually desired indoors. Boots, western wear, superhero, or circus accessories may be used outdoors with fewer limitations than may be necessary indoors. Since children's outdoor play is more active and dirtier than indoor play, outdoor dress-up materials must be sturdy enough to withstand frequent washing.

Capes are particularly popular as outdoor dress-up items and can be quickly made from a rectangle of fabric. Attach hook-and-loop closures to enable children to put on and remove the cape easily. Never use anything that ties at the neck; Velcro® enables quick release for safety. Hem the bottom and the cape is ready for use. A fake fur cape becomes an animal costume; any sheer fabric can be a bride or princess; black cotton material can be a witch or magician. And of course, superhero play will inevitably result from capes made of plain or printed fabrics (**Figure 13.13**).

StockPlanets/E+ via Getty Images

Figure 13-13 School-age children enjoy superhero play. What other dress-up props can suggest play themes for children?

Do not allow children to use climbing equipment while wearing loose dress-up clothing, as it might become entangled. Select a location for the dress-up materials that is well away from climbing equipment to reduce the temptation to combine the two. Avoid long dresses or other items that might induce a fall, since children are apt to run outdoors. To keep dress-up items reasonably clean, teach children to return them to a basket when they are not being worn.

Music and Movement

Since indoor music activities may be constrained by space and noise limits, take the music outside where children can be more actively engaged. Making original music using outdoor materials supports creativity; playground equipment and sticks make interesting sounds. Equipment manufacturers make outdoor equipment that involves music, such as xylophones and chimes. Adding music to your outdoor time need not be costly—it can be as simple as dancing with scarves or crepe paper streamers to music played on any portable device.

Art and Creative Expression

Fun, messy art activities can be conducted easily on the playground, where there is less concern about spillage. Fingerpainting on a table works well, and a water hose washes it all away when finished. Outdoor easels can be purchased, or an easel that a teacher is not using can be taken to the playground.

Another option is to attach cardboard to a fence to make an easel. The fence, too, provides a perfect place to put up a clothesline and hang paintings to dry. Here are additional options for outdoor art:

- Decorate sidewalks with colored chalk.
- Make crayon rubbings from natural objects.
- Let children remove their shoes and walk in paint, then walk onto paper to make footprint designs.
- Fill a squirt bottle with thinned tempera paint or water with food coloring, and let children spray the colors onto paper.
- Take playdough and clay to the playground to use on trays. Cinder blocks and a plank can provide working space if you do not have an outdoor table.

Discovery Journeys

Dancing on the Playground

Rae Pica, author of Experiences in Music and Movement *and numerous other books on learning through physical activity, shares her memories of music and movement on the playground, which led to her career as a keynote speaker, an author, and an advocate for recess and outdoor play in schools.*

Once upon a time, when asked their favorite subject in school, children overwhelmingly replied, "recess." Today, for many children, that is not an option. Schools have either limited recess time to the point where it offers little chance for play and creativity, or they have eliminated recess entirely.

I advocate for recess for many reasons, but among them are my memories. Although I enjoyed school itself, it was during elementary-school recess that I had the opportunity to express myself as I chose: choreographing dances to The Beatles' songs with my friend Kathy and performing them for the other kids.

I blush to think of the *hutzpah* (extreme confidence) I had then, but I suspect it was merely a precursor to my lifelong need for self-expression—as a writer, a keynote speaker, and an advocate for young children. Dancing on the playground was so much fun! And the positive reception from my classmates demonstrated the impact of having a "voice."

Not every child will have playground experiences that lead to future choices. But every child deserves the chance. Every child deserves that unstructured time… that research tells us they need in order to learn optimally.

Consider This

1. What do you remember about recess from your own childhood?
2. How does unstructured time benefit children?
3. Do you consider recess to be a privilege, right, or need for children?
4. What is your local school system's policy on recess?

Sand and Water Play

Sand and water play is inexpensive and provides valuable playful learning, engaging children and sustaining their interest for extended periods. Sand and water can involve all ages—toddlers through school-age children—and provide hours of play and learning. If sandboxes are not available, large dishpans, laundry tubs, new litter pans, or galvanized tubs may be used. To keep neighborhood cats from using the sand area for a litter box, cover it with a tarpaulin or other material when not in use. Clean the sand area periodically with a rake to remove sticks, rocks, and other accumulated debris. A small dustpan used as a shovel is the right size for small hands.

If you do not have a water table, select large plastic storage containers, dishpans, or infant bathers. To protect clothing, children can wear vinyl smocks or recycled shirts worn backwards. A square of plastic sewn on the front of a shirt can provide water protection. Another option is to just wear bathing suits or other clothing. After all, children will dry quickly in warm weather.

Alternating accessories provides variations in sand or water play. Possibilities are plastic bowls and funnels, or any plastic containers that can be used as a mold for damp sand. Most items appropriate for sand play are also useful for water play. In addition, add food coloring or bubbles to the water for a different experience. Both sand and water play can be relaxing for a child having a difficult time who needs a calming activity. Even toddlers enjoy sand and water play.

Setting up for Sand and Water Play

Allow plenty of space or limit the number of children to prevent crowding. Sand and water activities can even be designed for a single child as a solitary, calming location. Assure children that everyone will have turns. When children realize an activity will be regularly available, conflicts between everyone wanting to participate at once will subside. Be sure there are plenty of other exciting things for children to do.

Develop a few simple rules, such as "We keep the water in the pan," "We don't get our friends wet unless they say it's OK," and "Sand is for digging and molding, not for throwing." Usually, children will be so involved in the activities that misuse will be minimal.

For water play, put a few toy boats, corks, plastic jars, funnels, squeeze bottles, or poultry basters in a pan of water. Avoid glasses and cups since children will be tempted to drink from them. The following sections describe some special setups that allow children to imitate grown-up life.

Washing Dishes
Set up two dishpans side by side. Fill both with water, providing soap for one. Offer an assortment of small plastic dishes, a dish drainer, a dish mop or cloth, and a dish towel.

Bathing Dolls
Choose a simple, one-piece rubber doll without blinking eyes or rooted hair. Add a washcloth, some soap, and a small towel for young "parents" to bathe their baby. A baby bathtub is ideal for this activity.

Laundry Day
Gather an assortment of small cloth items such as handkerchiefs, doll clothes, scarves, or washcloths. Set up two dishpans of water. Add liquid soap for the realism that children like. Hang a clothesline and add clothespins. For a nostalgic touch, set up a washtub or dishpan and a small washboard. You will need to demonstrate and explain since children will probably not be familiar with washboards or clotheslines. Try some of the old-fashioned wooden clothespins without springs.

Toy or Chair Wash
Let children wash plastic toys, such as LEGO® or DUPLO®, in a dishpan with soapy water. Provide a second pan with clear water for rinsing. Offer sponges and scrub brushes to clean classroom chairs. Children enjoy real work and will clean the toys while having fun.

Fun With Sprinklers
Set up several sprinklers in a grassy area of the playground. Let children change into bathing suits and watch the excitement. Move the sprinklers periodically and water the lawn as an extra benefit.

Water Painting
Put out buckets of water and wide paintbrushes, and let children paint buildings, a wooden fence, a playhouse, or pictures on the sidewalk. Of course, the water "paint" dries and there is nothing there, but this does not hinder the motivation. The fun is in the process.

Blowing Bubbles
Mix bubble solution (**Figure 13.14**) and experiment with items to make bubbles. Some possibilities are colanders, spools, slotted spoons, new fly swatters, and children's plastic hangers (the type for two-piece outfits that have an opening). Pour the mixture into a dishpan for children to use. Bubbles can quickly gain the attention and engagement of children; keep the mixture handy and ready to use.

Other ideas for bubble blowers include strawberry baskets, funnels, plastic straws, pipe cleaners formed into hoops, plastic 6-pack rings, and so on. Expand on bubble play by holding a Bubble Festival. Set up different bubble stations and let children rotate among them.

Homemade Bubble Recipe

1 cup of Joy, Ivory, Dawn, or other high-suds hand dishwashing liquid
2 tablespoons of Karo syrup
6–10 cups of water

SDI Productions/E+ via Getty Images

Figure 13-14 Children of all ages and abilities can enjoy making bubbles from easily available ingredients. *What other tools can you think of to use to make bubbles?*

Language and Literacy

Outdoor time can offer an opportunity for quiet activities. Nature's soft sounds can be soothing and conducive to reading or enjoying a book. Find a shaded spot and make a reading area with beach towels or beanbag chairs. For a permanent area, install a porch swing or an umbrella table. A reading area provides a quiet place to relax, be alone, or be with a few friends. Just as indoors, teachers can read books aloud to children in small groups, or children can read themselves. Books might relate to outdoor experiences or a previous classroom activity. Many books with a theme of outdoor play can stimulate children to replicate activities or enact the story.

Science and Math

Outdoors can be a venue to promote emergent scientific and mathematical thinking. Looking at flowers and counting petals and leaves include science and math. Have a scavenger hunt and look for particular objects. Counting sets of seedpods or acorns brings more science and math to the outdoors. Children learn classification through seed collections, rocks to sort, or leaves to press in books.

If there is no place nearby for a nature walk, let children form circles on a grassy area with pieces of string. Give each child a magnifying glass and let them explore the area inside their circles to see what tiny nature items they can discover. Teach them how to look at bugs and other nature items safely.

Outdoors can lead to understanding science and nature. Children can see that rainwater evaporates and observe leaves blowing and limbs bending from the wind. They can throw things in the air to see if they glide or fall, or watch birds at a feeder or bath. Plants, with a mix of color, texture, fragrance, and softness, encourage multisensory experiences and novelty with seasonal changes.

Consider the experiences with aesthetic appreciation of the colors of the flowers, how the wind blows the leaves on the trees, or the aroma of freshly cut grass. Recognizing the beauty in nature is important for children's development. A growing body of research supports the importance of aesthetics in young children's lives.

Blocks and Construction

Blocks develop many science and math skills. Large blocks, crates, and planks provide for a larger version of block construction than is possible with unit blocks. However, even unit blocks can be brought out and used on pavement, a deck, or any flat surface covered with a sheet of vinyl flooring. Consider keeping an older set of blocks in external storage for outdoor use.

If you have no outdoor storage, keeping unit blocks in crates expedites transporting them to the playground. Limit the amount in each container to reduce weight and enlist the children's help or use wagons to transport.

Creative Outdoor Space

To best support development and learning, there are design elements to follow in establishing or equipping a playground (**Figure 13.15**). Arranging an outdoor environment requires as much consideration as indoors. The following are some of the factors to consider:

- an overall design with play zones that invite and integrate play over the whole area
- plenty of items for sand and water play, items for construction and artwork
- structures and props that encourage dramatic and social play
- vehicle pathways that go somewhere (slabs and linear sidewalks do not offer the challenge of a meandering path.)
- places to be alone or with a few friends
- surfaces, texture, and equipment to stimulate sensory learning
- climbing structures appropriate for the age groups with adequate fall-zone surfaces
- a variety of play opportunities that address all developmental domains
- consideration of supervision in the playground design (avoid blind spots and identify strategic locations for adults.)
- enough equipment and materials that children have choices of activities

Landscaping and Layout

The landscaping of a playground plays a role in safety. Make sure plants are nontoxic and that no toxic chemicals are present. Avoid plants such as holly, pyracanth, or others with thorns. Watch for roots that create tripping risks for running children. Any dead or diseased trees should be removed.

Dontstop/iStock/Getty Images Plus

Figure 13-15 This area of the playground contains permanent equipment and loose parts. What safety concerns have been addressed in this layout?

Children enjoy hills and changing levels. Variation in terrain provides opportunities and challenges for motor development. Hills and berms can add interest to children's play and often become a catalyst for creating games.

Planning starts with the size and shape, slope, drainage of the site, and analysis of conditions the weather will impose. An L-shaped playground may be hard to supervise since children can be out of adult sight. Hidden areas, such as a space behind a storage building, can create barriers to supervision. Define areas with clear pathways and traffic patterns so that children on one piece of equipment do not interfere with other activities.

Defined Areas

When planning a playground, create defined areas for play. For example, designate a place for riding toys away from running areas. Locate swings away from traffic patterns to avoid children walking in front of or behind swings. Arranging the playground involves consideration of location and traffic patterns just as the indoor environment does. Consider providing the following defined areas:

- quiet space—for calm, focused activities for a respite from active play
- open space—for running, cross-playground access, and group games
- active space—for busy, physical play that extends a wide range of skill levels
- nature area—for exploring natural elements, such as water, soil, leaves, trees, or a garden
- infant/toddler area—for age-appropriate activities so younger children do not compete with older children for activities

By providing defined spaces, you are planning for a balance of play activities. That does not mean that only quiet or active play will occur in the designated areas, but the arrangement of a quiet space permits a retreat. Think of a playground as a collection of spaces with potential for specific types of play.

☑ CHECKPOINT

1. What are some benefits to integrating outdoor play with other areas of the curriculum?
2. Why do you think sand and water play are popular with children?
3. How does the layout of the playground affect how children use it?

13.4 The Teacher's Role in the Outdoor Environment

The teacher's role in the outdoor environment is as important as it is inside. Planning, interacting with children, encouraging exploration, and implementing curriculum are all needed outdoors. Teachers can support the integration of their curriculum topics by taking advantage of outdoor time.

The most important playground safety feature for all ages is alert adults. In addition to noticing and addressing hazards, it is important that adults supervise the children and interact with them, moderating their activity when necessary. Maintain staff ratios and never leave children outside alone.

Access to climbing and other equipment adds an element of risk that requires alert and intentional supervision. The sections that follow discuss some health and safety considerations that are an integral part of the teacher's role.

Supervision

The key to a well-functioning and safe playground is well-trained staff who know how to make use of a developmentally appropriate outdoor learning environment while providing adequate supervision. Here are some suggested supervision guidelines:

- Always have at least two adults on the playground. One is available for general supervision if an issue requires an adult's focused attention.
- Use a **zone system** of supervision. Each adult covers a designated area of the playground (**Figure 13.16**), circulating but paying close attention to more risky areas such as climbing equipment.
- Teachers should position themselves in a place where they can see the entire playground or the area for which they are responsible.
- Teach children how to safely use equipment. Show them how to make sure their feet are secure on the surface, then reach up and take a firm hold with their hand before they step up.
- Avoid visiting with another adult and keep the focus on the children.
- Make sure all of the children come inside when outdoor time ends and are not left unattended. Having a schedule that requires one group to exit the playground before another group enters reduces the possibility of a child being left behind.

Fencing

Make sure the area is surrounded by a fence that is too high for children to climb over. There should be no gaps where it joins the building that children could squeeze through or become stuck in. Make sure the latches work and are either out of reach of children or require adults to open. Many states require self-closing latches that children cannot operate. Even if a state does not require them, teachers should consider one if parents must open the gate when they come to the center. The fence should go all the way to the ground. If the fence is wood, it should be free of splinters. Regular maintenance is necessary to keep fencing in good shape.

Hazards, Trash, and Debris

Each day, before taking the children out, teachers should walk around the play area and look for any hazards, such as damaged equipment. Discard any trash that may have blown in and remove sticks and rocks that children might use aggressively. Look at the

MBI/iStock/Getty Images Plus

Figure 13-16 This teacher is following a zone system for supervision by being responsible for supervising and interacting with children in this area of the playground. *Why is having two or more adults on the playground a desirable practice?*

playground from the child's eye level to see what enticing but unsafe things a curious child might see from their lower viewpoint. Look for animal droppings and ant hills while making the hazard walk.

Cushioning Surfaces

Shock-absorbing materials under swings, slides, and climbing equipment are required to cushion possible falls. These soft surfaces should extend well beyond the equipment, with edging to contain the material. Sand is a satisfactory surface if properly maintained at a depth of 8–12 inches. This can be difficult in situations where drainage washes sand away. Sand loses some of its safeguarding property when it is wet or packed. Sand is a very inviting play material for children, and they should not play under swings or climbing equipment. Have a sand play area elsewhere to reduce the temptation to play under equipment. Manufactured cushioning products and mats are available that meet safety requirements. Shredded tires provide an eco-friendly solution.

Grass is not considered a suitable cushioning surface under play equipment designed for climbing. Pea gravel is not recommended for infant and toddler areas because of children's tendency to put items in their mouths, ears, and noses.

Swings, Slides, and Climbers

There should be adequate space all around a swing so that children will not bump against another surface or hit swing supports when they lean back. Swings and attachments must be checked regularly and closely supervised to prevent misuse.

It is best if slides and climbers are in the shade and away from direct sunlight. Adults should check the temperature of a slide to make sure it is not too hot for the children to use. Equipment should have handholds where children climb. Steps should be wide and low, with platforms at the top of the steps, so several children can congregate with room to sit or turn around. Elaborate playground equipment intended for school-age children is not appropriate for preschoolers or toddlers. In fact, playground equipment for older children can be decidedly unsafe, since younger children often attempt to use it anyway.

Climbing structures do not need to be high to be fun and challenging for toddlers (**Figure 13.17**). Eighteen inches is an adequate height for toddlers. There are many manufactured climbers designed for toddlers and preschoolers, and some are portable and do not require permanent installation. Wooden climbers should be checked frequently for splinters.

Too Cold or Too Hot?

Deciding when the weather is inappropriate for outdoor time is a complex factor of temperature, humidity, air quality, pollen count, time of day, availability of shade, and other factors. Some outdoor enthusiasts say there is no bad weather, just inappropriate clothing.

Early learning programs should develop a policy addressing when they do not go outside or when they limit the time outdoors. The policy should include information on appropriate clothing so that children are prepared to participate whenever possible.

Ensure that children have access to drinking water outside. Children dehydrate more quickly when they play vigorously in the sun. Offer extra liquids in hot weather. Protect children's skin with sunscreen and hats. If you do not have trees on your playground, create shady places by adding covered areas. Consider the time of day and the length of time that you stay outside, especially during the summer.

Guidance in the Outdoors

Many indoor guidance methods are also appropriate outdoors. However, there are some strategies that may be needed more frequently outdoors. The following section considers specific strategies to help ensure a smoothly functioning playground.

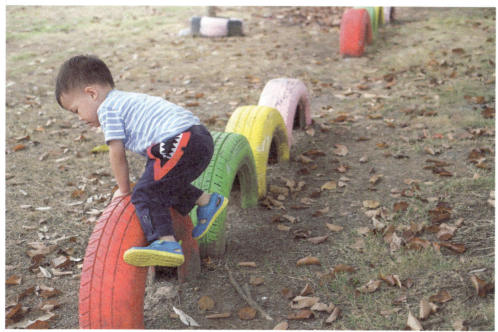

Figure 13-17 This early learning center has found an inexpensive way to provide for climbing by using tires. What other ways might recycled items be used on a playground?

Preventing Conflicts and Crowding

The major factor in providing guidance on the playground is to ensure there are enough appealing things to do. Insufficient equipment will increase conflicts over equipment use. Avoiding such conflicts is simple; provide plenty of interesting things to do. Have duplicates of popular toys for young children who may not share well, such as balls, buckets, or riding toys. Large items and objects that require two or more children to use can encourage cooperation.

To make sure there are enough interesting activities, determine the number of **play spaces** (an environment where play can take place) for children. Consider one play space as an available piece of equipment that will engage one child. For example, a two-seat swing set provides two play spaces because two children can swing at a time. A tricycle provides one play space since only one child can ride at a time. A climbing structure could include 6–8 play spaces, and a playhouse might accommodate 3–5 children, depending on their size.

There should be enough equipment or activities so that every child can be involved with an item or in a space but still have choices if they want to switch activities. As a rule of thumb, provide at least 50 percent more play spaces than the number of children using the playground at one time. Having plenty of play spaces increases the choices that a child has when wanting to change activities.

Ending Outdoor Time

Because children enjoy being outdoors, they may be reluctant to end the time outside. When it is time to stop playing and come indoors, two signals will help get the children's attention. First, raise one hand as a signal to gather together. Then, with the children who are first to join the line, start singing. When the others hear this second signal, they will quickly join in to help with the singing.

It is wise to give children notice that outdoor time is almost up. A signal such as a bell can indicate that they have five more minutes on the playground. Or give them a choice such as, "Are you ready to go in now, or would you rather have five more minutes?" They will undoubtedly select the five-more-minutes option, but they will cooperate because they made the choice.

✅ CHECKPOINT

1. How does having enough equipment affect safety?
2. Why is a zone system of supervision a good practice?
3. How does having one group exit the playground before another group enters constitute a safety practice?

13.5 Outdoors for Infants and Toddlers

Outdoor play is just as important for infants and toddlers as it is for older children. There are health benefits of fresh air, exercise, and sunlight, and opportunities to develop emerging gross motor abilities. Additionally, the outdoor environment can offer rich sensory experiences that children will not experience inside. There are plants to explore, new sounds, and unfamiliar smells of aromatic flowers or freshly cut grass. The light and temperature are different, and children experience the day-to-day changes. Being outdoors gives everyone a needed change of pace.

Gross motor activity dominates the play of infants and toddlers. They are busy learning the mechanics of their bodies and developing strength and coordination. Look for ways to provide for the development of the important gross motor skills of infants and toddlers.

Going for a walk outside using multiseat strollers or buggies is popular in settings for infants and toddlers. Children and adults alike enjoy such excursions. However, riding in a buggy should not be the only way that children get outside. Riding should not replace freely playing, since riding is more passive than active.

It is best to have an outdoor play space for infants and toddlers separate from that of older children (**Figure 13.18**). Most states require separation in their regulations. Older children's boisterous outdoor play can overwhelm and endanger babies and young toddlers. The needs and motor abilities of infants and toddlers are quite different from those of older children and require separate types of equipment. In fact, the needs of nonwalking infants are different from those of toddlers, who are clumsy but exuberant explorers. A case could be made for separating the play area for infants from that of toddlers as well, but for reasons of cost and space, many programs use a shared space. For example, one might have a grassy, shaded section for small babies, with many sensory objects available for exploration. Another area could be a small climber and swings for younger toddlers. A third area could include space for riding toys, sand play, and water play for older toddlers.

A shady area can even provide a place for napping. Consider having naptime outdoors when the weather is mild. Infants sleep well outside, and the fresh air is beneficial. For toddlers, rest mats or small cots work. Of course, you must still supervise children closely, even when they are asleep.

When designing an outdoor space and planning activities for infants and toddlers, start with the capabilities and interests of the children. What do the children enjoy doing indoors? Do they like riding toys? Are they using the furniture as support to pull up to a standing position? Do they enjoy things on which they can climb? Are they attracted to items that make noise? Think of ways to provide interesting and varied practice outdoors for those activities that the children often attempt indoors.

Textures and Sensory Variations

Babies are in the process of learning about the world through their senses. The outdoor space can be rich in sensory experiences. The light, shadows, wind, birds, butterflies, and textures of grass give a natural boost to the environment.

Think about how teachers can add to the textures of the outside play space. How many are there? Grass, concrete, sand, wood, water? What else can be added? A tree

sturti/E+ via Getty Images

Figure 13-18 A teacher helps a toddler learn to use the equipment in the toddler area of the playground. *Why is a separate area for infants and toddlers important?*

stump with bark and tree rings will be interesting for little fingers to explore. Large, smooth rocks, rubber tires, blankets, water, a small wooden deck, and indoor-outdoor carpeting are possibilities.

Patterns of Light and Shade

Trees create interesting shadows as leaves sway in the breeze. Add to the shadow patterns by hanging colored pieces of Plexiglas® or a crystal to make rainbows or casting colored light onto the ground. Crawling babies can see the world change color. Hang crepe paper or ribbon streamers from a tree and let the wind make them dance. Consider hanging large pieces of brightly colored shear fabrics for the light to shine through or using them as temporary shade structures. Shade is important for infants and toddlers with more sensitive skin. If natural shade is not available, canopies or other covered areas can be built on the playground.

Sounds and Smells

Wind chimes create a pleasant variety of sounds. Try bamboo, metal, and plastic to create different sounds. Make your own from pie tins or other metal items. Windsocks with streamers or decorative flags are beautiful to look at and provide rustling sounds in the breeze.

The sense of smell can be stimulated by flowers, but if ground space is limited, try window boxes or planters attached to fences. Wildflowers and other easy-to-grow flowers are a lovely gift of nature that delight children of all ages.

Space Considerations for Infants and Toddlers

Infants and toddlers need outdoor time regularly, and their needs are different from those of preschoolers. Infants will benefit from safe, shady spaces where they can crawl. A marvelous feature of your outdoor space is that it changes more than the inside. Help children notice these changes. See **Figure 13.19** for examples of outdoor play activities for infants and toddlers.

Gross Motor Play for Infants and Toddlers

For gross motor skills to develop as expected, children must have the time and space to move. The following sections discuss some ways that adults can ensure infants and toddlers have opportunities for movement as well as encouragement to develop important physical skills.

Tummy Time

Babies who are not yet crawling can still enjoy the outdoors. A clean blanket placed on the ground over grass will give them a nice, soft spot to stretch, reach for items, and practice rolling from tummy to back and over again (**Figure 13.20**). A baby will enjoy sitting supported on a teacher's lap, taking in the sights and sounds. If possible, separate babies from the careening toddlers and drivers of wheeled toys, as well as the curious pokes of older, more mobile infants.

Crawling and Creeping

Babies who are crawling or creeping will enjoy moving over textured materials. Make a "texture path" by providing a succession of different textures to crawl over and through. In addition to the natural textures presented by the playground, teachers can add pieces of fake fur, woven or rubber floor mats, throw rugs, soft blankets, vinyl, cardboard boxes, tunnels, and other items with interesting textures for babies to explore.

Outdoor Play Activities for Infants and Toddlers

Outdoor Equipment	Considerations
Climbing equipment	Provide safe, interesting climbing spaces. Be sure there is soft, cushioned material underneath.
Swings	Swings should be designed specifically for infants or toddlers. For infants, use swings that cradle them comfortably. Toddlers cannot predict the path of a swing and will often walk right in front of it. Make sure any swings are out of the flow of activity.
Permanently installed play equipment	These structures should be arranged so that children using them do not interfere with one another. Infants need protection from the activity of more mobile children.
Riding toys	There should be a smooth surface for riding toys, preferably a path. Design a trail that goes somewhere, such as around a tree, rather than just a straight line or circle.
Sand area equipment	Sand play gives toddlers ongoing opportunities to fill and dump, and they enjoy sand play for its sensory pleasure. Sand play requires close supervision on the part of teachers, but it is well worth it. Simply sit with the children and play with the sand next to them, modeling different things to do with sand.
Water play equipment	Water play in warm weather is endlessly interesting to both infants and toddlers. A dishpan of water will be eagerly explored. Add interesting things, such as a sponge, boats, and other water toys. Try special activities, such as letting children water the plants. Fill plastic containers, such as margarine tubs, with water and a little food coloring and freeze. Unmold it on a water table outside and place it in a sunny spot. Avoid wading pools because they are unsanitary for children in diapers or those not fully potty trained.

Goodheart-Willcox Publisher

Figure 13-19 This chart provides guidance in planning and establishing a playground for infants and toddlers. *Why is a separate outdoor play area desirable for these youngest children?*

Tatiana Dyuvbanova/iStock/Getty Images Plus

Figure 13-20 A blanket provides a surface for this infant to enjoy the change in environment outdoors. *What are additional considerations for taking infants and toddlers outdoors?*

Walking and Crawling on New Surfaces

Just walking on new surfaces can be challenging for just-beginning-to-walk toddlers. The grass and other surfaces are different from what the children are accustomed to inside. Exploring these new surfaces varies the experience of walking for toddlers. Putting small items around the playground that toddlers will want to get will encourage their newfound mobility as they meander over to the item they desire. The same is true of crawling babies on blankets or outdoor carpeted surfaces—they will work very hard to get an item that they want, increasing the opportunities to develop gross motor skills.

Cruising Around

Cruising is when children pull up to a standing position and walk along, holding onto something stable. There are many ways to include cruising opportunities in the outdoor environment. A good addition would be a "cruising rail," a low railing about 12–18 inches high, attached to posts or other structures, leading in interesting directions on the playground.

Climbing Up, Up, and Over

Climbing becomes a compulsive activity shortly after children learn to creep on all fours. There is a desire to climb up or over something and get on top. Consider adding variations in elevation, such as ramps. These could be built into a play structure or added as natural features to the playground. Vinyl ramps and blocks that can be used outdoors are commercially available.

Rolling Right Along

Toddlers dearly love pushing themselves along on wheeled toys. Keep safety and durability in mind when purchasing riding toys. Pay attention to the various developmental levels of the children. Some may need to just sit on the toy and push themselves around with their feet. Older toddlers will be ready for pedal toys. They need a smooth surface for riding toys and will have difficulty on grass.

Balls, Balls, and More Balls

Kicking a ball is a challenging task for a toddler who must balance on one leg momentarily to kick (**Figure 13.21**). Provide a variety of balls, from large beach balls to small tennis balls, to kick and throw. Toddlers love to chase after a ball that is rolled or thrown to them. They will bring it back over and over to repeat the fun.

Fine Motor Play for Infants and Toddlers

As infants and toddlers learn to control their bodies, fine motor skills are being developed as they learn to reach for, grasp, and release items in their environment.

Pointing and Touching

Encouraging children to "show me the…" motivates them to point at or touch objects, increasing control of their hands and fingers.

Filling, Carrying, and Dumping

Small wagons and carts to push are popular with toddlers, combining gross motor and fine motor play. Toddlers like to fill a container with small toys and empty it over and over again. They will also enjoy filling any container with a handle, carrying it around, and emptying it. Small sand buckets or plastic baskets are versatile and inexpensive additions to the outdoor environment. Many household items can be used by toddlers to fill and dump.

Manipulatives

Manipulatives can be taken outside for toddlers to use. A dishpan or tray helps to keep the parts together. Shape sorters, DUPLO®, snap beads, and many other manipulatives can be enjoyed outdoors.

More Activities for Infants and Toddlers

Almost anything that infants and toddlers can do inside, they can do outside. Infants and toddlers will enjoy music, eating, stories, pictures, and most other activities in the outdoor environment. Here are some favorites:

- Gather and jump in piles of leaves.
- Have a snack, picnic, or tea party on a blanket.
- Hide in a cardboard box or use it as a playhouse.
- Explore and investigate everything on the playground.

Hakase_/iStock/Getty Images Plus

Figure 13-21 A child is learning to balance and control her legs and feet to kick the ball. *What other ways do playground balls contribute to children's development?*

- Run, run, run—and run some more!
- Play peek-a-boo and hide-and-seek.
- Feel the rain when it starts to sprinkle.
- Play with mud and enjoy the squishy feel between their fingers.
- Splash in puddles with boots.
- Hang a Nerf ball on a string from a tree to swat at.
- Wash rocks in a dishpan.
- Capture the fun with a camera to share with their families.

☑ CHECKPOINT

1. Why are some adults reluctant to take groups of infants and toddlers outdoors?
2. What do you feel are the major benefits for infants and toddlers to be outdoors?
3. How would you address safety concerns?

13.6 Focus on Assessment of Program Practices

Various checklists are available to evaluate an outdoor play area. Many place an emphasis on safety, while others include criteria to be sure the area incorporates nature or expands opportunities for diverse learning experiences. The checklist in **Figure 13.24** focuses on the arrangement and equipment of the playground. Use it to determine what changes can improve the learning opportunities and functioning of outdoor time. Such a checklist can assist one in keeping the playground appealing to children.

Assessing Outdoor Time

Use this checklist to evaluate your playground according to the information in the text. Make a plan to improve areas if your playground does not adequately provide each experience for children. Rate how well your playground meets each criterion according to the following scale:

Not Met: 1   Playground is lacking in the criterion
Partially Met 2   Playground would benefit from improvements or additions
Fully Met: 3   Playground provides a significant amount of experiences that meet criteria

_____ The playground is highly multisensory—sight, sound, texture, temperature, movement, and aromas.
_____ It has an emphasis on nature and vegetation, including a garden or planting area.
_____ There are several types of surfaces and terrains.
_____ Provisions are made for shade if trees are absent or insufficient.
_____ A variety of spaces are available for different types of activities.
_____ There are places for refuge and contemplation.
_____ The materials and resources are age-appropriate.
_____ Many loose parts are available.
_____ Materials and space are flexible and responsive to what children choose to do.
_____ There are enough play spaces that children have many choices about what to do.
_____ The playground is familiar and easy for children to use independently.
_____ Transitions between inside and outside are orderly.
_____ Adults are comfortable and fully engaged with children.
_____ There is evidence of correlation with the curriculum.
_____ Storage is conveniently available for items to be rotated.
_____ Extra clothing is available for children who get muddy or wet or who need a jacket or sweater.
_____ A policy is in place and communicated to families regarding the weather's impact on outdoor time.
_____ The need for dressing children appropriately for outdoor play is communicated to families.
_____ Water is provided for children.

Goodheart-Willcox Publisher

Figure 13-22 This chart identifies ways to assess a playground to determine if improvements need to be made. *Why is assessment for playgounds an important process?*

✓ CHECKPOINT

1. What are some ways to ensure safety is assessed?
2. Why is it important to evaluate your playground for program quality?
3. How might you plan for needed improvements?

13.7 Family Matters

Memories of being outdoors as a child often include family experiences, as described in the Discovery Journeys feature "Fishing with My Father."

When families understand the value of outdoor time, they are less likely to be concerned about children getting dirty or soiling clothing. They are more apt to accommodate requests to provide extra clothes and dress children appropriately for the weather. Consider sending a newsletter like the one in **Figure 13.23** to families. Informing them of the program policy about outdoor play during enrollment can prevent misunderstandings later.

Dear Families,
Children need time outdoors. Inadequate time outdoors is affecting children in many ways. Those effects include hindrances to overall physical development, stamina, and strength. Obesity and resulting health problems, as well as missed opportunities to experience the benefits of nature, result from inadequate active play outside.

Each year we create a school garden with your help where children plant and care for vegetables and flowers, benefiting from experience in plant cultivation and growth. We allow the children to prepare and serve the items we grow as a part of our curriculum on healthy food.

Therefore, our program includes active outdoor time whenever weather permits. We ask that you dress children accordingly so they can fully participate in this important part of our curriculum. Appropriate clothing requires consideration of the weather and understanding that children will get dirty or wet at times. Why do we believe outdoor time is important for children? Here are some of the reasons:

When children play outdoors, they:
- use large muscles and increase their motor skills.
- develop a habit of being physically active.
- increase their overall health.
- develop overall coordination and physical skills.
- practice safety and caution.
- experience joy in achieving a skill.
- learn to take turns and share equipment.
- investigate and develop their curiosity in the world around them.
- grow in sensory awareness and appreciation of the beauty and order of nature.
- enjoy conversing with friends, building language skills.
- cooperate on projects such as constructing an obstacle course.

When children play in sand and water, they:
- find the materials relaxing and soothing.
- can relax with these materials and center their attention on a task.
- have an opportunity to play alone or with a few friends.
- learn about measuring.
- learn about pouring, measuring, and comparing quantities.

When children participate in gardening, they:
- begin to value how individuals can grow food.
- build skills and knowledge about how to grow and prepare healthy food.
- work on a project with others for a mutual goal.
- enjoy the sensory experience of working in the soil.
- see the results of their work and effort.
- enjoy preparing and eating the food they have been responsible for growing.

Thank you, as always!

Mr. Shay

Goodheart-Willcox Publisher; (illustration) 360 Production/Shutterstock.com

Figure 13-23 This family newsletter provides information about outdoor benefits, policies, and practices. *How does family communication and involvement support the outdoor part of your program?*

Discovery Journeys

Fishing with My Father

Dr. Sandra Duncan, noted author of The Honeycomb Hypothesis: How Infants, Toddlers and Two-Year-Olds Learn Through Nature Play *and consultant on numerous early childhood topics, shares her reminiscence of a favorite activity with her father.*

My dad was an avid fisherman. He liked to fish in all types of waters (oceans, lakes, ponds, rivers) for many kinds of fish. His favorite place, however, was a small freshwater lake in Michigan, where he fished for bluegills. My favorite place, as a young child, was right next to him, sitting on an oftentimes cold seat in a teeny-tiny, metal boat that once belonged to his father. Fishing with my dad was always something I considered an adventure.

We would get up early—sometimes even before sunrise—because my dad would tell me that the early bird gets the worm. I am not sure if I understood exactly what that phrase meant as a young child, but it didn't really matter. What mattered was that I was going to be with my dad for an entire day of fun and fishing on the lake. Off we would go in the old Woody station wagon, bouncing along the dirt road with the tiny boat strapped to the car's roof. Packed in the backseat of the Woody were our fishing gear, tackle, worms, and a net just in case we got lucky and managed to snag a "big one." The old wicker picnic basket, which had long seen good days, was filled with mommy-made provisions such as yummy PB&Js, homemade molasses cookies, and freshly squeezed lemonade stored in a huge Army-green thermos.

Once we got to our destination, my dad would lift off the small boat from the car's roof and drag it to the lake's edge, where he attached an outboard engine, which seemed no bigger than a postage stamp. I helped him load our gear and provisions—and away we would putt-putt to our special fishing hole. The hole was just off the far shore, straight out from the big weeping willow tree with the "V" trunk. I loved the challenge of throwing my line in the right spot, which was located right before the lily pads. It was exciting to feel that first tug on the line and watch the red and white plastic bobber duck below the waterline.

My dad told me all about the secret to catching fish. It was to watch for ripples to form around the plastic bobber, and this was the precursor to a fish bite. He taught me how to bait and take a fish off the hook, and even how to fry up the day's catch in a big cast iron skillet over an open campfire. But, in those long-ago days of fishing with my dad, I think he taught me far more lessons than just how to watch the red and white plastic bobber. In those special fishing moments, he taught me important lessons about the ways of life.

One life lesson my dad taught me was that patience doesn't always work. With fishing, you can sometimes wait…wait…and wait until your eyes cross, but your patience doesn't always reward you with a fish. And that's a good lesson. Even great work doesn't aways have a reward at the end of the day. Sometimes you can give your best effort and still not get the results you were hoping for. With age, I have come to realize that your best efforts are oftentimes rewarded on more of a personal and internal level rather than with confetti and cheers from others.

Another life lesson that fishing for bluegills taught me is to keep my eye on the goal (or, in this case, the bobber). When you take your eye off the bobber for a mere second, you might not see the ripples and, consequently, will not know the precise moment of when to jerk up the pole to catch the fish. I learned that life presents many opportunities; we just need to know when and how to look for them.

Consider This
1. What is it about being outdoors with family members that create lifelong memories?
2. How can we encourage families to share experiences in nature?
3. What memories do you have of your own outdoor time as a child?

✓ CHECKPOINT

1. Why is an outdoor policy important for a program?
2. What are the benefits from communicating the policy to families?
3. What are the factors to consider in deciding whether to go outdoors?

Chapter 13 Review and Assessment

Chapter Summary

13.1 **Describe why outdoor play is important for young children.**
- Nature deficit refers to a lack of experience with nature and has been linked to several negative consequences.
- Time outdoors in nature has been shown to have many positive effects on children.
- The playground can offer an expansion of the indoors while providing a level of physical activity that is not generally desirable indoors.
- Outdoor time in early learning programs can provide opportunities for young children to incorporate experiences in all developmental domains.
- Early learning programs can design their curriculum to include outdoor experiences.

13.2 **Identify what equipment and materials should be provided to support social, physical, emotional, and cognitive development.**
- The play options are expanded when there is variety in equipment, with loose parts supplementing permanently installed equipment.
- Loose parts are inexpensive ways to enrich the playground and ensure enough play spaces so that children always have choices about what they want to do.
- Although children will usually have their own ideas, the teacher can encourage diverse activities through suggestions and the materials that are made available.
- Many dramatic play possibilities occur with wheeled toys and props that relate to occupations that require transportation.
- Storage is important for a playground for maintaining equipment and providing variety.

13.3 **Explain how to integrate outdoor time with other curriculum areas.**
- Activities can correlate with curriculum themes and expand on ways to reinforce concepts and skills.
- Dramatic play outdoors can include dress up and other dramatic play activities.
- Music and movement on the playground can be as easy as dancing to music provided with any portable device.
- Many art activities can take place outdoors and can be easier to clean up.
- Sand and water play are engaging experiences. There are many variations for water play.
- Outdoors includes opportunities to experience the science of weather, plants, and other natural phenomena. Math opportunities can be provided through classification and other experiences.
- Wooden blocks will need to be transported since they can't be left outdoors. Larger blocks including crates and planks can be used outdoors.
- Reading books aloud outdoors can provide literacy experiences and suggest ideas to incorporate into play.
- The design and landscape of the playground will contribute to its success, convenience, and effectiveness. Various terrains and surfaces add interest and challenge.
- Defined areas provide zones for different types of activities and can control traffic flow and spacing.

13.4 **Describe the role of the teacher in maximizing outdoor experiences.**
- Adequate supervision is the major factor in safety.
- A zone system of supervision is useful in designating responsibilities for adults.
- Fences should be too high for climbing and have gates that children cannot open.
- Programs should have a policy addressing their outdoor procedures and a plan for meeting children's needs outside.
- The teacher is responsible for the upkeep and safety of the playground and should be on the lookout for hazards.
- Equipment should be appropriate for the age of the children using it, checked regularly, and supervised.
- Teaching children how to safely use equipment and guiding their behavior are important tasks.

- Signals or choices can help children cooperate with ending outdoor time.

13.5 Identify ways to provide outdoor time for infants and toddlers.
- Even infants and toddlers need time outdoors in an environment that addresses their needs.
- Special activities can be planned for outdoors, and many indoor activities can take place outside.
- The outdoors can be rich in sensory experiences for infants and toddlers.
- Shade and a separate space are desirable for infants and toddlers.
- Many outdoor activities can develop gross- and fine motor skills in infants and toddlers.

13.6 Describe one way to assess the outdoor environment for ongoing improvement.
- Checklists are useful tools for the assessment of outdoor environments.
- Assessment of the outdoor component of the program can help ensure safety and maintain or improve the quality of the playground and its role in the curriculum.
- Assessment helps keep the program dynamic and interesting for children.

13.7 Explain why and how to communicate with families about the benefits of outdoor time.
- Programs need to communicate the importance of outdoor time and help families understand the benefits.
- Families' cooperation is needed in dressing children appropriately and in following guidelines.
- The program will benefit from family involvement in such activities as planting a garden.

Recall and Application

1. Nature deficit refers to ____.
   A. climate change
   B. lack of time spent in nature
   C. the greenhouse effect
   D. urban areas that have fewer parks
2. **True or False.** Outdoor time is important because children need a break from learning.
3. **True or False.** Today, most children have plenty of time to play outdoors.
4. **True or False.** Outdoor play is important because children often do not get enough exercise.
5. **True or False.** Indoor activities can be expanded to the outdoors.
6. **True or False.** The playground should be planned entirely with a focus on group activities.
7. **True or False.** Playgrounds should include a variety of textures and surfaces.
8. Which of the following is *not* a key to effective use of space?
   A. Layout
   B. Space for movement
   C. Storage
   D. Extra fluorescent lighting
9. **True or False.** Only equipment purchased from reliable vendors should be on the playground to ensure that it is safe.
10. **True or False.** If you do not have equipment on your playground, you cannot have outdoor playtime.
11. **True or False.** Certain activities are best done outside because they are noisy or require more space.
12. The most important safety feature on the playground is ____.
    A. alert adults
    B. helmets
    C. foam flooring
    D. shade
13. **True or False.** Playgrounds should be checked regularly for safety hazards.
14. **True or False.** One good thing about outdoor time is that it does not have to be planned.
15. **True or False.** Infants and toddlers should not go outside because they might get sick or pick up things and put them in their mouths.
16. **True or False.** It is important that playground surfaces all be the same level.
17. **True or False.** If a playground is safe, there is nothing else to be assessed.
18. **True or False.** Checklists are one way to evaluate a playground.
19. **True or False.** Policies related to outdoor time need not be distributed to families.
20. **True or False.** Early childhood teachers can involve families in a number of ways regarding their children's outdoor time.

Part 4 Achieving Your Goals

Chapter 14: We All Belong: Becoming a Professional

Chapter 14

We All Belong: Becoming a Professional

Standards Covered in This Chapter

NAEYC

NAEYC—6a, 6b, 6c, 6d, 6e

DAP

DAP—6

Learning Outcomes

After reading this chapter, you should be able to:

14.1 Determine if a career in early childhood eductaion is the right choice for you.

14.2 Describe at least five ways that early childhood professionals commit to providing a safe and nurturing environment for young children.

14.3 Describe the role of professional organizations in early childhood education.

14.4 Define the issues of equity and equality.

14.5 Identify strategies for caring for oneself as a professional.

14.6 Explain how people use assessment in their daily lives.

14.7 Identify early childhood professionals' responsibilities to families.

Chapter opener image credit: kali9/E+ via Getty Images

Key Terms

accountability
advocacy
equity
ethics
universal precautions

Introduction

Many people focus on clothes or external factors when defining professionalism. Much of what is seen on the outside reflects what is felt within. How people dress may vary by career field, but how people see themselves and how they act is what will cause others to view them as professionals.

Most professions have standards that define them and are required to maintain employment for quality practice. These standards include:
- individual qualifications of education and experience.
- rules of conduct, such as a code of ethics.
- accountability requirements, such as continuing education, evaluation, research, and licensing.
- professional organizations that provide guidance and resources for best practices, such as establishing quality standards and systems for recognition of quality.

Professionalism is a way of respecting the dignity, worth, and uniqueness of each individual child, family member, and colleague. It is a way to assist children and adults in achieving their full potential in the context of relationships based on trust, respect, and positive regard.

How teachers act will determine how the community views them and why it is essential that the public recognizes the importance of the work that teachers do. This chapter will look closely at what constitutes a professional. The following are some characteristics that early childhood education professionals embody:
- **Always learning:** seeks to improve skills and increase knowledge by attending conferences and trainings, reading, reflecting on experiences, and evaluating success to stay abreast of new requirements and standards in the field; maintains a personal library or has access to resources related to child development and children's learning
- **Exceeds minimum standards:** has a formal certification or credential, such as a Child Development Associate (CDA®), and works to advance in a career.
- **Respects confidentiality:** does not discuss information concerning children and families except as defined by the *NAEYC Code of Ethical Conduct*; does not participate in gossip or other activities detrimental to colleagues and programs
- **Makes decisions based on knowledge and research:** considers facts, rather than conjecture, asks questions, gathers information, and consults with authorities when a decision must be made concerning a child or family situation
- **Displays responsible behavior:** arrives at work prepared and on time, completes required tasks, meets work expectations, and participates in activities of the organization
- **Acts ethically and respectably:** conducts oneself at work and outside of work in a manner that generates a good reputation and respect
- **Represented by professional organizations:** keeps up with and participates in the activities of professional organizations, such as the following:
  - National Association for the Education of Young Children (NAEYC)
  - Southern Early Childhood Association (SECA)
  - National Association of Family Child Care (NAFCC)
  - National Head Start Association (NHSA)
- **Service to the field:** serves the profession by contributing through activities that help to increase the quality of services, such as:
  - mentoring—helping train a new teacher through an on-site practicum
  - presenting at conferences—both local and national events
  - participating in leadership roles of professional organizations or their affiliates

Case Study

First, Do No Harm

As a profession with a great impact on the lives and well-being of children, leaders in the early childhood education field have applied the following principle, based on the medical profession's Hippocratic Oath (NAEYC 2016).

"Above all, we shall not harm children. We shall not participate in practices that are emotionally damaging, physically harmful, disrespectful, degrading, dangerous, exploitative, or intimidating to children."

Advocates seeking to reduce stress on young children from inappropriate testing, unrealistic expectations, and ill-advised practices not based on what is known about child development and how young children learn use the phrase to signify that early childhood professionals should avoid any practices known to be harmful to children. For example, discrimination or a lack of equal access to quality programs are harmful. Making decisions involving children without sufficient knowledge or facts, or without including appropriate individuals in the decision-making process, can be harmful.

If early childhood professionals are aware of harmful situations or the potential for harm, they must act to make changes. The importance of knowledge of child development in this field—and the critical role that such knowledge plays—means that early childhood professionals are in a position of responsibility.

Consider This
1. Why is precedence placed on the "do no harm" principle above all others?
2. How might this principle apply to your work with young children?
3. How might one avoid practices that could be harmful to children?

14.1 Is This Profession for You?

Early childhood can be a career choice with options for employment or a career stepping stone. Why are you considering working in the early childhood field? Do you want to make it a career, or do you aspire to some other area of employment? How passionate are you about children? What brings you satisfaction in your daily life? Here are some questions to ask yourself to assess your potential success in this field:
- Do you like being with children (**Figure 14.1**)?
- Do you enjoy interacting and conversing with children?

kali9/E+ via Getty Images

Figure 14-1 This third-grade teacher enjoys a humorous video with her class. How might a sense of humor be an asset in working with young children?

- Are you interested in learning about child growth and development?
- Are you working in early childhood eductaion while you pursue other studies such as a career in art or music or a degree in another field?
- Do you think of a job in this field as a version of babysitting?
- Do you show up and do your required tasks, or do you go beyond that and think about projects, look for books, or get excited about activities to share with children?
- Is a large pine cone a treasure to be collected for the science table or something that you step over on a hike?
- Do you enjoy sharing picture books with children, and do you have favorites you like to read aloud (**Figure 14.2**)?

When accepting a position in early childhood education, one's answers to these questions will reflect one's professionalism. Even if your reason for working with young children does not begin as a career choice, it may become one as you find the work meaningful and rewarding. Regardless of how one enters the field of early childhood education, advanced training and obtaining a certification or degree are important steps in having the skills and knowledge to do the best for children. Either way, education and ongoing skill development are linked to one's professionalism in the early childhood education field.

One usually thinks of being a teacher as the main role in early childhood education. Indeed, it is the most common role, but there are many other opportunities for working with children that can lead to a satisfying career. Most states have a type of career ladder of job responsibilities and requirements for people working as teachers in early childhood programs. The following sections review some of these options and requirements.

Career Options

Early childhood education employment opportunities range from direct care as home and center-based caregivers to college-level training and faculty positions to government-level administrative positions. The career path is not a typical ladder-type, where one moves upward from an entry-level position through the ranks to administration within a similar field.

FatCamera/E+ via Getty Images

Figure 14-2 A teaching intern shares a story with two 3-year-olds. Why is the ability to interact and communicate with children an important skill for prospective teachers?

Because many jobs in early childhood education are often within small programs, the typical hierarchy of job advancement is often impractical. The more common career ladder for those in early childhood education has been one where one moves from one setting to another as job opportunities become available. This system, unfortunately, has created high turnover in an area that needs stability. However, developments in the field have created a growing recognition of the need for individual programs to create career paths in their position structure. As the field seeks to reduce turnover and improve employment stability, directors are finding ways to offer career progression within their individual centers. They do this by establishing levels of employment, such as an entry-level teacher aide, a teacher, and a lead teacher with various responsibilities, and rates of pay as employees receive more training and experience. See **Figure 14.3** for an example of a typical progression in an early childhood education career based on education and training.

In addition to a career progression as a teacher or an administrator, there are numerous other possibilities for one with a degree or credential in early childhood education. See **Figure 14.4** for some of the possibilities.

These are some of the many career options in early childhood education. Some require advanced education or specialized training, while others require skills beyond teaching. Some of these career options are entrepreneurial in nature and require strong business expertise.

Many consider careers in early childhood education more of a career lattice than a ladder, since one can start at any level and advance based on education and achievement following employment. Increasingly, states are working to make it easy to move from one level to another through various incentives, such as scholarships and low- or no-cost training opportunities.

Job Requirements

Early childhood education in many states is a profession in progress. Although there are no mandated standards that apply to all people employed in programs for young children, educational requirements are becoming increasingly essential to enter the field.

Though requirements vary, experience does factor into many early childhood positions. Sometimes, experience is a substitute for more formal training. For instance, a person who has operated their own family child care business for many years may enter a program as a head teacher, even if they work toward a credential.

Possible Progression of a Career in Early Childhood Education

Position	Description
Classroom assistant or aide, beginning teacher	• Meets state licensing requirements with on-the-job training or clock-hour training
Head or lead teacher	• Child Development Associate (CDA®) credential™ • Two-year degree or diploma • College or technical school diploma or degree • State ancillary certificate • Specialized training (Montessori or HighScope)
Master teacher	• Specialized training or college credits • Two- or four-year college degree • Master's degree • Doctorate degree
Child care administration	• Specialized training (director's management or administration certificate or credential) • Two- or four-year college degree • Master's degree • Doctorate degree

Goodheart-Willcox Publisher

Figure 14-3 This chart shows a career progression for one early childhood education program. *Why is the ability to advance an important factor in making a career decision?*

Additional Career Paths in Early Childhood Education

Position	Description
Family child care provider	• An individual who provides a program of care and education for a small group of children in the provider's home
Specialist teacher or therapist	• Inclusion specialist • Speech or physical therapist • Bilingual specialist • Homeless services
Positions in large or multisite programs	• Specialist or curriculum coordinator • Marketing • Fundraising
College professor/Community college instructors	• Specialized credentials • Master's degree • Doctorate degree
Community-based positions	• Head Start leadership • Children's librarian • Military child care • State and licensing staff • Resource and referral or training agency positions • Children's service agencies (Children's Defense Fund, Child Welfare League of America, YWCA, and YMCA), advocacy or professional organizations, hospital-based Child Life programs
Private consultant	• Designing centers • Setting up new programs • Trainer
Entertainment or educational services	• School supply or book companies • Birthday and other party planning • Children's musician or performer • Commercial programs (Gymboree Play & Music, Mommy and Me, and Kindermusik) • Dancing or other skills instructor

Goodheart-Willcox Publisher

Figure 14-4 This chart identifies additional career options in working with young children. Can you think of other positions where an education in early childhood education, child development, or family and child studies would be desirable?

Continuing Education

Professionalism requires a commitment to continued growth and learning. Most states require a certain number of annual training hours for early childhood education personnel. Employers might also require even more ongoing training and tie their requirements to salary, employment incentives, and advancement, as seen in the military child care model.

The United States military child care system offers an excellent example of advancing "professionalism" through training. In 1989, the average turnover rate for staff employed in military facilities was 48 percent. High staff turnover is linked to low-quality care. Considerable effort went into changing this turnover rate and improving the quality of care being offered. In addition to better funding and standardized pay levels, salary increases became contingent upon the completion of training programs. This shift to a better-prepared workforce was further enhanced by adding curriculum specialists to the staff of each site. The responsibility of the curriculum specialist was to provide ongoing training about child development to teaching staff. Within four years, the staff turnover rate in military child care programs was cut in half, down to 24 percent. Improving quality required improving professionalism. As of the year 2000, 95 percent of military child care Centers (compared with 8 percent of civilian child care centers), had met NAEYC's accreditation standards, a nationally recognized standard of quality. The

Discovery Journeys

A Career Niche

Leslie Sinclair, who was hired in a child care resource and referral program, sent the following email to her employer years after she had moved to another state and assumed the position of director of another resource and referral program. Her note demonstrated to her employer the need for more recognition of the job prospects that a formal education in early childhood can offer. Here is her email:

"When you and I first met, I'd never heard of this early childhood niche career. Now this is my life's work. I appreciate all of the opportunities you have given me. As you can see, I am putting some of those skills to good use—or at least I try.

Your support of my application to the National Association of Child Care Resource & Referral Agencies (NACCRRA) Leadership Program put me in touch with people and projects I would not have known about otherwise. I've served on their membership committee and a couple of conference committees and continue to attend the symposium and see colleagues from that program. Surprisingly, most are still in the field. The connections I've made and the social aspect of the field add a valuable dimension to the experience. I just thought you should know the impact you had on my career."

Consider This
1. Why do you think that careers in early childhood outside of a classroom are less recognized?
2. How might one find out about options in their area?
3. What are some other jobs where knowledge of child development or education could be helpful?

---

military experience documents improved quality and workforce stability when attention is paid to creating a professional career for employees.

Licensing regulations usually specify a minimum amount of ongoing training. The requirements may cover certain topics, such as recognition of child abuse, basic health and safety, or appropriate guidance techniques. They may also require a number of clock hours of training in topics such as curriculum implementation, developmentally appropriate practices, and working with families. Often, states will provide or contract with organizations to make the training available for free or at an affordable cost.

Individual programs sometimes provide their own in-house training. Larger programs with several sites may hire an education specialist responsible for planning and providing training. In-house retreats and workshops are other means of offering continuing education.

Professional learning community groups are sometimes formed to work together to improve skills. These may be staff at a particular program who meet regularly to discuss topics and share ideas, or a group may consist of people from a variety of programs. Administrators, too, may have group meetings to share mutual concerns.

To learn more about continuing education requirements in your area, use the questions in **Figure 14.5** as a basis for inquiry.

Rules of Conduct

In addition to education and credentials, another aspect of professionalism is adherence to certain rules of conduct. These rules of conduct, which we refer to as ethics, are accepted concepts of appropriate actions related to one's profession or individual responsibilities. The *NAEYC Code of Ethical Conduct* is widely recognized in the early childhood education field. Following it, or some version of an ethical code, is a factor in one's sense of professionalism. The *NAEYC Code of Ethical Conduct* covers such areas as early childhood professionals' obligation to the children and families that they serve, their colleagues, and the profession as a whole.

- What are the continuing education or in-service requirements for early childhood professionals in your state?
- Does your employer or do employers in your area have annual educational requirements?
- Are these requirements based on "clock hour" training or achieving credentials?
- Why is it important to participate in those programs?
- What is available at your workplace or potential worksites?
- What community resources are available for increasing knowledge and skills in early childhood?

Goodheart-Willcox Publisher

Figure 14-5 Questions to ask about training and education requirements in your state. How does ongoing professional development enable one to be effective?

A code of ethics provides a guide for behavior and usually includes statements related to confidentiality and relationships. It can serve as a basis for decision-making and the selection of the best course of action in particular situations. A code can set standards of accountability and quality. As such, a code of ethics is an important part of professionalism.

Teaching Tip

Using Your Skills and Knowledge to Make Ethical Decisions

Here are some ethical issues involving the early childhood education field that you may face in your career. Why can situations like these not be good for children? How would you address these situations?

- A teacher in your program always asks the children to sit "Indian style." You feel it is not culturally appropriate because it encourages stereotypes of Native Americans.
- You accept a child with special needs into your group. Some other parents threaten to withdraw their children because they believe the child who is delayed will "hold their children back."
- A former teacher has asked you to provide a reference for a position in another program. You know she does not have the patience to work with young children.
- A child brings in a copy of their favorite book and asks if you can read it to the class. You review the book and find that it reinforces negative racial stereotypes.
- A coworker questions you about some difficulties that your assistant is having.

Accountability

In all professions, there are built-in expectations. Determining if expectations are being met is called **accountability**. Job performance evaluations, center-based evaluations, and regular licensing reviews are examples of accountability. When a problem is recognized through evaluation, specific steps should be taken to address the problem. Improvements may require a change in policy, practices, or environment, or they may highlight the need for additional training or better communication between teachers, between staff and administrators, or with parents.

Accountability within the profession of teaching is often tied to testing and students' scores. Because early childhood professionals work with very young children for whom formal testing is not appropriate, different means of measuring teacher accountability are preferred.

Ongoing Education and Staying Abreast of Research

Up-to-date knowledge of one's field is essential to performing as a professional. Information available changes constantly, and new research provides important data on how to best address the needs of children and families. Early childhood education is a profession that requires updated knowledge and skills, whether about growing concerns about equity, research on brain development, the effects of television and computer use, or new theories about strategies for teaching problem-solving skills. Because work with young children during critical formative years is so important, an early childhood professional's knowledge must be expanded through ongoing professional development.

It is easy to recognize the importance of research in a field such as medicine. New drugs and recommended protocols are constantly being developed. New medical devices are invented that can prolong life. Keeping up-to-date on research in the early childhood education field is necessary in a profession. For example, research on brain development has significantly impacted the field, as has research on the relationship between adult–child interactions and children's learning. Concerns about the amount of screen time have surfaced based on research related to its harmful effects and resulting reductions in human interactions.

Quality Linked to Education

Most research points to teacher–child relationships and a teacher's focused attention to children as key factors in program quality. However, higher education levels of teachers have also been found to be a quality indicator for early learning programs and children's progress.

Requirements for ongoing training hours exist in most states. Early childhood professionals can earn such credits through resource and referral agencies, community or technical college systems, state-approved workshop attendance, and a wide variety of special training seminars. Online training and a variety of alternative training, such as technical assistance, coaching, and mentoring, are becoming increasingly available.

Evaluations

There are many kinds of accountability evaluations. The most common are employee performance reviews. At preset intervals, such as every six months or once a year, each employee is given feedback on job performance. Based on the evaluation, a plan for improvement is agreed upon by the employee and supervisor. For example, a teacher with disruptive group times may be asked to take a workshop on group movement or music activities. Or, for a teacher having difficulty with transitions, a supervisor may suggest a resources or conference session on conducting smooth transitions.

It is important to view employment reviews not just as suggestions for improving areas of difficulty but also as a guideline for building on strengths and learning new skills. For example, a teacher who provides creative art experiences might be asked to share ideas with others at a staff meeting. One means of promoting accountability through training is by tying pay increases or incentives to advanced training and performance. Participation in a minimum number of training hours may be linked to pay increases or even be required for continued employment.

Other types of evaluation include those done by parents about the program or by staff as feedback to administrators. For example, the NAEYC and CDA® credential training program require parent questionnaires as part of the evaluation process. Accreditations set a quality standard for programs, and CDA® is a competency-based credential that documents a recognized level of performance.

Licensing and other regulations provide a type of accountability. Government regulators apply standards in areas such as health, safety, and the environment. Ideally, the creation of governmental standards and policies should have significant input from professionals within the early childhood education field to ensure that developmentally sound and feasible standards are required.

CHECKPOINT

1. How is accountability maintained in early childhood programs?
2. Why is a code of ethics important in any profession?

14.2 The Early Childhood Professional Commitment

In the *NAEYC Code of Ethical Conduct*, under "Principles" in Section I: Ethical Responsibilities to Children, under its first principle reads: "…we shall not harm children. We shall not participate in practices that are emotionally damaging, physically harmful, disrespectful, degrading, dangerous, exploitative, or intimidating, emotionally damaging, or physically harmful to children. This principle has precedence over all others in this Code" (NAEYC 2021).

What does this principle look like in action? Teachers prevent physical harm by paying constant attention to safety. They make sure there are no exposed cords or outlets, and no cups of hot coffee or tea within children's reach. They ensure the floor and play surfaces are clean and well maintained. These are just a few of the everyday signs of this principle in action.

Exploitation of children can be a horrific form of abuse, or it can be less obvious. Are children required to perform at unreasonable levels, such as reading or writing, before developmentally ready? Early academic pressure that excludes play and physical activity can be harmful and exploitive.

Emotional harm may be subtle. Are children encouraged in what they do, or are their efforts discounted and ridiculed? Are they helped to learn appropriate behavior, or are they humiliated by punishment and derogatory language? Consider how the following statements might influence a child's self-confidence:

"Give me that cup. You'll spill the milk."
"Look at the mess you made! You'll just have to clean it up!"
"Stop! You should never do that!"
"Go sit in time-out. You know better than to run inside!"
"How many times do I have to tell you to keep your hands to yourself?"

Each of these statements diminishes a child's self-esteem in some way. Are these statements or similar ones heard in your program?

As an early childhood professional, in what ways do you or your program live out this commitment? What do you do, or will you do, to prevent negative language in your work?

Values and Respect

Respect begins with self-respect. Valuing one's own needs and identity lies at the heart of a "culture of respect." If teachers within a program regard themselves as professionals and act in a respectful manner, the parents will respond to them with the respect they deserve in such an important career.

NAEYC lists several core values at the beginning of its *Code of Ethical Conduct*. One of these core values sums up the idea of a culture of respect as it applies to the early childhood education field. The core value states a commitment to:

Respect the dignity, worth, and uniqueness of each individual (child, family member, and colleague).

Respect should permeate the early childhood education profession (**Figure 14.6**). Because children are at the center of the early childhood education profession, providing respectful environments for children means considering their needs, abilities, and differences, as well as those of their families and of coworkers. Respect for children means attending to their developmental needs: physical, intellectual, emotional, and social. The context of children's needs includes their cultural, economic, or religious experiences.

Respect for families includes these same factors as well as offering opportunities for involvement, communication, and support. This respect is two-way. If staff members

Figure 14-6 A third-grade teacher greets each child respectfully as they enter the classroom. What are other ways teachers show respect for their young charges?

treat parents with respect, it is reasonable to expect that the same respect will be shown by parents to staff members.

Respect for colleagues requires sharing and teamwork. Competition or lack of respect between colleagues as expressed by negative actions such as gossiping, inappropriate comments, or unwillingness to do one's part or work as a team are harmful in an early learning environment.

Respect in early childhood education means going beyond nondiscrimination to actively foster inclusion. Inclusion means communicating respect and appreciation for differences while creating a sense of connection and belonging for all. Feeling good about oneself is the foundation of self-esteem.

Rotary International has a statement recited at the end of each Rotary club meeting that provides a course of action related to its mission of providing service to others, promoting integrity, and advancing world understanding, goodwill, and peace through the fellowship of business, professional, and community leaders. The statement has been paraphrased in a number of ways and can be a useful guide for respect and professionalism. It goes like this:

Of all of the things we think, say, and do,
- Is it the truth?
- Is it fair to all concerned?
- Will it build goodwill and better friendships?
- Will it be beneficial to all concerned?

What Parents See

What will demonstrate to a parent that an atmosphere of professionalism exists in a program? What are outward signs of a program committed to the higher ideals of the early childhood profession?

In the book *Positive Discipline for Preschoolers*, Roslyn Duffy and her co-authors provide a list to help parents when choosing an early learning program. They suggest parents should look for indicators of professionalism in three categories: (1) the physical facility, (2) the staffing, and (3) administration (**Figure 14.7**).

Indicators of a Quality Program

Indicator	Description
The center or home has...	• licenses that are displayed and current. • low rates of staff turnover. • local, state, and/or national accreditation. • a loving, child-centered environment.
The staff is...	• well trained in early childhood development. • working as a team. • staying up-to-date through training programs. • adequately paid.
The administrator...	• walks through the program with a checklist in hand. • looks for areas that need improvement. • make notes about the indications. • demonstrates professionalism.

Goodheart-Willcox Publisher

Figure 14-7 This chart provides an overview of what parents will see related to professionalism. *What other criteria might convey a professional first impression to a visitor?*

Appropriate Dress

How does one balance the need for a professional image with the need to be comfortable and at ease in an environment full of things that spill, stain, and tear? Developing a dress code that covers the unique needs in early childhood settings may be a difficult task. Yet, a neat, well-groomed, and appropriately dressed person will inspire confidence from parents and convey professionalism.

Appearance dramatically affects how a person and an early learning environment will be perceived by parents, students, the community, other child care workers, and prospective clients. Well-groomed employees project confidence and add credibility to the early learning center. Uniforms can provide a sense of organization and create coordinated and united impressions. The clothes one chooses to wear (or not wear) can affect their work attitude and their image.

Bare midriffs, see-through blouses, ripped jeans, too much jewelry, or suggestive logos are not desired. Most programs will not allow short shorts, halter tops, short skirts, and open-toe sandals. Some employees weigh a professional look against a cost-effective and easy-to-care-for wardrobe by wearing pants with a blouse or shirt. Wearing a skirt may not be practical in the up-and-down world of the early childhood classroom. Easy-to-care-for, washable clothing means professionals will not be as concerned if they get paint or other messy materials on it.

Many employees prefer to wear pants in an early childhood setting to slide down the slides or sit in the sandbox with children. A nice blazer or jacket can professionalize a pair of pants and a blouse or shirt for a more professional look when parents are arriving (**Figure 14.8**).

Special teacher aprons or smocks can look professional when kept clean and in good repair. There is an advantage to a program that provides aprons or smocks that identify the employees. If the program uses volunteers or has frequent visitors, such as parents or students, aprons or smocks can help parents know who is an employee and who is not.

Some programs discourage wearing regular T-shirts, particularly those with logos on them, unless the logo is a program logo. However, with fabric paints, appliques, and other decorations, one can do a lot to a simple T-shirt to make it attractive. Also, many programs do not accept sweatpants or sweatshirts.

Some programs develop a general code emphasizing professional dress rather than a specific set of guidelines. In those cases, the director may need to inform a staff member if the attire does not comply. The difficulty is that if the person dresses inappropriately,

Figure 14-8 A teacher waits outside her classroom ready to greet a group of parents for a meeting. *How does adding a blazer to casual attire provide a more professional appearance?*

unless they are asked to change, they will be inappropriately dressed for that day, and others, such as substitutes, may assume it is acceptable.

The bottom line is that if clothes interfere with work or do not inspire confidence from parents, then they are inappropriate. If one cannot get down on the floor without worrying about the consequences of their clothes, bend over without fear of exposure, or sit down next to a child and revel in fingerpainting, then the clothing is inappropriate. Here are some factors to consider when choosing attire for working in an early learning environment:

- the level of professionalism that the clothing portrays
- the different activities of one's day
- the comfort and functionality of the fabric style and fit
- the maintenance required, especially washability
- the cost

Required Continuing Education: The Basics

There are many special qualifications for those who work in the early childhood education field. Some of these are required for employment. Health requirements most often include CPR and first-aid training (**Figure 14.9**). Medication administration, food handling, or sanitation training may be required. Specialized trainings such as universal precautions, emergency response information, or disaster preparedness (such as fire or tornado drills) are other possibilities. For example, tornado drills are required in many states during the months that tornadoes are most apt to happen. State regulations may call for an evacuation plan in the event of electrical outages, floods, or other hazards.

Federal regulations mandate criminal background checks to ensure an employee has not been charged with crimes of violence or abuse. Certain criminal records can affect whether a person could be hired to work with young children. Many states also require training in recognizing the symptoms of abuse and neglect, knowledge of the law, and resources for addressing suspected abuse.

Practicing **universal precautions**, such as the use of plastic gloves when changing diapers or handling body fluids such as blood or vomit, is very important for people in

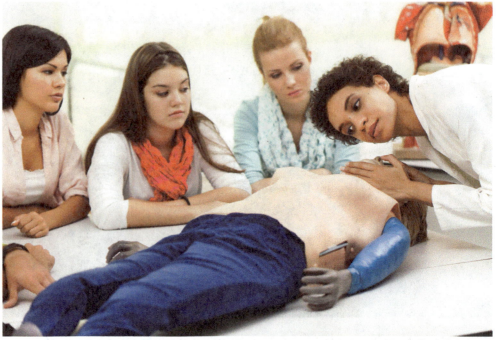

fotostorm/E+ via Getty Images

Figure 14-9 Apprentice teachers are learning CPR to prepare for work with children. What other emergency preparations are required in your state?

the early childhood education field. Because we work with children who may not be potty-trained and get upset tummies and frequent cuts and scrapes, we must know how to prevent the spread of disease and infection through contact transmission.

Monitoring fire safety and physical safety of environments for children is essential. Any emergency when many small children are present could quickly turn into a disaster. Proper safety precautions, such as wheels on cribs so nonwalking infants can be quickly evacuated, are lifesaving. Unprotected stairwells or open and accessible windows may present a danger of falling and must be made secure and safe.

Whatever the requirements, seeing that all employees are trained and can conduct the drills as required is the responsibility of both the administrators and employees. Doing so reflects professionalism.

Accreditation

One sign of professionalism is that of accreditation based on a set of standards that can be applied in different settings. An accredited program has demonstrated that it complies with those standards. Typically, accreditation sets standards that are developed from research and recognized as desirable to achieve a quality level of service. Accreditation differs from individual certification since it is based on program quality, not an individual achievement. It differs from licensing in that accreditation is designed to recognize quality, whereas licensing is a baseline of requirements for operation.

The largest and best-known accreditation for early childhood programs is provided through NAEYC. Over 10,000 programs have achieved NAEYC-accreditation.

NAEYC defines its accreditation as a "process through which early childhood professionals, families, and others concerned about the quality of early childhood education can evaluate programs, compare them with professional standards, strengthen the program, and commit to ongoing evaluation and improvement." NAEYC professional standards are widely accepted as a solid standard by which to evaluate a center's program. They were based on extensive research about what factors constitute quality.

There are other special accreditation and certifications available in the early childhood education field. For instance, programs such as those for Montessori educators, religious denominations, and family child care homes have organizations that offer special accreditation.

✓ CHECKPOINT

1. How does "we shall not harm children" apply to early childhood programs?
2. How is respect demonstrated in the early childhood field?
3. How does an accreditation system impact quality?

14.3 Professional Organizations and Resources

There are many organizations for people serving children and families. The following are some examples:
- Internationally, UNICEF, the World Forum on Early Care and Education, and Save the Children are examples of organizations or programs promoting the welfare of children worldwide.
- On the political level, the Children's Defense Fund has taken on the role of a major lobbying force in advocating for national legislation in support of families, especially those in poverty or most at-risk.
- On both the local and national levels, NAEYC is the acknowledged professional leader in the field of early childhood. This organization provides training, supports and disseminates research, and is at the forefront of early childhood professional development standards.

Consider what may be available in your area by answering the following questions:
- What organizations that are focused on serving children and families are available? Are there regional associations that you could join? Have you joined one, worked in support of the efforts of any early childhood group, or taken part in their activities?
- Do the organizations offer training, publications, and other resources to help you and the families you serve?

Consider making a commitment to join and participate in a professional organization. Such membership and involvement represent an important responsibility shared by all in the early childhood profession. We will now consider **advocacy** as a function of professionalism.

Advocacy

Being a professional means serving as an advocate for children and families, your program, and your profession. This section on advocacy will answer the following three questions: (1) What is advocacy? (2) Why is it important? and (3) How can I get started? We sometimes think of advocacy as a fearful and intimidating task, but at its base is speaking up for one's beliefs. There are many ways a person can be an advocate, even in daily work.

In the *NAEYC Code of Ethical Conduct*, under "Ideals" in Section IV: Ethical Responsibilities to Community and Society, the following ideals are listed:
- "…To work toward greater societal acknowledgement of children's rights and greater social acceptance of responsibility for the well-being of all children."
- "To support policies and laws that promote the well-being of children and families, and to work to change those that impair their well-being."

Both statements articulate a commitment to advocacy for children and their families. To advocate means to plead for or defend the cause of another—in this case, that of children and families. When a person begins to see oneself as an advocate for children and families, they take an important step toward true professionalism and lift themselves and the profession to a higher plane.

From the Field

Lareasa Addison

Early childhood educators know where students need to be developmentally; they are the experts. If children are not meeting their developmental milestones, it is up to the educator to advocate for the child to ensure that their needs are met so they can reach their fullest potential. I advocate for developmentally appropriate practices in my community by educating others on best practices and sharing research that supports best practices. I also seek out resources and partner with other organizations that might aid in implementing best practices.

Lareasa Addison
Assistant Principal at Wood View Elementary School
Valley View School District 365U
Bolingbrook, IL

Lareasa Addison

Figure 14-10

Another important factor in advocacy is taking part in the election process. Voting for candidates who support positions that you favor, voting for issues that you believe in, or voting against proposals that you feel are harmful is another obligation of advocacy. Whether the issue is an organizational or a public service election, an association policy, or a community proposal, taking the time to vote can make a difference in what is available for young children and their families.

Advocacy may seem daunting, but the steps to getting started are fairly simple. First, identify the issue and get the facts. Work with others interested in developing a strategy. What needs to be changed and why? Get to know the people involved and who has the decision-making power to change things.

Discovery Journeys

Rebecca Goes to Kindergarten

Rebecca is a 5-year-old girl with spina bifida. Although legally she is entitled to attend her local public school and be provided an aide, her parents were told that was not the practice in the school district, and she was offered a special class at a school some distance from her neighborhood. Rebecca's father researched the laws and was appalled that the school system had not implemented procedures to serve children in the least restrictive environment, as the law required. His networking with other families and, ultimately, the media resulted in a public forum of parents of children with special needs and top school system administrators.

On the night of the forum, many families described their frustrations with helping their children function in society and the challenges of having only a special class for them. The publicity and acknowledgment that the school system was not in compliance with legal requirements were apparent and brought pressure on the system to comply with the laws. The end result was that Rebecca was successfully enrolled in public school kindergarten with an aide to assist her. Rebecca's father's concern and advocacy for his own child helped numerous other families hold the school system accountable for fulfilling the legal requirements.

Consider This
1. How did the facts about the law help the families' advocacy efforts?
2. Can you think of other situations where one person has made a significant difference in what is available for children?
3. Why was it a good strategy to hold a public forum and include the media?

Professional advocacy means approaching problems in a calm, positive manner with a problem-solving approach. Consider the following scenarios. What would you do in the situations in **Figure 14.11**, **Figure 14.12**, **Figure 14.13**, and **Figure 14.14**?

Scenario 1

Your early childhood program is in a residential neighborhood. A person who is home all day has been complaining to the people on your street about the noise from your playground.

A parent hears about this from a friend and tells you what is happening. "Thank you for clueing us in to the problem. We'll need to think of some ways to become better friends with our neighbors," you tell her.

You come up with several ideas to try: you can send a newsletter to everyone in the area, have a picnic and invite neighbors, invite the neighbors to visit your program, or ask the local paper to do a story on what a good program you have. Some of these ideas may not work, but the process has been started.

Which of these might you try? What other ideas do you have to resolve the issue?

Goodheart-Willcox Publisher

Figure 14-11 Read this scenario. How would you respond? What are some other ways to address the issue?

Scenario 2

A homeowner's association in your city has just ruled that their policy against home businesses will be strictly enforced. This means that no family child care can be in the neighborhood, yet there is a serious shortage of infant care in your community. Parents are dismayed and worried about what this will mean for them. The parents are afraid their dependable and loving providers will not be able to continue caring for their children.

You ask for a few minutes at the next directors' meeting to discuss the issue with your colleagues. You work with others to form a committee that includes several parents and a city administrator. Your goal is to plan strategies to increase the availability of infant care.

What else might you try? What do you do next?

Goodheart-Willcox Publisher

Figure 14-12 Read this scenario. How would you respond? What are some other ways to address the issue?

Scenario 3

A teacher brings in an "English Only" leaflet that is being circulated in your neighborhood. It calls for a petition to do away with all bilingual services in the local school and community. You serve several families for whom English is a second language. You call a meeting with staff and parents to discuss a strategy. A parent suggests an "English Plus" leaflet supporting diversity. Staff and parents take on various responsibilities to work on the leaflet.

What do you do now? What other ideas do you have?

Goodheart-Willcox Publisher

Figure 14-13 Read this scenario. How would you respond? What are some other ways to address the issue?

> **Scenario 4**
> You and several others are asked to attend a public hearing on some proposed licensing changes. One person responds, "I wouldn't waste my time. You know their minds are already made up. They won't listen to us."
>
> Another responds, "I want to read the full proposal first. I hear there are some items that would be very difficult for us to implement. I need to let them know the problems and see what type of compromise might be worked out."
>
> Why is the second response a better example of advocacy and professionalism?

Goodheart-Willcox Publisher

Figure 14-14 Read this scenario. How would you respond? What are some other ways to address the issue?

Advocacy in Action: What Early Childhood Educators Can Do

Early childhood educators can choose from many courses of action once they make a commitment to become advocates for children, their families, and their profession. The following are ways that educators can become advocates:

- Share ideas for appropriate practice with other teachers and parents.
- Explain to administrators why certain practices are inappropriate for young children.
- Write a letter to the editor of a newspaper or magazine to respond to an article or a letter instead of complaining about how people do not understand the needs of children.
- Explain developmentally appropriate practice to parents and describe how children learn best through play rather than complaining that parents are pushing their children.
- Write to your state or federal legislators about a pending issue and share your experiences to point out needs rather than assuming someone else will write.
- Meet someone new who is interested in early childhood and ask them to join a professional group.
- Ask a friend to go with you to a legislator's town hall meeting instead of staying home because you do not want to go alone.
- Volunteer to represent your professional group in a coalition to speak about the educational needs of young children instead of waiting to be asked or declining because you have never done it before.
- Agree to serve on a legislative telephone tree rather than refusing because "my phone call will not matter anyway."
- Work and learn with others to develop a position statement on a critical issue instead of saying, "I don't really know much about this topic."
- Volunteer to speak at a school board meeting about NAEYC's "Guidelines for Developmentally Appropriate Practice in Action: Using Knowledge of Child Development and Learning in Context" position statement instead of resigning yourself to the idea that your school system does not understand much about early childhood education.
- Call or email your legislator on issues that matter to you. You know what young children need.
- Post information on social media about the needs of young children and appropriate practices.
- Provide materials to parents about screen time issues.

Teaching Tip

Roles Early Childhood Professionals Play
Early childhood professionals:
- establish cooperative relationships.
- use community resources.
- manage efficiently.
- organize space and materials.
- plan for daily activities.
- keep records.
- have a healthy attitude about power.
- keep confidences.
- protect children.
- provide good, quality care.
- respect parents' authority.
- support diversity and equity.
- improve themselves professionally.
- learn more about their profession.
- stand up for good programs and services for children and families.
- advocate for their profession.

Who Is Responsible?

In a profession, it is important to understand the responsibilities of all of those involved. In early childhood education, the responsibilities primarily rest on the program, teachers, and parents.

The Program's Responsibilities
The program has the responsibility to:
- meet all federal, state, local, and program requirements for health, nutrition, safety, emergency preparation, staffing patterns, program operation, and policies such as the release of children only to those designated in writing or the administration of medicine only when authorized by the parent or guardian.
- keep records of income, expenses, licenses, permits, insurance, and all other business and reporting information.
- request parental permission and involvement for developmental screening, photographs, and similar activities.
- discuss with parents the program's goals and objectives for the children's development and openly negotiate any areas of parental concern.
- maintain confidential records of children's development and progress and make these records available to parents and other professionals if authorized by the parents.
- report any suspected indicators of child abuse to the appropriate authorities.
- establish other policies where needed and apply them uniformly among staff, children, and parents (for example, policies about exclusion due to illness or notification of absences).

The Teachers' Responsibilities
Teachers have the responsibility to:
- plan and execute an appropriate curriculum based on the individual needs and interests of each child, considering language, culture, age, abilities, and all pertinent factors.
- ensure the safety and health of the child by following established policies and best practices.
- see that each child's needs are met while they are in the program.

- obtain parent permission whenever the child leaves the program premises during operating hours, such as on field trips.
- communicate with parents regarding a child's progress and needs.
- communicate with parents, if possible, in the language most comfortable for them.
- work with others as needed to implement intervention plans.

The Parents' Responsibilities:
Parents have the responsibility to:
- agree to follow all program policies.
- pay deposits and established fees for services as stated in the program's policies.
- provide any information about their child or the family that may affect decisions about the child.
- discuss any areas of concern with the appropriate staff member(s).
- work in cooperation with the staff to address any problems that occur.
- be involved with the staff, when possible, by volunteering or serving on policy boards or committees.

Although responsibilities may vary by programs or be assigned to different positions, the responsibilities described are components of a well-functioning, professional environment. In addition to knowledge of child development and education, there are other skills necessary for a career. We will now look at other important skills for one's success in the field.

Ancillary Skills for the Early Childhood Workforce

New performance standards and advanced technologies have changed the education requirements for the workforce of today. Skills that once were only needed by management personnel are now required of all workers. These new skills can be categorized as shown in **Figure 14.15**. How many of these skills do you possess? How are they relevant to work in the early childhood field?

These changes mean that the ways of working with children and the skills childhood professionals have typically focused on may need to change. Reflect on your life or work during the last few years. For each skill, think of a way you can improve yourself in that area. Then answer the following questions:
- How has technology changed the way you perform tasks?
- What changes have you seen in the skills you need to fulfill your responsibilities at work?
- What new skills have you had to learn to meet work responsibilities?

Academic Basics
- Reading
- Writing
- Computation

Adaptability Skills
- Learning how to learn
- Creative thinking
- Problem solving

Self-Management Skills
- Self-esteem
- Goal setting
- Motivation
- Dependability

Social Skills
- Interpersonal negotiation
- Teamwork

Communication Skills
- Listening
- Oral and written communication

Influential Skills
- Organizational effectiveness
- Leadership

Goodheart-Willcox Publisher

Figure 14-15 This chart includes ancillary skills important for working in an early childhood learning environment. *Can you think of other skills that would be helpful to anyone working in the early childhood field?*

Communication

The ability to communicate with children, coworkers, and families is an important skill for anyone who works in the field of early childhood education. Making positive changes or improving communication may often be necessary in your work. You will often be faced with the need to make on-the-spot decisions about how to best respond to situations that occur. It helps to think ahead and plan how you will handle them. Here are some typical examples of situations you may encounter that require good communication skills. What would you say in each of these situations to address them in a professional manner?

- A child gets wet playing in the water area, and you discover there are no extra clothes in her cubby. You look around and see other cubbies with few or no extra clothes as well.
    - Why might parents not be complying with your extra clothing policy?
    - What should you do about it?
- You sent permission slips for a neighborhood walk to parents about two weeks ago, but you have only seven of the ten permission slips that you need.
    - Why have so few been returned?
    - What should you do about it?
- In your newsletter, you ask families to provide healthy snacks for holiday treats. The first three holidays after your notice are all celebrated with iced cupcakes or cake and Kool-Aid or soda.
    - Why do you think families ignored your request?
    - How can you get families to plan more nutritious snacks?
- Your director gets a phone call from the local television station about staff qualifications for early childhood programs. They would like to interview her. She agrees and suggests they use your room as the setting.
    - Why do you think the director accepted the invitation for an interview?
    - What would you suggest that she say to the reporter?
    - What important information should she share with parents about quality?

☑ CHECKPOINT

1. What are the benefits of professional organizations in your area?
2. Have you ever talked to someone or taken an action that would be considered advocacy?
3. Why is advocacy important in the early childhood field?

14.4 Equity and Equality

One of the roles of a professional organization is to research and analyze issues and promote change to address those issues. Professional organizations often develop and issue position statements as an official stand on behalf of the organization. One such position statement issued by NAEYC is "Advancing Equity in Early Childhood Education." This document is based on extensive research into the imbalance of opportunities resulting from bias, background, or family status.

It is easy to confuse equality and equity, and indeed, there are similarities. However, important differences exist (**Figure 14.16**). Equality implies that resources are equally available; every child has access to a free public education at a specified age to learn academic skills. **Equity** connotes that resources are available as needed to achieve the identified goals of learning necessary academic skills. But does the availability of equality in public school admission lead to the goal of academic progress if the child is not provided a stable home, adequate nutrition, and the emotional support needed in order to be at ease in the school setting? Children come from a variety of circumstances and

Figure 14-16 Equality versus equity. *How does this illustration communicate the differences between these two concepts?*

have different strengths and needs, so distributing resources equally does not ensure all children have an equal opportunity to succeed.

Consider a child learning English as a second language who is struggling with reading in a mainly unfamiliar language. Allowing extra time to complete reading assignments would be equity because his situation has created not only a need to reach the goal of reading but also the need for the extra resource of time to reach that goal. The opportunities and the goal are equality; the extra time is equity.

Why is equity important in early childhood education? One increasing concern in the field is the need for all children to have access to quality early childhood programs, regardless of family situation. We have known the value of early childhood education for decades, yet it is still not realistically available to all. Children who start ahead tend to stay ahead, and those who start behind may stay behind.

The opportunity gaps begin before school. Not all children enter equally prepared. Children from low-income families are often already behind on language and other skills compared to peers from higher-income families. Addressing those inequities that young children face can help prevent the gaps from widening.

In an equitable system, each child gets what they need to reach their potential. If we believe that all children have the right to experiences that help them become valued members of society, then we have a professional obligation to speak up for equity.

In action, this means making sure we are using assessment strategies that authentically tell us what we need to know about a child's strengths and needs. It means planning for children as individuals, rather than planning for everyone to do the same thing. Differentiated instruction techniques enable teachers to customize lessons according to students' individual situations while still providing them with an equal chance of succeeding in the classroom environment. In early childhood, the use of learning centers is one way to provide for meeting individual needs.

☑ CHECKPOINT

1. Can you recall a situation where everyone got the same thing, but it wasn't what everyone needed?
2. How does the concept of fairness apply to equality and equity?

14.5 Taking Care of Yourself as a Professional

The day-to-day stress experienced by children and the adults responsible for them can be a challenge. The need for caring adults to listen, interpret, and explain events in appropriate and comforting ways is a challenge in our society today. Family arguments, financial stress, scheduling hassles, adult depression, violence, substance abuse, and even world events bombard us with stress. Young children's expressive language regarding their experiences may be limited. Stressful experiences may result in bad dreams, drawings, tears, tantrums, bedwetting, regression, or other behaviors. As a professional, one must learn to cope with the stress of both children and one's self.

When the preflight safety announcements are made on airlines, passengers are warned to secure their own oxygen mask before assisting others. Like those passengers, one must take care of one's own needs to be able to care for others. As professionals, we must first take care of ourselves. The constant presence of stress hormones begins to wear down the body's immunological system. Some or all of the following may occur when you are stressed:

- Your heartbeat increases to pump blood throughout the necessary tissues faster, carrying oxygen and nutrients to cells and clearing away waste products more quickly.
- As your heart rate increases, your blood pressure rises.
- Breathing may become rapid and shallow.
- Adrenaline and other hormones are released into the blood.
- Your pupils dilate to let in more light; all of your senses are heightened.
- Muscles tense for movement, either for flight or protective actions.
- Blood flow is constricted to the digestive organs and extremities and increased to the brain and major muscles.
- The body perspires to cool itself since increased metabolism generates more heat.

Stress response is appropriate if you are confronted by some threat to your life. However, most often in our society, stress results from a situation that is not life-threatening. Emotions, ideas, memories, and expectations can trigger stress. The effects of stress may be reduced or eliminated if one learns to rest the mind and body with deep breathing techniques and other strategies that reduce or even prevent many stress-related problems.

Stress affects not only our physical and emotional health but also those around us, especially our children. Young children can sense emotions. If we are happy and content with ourselves, our children become more relaxed and happier as well.

There are many stresses in our lives. We are the caretakers of not only our children, but also our spouses, parents, jobs, churches, and communities; in many respects, we are the primary caretakers of society. You need not give up all of your responsibilities to reduce stress, but you do need to recognize what things tend to "push your stress button" and learn to manage those areas of your life. You cannot control physical events, such as the sickness of a loved one, but you can control how you respond to those events.

Managing stress means coping with whatever life throws your way and not crumbling under the weight of the situation. You will find yourself constantly facing new challenges. Whether a child has the flu, a scrapped knee, or a tantrum, you will be faced with stress. If you learn how to manage your response to stress, then you will be able to enjoy more of the time with children and not fall apart whenever your day does not go according to your expectations.

There are ways to manage stress listed in **Figure 14.17**. Experiment to find what works best for you. Some people love yoga; others do not. Look at your interests to decide the best approach for stress reduction.

The nightly news reminds us frequently of the fragility of the human spirit but also of its potential to heal. Stress-management strategies and techniques are as essential to your own health as regular exercise, good nutrition, satisfying work, recreation, and close relationships.

Relaxation techniques	Hobbies and other interests	Support systems
Good nutrition	Journaling	Time with friends
Exercise	Play	

Goodheart-Willcox Publisher

Figure 14-17 This chart includes common methods for addressing stress. Which of these methods would you use?

> ### Teaching Tip
>
> **Eight Tips to Reduce Childhood Stress**
> 1. Daily quiet time alone without interruptions can be sacred.
> 2. Share some of your own successes with small stressful moments to demonstrate that everyone experiences and copes with stress. (For example, "Today I was frustrated with the traffic delays, so I thought about what fun we would have today. It cheered me up!")
> 3. Be ready to listen without judgment. Sometimes the open sharing and acceptance of concerns have a way of dissipating them.
> 4. Encourage drawing, artwork, and physical activities, which are healthy ways to discharge anxiety.
> 5. Monitor and restrict children's television, movie, and internet exposure. Psychological safety is as much your responsibility as fire prevention.
> 6. Look for good books to open up on subjects that children might need to talk about.
> 7. Remember how intuitive children are and that even when you think they do not understand the stress in others, they are sensing tension.
> 8. Give children language to communicate fears, questions, and secret wishes. Many skilled professionals, seminars, articles, and books can offer manageable strategies for preventing, assessing, and relieving stress in children.

Strategies for Stress Reduction

As changes in society put more stress on adults, there is an increased need to cope with those stresses and avoid creating a chaotic environment that can impact children's lives and their ability to function. We will look at popular strategies that are easy and inexpensive to implement.

Meditation

Meditation is a way to quiet the mind and relax. It not only calms your mind but also relaxes your muscles and energizes your body. Meditation can help you feel more rested. Books and videos are available to teach you how to meditate.

There is no set length of time you should meditate—choose whatever time is available and benefits you. You may find it easier to begin with short meditations and gradually increase the time. A few well-focused minutes of quietness can be effective.

Meditating may be difficult in the beginning. It is hard to sit quietly with yourself if you have never done so. Try starting your day with meditation before you get busy. Sit on the edge of your bed and do the meditation selected. Do this every morning for a week and see if you start your day feeling calmer than before.

Journaling

Writing down your thoughts can be a powerful way to deal with feelings. It can help focus attention and provide a creative outlet. Seeing your thoughts on paper often clarifies what things make you stressed and helps you identify ways to reduce the effect that the situations have on you. Journaling reduces stress by giving you a tool to channel your thoughts and feelings.

All you need is a spiral notebook. The point of writing down your thoughts is for you to be completely honest. These are your private thoughts. By putting your thoughts on paper, you can work with them more effectively.

What should you write in your journal? Simply put, anything you want. You may choose to address a weekly topic or whatever is of concern to you. It is more about writing down whatever comes to your mind than following a rigid format.

Get Creative

As adults, we often lose that natural sense of creative expression as we take on responsibilities in life: work, family, bills, and so forth. Reconnect with your childhood creative energy and tap into a wonderful stress reducer. Think of an activity you enjoy—crafting, painting, writing stories or poetry, composing music, or dancing. Even gardening, cooking, and decorating all have creative elements. Using your creative energies allows you to focus on something positive, providing you with a much-needed break from your daily routine.

Get involved in activities you like. Turn on some music and dance, plant a flower, bake some cookies—look for creative opportunities.

Yoga

There are several forms of yoga for you to select from—some have religious undertones and others do not—so shop around for a method that suits your goals, interest level, and resources. Yoga involves holding a series of "postures," either sitting or standing (**Figure 14.18**). At its heart, yoga is simply a form of gentle exercise that combines stretching, breathing, and self-reflection. If classes are not available, there are many videos on the Internet that demonstrate yoga techniques.

FreshSplash/E+ via Getty Images

Figure 14-18 A teacher practices yoga, a popular means of reducing stress and building good health. What are some ways yoga can help one fulfill the responsibilities required of early childhood personnel?

Exercise
When you exercise, your brain releases chemicals that make you feel good. Besides reducing stress and getting in better physical condition, exercise also provides natural energy. You might think exercise will tire you out, but it can actually give you more energy throughout the day. Exercise gets your blood pumping and allows your cells to take in greater amounts of oxygen.

Case Study

Scenarios You May Face
The following situations are issues that you are likely to face as an early childhood professional. Use the questions following the situations to consider the best course of action and to think about how you might respond.

Ms. Stanley
Ms. Stanley is a new mother. She has called your center to inquire about enrolling her infant girl, who is 3 months old. She asks, "What do you charge? I've called three places already, and they all want way too much just to care for an infant! I don't know why babysitting has to be so expensive."

Mr. Jason
Mr. Jason has custody of his preschool son, and he works evenings. He asks, "I have to hire someone to keep him in the evenings, too. Why can't you just have someone stay late with him?"

Ms. Brenton
Ms. Brenton stops by to visit your center. She has a 3-year-old girl. She says, "I know my daughter will learn what she needs to know when she gets to kindergarten because we work with her a lot. I just want a place where someone will watch her."

Ms. Charlton
Ms. Charlton has a kindergarten child who needs after-school and summer care. She says, "My 5-year-old doesn't want to just play. What do you do with them all day?"

Ms. Alford
One day, Ms. Alford, whose child has been in your center for six months, says, "This will be his last week. I'm going to put him in ABC Day Care. They charge less, and I'm having a hard time paying."

You have a ratio of six 1-year-olds to each teacher, and you know that ABC has a one-to-eight ratio and almost no equipment. You also know that the staff there rarely goes to training.

Mr. Daniel
Mr. Daniel arrives to pick up his infant. You tell him about a parent meeting you have scheduled to discuss appropriate activities for infants. He says he's not coming and asks, "What can you do all day with babies? All they need is to be fed and changed."

Ms. Williamson
Ms. Williamson has custody of her grandson, 2-year-old Taylor. Ms. Williamson does not work, so she just wants to enroll her grandson for two days a week. You explain that right now, you do not have room for another 2-year-old, but she insists that you take him anyway because "What's one more when it's just two days a week?"

Consider This
1. Why do you think Ms. Stanley expected the cost to be less?
2. How might you help Ms. Stanley understand why the cost is necessary to provide a quality program?
3. What would it cost to have someone stay with Mr. Jason's child?
4. How might regulations make it difficult for someone to stay with Mr. Jason's child?
5. What could you do to help Mr. Jason?
6. What are some ways you can explain the importance of the experiences you provide in your program to Ms. Brenton?
7. How can you explain to Ms. Brenton what her child can learn in your program?
8. How might you explain the value of play for young children to Ms. Charlton?
9. What can you tell Ms. Charlton about your program?
10. Is it a good idea to tell Ms. Alford what you know about ABC? Why or why not?
11. Is there a system of financial aid that can help Ms. Alford?
12. How can you explain to Mr. Daniel the importance of the caring, responsive environment you provide?
13. What can you tell Mr. Daniels about the activities you provide?
14. What would you say to Ms. Williamson about the importance of ratios?
15. What might you do to help Ms. Williamson?

While we all know that regular exercise is good for us, it can be hard to find time for it. But working exercise into your routine is good for your mind and body. You do not need to go to a gym or buy expensive equipment. Walking is an easy way to get started. It is self-paced and gives you a chance to think and reflect while you walk. If you walk outdoors, the fresh air and sunshine provide additional benefits. Listening to music or podcasts or walking with a friend can increase the pleasure of walking.

Other options can include exercise or dance classes available through videos and online. Line dancing is repetitious, easy to learn, and ranges from beginner to advanced, offering versions for all skill levels.

Take part in activities with the children. Strike up a dance routine to the tune of children's music and enjoy moving to the beat with them.

Play

We know the value of play for children, but consider the stress-reducing influence of play for adults. It is easier to think about the many things you need to do than to focus on the moment. Playing is more fun if you let go of everything else and give a child your undivided attention. It is a great feeling when you can return to your childhood feelings and enjoy the simple act of play.

☑ CHECKPOINT

1. Which of the strategies for coping with stress might you use?
2. What are some factors that contribute to stress in working with children?
3. How does taking care of yourself benefit children?

14.6 Focus on Assessment

Assessment is a formal process of determining how a process can be improved. When we evaluate something, we figure out what is working well, what is not working, and what might be done to make it better. We evaluate in our daily lives in many ways. We look to see how well a new product works or if one piece of equipment functions better than another. The process of evaluation in our daily lives often follows a format such as the one described in the following section.

Three-Layer Format for Assessment

Think of the process of assessment as a three-layer format. People use this system often in their daily activities. Consider a new recipe we tried for meatloaf that we have just taken from the oven. We notice it smells very good, so we cut into it to see if it is cooked properly. Is it too pink in the center, cooked too much, not cooked enough, or just right? We check with a thermometer. We take a bite to see if it tastes as good as it smells. We decide it could use a bit more salt and pepper.

The information presented is an evaluation in three layers. The top layer would be what we liked:

"The meatloaf smells really wonderful."

The next layer would be what was right and what we thought could use improvement:

"The meatloaf is cooked just right. The temperature is correct. But it could use a bit more salt and pepper."

The final layer would be what could be done to make it better:

"Next time, I'll put a little more salt and pepper in the meat mixture."

We would even make notes on the recipe about the additional salt and pepper so we could remember to make the change the next time we use the meatloaf recipe.

Without going through a process of evaluation, our recipe would not be exactly what we wanted. The assessment process helps us improve what we do. This layered approach works well in evaluations of all types. See **Figure 14.19** for things a director might say when they are evaluating and providing feedback to a lead teacher. The teacher agrees that this might work and makes a note about the suggestions so they can consider what they will do differently.

This process has many additional possibilities, including asking the teacher for their ideas on how the situation is working and whether they want to change it, but the basic system is to determine what is working, what could work better, and how to make it better.

In many cases where a problem is found, a change is needed to meet the center's policies or philosophy. Simply saying that a practice must change without giving the employee support or guidance about how to change it leaves the process unclear. The person affected might suggest a better way themselves or need someone to suggest a solution. In any case, the goal is improvement.

Evaluations can be formal or informal. Formal evaluations often use rating sheets, checklists, or scales. Several versions of one commonly used scale, the *Early Childhood Environment Rating Scale®*, are available (ERSI n.d.). These scales help to evaluate programs for children in different age groups and settings.

For example, the *Infant/Toddler Environment Rating Scale®* (ERSI n.d.) is used to assess centers caring for children up to 30 months of age. Using a rating of 1 to 7, with 1 being less adequate than custodial care and 7 being the highest quality possible, a person using the scale can evaluate 39 different items.

The scale identifies these seven categories (or close variations of them):

- **Space and Furnishings for Care and Learning** looks at indoor furniture as well as outdoor play and privacy spaces.
- **Basic Care** evaluates routines such as diapering, meals, or arrival and departure practices.
- The **Language and Reasoning Learning Activities checks** for art, music, and block play as well as dramatic play, the schedule of activities, and use of television.
- **Social Development** rates things such as discipline and cultural awareness.
- **Adult Needs** considers the relationships with parents as well as professional growth opportunities.
- **Supplementary Items,** the final category, includes resources and tools related to providing care for children with special needs such as adaptations of equipment and activities or special caregiver training to show teachers how to provide care for children with special needs.

Layer One
"The song you opened circle time with is really fun, and I saw how the children all joined in singing it."
Layer Two
"I noticed that the children took quite a while to come together for circle time. Is that a typical problem?"
The teacher acknowledges that it is common.
Layer Three
"I've found that playing a song while children are gathering together gives them a helpful clue about how long they have to get seated. Is that something you could try?"

Goodheart-Willcox Publisher

Figure 14-19 A three-layer evaluation helps one look at a situation to see how it can be improved. What are some ways you use the three-layer approach in your daily life?

Based on the ratings, and which items received the lowest scores, it will be clear where changes are needed. This is only one example of a formal evaluation tool that helps a teacher identify what works and what needs work. The next step would be to figure out what to do to make improvements.

Personnel Evaluations

Staff and administrators need to know how they are doing. Individual evaluations, personnel evaluations, or job reviews are ways to show them. The more respectful the environment, the less threatened people will feel about evaluations. Regular evaluations every six months or once a year are common and, when expected in advance, will not seem punitive and more likely be viewed as helpful.

Center-Wide Assessments

Evaluations can be personal, as with employee reviews, or they can be center-wide to assess the program. A center-wide evaluation should include feedback from the families and the staff. Often, a center takes part in such a review when becoming accredited or re-accredited.

There is also a regulatory level for center-wide evaluations. City or state agencies conduct observations of programs at regular intervals. When needs are recognized, a plan of action is developed, and the center is given a specified time by which changes must be made. For example:

- **Observation:** A water fountain is not working.
- **Plan of Action:** The repairs to the fountain will need to be scheduled and completed within the next week. Arrangements have been made to provide children with a pitcher of water and paper cups.

When areas needing improvement are identified and solutions are proposed, ensuring that the changes take place is essential. When this is done, everyone is reassured that the activities of the center are conducted smoothly and effectively. Thus, there are measures in place that will correct problems when they turn up. Even if an evaluation shows overall outstanding results, it is important to remember that even the best programs have room for improvement. The evaluation component of professionalism includes continually working for higher quality and ongoing improvement.

Self-Evaluation

In addition to evaluating the program components, self-evaluation can help one identify areas of strength and need improvement. The following is a list of personal characteristics that are important when working with young children:

- Warm and caring personality
- Flexible and adaptable
- Respect for children, parents, and other staff
- Accepting of diverse ideas and values
- Actively listen to others
- Honest
- Enthusiastic about working with children
- Adequate energy and stamina
- Creative and curious
- Patient
- Remaining calm in difficult situations
- Inner strength
- Making decisions based on knowledge and facts, not opinions
- Constantly learning
- Recognizing children's strengths and areas in which they need to improve

☑ CHECKPOINT

1. What is the difference between a personnel assessment and a center-wide assessment?
2. How can assessments be used to evaluate early learning environments?

14.7 Family Matters

As professionals, what are our responsibilities to families? First of all, we must develop mutual trust with families served. We can do this by looking for the families' strengths and building upon them. This requires us to respect the dignity of each family's culture and beliefs, their values about child-rearing, and their right to make decisions for their children (**Figure 14.20**).

We are responsible for helping interpret each child's progress in ways that families may understand and appreciate the programs in which their children grow. We want to help family members improve their understanding of children and enhance their skills as parents. Developing these understandings means that we must communicate with families in a clear and positive way.

Professionally managing family relations includes ensuring that families are informed about policies and procedures. Families must understand policies and procedures in order to comply with them. Part of every early childhood professional's job is to create an atmosphere that families find inclusive and nonjudgmental.

Respecting Families' Authority

Being a professional means having respect for families' authority over their children and viewing yourself as part of a team working with their child. You have expertise and knowledge that you may want to share with them, yet it is important to understand that

Phynart Studio/E+ via Getty Images

Figure 14-20 A program director talks to a parent considering enrollment about her expectations for her child. What are questions the director might ask to learn more about the family and their needs?

Discovery Journeys

Lessons in Listening

Roslyn Duffy, author, counselor, speaker, and noted advocate for families and children, reminds us that a professional is always learning and shares with us how she learned to listen to families. She shares her growth in professionalism and her reason for becoming an advocate for families.

Mistakes are often my main learning style, and I've made plenty! Here are two mistakes and what I learned from them:

Mistake #1

A 2-year-old boy had attended our school for about six weeks when staff became concerned that he had language delays. As director, I met with his parents and explained our worries, noting that he never spoke at school. They responded with astonishment. "But he talks nonstop at home!"

Lesson #1: Ask, don't tell.

A better question would have been, "Do you have concerns about your son's language development?"

Lesson #2: Don't assume.

Early childhood professionals don't automatically know more than parents about their child.

Mistake #2

Another child wasn't really communicating or relating to her teachers or classmates. After sharing our concerns, along with a resources list, her mother said, "Why would you believe we hadn't noticed or done anything?"

Whoops! (Previous lessons not yet well-learned!)

She proceeded to outline interventions, counselors, and therapists they had worked with. Why hadn't they told us? They didn't want their child labeled, they said.

Lesson #3 Have faith in families.

It is possible to be right—and still get it wrong. Sadly, I assumed and didn't ask—but my demonstrated lack of faith and trust in this child's parents was the bigger lesson.

Consider This

1. Think of a situation in which you were not listened to by a person in authority. How did it make you feel?
2. Consider a time you assumed something that turned out not to be correct? What did you learn from the incorrect assumption?
3. How is acknowledging and learning from mistakes important in professionalism?

---

the families' values, ways of relating to their children, and even living arrangements may differ from yours. Think about the following situations and how you might communicate your concerns to the parents in a helpful and respectful way.

- Parents insist on dressing their 4-year-old in an expensive white shirt almost every day, and they want him to stay clean.
- A child clearly has not been bathed in several days. Her hair is tangled, and her fingernails are imbedded with dirt. She is developing a rash.
- One 2-year-old boy has been biting other children. You know you should speak to his parents about it, but you also know that if you do, they will probably spank him.
- Each morning, one parent stops in the driveway, honks the horn, and then sends her child alone up to your door. You have reminded her twice that parents are required to bring children inside.

Case Study

Professional Obligations

Those who work with young children have unique skills and knowledge that are needed by society. Those unique skills were shared with Allie's community during a natural disaster that uprooted families. When their hometown was hit by an unprecedented storm one hot summer, numerous families were displaced from flooding and lack of power. Shelters were opened by several nonprofit agencies to help those families, welcoming hundreds who were unable to remain in their homes due to the flooding and lack of power in the sweltering temperatures.

Allie, a kindergarten teacher, who was off for summer break, saw on the news the first morning that the shelters opened. The newscast showed hundreds of cots spread out in a local college gym for distressed families. Children were milling about aimlessly. Her first thought was that distressed families and children with nothing to do was not a good situation. She had an idea of what she could do to help. She called the organization sponsoring the shelter and offered to volunteer to arrange activities for the children. She was enthusiastically welcomed. Texting a number of coworkers, she found several available and willing to help but was disappointed by a few who replied in various ways: "I'm off on summer break" or "I'm not going to do that as a volunteer."

For the rest of the week, until families were able to return home or make alternate arrangements, Allie and a group showed up every morning with games, stories, toys, and art supplies to engage children and give adults a much-needed respite during this stressful time.

In a conversation in the lounge after returning to school, Allie told the group she felt an obligation to use her skills to help those families and children in need. "We know what children like, how to talk to them, and how to quickly get activities organized," she explained. "There were nurses, doctors, social workers, and counselors who came. Why shouldn't we? Don't we also have an obligation to use our skills for the public good when we can?"

Consider This
1. How do you feel about Allie's statement?
2. What are some obligations of a profession to a community?
3. What are your thoughts about those who would not volunteer?

☑ CHECKPOINT

1. What are some ways early childhood professionals can show respect for families?
2. What are some areas where families' ideas about rearing children may differ?

Chapter 14 Review and Assessment

Chapter Summary

14.1 **Determine if a career in early childhood education is the right choice for you.**
- A professional is defined not by how one is dressed but by how one performs and acts.
- A profession is typically a field of work where there are individual qualifications of education or experience, rules of conduct, and accountability requirements, such as licensing or ongoing education.
- A professional will pursue earning the needed credentials, expand their knowledge and understanding of their chosen field, and continue to learn new skills.
- Career options in early childhood education exist in addition to those of a classroom teacher in a public or private school. A person with a degree in early childhood education or a closely related field may choose employment in governmental or community-based areas where knowledge of working with children is important. Entrepreneurial opportunities as a consultant or business owner are other possibilities.
- Continuing education is required and may be achieved in a variety of ways. In-house training, workshops, staff meetings, and seminars are options.

14.2 **Describe at least five ways that early childhood professionals commit to providing a safe and nurturing environment for young children.**
- Appropriate dress for early childhood is usually casual but does require attention to cleanliness, neatness, and appropriateness for the tasks involved in working with young children.
- NAEYC accreditation is a measure of professionalism, as it documents the achievement of a quality program.

14.3 **Describe the role of professional organizations in early childhood education.**
- There are a number of professional organizations that provide resources for the field of early childhood education.
- NAEYC is the major professional organization in the field of early childhood education.
- Advocacy is an important function of a profession.
- Advocacy can be informal, such as having a conversation with a parent about how children learn, or formal, such as testifying before a legislative committee on licensing standards.
- In the early childhood education profession, the program, teachers, and parents all have different responsibilities.
- New performance standards and advanced technologies have changed the number and level of skills needed by today's early childhood professionals.
- The ability to communicate with children, families, and coworkers is important in the field of early childhood education.

14.4 **Define the issues of equity and equality.**
- NAEYC's position statement on equality is the official stance of the organization.
- Equity is not the same as equality and is an important concern in the early childhood education field today.
- Equity means that all children get what they need, regardless of their family circumstances.

14.5 **Identify strategies for caring for oneself as a professional.**
- When we feel stress, it affects others around us, including children.
- Managing stress is an important skill for anyone who works in early childhood.
- Some ways to manage stress are meditation, journaling, crafts, cooking, gardening, and exercising. Taking part in playful activities can also be a good stress reducer.

14.6 **Explain how people use assessment in their daily lives.**
- Assessment is important for success in all fields, and equally so in early childhood education.
- People use assessment regularly in their daily lives but may not recognize it as such.
- At its basis, assessment is looking at what is happening, determining if what is happening is as it should be, and, if not, designing a plan to improve.

- Assessment helps one identify strengths and skills that can be built on for ongoing improvement.
- Assessment can be center-wide to look at the environment, curriculum, and overall operation. It can include personnel evaluations and self-evaluations as well as assess individual performance.

14.7 Identify early childhood professionals' responsibilities to families.
- Good relationships with families are important not only as customers but in their role in their children's education.

Recall and Application

1. A career _____ is a means of advancing in one's career through additional training and experience.
   A. advocacy
   B. ladder
   C. journal
   D. accreditation
2. **True or False.** Once one meets the requirements to work in the early childhood education field, no other training or education is needed.
3. **True or False.** "Do no harm" means only to not hit children or use physical punishment.
4. **True or False.** Appropriate dress is the most important criterion in professionalism.
5. _____ is an important indicator of quality.
   A. Accreditation
   B. Advocacy
   C. Journaling
   D. Evaluation
6. **True or False.** Learning to cope with stress is an important component of being a professional.
7. Speaking up for quality in programs is an example of _____.
   A. accreditation
   B. advocacy
   C. evaluation
   D. journaling
8. **True or False.** Only professional lobbyists should be involved in advocacy.
9. Advocacy may involve each of the following except _____.
   A. lobbying the legislature
   B. filing a complaint with a city office
   C. handing out brochures about quality care
   D. shouting at a parent
10. **True or False.** Equity is the same as equality.
11. **True or False.** To be fair, all children should participate in the same experiences.
12. **True or False.** Most stress-reduction strategies are too expensive to be practical.
13. **True or False.** Early childhood teachers only need to be concerned about stress response in children.
14. Which of the following is *not* a good way to deal with stress?
    A. Ignore it, and it will go away.
    B. Exercise or do activities such as yoga.
    C. Take part in hobbies you enjoy.
    D. Practice meditation.
15. **True or False.** The purpose of assessment is to determine what can be improved.
16. **True or False.** We often use assessment in our daily lives.
17. **True or False.** Asking a child's parents if they share concerns about a child's behavior shows respect for the parent and the child.
18. **True or False.** Sharing information with families is a criterion for early childhood professionals.

Glossary

A

accessible. Equipment or toys should allow use by children of differing abilities. (3)

accommodation. Adjustment that allows a child with a disability to participate in a program in a way that matches the child's learning strengths and abilities. (3)

accountability. Determining if expectations are being met. (14)

adaptable. Toy that a child can do something playful with, even if it is not the same activity. (3)

advocacy. To plead or defend the case of another. (14)

aesthetics. Refer to a set of values relating to the appreciation of beauty and nature. (2)

affirmation. Acknowledging that something is true. (1)

analytical. Reasoning. (11)

anticipation. Prediction of what might happen based on knowledge of children's behavior. (5)

artifact. Example of an item that a child has created. (7)

associative play. Emerges around age 4 to 4½ as children begin to acknowledge one another as they play. (4)

attributes. Characteristics of an item. (12)

authentic assessment. Involves considering a child's ability to apply knowledge and skills in real-life situations or scenarios. (7)

B

bibliotherapy. A system of using books and reading materials to aid in understanding emotions. (8)

blended family. A family consisting of a couple and their children from this and all previous relationships. (6)

C

child-directed learning. Children carry out an activity as they wish, but within a framework provided by an adult who provides the resources from which to choose. (1)

child-initiated learning. Focuses on each child's interests, abilities, and learning styles, placing the teacher in the role of facilitator rather than the director of learning. (1)

childproofing. Thorough process of ensuring that an area has minimum risk to a child, including placing latches on cabinets and covers on electrical outlets. (5)

classification. Involves grouping and sorting according to categories, such as size, shape, color, or use. (10)

closed question. One that has a specific, expected answer. (1)

cognition. Thinking, understanding, reasoning, analysis, and problem solving. (3)

collage. Artwork made of gluing or pasting materials on a flat surface. (11)

communication loop. Usually involves a statement and a reaction that may continue back and forth. (8)

comparison. Analysis of similarities and differences in objects. (10)

constructive play. Involves any of the common construction toys, such as LEGO®, DUPLO®, unit blocks, magnetic tiles, and similar items that are often used in a manipulative area. (4)

constructivist learning. Learning that emphasizes the active role of learners in building their own understanding. (1)

context. Setting and circumstances, to adapt actions appropriately. (5)

convergent thinking. Looking to find the right answer. (4)

cooperative play. Occurs from about 4½ years of age and involves interaction and cooperation between children in social groups. (4)

creative play. Involves children using common, everyday materials in new and unusual ways. (4)

creativity. Involves the use of one's imagination and seeing new possibilities. (11)

criteria. Age range at which such skills are typically mastered by children. (7)

D

developmentally appropriate practice (DAP). Promotes optimal learning and development for children. (1)

divergent thinking. Process of looking at many ideas, much like brainstorming, to generate new ideas or find solutions. (4)

documentation board. Helps children organize information into chronological order and represent events that have already taken place. (9)

dramatic play. Form of play in which children create scenarios. (4)

dyad. Two children at a time. (2)

E

ecology. Impact of humans on the Earth. (9)

economics. Study of scarcity and implications for the use of resources, production of goods and services, and growth of production and welfare over time. (9)

emergent literacy. Term used to describe the way children's literacy develops over time, beginning in infancy, as a result of their experiences with spoken language, books, and print. (8)

Note: The number in parentheses following each definition indicates the chapter in which the term can be found.

emergent writing. Refers to a child's growing ability to use marks to represent words. (8)
empathy. Ability to feel the emotions of others. (9)
engineering. Process of building machines and structures. (10)
environment. Furniture and materials in a room and how they are arranged. (2)
environmental print. Refers to the words and signs that are all around us. (8)
equity. Resources are available as needed to achieve the identified goals. (14)
ethics. The rules of conduct. (14)
experience chart. Written stories compiled by children describing an event that the class has experienced. (10)
exploration. Children examining an object to see what it does and what they can do with it. (10)

F

Family Engagement Assessment and Planning Tool (FEAP-T). Program developed by the National Center for Children in Poverty (NCCP) in partnership with the Georgia Department of Early Care and Learning to help program staff identity specific, measurable actions they could take to strengthen family engagement practices. (6)
fantasy play. Often seen as a part of social play when children pretend. (4)
feedback loop. Back-and-forth exchanges between a teacher and a child that increase a child's understanding of a topic or performance of a skill. (1)
fidelity. Using the curriculum and following teaching practices consistently and accurately, as the developers intended. (1)
field guide. A book with illustrations and descriptions to identify plants or animals. (13)
fill and dump. Process in which toddlers will repetitively fill a container and dump out the contents. (4)
fine motor development. The use of smaller muscles in fingers and hands. (13)
fine motor skills. Developed during constructive play since children use their hands to manipulate the items. (4)
formative. To be used to understand each child and plan for the child's expanded learning based on what has been documented. (7)

G

games with rules. More formal type of play that is common during middle childhood in which the players must agree to follow an understood set of regulations or principles. (4)
graphing. Pictorially representing numbers on a chart. (12)
gross motor development. The development of large muscles. (13)

H

heterogenous. Programs in which peers with a range of abilities and needs are grouped together. (3)

homogenous. Programs in which children with similar diagnoses are grouped together. (3)
hypothesis. Asking a "what-if" question or making an estimate of what you believe is true. (7)

I

implicit bias. Attitude that is unintentional and not recognized by the individual. (7)
inclusion. Act or practice of combining in the same room children who have disabilities or exceptionalities with children who do not have disabilities or exceptionalities. (3)
indirect guidance. Sounds, objects, visuals, and people in a child's environment that affect their behavior. (2)
inference. Educated guess about an object or event based on data or observations. (10)
interlacing. Includes any type of weaving, lacing, knotting, or sewing, or any means of creating by attaching materials in such a manner. (11)

L

labeling. Giving a name to a shape. (12)
language. Any system used to communicate and share information, ideas, and feelings. (8)
language. Both receptive and expressive abilities. (3)
learning center. Distinct place where small groups of children can engage in self-selected activities. (2)
LGBTQ+. Acronym for lesbian, gay, bisexual, transgender, queer or questioning, and other terms to describe a person's sexual orientation or gender identity. (6)
literacy. Ability to read and write. (8)
loose parts. Materials that can be moved, carried, combined, put together, and taken apart in a variety of ways. (13)

M

mandated reporter. Person who is required by law to report suspected abuse or neglect. (5)
media. Materials used. (11)
model. Sample. (11)
modification. Change to what a child is taught or expected to do in the learning environment. (3)
motor coordination. Gross and fine motor skills, including jumping, hopping, throwing, catching, drawing, and stacking. (3)
multicultural. Having multiple cultures. (6)
multiple intelligences. Theory that claims that humans have different ways of processing information rather than a single general ability. (1)
multiracial. Having parents or ancestors from different racial or ethnic backgrounds. (6)
myopia. Nearsightedness. (13)

N

narrative skills. Involve the ability to tell a story or describe a sequence of events to others. (8)

National Association for the Education of Young Children (NAEYC). A large nonprofit association in the United States representing early childhood education teachers, paraeducators, center directors, trainers, college educators, families of young children, policymakers, and advocates. (1)

natural environment. Places where a child would be or go if they did not have disabilities. (3)

nature-deficit disorder. Describes how humans, especially children, are spending far less time outdoors, and this is resulting in a wide range of behavioral and other issues. (13)

O

observation. Consists of using the five senses to gather information to understand how things work. (10)

one-to-one correspondence. Counting a group of objects by assigning one number to each object and only counting each object once. (12)

onlooker play. Child shows interest in or watching what other children are doing without attempting to enter the activity. (4)

open-ended question. A question that does not have a specific, single, correct answer. (1)

P

paradigm. Model or system based on real-world practical applications. (10)

parallel play. Occurs at about 2 to 3 years of age, where many children enjoy playing alongside another child and engage in similar or identical activities. (4)

parallel talk. Describing what children are doing as they are doing it. (1)

parrot. When a child uses a word they don't understand. (12)

people-first language. Referring to a child before using any other descriptive characteristics, and referring to a child's disability only when it is relevant and necessary. (3)

phonological awareness. Sensitivity to sound. (8)

physical play. Consists of activities that involve movement, especially gross motor skills that involve the use of children's larger muscles. (4)

picture symbol chart. Reminder to prompt children. (2)

pinch point. Place where a body part, such as fingers, can be caught between pieces of equipment. (5)

pitch. Highness or lowness of a musical tone, so the use of high and low movements is appropriate. (11)

play. Foundation for learning in which children acquire the skills and knowledge to prepare them for adult life, including the development of imagination and problem-solving skills. (4)

play space. An environment where play can take place. (13)

portfolio. Collection of observation records and artifacts. (7)

positioning. Providing a child with external supports to help compensate for instability. (3)

prediction. Reasonable guess or estimation of what will happen under specified circumstances. (10)

pretend play. Form of play in which children create scenarios. (4)

process skills. Skills that scientists use in their work, and the competencies in solving scientific problems. (10)

prop box. Container of related materials for use in dramatic play that can be used alone or as the basis for setting up a learning center. (4)

props. Materials and supplies that children arrange in play setups to suggest play ideas and relate play to curriculum themes. (4)

proximity. Nearness in space, time, or relationship. (4)

Q

qualitative measure. Type of measurement that involves judgment. (7)

quantitative. Relates to the determination of quantity and involves using numbers, distances, time, volumes, or weights. (10)

R

rebus. An instruction card using pictures to show the steps in a task. (12)

recording. Information that is documented by teachers about what children do and say as events happen. (7)

rhythm. Consists of the concepts of beat and meter. (11)

rhythmic. Repeated. (11)

role play. Form of play in which children create scenarios. (4)

role. Identity that a child assumes in play. (4)

rough and tumble play. Involves running, jumping, pretend wrestling, or other physical contact between two children, usually accompanied by loud noises. (4)

S

scaffolding. Process of giving children a little help when needed but stopping short of doing a task for them. (1)

science. Refers to the process of methodically exploring through observation and experiment; it involves paying attention to what exists or is happening, predicting what might happen if specific changes are made or actions are taken, testing predictions under controlled conditions to see if they are correct, and trying to make sense of the experiences. (10)

scope and sequence. Outlines what the early childhood curriculum focuses on and how the plans and materials support children at different stages of development. (1)

screen time. Time using tablets, smartphones, televisions, video games, and other screen items. (10)

self-help. Dressing, washing, eating, and toileting. (3)

self-talk. Describing what you are doing as you are doing it. (1)

sensorimotor play. A type of play in which children experiment with body movements and objects. (4)

seriation. Arranging objects by size, or in some instances, characteristics. (12)

social interaction. Response to social cues, initiating peer contact, and participating in group play. (3)

social play. Includes activities with others. (4)

socio-dramatic. Play that includes elements of imitative play and make-believe play; however, it stands apart from the earlier stages in that it requires verbal interaction between two or more children as well as the ability to make plans. (4)

solitary play. Occurs typically between 3 months and 2½ years of age and involves children playing alone, often with a toy. (4)

STEAM. Depicts the interrelationship of the arts with the technical and scientific fields. (10)

STEM. Science, technology, engineering, math. (10)

stereotyping. Perception that groups of people will all have characteristics in common. (9)

supervision. Process of overseeing or guiding a person, an object, or an action. (5)

symmetry. Balanced proportions, similarity of placement. (12)

T

teachable moment. Interaction where children acquire knowledge by asking a specific question of their teachers. (1)

teacher-directed learning. Children participate in activities designed and overseen by the teacher. (1)

teacher-initiated learning. Teacher starts and controls the activity. (1)

technology. Application of scientific knowledge for practical purposes. (10)

tempo. Speed at which music is performed. (11)

three-dimensional. Having width, height, and depth. (11)

tinkering. Playing around with materials, becoming familiar with their properties and what they can do. (10)

transferable. Abilities that are necessary to many disciplines and reflective of the behavior of scientists. (10)

transition. Switching from one area or activity to another. (11)

tummy time. Playtime for infants placed on a quilt or blanket on the floor. (2)

U

universal precautions. Safety measures. (14)

unoccupied play. Characterized by a child's lack of focus, no obvious story line, and absence of language use. (4)

V

variable. Characteristic in an investigation that should be consistent to conduct an experiment. (10)

visual perception. Ability to perceive one's surroundings through the light that enters one's eyes. (4)

visual schedule. Schedule with photographs representing major events of the day with time and simple text and can be utilized by children as young as 2 years old. (1)

Z

zone system. Supervision system where each adult covers a designated area of the playground, circulating but paying close attention to more risky areas such as climbing equipment. (13)

Reference List

Chapter 1

National Association for the Education of Young Children (NAEYC). (n.d.). *Principles of child development and learning and implications that inform practice.* https://www.naeyc.org/resources/developmentally-appropriate-practice

NAEYC. (2003). *Early childhood curriculum, assessment, and program evaluation.* https://www.naeyc.org/sites/defaults/files/globally-shared/downloads/PDFs/resources/position-statements/CAPEexpand.pdf

NAEYC. (2020). *Developmentally appropriate practice (DAP) position statement.* https://www.naeyc.org/resources/position-statements/dap/contents

United States Department of Health and Human Services. (2022). National Center on Early Childhood Development, Teaching, and Learning (NCECDTL). https://hhs.gov

Chapter 2

Duncan, S., DeViney, J., Harris, S., Rody, M. A., & Rosenberry, L. (2010). *Inspiring spaces for young children.* Lewisville, NC: Gryphon House.

The IRIS Center. (2015). *Page 3: Social environment.* https://iris.peabody.vanderbilt.edu/module/env/cresource/q1/p03/#content

Lally, J. R., Mangione, P. L., & Signer, S. (2004). *Space to grow: Creating a child care environment for infants and toddlers (2nd ed.).* Sacramento, CA: California Department of Education.

Luckenbill, J., Subramaniam, A., & Thompson, J. (2019). *This is play: Environments and interactions that engage infants and toddlers.* Washington, DC: National Association for the Education of Young Children.

Michigan Department of Education. (2020). *Key elements of high-quality early childhood learning environments: Preschool (Ages 3-5).* https://www.michigan.gov/-/media/Project/Websites/mde/gsrp/standards/Key_Elements_of_High-Quality_Early_Childhood_Learning_Environments_Preschool_Ages_3-5.pdf?rev=e2bd1168c1be47e8a650c596ed3c65c

NAEYC. (2016). *Building environments that encourage positive behavior: The preschool behavior self-support assessment.* https://www.naeyc/pubs/yc/mar2016/building-environments-encourage-positive-behavior-preschool

Chapter 3

Americans with Disabilities Act, 42 U.S.C. § 12101 et seq. (1990). https://www.ada.gov/pubs/adastatute08.htm

Civil Rights Act of 1964, Pub. l. No. 88-352, 78 Stat. 241 (1964). https://www.govinfo.gov/content/pkg/STATUTE-78/pdf/STATUTE-78-Pg241.pdf#page=12

Division for Early Childhood (DEC) and NAEYC. (2020). *Early childhood inclusion (Joint position statement).* https://www.naeyc.org/sites/default/files/globally-shared/downloads/PDFs/resources/position-statements/ps_inclusion_dec_naeyc_ec.pdf

Education for All Handicapped Children Act of 1975, Pub. L. No. 94-142, 89 Stat. 773 et. seq. (1975). https://www.govinfo.gov/content/pkg/STATUTE-89/pdf/STATUTE-89-Pg773.pdf

Education of the Handicapped Act Amendments of 1983, Pub. L. No. 98-199, 97 Stat. 1357 et. seq. (1983). https://www.govinfo.gov/content/pkg/STATUTE-97/pdf/STATUTE-97-Pg1357.pdf

Education of the Handicapped Act Amendments of 1986, Pub. L. No. 99-457, 100 Stat. 1145 et. seq. (1986). https://www.govinfo.gov/content/pkg/STATUTE-100/pdf/STATUTE-100-Pg1145.pdf

Education of the Handicapped Act Amendments of 1990, Pub. L. No. 100-476, 104 Stat. 1103 et. seq. (1990). https://www.govinfo.gov/content/pkg/STATUTE-104/pdf/STATUTE-104-Pg1103.pdf#page=49

Individuals with Disabilities Education Act Amendments of 1997, Pub. L. No. 105-17, 111 Stat. 37 et seq. (1997). https://www.congress.gov/105/plaws/publ17/PLAW-105publ17.pdf

Individuals with Disabilities Improvement Act of 2004, Pub. L. No. 108-466, 118 Stat. 2647 (2004). https://ies.ed.gov/ncser/pdf/pl108-446.pdf

Molina Roldán, S., Marauri, J., Aubert, A., & Flecha, R. (2021). How inclusive interactive learning environments benefit students without special needs. *Frontiers in Psychology.* https://www.ncbi.nlm.nih.gov/pmc/articles/PMC8116690/

Research and Training Center on Independent Living. (2020). *Guidelines: How to write about people with disabilities, 9th ed.* Lawrence, KS: The University of Kansas.

Rosa's Law, Pub. L. No. 111-256, 124 Stat. 2643 (2010). https://www.govinfo.gov/content/pkg/PLAW-111publ256/pdf/PLAW-111publ256.pdf

Willis, C. (2015). *Teaching young children with autism spectrum disorder.* Lewisville, NC: Gryphon House.

Chapter 4

Smith, P. & Boulton, M. (1990). Rough-and-tumble play, aggression and dominance: Perception and behaviour in children's encounters. *Human Development.* https://www.jstor.org/stable/26767253

Chapter 5

Centers for Disease Control and Prevention (CDC). (2022). *Health effects of lead exposure.* https://www.cdc.gov/nceh/lead/prevention/health-effects.htm

Child Welfare Information Gateway. *State laws on child abuse and neglect.* US Children's Bureau, Administration for Children & Families, US Department of Health and Human Services (HHS). https://www.childwelfare.gov/topics/systemwide/laws-policies/can/

NAEYC. (2020). *Developmentally appropriate practice (DAP) position statement.* https://www.naeyc.org/resources/position-statements/dap/contents

NAEYC. (2022). *Early learning program accreditation standards, assessment, and items.* https://www.naeyc.org/sites/default/files/globally-shared/downloads/PDFs/accreditation/early-learning/2022elpstandardsandassessmentitems-compressed.pdf

National Institute of Arthritis and Musculoskeletal and Skin Diseases (NIAMS). (2019). *Back pain.* https://www.niams.nih.gov/health-topics/back-pain

National Program for Playground Safety (NPPS). (n.d.). *S.A.F.E.™ framework for playground safety.* https://www.playgroundsafety.org/safe

Chapter 6

The American Academy of Child & Adolescent Psychiatry (AACAP). (2023). *Multiracial children.* htpps://www.aacap.org/AACAP/Families_and_Youth/Facts_for_Families/FFF-Guide/Multiracial-Children-071.aspx

American Academy of Pediatrics (AAP). (2022). *Promoting the well-being of children whose parents are gay or lesbian.* https://publications.aap.org/pediatrics/article/131/4/827/31789/Promoting-the-Well-Being-of-Children-Whose-Parents?autologincheck=redirected

The Annie E. Casey Foundation (AECF) (2020). *Child poverty.* https://www.aecf.org/topics/child-poverty

Duffy, R. (1997). *Parents' perspectives on conferencing.* Exchange Press. https://www.exchangepress.com/article/parents-perspective-on-conferencing/5011640/

Kinsner, K. (2021). *Separation anxiety.* Zero to Three. https://www.zerotothree.org/resources/3919-separation-anxiety

Martoma, J. (2023). *Parental incarceration is a silent epidemic more common than childhood asthma.* he New York Times. https://www.nytimes.com/2023/06/26/learning/parental-incarceration-is-a-silent-american-epidemic-more-common-than-childhood-asthma.html

Nguyen, U. S., Smith, S., & Granja, M. R. (2018). *Helping early care and education programs assess family engagement practices and plan improvements: Results of the Georgia family engagement planning tool pilot.* New York, NY: National Center for Children in Poverty, Mailman School of Public Health, Columbia University.

Paris, R., DeVoe, E., Ross, A., & Acker, M. (2010). When a parent goes to war: Effects of parental deployment on very young children and implications for intervention. *American Journal of Orthopsychiatry*, 80 (4), 610–618. https://doi.org/: 10.1111/j.1939-0025.2010.01066

Prison Fellowship. (n.d.). *Impact of incarceration on children.* https://www.prisonfellowship.org/resources/training-resources/family/ministry-basics/impact-of-incarceration-on-children/

What We Know Project. (2015). *What does the scholarly research say about the well-being of children with gay or lesbian parents?* Cornell University. https://whatweknow.inequality.cornell.edu/topics/lgbt-equality/what-does-the-scholarly-research-say-about-the-wellbeing-of-children-with-gay-or-lesbian-parents/

Chapter 7

NAEYC. (n.d.) *DAP: Observing, documenting, and assessing children's development and learning.* https://www.naeyc.org/resources/position-statements/dap/assessing-development

NAEYC. (2020). *Developmentally appropriate practice (DAP) position statement.* https://www.naeyc.org/resources/position-statements/dap/contents

NAEYC (2020) *Statement from NAEYC on implicit bias research.* https://www.naeyc.org/about-us/press-releases/statement-naeyc-implicit-bias-research

Chapter 8

Harms, T., Clifford, R., & Cryer, D. (2014). *The early childhood environment rating scale, 3rd ed.* New York, NY: Teachers College Press.

Hart, B. & Risley, T. R. (2003). The early catastrophe: The 30 million word gap by age 3. *American Educator*, Vol. 27, No. 1. https://www.aft.org/ae/spring2003/hart_risley

Hart, B. & Risley, T. R. (2008). *Meaningful differences in the everyday experience of young American children.* Baltimore, MD: Brookes Publishing.

Sparks, S. (2015) *Key to vocabulary gap is quality of conversation, not dearth of words.* https://www.edweek.org/ew/articles/2015/04/22/key-to-vocabulary-gap-is-quality-of.html

Uttal, D., & Yuan, L. (2014). Using symbols: Developmental perspectives. *Wiley Interdisciplinary Reviews: Cognitive Science.* Vol. 5, No. 3, 295–304. https://wires.onlinelibrary.wiley.com/doi/abs/10.1002/wcs.1280

Chapter 9

Brillante, P. & Mankiw, S. (2015). *A sense of place: Human geography in the early childhood classroom.* Young Children, Vol. 70 H, No. 3. https://www.naeyc.org/resources/pubs/yc/jul2015/sense-of-place-human-geography

National Council for the Social Studies (NCSS). (2019). *Early childhood in the social studies context.* https://www.socialstudies.org/position-statements/early-childhood-social-studies-context

Neill, P. (2018). *Going from me to we: Social studies in preschool.* Newsletter Extensions, Vol. 29, No. 1. https://image.highscope.org/wp-content/uploads/2018/08/16053918/166.pdf

Chapter 10

American Academy of Pediatrics (APA). (2023). *Screen time guidelines.* https://www.aap.org/en/patient-care/media-and-children/center-of-excellence-on-social-media-and-youth-mental-health/social-media-and-youth-mental-health-q-and-a-portal/middle-childhood/middle-childhood-questions/screen-time-guidelines/

McComas, W. (2014). STEM: Science, technology, engineering, and mathematics. In: McComas, W. F. (eds) *The Language of Science Education.* SensePublishers, Rotterdam. https://doi.org/10.1007/978-94-6209-497-0_92

NAEYC. (2020). *Developmentally appropriate practice (DAP) position statement.* https://www.naeyc.org/resources/position-statements/dap/contents

National Association for Research in Science Training (NARST). (n.d.). *The science process skills.* https://narst.org/research-matters/science-process-skills

US Department of Education (USDE). (2022). *Science, technology, engineering, and math, including computer science.* https://www.ed.gov/stem

Chapter 11

Mayesky, M. (2002). *Creative activities for young children.* Clifton Park, NY: Delmar Learning.

National Gallery of Art. (n.d.). *The elements of art.* https://www.nga.gov/education/teachers/lessons-activities/elements-of-art.html

Sarrazin N. (2016). *Music and the child.* https://open.umn.edu/opentextbooks/textbooks/283.

Chapter 12

Copley, J. (n.d.). *Assessing mathematical learning: Observing and listening to children.* https://ccie-catalog.s3.amazonaws.com/library/5015147.pdf

Geist, E. (2016). *Support math readiness through math talk.* https://www.naeyc.org/our-work/families/support-math-readiness-through-math-talk

Chapter 13

Brussoni, M., Olsen, L. L., Pike, I., & Sleet, D. A. (2012). Risky play and children's safety: Balancing priorities for optimal child development. *International Journal of Environmental Research and Public Health.* 30;9(9):3134–48. doi: 10.3390/ijerph9093134.

Kuo, M., Barnes, M., & Jordan, C. (2019). Do experiences with nature promote learning? Converging evidence of a cause-and-effect relationship. *Frontiers in Psychology.* 10:305. https://doi.org/: 10.3389/fpsyg.2019.00305

Louv, R. (2005). *Last child in the woods: Saving our children from nature-deficit disorder.* Algonquin Books.

Oh, B., Lee K. J., Zaslawski, C., Yeung, A., Rosenthal, D., Larkey, L. & Back, M. (2017). Health and well-being benefits of spending time in forests: Systematic review. *Environmental Health and Preventive Medicine.* Med. 2017 Oct 18;22(1):71. https://doi.org/: 10.1186/s12199-017-0677-9.

Chapter 14

Environment Rating Scales Institute (ERSI). (n.d.). *Early childhood environment rating scale®, revised (ECERS-R).* https://www.ersi.info/ecers.html

Environment Rating Scales Institute (ERSI). (n.d.). *Infant/toddler rating scale®, third edition (ITERS-3).* https://www.ersi.info/iters3.html

NAEYC. (2020). *Developmentally appropriate practice (DAP) position statement.* https://www.naeyc.org/resources/position-statements/dap/contents

NAEYC. (n.d.). *Code of ethical conduct and statement of commitment.* https://www.naeyc.org/resources/position-statements/ethical-conduct

Index

30-million-word gap, 242–43

A

AAP. *See* American Academy of Pediatrics
ABC, acronym, 147–48
abuse, 162–63
accessible, 90
accidents, responding to, 155–57
accommodations, 87
accountability, 454
accreditation, 460–61
active play area, 56
activities
    considering, 90–91
    fine motor play for, 440
ADA. *See* Americans with Disabilities Act (ADA)
adaptable, 90
adaptation, curriculum, 37–38
adaptive equipment, 91
ADHD. *See* attention-deficit/hyperactivity disorder
adoptive families, 187–88
advocacy, 461
    in action, 464
    as professional resources, 461–63
    responsibilities, 465–66
aesthetics, 61–63, 349
affirmation, 19
age-appropriate language, 128
age-appropriateness, SAFE, 146
allergies, 172
aluminum foil sculptures, 357
American Academy of Pediatrics (AAP), 308
American Psychological Association (APA), 308
Americans with Disabilities Act (ADA), 86–87
analytical, 338
analytical skills, developing, 18
ancillary skills, 466
anecdotal records, 218–23
animals, 317
anticipation, 146
anticipation, ANC, 148
APA. *See* American Psychological Association
appropriate dress, 458–59

appropriate language, applying, 83
art, 313
    assessment, 373–74
    families, 374–76
    outdoor play and, 427
    talking about, 364–65
art and creative expression center, 55
art and music, STEAM
    benefits, 341–45
    curriculum, 345–51
    stages of development, 352–62
    teacher's role, 363–72
    for young children, 338–45
art area, setting up, 364
art fair, 374
artifacts, 223
artwork, displaying, 365–67
assessment
    center-wide assessment, 475
    evaluating program as whole, 235–36
    families and, 237–38
    fidelity, 44–45
    guiding behavior using, 229–35
    mathematics, 405–6
    outdoor play, 441–42
    personnel evaluations, 475
    for planning and language, 209–10
    portfolios, 223–27
    published, 225
    purpose of, 208
    recording observations, 212–23
    social studies, 297
    STEM programs, 329–31
    teacher's role in, 227–29
    technology options, 234–35
    three-layer format for, 473–75
    using systematic approach in, 228–29
assessment–planning–learning cycle, 210
associative play, 115
attention, 98
attention span, 341
attention-deficit/hyperactivity disorder (ADHD), 101
attention, gaining and holding, 348
attributes, 390
authentic assessment, 226
authority, respecting, 476–78
autism spectrum disorder, 101
autonomy, supporting, 19

B

back injury, preventing, 157–59
balls, 440
barriers, family involvement, 180–82
basic learning centers, 54–56
beanbags, 425
behavior, ABC, 148
behavior, guiding, 229–35
    concerns, 231
    implicit biases, 229
    intervention, 233–34
    rapid change and expectations, 232–33
    three Ws, 230–31
benefits of inclusion, 81–82
bibliotherapy, 263
blended families, 190–91
block and construction center, 55
block play, guidelines for, 393
blocks, 430–31
bodies, 315–16
book bag guide, 269–70
books
    inspiring play using, 137
    staff use of, 267
box construction, 357
brain development, 5
bubbles, blowing, 429
bulletin boards, 366

C

Caldecott Medal, 259
car race, 402–3
cardiopulmonary resuscitation (CPR), 153
careers, 449–50
    accountability, 454
    continuing education, 452–53
    evaluations, 455
    job requirements, 451
    ongoing education, 455
    options, 450–51
    quality linked to education, 455
    rules of conduct, 453–54
    staying abreast of research, 455
caregivers, male, 183–84
carrying, 440
center-wide assessment, 475
cerebral palsy, 101

chair, washing, 429
Charlotte Zolotow Award, 259
checklists, 149, 213–16
child development knowledge, 98–102
    attention, 98
    cognition, 98
    common disabilities, disorders, and delays, 101
    directory of conditions, 100
    language, 98
    making a referral, 100–102
    motor coordination, 98
    self-help, 98
    social interaction, 98
    stages, 99
child protective services, 163
child with disabilities, welcoming, 93–94
child-directed learning, 27
child-initiated learning, 27
childproofing, 154–55
children
    child abuse and neglect, 162–63
    encouraging to use language, 267
    encouraging use of books, 268
    exploration of materials, 6–11
    helping, 201–2
    helping to expand vocabulary, 267
    keeping physically healthy, 160–62
    nutrition and, 164–72
    safe habit development, 154
    talking about art of, 364–65
children's behavior, 65–66, 69–72
children's learning, domains of, 7
Children's Book Award, 259
circle time, 34, 51
classification, 305
classifying, 385–86
classroom
    benefits of inclusion in, 81–82
    inclusion in, 80–84
    integration of science, technology, and engineering in, 311–15
    management of music in, 347–50
    sample activities, 318–22
    themes, 315–18
cleaning, 162
climbers, 434
climbing, 439
closed question, 18
clothesline, 366
clothing, protecting, 367
cognition, 98
cognitive development, 12–13, 417–18
    encouraging exploration and discovery, 21
    problem solving, 21–24
    promoting, 21–24
cognitive domain, skills in, 112

collage, 343
colored dough, 356
commitment, early childhood professional
    accreditation, 460–61
    appropriate dress, 458–59
    required continuing education, 459–60
    values and respect, 456–57
    what parents see, 457–58
communication, 467
    importance of, 191–96
    improving, 179
communication loop, 252–53
community helpers, 318
community, people in, 282
comparing, 386
comparison, 305
complaints, responding, 195
concepts, 36
    clarifying, 18
    integrating, 20
concern, assessing, 231–32
conditions, directory of, 100
construction, 430–31
constructive play, 117–18
constructivist learning, 13
container weaving, 358
containers, 358
context, ABC, 148
continuing education, 452–53, 459–60
convenience, environment, 52–53
convergent thinking, 123
conversations, holding, 16–17
cooperative, 90
cooperative play, 116
counting, 384–85
CPR. See cardiopulmonary resuscitation
crafts, 340
crawling, 438
creating, 372
creating, including opportunities for, 20
creative domain, skills in, 112–13
creative expression, 471
creative outdoor space, 431–32
creative play, 123
creative process, 340–41
creativity, cultivating, 339
creeping, 438
criteria, 218
crowding, 435
cruising around, 439
cultural background, families, 182–83
    adoptive families, 187–88
    blended families, 190–91
    divorced families, 190–91
    father and male caregivers, 183–84
    foster families, 185–86

    homeless families, 185–86
    incarcerated families, 188–89
    kinship care, 184–85
    LGBTQ+ parents, 186
    military families, 186–87
    multicultural families, 189–90
    multigenerational families, 184–85
    multiracial families, 189–90
    single parents, 183
    teen parents, 185
curriculum
    adaptations, 37–38
    art and music, 345–51
    choosing, 30
    components, 32–36
    concepts, 36
    developmentally appropriate practice (DAP), 25–32
    effectiveness of, 24–25
    emergent, 31
    fidelity, 41–45
    food preparation, 168–70
    guidance for differentiating instruction, 37
    implementing, 38–45
    for infants and toddlers, 38
    language throughout, 248–55
    outdoor play and, 426–32
    purchased prepackaged, 30–31
    quality curriculum, 28–30
    schedules and routines, 32–35
    theme-based, 31
    themes, 35–36
    types, 30–31

D

daily experiences, planning for, 39–41
dance, 214
DAP. See developmentally appropriate practice
deafness, 101
debris, 433–34
DEC. See Division for Early Childhood
decisions, making, 285
democracy, 284–85
describing, 359
development, planning for, 19–21
developmental milestones, 98
developmental scales, 217–18
developmentally appropriate concepts, social studies, 276
    becoming good citizen, 282
    community, 280–82
    community resources, 286–89
    democracy and government, 284–85
    ecology, 283–84

developmentally appropriate concepts, social studies *(continued)*
   economics of work, 282–83
   family, 277
   friends and neighbors, 278
   geography, 282
   history, 286
   learning empathy, 279
   making decisions, 285
   myself, 277
   people in community, 282
   specific social skills, 279–80
   valuing self and others, 278
developmentally appropriate play activities, 123–32
   creative play, 123
   dramatic play, 124–25
   support and guide during play, 125–32
developmentally appropriate practice (DAP), 25–32
   age-appropriate, 26
   child-directed learning, 27
   child-initiated learning, 27
   choosing curriculum, 28–30
   culturally appropriate, 26
   finding out children's interests, 31
   individually appropriate, 26
   quality curriculum, 28–30
   teacher-directed learning, 27
   teacher-initiated learning, 27
   term, 27
   types of curricula, 30–31
difficult issues, talking about, 194–95
digital media, 340
digital portfolios, 224–25
direct vocabulary learning, 248
disease, preventing spread of, 160–62
dishes, washing, 429
disinfecting, 162
distance, 391–92
divergent thinking, 123
diversity. *See* cultural background, families
Division for Early Childhood (DEC), 80
divorced families, 190–91
documentation boards, 286
dolls, bathing, 429
domains, skills in
   cognitive, 112
   creative, 112–13
   physical, 109
   social-emotional, 110–12
Down syndrome, 101
dramatic play, 124–25
   curriculum areas, 426–27
   wheeled toys, 424–25
drills, 153
dumping, 440
DVDs, 61
dyads, 67

E

early childhood education
   ancillary skills for workforce, 466–67
   career progression in, 451–52
   engineering, 309–11
   key theorists and, 12–15
   learning environment, 49–76
   math recognition, 382
   professional commitment, 456–61
   science, 304–7
   STEAM and, 302–4
   technology, 407–9
Early Childhood Environment Rating Scale, 474
Early Childhood Inclusion, 80
easel painting, 358–59
easels, 358
ecology, 283–84
economics of work, 282–83
emergencies, responding to, 155–57
emergency preparedness, 152–53
emergent curriculum, 31
emergent literacy, 263
   by age, 263–65
   and emergent writing, 265–66
   special language and literacy issues, 267
emergent writing, 265–66
emotional disturbance, 101
empathy, learning, 279
encouragement, 19
engagement, encouraging, 19
engagement, families, 178–204
   assessment of program practices, 203–4
   cultural background and diversity, 182–91
   importance of communication, 191–96
   involving families in program, 196–203
   positive family-program relationships, 179–82
engineering, 309
   in early childhood education, 309–10
   math and, 402–3
environment, 50
   assessment, 74–76
   considering, 89
   families and, 75–76
   interacting with children, 73–74
   learning centers, 53–65
   maintenance, 72
   materials, 73
   physical environment, 50–53
   room arrangement and children's behavior, 65–66
   social and emotional environment, 66–72
   teacher's role, 72–74
environmental print, 257–58
epilepsy, 101
equality, 467–68
equipment maintenance, SAFE, 147
equipment, outdoor play, 420–21
   storage, 425–26
   supplementing permanently installed equipment, 421–25
equity, 467–68
esoteric terms, 192
evacuation, 153
evaluation, environment, 74
evaluations, 455
exercise, 472–73
expansion, 252
experience charts, 312
experiences, 254
exploration, 304
   encouraging, 21
   motivating, 323
expressive language, 244–46

F

falls, SAFE, 147
families, 75–76
   art, 374–76
   assessment and, 237–38
   common reactions, 104
   cultural background and diversity, 182–91
   engaging, 178–204
   food safety, 172–74
   generations and, 290
   helping, 200–201
   involving, 102–3
   language and literacy, 269–70
   mathematics and, 406–9
   matters involving, 103–5
   multigenerational, 184–85
   music, 374–76
   outdoor play and, 442–43
   respecting authority of, 476–78
   responsibilities to, 476–78
   science, technology, engineering, and mathematics, 331–33
   social studies, 297–98
   supporting, 104–5
   understanding playful learning, 141–42

Family Engagement Assessment and Planning Tool (FEAP-T), 203
family meeting, planning and holding, 197–98
family-program relationships, 179–82
fantasy play, 118
fathers, 183–84
FEAP-T. *See* Family Engagement Assessment and Planning Tool
feedback loops, 16
feelings, incarcerated parents, 188
fencing, 433
fidelity, 41–45
field guide, 416
field trips, 287–89
fill and dump, 121
filling, 440
fine motor
    development, 418
    play, 440
    skills, 117
fire prevention, 153
first aid, 153
first impression, 179–80
flower garden, 320
food
    eating too little/too much, 170–72
    math and preparation of, 394–96
    security, 165–66
formative, 228
foster families, 185–86
fractions, understanding, 391
frames, 366
friendships, nurturing, 67–69

G

games with rules, 118–19
Gardner, Howard, 15
general arrangements, classroom considerations, 58
generations, 290
geography, learning, 282
geometry, 390–91
good citizen, becoming, 282
government, 284–85
grandfamilies, 184
graphing, 387–88
grids, 217
grill weaving, 358
gross motor
    development, 416
    play, 438–40
group programs, learning in, 11
group time, 34, 51
guidance, outdoors, 434–35

H

Hart, Betty, 242
hats, 357
hazards, 433–34
health, 160–64
    child abuse and neglect, 162–63
    physical, 160–62
hearing loss, 101
heterogenous, 84
high-quality children's literature, 258
history, 286
holidays, 291–92
homeless families, 185–86
homemade ice cream, 321
homogenous, 84
housekeeping, 426–27
housekeeping and dramatic play center, 55
hygienic diapering, 161
hypothesis, 210, 395

I

IDEA. *See* Individuals with Disabilities Education Act
IEP. *See* Individualized Education Program (IEP)
implementation, curriculum, 38–45
    curriculum fidelity, 41–45
    daily experiences, 39–41
implicit biases, 229
incarcerated families, 188–89
inclusion, 80
    assessing child's needs, 92–93
    benefits of, 81–82
    in classroom, 80–84
    positioning, 94
    social interactions, 96–97
    structural adaptation, 94–96
    taking steps toward, 92–98
    welcoming child with disabilities, 93–94
inclusive classroom, 80–84
    benefits of inclusion, 81–82
    child development knowledge, 98–102
    creation of, 89–91
    family matters, 103–5
    focus on assessment of program practices and involving families, 102–3
    importance of language in, 83
    people-first language, 80
    taking steps toward inclusion, 92–98
    teaching, 84
inclusive education, special education laws for, 84–89

independence, supporting, 19
indirect guidance, 57, 71–72
indirect vocabulary learning, 248
individual children, questions to help assessing, 88–89
Individualized Education Program (IEP), 85
Individuals with Disabilities Education Act (IDEA), 84–86
indoor environment, 50
indoors, safety, 153–57
    accidents or emergencies, 155–57
    childproofing, 154–55
    safe habit development, 154
Infant/Toddler Environment Rating Scale, 474
infants
    activities for, 440–41
    age-appropriate language, 127
    art and music for, 351
    brain development in, 5
    classroom considerations for, 58–59
    curriculum for, 38
    emergent literacy, 263–64
    fine motor play for, 440
    friendship opportunities for, 68–69
    gross motor play for, 438–40
    learning centers for, 59
    learning characteristics of, 7
    math for, 400–402
    outdoor play for, 436–40
    reading to, 260
    selecting children's books, 258
    sensorimotor play of, 120–21
    space considerations, 437–41
    talking to, 246
inference, 305
informal measurement, 393
informal methods, 221–23
information
    interpreting and using, 229
    providing, 18
Instructions for Scoring: The Infant/Toddler Environment Rating Scale-3™ (ITERS-3™), 140
instrument, playing, 370
intellectual disability, 101
interactions supporting learning, 15–21
    planning for development and learning, 19–21
    steps to quality interactions, 16–19
interactions, assessing, 75
interactive, 90
interest areas, 53
interest centers, 53
interlacing, 358
intervention, 233–34

ITERS-3™. *See* Instructions for Scoring: The Infant/Toddler Environment Rating Scale-3™

J
jargon, 192
journaling, 470–71

K
keeping clean, 366
kindergarteners, age-appropriate language with, 127
kinship care, 184–85

L
labeling, 359, 390
landscaping, 431–32
language, 98
    advancing, 20–21
    assessing program practices, 267–68
    defined, 243
    development, 243–46
    expressive, 244–46
    importance of, 83
    mathematics, 402
    outdoor play, 430
    receptive, 244–46
    science, engineering, and technology in classroom, 312–13
    sequence of development of, 243–44
    sharing with families, 269–70
    30-million-word gap, 242–43
language skills, art and music, 342
language throughout curriculum, 248–49
    experiences, 254
    high-quality children's literature, 258
    language first, 253
    literacy, 253
    narrative skills, 254
    objects, 253–54
    phonological awareness, 254
    sequencing, 254
    stimulation techniques, 249–53
    symbols, 255
laundry day, 429
layout, 431–32
leadership, supporting, 19
learning
    child-directed, 27
    child-initiated, 27
    teacher-directed, 27
    teacher-initiated, 27
learning centers, 52–53
    aesthetics, 61–63
    basic, 54–56
    classroom considerations, 58–59
    components, 54–56
    developmentally appropriate toys and equipment, 59–61
    establishing and arranging, 57–58
    supervision and safety, 63–65
learning characteristics, 6–11
    domains, 7
    group programs, 11
    infants, 7
    preschoolers, 10
    school-age, 10–11
    toddlers, 7–9
learning disabilities, 101
learning, planning for, 19–21
length, 391–92
LGBTQ+ parents, 186
libraries, 286–87
library and listening center, 55
library center, creating, 261–62
light, 437
listening, 370
literacy, 242, 253
    assessing program practices, 267–68
    bibliotherapy, 263
    daily activities promoting, 256
    emergent, 263–67
    environmental print, 257–58
    holding conversations about books, 261
    library center, 261–62
    mathematics and, 402
    outdoor play, 430
    reading aloud, 259–62
    science, engineering, and technology in classroom, 312–13
    sharing with families, 269–70
    when to read to children, 261
loose parts, 421
    activities, 422
    beanbag activities, 425
    dramatic play activities with wheeled toys, 424
    integrating into curriculum, 422

M
magnets, 366
maker or tinkering center, 56
mandated reporter, 162
manipulatives, 399–400, 440
materials, 19
    exploration of, 6–11
    organizing, displaying, and storing, 73
    providing/organizing, 133
math and manipulative center, 55, 403–4
math awareness, developing, 381
math-rich environment, creating, 394
mathematical concepts, 382–84
    counting, 384–85
    geometry, 390–91
    measurement, 391–93
    number awareness, 384–85
    quantitative and qualitative concepts, 385–90
    recognition, 384–85
mathematics, 313
    assessment and, 405–6
    combining language and literacy with, 402
    engineering and, 402–3
    extending math learning, 397
    families and, 406–9
    math awareness development, 381
    mathematical concepts, 382–93
    one-to-one correspondence, 380
    outdoor play, 430
    supporting math learning, 397–99
    teacher's role, 394–404
    vocabulary of, 397
measurement, 391–93
media, 338
meditation, 470
military families, 186–87
mishaps, preventing, 367
modalities, 19
modifications, 88
money, value of, 388–89
Montessori Method, 15
Montessori, Maria, 14–15
mood, 368
morning meetings, 34, 51
motor coordination, 98
movement, music and, 350
moving, 370
multicultural families, 189–90
multicultural program, 294–96
multigenerational families, 184–85
multiple intelligences, 15
multiracial families, 189–90
museums, 286–87
music, 314
    assessment, 373–74
    creating and using invented songs, 371–72
    elements of, 368–70
    families, 374–76

movement and, 427
　musical experiences, 370–71
　outdoor play and, 427
　your role in, 367–70
music and movement center, 56
music center, 369–70
music day, 374
myopia, 414

N

NAEYC Early Learning Program Accreditation Standards and Assessment Items, 204
NAEYC. *See* National Association for the Education of Young Children
narrative skills, 254
National Association for the Education of Young Children (NAEYC), 26
National Science Foundation (NSF), 302
natural environment, 86
nature exposure, benefits of, 414–15
nature-deficit disorder, 412–13
　causes, 413
　results, 414
needs, assessing, 92–93
neglect, 162–63
newsletters, 269
note-taking, 213
NSF. *See* National Science Foundation
number awareness, 384–85
nutrition, 164–72
　characteristics of healthy children, 164
　education, 166–67
　food preparation in curriculum, 168–70
　food security, 165–66

O

object permanence, 200
objectives, stating, 19
objectivity, maintaining, 220
objects, 253–54
observations, 304
　anecdotal records, 218–23
　checklists, 213–16
　developmental scales, 217–18
　grids, 217
　guiding behavior using, 229–35
　note-taking, 213
　recording, 212–13
　tallies, 213–16
　technology options, 234–35
　tool for assessment, 210
one-to-one correspondence, 380
ongoing education, 455
onlooker play, 115
open-door policy, 198–99
open-ended questions, 18, 252
ordering, 386
organizations, professionals. *See* resources, professionals
outdoor environment, 50
outdoor play
　art and creative expression, 427–28
　assessment of program practices, 441–42
　blocks and construction, 430–31
　creative outdoor space, 431–32
　developmental benefits, 416–17
　ending, 435
　equipment and materials, 420–25
　families, 442–43
　housekeeping and dramatic play, 426–27
　importance of, 412–20
　integrating with other curriculum areas, 426–32
　language and literacy, 430
　music and movement, 427
　sand and water play, 428–29
　science and math, 430
　teacher's role, 432–35
outdoors, safety, 146–53
　ABC, 147–48
　checklists, 149
　emergency preparedness, 152–53
　keys to playground safety, 149
　maintenance, 150–51
　monitoring, 150–51
　SAFE, 146–47
overweight, 171

P

pace, providing change of, 348
paint, 358
paper, 358
paper plate weaving, 358
paradigm, 303
parallel play, 115
parallel talk, 17–18, 251
paraprofessional, 93
parent conferences, 192–95
parent–teacher conferences, guidelines, 193–94
parents
　book bag guide for, 269–70
　term, 178
　viewing world of, 180
parks, 286–87
parrot, 384
pathways, 319
patterns, recognizing and creating, 386–87
people-first language, 80
percentages, understanding, 391
permanently installed equipment, 421–25
personnel evaluations, 475
phonological awareness, 254
photography activities, 321–22
physical development, 343, 418–20
physical domain, skills in, 109
physical environment, 50–53
physical health, 160–62
physical play, 116–17
physiological needs, 164
Piaget, Jean, 12–13
picture symbol charts, 52
pinch points, 153
pitch, 368
planning for development and learning, 19–21
planning, fidelity, 43–44
plants, 317
play, 314–15
　adults' role in, 133–38
　approaches, 125
　associative, 115
　characteristic of children ages 1 to 8, 126–27
　constructive, 117–18
　cooperative, 116
　creative, 123
　cultural influences of, 121–22
　defined, 108
　developmentally appropriate play activities, 123–32
　dramatic, 124–25
　fantasy, 118
　focus on assessment of program practices, 138–41
　games with rules, 118–19
　importance of, 108–13
　modeling love of, 134–36
　onlooker, 115
　parallel, 115
　physical, 116–17
　rough and tumble, 120
　sensorimotor, 120–21
　skills in cognitive domain, 112
　skills in creative domain, 112–13
　skills in physical domain, 109
　skills in social-emotional domain, 110–12
　social, 117
　solitary, 114
　stages of, 114–16
　stress reduction, 473

play *(continued)*
   support and guide during, 125–32
   types of, 116–21
   understanding playful learning, 141–42
   unoccupied, 114
   using books to inspire, 137
   using themes in planning for, 136
play spaces, 435
playground safety, 149
playground setting, nature in, 415–16
playing, 372
pleasure, 343–44
pointing, 440
portfolios
   components, 224
   defined, 223
   digital portfolios, 224–25
   making and using, 223–24
   published assessment, 225
   screening tools, 225
   standardized tests, 225–26
positioning, 94
pre-reading skills, art and music, 343
prediction, 304
preparation, food, 168–70
preschoolers
   age-appropriate language, 127
   emergent literacy, 264–65
   learning characteristics of, 10
   reading to, 261
   selecting children's books, 258
   talking with, 247
   term, 4
pretend play, 124
prewriting skills, art and music, 343
print, becoming familiar with, 268
prisms, 319
private spaces, creating, 69–70
probability, 390
problem solving, developing skills for, 21–24
procedures, 359
process skills, 304
processes, art, 354–55
   applying, 356
   constructing, 357
   easel painting, 358–59
   forming, 356–57
   interlacing, 358
   materials that children can use to paint, 360
professionals
   assessment, 473–76
   career choice, 449–56
   early childhood professional commitment, 456–61
   equity and equality, 467–68
   organizations and resources, 461–67
   possible progression of career in early childhood education, 451–52
   responsibilities to families, 476–78
   self-care, 469–73
program practices, focus on assessment, 102–3
prop boxes, 133, 134
props, 133
prosocial behavior and social skills, 294
proximity, 129
published assessment, 225
purchased prepackaged curriculum, 30–31
purposeful music, 350

Q

qualitative measure, 214
quality linked to education, 455
qualitative concepts
   classifying, 385–86
   comparing, 386
   graphing, 387–88
   money value, 388–89
   ordering, 386
   patterns, 386–87
   probability, 390
   seriation, 386
   sorting, 385–86
   statistics, 390
quantitative, 305
quantitative concepts
   classifying, 385–86
   comparing, 386
   graphing, 387–88
   money value, 388–89
   ordering, 386
   patterns, 386–87
   probability, 390
   seriation, 386
   sorting, 385–86
   statistics, 390
questions
   asking, 17
   individual child assessment, 88–89

R

rainbows, 319
ramps, 319
rapid change and expectations, 232–33
reading aloud, 259–62
real world, making connections to, 20
reasonable accommodations and modifications, 87–89
reasoning skills, developing, 18
rebus, 395
receptive language, 244–46
recognition, 384–85
recording, 213
recreation opportunities, 286–87
referral, making, 100–102
relaxation, music for, 348–49
research, staying abreast of, 455
resources, community, 286–89
resources, professionals
   advocacy, 461–66
   ancillary skills, 466
   communication, 467
responsibilities, advocacy, 465–66
rhythm, 369
rhythmic, 345
Risley, Todd, 242
role play, 124
roles, 124
rolling, 439
room arrangement, 65–66
   guidelines, 50–53
   making the environment convenient, 52–53
   providing for whole group, small group, and individual activities, 51–52
rough and tumble play, 120
routines, 32–35, 70–71
rules of conduct, 453–54

S

safe habits, helping children develop, 154
SAFE, acronym, 146–47
safety, 63–65
   health, 160–64
   indoors, 153–57
   nutrition, 164–72
   outdoors, 146–53
   teacher self-care, 157–60
   transportation, 151–52
   water, 150–51
safety, monitoring, 133
sand, 428–29
sand, water, and sensory area, 56
sanitizing, 162
scaffolding, 14, 20
schedules, 32–35, 70–71, 347
schemas, 13
schemes, 12
school-age children, 265
   learning characteristics, 10–11
   reading to, 261
   selecting children's books, 258
   talking with, 247
   term, 4

science, 304
    outdoor play, 430
science and discovery center, 56
science and tinkering centers
    establishing, 325–26
    goals, 326–27
    items and equipment, 327–29
science, technology, engineering, and mathematics (STEM), 302–3
    assessment, 329–31
    in classroom, 311–22
    engineering, 309–11
    families and, 331–33
    mathematics, 380–409
    science, 304–7
    science and tinkering centers, 325–29
    teacher's role, 322–24
    technology, 307–9
scope and sequence, 43
screen time, 307
screening tools, 225
seasonal themes, 317–18
self-care
    as professional, 469–73
    strategies for stress reduction, 470–73
    teachers, 157–60
self-evaluation, 475
self-expression, 343–44
self-help, 98
self-talk, 17–18, 249–51
sensorimotor play, 120–21
sensory art experience, benefits of, 361
sensory variations, 436–37
separation anxiety, understanding, 199–203
sequence, 392–93
sequences, 254
seriation, 381, 386
shade, 437
shaken baby syndrome, 163
shapes, recognizing, 390
singing, 367, 370, 371–72
single parents, 183
skipped-generation families, 184
slides, 434
small appetites, 171
smells, 437–38
smocks, 359
social and emotional environment, 66–72
    children's behavior, 69–72
    nurturing friendships, 67–69
social interaction, 96–98
social play, 117

social studies
    assessment of program practices, 297
    cultural aspects, 290–93
    developmentally appropriate concepts, 276–89
    supporting concepts, 296
    teacher's role in, 293–97
    for young children, 274–75
social-emotional development, 417
social-emotional domain, skills in, 110–12
social-emotional skills, art and music, 343
socio-dramatic, 116
solitary play, 114
sorting, 385–86
sounds, 437–38
space concept, understanding, 390–91
special education laws
    Americans with Disabilities Act (ADA), 86–87
    Individuals with Disabilities Education Act (IDEA), 84–86
    reasonable accommodations and modifications, 87–89
    timeline of legal protections, 85
specific feedback, giving, 18
speech and language impairments, 101
spina bifida, 101
sprinklers, 429
stages of development, art and music, 352–54
    art processes, 354–60
    benefits of sensory art experience, 361
    children's music skills, 361–62
stages of play, 114–16
standardized tests, 225–26
standards, fidelity, 44–45
statistics, 390
STEAM, 302–4
    art and music, 337–76
    science, technology, and engineering, 302–33
STEM. See science, technology, engineering, and mathematics
steps to quality interactions
    asking questions, 18
    clarifying concepts, 18
    developing analytical/reasoning skills, 18
    expanding on what children know, 18
    explaining new vocabulary, 18
    feedback loops, 16
    holding conversations, 16–17

    offering encouragement and affirmation, 19
    parallel talk, 17–18
    prompting thought processes, 19
    providing information, 18
    self-talk, 17–18
    specific feedback, 18
stereotyping, 290
stimulation techniques, language
    communication loop, 252–53
    expansion, 252
    open-ended questions, 252
    parallel talk, 251
    self-talk, 249–51
storage, playground, 425–26
stress reduction, strategies for, 470–73
stress, coping with, 160
structural adaptation, 94–96
Styrofoam weaving, 358
sufficient time, allowing, 133–34
sun, safety, 151
supervision
    in outdoor environment, 432–33
    planning for, 63–65
    SAFE, 146
support and guide during play, 125–32
support, incarcerated parents, 188–89
surfaces, cushioning, 434
surfaces, walking and crawling on, 439
sweet potato plants, 319–20
swings, 434
symbols, 255
symmetry, 390

T

table toys, 399–400
take-home bags, 406–9
taking art outside, 366
tallies, 213–16
taping, 366
Tax Reduction to Remove Architectural and Transportation Barriers to People with Disabilities and Elderly Individuals, 92
teachable moments, 35–36
teacher-directed learning, 27
teacher-initiated learning, 27
teachers
    mathematics, 394–404
    outdoor play, 432–35
    role in assessment, 227–29
    role in fostering language and literacy skills, 246–59
    role in learning environment, 72–74
    role in playful learning, 133–38

teachers *(continued)*
    role in science, technology, engineering, and mathematics, 322–24
    self-care of, 157–60
    social studies, 293–97
technology, 307
    incorporating math learning in, 403
technology options, assessment, 234–35
teen parents, 185
temperature, 434
tempo, 368
textures, 436–37
theme-based curriculum, 31
themes, 35–36
Theodor Seuss Geisel Medal, 259
theorists, 12–15
thought processes, prompting, 19
thoughtful questions, asking, 323
three Ws, 230–31
three-dimensional, 356
three-layer format, assessment, 473–75
time, 392–93
tinkering, 309
toddlers
    activities for, 440–41
    age-appropriate language, 127
    art and music for, 351
    brain development in, 5
    classroom considerations for, 58–59
    curriculum for, 37
    emergent literacy, 264
    friendship opportunities fo, 68–69
    learning centers for, 59
    learning characteristics of, 7–9
    math for, 400–402
    outdoor play for, 436–40
    reading to, 260–61
    selecting children's books, 258
    sensorimotor play of, 120–21
    space considerations, 437–41
    talking to, 246–47
    term, 4
touching, 440
toys
    developmentally appropriate toys, 59–61
    selecting and adapting, 89–90
transferable, 304
transitions, 347–48
transportation
    safety, 151–52
    science, technology, and engineering, 318
trash, 433–34
traumatic brain injury, 101
tummy time, 58, 438

U

unit blocks, 393
United States Department of Agriculture (USDA), 320
United States, special education laws of, 84–88
universal precautions, 459
unoccupied play, 114
unplanned opportunities, 323–24
USDA. *See* United States Department of Agriculture

V

variables, 305
variety, providing, 367
vegetable garden, 320
Vgotsky, Lev, 13–14
video access, 198–99
visual impairments, 101
visual perception, 112
visual schedule, 32, 286
vocabulary learning, 248
vocabulary, explaining, 18
volume, 368, 391–92

W

water painting, 429
water play, 428–29
water, safety, 150–51
wave jars, 320
weight, 391–92
wheeled toys, 424–25
writing center, 56
writing, stages of, 265–66

Y

yoga, 471
young children
    art and music for, 338–45
    creativity and, 339
    food preparation and, 170
    importance of play for, 108–13
    nutrition for, 164–72
    outdoor play for, 412–20
    responses of, 187
    social studies for, 274–75
    STEAM for, 322
    steps to quality interactions with, 16–19
yourself, helping, 203

Z

zone of proximal development (ZPD), 14
zone system, 433
ZPD. *See* zone of proximal development